**THIRD EDITION**

# CRITICAL ISSUES IN POLICING

# THIRD EDITION

# CRITICAL ISSUES IN POLICING

## CONTEMPORARY READINGS

## ROGER G. DUNHAM
*University of Miami*

## GEOFFREY P. ALPERT
*University of South Carolina*

WAVELAND
PRESS, INC.

Prospect Heights, Illinois

For information about this book, write or call:
Waveland Press, Inc.
P.O. Box 400
Prospect Heights, Illinois 60070
(847) 634-0081

# Contents

# Preface

The third edition of *Critical Issues* includes many updated and new articles reflecting changes that have evolved in policing during the past five years. We are pleased that the authors we asked to update their material were willing to do so with dedicated attention, and we are proud to include the new articles that introduce fresh ideas on current topics.

It is instructive to view policing as an elastic profession. That is, it changes shape, often appears different than it has in the past, may have a shift in focus but seems to return to an original shape and function. The new and different look of the third edition of *Critical Issues* reflects that elasticity. Police work must be in concert with the community if it is to be successful. The agents of formal social control must rely upon citizens, or agents of informal social control, to perform successfully their duties, gain respect and earn a sense of satisfaction.

In choosing our topics for *Critical Issues*, we selected those which have the broadest application. Rather than limiting the scope of our material to large, urban, suburban, rural or small departments, we have selected issues that are applicable to all. As in *Policing Urban America*, a text designed to accompany *Critical Issues*, we are emphasizing the importance of involving community members in decisions concerning law enforcement—including tasks, objectives and goals.

One of the major roles played by citizens is to help identify what is a proper measure of performance in law enforcement. In the past, the ultimate measure of police success has been an evaluation of the crime rates. It seems that the comments made by Durkheim, as well as contemporary researchers, that a change in the rate of crime is influenced by factors beyond the control of police, has fallen on deaf ears. Politicians and police officials still take credit when the reported crime rate decreases and are blamed when the reported rate of crime increases. The use of reported crimes as a measure of success for police demonstrates an unsophisticated understanding of the role and scope of police services. While different styles of policing can affect many performance measures including response time and the nature and extent of community contacts, understanding changes in the rates of crime requires a far more sophisticated analysis.

Hopefully, we will soon see a switch from holding police responsible for crime rates to holding them accountable for specific tasks and objectives and the general goal of law enforcement: promoting secure communities. In that spirit, we have revised *Critical Issues* to include information on the tasks, objectives and the law enforcement goal of promoting community security.

# Acknowledgments

We are indebted to many people for their contributions to this collection. The collaboration and friendship of our colleagues who wrote the excellent articles in this book are sincerely appreciated. Our wives, Vicki Dunham and Margaret Alpert, offered patience, support and understanding. Our collective nine children provided both incentive and distraction. Thanks to the many colleagues who have used the second edition in the classroom and offered suggestions for the revision. This work was a cooperative effort and we thank everyone who generously shared their time, knowledge, and expertise.

# 1

# The Foundation of the Police Role in Society

What is the basic role of the police in our society? What do we expect them to do, and not to do? And how does this correspond to their actual day-to-day behavior? If the police "get out of line" or begin using their authority in ways deemed inappropriate by a majority of citizens, do we have the right or ability to control their behavior? To answer these questions, we must understand that the police are an integral part of government. In fact, they are located at the point of interface between government and the private lives of individual citizens (Pollock, 1994). The police represent and implement the government's right to use coercion and force to guarantee certain behaviors from its citizens (such as the payment of taxes and obeying the law).

Carl Klockers (1984) has described police control as having four major elements: authority, power, persuasion, and force. Authority is the unquestionable entitlement to be obeyed. Power is held by the organization, is drawn upon by the individual officer and implies that if there is resistance, it will be defeated. Persuasion involves the use of symbols, words, and arguments to convince the individual that he or she ought to comply with the rules. Force involves something very different from the other elements of control: physical control. The other three elements rely mostly on mental or psychological control, with the underlying threat of force. All of these elements of control are used by the police, but the ultimate right to use force is what makes police unique.

## The Police Right to Use Force

Where do the police get the right to use force to control citizens? Ideally, they get it from the citizenry through a governmental right invested in federal, state, and local governing bodies. Although we may wonder if we really need all the government we have, and may fear the tremendous power vested in it, most of us realize that governments are a necessary feature of modern societies.

Mancur Olsen (1965) made the argument that governments are unavoidable features of human societies. He argued that we need public goods (e.g., public safety), and that public goods can only be created by coercion. It is through the formation of a state or government that force is legitimized to coerce citizens into contributing to public goods. Fortunately, it is not necessary to apply force most of the time, as long as there always is a credible threat of force.

Richard Quinney (1970:9–10) has said that "society is held together by force and constraint . . . [that] values are ruling rather than common, enforced rather than accepted, at any given point in time." Although other institutional means exist to officially establish sets of values and rules (e.g., laws and fines), they mean little without some method of enforcement. To enforce the rules, we have created the social institution of police and authorized it to use physical force. In fact, the police are the only ones given the right to use physical force, and are the only ones that have a legitimate right to do so. In a sense, the government must use organized coercion to prevent private coercion (Quinney, 1970).

In sum, we need the police to have a civilized society, to ensure safety from being harmed by insiders, and to make sure we contribute to other needed public goods. In his *Leviathan*, Thomas Hobbes tried to describe what life would be like in a condition of anarchy.

> Hereby it is manifest, that during the time men live without a common power to keep them all in awe, they are in that condition which is called war . . . where every man is enemy to every man . . . In such condition, there is no place for industry: because the fruit thereof is uncertain: and consequently no agriculture . . . no society; and which is worst of all, continual fear, and danger or violent death; and the life of man, solitary, poor, nasty, brutish, and short.

While Olsen demonstrated that we need the state, throughout human history the state has often been an institution of repression. It seems to be in the disposition of most individuals, that when they are put in positions of authority and given that right to use force to maintain society, they will begin to use that power and authority to exploit others. Most citizens will give in to the human temptation to use the power and force to benefit themselves individually. This has been called the great dilemma of the state: how to have the state and keep it tame, or from exploiting its citizens (Stark, 1996). This is also the great dilemma of policing. How can we authorize a police force to maintain our safety, ensure that our laws are obeyed, and keep officers from using that force illegitimately? Most of the important issues concerning the police emanate from this basic dilemma. The greatest issues surrounding the police are misuse of force, police corruption, and fair methods to control these problems. Taming the police is a major aspect of the distinction between a police state and a democratic state. In a police state the citizens do not have adequate control over the police. The police are therefore able to use their monopoly on physical force to exploit citizens. In a democratic state, the people have maintained more control over the police, so that the police cannot exploit them.

## The Social Contract

In discussing what has been termed the social contract, Jeffrey Reiman (1985) explains that democracy does not guarantee that the judgments of public officials, such as the police, will uniformly replicate those of the public. The power is delegated and must be exercised according to the judgment of the individuals to whom it is delegated. However, Reiman makes clear that "the public has a right to spell out the criteria by which the judgments should be made, and to insist on both competence and good faith in the application of those criteria" (1985:237). He defines the social contract as "embodying a general test of the legitimacy of the acts and rules of public agencies of law enforcement, namely, that such acts or rules must be such that the limits on citizens' freedom that they bring must result in a net increase of that freedom all told" (p. 246). His test gives us a way to exercise public control over the police right to use force. To refuse to give the police the right to use force to enforce the law would undermine our laws and freedom and compel us to devote much of our time and effort to self-protection. Thus, according to Reiman, the public surrenders its right to use force and loans that right to the police to use it in the name of the group and to protect each member of the group against the use of force by other members. The sacrifice of this individual right results in a gain in real and secure freedom to live with minimal fear of victimization by others.

The real issue for citizens is, when they delegate the right to use force to the police and thereby create the potential of being harmed by the police misusing that force, do they really *decrease* their personal likelihood of harm given the reduction of victimization by other members? In a video series on the U.S. Constitution, entitled *Law and Order*, a victim of police misuse of authority, who later was able to obtain justice in the courts, said that he would still vote to give the police greater authority and risk the potential for misuse, than to have to fend off violent offenders in his community. He felt that with the police he at least had a chance for justice in the courts (*Law and Order*, 1987).

An argument against the social contract theory is that the police have always been instruments of the dominant class, and seldom look out for the interests of all citizens equally. In fact, historically the police have been extremely partisan toward those in power by looking out for their interests and by enforcing laws against opposing classes and groups. However, the idea of citizens actually delegating power and authority to the police has some historical support. Samuel Walker, a police scholar, attributes the rapid social change in the early to mid 1800s to the breakdown of the old system of law enforcement, and the need to establish modern police forces (Walker, 1992). When many thought the best solution to social disorder, rampant during this time, was to create modern police forces modeled after the newly formed London police, Americans showed great uncertainty and hesitated to create them.

> Despite the breakdown in law and order, Americans moved very slowly in creating new police forces. New York City did not create a new police force until 1845, eleven years after the first outbreak of riots. Philadelphia followed a more erratic course. Between 1833 and 1854, in the face of recurring riots, the city wrestled with the problem of police reform before finally creating a consolidated, citywide police force on the London model. These delays reflected deep public uncertainty about modern police methods. For many Americans, police officers dispersed throughout the community brought to mind the hated British colonial army. Others were afraid that rival politicians would fight for control of the police department to their own partisan advantage—a fear that proved to be correct. (Walker, 1992:7–8)

The dilemma created by the desire for police protection and the fear of losing control of the police was a factor in deciding whether or not to establish the modern police forces in American cities. The notion that the police received their authority and right to use force from the citizens of the young democracy was as much a part of policing in America as the subsequent partisan policing and corruption.

Beyond the historical validity of this democratic model of police in society, it is a valuable standard or ideal for modern policing. Just as much of our constitution remains an unfilled ideal, a democratic model of policing could provide a framework for improving the police. In fact, the history of the American police, especially since the 1960s, supports the idea that policing is progressively moving closer to this ideal.

Following this model, Reiman (1985) outlines the implications of the social contract perspective for modern policing. He argues that "any coercive practice by legal agents that constricts and endangers the freedom of the citizenry, rather than expanding and securing it, reproduces the very condition of the state of nature that coercive legal agencies are meant to remedy" (p. 240). In other words, if the police use their authority and force in an exploitive fashion, it would literally undermine their own justification, because it would subject citizens to precisely the sort of risks they were given special powers to prevent. Reiman continues, "if law enforcement threatens rather than enhances our freedom, the distinction between crime and criminal justice is obliterated" (p.241).

This view of the police is consistent with the idea of legitimate public power in which the power flows from the citizens to the police. To make this a reality, Reiman argues that the police must be accountable for their use of public power, and accountable to the wider public, not just to other law enforcement agents. For force to be legitimate, he maintains, it must be viewed as owned by the public and loaned to police officers for specific reasons, and it must be exercised under specific conditions (Reiman, 1985).

Throughout this book, many of the issues examined (especially the hotly debated ones) will tie into the dilemma of policing as we have discussed it. Hopefully this general analysis will help to set a valuable framework and foundation for thinking about the many topics covered in the book.

## How Americans View the Police

The social contract perspective discussed above demonstrates the tie between the police and the public based on a moral or philosophical argument. Beyond this basis for authority, the police have learned that they need a cooperative public to be effective in controlling crime and maintaining order. This has been termed the "co-production of police services" (Reiss, 1971). It has been found that between 75 and 85 percent of police-citizen encounters are generated by citizens calling for police services. Recent trends in policing strategy focus more and more on citizen involvement and cooperation with the police (for example, community-based policing and problem-solving policing). This trend has sensitized the police to the importance of citizens' attitudes toward the police and how they go about doing their job. Favorable attitudes toward the police are crucial to the success of this new wave of policing strategies.

A brief review of some recent studies on how Americans view the police can set the stage for understanding the critical link between the police and citizens. First, it is interesting to note that the general public is surprisingly satisfied with the quality of police work. On the average, between 70 and 75 percent of the public think that the police are doing a very good or fairly good job, and rate police service as excellent or good. A slightly higher percentage of the public (around 80 percent) hold favorable impressions of the police, and have confidence in them (Huang and Vaughn, 1996).

While general support for the police has been consistently high, attitudes differ among diverse demographic groups, and according to the type of experiences people have had with the police. Race or ethnic group membership has been a strong predictor of attitudes toward the police. African Americans are usually less positive about the police, and hold more antagonistic attitudes toward the police than do whites. African Americans generally score about 25 percentage points lower on favorable attitudes toward the police, and on their ratings of police services (Huang and Vaughn, 1996). In fact, lower income African Americans living in the inner city have the least favorable attitudes toward the police.

Hispanics, with the exception of Cubans in Miami, usually are more favorable toward the police than African Americans, but less favorable than whites. The Cubans in Miami hold more favorable attitudes toward the police than all others, with the exception of recent immigrants (Alpert and Dunham, 1988).

Generally, people younger than 30 years of age have more negative attitudes toward the police than do other age groups (Sullivan et al., 1987). This is especially true of adolescents, and has been attributed to this group having more negative encounters with the police than others, and having a low level of identification with law enforcement officers.

Political ideology even has an impact on how favorably people view the police. Conservatives and Republicans generally hold more favorable attitudes toward the police than Democrats. Socioeconomic status is another variable that helps explain variations in attitudes toward the police. It is the lower-income people who hold least favorable attitudes of the police. This relationship holds up even within ethnic groups. For example, whites generally hold more favorable attitudes toward the police than African Americans. However, middle-class whites are more favorable toward police than are lower-class whites, and the same is true for African Americans. Higher social class is associated with more positive attitudes (Huang and Vaughn, 1996).

In addition to demographic factors having an influence on attitudes toward the police, the types of contacts and experiences people have with the police seem to play a major role in how positively or negatively they view the police. Generally, positive contacts and experiences with the police result in positive attitudes, and negative contacts lead to negative attitudes. Also, contacts initiated by the citizen, such as calls for police services, tend to be more positive than contacts where the police initiate the contact, such as giving a traffic ticket. The impact of contacts with the police are so strong in determining attitudes toward the police and police services that many believe that negative contacts explain why some groups have such negative attitudes about the police (such as African Americans and teenagers). These groups have many more negative contacts with the police than the general population. For example, African Americans and teenagers perceive the police as less friendly, less fair, and even less prompt when compared with the evaluations of the police by other groups. The same is true for perceptions of the police use of force. African Americans are much more likely than others to think that the police are allowed to use too much force, and to view police abuse of force as a problem. Huang and Vaughn (1996:41) report from their research that, "older, middle-income, rural, and conservative respondents tended to have more favorable perceptions about police use of force than did younger, urban, and liberal ones."

Huang and Vaughn (1996) conclude from their extensive research that direct police contacts were more important than demographic variables in explaining most attitudes toward the police. For example, African Americans and youth who experienced positive contacts with the police were as likely as others to report the police to be friendly, prompt, and effective at crime control. There were some exceptions: when experiences with the police were taken into account, African Americans still believed that they were treated unfairly and that the police used too much force.

Current trends in policing have emphasized the relationship between the police and citizens, so that police administrators are becoming more and more sensitized to the value of a positive and supportive citizenry. Many police administrators have found that positive contacts and good policing can overcome negative attitudes of citizens and are making strong efforts to foster a conciliatory atmosphere and to develop programs and strategies to cultivate positive police-citizen encounters as much as possible. While there is still much room for improvement, all of this leads to more police accountability to citizens.

It is noteworthy, in spite of the fact that the role of the police officer has become increasingly complex and that citizens' expectations of the police continue to broaden, that attitudes citizens hold toward the police and toward how well they do their job are generally positive.

## The Increasing Complexity of the Police Role

If we were asked to identify the most apparent changes in modern policing during the twentieth century, the raised level of expectations by citizens of the police would most certainly rank among the top. August Vollmer, police chief of Berkeley, California from 1905–1932, and one of the first great reformers, once observed:

> The citizen expects police officers to have the wisdom of Solomon, the courage of David, the strength of Samson, the patience of Job, the leadership of Moses, the kindness of the Good Samaritan, the strategical training of Alexander, the faith of Daniel, the diplomacy of Lincoln, the tolerance of the Carpenter of Nazareth, and finally, an intimate knowledge of every branch of the natural, biological, and social sciences. If he had all these, he might be a good policeman! (cited in Bain, 1939)

As problems of social control have grown and become more complex, so have the actions and reactions required of the police. Unfortunately, the tendency has been to proliferate new agencies to meet specific needs rather than to consolidate or to improve the effectiveness of existing organizations. The result has been an increasingly complex and uncoordinated development of law enforcement, mired in the multiplicity of agencies and the overlapping of jurisdiction and responsibility. Simultaneous with these developments has been the growing complexity of police functions, and the growing public expectation of a more professionalized and competent police force. All of this has made the study of modern policing an exciting, yet difficult topic.

There is a great deal of confusion over the terms, "policing" and "law enforcement." These terms are often seen as interchangeable. In the common usage, a police officer is a law enforcement officer, but a law enforcement officer is not always a police officer. Another important distinction is that many law enforcement officers are not involved in traditional police work such as patrolling, traffic enforcement, service calls, and so on. For example, a private security guard or store detective may spend considerable time trying to detect crimes, but he or she is not a police officer. In the same light, a detective for a police department, or an agent of one of many state or federal law enforcement agencies, may have police power and authority, but does not participate in traditional police work.

Law enforcement, whether practiced by a specialist sitting in front of a computer terminal or investigating a crime scene, or by the general practitioner cruising in his or her car or walking the beat, has an important role to play in American society. It is a most difficult chore to separate police work from that of law enforcement, as they overlap in many situations. But it is the work of the local, uniformed officer that represents the major portion of police work and consequently the major emphasis of this book.

Police agencies and departments come in all sizes and many shapes. The federal government supports more than fifty law enforcement agencies, including the Federal Bureau of Investigation (FBI); the Drug Enforcement Agency (DEA); the United States Marshals Service; the United States Secret Service; the Bureau of Alcohol, Tobacco, and Firearms (ATF); and the United States Customs Service, among others. There are close to 60,000 federal law enforcement personnel who work for these agencies. While it may be necessary to refer to the work of these and other agencies, we will focus our attention on the local police in urban America.

According to the most recent Uniform Crime Reports (the report compiled by the Federal Bureau of Investigation that summarizes national crime statistics and data on law enforcement personnel), there are almost 700,000 sworn police officers and civilians in state and local police. The numbers range from approximately 25,000 sworn officers and a budget of about one billion dollars in New York, to numerous rural areas that employ only one officer, who may work part-time. It is interesting to note that more than 90,000 officers and civilians work in the ten largest departments, but there are more than 10,000 police departments with ten or fewer employees. American police officers work for a large *number* of departments, but these are mostly small departments with approximately five sworn officers. The focus of this book is on the larger urban departments and their problems.

## Outline of the Book

The purpose of this anthology is to provide a selection of readings which covers policing comprehensively, yet focuses on specific topics and issues. The readings are selected to provide greater insight and depth than is possible in a general text, and to expose the student to a variety of experts and specialists from several disciplines who study the police. For each section, we have provided a short introduction which summarizes the major themes and issues in the readings.

In Section I, "Introduction and Historical Overview," we provide a socio-historical overview of policing, focusing on the social context in which the police function. A review of history is necessary to understand more completely the present and the future, and to put police work in the larger context of the social control functions of our society. As one form of social control, the police appear fairly recently in the history of society's attempts to control aberrant behavior. Specifically, policing represents the government's entry into the business of social control. Boston, in 1838, was the first major American city to sponsor a police force. New York followed closely behind Boston by establishing the first large police department in America.

Our rapidly changing society led to many changes in policing. Changes which greatly impacted police work include the invention of the telegraph, the two-way radio and the police car. These changes, among others, have led to the impersonalization of police work and the eroding of the bond between the police officer and the citizen. The disappearance of the officer on the "beat" who knew his neighborhoods and had earned the confidence of citizens was followed by the appearance of an unknown officer behind the tinted glass of a patrol car, who often fears getting out on the street without backup and applies the law in an extremely bureaucratic fashion. The accumulation of these and other changes in American policing have led to the issues and dilemmas facing police officers and administrators today.

In Section II, "Selection, Training and Socialization," articles are included which point out the significance and impact of these functions. Police work is a labor-intensive service industry, in which approximately 80 percent of the budget is devoted to personnel costs. The most significant investment a police department can make is in recruiting, selecting and training its personnel. Careful and knowledgeable recruitment and selection can save the department many costly and embarrassing problems by eliminating the recruits who are likely to fail or to become problem officers.

The first critical decision is the selection of a recruit. Many may apply, but not all applicants possess the personality and aptitude to make good police officers. There are several methods which are used to screen applicants. Psychological screening is the traditional method by which candidates are permitted to enter into the academy. If candidates demonstrate that they are unfit for police work, they are prevented from attending the preservice academy. Progressive agencies have employed a multi-hurdle approach to the selection of police recruits. That is, applicants must take a battery of tests, a physical examination and a lie detector test. Further, a background investigation will be completed, and only after a personal interview will a candidate be accepted into an assessment center. Here, a candidate will role-play a number of stressful scenarios and exercises under the watchful eyes of several observers to determine if the candidate has the potential for handling the situations he or she will likely encounter as a police officer. These assessment centers can also be used for promotional purposes. Although the purpose of the assessment is to determine the applicant's aptitude for police work, it does not rely on formal education.

In the 1990s an increasing emphasis is being placed on college education as a prerequisite for police work. In fact, the state of Minnesota has developed a combined curriculum which leads to a bachelor's degree and police officer certification. The findings of some studies indicate that the college-trained officer is less cynical, less prejudiced, less authoritarian, less hostile and less likely to use force than the non-college-educated officer. On the other side of the argument, college-educated officers are viewed by many as prone to dissatisfaction with the job, show a higher turnover rate, and may exhibit hostility toward non-college-educated officers. In spite of the controversy, many departments are requiring some college education and are placing college-educated officers in preferential assignments and first in line for promotions.

The police academy provides the basic training for the new police recruit. More than a century ago, it was discovered that although very little training was required of police officers, *good* police work required considerable knowledge and skills. To correct this inconsistency, efforts were made to formalize a model for police training around the country. The police academy was instituted to fill this void. Police academies throughout the country emphasize the technical aspects of police work, but also cover topics such as human relations skills, intercultural communication, the structure and functions of the criminal justice system, and the organization of police departments. In addition to training received in the police academy, officers gain valuable training in the field from more senior officers. This type of on-the-job training is supplemented by in-service training which continues throughout the officer's career.

This section also deals with one of the most interesting aspects of police work: socialization. As in other professions, the police go through a rigorous socialization process which results in the development of distinct attitudes and beliefs among officers. Many students of the police refer to this as the police subculture and the police personality. One aspect of the police personality which has received considerable attention is authoritarianism. This is a complex domain of personality traits which includes an exaggerated concern for authority, punitiveness, conservatism, and rigid adherence to rules and values. Included in this personality constellation is a need for order and routine, inflexibility and a proclivity to stereotype groups different from one's own group. This personality type raises some concern when present among police officers because it is linked to toughness, aggressiveness and cynicism among officers. An outgrowth of the authoritarian personality is its relationship to prejudice. Individuals with authoritarian personalities often have unfavorable attitudes about people belonging to groups other than their own and are likely to stereotype members of these groups. These traits, when present in police officers, have obvious implications for fair and equal treatment under the law.

The police subculture has an impact similar to a double-edged sword: it is extremely functional for the survival of officers and for the effectiveness of police work, yet it has been criticized for the tremendous pressure it exerts on officers to be loyal to the group. The pressure for loyalty and complete conformity among officers can create ethical dilemmas when it is used to cover up mistakes or to help officers in trouble with the system.

Included in this section is a discussion of styles of policing, and the ways police exercise discretion in fulfilling their police responsibilities. Police styles develop in response to the social environment in which the police operate, the individual officer's personality characteristics, and the political demands imposed on the department and on individual officers. Individual police officers develop personal styles of carrying out their tasks and responding to various problems. As these ways of approaching and dealing with demands and problems develop into patterns which dominate a particular department or unit, they are referred to as institutionalized characteristics and styles of policing. There is a great deal of variation among the institutionalized styles of police departments. It is difficult to determine which comes first: individual styles which begin to fall into distinct patterns that develop into institutional styles, or institutional patterns which socialize new recruits into particular styles. In reality, each has an influence on the other.

In recent years, there has been a call for changes in police style. An increasing emphasis on the professionalization of the police, on decreasing the fear of being victimized, and on safety and security of the community has focused attention on police style and measures of effectiveness. Unfortunately, different types of communities desire different styles and levels of policing, adding another complexity to these issues of police-community relations. The understanding of this complexity has led to a call for community-oriented policing based on the characteristics of the particular community and its citizens.

Section III, "Management and Organization," includes selections which outline various managerial and organizational characteristics of police departments. Since police departments have such unique characteristics and functions when compared to other institutions in our society, we would expect the organization and management of these units to be quite different from other institutions. Police departments are charged with maintaining order and are authorized to use force when necessary. This fact alone does more to shape the organization and management of police departments than anything else.

Police departments are organized in a style similar to the military, using military ranks to designate authority, such as captain, lieutenant, sergeant, and so on. Most traditional departments are organized around a highly structured bureaucratic model with specialized units and a well-developed division of labor. The police bureaucracy is characterized by a high degree of formalization and specification of rules and procedures. This is usually an attempt to control discretion of officers in the controversial situations they may face, and especially in the use of force. Because of the detailed division of labor and the delegation of authority and responsibility to the various parts of a police organization, a chain of command is created. The chain of command is the route or channel along which authority and responsibility flow. Police responsibility and authority are generally very sensitive subjects, so most departments adhere to a "unity of command" principle which maintains that each person in the organization is accountable to only one superior. Although agencies may differ in their emphasis, certain characteristics of organization and management are common among most departments.

As a response to the movement involving community-oriented policing and the need to decentralize authority, many agencies have changed their organizational structure drastically and quickly. One consequence of these rapid changes has been an emphasis on community expectations and a decrease in bureaucratic management. A solid bureaucracy and strong community interaction are both required for effective and efficient management (Reiss, 1992).

Section IV, "Police Deviance: Corruption and Controls," deals with an important topic of policing. There has always existed a concern about the control of those powers given by the state to the police, authorizing them to use force in the name of the state. When extensive power is given, there is the potential for corruption and misuse or abuse of that power. Over the years, police organizations have become more and more bureaucratic in an effort to control this high level of power, authority and discretion. As a result, there has been an improvement in efforts to control all types of police deviance.

Unfortunately, there will always be two elements which result in corruption of our police: opportunity and greed. Police deviance is a type of occupational deviance, deviance that is made possible by an opportunity structure associated with a particular occupation. Police officers, by the nature of their work, are constantly being exposed to opportunities for misconduct. Even in the most crime-free areas, there are opportunities to base arrest decisions on extra-legal criteria, or to accept money for not issuing a traffic ticket, or to use one's authority against someone or some group which one does not like. The police officer's role is one that provides a wider range of deviance-inducing situations than most other occupations.

Additionally, organizational deviance is an issue of concern for the police. Organizational deviance is that which extends beyond acts of individuals to deviant acts sanctioned by the organization. For example, the Special Investigative Section of the Los Angeles Police Department has come under attack by a movie titled *S.I.S.* Similarly, a former detective with L.A.P.D.'s Organized Crime Intelligence Division (OCID) has written a book titled, *L.A. Secret Police: Inside the LAPD Elite Spy Network* (1992), detailing the unethical and illegal acts of that division. The implied allegations, if true, paint a sordid picture of police activities in Los Angeles.

It is central to a police department's public image and survival to have a system for controlling police deviance and corruption that is both known and trusted by community members. Although much of the focus on controlling police deviance involves negative discipline, it is much more effective to focus on the positive. For example, it has been found that there are three main elements to an effective system of discipline. First, a department must have a well-formulated and consistent set of rules and procedures. Second, the rules and procedures must be communicated fully and effectively to the officers at all levels through proper training. Finally, proper supervision and leadership within the department can help to ensure conformity to the rules and to the maintenance of a good working environment. Focusing on positive aspects of discipline will serve as a preventive effort, which is more effective than focusing on the problems after they happen.

In Section V, "Minorities in Policing," the articles focus on the representation of minority groups in police work and the implications of any discrimination, both upon members of minority groups and upon the effectiveness of policing. The readings include reviews of the major issues as well as experiences of a female officer who has endured the process yet advanced through the ranks. These ordeals demonstrate why minorities have had problems integrating into the police work force and why change has been so slow.

The potential impact of minorities in policing has not yet been realized. The United States Civil Rights Commission stated in its report, *Who is Guarding the Guardians?* (1982), that police agencies were under-utilizing minorities and women and that this under-representation was hampering the ability of police departments to function at their most effective levels. If police agencies do not represent the ethnic characteristics of those they police, they have a difficult time earning the respect of the citizens in the community, and actually may increase the incidence of perceived or real prejudice or discrimination. This in turn increases the chances of racially-based trouble and violence. Many students of the police as well as civil rights groups argue that minority representation in police departments is an important factor in improving relations between the police and members of minority communities. However, it has been found in many cities that if hiring, making assignments and giving promotions are done for affirmative action purposes first, and not as rewards for competence and performance, a number of unintended consequences will likely occur. These side effects include an increase in confusion, and a decrease in morale among officers in the department. This can lead to a decrease in loyalty and trust given to the department and to the public.

If such procedures result in a lowering of the quality and qualifications of officers generally, mistakes and poor judgment will often cost the department in the long run. Social, political and economic considerations must be balanced with the impact that hiring and promotion practices will have on the department and its ability to function effectively.

The selections in Section VI, "Community-Based Policing," were chosen to provide the reader with the basics of the discussions concerning community-based policing philosophies and strategies. These arguments for community-based policing evolve from the idea that the community is a major source of social integration in our large-scale and impersonal society. These "natural areas," as they were called by early students of the city, provide residents with an alternative means of relating to the larger, complex society. Communities influence individual behavior, which usually functions to maintain informal social control of members. It is argued that the formal social control system of the police, which is based on written rules and laws and prescribed punishments, cannot be fully effective without being closely integrated with the informal control system in the community. The effectiveness of the formal control system (i.e., the police), depends on citizens to initiate and assist in the enforcement of norms and laws. The formal means of control, then, becomes a backup or support of local enforcement. If neighborhood residents view the police as outsiders, and the arrest situation as the imposition of unfair or biased rules on fellow citizens, then the normal, negative social stigma of arrest is absent, and the informal control system works against the formal system. This condition can seriously limit the effectiveness of the police.

Community-based policing is a strategy to maximize the integration of the formal control system of the police with the informal control system of the community. Emphasis is placed on building bonds of communication, interaction and mutual input between the community and the police, which will develop strong bonds of mutual trust and support.

Although there is an emphasis on community-oriented or community-driven programs, the crime-fighting function of police work must not be lost (Moore, 1992). Rather, innovative departments have linked their techniques of police work to their styles of fighting crime. Whether it is the identification of high-crime locations, known as "hot-spots," or an innovative strategy to reduce the level of crime in these areas, i.e., problem-oriented policing, the police are showing their involvement and respect for the communities which they serve.

In Section VII, "Use of Force," selections deal with an issue that traditionally has been one of the most controversial aspects of police work. We have given the police the right to use force to maintain order and to enforce the law. However, this is not a blanket authority. Police officers have many constraints on exactly when and under which conditions they may legitimately and lawfully use force. A mistake in job performance which merely creates an inconvenience in most occupations may result in an officer being suspended from the job, sued or possibly even arrested for committing a crime. In the normal course of fulfilling legitimate duties, an officer is often placed in legal jeopardy.

The beating of Rodney King in Los Angeles has become a referent to police use of force. This event, as no other, has focused our attention on police violence and public response to it. Although the events surrounding the beating death of Arthur McDuffie in Miami were hauntingly similar, they lacked one ingredient: a videotape. The technology and practice of capturing events on videotape has become a valuable tool for law enforcement, its training and accountability (Alpert et al., 1992).

It is little wonder that the use of force is such a controversial aspect of police work. Over the years, citizens have complained about excessive police force, and this has led to sporadic reform movements that have helped curtail abuse of this important tool for maintaining law and order.

> Reforms in this area have mostly consisted of minor adjustments to a system that needs an overhaul. We need to think differently about police use of force, not just tinker around with the timing and degree. Too much attention has been placed on specific beatings or shootings, while insufficient attention has been paid to the ways in which police control citizens. (Alpert and Dunham, 1988:158)

Until the police change their training philosophy concerning the use of force, and accept the role of controlling without it, problems related to the use of force will continue to plague our society. The latest concept in training is commonly called "violence reduction," "restraint" or "avoidance training." This new philosophy of training puts an emphasis on the need to reduce violence and the excessive use of force, and differs from earlier training by stressing communication and restraint, rather than traditional, violent responses. Restraint training stresses tactical knowledge and the use of concealment strategies to avoid being placed in a situation which has a high probability of violence.

The subject of Section VIII, "The Hazards of Police Work," is perhaps the greatest concern of the police officer. Police work incorporates several characteristics which present a unique set of personal hazards. Research has indicated that there is an unusual amount of stress generated by police work. This is due to the ever-present threat of danger to the officer and to others, and the potential or actual use of force. This high level of stress has been associated with the relatively frequent occurrence among police officers of such personal problems as divorce, alcoholism, and suicide.

There are no simple solutions to the complex problems associated with police work. The most reasonable approach is to reduce stress as much as possible by changing stress-producing aspects of the police bureaucracy, procedures and operations. However, in spite of any attempts to reduce stress, it will always be an inherent part of police work. The alternative strategy is to help officers cope with the everyday stress they experience, and to develop programs and services to help the officer cope in specific stress-producing situations (e.g., when an officer is involved in a shooting or responding to a domestic violence call).

A positive development is that police administrators are becoming more sensitive to the personal hazards of police work and their effect on the individual officer. This increased awareness is resulting in attempts to reduce stress when possible, and the provision of services to help officers cope with the highly charged police role.

The chapters that follow provide an exciting selection of readings which offer valuable insights into many of the important issues concerning the police role and police work. We will begin with a historical overview of policing.

## References

Alpert, Geoffrey and Roger Dunham. 1988. *Policing Multi-Ethnic Neighborhoods*. New York: Greenwood Press.

Alpert, Geoffrey, P. William Smith and Daniel Watters. 1992. "Implications of the Rodney King Beating," *Criminal Law Bulletin* 28:469–78.

Bain, Read. 1939. The Policeman on the Beat, *Science Monthly* 48:5.

Huang, W. S. Wilson and Michael Vaughn. 1996. Support and Confidence: Public Attitudes Toward the Police. In *Americans View Crime and Justice: A National Public Opinion Survey*, edited by Timothy Flanagan & Dennis Longmire. Thousand Oaks, CA: Sage Publications.

Klockers, Carl. 1984. Blue Lies and Police Placebos. *American Behavioral Scientist*. 4(27): 529–44.

*Law and Order*. 1987. Princeton, NJ: Films for the Humanities.

Moore, Mark. 1992. Problem-Solving and Community Policing. In *Modern Policing*, edited by Michael Tonry and Norval Morris (pp. 99–158). Chicago: University of Chicago Press.

Olsen, Mancur. 1965. *The Logic of Collective Action*. Cambridge: Harvard University Press.

Pollock, Joycellyn. 1994. *Ethics in Crime and Justice: Dilemmas and Decisions*. 2d ed. Belmont, CA: Wadsworth.

Quinney, Richard. 1970. *The Social Reality of Crime*. Boston: Little, Brown, and Company.

Reiman, Jeffrey. 1985. The Social Contract and the Police Use of Deadly Force. In *Moral Issues in Police Work*, edited by Frederick A. Ellison and Michael Feldberg. Savage, Maryland: Rowman & Littlefield Publishers.

Reiss, A. J. 1971. *The Police and the Public*. New Haven: Yale University Press.

Reiss, Albert. 1992. Police Organizations in the Twentieth Century. In *Modern Policing*, edited by Michael Tonry and Norval Morris (pp. 51–97). Chicago: University of Chicago Press.

Rothmiller, M. 1992. *L.A. Secret Police: Inside the LAPD Elite Spy Network*. New York: Pocket Books.

Stark, Rodney. 1996. *Sociology*, 6th ed. New York: Wadsworth Publishing Company.

Sullivan, Peggy, Geoffrey Alpert and Roger Dunham. 1987. "Attitude Structures of Different Ethnic and Age Groups Concerning Policing." *Journal of Criminal Law and Criminology*, 78:501–21.

United States Civil Rights Commission. 1982. "Who is Guarding the Guardian?" Washington, D.C.: United States Printing Office.

Walker, Samuel. 1992. *The Police in America*, 2d ed. New York: McGraw-Hill.

# Section I

## Introduction and Historical Overview

As we have discussed in the first article, American police, like many other social institutions, have evolved over time into what they are today. This slow but certain evolution will continue as American law enforcement is influenced by its current and future social environment. Our objective in this section is to provide some historical perspective to our study of the police in America. Of course, we will only be able to scratch the surface in our few selections. Craig Uchida's article, "The Development of the American Police: An Historical Overview," takes us from the colonial period of law enforcement to the present. Professor Uchida provides us with an in-depth analysis of the changes in emphasis and form that have occurred in policing over this period of time. His article is divided into the various reform movements which have molded and changed police into our modern day departments.

In 1993, the Law Enforcement Management and Administrative Statistics (LEMAS) program of the Bureau of Justice Statistics surveyed a nationally representative sample of local and sheriff's departments. The LEMAS reports (the second article in this section) present data on personnel, duties of sworn personnel, expenditures and pay, operations, equipment, computers and information systems, and policy directives. These data are very helpful in analyzing and understanding the police working environment as well as in assessing the current and future needs of law enforcement agencies. Due to space limitations, we have omitted small portions of the reports, some of the tables, and the methodology sections.

In the selection, "Police in the Laboratory of Criminal Justice," Lawrence Sherman argues that traditional policing strategies have not progressed over the centuries of policing, and are similar to "leeching out bad blood to cure diseases." He discusses the limitations of traditional methods for controlling violent crime and makes policy recommendations for improved nontraditional strategies. Although this article was written in 1983, many valuable ideas, applicable in current contexts, are included which stimulate the reader to think critically about various programs and policies for policing and dealing with crime.

17

# The Development of the American Police
## An Historical Overview

*Craig D. Uchida*

## Introduction

During the past 20 years, scholars have become fascinated with the history of police. A plethora of studies have emerged as a result. Early writings were concerned primarily with descriptions of particular police agencies. Roger Lane (1967) and James F. Richardson (1970) broke new ground in describing the origins of policing in Boston and New York, respectively. Since that time, others have followed suit with narratives of police organizations in St. Louis (Maniha, 1970; Reichard, 1975), Denver (Rider, 1971), Washington, DC. (Alfers, 1975), Richmond (Cei, 1975), and Detroit (Schneider, 1980).

Other authors have focused on issues in policing. Wilbur R. Miller (1977) examined the legitimation of the police in London and New York. Samuel Walker (1977) and Robert Fogelson (1977) concentrated on professionalism and reform of errant police in the 19th and 20th centuries. Eric Monkkonen (1981) took an entirely different approach by using quantitative methods to explain the development of policing in 23 cities from 1860 to 1920.[1]

Overall these histories illustrate the way in which police have developed over time. They point out the origins of concepts like crime prevention, authority, professionalism and discretion. In addition, these historical analyses show the roots of problems in policing, such as corruption, brutality, and inefficiency.

The major purpose of this selection is to examine the development of the police since 900 A.D. and more specifically, to determine whether the role of the police has changed in American society over a period of about 300 years. This is not an easy task. The debate over the "true" or "proper" police function is an ongoing one and cannot itself be resolved in a selection

Prepared especially for *Critical Issues in Policing* by Craig D. Uchida.

such as this.[2] However, by describing the various roles, activities, and functions of law enforcement over time, we can at least acquire a glimpse of what the police do and how their activities have varied over time. To do so, we rely on a number of important contributions to the study of the history of police.

The selection is divided into seven parts and basically covers the history of law enforcement and the role of the police from colonial America to the present. Part I examines the English heritage of law enforcement and its effect on colonial America. The colonists relied heavily on the mother country for their ideas regarding community involvement in law enforcement.

Part II examines the problems of urban centers in the 18th and 19th centuries and turns to the development of the full-time uniformed police in England and America. The preventive approach to law enforcement became central to the police role in both London and American cities. Part III is concerned with police activity in 19th century American cities. Patrol work and officer involvement in corruption are discussed.

In Part IV the reform movement of the Progressive Era is examined. From 1890 to 1920 reformers attempted to implement social, economic, and political change in the cities. As part of city government, police departments were targets of change as well.

In Part V we study a second reform era. From 1910 to 1960 chiefs became involved in a movement to professionalize the police. Part VI covers the riots and disorders of the 1960s and their immediate effect on policing across the country. Finally, in Part VII, we discuss the long-term legacy of the 1960s. That is, we examine the developments of the police since 1969 in terms of research and public policy.

## I. Communities, Constables, and Colonists

Like much of America's common-law tradition, the origins of modern policing can be linked directly to its English heritage. Ideas concerning community policing, crime prevention, the posse, constables, and sheriffs developed from English law enforcement. Beginning at about 900 A.D., the role of law enforcement was placed in the hands of common, everyday citizens. Each citizen was held responsible for aiding neighbors who might be victims of outlaws and thieves. Because no police officers existed, individuals used state-sanctioned force to maintain social control. Charles Reith, a noted English historian, refers to this model of law enforcement as "kin police" (Reith, 1956). Individuals were considered responsible for their "kin" (relatives) and followed the adage, "I am my brother's keeper." Slowly this model developed into a more formalized "communitarian," or community-based police system.

After the Norman Conquest of 1066, a community model was established, which was called frankpledge. The frankpledge police system required that every male above the age of twelve form a group with nine of his neighbors called a tything. Each tything was sworn to apprehend and deliver to court any of its members who committed a crime. Each person was pledged to help protect fellow citizens and, in turn, would be protected. This system was "obligatory" in nature, in that tythingmen were not paid salaries for their work, but were required by law to carry out certain duties (Klockars, 1985:21). Tythingmen were required to hold suspects in custody while they were awaiting trial and to make regular appearances in court to present information on wrong-doing by members of their own or other tythings. If any member of the tything failed to perform his required duties, all members of the group would be levied severe fines.

Ten tythings were grouped into a hundred, directed by a constable (appointed by the local nobleman) who, in effect, became the first policeman. That is, the constable was the first official with law enforcement responsibility greater than simply helping one's neighbor. Just as the tythings were grouped into hundreds, the hundreds were grouped into shires, which are similar to counties today. The supervisor of each shire was the shire reeve (or sheriff), who was appointed by the king.

Frankpledge began to disintegrate by the 13th century. Inadequate supervision by the king and his appointees led to its downfall. As frankpledge slowly declined, the parish constable system emerged to take its place. The Statute of Winchester of 1285 placed more authority in the hands of the constable for law enforcement. One man from each parish served a one-year term as constable on a rotating basis. Though not paid for his work, the constable was responsible for organizing a group of watchmen who would guard the gates of the town at night. These watchmen were also unpaid and selected from the parish population. If a serious disturbance took place, the parish constable had the authority to raise the "hue and cry." This call to arms meant that all males in the parish were to drop what they were doing and come to the aid of the constable.

In the mid-1300s the office of justice of the peace was created to assist the shire reeve in controlling his territory. The local constable and the shire reeve became assistants to the justice of the peace and supervised the night watchmen, served warrants, and took prisoners into custody for appearance before justice of the peace courts.

The English system continued with relative success well into the 1700s. By the end of the 18th century, however, the growth of large cities, civil disorders and increased criminal activity led to changes in the system.

## Law Enforcement in Colonial America

In colonial America (17th and 18th centuries), policing followed the English systems. The sheriff, constable, and watch were easily adapted to the colonies. The county sheriff, appointed by the governor, became the most important law enforcement agent particularly when the colonies remained small and primarily rural. The sheriff's duties included apprehending criminals, serving subpoenae, appearing in court and collecting taxes. The sheriff was paid a fixed amount for each task he performed.

Since sheriffs received higher fees based on the taxes they collected, apprehending criminals was not a primary concern. In fact, law enforcement was a low priority.

In the larger cities and towns, such as New York, Boston, and Philadelphia constables and the night watch performed a wide variety of tasks. The night watch reported fires, raised the hue and cry, maintained street lamps, arrested or detained suspicious persons, and walked the rounds. Constables engaged in similarly broad tasks, such as taking suspects to court, eliminating health hazards, bringing witnesses to court, and so on.

For the most part, the activities of the constables and the night watch were "reactive" in nature. That is, these men responded to criminal behavior only when requested by victims or witnesses (Monkkonen, 1981). Rather than preventing crime, discovering criminal behavior, or acting in a "proactive" fashion, these individuals relied on others to define their work. Public health violations were the only types of activity that required the officers to exercise initiative.

## II. Preventive Police: Cops and Bobbies

The development of a "new" police system has been carefully documented by a number of American and English historians. Sir Leon Radzinowicz (1948–1968), Charles Reith (1956) and T. A. Critchley (1967) are among the more notable English writers. Roger Lane (1967), James F. Richardson (1970), Wilbur R. Miller (1977), Samuel Walker (1977), and Eric Monkkonen (1981) represent a rather diverse group of American historians who describe and analyze a number of early police departments. Taken together these works present the key elements of the activities of the first English and American police systems that used the preventive model.

During the mid- to late-1700s the growth of industry in England and in Europe led to rapid development in the cities. London, in particular, expanded at an unprecedented rate. From 1750 to 1820 the population nearly doubled (Miller, 1977) and the urban economy became more complex and specialized. The Industrial Revolution led to an increase in the number of factories, tenements, vehicles, and marketplaces. With industrial growth came a breakdown in social control, as crime, riots, disorder, and public health problems disrupted the city. Food riots, wage protests, poor sewage control, pickpockets, burglars, and vandals created difficulties for city dwellers. The upper and middle classes, concerned about these issues, sought more protection and preventive measures. The constable-watch system of law enforcement could no longer deal successfully with the problems of the day, and alternative solutions were devised.

Some of the alternatives included using the militia; calling out the "yeomanry" or cavalry volunteers for assistance; swearing in more law-abiding citizens as constables; or employing the army to quell riot situations (Richardson, 1974:10). However, these were short-term solutions to a long-term problem.

Another proposal was to replace the constable-watch system with a stronger, more centralized police force. Henry and John Fielding (magistrates in the 1750s), Patrick Colquhoun (a magistrate from 1792 to 1818), and philosopher Jeremy Bentham and his followers advocated the creation of a police force whose principal object was the prevention of crime. A preventive police force would act as a deterrent to criminals and would be in the best interests of society. But the idea of a uniformed police officer was opposed by many citizens and politicians in England. An organized police too closely resembled a standing army, which gave government potentially despotic control over citizens and subjects. The proponent of a police force eventually won out, based primarily on the disorder and fear of crime experienced by London residents. After much debate in the early 1800s, the London Metropolitan Police Act was finally approved by Parliament in 1829 (see Critchley, 1967 and Reith, 1956).

The London Metropolitan Police Act established a full-time, uniformed police force with the primary purpose of patrolling the city. Sir Robert Peel, Britain's Home Secretary, is credited with the formation of the police. Peel synthesized the ideas of the Fieldings, Colquhoun and Bentham into law, convinced Parliament of the need for the police, and guided the early development of the force.

Through Peel and his two police commissioners, Charles Rowan and Richard Mayne, the role of the London police was formulated. Crime prevention was the primary function, but to enforce the laws and to exert its authority, the police had to first gain legitimacy in the eyes of the public. According to Wilbur R. Miller (1977) the legitimation of the London police was carefully orchestrated by Peel and his associates. These men recognized that in order to gain authority police officers had to act in a certain manner or the public would reject them. To gain acceptance in the eyes of the citizen, Peel and his associates selected men who were even-tempered and reserved; chose a uniform that was unassuming (navy blue rather than military red); insisted that officers be restrained and polite; meted out appropriate discipline, and did not allow officers to carry guns. Overall, the London police emphasized their legitimacy as based on *institutional* authority—that their power was grounded in the English Constitution and that their behavior was determined by rules of law. In essence, this meant that the power of the London "bobby" or "Peeler" was based on the institution of government.

American cities and towns encountered problems similar to those in England. Cities grew at phenomenal rates; civil disorders swept the nation, and crime was perceived to be increasing. New York, for example, sprouted from a population of 33,000 in 1790 to 150,000 in 1830. Foreign immigrants, particularly Irish and Germans, accounted for a large portion of the increase. Traveling to America in search of employment and better life-styles, the immigrants competed with native-born Americans for skilled and unskilled positions. As a result, the American worker saw the Irishman and German as social and economic threats.

Other tensions existed in the city as well. The race question was an important one in the northern cities as well as on the southern plantations. In fact, historians have shown that hostility to blacks was just as high in the North as in the South (Litwack, 1961). Those opposed to slavery (the abolitionists) were often met by violence when they attempted to speak out against it.

Between the 1830s and 1870s, numerous conflicts occurred because of ethnic and racial differences, economic failures, moral questions, and during elections of public officials. In New York, 1834 was designated the "Year of the Riots" (Miller, 1977). The mayoral election and anti-abolitionist sentiment were the two main reasons for the disorders. Other cities faced similar problems. In Philadelphia, the Broad Street Riot of 1837 involved almost 15,000 residents. The incident occurred because native-born volunteer firemen returning from a fire could not get by an Irish funeral procession. In St. Louis in 1850, a mob destroyed the brothels in the city in an attempt to enforce standards of public decency. To quell most of these disturbances, the local militia was called in to suppress the violence, as the constables and the night watch were ineffectual.

At the same time that the riots occurred, citizens perceived that crime was increasing. Homicides, robberies, and thefts were thought to be on the rise. In addition, vagrancy, prostitution, gambling, and other vices were more observable on the streets. These types of criminal activities and the general deterioration of the city led to a sense of a loss of social control. But in spite of the apparent immediacy of these problems, replacements for the constable-watch police system did not appear overnight.

The political forces in the large industrial cities like New York, Philadelphia, Boston, and others precluded the immediate acceptance of a London-style police department. City councils, mayors, state legislatures, and governors debated and wrangled over a number of qustions and could not come to an immediate agreement over the type of police they wanted. In New York City for example, although problems emerged in 1834, the movement to form a preventive police department did not begin until 1841; it was officially created in 1845, but officers did not begin wearing uniforms until 1853.

While the first American police departments modeled themselves after the London Metropolitan Police, they borrowed selectively rather than exactly. The most notable carryover was the adoption of the preventive patrol idea. A police presence would alter the behavior of individuals and would be available to maintain order in an efficient manner. Differences, however, between the London and American police abounded. Miller (1977), in his comparative study of New York and London police, shows the drastic differences between the two agencies.

The London Metropolitan Police was a highly centralized agency. An extension of the national government, the police department was purposely removed from the direct political influence of the people. Furthermore, as noted above, Sir Robert Peel recruited individuals who fit a certain mold.

Peel insisted that a polite, aloof officer who was trained and disciplined according to strict guidelines would be best suited for the function of crime prevention. In addition, the bobbies were encouraged to look upon police work as a career in professional civil service.

Unlike the London police, American police systems followed the style of local and municipal governments. City governments, created in the era of the "common man" and democratic participation, were highly decentralized. Mayors were largely figureheads; real power lay in the wards and neighborhoods. City councilmen or aldermen ran the government and used political patronage freely. The police departments shared this style of participation and decentralization. The police were an extension of different political factions, rather than an extension of city government. Police officers were recruited and selected by political leaders in a particular ward or precinct.

As a result of the democratic nature of government, legal intervention by the police was limited. Unlike the London police which relied on formal institutional power, the American police relied on informal control or individual authority. That is, instead of drawing on institutional legitimacy (i.e., parliamentary laws), each police officer had to establish his own authority among the citizens he patrolled. The personal, informal police officer could win the respect of the citizenry by knowing local standards and expectations. This meant that different police behavior would occur in different neighborhoods. In New York, for example, the cop was free to act as he chose within the context of broad public expectations. He was less limited by institutional and legal restraints than was his London counter part, entrusted with less formal power, but given broader personal discretion.

## III. Police Activity in the 19th Century

American police systems began to appear almost overnight from 1860 to 1890 (Monkkonen, 1981). Once large cities like New York, Philadelphia, Boston, and Cincinnati had adopted the English model, the new version of policing spread from larger to smaller cities rather quickly. Where New York had debated for almost ten years before formally adopting the London-style, Cleveland, Buffalo, Detroit, and other cities readily accepted the innovation. Monkkonen explains that the police were a part of a growing range of services provided by urban administrations. Sanitation, fire, and health services were also adopted during this period, and the police were simply a part of that natural growth.

Across these departments, however, differences flourished. Police activity varied depending upon the local government and political factions in power. Standards for officer selection (if any), training procedures, rules and regulations, levels of enforcement of laws, and police-citizen relationships differed across the United States. At the same time, however, there were some striking similarities.

## Patrol Officers

The 19th century patrolman was basically a political operative rather than a London-style professional committed to public service (Walker, 1977). Primarily selected for his political service, the police officer owed his allegiance to the ward boss and police captain that chose him.

Police officers were paid well but had poor job security. Police salaries compared favorably with other occupations. On average in 1880, most major cities paid policemen in the neighborhood of $900 a year. Walker (1977) reports that a skilled tradesman in the building industry earned about $770 a year, while those in manufacturing could expect about $450 a year. A major drawback, however, was that job security was poor, as their employment relied on election day events. In Cincinnati, for example, in 1880, 219 of the 295 members of the force were dismissed, while another 20 resigned because of a political change in the municipal government. Other departments had similar turnover rates.

New officers were sent out on patrol with no training and few instructions beyond their rule books. Proper arrest procedures, rules of law, and so on were unknown to the officers. Left to themselves, they developed their own strategies for coping with life in the streets.

## Police Work

Police officers walked a beat in all types of weather for two to six hours of a 12-hour day. The remaining time was spent at the station house on reserve. During actual patrol duty, police officers were required to maintain order and make arrests, but they often circumvented their responsibilities. Supervision was extremely limited once an officer was beyond the station house. Sergeants and captains had no way of contacting their men while they were on the beat, as communications technology was limited. Telegraph lines linked district stations to headquarters in the 1850s, but call boxes on the beat were not introduced until late in the 19th century, and radio and motorized communications did not appear until the 1900s (Lane, 1980). Police officers, then, acted alone and used their own initiative.

Unfortunately, little is known about ordinary patrol work or routine interactions with the public. However, historians have pieced together trends in police work based on arrest statistics. While these data have their limitations, they nonetheless provide a view of police activity.

Monkkonen's work (1981) found that from 1860 to 1920 arrests declined in 23 of the largest cities in the United States. In particular, crimes without victims, such as vice, disturbances, drunkenness, and other public order offenses, fell dramatically. Overall, Monkkonen estimated that arrests declined by more than 33% during the 60-year period. This trend runs contrary to "common sense notions about crime and the growth of industrial cities, immigration and social conflict" (p. 75). Further analysis showed that the decline occurred because the police role shifted from one of controlling the "dangerous class" to one of controlling criminal behavior only. From 1860 to 1890, Monkkonen argues, the police were involved in assisting the poor, taking in overnight lodgers, and returning lost children to their parents or orphanages. In the period of 1890 to 1920, however, the police changed their role, structure, and behavior because of external demands upon them. As a result, victimless arrests declined, while assaults, thefts, and homicide arrests increased slightly. Overall, however, the crime trend showed a decrease.

## Police Corruption and Lawlessness

One of the major themes in the study of 19th century policing is the large-scale corruption that occurred in numerous departments across the country. The lawlessness of the police—their systematic corruption and nonenforcement of the laws—was one of the paramount issues in munici-pal politics during the late 1800s.

Police corruption was part of a broader social and political problem. During this period, political machines ran municipal governments. That is, political parties (Democrats and Republicans) controlled the mayor's office, the city councils and local wards. Municipal agencies (fire depart-ments, sanitation services, school districts, the courts, etc.) were also under the aegis of political parties. As part of this system, political patron-age was rampant. Employment in exchange for votes or money was a com-mon procedure. Police departments in New York, Chicago, Philadelphia, Kansas City, San Francisco, and Los Angeles were filled with political appointees as police officers. To insure their employment, officers followed the norms of the political party, often protecting illicit activities conducted by party favorites.

Corrupt practices extended from the chief's office down to the patrol officer. In New York City, for example, Chief William Devery (1898–1901) protected gambling dens and illegal prize fighting because his friend, Tim Sullivan (a major political figure on the Lower East Side), had interests in those areas. Police captains like Alexander "Clubber" Williams and Timo-thy Creeden acquired extensive wealth from protecting prostitutes, saloon-keepers, and gamblers. Williams, a brutal officer (hence, the nickname Clubber), was said to have a 53-foot yacht and residences in New York and the Connecticut suburbs. Since a captain's salary was about $3,000 a year in the 1890s, Williams had to collect from illegal enterprises in order to maintain his investments.

Because police officers worked alone or in small groups, there were ample opportunities to shake down peddlers and small businesses. Detec-tives allowed con men, pickpockets, and thieves to go about their business in return for a share of the proceeds. Captains often established regular payment schedules for houses of prostitution depending upon the number of girls in the house and the rates charged by them. The monthly total for police protection ranged between $25 and $75 per house plus $500 to open or re-open after being raided (Richardson, 1970).

Officers who did not go along with the nonenforcement of laws or did not approve of the graft and corruption of others found themselves transferred to less-than-desirable areas. Promotions were also denied; they were reserved for the politically-astute and wealthy officer (promotions could cost $10,000 to $15,000).

These types of problems were endemic to most urban police agencies throughout the country. They led to inefficiency and inequality of police services.

# IV. Reform, Rejection, and Revision

A broad reform effort began to emerge toward the end of the 19th century. Stimulated mainly by a group known as the Progressives, attempts were made to create a truly professional police force. The Progressives were upper-middle class, educated Protestants who opposed the political machines, sought improvements in government, and desired a change in American morality. They believed that by eliminating machine politics from government, all facets of social services, including the police, would improve.

These reformers found that the police were without discipline, strong leadership, and qualified personnel. To improve conditions, the progressives recommended three changes: 1) the departments should be centralized; 2) personnel should be upgraded; and 3) the police function should be narrowed (Fogelson, 1977). Centralization of the police meant that more power and authority should be placed in the hands of the chief. Autonomy from politicians was crucial to centralization. Upgrading the rank-and-file meant better training, discipline, and selection. Finally, the reformers urged that police give up all activities unrelated to crime. Police had run the ambulances, handled licensing of businesses, and sheltered the poor. By concentrating on fighting crime, the police would be removed from their service orientation and their ties to political parties would be severed.

From 1890 to 1920 the Progressive reformers struggled to implement their reform ideology in cities across the country. Some inroads were made during this period, including the establishment of police commissions, the use of civil service exams, and legislative reforms.

The immediate responses to charges of corruption were to create police administrative boards. The reformers attempted to take law enforcement appointments out of the hands of mayors and city councilmen and place control in the hands of oversight committees. The Progressives believed that politics would be eliminated from policing by using this maneuver. In New York, for example, the Lexow Committee, which investigated the corrupt practices of the department, recommended the formation of a bipartisan Board of Police Commissioners in 1895. Theodore

Roosevelt became a member of this board, but to his dismay found that the commissioners were powerless to improve the state of policing. The bipartisan nature of the board (two Democrats and two Republicans) meant that consensus could not be reached on important issues. As a result, by 1900 the New York City police were again under the influence of party politics. In the following year the board of commissioners was abolished and the department was placed under the responsibility of a single commissioner (Walker, 1977). Other cities had similar experiences with the police commission approach. Cincinnati, Kansas City, St. Louis, and Baltimore were among those that adopted the commission, but found it to be short-lived. The major problem was still political—the police were viewed as an instrument of the political machine at the neighborhood level and reformers could not counter the effects of the Democratic or Republican parties.

Civil service was one answer to upgrading personnel. Officers would be selected and promoted based on merit, as measured by a competitive exam. Moreover, the officer would be subject to review by his superiors and removal from the force could take place if there was sufficient cause. Civil service met with some resistance by officers and reformers alike. The problem was that in guarding against the effects of patronage and favoritism, civil service became a rigid, almost inflexible procedure. Because it measured abstract knowledge rather than the qualities required for day-to-day work, civil service procedures were viewed as problematic. Eventually, the program did help to eliminate the more blatant forms of political patronage in almost all of the large police departments (Walker, 1977).

During this 30-year period, the efforts of the Progressive reformers did not change urban departments drastically. The reform movement resulted, in part, in the elimination of the widespread graft and corruption of the 1890s, but substantive changes in policing did not take place. Chiefs continued to lack power and authority, many officers had little or no education, training was limited, and the police role continued to include a wide variety of tasks.

Robert Fogelson (1977) suggests several reasons for the failure of reform. First, political machines were too difficult to break. Despite the efforts by the Progressives, politicians could still count on individual supporters to undermine the reforms. Second, police officers themselves resented the Progressives' interventions. Reformers were viewed by the police as individuals who knew little about police work and officers saw their proposals for change as ill-conceived. Finally, the reforms failed because the idea of policing could not be divorced from politics. That is, the character of the big-city police was interconnected with policymaking agencies that helped to decide which laws were enforced, which public was served, and whose peace was kept (Fogelson, 1977). Separating the police completely from politics could not take place.

## V. The Emergence of Police Professionalism

A second reform effort emerged in the wake of the failure of the Progressives. Within police circles, a small cadre of chiefs sought and implemented a variety of innovations that would improve policing generally. From about 1910 to 1960 police chiefs carried on another reform movement, advocating that police adopt the professional model.

The professional department embodied a number of characteristics. First, the officers were experts; they applied knowledge to their tasks and were the only ones qualified to do the job. Second, the department was autonomous from external influences, such as political parties. This also meant that the department made its own rules and regulated its personnel. Finally, the department was administratively efficient, in that it carried out its mandate to enforce the law through modern technology and business-like practices. These reforms were similar to those of the Progressives, but because they came from within police organizations themselves, they met with more success.

Leadership and technology assisted the movement to professionalize the police. Chiefs like Richard Sylvester, August Vollmer, and O. W. Wilson emphasized the use of innovative methods in police work. Samuel Walker (1977) notes that Sylvester, the chief of the Washington, D.C., police, helped to establish the idea of professionalism among police chiefs. As president of the International Association of Chiefs of Police (IACP), Sylvester inculcated the spirit of reform into the organization. He stressed acceptance of technological innovations, raised the level of discussion among chiefs to include crime control ideas, and promoted professionalism generally.

The major innovator among the chiefs was August Vollmer, chief of the Berkeley, California, police. Vollmer was known for his pioneering work in developing college-level police education programs, bicycle and automobile patrols, and scientific crime detection aids. His department was the first to use forensic science in solving crimes.

Vollmer's emphasis on the quality of police personnel was tied closely to the idea of the professional officer. Becoming an expert in policing meant having the requisite credentials. Vollmer initiated intelligence, psychiatric, and neurological tests by which to select applicants. He was the first police chief to actively recruit college students. In addition, he was instrumental in linking the police department with the University of California at Berkeley. Another concern of Vollmer's dealt with the efficient delivery of police services. His department became the first in the nation to use automobiles and the first to hire a full-time forensic scientist to help solve crimes (Douthit, 1975).

O. W. Wilson, Vollmer's student, followed in his mentor's footsteps by advocating efficiency within the police bureaucracy through scientific techniques. As chief in Wichita, Kansas, Wilson conducted the first systematic study of one-officer squad cars. He argued that one-officer cars were efficient, effective, and economical. Despite arguments from patrol officers that their safety was at risk, Wilson claimed that the public received better service with single-officer cars.

Wilson's other contributions include his classic textbook, *Police Administration* which lays out specific ideas regarding the use of one-man patrol cars, deployment of personnel on the streets, disciplinary measures, and organizational structure. Later in his career, Wilson accepted a professorship at the University of California at Berkeley where he taught and trained law enforcement officers. In 1947 he founded the first professional school of criminology.

Other chiefs contributed to the professional movement as well. William Parker changed the Los Angeles Police Department (LAPD) from a corrupt, traditional agency to an innovative, professional organization. From 1950 to his death in 1966, Parker served as chief. He was known for his careful planning, emphasis on efficiency, and his rigorous personnel selection and training procedures. His public relations campaigns and adept political maneuvers enabled him to gain the respect of the media and community. As a result, the LAPD became a model for reform across the country.

Technological changes also enabled the police to move toward professionalism. The patrol car, two-way radio, and telephone altered the way in which the police operated and the manner in which citizens made use of the police. Motorized patrol meant more efficient coverage of the city and quicker response to calls for service. The two-way radio dramatically increased the supervisory capacity of the police; continuous contact between sergeant and patrol officer could be maintained. Finally, the telephone provided the link between the public and the police. Though not a new invention, its use in conjunction with the car and two-way radio meant that efficient responses to calls for service could be realized.

Overall, the second reform movement met with more success than the Progressive attempt, though it did not achieve its goal of professionalization. Walker (1977) and Fogelson (1977) agree that the quality of police officers greatly improved during this period. Police departments turned away the ill-educated individual, but at the same time failed to draw college graduates to their ranks. In terms of autonomy, police reformers and others were able to reduce the influence of political parties in departmental affairs. Chiefs obtained more power and authority in their management abilities, but continued to receive input from political leaders. In fact, most chiefs remained political appointees. In terms of efficiency, the police moved forward in serving the public more quickly and competently. Technological innovations clearly assisted the police in this area, as did streamlining the organizations themselves. However, the innovations also created problems. Citizens came to expect more from the police—faster response times, more arrests, and less overall crime. These expectations, as well as other difficulties, led to trying times for the police in the 1960s.

# VI. Riots and Renewal

Policing in America encountered its most serious crisis in the 1960s. The rise in crime, the civil rights movement, anti-war sentiment, and riots in the cities brought the police into the center of a maelstrom.

During the decade of the 1960s crime increased at a phenomenal rate. Between 1960 and 1970 the crime rate per 100,000 persons doubled. Most troubling was the increase in violent crime—the robbery rate almost tripled during these ten years. As crime increased, so did the demands for its reduction. The police, in emphasizing its crime fighting ability, had given the public a false expectation that crime and violence could be reduced. But with the added responsibility of more crime, the police were unable to live up to the expectation they had created. As a result, the public image of the police was tarnished.

The civil rights movement created additional demands for the police. The movement, which began in the 1950s, sought equality for black Americans in all facets of life. Sit-ins at segregated lunch counters, boycotts of bus services, attempts at integrating schools, and demonstrations in the streets led to direct confrontations with law enforcement officers. The police became the symbol of a society that denied blacks equal justice under the law.

Eventually, the frustrations of black Americans erupted into violence in northern and southern cities. Riots engulfed almost every major city between 1964 and 1968. Most of the disorders were initiated by a routine incident involving the police. The spark that ignited the riots occurred on July 16, 1964, when a white New York City police officer shot and killed a black teenager. Black leaders in the Harlem ghetto organized protests demanding disciplinary action against the officer. Two days later, the demonstrators marched on precinct headquarters, where rock-throwing began. Eventually, looting and burning erupted during the night and lasted for two full days. When the riot was brought under control one person was dead, more than 100 injured, almost 500 arrested, and millions of dollars worth of property destroyed. In the following year, the Watts riot in Los Angeles led to more devastation. Thirty-four persons died, a thousand were injured, and 4,000 arrested. By 1966, 43 more riots broke out across the country, and in 1967 violence in Newark and Detroit exceeded the 1965 Watts riot. Disorders engulfed Newark for five days, leaving 23 dead, while the Detroit riot a week later lasted nearly seven days and resulted in 43 deaths with $40 million in property damages.

On the final day of the Detroit riot, President Lyndon Johnson appointed a special commission to investigate the problem of civil disorder. The National Advisory Commission on Civil Disorders (The Kerner Commission) identified institutional racism as the underlying cause of the rioting. Unemployment, discrimination in jobs and housing, inadequate social services, and unequal justice at the hands of the law were among the problems cited by the commission.

Police actions were also cited as contributing to the disorders. Direct police intervention had sparked the riots in Harlem, Watts, Newark, and Detroit. In Watts and Newark the riots were set off by routine traffic stops. In Detroit a police raid on an after-hours bar in the ghetto touched off the disorders there. The police thus, became the focus of national attention.

The Kerner Commission and other investigations found several problems in police departments. First, police conduct included brutality, harassment, and abuse of power. Second, training and supervision was inadequate. Third, police-community relations were poor. Fourth, the employment of black officers lagged far behind the growth of the black population.

As a means of coping with these problems in policing (and other agencies of the criminal justice system) President Johnson created a crime commission and Congress authorized federal assistance to criminal justice. The President's crime commission produced a final report that emphasized the need for more research, higher qualifications of criminal justice personnel, and greater coordination of the national crime-control effort. The federal aid program to justice agencies resulted in the Office of Law Enforcement Assistance, a forerunner of the Law Enforcement Assistance Administration (LEAA).

## VII. The Legacy of the '60s

The events of the 1960s forced the police, politicians, and policymakers to re-assess the state of law enforcement in the United States. For the first time, academicians rushed to study the police in an effort to explain their problems and crises. With federal funding from LEAA and private organizations, researchers began to study the police from a number of perspectives. Sociologists, political scientists, psychologists, and historians began to scrutinize different aspects of policing. Traditional methods of patrol deployment, officer selection, and training were questioned. Racial discrimination in employment practices, in arrests, and in the use of deadly force were among the issues closely examined.

In addition, the professional movement itself came into question. As Walker notes, the legacy of professionalization was "ambiguous" (Walker, 1977:167). On one hand, the police made improvements in their level of service, training, recruitment, and efficiency. On the other hand, a number of problems remained and a number of new ones emerged. Corruption scandals continued to present problems. In New York, Chicago, and Denver systematic corruption was discovered. Political parties persisted in their links to policing.

The professional movement had two unintended consequences. The first involved the development of a police subculture. The second was the problem of police-community relations. In terms of the subculture, police officers began to feel alienated from administrators, the media, and the public and turned inward as a result. Patrol officers began to resent the police hierarchy because of the emphasis on following orders and regulations. While this established uniformity in performance and eliminated some abuses of power, it also stifled creativity and the talents of many officers. Rather than thinking for themselves (as professionals would) patrol officers followed orders given by sergeants, lieutenants, or other ranking officers. This led to morale problems and criticism of police administrators by the rank and file.

Patrol officers saw the media and the public as foes because of the criticism and disrespect cast their way. As the crime rate increased, newspaper accounts criticized the police for their inability to curtail it. As the riots persisted, some citizens cried for more order, while others demanded less oppression by the police on the streets. The conflicting messages given to the patrol officers by these groups led to distrust, alienation, and frustration. Only by standing together did officers feel comfortable in their working environment.

The second unintended consequence of professionalism was the problems it generated for police-community relations. Modern technology, like the patrol car, removed the officer from the street and eliminated routine contact with citizens. The impersonal style of professionalism often exacerbated police-community problems. Tactics such as aggressive patrol in black neighborhoods, designed to suppress crime efficiently, created more racial tensions.

These problems called into question the need for and effectiveness of professionalism. Some police administrators suggested abandoning the movement. Others sought to continue the effort while adjusting for and solving the difficulties. For the most part, the goal of professionalization remains operative. In the 1970s and 1980s, progressive police chiefs and organizations continue to press for innovations in policing. As a result, social science research has become an important part of policymaking decisions. By linking research to issues like domestic violence, repeat offenders, use of deadly force, training techniques, and selection procedures, police executives increase their ability to make effective decisions.

## Concluding Remarks

This chapter has examined the history of American police systems from the English heritage through the 20th century. Major emphasis has been placed on the police role, though important events that shaped the development of the police have also been discussed. As can be seen through this review, a number of present-day issues have their roots in different epochs of American history. For example, the idea of community policing can be traced to the colonial period and to medieval England. Preventive patrol, legitimacy, authority, and professionalism are 18th and 19th century concepts. Riots, disorders, and corruption are not new to American policing; similar events occurred in the 19th century. Thus, by virtue of studying history, we can give contextual meaning to current police problems, ideas, and situations. By looking at the past, present-day events can be better understood.

## Notes

1 This list of police histories is by no means a comprehensive one. A vast number of journal articles, books and dissertations have been written since the 1960s.

2 A number of scholars have examined the "police function," particularly in the last 20 or so years. Among the most well-known are Wilson (1968), Skolnick (1966), Bittner (1971), and Goldstein (1977). Each of these authors prescribes to a different view of what the police should and should not do.

## References

Alfers, Kenneth G. 1975. "The Washington Police: A History, 1800–1886." Ph.D. Dissertation. George Washington University.

Bittner, Egon. 1970. *The Functions of the Police in Modern Society*. Chevy Chase, Maryland: National Institute of Mental Health.

Cei, Louis B. 1975. "Law Enforcement in Richmond: A History of Police Community Relations, 1737–1974." Ph.D. Dissertation. Florida State University.

Critchley, T. A. 1967. *A History of Police in England and Wales*. Montclair, New Jersey: Patterson Smith.

Douthit, Nathan. 1975. "August Vollmer: Berkeley's First Chief of Police and the Emergence of Police Professionalism." *California Historical Quarterly* 54 Spring: 101–24.

Fogelson, Robert. 1977. *Big-City Police*. Cambridge: Harvard University Press.

Goldstein, Herman. 1977. *Policing a Free Society*. Cambridge: Ballinger Press.

Klockars, Carl. 1985. *The Idea of Police*. Beverly Hills: Sage Publications.

Lane, Roger. 1967. *Policing the City: Boston, 1822–1885*. Cambridge: Harvard University Press.

_____. 1980. "Urban Police and Crime in Nineteenth-Century America," in Michael Tonry and Norval Morris (eds.), *Crime and Justice: An Annual Review of Research*, Vol. 2. Chicago: University of Chicago Press.

Litwack, Leon. 1961. *North of Slavery*. Chicago: University of Chicago Press.

Maniha, John K. 1970. "The Mobility of Elites in a Bureaucratizing Organization: The St. Louis Police Department, 1861–1961." Ph.D. Dissertation. University of Michigan.

Miller, Wilbur R. 1977. *Cops and Bobbies: Police Authority in New York and London, 1830–1870*. Chicago: University of Chicago Press.

Monkkonen, Eric H. 1981. *Police in Urban America, 1860–1920*. Cambridge: Cambridge University Press.

Radzinowicz, Leon. 1948–1968. *History of the English Criminal Law*, Vol. 1–4. New York: MacMillan.

Reichard, Maximilian I. 1975. "The Origins of Urban Police: Freedom and Order in Antebellum St. Louis." Ph.D. Dissertation. Washington University.

Reith, Charles. 1956. *A New Study of Police History*. Edinburgh.

Richardson, James F. 1970. *The New York Police: Colonial Times to 1901*. New York: Oxford University Press.

_____. 1974. *Urban Police in the United States*. Port Washington, New York: Kennikat Press.

Rider, Eugene F. 1971. "The Denver Police Department: An Administrative, Organizational, and Operational History, 1858–1905." Ph.D. Dissertation. University of Denver.

Schneider, John C. 1980. *Detroit and the Problems of Order, 1830–1880*. Lincoln: University of Nebraska Press.

Skolnick, Jerome. 1966. *Justice Without Trial: Law Enforcement in Democratic Society*. New York: John Wiley and Sons.

Walker, Samuel. 1977. *A Critical History of Police Reform: The Emergence of Professionalism*. Lexington, Massachusetts: D.C. Heath and Company.

Wilson, James Q. 1968. *Varieties of Police Behavior: The Management of Law and Order in Eight Communities*. Cambridge: Harvard University Press.

# 3

# LEMAS Reports—1993

*U.S. Department of Justice*

## Local Police Departments

During 1993, the Bureau of Justice Statistics (BJS) as a part of its Law Enforcement Management and Administrative Statistics (LEMAS) program, surveyed a nationally representative sample of the more than 17,000 state and local law enforcement agencies operating nationwide. This report presents data describing the more than 12,000 general purpose local police departments operated by municipal or county governments in terms of their personnel, expenditures and pay, operations, equipment, computers and information systems, and policies.

This is the third LEMAS survey. Data from the previous surveys in 1987 and 1990 are used for comparison purposes in this report. Major findings include the following:

- As of June 30, 1993, local police departments in the United States had an estimated 474,072 full-time employees, 3 percent more than in 1990. Among this total were 373,554 sworn personnel, including approximately 230,000 uniformed officers whose regularly assigned duties included responding to calls for service.
- About 80 percent of U.S. residents were served by a local police department at either the municipal or county level, and there were approximately 21 full-time local police officers employed for every 10,000 residents served.
- For fiscal year 1993, local police departments had total operating expenditures of $24.3 billion, compared to $20.6 billion in 1990, a 6 percent increase after controlling for inflation. Operating expenditures averaged $62,600 per sworn officer, $48,200 per employee, and $131 per resident for 1993.

Excerpted from Brian A. Reaves, *Bureau of Justice Statistics Local Police Departments*, (Washington, D.C.: U.S. Department of Justice, April 1996) and Brian A. Reaves and Pheny Z. Smith, *Bureau of Justice Statistics Sheriffs' Departments 1993* (Washington, D.C.: U.S. Department of Justice, June 1996).

- Women comprised 8.8 percent of all full-time local police officers in 1993, compared to 8.1 percent in 1990 and 7.6 percent in 1987. Black officers accounted for 11.3 percent of the total in 1993, compared to 10.5 percent in 1990 and 9.3 percent in 1987. The percentage of Hispanic officers was 6.2 percent in 1993, up from 5.2 percent in 1990 and 4.5 percent in 1987.

- Twelve percent of local police departments required new officer recruits to have at least some college education in 1993, compared to about 6 percent in 1990. Eight percent of departments had some type of degree requirement, with 1 percent requiring a 4-year degree.

- The average number of training hours required of new local police officer recruits in 1993 ranged from over 1,100 hours in departments serving a population of 100,000 or more to under 500 in those serving fewer than 2,500 residents.

- Eighty-four percent of local police departments authorized their regular field officers to use semiautomatic sidearms in 1993, up from 73 percent in 1990. Departments authorizing semiautomatic sidearms employed 96 percent of all local police officers in 1993, compared to 91 percent in 1990.

- In 1993, a third of all local police departments, including nearly half of those serving a population of 1 million or more, required all regular field officers to wear protective body armor while on duty. Departments with such a requirement employed 41 percent of all local police officers in 1993, compared to 32 percent in 1990.

- Nearly all local police departments authorized the use of one or more types of impact devices as a nonlethal weapon, most commonly in the form of a PR-24 baton (59 percent) or traditional baton (58 percent). Three-fourths of departments authorized the use of chemical agents, with pepper spray (59 percent) the type most commonly authorized.

- Sixty-eight percent of local police departments participated in a 911 emergency telephone system during 1993, and 41 percent had an enhanced 911 system. Departments with a 911 system employed 89 percent of all local police officers in 1993, compared to 65 percent in 1990.

- In addition to traditional law enforcement duties, some local police departments were responsible for court-related functions such as providing court security (19 percent) or serving civil process (11 percent), and 5 percent operated a jail. Among the numerous other special functions performed by local police departments were animal control (49 percent), and emergency medical services (20 percent).

- Two-thirds of local police departments were using computers in 1993, compared to half in 1990. Departments using computers employed 95 percent of all local police officers in 1993. Departments that used laptop computers or mobile terminals employed twice as many officers in 1993 (60 percent) as in 1990 (30 percent).

## Personnel

During 1993 an estimated 17,120 publicly funded state and local law enforcement agencies were operating in the United States (table 1). The estimated 12,361 general purpose local police departments accounted for 72 percent of this total. Municipal governments operated over 99 percent of these local police departments. Although county police departments comprised less than 1 percent of all local police departments, they employed about 7 percent of all local police officers.

**Table 1    Employment by state and local law enforcement agencies in the United States, 1993**

| Type of agency | Number of agencies | Number of employees | | | | | |
| | | Full-time | | | Part-time | | |
| | | Total | Sworn | Civilian | Total | Sworn | Civilian |
|---|---|---|---|---|---|---|---|
| Total | 17,120 | 828,435 | 622,913 | 205,522 | 87,875 | 42,890 | 44,985 |
| Local police | 12,361 | 474,072 | 373,554 | 100,518 | 58,146 | 28,186 | 29,960 |
| Sheriff | 3,084 | 224,236 | 155,815 | 68,421 | 19,660 | 11,048 | 8,612 |
| State police | 49 | 76,972 | 51,874 | 25,098 | 845 | 228 | 617 |
| Special police | 1,626 | 53,156 | 41,670 | 11,485 | 9,224 | 3,428 | 5,796 |

Note: Consolidated police-sheriff agencies are included under the local police category.
The special police category includes both State-level and local-level agencies.
Data are for the pay period that included June 30, 1993.

Local police departments employed an estimated 474,072 persons full time and another 58,146 on a part-time basis as of June 30, 1993. An estimated 373,554 (79 percent) of full-time local police employees were sworn officers, representing 60 percent of all full-time state and local sworn personnel nationwide. Local police departments had an estimated 100,518 full-time civilian employees in 1993, about half of all full-time state and local civilian law enforcement employees nationwide.

The number of local police employees in 1993 was up by about 14,000, or 3.1 percent, from 1990 and by about 27,000, or 6.1 percent, compared to 1987. For all state and local law enforcement agencies, there was an increase of about 35,000, or 4.5 percent, over 1990 levels and 69,000, or 9.2 percent, compared to 1987.

While 38 local police departments employed 1,000 or more sworn officers, nearly 6,400 (52 percent of all departments) employed fewer than 10 officers (table 2). Nearly twice as many departments employed only 1 full-time or part-time officer as employed 100 or more officers (7 percent versus 4 percent).

Table 2   Local police departments, by number of sworn personnel, 1993

| Number of sworn personnel* | Agencies | | Full-time sworn personnel | |
|---|---|---|---|---|
| | Number | Percent | Number | Percent |
| Total | 12,361 | 100% | 373,554 | 100% |
| 1,000 or more | 38 | 0.3% | 118,460 | 31.7% |
| 500-999 | 38 | 0.3 | 27,351 | 7.3 |
| 250-499 | 86 | 0.7 | 29,344 | 7.9 |
| 100-249 | 326 | 2.6 | 46,983 | 12.6 |
| 50-99 | 692 | 5.6 | 45,779 | 12.3 |
| 25-49 | 1,443 | 11.7 | 45,160 | 12.1 |
| 10-24 | 3,361 | 27.2 | 40,913 | 11.0 |
| 5-9 | 2,940 | 23.8 | 13,906 | 3.7 |
| 2-4 | 2,587 | 20.9 | 5,065 | 1.4 |
| 1 | 851 | 6.9 | 594 | 0.2 |

Note: Detail may not add to total because of rounding.
*Includes both full-time and part-time employees.

Despite the large number of small police departments, they accounted for a small proportion of local police officers. Just 1 in 19 full-time local police officers were employed by a department with fewer than 10 sworn employees. In contrast, about 3 in 5 worked for a department with 100 or more officers, and nearly 1 in 3 worked for a department with 1,000 or more officers.

About half of all full-time local police officers worked for a department serving a population of 100,000 or more, and a fifth were employed by the 12 departments that served a population of 1 million or more (table 3). About 1 in 7 officers were employed by the more than 9,000 departments serving a population under 10,000.

On average, departments serving a population of 1 million or more had about 8,000 full-time employees, including about 6,300 full-time sworn officers. These departments did not employ any part-time officers. Departments in the smallest towns (under 2,500 in population) employed an average of 3 full-time sworn officers, and 2 part-time officers.

On average, local police departments employed about 2.1 full-time officers for every 1,000 residents. By population category, this ratio ranged from 1.7 for departments serving 50,000 to 99,999 residents to 2.6 among departments serving a population of 1 million or more.

### Duties of sworn personnel.

*Departments with 100 or more officers.* About 10 percent of the officers in departments with 100 or more sworn personnel primarily performed duties outside the area of field operations. About half of these offic-

Table 3   Local police departments and full-time sworn personnel, by size of population served, 1993

| Population served | Agencies | | Full-time sworn personnel | |
|---|---|---|---|---|
| | Number | Percent | Number | Percent |
| All sizes | 12,361 | 100% | 373,554 | 100% |
| 1,000,000 or more | 12 | 0.1% | 75,496 | 20.2% |
| 500,000-999,999 | 27 | 0.2 | 37,856 | 10.1 |
| 250,000-499,999 | 45 | 0.4 | 33,261 | 8.9 |
| 100,000-249,999 | 147 | 1.2 | 39,057 | 10.5 |
| 50,000-99,999 | 340 | 2.7 | 40,493 | 10.8 |
| 25,000-49,999 | 703 | 5.7 | 42,864 | 11.5 |
| 10,000-24,999 | 1,662 | 13.4 | 47,405 | 12.7 |
| 2,500-9,999 | 4,099 | 33.2 | 42,879 | 11.5 |
| Under 2,500 | 5,327 | 43.1 | 14,243 | 3.8 |

Note: Detail may not add to total because of rounding.

ers worked in administrative areas (5 percent), including finance, personnel, and internal affairs.

Another 4 percent of the officers in these larger departments provided technical support services. These sworn personnel primarily performed duties related to dispatch, recordkeeping, data processing, communications, fleet management, and training.

Among the 90 percent of officers classified as working in field operations, an estimated 3 in 4 were uniformed officers whose regularly assigned duties included responding to calls for service. The other fourth included supervisors and those whose primary duties were investigative in nature, such as detectives. Other examples of field operation officers whose primary duties did not include responding to calls for service included those assigned to special operations or traffic-related duties.

*All departments.* Overall, an estimated 252,000 local police officers, 67 percent of all such officers nationwide, were uniformed personnel whose regularly assigned duties included responding to calls for service.

The percentage of full-time sworn personnel in local police departments who were uniformed officers assigned to respond to calls for service was highest in jurisdictions with fewer than 25,000 residents.

Possible explanations for this pattern include the fact that smaller departments have less need for administrative personnel such as those handling budgetary and personnel matters. Smaller departments also tend to be less technologically advanced and may need fewer employees for technical support duties related to computerized functions. Smaller departments also often rely on larger departments for their training needs rather than employ personnel to handle such duties.

**Table 4   Sex of full-time sworn personnel in local police departments, by size of population served, 1993**

| Population served | All sworn employees | | |
|---|---|---|---|
| | Total | Male | Female |
| All sizes | 100% | 91.2% | 8.8% |
| 1,000,000 or more | 100% | 85.4% | 14.6% |
| 500,000-999,999 | 100 | 87.6 | 12.4 |
| 250,000-499,999 | 100 | 88.1 | 11.9 |
| 100,000-249,999 | 100 | 91.0 | 9.0 |
| 50,000-99,999 | 100 | 93.0 | 7.0 |
| 25,000-49,999 | 100 | 94.8 | 5.2 |
| 10,000-24,999 | 100 | 95.0 | 5.0 |
| 2,500-9,999 | 100 | 95.6 | 4.4 |
| Under 2,500 | 100 | 97.2 | 2.8 |

Note: Detail may not add to total because of rounding.

In some small departments it may also be more common for sworn personnel to handle multiple areas of responsibility, including but not limited to responding to calls for service.

### Race and sex of officers.

Women comprised 8.8 percent of all local police officers nationwide in 1993 (table 4). The percentage of women officers was highest in large jurisdictions, including 15 percent of officers in jurisdictions of 1 million or more in population, and 12 percent in jurisdictions with at least 250,000 residents but fewer than 1 million. About 3 percent of officers in departments serving fewer than 2,500 residents were women, as were about 5 percent of those serving a population of at least 2,500 but less than 50,000.

The estimated 32,849 female local police officers employed in 1993 represented an increase of about 3,500 over the number in 1990 and about 5,800 over 1987. Women also comprised a higher percentage of the total local police force in 1993 (8.8 percent) than in 1990 (8.1 percent) or 1987 (7.6 percent).

About 302,000, or 81 percent, of full-time local police officers were non-Hispanic whites in 1993 (table 5). This represented a decrease from 1990 (83 percent) and 1987 (85 percent). The number of white male local police officers in 1993 was estimated to be 281,057, a decrease of about 20,000 from 1990 and about 22,000 from 1987. In contrast, the estimated 71,244 minority officers in 1993 was larger than the 61,710 in 1990 and the 51,872 in 1987.

The estimated 42,212 black local police officers in 1993 represented an increase of about 4,000 over 1990 and about 9,000 over 1987. The percentage of local police officers who were black was 11.3 percent in 1993, compared to 10.5 percent in 1990 and 9.3 percent in 1987.

Hispanics also comprised a larger percentage of local police officers in 1993 (6.2 percent) than in earlier years (5.2 percent in 1990, 4.5 percent in 1987). The number of Hispanic officers in 1993 (23,309) was 23 percent greater than in 1990 (18,876) and 46 percent greater than in 1987 (15,988).

Table 5 Race and ethnicity of full-time sworn personnel in local police departments, by size of population served, 1993

| Population served | Total | Percent of full-time sworn employees who are: | | | | | | | | | | | |
|---|---|---|---|---|---|---|---|---|---|---|---|---|---|
| | | White | | | Black | | | Hispanic | | | Other | | |
| | | Total | Male | Female | Total | Male | Female | Total | Male | Female | Total | Male | Female |
| All sizes | 100% | 80.9% | 75.2% | 5.7% | 11.3% | 9.1% | 2.2% | 6.2% | 5.5% | .7% | 1.5% | 1.4% | .1% |
| 1,000,000 or more | 100% | 69.2% | 61.7% | 7.5% | 17.7% | 12.8% | 4.9% | 12.0% | 10.0% | 2.0% | 1.2% | 1.0% | .2% |
| 500,000-999,999 | 100 | 66.2 | 60.1 | 6.1 | 21.0 | 16.1 | 5.0 | 7.0 | 6.1 | .9 | 5.8 | 5.4 | .4 |
| 250,000-499,999 | 100 | 71.9 | 64.5 | 7.4 | 17.7 | 14.3 | 3.4 | 9.0 | 8.2 | .9 | 1.4 | 1.2 | .2 |
| 100,000-249,999 | 100 | 80.6 | 74.2 | 6.3 | 12.4 | 10.4 | 2.1 | 5.4 | 4.9 | .4 | 1.6 | 1.5 | .1 |
| 50,000-99,999 | 100 | 86.3 | 80.7 | 5.5 | 7.2 | 6.3 | .9 | 5.1 | 4.7 | .5 | 1.4 | 1.3 | .1 |
| 25,000-49,999 | 100 | 89.8 | 85.1 | 4.6 | 5.4 | 5.0 | .5 | 4.3 | 4.1 | .2 | .6 | .6 | -- |
| 10,000-24,999 | 100 | 91.6 | 87.1 | 4.5 | 5.1 | 4.8 | .3 | 2.6 | 2.5 | .1 | .6 | .6 | -- |
| 2,500-9,999 | 100 | 92.8 | 88.9 | 3.9 | 4.1 | 3.8 | .3 | 2.6 | 2.4 | .1 | .5 | .5 | -- |
| Under 2,500 | 100 | 91.7 | 89.3 | 2.3 | 5.3 | 5.0 | .3 | 1.9 | 1.8 | .1 | 1.2 | 1.1 | .1 |

Note: Detail may not add to total because of rounding.
-- Less than .05%.
*Includes Asians, Pacific Islanders, American Indians, and Alaska Natives.

Table 6　Minimum educational requirement for new officer recruits in local police departments, by size of population served, 1993

| Population served | Total with requirement | Percent of agencies requiring a minimum of: | | | |
|---|---|---|---|---|---|
| | | High school diploma | Some college* | 2-year college degree | 4-year college degree |
| All sizes | 97% | 86% | 4% | 7% | 1% |
| 1,000,000 or more | 100% | 75% | 25% | 0% | 0% |
| 500,000-999,999 | 100 | 85 | 11 | 4 | 0 |
| 250,000-499,999 | 98 | 73 | 13 | 9 | 0 |
| 100,000-249,999 | 100 | 81 | 9 | 3 | 2 |
| 50,000-99,999 | 100 | 72 | 11 | 17 | 7 |
| 25,000-49,999 | 100 | 78 | 9 | 9 | 1 |
| 10,000-24,999 | 98 | 84 | 5 | 7 | 4 |
| 2,500-9,999 | 100 | 90 | 2 | 7 | 3 |
| Under 2,500 | 94 | 85 | 4 | 5 | 1 |

Note: Detail may not add to total because of rounding.
*Nondegree requirements

**Education and training requirements for new officers.** Nearly all (97 percent) local police departments had a formal education requirement for new officer recruits (table 6). The typical minimum educational requirement for new local police officers was completion of high school (86 percent). In 1993, 12 percent of local police departments, twice as many as in 1990, required at least some college coursework. About 1 percent required new officers to have a 4-year college degree, and 7 percent required a 2-year degree.

Ninety-nine percent of all local police officers were employed by a department that required at least a high school diploma of new recruits, and 15 percent worked for a department that required at least some college.

In 90 percent of local police departments, employing 99 percent of all local police officers, new officer recruits were required to complete formal training (table 7). Nearly all (95 percent) of the departments serving a population of 2,500 or more required training, while 83 percent of the departments in towns of under 2,500 had a training requirement.

On average, local police departments required 640 training hours of their new officer recruits, including 425 classroom training hours and 215 field training hours. Training requirements were more stringent in larger jurisdictions than smaller ones—ranging from over 1,100 total hours in departments serving a population of 100,000 or more to under 500 hours in jurisdictions with fewer than 2,500 residents.

The average number of required classroom training hours was highest in departments serving 1 million or more residents (865 hours), while the most field training was required by departments serving a population

| Table 7 Training requirements for new officer recruits in local police departments, by size of population served, 1993 | | | |
|---|---|---|---|
| | | Average number of hours required | |
| | Percent of agencies requiring | | |
| Population served | training | Class-room | Field |
| All sizes | 90% | 425 | 215 |
| 1,000,000 or more | 100% | 865 | 311 |
| 500,000-999,999 | 100 | 757 | 396 |
| 250,000-499,999 | 100 | 727 | 551 |
| 100,000-249,999 | 99 | 630 | 498 |
| 50,000-99,999 | 100 | 494 | 435 |
| 25,000-49,999 | 100 | 492 | 393 |
| 10,000-24,999 | 98 | 468 | 305 |
| 2,500-9,999 | 93 | 455 | 204 |
| Under 2,500 | 83 | 352 | 105 |

Note: Computation of average number of training hours required excludes departments not requiring training.

of 250,000 to 499,999 (551 hours). When departments are weighted according to number of officers employed, it is estimated that the average new local police recruit in 1993 was required to undergo nearly 1,000 hours of training, with two-thirds of it in the classroom.

*Applicant and employee drug testing.* Twenty-eight percent of local police departments, employing 64 percent of all local police officers, required that all applicants for sworn positions be tested for illegal drug use (table 8). A majority of the departments serving a population of 50,000 or more required a drug test of all officer applicants, as did about half of those in jurisdictions with at least 10,000 but fewer than 50,000 residents. Departments in small jurisdictions were the least likely to test all officer applicants for drugs: 28 percent of departments serving a population of 2,500 to 9,999 and 15 percent of those serving fewer than 2,500 residents had such a requirement.

Overall, about a fourth of local police departments had a drug testing program for their regular field officers, and a majority (58 percent) of local police officers were employed by a department that had some type of drug testing program for regular field officers.

Unlike applicant testing programs, testing requirements for regular field officers were rarely mandatory. Just 3 percent of local police departments, employing 4 percent of all officers, had a mandatory requirement that all regular field officers be tested for drugs. Most common was a drug testing program that required testing of officers suspected of using illegal drugs—16 percent of local police departments employing 43 percent of all officers had such a drug testing program. Half this many departments had a random selection drug testing program (8 percent). Departments with random selection drug testing for regular field officers employed 28 percent of all local police officers.

## Expenditures and Pay

*Operating expenditures.* The total annual operating expenditure by local police departments during fiscal year 1993 was $24.3 billion, an

Table 8  Drug testing of applicants for sworn positions and regular field officers in local police departments, by size of population served, 1993

| Personnel category and population served | Percent of agencies with a drug testing program | | | |
|---|---|---|---|---|
| | Any type of testing program | Mandatory (all are tested) | Random selection process | Use of drugs is suspected |
| **Applicants for sworn positions** | | | | |
| All sizes | 33% | 28% | 3% | 5% |
| 1,000,000 or more | 92% | 83% | 8 | 7 |
| 500,000-999,999 | 70 | 66 | 7 | 7 |
| 250,000-499,999 | 89 | 87 | 2 | 7 |
| 100,000-249,999 | 68 | 64 | 1 | 6 |
| 50,000-99,999 | 60 | 56 | 2 | 11 |
| 25,000-49,999 | 53 | 50 | – | 5 |
| 10,000-24,999 | 52 | 49 | 2 | 6 |
| 2,500-9,999 | 32 | 28 | 3 | 5 |
| Under 2,500 | 22 | 15 | 5 | 5 |
| **Regular field/patrol officers** | | | | |
| All sizes | 24% | 3% | 8% | 16% |
| 1,000,000 or more | 92% | 0% | 58% | 75% |
| 500,000-999,999 | 59 | 4 | 26 | 51 |
| 250,000-499,999 | 84 | 4 | 35 | 73 |
| 100,000-249,999 | 62 | 3 | 29 | 48 |
| 50,000-99,999 | 46 | 2 | 13 | 39 |
| 25,000-49,999 | 42 | 2 | 6 | 36 |
| 10,000-24,999 | 34 | 2 | 6 | 29 |
| 2,500-9,999 | 27 | 4 | 10 | 17 |
| Under 2,500 | 14 | 3 | 6 | 6 |

–Less than .5%.
Note: Some agencies had more than 1 type of testing program.

increase of 18 percent over 1990. After controlling for inflation, the increase was about 6 percent. These figures do not include capital expenditures such as those for equipment purchases or construction projects. Local police accounted for 58 percent of the $41.9 billion in total operating expenditures for all state and local law enforcement agencies during fiscal year 1993.

Local police operating expenditures averaged about $2 million per department, ranging from an average of about $427,000,000 for departments serving a population of 1 million or more, to $107,000 in those serving fewer than 2,500 residents (table 9).

Overall, the operation of local police departments for the year cost $131 per resident served. Departments serving a population of 1 million or more cost the most to operate, about $194 per resident, and those in

**Table 9   Operating expenditures of local police departments, by size of population served, 1993**

| Population served | Operating expenditures, fiscal year 1993 | | | | |
| --- | --- | --- | --- | --- | --- |
| | Total | Per agency | Per sworn officer | Per employee | Per resident |
| All sizes | $24,263,852,000 | $1,963,000 | $62,600 | $48,200 | $131 |
| 1,000,000 or more | $5,121,639,000 | $426,803,000 | $67,800 | $52,200 | $194 |
| 500,000-999,999 | 2,923,851,000 | 108,291,000 | 77,200 | 58,600 | 148 |
| 250,000-499,999 | 2,258,447,000 | 50,188,000 | 67,700 | 50,100 | 141 |
| 100,000-249,999 | 2,768,374,000 | 18,832,000 | 70,600 | 52,000 | 129 |
| 50,000-99,999 | 2,870,655,000 | 8,443,000 | 70,400 | 52,100 | 124 |
| 25,000-49,999 | 2,823,516,000 | 4,028,000 | 64,600 | 50,400 | 116 |
| 10,000-24,999 | 2,709,979,000 | 1,631,000 | 54,900 | 43,400 | 104 |
| 2,500-9,999 | 2,215,401,000 | 540,000 | 45,800 | 36,600 | 101 |
| Under 2,500 | 571,991,000 | 107,000 | 29,400 | 25,300 | 88 |

Note: Figures are for fiscal year ending June 30, 1993, or the most recent fiscal year completed prior to that date. Figures do not include capital expenditures such as equipment purchases or construction costs. Computation of per officer and per employee averages include both full-time and part-time employees, with a weight of 0.5 assigned to part-time employees. Total and per agency figures are rounded to the nearest $1,000, per officer and per employee figures to the nearest $100, and per resident figures to the nearest $1.

the smallest jurisdictions (under 2,500 residents) cost the least, $88 per resident.

Nationwide, local police departments cost about $63,000 per sworn officer to operate for the year, with departments serving a population of 50,000 or more costing more than this, and departments serving fewer than 25,000 residents costing less. Departments serving a population of 500,000 to 999,999 had the highest per-officer operating expenditure, about $77,000. This was more than twice the per officer expenditure for departments serving fewer than 2,500 residents ($29,400).

After controlling for inflation, per officer operating costs were up from about $67,000 in 1990 to about $70,000 in 1993 for departments serving a population of 250,000 or more. A similar increase was seen among departments serving 10,000 to 49,999 residents (from $57,000 to $59,000) and departments serving fewer than 10,000 residents (from $39,000 to $41,000). Departments serving a population of 50,000 to 249,999 experienced the largest increase, from $62,000 per officer in 1990 to $70,000 per officer in 1993.

**Salaries.** The average base starting salary offered by local police departments to entry-level officers was $21,300 in 1993 (table 10). This was an increase of 12.6 percent compared with 1990, or 1.9 percent after controlling for inflation. Departments in jurisdictions with 10,000 or more residents had an average starting salary that was higher than the overall average, ranging from $24,600 (population served of 10,000 to 24,999) to $28,200 (population served of 1 million or more). The average for departments serving a population of 2,500 to 9,999 was about the same as the overall average, and departments serving a population under 2,500 paid

Table 10    Average base starting salary for selected positions in local police departments, by size of population served, 1993

| Population served | Average base starting salary, 1993 | | |
| --- | --- | --- | --- |
| | Entry-level officer | Sergeant | Chief of police |
| All sizes | $21,300 | $28,500 | $34,600 |
| 1,000,000 or more | $28,200 | $44,600 | $91,700 |
| 500,000-999,999 | 28,000 | 39,100 | 78,400 |
| 250,000-499,999 | 27,000 | 37,600 | 68,900 |
| 100,000-249,999 | 27,800 | 37,800 | 64,900 |
| 50,000-99,999 | 28,000 | 39,500 | 62,300 |
| 25,000-49,999 | 26,900 | 37,300 | 54,900 |
| 10,000-24,999 | 24,600 | 33,400 | 47,100 |
| 2,500-9,999 | 21,200 | 27,500 | 34,700 |
| Under 2,500 | 17,400 | 20,800 | 22,900 |

Note: Salary figures have been rounded to the nearest $100. Computation of average salary excludes agencies with no full-time employee in that position.

entry-level officers an average starting salary of $17,400 per year, about $4,000 below the overall average. When departments are weighted according to number of officers employed, the average entry-level salary for local police officers in 1993 was about $26,000.

By department, the average starting salary for sergeants was $28,500, with sergeants in the largest jurisdictions starting at $44,600 on average, about twice as much as in departments in the smallest jurisdictions ($20,800).

The overall average base starting salary for chiefs of local police departments was $34,600; however, the chiefs of departments in jurisdictions with 10,000 or more residents had an average starting salary that was considerably higher. The average starting salary for local police chiefs was highest in jurisdictions with 1 million or more residents ($91,700) and lowest in departments serving a population of under 2,500 ($22,900).

## Operations

*Crime investigation.* Nearly all local police departments had primary responsibility for investigating at least some types of crimes occurring in their jurisdiction. All departments in jurisdictions with a population of 250,000 or more had primary responsibility for investigating homicides and other violent crimes such as rape, robbery, or assault. Nearly all departments serving a population of 10,000 or more had primary responsibility for homicide investigation, but 11 percent of those serving a population of 2,500 to 9,999 and 30 percent of those serving fewer than 2,500 residents reported they did not have primary responsibility for such investigations. In jurisdictions under 2,500 in population, about 1 in 7 local police departments did not have primary responsibility for the investigation of any violent crimes.

About three-fourths of all local police departments had the primary role in arson investigations. Nearly all departments had primary responsibility for the investigation of other property crimes such as burglary, motor vehicle theft, or larceny. By population category, departments in jurisdictions with fewer than 2,500 residents were the least likely to have primary investigative responsibility for arson (66 percent) or other property crimes (94 percent).

*Investigative support functions.* A majority of the departments serving a population of 10,000 or more were responsible for fingerprint processing, including over three-fourths of those serving a population of 50,000 or more. About three-fourths of local police officers nationwide were employed by a department that was responsible for fingerprint processing.

Overall, few local police departments were responsible for laboratory testing of substances (2 percent) or ballistics testing (1 percent); however, 75 percent of departments serving a population of 1 million or more were responsible for these functions, as were over 40 percent of the departments in jurisdictions with 250,000 to 999,999 residents.

*Drug and vice enforcement.* Eighty percent of all local police departments, including over 90 percent of those serving 25,000 or more residents, had primary drug enforcement responsibility in their jurisdiction. These departments employed 93 percent of all local police officers. Departments in jurisdictions of less than 2,500 in population (72 percent) were the least likely to have primary drug enforcement responsibility. In some cases, departments without primary drug enforcement responsibility reported they shared that responsibility with other law enforcement agencies. Often this was through participation in a multi-agency drug enforcement task force.

About half of all local police departments were responsible for vice enforcement, including over 90 percent of the departments serving a population of 50,000 or more. Departments in jurisdictions with fewer than 2,500 residents (33 percent) were the least likely to have vice enforcement responsibilities. Overall, local police departments responsible for vice enforcement employed 86 percent of all local police officers.

*Patrol and response.* Ninety-seven percent of local police departments, including all those serving a population of 50,000 or more, provided routine patrol services for their jurisdiction. At least 95 percent of the departments in all population categories provided patrol services, and 99.6 percent of all local police officers worked for a department with routine patrol responsibilities.

Nearly all (93 percent) local police departments reported they had primary responsibility for receiving calls for service from citizens. The percentage of departments that handled service calls directly was at least 90 percent in all population categories, and 97 percent of all officers were employed by these departments.

About half of local police departments had responsibility for dispatching calls for service to officers in the field. Police departments in larger jurisdictions were the most likely to perform dispatch services. Over

90 percent of those serving a population of 250,000 or more were responsible for dispatching calls for service, as were over 80 percent of those serving at least 10,000 but fewer than 250,000 residents. Nearly two-thirds of the departments serving 2,500 to 9,999 residents (63 percent) had dispatch responsibilities, while a fourth of the departments serving fewer than 2,500 residents had primary responsibility for dispatching calls for service.

*911 Emergency telephone system.* In 1993 about two-thirds of all local police departments participated in an emergency telephone system whereby one of their units could be dispatched in response to a citizen call to 911 or its equivalent. This was a significant increase from 1990 when about half of all departments had a 911 system, and twice the proportion of agencies reporting 911 participation in 1987. Local police departments with a 911 system employed 89 percent of all officers in 1993, compared to 65 percent in 1990.

In contrast to 1990, a majority of the departments with a 911 system in 1993 reported their system was an enhanced system, capable of pinpointing the location of a caller automatically. In 1993, enhanced 911 systems were operating in 41 percent of all local police departments, while 27 percent reported they had a basic 911 system. In 1990, 18 percent had an enhanced system and 30 percent a basic system.

*Traffic-related functions.* Nearly all local police departments were responsible for traffic-related functions such as enforcement of traffic laws (99 percent), accident investigation (98 percent), or traffic direction and control (90 percent). In all population categories, at least 97 percent of the departments were responsible for enforcing traffic laws and investigating accidents. At least 93 percent of the departments in each population category from 2,500 to 249,999 were responsible for traffic direction and control.

*Jail- and court-related functions.* Nationwide, 5 percent of local police departments, employing 11 percent of all local police officers, operated a jail in 1993. Nearly a fourth of departments serving a jurisdiction with 100,000 to 499,999 residents operated a jail. Nearly 1 in 5 local police departments provided court security, and about 1 in 9 served civil process papers such as summonses.

*Lockup facilities.* In addition to various law enforcement functions, local police departments in some jurisdictions were also responsible for functions related to jail or court operations. About 1 in 4 local police departments were operating at least one lockup facility in 1993. Lockup facilities are temporary holding facilities operated separately from a jail with a limited holding time. An average maximum holding time of 22 hours was reported by the local police departments that operated a lockup facility.

A majority of the departments serving a population of 500,000 or more and those serving a population of 10,000 to 49,999 were operating at least 1 lockup facility. Departments serving a population of under 2,500 (6 percent) were the least likely to be operating a lockup. Overall, 41 percent of local police officers were employed by a department that operated at least one lockup.

*Special public safety functions.* Another important area of responsibility for many local police departments involves the performance of special functions related to public safety. Examples of such functions include animal control, search-and-rescue operations, emergency medical services, civil defense, and fire services.

Of these functions, the one performed by the most local police departments in 1993 was animal control. A third of all local police departments, employing two-fifths of all officers, were responsible for performing search-and-rescue operations. Twenty percent of local police departments were the primary provider of emergency medical services in their jurisdiction; however, no departments serving a population of 250,000 to 499,999 had this responsibility. About 16 percent of local police departments were responsible for civil defense functions in their jurisdiction. In about 9 percent of local police departments, fire services were a part of the agency's overall responsibility; however, no departments serving a population of 250,000 or more provided fire services.

*Training academy operation.* An important area of responsibility for about 600 local police departments nationwide was the operation of a training academy. Although just 5 percent of all local police departments operated a training academy, these departments employed 46 percent of all local police officers. A large majority of departments serving a population of 250,000 or more operated a training academy, as did about half of those in jurisdictions with 100,000 to 249,999 residents. Less than 10 percent of local police departments serving a population of under 50,000 operated a training academy.

## Equipment

*Sidearms.* In 1993, 84 percent of local police departments, employing 96 percent of all local police officers, authorized the use of some type of semiautomatic weapon as an officer sidearm.

Well over 90 percent of departments serving a population of 25,000 or more authorized semiautomatic weapons in 1993, as did 90 percent of those serving a population of 2,500 to 24,999. Departments serving a population of under 2,500 (73 percent) were the least likely to authorize the use of semiautomatic sidearms by officers.

As in 1990, the 9mm semiautomatic was the most popular type of local police sidearm, with 69 percent of departments authorizing its use by officers. Thirty-one percent of departments authorized .45-caliber semiautomatic sidearms. Smaller percentages authorized 10mm and .380-caliber semiautomatics. Just over half (55 percent) of local police departments authorized the use of revolvers by officers, with .357-caliber (45 percent) and .38-caliber (30 percent) revolvers being the types most commonly authorized.

An estimated 62 percent of local police departments supplied sidearms to their regular field officers, and another 4 percent provided a cash allowance to officers for the purchase of sidearms.

***Body armor.*** Sixty-five percent of local police departments, employing 73 percent of all officers, supplied protective body armor to their regular field officers. An additional 5 percent, employing 9 percent of all officers, provided a cash allowance for armor. At least 80 percent of the departments in each population category from 2,500 up either supplied body armor or provided a cash allowance for it. Departments serving a population of under 2,500 were the least likely to supply armor (51 percent) or to provide a cash allowance for its purchase (2 percent).

A third of local police departments, employing about two-fifths of all officers, required all regular field officers to wear body armor while on duty and an additional 4 percent of departments (employing 8 percent of all officers) required some of their officers to do so. About half of local police officers were employed by a department that required either some or all regular field officers to wear protective armor while on duty. Overall, the percentage of local police departments requiring all or some regular field officers to wear body armor increased from 27 percent in 1990 to 37 percent in 1993.

***Nonlethal weapons.*** Nearly all (99 percent) local police departments, authorized their field officers to use one or more types of nonlethal weapons. Impact devices were the type most commonly authorized: 93 percent of all departments, employing 98 percent of all officers, authorized this type of weapon. The second most popular category of nonlethal weapon, chemical agents, was authorized by 76 percent of all departments. These departments employed 89 percent of all officers.

The types of impact devices most frequently authorized were PR-24 batons (59 percent) and traditional batons (58 percent), followed by collapsible batons (39 percent).

Pepper spray (59 percent) was the most popular chemical nonlethal weapon, and was the only nonlethal weapon other than PR-24 and traditional batons to be authorized by a majority of local police departments. About 28 percent of local police departments authorized the use of tear gas by officers. A sixth of local police departments authorized the use of stun guns. About 1 in 12 authorized the use of flash/bang grenades, including the majority of those serving a population of 100,000 to 999,999.

***Vehicles.*** Nationwide, local police departments operated about 47 cars per 100 sworn personnel. The ratio of cars to officers was lowest in jurisdictions with a population of 1 million or more, with about 24 per 100 officers. An estimated 38 percent of the cars operated by local police departments were unmarked. The proportion of cars that were unmarked ranged from half in departments serving a population of 1 million or more, to a sixth in departments serving a population of under 2,500.

Forty-two percent of local police departments allowed sworn personnel to take marked vehicles home. In most of these departments, officers were allowed only to drive the vehicle to and from work (32 percent).

Overall, only small percentages of local police departments operated off-land vehicles such as boats (4 percent), helicopters (1 percent), or planes (less than 1 percent); however, many departments serving larger jurisdictions operated such vehicles.

## Computers and Information Systems

*Types of computers used.* All local police departments serving a population of 50,000 or more, and nearly all those in jurisdictions with 10,000 to 49,999 residents were using 1 or more types of computers in 1993. About 4 in 5 departments serving a population of 2,500 to 9,999 were using computers, as were about 2 in 5 departments serving a population under 2,500. Overall, two-thirds of local police departments were using computers in 1993, compared to about half in 1990. The percentage of all local police officers employed by a department that used computers of some type was 95 percent in 1993, compared to 90 percent in 1990.

Personal computers were used by 54 percent of local police departments in 1993. This represented an increase over 1990 when 40 percent of departments were using personal computers. All departments serving a population of 500,000 or more were using personal computers in 1993, as were 98 percent of those serving a population of 100,000 to 499,999.

About a third of local police departments were using a mainframe computer during 1993, compared to a fifth in 1990. A majority of the departments serving a population of 10,000 or more were using a mainframe in 1993, including all departments serving a population of 1 million or more. A majority of departments serving a population of 250,000 or more were using mini-computers in 1993, as were about half of the departments serving a population of 50,000 to 249,999. Although just 10 percent of all local police departments were using laptop computers in 1993, these departments employed about half of all local police officers.

About 7 percent of local police departments were using mobile digital terminals in 1993, twice the percentage that were using them in 1990. Most departments using mobile terminals were using the car-mounted type with about 1 in 7 using hand-held terminals.

Overall, 14 percent of local police departments were using either laptop computers or mobile digital terminals in 1993, compared to 5 percent in 1990. Although departments in larger jurisdictions continued to be more likely than those in smaller jurisdictions to use laptops and mobile terminals, significant increases in their use were seen in all population categories from 1990 to 1993.

*Computer functions.* An estimated 53 percent of all local police departments, employing 88 percent of all officers, were using computers for record keeping in 1993 (table 11). This included over 90 percent of the departments serving a population of 50,000 or more. More than a fourth of all local police departments, including a majority of those serving a population of 25,000 or more, also used computers for criminal investigations (41 percent), budgeting (31 percent), crime analysis (29 percent), or dispatch (29 percent). A majority of departments serving a population 100,000 or more also used computers for fleet management, manpower allocation, and research purposes during 1993.

About three-fourths of all local police officers worked for a department that used computers for criminal investigations, crime analysis, and dispatch, and just over half were employed by a department that used computers for budgeting, fleet management, manpower allocation, and research.

Table 11 **Selected functions of computers in local police departments, by size of population served, 1993**

| Population served | Percent of agencies using computers for: | | | | | | | | |
|---|---|---|---|---|---|---|---|---|---|
| | Record-keeping | Criminal investigations | Budgeting | Crime analysis | Dispatch | Fleet management | Manpower allocation | Research/statistics | Jail management |
| All sizes | 53% | 41% | 31% | 29% | 29% | 17% | 16% | 14% | 4% |
| 1,000,000 or more | 100% | 83% | 92% | 100% | 83% | 100% | 75% | 83% | 42% |
| 500,000-999,999 | 100 | 85 | 85 | 89 | 93 | 82 | 81 | 89 | 22 |
| 250,000-499,999 | 96 | 89 | 87 | 96 | 88 | 80 | 80 | 80 | 11 |
| 100,000-249,999 | 94 | 92 | 81 | 92 | 90 | 52 | 64 | 65 | 25 |
| 50,000-99,999 | 92 | 82 | 78 | 81 | 82 | 42 | 51 | 45 | 20 |
| 25,000-49,999 | 88 | 74 | 64 | 66 | 77 | 30 | 52 | 34 | 12 |
| 10,000-24,999 | 82 | 73 | 49 | 58 | 58 | 36 | 25 | 25 | 7 |
| 2,500-9,999 | 64 | 47 | 35 | 30 | 30 | 19 | 17 | 12 | 3 |
| Under 2,500 | 27 | 16 | 12 | 8 | 7 | 5 | 3 | 4 | 1 |

*Computerized files.* Local police were also more likely to be maintaining computerized information files in 1993 than they were in 1990. For example, 55 percent of all local police departments were maintaining computerized files on arrests compared to 39 percent in 1990, and nearly half of all departments were maintaining files on traffic citations (46 percent) and calls for service (45 percent) compared to about a third for each in 1990.

At least a third of all local police departments were also maintaining the following types of computerized information files during 1993: traffic accidents (42 percent), stolen property (39 percent), warrants (36 percent), summary Uniform Crime Reports (35 percent), criminal histories

(34 percent), agency personnel (34 percent), and stolen vehicles (34 percent).

## Policy Directives

Nearly all local police departments serving a population of 2,500 or more maintained written policy directives on the use of deadly force, pursuit driving, and employee conduct and appearance (table 12). About three-fourths of the departments serving a population under 2,500 had policy directives covering these subjects as well.

Overall, departments with a policy directive on deadly force employed 99 percent of all officers, and those with directives on pursuit driving, and employee conduct and appearance employed 98 percent of all officers. At least two-thirds of all local police departments also had policy directives that addressed the handling of domestic disputes, juveniles, citizen complaints, and off-duty employment by officers. At least 88 percent of the departments in each population category of 10,000 or more had a directive on these matters.

Departments with a policy directive pertaining to off-duty employment employed 93 percent of all local police officers nationwide and more than 80 percent of officers were employed by a department with a policy directive on the handling of juveniles, citizen complaints, and domestic disputes. About half of local police departments had a written policy directive pertaining to the handling of mentally ill persons and to the conducting of strip searches. Nearly half had a directive on the use of confidential funds, and a third maintained a directive pertaining to employee counseling assistance.

## Sheriffs' Departments

As previously mentioned, during 1993 an estimated 17,120 publicly funded state and local law enforcement agencies were operating in the United States (table 1). Excluding a small number of consolidated police-sheriff agencies, there were 3,084 sheriffs' departments, all operated by counties and independent cities. Major findings include the following:

- As of June 30, 1993, sheriffs' departments in the United States had an estimated 224,236 full-time employees, 10 percent more than in 1990. This total included 155,815 sworn 68,421 civilian employees.
- Nearly all sheriffs' departments were responsible for performing court-related functions such as serving civil process (97 percent) and providing court security (93 percent). About 9 in 10 investigated crimes (92 percent), responded to calls for service (91 percent), and provided routine patrol services (88 percent).
- Many sheriffs' departments also had primary responsibility for dispatching calls for service (80 percent), operating a jail (79 percent), drug enforcement (78 percent), traffic enforcement (77 percent), and search and rescue operations (65 percent).

**Table 12 Selected subject areas of written policy directives maintained by local police departments, by size of population served, 1993**

| Population served | Percent of agencies maintaining a written policy directive pertaining to: | | | | | | | | | | | | |
|---|---|---|---|---|---|---|---|---|---|---|---|---|---|
| | Deadly force | Pursuit driving | Employee conduct and appearance | Domestic disputes | Juveniles | Citizen complaints | Off-duty employment | Mentally ill persons | Strip searches | Confidential funds | Employee counseling | Homeless persons | Private security firms |
| All sizes | 89% | 87% | 87% | 81% | 78% | 76% | 68% | 53% | 50% | 43% | 33% | 21% | 20% |
| 1,000,000 or more | 100% | 100% | 100% | 100% | 100% | 100% | 100% | 100% | 100% | 100% | 100% | 58% | 42% |
| 500,000-999,999 | 100 | 100 | 100 | 96 | 100 | 96 | 100 | 96 | 82 | 82 | 93 | 33 | 55 |
| 250,000-499,999 | 100 | 100 | 100 | 98 | 100 | 100 | 98 | 93 | 73 | 93 | 93 | 31 | 40 |
| 100,000-249,999 | 100 | 100 | 99 | 95 | 97 | 97 | 99 | 85 | 71 | 86 | 90 | 23 | 25 |
| 50,000-99,999 | 99 | 99 | 99 | 96 | 93 | 97 | 94 | 81 | 82 | 83 | 84 | 29 | 18 |
| 25,000-49,999 | 100 | 100 | 100 | 92 | 93 | 91 | 95 | 67 | 65 | 70 | 73 | 27 | 29 |
| 10,000-24,999 | 99 | 98 | 97 | 93 | 90 | 88 | 91 | 76 | 76 | 60 | 51 | 27 | 22 |
| 2,500-9,999 | 96 | 95 | 94 | 87 | 84 | 82 | 77 | 54 | 54 | 49 | 32 | 19 | 22 |
| Under 2,500 | 78 | 75 | 75 | 70 | 66 | 64 | 47 | 41 | 35 | 25 | 16 | 19 | 15 |

- For fiscal 1993, sheriffs' departments had operating expenditures of $10.7 billion. This was 6 percent more than 1990 after adjusting for inflation. Operating expenditures averaged $66,500 per sworn officer, $45,900 per employee, and $45 per resident for 1993.

- Overall, 16.9 percent of the full-time sworn personnel employed by sheriffs' departments in 1993 were members of a racial or ethnic minority. This was an increase compared to 1990 (15.5 percent) and 1987 (13.4 percent). Blacks accounted for 10 percent of sworn personnel in 1993, and Hispanics comprised about 6 percent.

- In 1993, 8 percent of sheriffs' departments required new deputy recruits to have completed at least some college course work, compared to about 4 percent in 1990. Less than 1 percent of all departments required a 4-year degree; however, 5 percent required a 2-year degree.

- New deputy recruits were required to undergo an average of about 750 hours of training in 1993. The average requirement ranged from about 900 hours among departments serving a population of 1 million or more, to about 450 hours in those serving fewer than 10,000 residents.

- Eighty-two percent of sheriffs' departments authorized their regular field officers to use semiautomatic sidearms in 1993, up from 74 percent in 1990. Departments authorizing semiautomatic sidearms employed 91 percent of all sheriffs' officers in 1993, compared to 83 percent in 1990.

- Nearly all (97 percent) sheriffs' departments authorized the use of nonlethal weapons by officers. Impact devices such as batons were authorized by 85 percent of all departments. Chemical agents were authorized by 77 percent, with pepper spray (56 percent) the type most commonly approved.

- Thirty percent of sheriffs' departments required all of their regular field officers to wear protective body armor while on duty during 1993, up from 21 percent in 1990. Departments with such a requirement employed 35 percent of all sheriffs' officers in 1993, compared to 23 percent in 1990.

- Sixty-five percent of sheriffs' departments participated in a 911 emergency telephone system during 1993, a considerably higher percentage than in 1990 (42 percent) and more than twice as many as in 1987 (28 percent).

- A majority of the 911 systems that sheriffs' departments participated in during 1993 were enhanced systems, capable of pinpointing the source of a call automatically. Overall, 36 percent of sheriffs' departments had an enhanced system in 1993, compared to 11 percent in 1990 and 8 percent in 1987.

- An estimated 62 percent of sheriffs' departments were maintaining computerized files on warrants in 1993, up from 47 percent in 1990.

A majority of departments (58 percent) also maintained computer-ized arrest information during 1993, compared to 42 percent in 1990.

## Personnel

As of June 30, 1993, sheriffs' departments had an estimated 224,236 full-time employees. They employed an additional 19,660 persons on a part-time basis. About 156,000, or 69 percent, of full-time sheriffs' depart-ment employees were sworn officers. This represented a fourth of all state and local officers nationwide. The estimated 68,421 civilian sheriffs' department personnel in 1993 accounted for a third of all nonsworn state and local law enforcement employees in the United States.

There were about 20,000, or 9.9 percent, more full-time employees in sheriffs' departments in 1993 than in 1990, and about 47,000, or 26.6 percent, more than in 1987. When only sworn personnel are considered, employment by sheriffs' departments increased by about 14,000 officers, or 10.2 percent, from 1990 to 1993 and by about 33,000, or 27.2 percent, from 1987 to 1993.

Nationwide, there were 17 sheriffs' departments that employed 1,000 or more sworn officers (0.6 percent), and more than 300 that employed at least 100 officers (10.3 percent) (table 13). Nearly 1,000 sheriffs' depart-ments employed fewer than 10 officers (31.2 percent), including 19 with just one sworn officer (0.6 percent). About a fifth of all full-time sheriffs' officers were employed by a department with 1,000 or more officers, and two-thirds were employed by a department with at least 100 officers. Sher-iffs' departments that employed fewer than 10 officers accounted for about 3 percent of all sheriffs' department sworn personnel nationwide.

On the average, sheriffs' departments nationwide had 73 full-time employees including 51 sworn personnel and 22 civilian employees (table 14). The size of departments varied greatly depending on the jurisdiction population: Sheriffs' departments in jurisdictions with a population of 1 million or more had an average of 1,936 full-time employees, including 1,233 sworn officers and 703 civilian employees. In contrast, sheriffs' departments in jurisdictions with fewer than 10,000 residents employed an average of 6 full-time sworn officers, and 3 full-time civilians.

## Functions of Sheriffs' and Police Departments and Their Officers

Among the 156,000 full-time sworn personnel employed by sheriffs' departments in 1993, about 60,000 were uniformed officers whose reg-ularly assigned duties included responding to calls for service. This amounted to 39 percent of sheriffs' department sworn personnel handling calls for service, compared to 63 percent of officers in local police depart-ments (table 15). This difference is attributable to the fact that, relative to local police, sheriffs' departments are much more likely to be responsible

Table 13   Sheriffs' departments, by number of sworn personnel, 1993

| Number of sworn personnel* | Agencies | | Full-time sworn personnel | |
|---|---|---|---|---|
| | Number | Percent | Number | Percent |
| Total | 3,084 | 100.0% | 155,815 | 100.0% |
| 1,000 or more | 17 | .6% | 32,045 | 20.6% |
| 500-999 | 24 | .8 | 15,010 | 9.6 |
| 250-499 | 77 | 2.5 | 26,775 | 17.2 |
| 100-249 | 199 | 6.4 | 29,022 | 18.6 |
| 50-99 | 307 | 10.0 | 18,735 | 12.0 |
| 25-49 | 564 | 18.3 | 16,596 | 10.7 |
| 10-24 | 936 | 30.4 | 12,782 | 8.2 |
| 5-9 | 602 | 19.5 | 3,811 | 2.4 |
| 2-4 | 340 | 11.0 | 1,028 | .7 |
| 1 | 19 | .6 | 10 | — |

Note: Detail may not add to total because of rounding.
*Includes both full-time and part-time employees.
—Less than 0.5%.

Table 14   Sheriffs' departments and full-time sworn personnel, by size of population served, 1993

| Population served | Agencies | | Full-time sworn personnel | |
|---|---|---|---|---|
| | Number | Percent | Number | Percent |
| All sizes | 3,084 | 100.0% | 155,815 | 100.0% |
| 1,000,000 or more | 25 | .8% | 31,266 | 20.1% |
| 500,000-999,999 | 63 | 2.0 | 24,483 | 15.7 |
| 250,000-499,999 | 96 | 3.1 | 21,504 | 13.8 |
| 100,000-249,999 | 260 | 8.4 | 27,442 | 17.6 |
| 50,000-99,999 | 376 | 12.2 | 19,144 | 12.3 |
| 25,000-49,999 | 616 | 20.0 | 15,244 | 9.8 |
| 10,000-24,999 | 916 | 29.7 | 12,146 | 7.8 |
| Under 10,000 | 731 | 23.7 | 4,585 | 2.9 |

Note: Detail may not add to total because of rounding.

Table 15 Percentage of Sheriffs' and local police departments performing different functions

| Function | Percent of agencies | |
| --- | --- | --- |
| | Sheriffs' | Local police |
| Receiving calls for service | 91% | 93% |
| Crime investigation | 92 | 97 |
| Routine patrol | 88 | 97 |
| Process serving | 97 | 11 |
| Court security | 93 | 19 |
| Jail operations | 79 | 5 |
| Search and rescue | 65 | 33 |
| Dispatching calls for service | 80 | 52 |
| Fingerprint processing | 55 | 41 |
| Enforcing traffic laws | 77 | 99 |
| Accident investigation | 69 | 98 |
| Traffic direction and control | 64 | 90 |

for activities related to jail and court operations. More often than not, these responsibilities are in addition to traditional law enforcement duties.

*Race and sex of officers.* Of the estimated 155,518 full-time sworn personnel employed by sheriffs' departments in 1993, an estimated 22,657, or 1 in 7, were women. The percentage of female officers varied slightly across population sizes, ranging from about 16 percent in jurisdictions with a population of 100,000 to 999,999 to just under 12 percent in jurisdictions with a population of 10,000 to 49,999 (table 16).

Compared to 1990, the number of female officers was up by less than a thousand, and the percentage of all sheriffs' officers represented by women was down slightly from 15.4 percent to 14.6 percent. However, there were about 7,200 more female officers in 1993 than in 1987, when 12.6 percent of sheriffs' officers were women.

In 1993, about a sixth of full-time sheriffs' officers were members of a racial or ethnic minority, with the percentage of minority officers higher in jurisdictions with a population of 500,000 or more (table 17). Overall, the number of sheriffs' officers who were members of a racial or ethnic minority in 1993 (26,367) was about 20 percent greater than in 1990 (21,290) and about 61 percent greater than in 1987 (16,420).

Blacks accounted for 10 percent of all sheriffs' officers in 1993, with departments serving a population of 500,000 to 999,999 employing the highest percentage of black officers (14.1 percent). About 6 percent of sheriffs officers nationwide were Hispanic, with departments serving a population of 1 million or more having the most Hispanic officers (13.3 percent).

The estimated 15,621 full-time black officers employed in 1993 represented an increase of 1,762 compared to 1990 and 5,450 compared to 1987. The percentage of black officers in 1993 (10.0 percent) was about

Table 16   Sex of full-time sworn personnel in sheriffs' departments, by size of population served, 1993

| Population served | All sworn employees | | |
|---|---|---|---|
| | Total | Male | Female |
| All sizes | 100% | 85.5% | 14.5% |
| 1,000,000 or more | 100% | 85.5% | 14.5% |
| 500,000-999,999 | 100 | 84.0 | 16.0 |
| 250,000-499,999 | 100 | 83.6 | 16.4 |
| 100,000-249,999 | 100 | 84.3 | 15.7 |
| 50,000-99,999 | 100 | 86.6 | 13.4 |
| 25,000-49,999 | 100 | 88.5 | 11.5 |
| 10,000-24,999 | 100 | 88.2 | 11.8 |
| Under 10,000 | 100 | 86.8 | 13.2 |

Note: Detail may not add to total because of rounding.

the same as in 1990 (9.8 percent), but up significantly from 1987, when 8.3 percent of all sheriffs' officers were black.

There were an estimated 8,979 Hispanic officers employed by sheriffs' departments in 1993. This was 35 percent more than in 1990 (6,647) and 70 percent more than in 1987 (5,269). The percentage of sheriffs' officers represented by Hispanics in 1993 (5.8 percent) represented an increase over 1990 (4.7 percent) and 1987 (4.3 percent) levels.

***Education and training requirements for new officers.*** Nearly all (97 percent) sheriffs' departments had a formal education requirement for new officer recruits in 1993 (table 18). The typical minimum educational requirement was completion of high school (89 percent). About 8 percent of departments, twice as many as in 1990, required at least some college course work of new deputy recruits. Although less than 1 percent of sheriffs' departments required new deputy recruits to have a 4-year college degree, 5 percent did require a 2-year degree. Overall, 99 percent of sheriffs' officers nationwide were employed by a department that required new deputies to have at least a high school diploma, including 7 percent who were employed by a department that required them to have at least some college.

An estimated 90 percent of all sheriffs' departments, employing 97 percent of all officers, required new deputy recruits to complete formal training (table 19). All of the departments serving a population of 500,000 or more and more than 90 percent of those serving a population of 25,000 to 499,999 required training. The percentage of departments in smaller jurisdictions that required training was slightly lower—86 percent in jurisdictions with a population of 10,000 to 24,999, and 83 percent in jurisdictions with fewer than 10,000 residents.

On average, sheriffs' departments required 565 training hours of new deputy recruits, with about two-thirds of the training in the classroom. Sheriffs' departments in jurisdictions with 1 million or more residents (901 hours), required about twice as many training hours of new recruits as those serving a population of less than 10,000 (451 hours). Classroom training requirements were most stringent among departments serving a population of 1 million or more (an average of 615 hours), while departments serving a population of 250,000 to 999,999 (about 330 hours) required the most field training hours on average.

## Table 17 Race and ethnicity of full-time sworn personnel in sheriffs' departments, by size of population served, 1993

| Population served | Total | Percent of full-time sworn employees who are: | | | | | | | | | | | |
| --- | --- | --- | --- | --- | --- | --- | --- | --- | --- | --- | --- | --- | --- |
| | | White | | | Black | | | Hispanic | | | Other[a] | | |
| | | Total | Male | Female | Total | Male | Female | Total | Male | Female | Total | Male | Female |
| All sizes | 100% | 83.1% | 72.1% | 11.0% | 10.0% | 7.4% | 2.7% | 5.8% | 5.0% | .8% | 1.1% | 1.0% | .1% |
| 1,000,000 or more | 100% | 73.1% | 63.6% | 9.5% | 11.4% | 8.4% | 3.0% | 13.3% | 11.5% | 1.8% | 2.2% | 2.0% | .2% |
| 500,000-999,999 | 100 | 78.9 | 67.5 | 11.4 | 14.1 | 10.3 | 3.9 | 5.5 | 5.0 | .6 | 1.5 | 1.2 | .2 |
| 250,000-499,999 | 100 | 83.3 | 70.8 | 12.5 | 11.0 | 8.0 | 3.0 | 4.7 | 4.0 | .7 | 1.0 | .8 | .2 |
| 100,000-249,999 | 100 | 85.8 | 73.9 | 11.9 | 10.7 | 7.4 | 3.2 | 2.9 | 2.4 | .5 | .6 | .5 | — |
| 50,000-99,999 | 100 | 90.5 | 79.2 | 11.3 | 6.3 | 4.7 | 1.6 | 2.4 | 2.1 | .4 | .8 | .6 | .1 |
| 25,000-49,999 | 100 | 89.8 | 79.9 | 9.9 | 6.1 | 4.7 | 1.4 | 3.5 | 3.3 | .2 | .6 | .6 | — |
| 10,000-24,999 | 100 | 87.7 | 78.0 | 9.8 | 7.9 | 6.6 | 1.2 | 3.9 | 3.1 | .8 | .5 | .5 | — |
| Under 10,000 | 100 | 90.1 | 79.0 | 11.2 | 4.8 | 3.4 | 1.3 | 4.1 | 3.4 | .7 | 1.0 | 1.0 | — |

Note: Detail may not add to total because of rounding.
[a]Includes Asians, Pacific Islanders, American Indians, and Alaska Natives.
—Less than 0.05%

Table 18    Minimum educational requirement for new officer recruits in sheriffs' departments, by size of population served, 1993

| Population served | Total with requirement | Percent of agencies requiring a minimum of: | | | |
|---|---|---|---|---|---|
| | | High school diploma | Some college* | 2-year college degree | 4-year college degree |
| All sizes | 97% | 89% | 2% | 5% | – |
| 1,000,000 or more | 100% | 96% | 4% | 0% | 0% |
| 500,000-999,999 | 93 | 83 | 6 | 2 | 2 |
| 250,000–499,999 | 100 | 88 | 7 | 3 | 1 |
| 100,000-249,999 | 100 | 88 | 2 | 10 | – |
| 50,000-99,999 | 99 | 89 | 5 | 2 | 2 |
| 25,000–49,999 | 97 | 88 | 1 | 7 | 0 |
| 10,000-24,999 | 95 | 89 | 1 | 5 | 0 |
| Under 10,000 | 98 | 92 | 1 | 5 | 0 |

Note: Detail may not add to total because of rounding.
*Nondegree requirements
–Less than 0.5%

Table 19    Training requirements for new deputy recruits in sheriffs' departments, by size of population served, 1993

| Population served | Percent of agencies requiring training | Average number of hours required | |
|---|---|---|---|
| | | Class-room | Field |
| All sizes | 90% | 366 | 199 |
| 1,000,000 or more | 100% | 615 | 286 |
| 500,000-999,999 | 100 | 414 | 331 |
| 250,000-499,999 | 96 | 411 | 336 |
| 100,000-249,999 | 96 | 388 | 255 |
| 50,000-99,999 | 98 | 414 | 242 |
| 25,000–49,999 | 92 | 357 | 239 |
| 10,000-24,999 | 86 | 343 | 155 |
| Under 10,000 | 83 | 342 | 109 |

Note: Computation of average number of training hours required excludes departments not requiring training.

Compared to 1990, the average number of training hours required of new deputy recruits in 1993 was up significantly in most sheriffs' departments. Departments serving a population of less than 25,000 required an average of 416 hours of training in 1993, compared to 346 in 1990. Among departments serving a population of 25,000 to 99,000, the average training requirement was up by more than 100 hours, from 474 hours in 1990 to 579 hours in 1993. Departments serving a population of 100,000 to 499,999 increased their average requirement by nearly 100 hours, from 553 hours to 646 hours. Among departments serving 500,000 or more residents, training requirements for new recruits remained about the same, averaging just under 800 hours.

*Applicant and employee drug testing.* A fourth of all sheriffs employing half of all officers, required that all applicants for sworn positions be tested for illegal drug use (table 20). A majority of the departments serving a population of 500,000 or more required a drug test of all officer applicants, as did 41 percent of those serving a population of 100,000 to 499,999. Applicants for officer positions were least likely to be tested for drugs in small jurisdictions: 18 percent of departments serving a population of 10,000 to 24,999 and 12 percent of those serving fewer than 10,000 residents had a mandatory drug testing requirement for applicants.

Overall, about a fourth of sheriffs' departments, employing about half of all sheriffs' officers, had some type of drug testing program that included regular field officers. Drug testing programs that were mandatory for all regular field officers were reported by 6 percent of sheriffs' departments, employing 5 percent of all officers. More common were testing programs limited to officers suspected of using illegal drugs (13 percent) or to those selected through a random selection process (12 percent). Nearly half of the departments serving a population of 500,000 or more tested regular field officers suspected of using illegal drugs and 39 percent of all sheriffs' officers nationwide were employed by a department with such a program. Departments with a random selection testing program for regular field officers employed 24 percent of all officers nationwide.

## Expenditures and Pay

*Operating expenditures.* The total annual operating expenditure of sheriffs' departments during fiscal year 1993 was $10.7 billion, an increase of 17 percent compared to 1990. After controlling for inflation, the net increase in spending was about 6 percent. (These figures do not include capital expenditures such as those for equipment purchases or construction projects.) Sheriffs' departments accounted for 26 percent of the $41.9 billion in total operating expenditures for all state and local law enforcement agencies during fiscal year 1993.

Operating expenditures averaged about $3.5 million per sheriffs'

Table 20   Drug testing of applicants for sworn positions and regular field officers in sheriffs' departments, by size of population served, 1993

| Personnel category and population served | Percent of agencies with a drug testing program | | | |
|---|---|---|---|---|
| | Any type of testing program | Mandatory (all are tested) | Random selection process | Use of drugs is suspected |
| **Applicants for sworn positions** | | | | |
| All sizes | 30% | 25% | 5% | 5% |
| 1,000,000 or more | 55% | 50% | 5% | 9% |
| 500,000-999,999 | 66 | 65 | 3 | 6 |
| 250,000-499,999 | 46 | 41 | 1 | 8 |
| 100,000-249,999 | 46 | 41 | 4 | 6 |
| 50,000-99,999 | 38 | 36 | 2 | 9 |
| 25,000-49,999 | 34 | 29 | 5 | 4 |
| 10,000-24,999 | 24 | 18 | 4 | 6 |
| Under 10,000 | 20 | 12 | 7 | 3 |
| **Regular field/patrol officers** | | | | |
| All sizes | 26% | 6% | 12% | 13% |
| 1,000,000 or more | 50% | 5% | 14% | 45% |
| 500,000-999,999 | 54 | 3 | 15 | 49 |
| 250,000-499,999 | 44 | 4 | 12 | 36 |
| 100,000-249,999 | 42 | 4 | 16 | 23 |
| 50,000-99,999 | 37 | 4 | 17 | 20 |
| 25,000-49,999 | 28 | 9 | 14 | 13 |
| 10,000-24,999 | 20 | 6 | 10 | 9 |
| Under 10,000 | 15 | 4 | 7 | 5 |

Note: Some agencies had more than 1 type of testing program.

department for fiscal 1993, ranging from an average of $132,467,000 for departments serving a population of 1 million or more, to $273,000 among those serving fewer than 10,000 residents (table 21). The overall operating cost per resident was $45, with departments in jurisdictions with a population of 1 million or more costing the most to operate, $60 per resident, followed by those in jurisdictions with fewer than 10,000 residents at $48 per resident. Departments in jurisdictions with a population of 25,000 to 49,999 residents had the lowest per resident cost—$34.

Nationwide, sheriffs' departments cost $66,500 per sworn officer to operate for fiscal 1993, ranging from $104,700 per officer in jurisdictions with more than 1 million residents to $39,500 per officer in jurisdictions with fewer than 10,000 residents. Overall, employee salaries and benefits accounted for about $4 of every $5 in sheriffs' department operating expenditures.

Table 21  Operating expenditures of sheriffs' departments, by size of population served, 1993

| Population served | Operating expenditures, fiscal year 1993 | | | | |
|---|---|---|---|---|---|
| | Total | Per agency | Per sworn officer | Per employee | Per resident |
| All sizes | $10,732,086,000 | $3,480,000 | $66,500 | $45,900 | $45 |
| 1,000,000 or more | $3,311,663,000 | $132,467,000 | $104,700 | $66,600 | $60 |
| 500,000-999,999 | 1,726,039,000 | 27,397,000 | 69,000 | 48,200 | 41 |
| 250,000-499,999 | 1,474,363,000 | 15,358,000 | 67,300 | 46,400 | 43 |
| 100,000-249,999 | 1,698,813,000 | 6,534,000 | 60,300 | 41,900 | 42 |
| 50,000-99,999 | 1,015,455,000 | 2,701,000 | 50,700 | 37,100 | 38 |
| 25,000-49,999 | 739,475,000 | 1,200,000 | 44,700 | 31,800 | 34 |
| 10,000-24,999 | 566,436,000 | 618,000 | 43,600 | 30,800 | 39 |
| Under 10,000 | 199,842,000 | 273,000 | 39,500 | 27,600 | 48 |

Note: Figures are for the fiscal year ending June 30, 1993, or the most recent fiscal year completed prior to that date. Figures do not include capital expenditures such as equipment purchases or construction costs. Computation of per officer and per employee averages include both full-time and part-time employees, with a weight of .5 assigned to part-time employees. Total and per agency figures are rounded to the nearest $1,000, per officer and per employee figures to the nearest $100, and per resident figures to the nearest $1.

**Salaries.** The average base starting salary offered by sheriffs' departments to entry-level deputies was about $19,300 in 1993 (table 22). Departments in jurisdictions with 50,000 or more residents had an average starting salary that was higher than the overall average, ranging from $20,600 (population of 50,000 to 99,999) to $28,300 (population served of 1 million or more). The average starting salary for deputies in departments serving a population of less than 10,000 was about $2,000 below the overall average.

Salaries for the positions of sergeant and sheriff increased with jurisdiction size in a pattern similar to that for entry-level officers. By department, the average starting salary for sergeants was $24,400, with sergeants in the largest jurisdictions starting at $40,200 on average, about twice as much as in departments in the smallest jurisdictions ($20,600).

The overall average base starting salary for sheriffs in 1993 was $37,700, but sheriffs in jurisdictions with 100,000 or more residents had a starting salary that was considerably higher. The average starting salary for sheriffs in jurisdictions with 1 million or more residents was $89,800, more than 3 times as much as in jurisdictions with a population of less than 10,000 ($26,700).

## Operations

**Crime investigation.** About 9 in 10 sheriffs' departments had primary responsibility for investigating violent crimes occurring in their jurisdiction. Departments in jurisdictions with a population of less than

**Table 22    Average base starting salary for selected positions in sheriffs' departments, by size of population served, 1993**

| Population served | Average base starting salary, 1993 | | |
|---|---|---|---|
| | Entry-level deputy | Sergeant | Sheriff |
| All sizes | $19,300 | $24,400 | $37,700 |
| 1,000,000 or more | $28,300 | $40,200 | $89,800 |
| 500,000-999,999 | 23,900 | 33,300 | 67,200 |
| 250,000-499,999 | 23,400 | 31,900 | 63,800 |
| 100,000-249,999 | 22,200 | 28,600 | 53,500 |
| 50,000-99,999 | 20,600 | 26,200 | 42,400 |
| 25,000-49,999 | 19,200 | 23,900 | 37,900 |
| 10,000-24,999 | 18,500 | 22,900 | 33,800 |
| Under 10,000 | 17,400 | 20,600 | 26,700 |

Note: Salary figures have been rounded to the nearest $100. Computation of average salary excludes departments with no full-time employee in that position.

100,000 were more likely to be responsible for investigating violent crimes than those in larger jurisdictions. Departments serving a population of 500,000 to 999,999 were the least likely to be the primary investigative agency for violent crimes.

Ninety-two percent of sheriffs' departments had primary responsibility for investigating property crimes such as burglary, larceny, or motor vehicle theft. As with violent crimes, departments serving a population of 500,000 to 999,999 were the least likely to be responsible for investigating property crimes, and those serving fewer than 100,000 residents were the most likely to handle such investigations.

Eighty percent of sheriffs' departments were responsible for investigating arson incidents. An estimated 22 percent of sheriffs' departments were responsible for the investigation of environmental crimes, with only a slight variation by population category.

*Investigative support functions.* Some sheriffs' departments had primary responsibility for investigative support functions such as fingerprint processing, laboratory testing of substances, or ballistics testing. A majority were responsible for fingerprint processing (55 percent), including about two-thirds of those in jurisdictions with a population of 1 million or more, or a population of 100,000 to 499,999. Nearly three-fourths (71 percent) of sheriffs' officers nationwide were employed by a department that was responsible for fingerprint processing.

Overall, few sheriffs' departments were responsible for laboratory testing of substances (5 percent) or ballistics testing (2 percent). Departments in jurisdictions with a population of 1 million or more were the most likely to be responsible for these functions: 38 percent conducted laboratory tests of substances and 33 percent conducted ballistics tests. Less than 10 percent of the departments in jurisdictions with a population of less than 250,000 performed these functions.

*Drug and vice enforcement.* An estimated 78 percent of all sheriffs' departments had primary responsibility for drug enforcement in their jurisdiction, and these departments employed 78 percent of all sheriffs' officers nationwide. Departments in jurisdictions with a population of less than 25,000 (85 percent) were the most likely to be responsible for drug enforcement, while those in jurisdictions with 500,000 to 999,999 residents (47 percent) were the least likely.

About half of all sheriffs' departments, employing two-thirds of all sheriffs' officers, had primary vice enforcement responsibilities. By population category, slightly more than half of the departments in jurisdictions with a population of 1 million or more or a population of 25,000 to 499,999 were responsible for vice enforcement. Slightly less than half of the departments in other population categories were responsible for vice enforcement.

*Patrol and response.* Eighty-eight percent of all sheriffs' departments were responsible for providing routine patrol services in their jurisdiction. About 90 percent of the departments in jurisdictions with a population of less than 50,000 provided patrol services. Except for departments serving a population of 500,000 to 999,999 (53 percent), a large majority of the departments serving other jurisdiction sizes also provided patrol services. Nationwide, 86 percent of all sheriffs' officers were employed by a department that performed patrol services.

About 9 in 10 sheriffs' departments reported they had primary responsibility for receiving calls for service from citizens. The percentage that received service calls was 90 percent or higher in all population categories less than 100,000. About 4 in 5 sheriffs' departments also had responsibility for dispatching calls for service to officers in the field, with departments serving a population of less than 50,000 the most likely to perform dispatch services.

*911 Emergency telephone system.* In 1993, 65 percent of all sheriffs' departments participated in an emergency telephone system whereby one of their units could be dispatched as a result of a citizen call to 911 or its equivalent. This was a significant increase from 1990 when 42 percent of all sheriffs' departments were 911 participants, and more than twice the percentage of departments reporting 911 participation in 1987.

In 1993, slightly over half of the sheriffs' departments with a 911 system reported their system was an enhanced system, capable of pinpointing the location of a caller automatically. The percentage of sheriffs' departments that had an enhanced 911 system in 1993 (36 percent) was about 3 times greater than in 1990 (11 percent), and about 4 times greater than in 1987 (8 percent).

*Traffic-related functions.* About three-fourths of sheriffs' departments were responsible for the enforcement of traffic laws (77 percent), while about two-thirds handled accident investigation (69 percent), and traffic direction and control (64 percent). At least half of the departments in each population category under 500,000 had traffic-related responsibilities, with departments serving a population of less than 100,000 the most likely to perform such duties. More than 80 percent of the departments serving a population of less than 10,000 were responsible for traffic enforcement (84 percent) and accident investigation (81 percent).

***Jail- and court-related functions.*** To a much greater extent than their local police counterparts, sheriffs' departments were responsible for functions related to court and jail operations. Nearly all sheriffs' departments had primary responsibility for serving civil process (97 percent) and providing court security (93 percent), while 79 percent operated a jail. For a large majority of departments, these duties were in addition to traditional law enforcement responsibilities.

Nearly all of the sheriffs' departments serving a population of less than 1 million were responsible for serving civil process. Nationwide, 92 percent of all sheriffs' officers were employed by a department that handled process serving.

More than 90 percent of the departments serving a population of less than 500,000 provided court security services, as did 88 percent of those serving a population of 500,000 to 999,999. Departments in jurisdictions with a population of 1 million or more (68 percent) were the least likely to provide court security.

***Special public safety functions.*** Another important area of responsibility for sheriffs' departments in 1993 involved the performance of special functions related to public safety. Examples of such functions included search and rescue, animal control, civil defense, emergency medical services, and fire services. About two-thirds of all departments were responsible for search and rescue, including a majority of the departments in all population categories except 500,000 to 999,999. The percentage of sheriffs' departments responsible for search and rescue operations was highest among those serving a population of less than 10,000 (73 percent).

About a fourth of sheriffs' departments had primary responsibility for animal control. Twenty-two percent of all sheriffs' departments were responsible for civil defense functions, including 34 percent of those in jurisdictions with fewer than 10,000 residents. Smaller percentages of sheriffs' departments provided emergency medical services (13 percent) or fire services (8 percent). None of the departments in jurisdictions with 1 million or more residents was responsible for providing these services.

***Training academy operation.*** Another area of responsibility for 9 percent of sheriffs' departments was the operation of a training academy. Although just 1 in 11 departments operated their own training academy, these departments employed 38 percent of all sheriffs' officers. Two-thirds of the departments in jurisdictions with a population of 1 million or more operated a training academy, as did nearly half of those in jurisdictions with 500,000 to 999,999 residents.

## Equipment

*Sidearms.* In 1993, 82 percent of sheriffs' departments, employing 91 percent of all sheriffs' officers, authorized the use of some type of semi-automatic weapon as a sidearm. These figures represent increases compared to 1990, when 73 percent of departments, employing 83 percent of all officers, authorized semiautomatic sidearms.

Sheriffs' departments serving a population of 1 million or more (96 percent) were the most likely to authorize semiautomatic sidearms in 1993. Such weapons were least likely to be authorized by departments in jurisdictions with a population of less than 25,000, where just under 80 percent of departments authorized them.

As in 1990, the 9mm semiautomatic was the most popular type of sheriffs' sidearm, with 65 percent of sheriffs' departments authorizing its use by officers. Forty-two percent of departments authorized .45-caliber semiautomatic sidearms. About two-thirds (65 percent) of sheriffs' departments authorized the use of one or more types of revolvers by officers, with .357-caliber (57 percent) and .38-caliber (34 percent) revolvers the types most commonly authorized.

A majority (58 percent) of sheriffs' departments supplied sidearms to officers, and another 5 percent provided a cash allowance to officers for the purchase of sidearms. At least 70 percent of the departments in each population category of 50,000 or more supplied sidearms, compared to 44 percent of those serving a population of less than 10,000.

*Body armor.* Sixty-eight percent of sheriffs' departments, employing 76 percent of all officers, supplied protective body armor to their regular field officers. In 1993, 35 percent of sheriffs' departments required at least some of their regular field officers to wear protective armor while on duty. These agencies employed nearly half of all sheriffs' officers. The percentage of sheriffs' departments requiring all regular field officers to wear body armor increased from 21 percent in 1990 to 30 percent in 1993. Such an increase was seen in all population categories.

*Nonlethal weapons.* In nearly all sheriffs' departments (97 percent), officers were authorized to use one or more types of nonlethal weapons. Impact devices such as batons were the type most commonly authorized: 85 percent of all departments, employing 94 percent of all officers, authorized this type of nonlethal weapon. The second most popular category of nonlethal weapon, chemical agents, were authorized by 77 percent of all departments. These departments employed 84 percent of all officers. About a fourth of all departments, employing about a third of all officers, authorized the use of one or more types of electrical devices as nonlethal weapons.

Among chemical agents, pepper spray (56 percent) was the one most commonly authorized. Overall, 64 percent of sheriffs' officers were employed by a department that authorized the use of pepper spray. Traditional batons (52 percent) and PR-24 batons (51 percent) were the only nonlethal weapons other than pepper spray authorized by at least half of all sheriffs' departments.

Thirty-five percent of sheriffs' departments authorized the use of tear gas. Departments were more likely to authorize tear gas in the personal issue size (27 percent) than in the bulk form (15 percent). About half of the officers were employed by a department that authorized the use of tear gas in one or more forms.

About a fourth of sheriffs' departments authorized the use of stun guns. Fifteen percent authorized the use of flash/bang grenades, including a majority of those serving a population of 500,000 or more. Just 10 percent of all departments authorized the use of carotid holds or choke holds; however, nearly half of the departments serving a population of 1 million or more (47 percent) authorized officers to use a carotid hold.

**Vehicles.** Nationwide, sheriffs' departments operated about 52 cars per 100 sworn personnel. The ratio of cars to officers increased as population decreased, ranging from 29 cars per 100 officers in jurisdictions with 1,000,000 or more residents to more than 70 per 100 in jurisdictions with fewer than 25,000 residents. An estimated 37 percent of the cars operated by sheriffs' departments were unmarked. The proportion of cars that were unmarked ranged from about half in jurisdictions with a population of 500,000 or more to about a fourth in jurisdictions with a population of less than 25,000.

Eighty-four percent of sheriffs' departments, employing 73 percent of all sheriffs' officers, allowed sworn personnel to take marked vehicles home. In a large majority of the sheriffs' departments that allowed marked vehicles to be taken home, officers were allowed only to drive the vehicle to and from work.

An estimated 30 percent of sheriffs' departments operated at least 1 boat, including 56 percent of those serving a population of 1 million or more. Nearly half of the departments in jurisdictions with a population of at least 50,000 but less than 1 million also operated 1 or more boats. Small percentages of sheriffs' departments operated airplanes (5 percent) or helicopters (3 percent); although about 1 in 3 departments in jurisdictions with a million or more residents did so.

## Computers

**Types of computers used.** An estimated 82 percent of all sheriffs' departments were using 1 or more types of computers in 1993, compared to 63 percent in 1990. Well over 90 percent of the departments in jurisdictions with 50,000 or more residents were using computers, including all departments serving a population of 1 million or more. The percentage of all sheriffs' officers nationwide that were employed by a department using computers increased from 89 percent in 1990 to 96 percent in 1993.

The type of computer most commonly used by sheriffs' departments in 1993 was the personal computer, used by two-thirds of all departments. This represented an increase compared to 1990 when just under half of all departments were using personal computers. A majority of the departments in each population category were using personal computers with the exception of those serving fewer than 10,000 residents (49 percent). Overall, sheriffs' departments using personal computers in 1993 employed 87 percent of all sheriffs' officers.

Nearly half of all sheriffs' departments were using a mainframe computer (47 percent) in 1993 compared to just under a third in 1990. At least two-thirds of the departments in each population category of 50,000 or more were using a mainframe in 1993, including 91 percent of those serving a population of 1 million or more. About 1 in 6 departments were using a minicomputer, including a majority of those in jurisdictions with a population of 500,000 or more. Departments using mainframes employed 73 percent of all officers in 1993, and those using minicomputers about 42 percent.

More than 3 times as many sheriffs' departments were using laptop computers in 1993 (17 percent) as in 1990 (5 percent). An estimated 4 percent of sheriffs departments were using mobile digital terminals in 1993, with about three-fourths of these departments using the car-mounted type and a fourth the handheld variety. Overall, 18 percent of sheriffs' departments were using either laptop computers or mobile digital terminals in 1993 compared to 6 percent in 1990.

**Computer functions.** An estimated 65 percent of sheriffs' departments, employing 88 percent of all officers, were using computers for recordkeeping in 1993 (table 23). This included more than 90 percent of the departments serving a population of 500,000 or more and more than 80 percent of those serving a population of 50,000 to 499,999. About half of all sheriffs' departments utilized computers for criminal investigations (52 percent) or jail management (47 percent). A majority of the departments serving a population of 25,000 or more used computers for these purposes. Other functions for which computers were used by more than a third of sheriffs' departments included dispatch (41 percent) and budgeting (37 percent). About a fourth of sheriffs' departments used computers for crime analysis or fleet management.

**Computerized files.** Nearly two-thirds of sheriffs' departments (62 percent) were maintaining computerized files on warrants in 1993, and a majority (58 percent) had computerized arrest files. More than two-thirds of the departments in each population category of 50,000 or more had computerized arrest files in 1993, and more than three-fourths of the departments in each of these population categories had computerized warrant information.

Nearly half of all sheriffs' departments had computerized files on stolen property (48 percent) and criminal histories (46 percent). A majority of the departments serving a population of 50,000 or more maintained computerized criminal history information during 1993, including 87 percent of those serving a population of 1 million or more.

Table 23   Selected functions of computers in sheriffs' departments, by size of population served, 1993

| Population served | Record-keeping | Criminal investigations | Jail management | Dispatch | Budgeting | Crime analysis | Fleet management | Manpower allocation | Research/statistics |
|---|---|---|---|---|---|---|---|---|---|
| | | | | Percent of agencies using computers for: | | | | | |
| All sizes | 65% | 52% | 47% | 41% | 37% | 25% | 23% | 15% | 13% |
| 1,000,000 or more | 95% | 73% | 79% | 61% | 78% | 47% | 55% | 51% | 37% |
| 500,000-999,999 | 94 | 56 | 67 | 53 | 68 | 40 | 46 | 44 | 27 |
| 250,000-499,999 | 81 | 62 | 61 | 56 | 75 | 61 | 42 | 37 | 36 |
| 100,000-249,999 | 84 | 68 | 63 | 60 | 68 | 53 | 40 | 26 | 24 |
| 50,000-99,999 | 87 | 75 | 72 | 59 | 59 | 37 | 41 | 21 | 19 |
| 25,000-49,999 | 71 | 52 | 53 | 43 | 38 | 28 | 22 | 15 | 12 |
| 10,000-24,999 | 56 | 46 | 42 | 37 | 22 | 17 | 15 | 11 | 8 |
| Under 10,000 | 49 | 40 | 25 | 26 | 24 | 11 | 13 | 9 | 8 |

Other types of computerized information files maintained by at least a third of all sheriffs' departments in 1993 included calls for service (42 percent), agency personnel (41 percent), stolen vehicles (41 percent), summary Uniform Crime Reports (37 percent), traffic citations (36 percent), inventory (35 percent), and summonses (34 percent). Less than a third of sheriffs' departments reported that they maintained computer files containing information on the following: traffic accidents (29 percent), evidence (29 percent), vehicle registration (28 percent), payroll (26 percent), driver's license information (26 percent), incident-based Uniform Crime Reports (24 percent), and fingerprints (7 percent). A majority of the departments in jurisdictions with a population of 1 million or more maintained computerized files on evidence and fingerprints.

## Policy Directives

An estimated 90 percent of all sheriffs' departments maintained a written policy directive on the use of deadly force, including 94 percent or more of those in each population category of 25,000 or more (table 24). More than 80 percent had written directives pertaining to employee conduct and appearance (86 percent), and pursuit driving (83 percent). Overall, departments with a policy directive on deadly force employed 97 percent of all sheriffs' officers nationwide; those with a directive on employee conduct and appearance, 95 percent of all officers; and those with a directive on pursuit driving, 89 percent of all officers.

More than three-fourths of all sheriffs' departments had written policy directives pertaining to the handling of juveniles (79 percent) and domestic disputes (78 percent). At least two-thirds had policy directives that addressed strip searches (72 percent), off-duty employment by officers (70 percent), citizen complaints (69 percent), and mentally ill persons (67 percent).

Table 24 Selected subject areas of written policy directives maintained by sheriffs' departments, by size of population served, 1993

Percent of agencies maintaining a written policy directive pertaining to:

| Population served | Deadly force | Code of conduct | Pursuit driving | Juveniles | Domestic disputes | Strip searches | Off-duty employment | Citizen complaints | Mentally ill persons | Confidential funds | Employee counseling | Private security firms | Homeless persons |
|---|---|---|---|---|---|---|---|---|---|---|---|---|---|
| All sizes | 90% | 86% | 83% | 79% | 78% | 72% | 70% | 69% | 67% | 57% | 36% | 24% | 23% |
| 1,000,000 or more | 100% | 100% | 87% | 92% | 80% | 83% | 100% | 92% | 74% | 79% | 100% | 23% | 19% |
| 500,000-999,999 | 98 | 89 | 80 | 79 | 66 | 72 | 88 | 76 | 76 | 50 | 72 | 17 | 20 |
| 250,000-499,999 | 100 | 99 | 81 | 86 | 74 | 87 | 90 | 81 | 71 | 61 | 86 | 19 | 14 |
| 100,000-249,999 | 97 | 95 | 87 | 82 | 76 | 85 | 87 | 77 | 75 | 67 | 51 | 19 | 14 |
| 50,000-99,999 | 96 | 95 | 89 | 82 | 83 | 80 | 85 | 70 | 67 | 66 | 52 | 34 | 15 |
| 25,000-49,999 | 94 | 90 | 86 | 79 | 81 | 68 | 74 | 72 | 69 | 61 | 30 | 22 | 23 |
| 10,000-24,999 | 87 | 84 | 83 | 76 | 80 | 70 | 66 | 70 | 67 | 59 | 32 | 25 | 29 |
| Under 10,000 | 82 | 76 | 77 | 78 | 72 | 66 | 53 | 58 | 61 | 43 | 22 | 21 | 25 |

# 4

# Police in the Laboratory of Criminal Justice

*Lawrence W. Sherman*

## Police Thinking About Violent Crime

Traditional police thinking about crime has put the cart before the horse: it has tried to make crime problems respond to police strategies, rather than crafting strategies to fit the crime problems. Ever since Patrick Colquhoun's eighteenth century treatise[1] laid out the basic strategy of uniformed civilians patrolling the streets to deter crime by the threat of arrest, police have attempted to apply that strategy to all forms of crime. For those crimes that police did not observe and intercept in progress, the even older strategy of detective investigations was the preferred approach. For almost two centuries Anglo-American police work has been little more than these two strategies in search of problems. Just as the eighteenth century physicians prescribed leeching out bad blood for almost all kinds of diseases, eighteenth century police thinkers prescribed patrol and investigations as the cures for all kinds of crime. When it became apparent that leeching did not work with all diseases (if any) physicians moved beyond this crudely simple approach to test more refined and specific strategies for curing different diseases. But the spirit of scientific inquiry that guided the physicians bypassed the police, leaving them with little else but eighteenth century theories until about 1970. Only as a result of federal and foundation funding was scientific diagnosis, theory-building and experimentation brought to bear on police strategies for fighting crime.

Even then, however, the research and testing was driven by basic strategies rather than by diagnosis of the problems. One study, for example, tested the effects of preventive patrol on hundreds of types of crime as well as on public perceptions of safety—and found it lacking.[2] We have

Kenneth Feinberg, ed., *Violent Crime in America* (National Policy Exchange: Washington, DC, 1983), pp. 26–43. Reprinted with permission of the publisher.

tested the ability of detectives to solve all kinds of crimes and arrest suspects—and found it lacking.[3] But only recently have we implemented the "crime-specific" or problem-oriented philosophy first suggested a decade ago, testing what police can do about robbery of the elderly, violence between married couples or burglaries of detached houses unoccupied during business hours.

The traditional failure to begin with problems, rather than received strategies, is part of our more general tendency to confuse two very different problems: how to reduce *crime* and what to do about *criminals*. The two problems have been comingled on the mistaken assumption that punishing criminals is the primary, or perhaps only, method of reducing crime. It is not. There is much more to preventing crime than deterring potential criminals. Reducing opportunities for criminal access to vulnerable places, people and things is probably far more important for preventing crime and should be a major factor in constructing specific police strategies for specific crime problems. But if one begins with strategies focused only on the apprehension and punishment of criminals, the potential for crime prevention may never be fulfilled. Traditional police thinking is analogous to a strategy for reducing cancer that relies solely on surgery and treatment of those who already have cancer, with no attention to reducing cigarette smoking or other factors predisposing people to cancer.

Reformers have tried for years to improve police effectiveness at fighting crime. But the focus on strategies rather than specific problems produced a misguided reform agenda. Rather than trying new and different strategies for fighting crime, police reformers devoted most of their energy to altering the inputs for those strategies. Like most other thinkers in the era of good government reform, they believed in making government more "businesslike." They blamed the failure of patrol and investigations on poorly educated police officers, inadequately trained police managers, inflexible civil service systems, weak disciplinary controls and political interference.[4] To be sure, all of these inputs are major organizational problems in policing. But even with the best inputs possible, it is by no means clear that the two very blunt and general strategies of patrol and investigations are the best ways to deal with the myriad of crime problems that have very different causes and characteristics.

Consider motorized police patrol. Patrol may be a good way to deter strong arm robberies on the street and enforce minimal standards of civility in public places (such as not urinating on walls). But patrol makes little sense as a strategy for combatting rape by a victim's acquaintance inside a house or robberies in office building elevators. Police *can* address these problems of violent crime in private places, but not through patrol.

A more sensible approach to policing violent crime would conform to the following model:

- Map out the nature of the problems, classifying them into different categories and sub-categories according to their most important characteristics.

- Determine the possible *causes* of each sub-category of a violent crime problem, separating those causes that police can affect and those causes that are beyond police control.
- List all of the possible police tactics or strategies that could affect any of the causes of the specific crime problem and develop an overall strategy that focuses on what appear to be the most potent (yet tractable) causes.
- Conduct field experiments to test the strategy and measure its effect on the specific crime problem.

## Thinking More About the Crime Problem

Just as biology describes each specific genus and species, a science of crime control must differentiate all the types of crime. Legal labels are not sufficient. The different behaviors encompassed within the legal definition of robbery, for example, are far too diverse for designing a robbery reduction strategy. All of them involve the use of force to obtain property from a victim. But there are many types of robberies: purse snatching by juveniles, bank robberies with bomb threats, midnight liquor store holdups with sawed off shotguns and planned ambushes of armored cars.

Each of these specific types of robberies may have different specific causes. Purse snatching by juveniles may be caused by the breakdown of the family in poor neighborhoods. The bank robberies may be caused by layoffs at a local factory or other short run economic problems. The liquor store and armored car holdups may be caused, in part, by the easy traffic in illicit weapons.

Some of the causes are clearly beyond police control: poverty, broken families, factory layoffs. They are the kinds of "intractable" factors that some people have accused sociologists of emphasizing in developing causal models. While these factors may have the greatest explanatory power in accounting for violent crime, it is pointless for the police to consider them in developing a crime reduction strategy. All police can do is focus on factors they have some ability to control, even if those factors are further down the list of leading causes of that type crime. Intercepting the traffic in weapons, for example, may help reduce the frequency of holdups using heavy armament, even though economic factors may be the major cause of such crimes.

To be sure, the causes of crime are by no means clear for any type of crime, let alone their rank order of importance. But it is not necessary (although it is certainly helpful) to know the causes of crime in order to reduce it. By making informed guesses about the causes of a type of crime and intervening in accord with those guesses, the police may discover what works to reduce that type of crime.

The process of breaking crime problems down into categories can proceed along several dimensions relevant to both causation and control. The nature of the relationships between victims and offenders, for example, provides a dimension along which most legal categories of crime can be subdivided: family, acquaintances and strangers. Police have almost no difficulty in apprehending suspects in family homicides, but they have great difficulty in apprehending suspects in stranger homicides. Another characteristic is the place in which crimes occur: public, semi-private (offices or commercial establishments) or private; high crime or low crime area, and locations in which cash is kept. A third characteristic, one that the law relies on heavily, is the tool of violence that is used in the crime: gun, knife, bomb, fist, club. Many other characteristics may be important for particular types of offenses.

The exact combinations of these characteristics vary widely within and across cities. Some cities have almost no homicide or arson; others are plagued with it daily. Some parts of a city may almost never see a robbery while other parts suffer almost all the robberies in the city. That is why there can be no one national or city-wide strategy to reduce crime. Rather, police strategies for reducing violent crime must be highly localized. What is appropriate for one neighborhood—or even one block—may not be appropriate for another area.

Police thinking about violent crime should begin with a crime analysis of small areas. Unfortunately, crime analysis has been concentrated at the city-wide level, since the only purpose of crime statistics has been to provide political accountability of the police department as a whole. Police precinct commanders, district sergeants and beat patrol officers have only recently (and only in some police agencies) been able to gain access to computerized data analysis of crime problems in their localized areas. Even now, the statistical categories into which crimes are grouped are not informative enough to help design a crime reduction strategy. The relationship between the victim and offender, for example, is often omitted from statistical tabulations for many types of crime. The absence of these breakdowns can be dangerously misleading. An overall decline in aggravated assault, for example, may mask a sharp increase in knife fights between Laotian and Cuban immigrants.

Manual analysis of crime reports, however, can pick up almost any important characteristic. If enough models of this procedure are created and publicized, police managers will be able to perform their own detailed crime analysis and draw on a range of tested crime reduction strategies, just as doctors draw from a range of tested treatments of disease based on their diagnoses of patients' symptoms. The crime analysis and diagnosis is the easy part. The hard part is developing and testing the crime reduction strategies.

## Thinking About Crime Prevention

Even though patrol and investigations are blunt tools, we should not be too quick to abandon them. One reason is that it is hard to think of many alternative approaches that do not embody the basic ideas of patrol and detective work. Another reason is that the number of studies suggesting the ineffectiveness of these strategies is too small to be conclusive. Finally, even if patrol and investigations are indeed ineffective as they are currently organized and performed, that does not mean that they cannot be effective if they are performed differently.

For thousands of years, human societies have used three basic crime prevention strategies: watching, walling and wariness. The tactics have varied enormously, but the basic theory of each strategy has remained constant. *Watching* a potential crime target is an attempt to deter potential criminals by the threat of immediate apprehension, as well as a way of making sure that apprehension takes place—often (but not always) before the attempt to commit a crime can be completed. Some people (like the President) or places (like Fort Knox) are watched all the time; others (like suburban homes) are watched infrequently and haphazardly by public police, although with increasing intensity by volunteer neighbors or paid private police. *Walling* is the use of physical devices to try to bar potential criminals from access to potential crime targets. *Wariness* is any change in someone's life-style or behavior intended to reduce their risk of criminal attack.

Historically, police have concentrated their efforts on watching. But their approach to watching has changed drastically over the past thirty years arguably to great detriment. On the other hand, they have recently taken a more active role in helping private citizens pursue strategies of walling and wariness.

The decline of police watching was an almost inevitable response to the suburbanization of America and the rise of the automobile. As the population spread into lower density housing, police patrols on foot became less efficient as a means of watching people and property. The police adopted automobile patrol as a way of watching more locations during each tour of duty. But there is no way to watch as many suburban homes and people simultaneously as could the foot patrol officers in high density neighborhoods.

Not only do police subject homes and people to less watching in cars than they did on foot, they employ a very different kind of watching. Patrol officers on foot among citizen pedestrians learn a great deal about the social context of the events they watch: the bondings of friendship, love, jealousy, kinship, gang membership, business and other relationships that can prevent or give rise to crime. Patrol officers in cars do not take the time to chat about such gossip nor do they develop the personal relationships with storekeepers, members of the clergy and others who can supply such information. With a rich knowledge of the social context of what they are watching, foot patrol officers have an excellent basis for determining what is suspicious and requires investigation. Patrol officers in cars do not know enough of the social context of an area to distinguish the normal from the abnormal, the mundane from the suspicious. The watching police provide in cars, stripped of contextual knowledge of the area, is necessarily so superficial that one may question whether it is truly watching at all.

It is not surprising that there is strong public support in many cities for a return to more foot patrol—to police officers you can get to know and talk to on the street rather than faceless uniforms inside a passing car. The growth in car patrols has coincided with an apparent decline in public confidence in the public police. At a time when private police companies are booming, selling their services to neighborhoods wanting extra watching services, voters have generally turned down propositions to increase local taxes to hire more public police. But in Flint, Michigan, a city suffering a serious unemployment problem, voters approved a tax increase to continue an experimental foot patrol program that had been funded for several years by the Mott Foundation.

Yet the police are deterred from a widespread reassignment of personnel to foot patrol by an equally strong public demand: that police respond to requests for emergency assistance within two to five minutes of citizen phone calls. Maintaining this rapid response, "dial-a-cop" capacity can only be accomplished by assigning most patrol officers to stay in their cars most of the time to wait for a call to come in. The emphasis on rapid response has several unfortunate consequences. It destroys police interest in watching as a crime prevention strategy, displacing it with *waiting* for an emergency call as the primary purpose of patrol. A great deal of time is wasted as a result. Just as firemen relax waiting for a fire, police often pass the time of day or run errands while waiting for a call. When a call occurs, they attempt to "handle" the call as quickly as possible and return to their cars to await the next call. This fosters a view of police work as merely a matter of managing situations and their immediate consequences, rather than focusing on the long-term implications of a situation for future crimes in the same relationship or location.

Ironically, the calls the police spend so much time waiting to occur are very rarely reports of serious crime. Many of them are minor problems of disorder or requests for police service that police label "garbage" calls. They are not the "real" police work of catching criminals. A good case can be made for the prospect that many of these minor problems could turn into serious crime and that police could take advantage of these situations to prevent it. Nonetheless, maintaining the rapid response capacity for a large number of minor calls, and only rarely for true emergencies, is a wasteful, inefficient and expensive policy. If the police are to improve their performance at *preventing* crime, they will have to find a way to wean the public from rapid police response to non-emergency calls.

Although police have been forced by the telephone and the automobile to abandon the traditional watching strategy, they have made some progress in helping the public do better at walling out access to criminals and developing wariness in their life-styles to prevent crime. Special crime prevention officers have taken advanced courses on locks, windows, landscaping, lighting and other aspects of physical security. Some of them have also been exposed to suggestions for what citizens should do if they are attacked by burglars, muggers or rapists, and how to avoid such attacks in the first place. These specialists convey the information on request at civic meetings, in schools and to families that have been victimized.

Three major limitations hinder this work as a crime prevention strategy. First, these public education officers are defined as public relations people whose primary job is to sell the police department. Since public relations is a marginal function, very few officers are assigned to it (in order to preserve resources for the rapid response to non-emergencies). Secondly, the advice they give citizens may well be wrong. There is little evidence, for example, that better locks or burglar alarms reduce the risks of burglary. Much more research is needed before any advice on walling or wariness can be given with more confidence. Third, the advice is rarely grounded in localized crime analysis, anchoring it to the specific kinds of crimes recently occurring in a particular block or neighborhood. Without a focus on the precise nature of local crime problems, citizens may be misguided into preventing the wrong kind of crime for their neighborhood.

Lack of analysis plagues police efforts at catching criminals as well as preventing crime. The most wasteful police activity aimed at apprehending criminals—detective investigations—was guided by almost no analysis until very recently. Most cases received roughly equal levels of effort, regardless of the likelihood of their leading to an arrest. Research produced a list of "solveability factors" that let detectives decide very quickly whether they should try to investigate a burglary or close the case as unsolveable, and this decision model has been widely adopted.[5] But most police efforts to catch criminals are still reactive to events on a case by case basis, with little focus on the setting of priorities for specific places, suspects or victims.

Research has shown, for example, that a small proportion of criminals account for a large portion of all violent crimes. But few cities have even attempted to identify the local major repeat offenders, let alone focus police resources on apprehending them. There is a national "ten most wanted criminals list," but few cities or police precincts maintain such a list of *local* criminals. The prevailing approach to criminal investigations is dominated by a reactive philosophy: handling the most recent event is the highest priority. Attempting to intercept criminals in the act based on analysis of past crimes is, in most agencies, a very low priority.

## Policing and Preventing Violent Crime

Given this diagnosis of the flaws in current police strategies for reducing violent crime, what prescriptions can be offered? It is very hard to make any promises that different strategies will work better. But many new ideas for both preventing violent crime and catching violent criminals deserve to be tested. All of them presume a much greater level of analysis, planning and setting of priorities than police currently employ.

Following the approach described earlier, there are at least three different ways for police to focus their efforts at preventing violent crime in highly localized areas. Each of them is both a cause and a predictor of violence. One is violent or potentially violent *relationships* among people. Another is *places* that have a high potential for violent crimes. A third is the injuries caused by violent attacks committed with *weapons,* such as handguns or while the perpetrator is under the influence of alcohol.

## Violent Relationships

The victim-offender relationships in violent crime are often distinguished by whether they were *acquaintances* or *strangers.* Acquaintance crimes generally appear to be caused by passion rather than the desire to obtain some other goal, such as theft. Acquaintance violence is an end in itself, while stranger violence is more often a means to an end. To this dichotomy we can add "business" violence, which often takes place among acquaintances for the instrumental purposes of enforcing discipline or collecting debts.

*Acquaintance Violence.* If police assume that most acquaintance violence is an expression of passionate emotions, then they can use police data to predict many relationships that become violent. They are in the best position to do this with domestic disputes, child abuse and other crimes which produce a series of calls to police over a long period of time. They are less well equipped to do this with crimes that develop out of more transient relationships, such as youth gang rivalries or unpleasant encounters in public taverns leading to threats of violence. They are least able to do this with newly formed relationships, such as a blind date that can turn into rape. These differences in sources of intelligence suggest different methods for identifying and intervening in potentially violent (or already violent) relationships.

*Domestic Violence.* Lover's quarrels are a classic source of homicides and serious assaults. But police see the quarrels, often many times, long before they turn violent. Research by Kansas City (Mo.) police found that 85 percent of the homicides among cohabitating men and women had been preceded by at least one police intervention in a domestic quarrel, and that some 50 percent of the couples had five or more police interventions in their quarrels.[6] These figures suggest a tremendous potential for police to take action to prevent a homicide or serious assault. But it is hard to say exactly how this can be done without more research on two key issues: identifying which couples may become seriously violent and determining which forms of intervention are most effective (under different circumstances) in reducing the likelihood of violence.

The fact that most incidents of domestic violence have been preceded by police intervention does not mean that most police interventions will be followed by serious violence. There are no reliable studies of the question, but available evidence suggests that most couples police visit as a result of a domestic disturbance call do not develop into serious violence. If this is generally true then it would be hard to justify police or other agencies taking any more intrusive action than they already do. Unless the specific couples likely to become more violent can be predicted with a high level of accuracy, then intrusive interventions (such as frequent visits to the home) would be applied to many couples for whom the interventions are unnecessary and unwarranted by any balancing test of individual freedom and the protection of others. Even if the violence-prone couples could be identified with great accuracy, there would be substantial civil liberties questions about any interventions (such as long jail terms for a third simple assault) that would not be applied to others guilty of the same offenses who had not been classified into a high risk group.

Perhaps the best police can do is deal with each situation as it occurs. But there is substantial disagreement on how to do even that. Police officers have historically preferred to do little, if anything, about domestic situations, even when minor violence has occurred. In the late 1960s and early 1970s many police officers were exposed to training by clinical psychologists in "family crisis intervention." During that training they were urged to take an active role as mediators or arbitrators of the disputes. The psychologists providing the training urged the police not to make arrests if at all possible, since an arrest might leave a more lasting scar in the relationship. But in the mid 1970s, some feminist groups began to lobby for police to use their arrest authority much more often. Where the legal constraints requiring police to witness misdemeanors before making arrests posed an obstacle, these groups lobbied the state legislatures to pass specific exceptions to that rule for domestic violence.[7]

None of these debates over the best response to domestic violence, however, produced any hard evidence to support any of the positions. Police argued that arrests could backfire and cause more serious violence as soon as the couple was reunited, but they could only offer anecdotes as evidence. The psychologists only offered theory, and no data, to support their recommendation for mediation. The feminists cited the deterrence principle to support their claims for arrest, assuming that punishment would reduce rather than encourage violence. In the court of public policy analysis, the cases of all three positions were weak and unproven.

This debate is a prime example of the vital need for research on police methods and particularly for experimental research. With a similar debate over medical treatments, the customary practice would be to conduct experiments in which three equivalent groups of couples would each receive one of the three treatments. A follow-up study would then measure the seriousness and frequency of violence in the couples' relationships in each treatment group. The treatment that produced the lowest average level of violence would "win" the test and the debate, at least until the experiment was replicated or modified under different conditions.

This kind of experiment would not have been conducted by an American police agency ten years ago. But from early 1981 to mid 1982, the Minneapolis Police Department conducted just such an experiment with the

Police Foundation under funding from the National Institute of Justice. And when the results are available in mid-1983, the research will provide the basis for national recommendations about how police can be most effective in reducing long-term violence in domestic relationships among lovers.

*Child Abuse.* Child abuse could be the subject of similar research except for the fact that there is little debate over police policy. Few clear alternatives have been formed. Much child abuse never gets seen by police, hospitals or teachers. When cases come to police attention, they are usually so serious that prosecution is warranted if the parent can be identified as the cause. But for younger children who cannot talk, the cause may be ambiguous. The child "fell down the steps," for example, and no witnesses can dispute the parent's claim in that particular case.

A pattern of serious injury to an infant or older child, however, could provide the basis for court intervention. The problem is creating the data system that would compile evidence of such a pattern. Cooperation of police, hospitals and perhaps schools would be required to produce comprehensive injury histories of children. With data from these multiple sources, it might be possible to produce a list of high risk cases that police should investigate.

Here again, however, there are major civil liberties questions. Many people would resist the privacy intrusions a "child abuse data system" would constitute. The potential for mistaken investigation of nonviolent parents of accident-prone children should not be taken lightly. Even though such a system might literally prevent many children from being murdered, we should think long and hard before mounting such a widespread surveillance net encompassing parents and children.

Moreover, once a case is identified as a likely child abuse problem, the possible interventions are not at all clear. The consequences of removing a child from home are serious and far reaching. It is hard for police or judges to assess whether the risks of parental violence outweight the risks of parental deprivation. A major long-term research effort would be needed to answer the question, and even that would raise a host of moral issues concerning the rights of human subjects of research.

*Youth Gangs.* A large proportion of violent crime is committed by juvenile males in groups. Some of it is committed against other gangs, some of it is committed against targets of extortion, such as shopkeepers and some of it is committed against targets who are strangers to the gangs. The likely targets of gang violence can vary over relatively short time spans, and police need to keep current on these changes.

In cities where gangs have created major violence problems, such as New York and Chicago, special gang units have been established to monitor their activity. Some of these units have attempted to deter gang violence through harassment, with little success. Even when gang leaders have been locked up, the gangs have persisted despite, or perhaps because of, visible police monitoring.

What appears to be a less common approach could be tested for its possibly greater effectiveness: covert monitoring of gang plans, followed by interception of gang crimes in the act. The use of paid informants, while common for narcotics enforcement, has rarely been applied to gathering intelligence about gang violence. It is doubtless a high risk strategy, given the penalties a gang would levy against an informant. But secrecy provisions in gangs are less than airtight; girlfriends, relatives and others may come to possess information the police could purchase to stop gang violence from happening. Whether the strategy would work can only be determined by trying it out experimentally.

*Taking Threats Seriously.* Many crimes among acquaintances are committed as "punishment." The criminal's motive is to punish the victim for the victim's affront to the criminal's honor. Bar patrons ejected for intoxication, for example, often retaliate by bombing or setting fire to the bar. Indeed, a large part of the arson problem is arson-for-revenge, not arson-for-profit. Another example is ambush homicides, which can result from a fight in which one party loses badly but lives to settle the score.

Police often witness threats to carry out those offenses. Police may be present when the bar patron is evicted, or they may break up a fight that the aggrieved party was losing. They are accustomed to hearing the threats and think little of them. Threats are just a way of blowing off steam, of saving face in public. Most of the time the police may be right. Most threats may be idle talk, with no subsequent attempt to implement them. But some threats are carried out and that may be sufficient reason for police to stop ignoring them and start taking threats seriously.

Police need not be able to distinguish real and fake threats to take action. They could simply establish a data bank for "threat control," and let the fact be widely known in the community. Any time someone makes a threat to commit violence, they would be (minimally) cited for the common law offense of assault, which is technically just a threat. The incident would generate a threat report that would be filed by the names of the threatener and the target, and by the nature of the threat (shoot, bomb, knife, or whatever). If anything happens to the target, or if a crime embodied in the threat occurs (like a bombing), then the threatener will be a prime suspect. If police warn the threatener as soon as the threat is made, the mere existence of the data bank may deter the crime.

The development of a threat control data bank would also provide the basis for sophisticated analyses of the circumstances under which threats are likely to be carried out. This kind of analysis could lead to formulas guiding police to take more active intervention with high risk threats. Guarding the target or putting the threatener under surveillance are obvious, if expensive, forms of intervention that could prevent a homicide. They may only be needed until tempers cool down. A threat control data bank could provide enough analysis to plan the intervention with minimal waste of police resources.

Once again, this plan may raise civil liberties concerns. But since a threat is a crime in itself, it is hard to object to police keeping records of past crimes. If there is no trial and conviction, there are appropriate concerns about accuracy and dissemination of these records. But all citizens could be given the right to review any file involving themselves and the data could be strictly limited to this and no other purpose.

*Acquaintance Rape.* This crime best exemplifies the challenge to police of no advance warning of a potentially violent relationship. A large portion of all rapes—over half by some estimates—occur among acquaintances. Blind dates, sister's (or mother's) boyfriends, classmates and even husbands are all potential rapists. Police have no way of monitoring all of these relationships (which is as it should be) nor of predicting which of them might lead to a rape. What then can they do to prevent such rapes?

Public education in "wariness" strategies is the most likely answer, despite the problems noted earlier. Common sense advice like meeting blind dates in a public place or avoiding private situations with friends and relatives might be very helpful. Less reliable is advice about what to do if a rape attempt begins, since there is no good evidence about the relative risks or resisting or cooperating. But the various schools of thought could be presented to allow women to make up their own minds.

One may deplore the breakdown of male-female trust that a public education effort on this topic might engender. But any effort to make people more wary of potential criminal attack necessarily asks them to trust others less: lock your doors, don't talk to strangers, don't pick up hitchhikers. The message that acquaintances may be more dangerous than strangers is a tragic but important message to convey.

**Stranger Violence.** Stranger-to-stranger violence is probably harder for police to predict and prevent than acquaintance violence. Most of what the police can do should come from a different analytic focus: on violent places or tools or on catching violent criminals. But there is a great deal they can do to prevent opportunities for stranger violence. Once again, the most effective strategy may be public education.

The municipal police command an enormous amount of respect for their expertise about how people can protect themselves from crime. If they were to use that prestige in an extensive public education campaign, they might be able to make many people more wary and better walled. No one medium would be sufficient. Donated television time, newspaper space, community group meetings, church fellowships, boy scouts and other social networks should all be used. Even free classes at the local police station could be offered on a regular basis. The message should be broad but it should also be sophisticated. A dog taking a bite out of crime, the focus of one current national public relations effort, does not inform citizens in very much detail about how to protect themselves.

The problems that remain are the substance of the message. Our knowledge is incomplete on many key questions. Until more research is done, police would have to be very careful to avoid topics lacking reliable data. There are, however, enough clearly supported recommendations to fill a public education campaign, such as:

- lock your doors and windows
- try to have someone stay in your home as much as possible
- do not walk outside alone after 11:00
- live on a side street, not a main thoroughfare

## Violent Places

Police could gain considerably by focusing their limited enforcement efforts on violent places. Violent crime analysis showing the location of the most violent places would help to set priorities. The analysis could be done in several different ways: by specific address, by type of structure or establishment, or by neighborhood.

*Violent Bars.* An analysis of all licensed bars in a city might reveal that five or ten of them account for half of the major assault incidents occurring in bars. If this is the case then the police might be able to ask the alcoholic beverage control authorities to revoke the liquor licenses on those premises.

An analysis might also show a relatively high frequency of weapons crimes (both robbery and assault) in bars generally. Such findings might enable police to ask the city council to legislate a requirement that all licensed premises with a certain minimum history of violent offenses install an airport-style metal detector entry gate, with a guard monitoring the gate and searching anyone who trips the detector buzzer. The old western saloons required that all guns be checked at the door. Some of our modern saloons are no less violent and no less armed.

*Violent Cash Repositories.* The same requirement might be imposed upon places that are well known sources of cash: banks, all-night grocery stores, liquor stores. Any location that has had at least two hold-ups in the past year might be required by law to install metal detectors, if only as a protection for employees and customers. Whether the metal detectors should be monitored by armed, unarmed or any guards at all is an issue of economics as well as safety, since convenience stores often operate with only one employee on duty. But the law mandating the gun screening could be tested on a provisional basis with an early initial expiration date.

In addition to preventing holdups of cash repositories, police could refine their methods of interception of such robberies through stakeout techniques. Police have conducted surveillance on repeat holdup locations with waxing and waning enthusiasm for years. Great doubts persist about whether the long hours of waiting are a waste of time, and whether the interruption by police creates more violence than would otherwise have occurred. But when a rash of holdups occurs, it is one of the most tangible responses a police manager can make to the pressure to "do something."

The questions about the costs and benefits of stakeouts can be easily resolved through a field experiment. Using local crime analysis, police could compile a list of repeat holdup locations that would be eligible for a stakeout team to monitor, from either inside or outside. Half of the list could then be randomly selected to receive stakeouts (although not all at once) and the others would receive no extra police attention. After a given period, the costs and benefits associated with the stakeout group and the control group could be measured and compared: lives lost, injuries, police personnel costs, arrests and convictions, funds lost from the establishments. If this experiment were replicated, police nationally would have a fairly reliable basis for judging whether to employ stakeout units in their own communities.

**Homes.** The most promising approach to preventing stranger attacks in homes is organizing citizens to watch each other's homes for suspicious circumstances. A high level of surveillance of homes by neighbors who call the police if circumstances warrant can increase the chances that a burglary will be intercepted by police, preventing loss of property. There are many more citizens than police, and their volunteered eyes and ears cost the taxpayer nothing.

The major problem with this approach is maintaining citizen interest in watching out for crime. Since the invention of the television, citizens have had a more stimulating alternative to looking out the window at life on the street. Watching for crime is boring enough in the center city, let alone in low-density suburbs. Citizen watches have been organized (by police or civilian community organizers) without assigning specific responsibilities for specific days and times to specific people. Since everyone is responsible for watching all the time, it can happen that no one is responsible for watching any of the time. The programs are often organized in the wake of some particularly serious local crime that stirs citizen interest. As the fear produced by that event fades away, so may the volunteer efforts to watch out for crime.

Police might be able to solve the maintenance of interest problems in citizen watch by taking a stronger leadership role in organizing citizen efforts. Each crime watch block club could be assigned one police officer to work with on a permanent basis. The officer would meet with the club several times a year to help plan specific watching schedules for each resident, discuss local crime problems and give a report on most recent crime analysis for that block and neighborhood. These officers could be called the "cop-of-the-block" and could be evaluated on how well they stimulate and maintain citizen interest in watching each other's homes.

This idea, like all the ideas presented so far, requires a rigorous evaluation before police departments should invest substantial resources in such a strategy. An experimental design comparing the burglary rates of blocks with a cop-of-the-block to blocks without one would demonstrate the benefits. The costs would be eight to twelve officer hours per year per block. Not all blocks would be appropriate for this strategy, but a careful experimental evaluation would distinguish the types of blocks and areas for which the strategy might make the most sense.

*Disorderly Neighborhoods.* Just as individual criminals and victimized places (such as bank locations) have careers and histories in crime, so do neighborhoods. A neighborhood may begin its existence as a low-crime neighborhood and stay that way for years. But with changes in a city's housing stock and economy, a low-crime neighborhood may "decay" into a high-crime neighborhood.

One of the main harbingers of a transition to a high crime rate may be a rise in public disorder.[8] Wilson and Kelling have argued that the appearance of disorder, which has been demonstrated to cause public fear of crime, may undermine a neighborhood's defenses to serious crime itself. A neighborhood full of panhandlers, prostitutes, inebriates, rowdy juveniles and recently released mental patients may soon become a neighborhood full of armed robbers, auto thieves and rapists. Kobrin and Schuerman's study of historical trends in crime rates in Los Angeles communities supports this thesis, showing that the "tipping point" into a high crime rate condition is typically preceded by a surge in minor juvenile offenses—the kind of offenses that produce a public appearance of disorder.[9]

What can the police do to reduce public disorder and keep neighborhoods from attracting serious crime? The specific strategies may vary depending on the type of order problem. The important point is to focus on the problem analytically as neighborhood careers in crime. The most productive investments may be in neighborhoods in which a new disorder problem has appeared. Whatever the problem, there is a response that can at least be tried and tested:

- *Prostitutes*—Police might set up roadblocks to keep non-residents' cars out of the streets the prostitutes are "invading," cutting off their customers and their incentives to cruise there.
- *Panhandlers*—Police could aggressively enforce harassment statutes, letting potential panhandlers know they should stay clear of this area.
- *Inebriates*—Police could examine the sources of the liquor, and enlist local bars' and liquor stores' support in refusing to sell liquor to known public inebriates.
- *Drug Dealers*—Police could assign foot patrols to the prime drug dealing locations, conspicuously watching for any attempts to conduct business.

With support from the National Institute of Justice, the Police Foundation will soon be planning a series of experiments in which police attempt to make disorderly neighborhoods orderly. These other approaches will be tested for their short-range effectiveness at reducing disorder, as well as for their long-range effectiveness in minimizing any increase in the crime rate.

Another approach police should consider in preventing crime in neighborhoodds is redesign of street traffic patterns. Recent research suggests that areas with through traffic are associated with higher crime than quieter areas more isolated from main thoroughfares. Not all areas can be sheltered from traffic, or else transportation would be snarled. But crime analysis could guide a series of recommendations to the city council for changes in traffic engineering that could reduce opportunities for crime.

One of the most striking examples of this approach was evaluated in Hartford.[10] Entire blocks were closed off to all but the residents, creating much greater familiarity and social control. In combination with several other crime prevention strategies, blocking off the streets was credited with a significant reduction in the burglary rate.

## Tools of Violence

Police can also find ways to prevent violent crime by focusing on the "tools" used in committing the crimes or the factors that predispose people to committing a crime. Two of the most powerful criminogenic tools or substances are guns and alcohol. Police can do much more to control both and thereby reduce violent crime.

*Carrying Guns.* It is fairly clear that an attack with a gun is more likely to be fatal than an attack with a knife or lesser weapon. Regardless of the right to *own* guns, the right to *carry* concealed guns in public places has been restricted in many areas precisely because of this greater killing power. The mandatory one-year sentence for mere illegal *carrying* (regardless of use) of a concealed weapon in Massachusetts appeared to deter both carrying and the frequency of the crimes committed with guns.[11] These findings suggest that an aggressive police enforcement effort aimed at gun carrying might have an even greater impact on gun crime.

Unfortunately, the police have taken a very reactive posture towards the detection of illegally carried concealed weapons. They may seize such weapons if discovered in the course of an interrogation for another offense, but rarely do police go out looking for people carrying guns. Given our constitutional rights regarding unreasonable searches, many would no doubt applaud this reactive posture.

But there are ways the police can look for illegal guns without violating the Constitution. They may be able to train dogs, who now smell luggage for drugs, to smell the gunpowder and oil in guns. The dogs need not be German shepherds or dobermans; poodles and other non-threatening breeds can suffice. When a dog (on a leash) has identified a pedestrian with the tell-tale smell, the police officer would then have probable cause to ask for a concealed weapon license and conduct a search.

Another approach would be to give police administrative powers to conduct hand-held metal detector searches for concealed guns on a random, nondiscriminatory basis but without probable cause. The fruits of such searches would be seized and destroyed but no criminal charges would be pressed. The constitutional protection would therefore probably not apply and no record or penalty would be created. Just as housing inspectors conduct random inspections without a warrant to enforce the housing code (for compliance, not punishment) police could use this procedure to reduce the threat of concealed weapons in public.

The least intrusive and most preferred approach to gun detection would be the development of a new hand-held instrument that would tell police whether a person is carrying a concealed weapon. This kind of device would help inform police in general enforcement situations who is carrying a gun. It would also help police patrol the streets in plainclothes (with uniform backup) looking for people carrying concealed weapons. The basic sonar technology for such a device now exists. All it lacks is venture capital or federal funding to apply the technology to this particular problem.

*Driving with Alcohol.* We should not hesitate to call drunken driving a violent crime. The results of this behavior kill some 26,000 people a year, far more than those killed by "intentional" homicide. If police can reduce the number of drunken drivers on the highways, as they have in several European countries through aggressive enforcement, then they can save thousands of lives.

The licensing of auto driving gives police a legal basis for highly intrusive enforcement efforts. One of the most controversial is the roadblock sobriety check. In Montgomery County, Maryland police have used this approach with conflicting judicial opinions about its legality. By asking each driver a few questions, police can make an initial sobriety determination and move on to a more precise measure, such as breathanalyzer tests, if the facts warrant it. If such roadblocks were widely used in the evenings or other prime drunk driving times, they would greatly increase the drinking driver's chances of getting caught. If general deterrence theory is correct, this would reduce the frequency of drunk driving. The only way to test the theory is to experiment.

## Incarcerating Violent Criminals

The police can make substantial gains in apprehending criminals as well as in preventing crime. Moreover, assuming that incarcerating criminals reduces crime through general deterrence and incapacitation of the repeat offender, police should help crime reduction by doing more to insure that the criminals they arrest are convicted and sentenced. To do that, police need to develop better ways of identifying and catching violent criminals, as well as developing the evidentiary basis needed for a conviction.

## Identifying Violent Criminals

If police are going to focus limited resources on a small group of violent repeat offenders then it is extremely important that they pick the right offenders. Previous police methods have been inadequate to the task. One approach has been to pick people suspected of recent dramatic crimes, such as a child molestor. This approach ignores the repeat offender who may commit two hundred mundane robberies a year. Another approach, slightly more systematic, looks at the number of felony arrests or convictions local suspects have acquired over the past six months or year. This approach may reveal little more than the number of times the suspects were caught and may miss entirely some of the more active criminals.

Other methods of identifying violent offenders might include use of informants or general intelligence gathering from citizens. Parole notifications to local police about the release of repeat convicts returning to the area may also provide more names for the pool. The problem is not in getting the names of possible repeat offenders but in picking out the ones who are committing the most crimes and who deserve the highest priority.

One other possible solution to this problem is to test several different methods of selecting targets, interview all of the targets and then compute the average rate of self-reported crime per week for each group of targets.

## Apprehending Violent Criminals

Once they have identified violent criminals, police must be able to catch them with evidence of their crimes. This is no easy matter. Witnesses are often reluctant to testify and they may leave little physical evidence behind. The best evidence can be obtained by having police observe them commit (or attempt) crimes in progress so that the police themselves can offer eyewitness testimony. But efforts to "tail" career criminals covertly have been largely unsuccessful to date.

The first evaluated program for watching repeat offenders was the Kansas City (Mo.) Police Department's "Perpetrator-Oriented-Patrol." This program suffered from department rules calling for short haircuts for the officers conducting the surveillance, the necessity of driving "obvious" unmarked police cars that could only be refueled at the police garage and other obstacles to maintaining secrecy.[12] A recent program in New York City, the surveillance teams of the Felony Augmentation Project, suffered from similar difficulties. White middle-aged men in Harlem trying to follow around black males have some clear problems in maintaining their covers.

A more promising version of the 24-hour-a-day offender surveillance strategy is the Repeat Offender Project of the Washington, D.C. police. This project seems to have solved most of the logistic and personnel problems of maintaining secrecy. But it also confronts the standard problems of surveillance: boredom, high manpower costs, difficulties in locating the targets. It is unclear yet whether ROP will produce more arrests of targeted repeat offenders. But a Police Foundation evaluation funded by the National Institute of Justice will soon address that question.

There are other methods short of following suspects around the clock with a specialized unit. A police precinct in Brooklyn has started its own "most wanted" list, with pictures on the station house wall. Minneapolis has mounted a targeted criminal program on a city-wide basis. These strategies involve all patrol officers in looking for serious criminals against whom arrest warrants have already been issued. Their effectiveness awaits careful evaluation.

## Making Charges Stick

Police have historically viewed their responsibilities as ending when they have made an arrest. Recent research suggests, however, that what police do both before and *after* an arrest has a substantial impact on the likelihood of the arrest resulting in a conviction. A study of the Washington, D.C. police showed that some 15 percent of the officers made over half the arrests resulting in convictions.[13]

A follow-up study in several cities suggested that the high arrest rate officers did much more work in seeking out witnesses, safeguarding physical evidence and preparing cases for prosecution. Conversely, most officers do very little of these tasks in their initial investigations and most of their felony arrests fail to result in a conviction. The "fallout" rate of arrests is substantial and perhaps unnecessarily high.

The New York City police have addressed this problem in two different programs. One is a specialized, city-wide felony arrest case augmentation team. Each time a career criminal on a pre-determined list is arrested for any offense, a special investigatory team gathers all the evidence possible in order to try to insure that a conviction and prison sentence will result. This approach has yet to be rigorously evaluated. The other program is a precinct level strategy for all arrests, designed to improve the quality of case preparation before the case is submitted to the prosecutors. This experimental program in the Bronx has been evaluated by the Vera Institute of Justice.[14] It appears to produce greater effectiveness in obtaining prosecution and convictions compared to the normal procedures in a comparison precinct. Either of these projects could become models for other police agencies around the country.

## Incentives for Incarceration

It is not surprising that few police officers have paid any attention to whether their arrests resulted in conviction or incarceration. It made no difference in salaries, promotions, evaluations or peer group perceptions. Until very recent improvements in court information systems, police supervisors had no way of even knowing their officers' "success" rates in court—nor did the officers themselves.

The advent of PROMIS (Prosecution Management Information Systems) has made it possible to examine convictions in evaluating police officers. But few police agencies have moved to incorporate such data in personnel evaluations—nor should they without thinking it through very carefully. Convictions are not unambiguously a good thing. Convictions for minor offenses may clog the system and use up precious resources needed for targeting more serious criminals. Convictions or cases involving minor disputes may be counterproductive to the reduction of further violence. We must avoid the temptation of blindly rewarding all arrests resulting in convictions and incarceration, just as we must move away from blindly rewarding all arrests.

Nonetheless, police managers can do much more to stem the hemorrhaging of arrests of serious criminals from the presecution process. Better attention to case building and constitutional criminal procedure should result in more convictions of repeat offenders. Police organizations should find some way to reward such good work.

## Public Policy Conclusions

This agenda for police action against violent crime is comparatively modest. It calls for no new expenditures of local or federal funds. It calls for no difficult-to-pass legislation, such as a national handgun ban. It asks for no Supreme Court decisions removing restraints on police conduct. It merely calls for a careful and thorough testing of new ways of doing police work.

### Violent Relationships

*Domestic Violence.* State Legislatures should exempt domestic violence from the "in-presence" requirement for police to make misdemeanor arrests. Police should analyze their repeat call data and arrest histories to identify repeat offenders and experiment with different strategies of forestalling serious violence.

*Child Abuse.* Police, hospitals and schools should consider pooling their information to produce a list of high risk cases police might investigate but with great sensitivity to the civil liberties problems such a list would create.

*Youth Gangs.* Police should experiment with using paid informants to give advance warning of gang crimes.

*Threats of Violence.* Police should establish a record of all threats of violence, making the threatener a prime suspect if the threatened arson, bombing or murder actually occurs.

*Acquaintance Rape.* Police should mount public education campaigns to make women more wary of private encounters with acquaintances.

## Violent Places

*Violent Bars and Stores.* Police should ask legislative authorities to require the installation of metal detectors at the entrances to business premises with a recent history of violent incidents. These violence-prone businesses should also be subjected to police stakeouts but with careful experimental evaluations to assess the costs and benefits of this technique.

*Disorderly Neighborhoods.* Police should try to counteract the tendency of disorderly neighborhoods to attract violence by reducing disorder. Foot patrols and other special efforts should be used to combat prostitutes, panhandlers, drunks and drug dealers.

## Tools of Violence

*Concealed Weapons.* Police should try using dogs to patrol public places sniffing for people carrying concealed weapons illegally. Police might also seek administrative authority to conduct searches for concealed weapons with hand-held metal detectors. The goal would be to seize the guns rather than arrest the carriers.

*Drunken Driving.* Police should try frequent roadblocks to determine whether each driver checked is sober.

## Career Criminals

*Identifying Career Criminals.* Police should test the effectiveness of different methods of identifying career criminals to see which methods are most effective in selecting the most active and violent offenders for special attention.

*Apprehending Career Criminals.* Police should experiment with surveillance, decoys, "most wanted" lists and other ways of focusing attention on the repeat violent offenders who account for a disproportionately large share of violent crime.

*Convicting Career Criminals.* Police should emphasize initial investigations more in order to increase the chances of arrests resulting in convictions. Post arrest investigations for career criminals should also be tried to overcome any weaknesses in case preparation.

Two public policy choices must be made to support this agenda and see it through. First, the funding for the National Institute of Justice must be maintained if any of these new ideas are to be tested. Discretion in policing provides boundless opportunities for experimentation. This, in turn, holds out the promise of establishing a scientific practice of police work.

The other public policy choice implicit in this agenda is far more difficult. It is an issue for municipal politics, one that few police chiefs or mayors would be eager to take on. That choice is the abandonment of the wasteful dial-a-cop system, in which waiting for a call is made the highest priority of a policy agency. This agenda demonstrates the wide range of proactive police strategies that can be substituted for the dial-a-cop system. Research may show them all to be ineffective. But the present system seems to do so little to fight violent crime that alternatives seem to be well worth exploring.

Even this choice is objectively quite modest. All it requires is a cutback of current patrol (and perhaps detective) strength by about two-thirds. The police must retain some reactive capacity for life-threatening emergencies. But they can well afford to abandon house call service for filling out crime reports—if the public will permit it. The resources freed up by that cutback could be tightly managed and sharply focused to attack specific crime problems, guided constantly by updated crime analyses. That small portion of the population which calls the police would not get as much hand holding, but the entire population might benefit from much lower crime rates.

This choice is not a precondition for testing these ideas. None of the ideas, taken separately, requires much manpower. But if many of the separate ideas work, a police agency reorganized for proactive crime fighting will be able to make the best use of them.

One final note. This agenda addresses the actual incidence of violent crime and not the fear of violence. Fear is a separate and in some ways equally important problem. Many of the strategies suggested here for reducing crime (such as public education campaigns) may have the paradoxical effect of increasing the fear of crime, at least in the short run. Others, such as foot patrol, may be more successful at reducing fear than at reducing the actual incidence of crime.

As long as fear affects decisions about where to live and the general quality of life, we must not lose sight of it in choosing strategies to combat crime. Evaluation research should continue to measure the effects of new strategies on fear as well as crime. And where tradeoffs may exist between reducing one or the other, we must be prepared to make difficult choices.

## Footnotes

[1] P. Colquhoun, *Treatise on the Police of the Metropolis* (7th ed. London 1806 & photo. reprint 1969).

[2] G. L. Kelling, T. Pate, D. Dieckman & C. Brown, *The Kansas City Preventive Patrol Experiment* (Police Foundation, 1974).

[3] P. Greenwood, *The Criminal Investigation Process* (The Rand Corporation, 1975).

[4] This critique draws heavily on the writings of University of Wisconsin Law Professor Herman Goldstein. *See also* R. Fogelson, *Big City Police* (1977).

[5] J. E. Eck, *Managing Case Assignments: The Burglary Investigation Decision Model Replication* (Police Executive Research Forum, 1979).

[6] Police Foundation, *Domestic Violence and the Police: Studies in Detroit and Kansas City* (Police Foundation, 1977).

[7] For an up-to-date list of the states which have enacted this change, contact the Center for Women's Policy Studies, 2000 P St., N.W., Washington, D.C. 20036.

[8] J. Q. Wilson & G. L. Kelling, "*Broken Windows: The Police and Neighborhood Safety*" (Atlantic Monthly, Vol. 243, March 1982).

[9]S. Kobrin & L. Schuerman, *Interaction Between Neighborhood Change and Criminal Activity: Interim Report* (Social Science Research Institute, University of California, 1981).

[10]F. J. Fowler, *Reducing Residential Crime and Fear: The Hartford Neighborhood Crime Prevention Program* (National Institute of Justice, 1979).

[11]D. Rossman, et al., *The Impact of the Mandatory Gun Law in Massachusetts* (Boston University School of Law, 1979).

[12]T. Pate, et al., *Three Approaches to Criminal Apprehension in Kansas City* (Police Foundation, 1976).

[13]B. Forst, et al., *What Happens After Arrest?: A Court Perspective of Police Operating in the District of Columbia* (Institute for Law and Social Research, 1977).

[14]J. E. McElroy, C. A. Cosgrove & M. Farrell, *Felony Case Preparation: Quality Counts* (Vera Institute, 1981).

# Section II

## Selection, Training and Socialization

As a result of the trend for increasing accountability of police departments and public oversight of policy making, issues of officer selection, training and socialization have moved into the forefront of police research. Because of the labor-intensive nature of police work, the most significant investment police departments make is in the recruitment, selection and training of their personnel. The readings in this section provide students with a working knowledge of issues involving police personnel and of the images the police project as a result of their socialization into the world of policing.

Our first selection, "Police Psychology: A Profession with a Promising Future," discusses the origin and history of psychological testing in police agencies. The author conducted a survey of police psychologists in the field currently and discovered that pre-employment screening consumed the largest percentage of their time. This finding is not surprising considering how important it is to make sure the applicant is well suited for police work.

Bayley and Bittner provide insight into the process of learning how to be an effective police officer in article six, "Learning the Skills of Policing." Given the complex nature of policing today, the authors analyze the benefits of learning the police craft through experience as opposed to formal training. Even after extensive formal training, it is necessary for young police officers to gain field experience.

In our seventh article, "Field Training for Police Officers," Michael McCampbell gives a detailed account of the state of the art field-training programs. The major purpose behind proper selection, appropriate training and socialization is to provide the police officer with the ability to use his or her power of discretion in a professional manner.

Professor Laure Weber Brooks presents an exhaustive, up-to-date review of the current research on police discretionary behavior, emphasizing the factors that affect police officers' behavioral choices.

In article nine, John Van Maanen provides an overview of the process of "making rank" in a police department. He points out that the passage from police officer to police sergeant, a neglected topic of study, is unpredictable, individual, informal and disjunctive.

The final article of this section, by Peter Manning, explores how the mass media (television in particular) create dramatic images of the police and how these images affect how the police view themselves.

# Police Psychology
## A Profession with a Promising Future

*Curt R. Bartol*

Police psychology is a profession within the larger profession of forensic psychology. Forensic psychology refers to the production and application of psychological knowledge to the civil and criminal justice systems. Police psychology refers to the production and application of psychological knowledge specifically related to law enforcement.

The term "police psychology" appears too narrow in its scope, however, because the word "police" appears to exclude other law enforcement agents, such as deputy sheriffs, fish and wildlife officers, marshals, or constables. Ted Blau (1994), a psychologist and deputy sheriff in the Manatee County (Florida) Sheriff's Department, may have felt the same way when he called his book *Psychological Services for Law Enforcement*. The term "law enforcement" also has its critics, however, particularly those who argue that police enforce the law selectively and minimally. The real work of "police" is maintaining order, keeping the peace, or being co-producers, with citizens, of public safety. Rather than weigh in heavily in favor of one or the other term, the less cumbersome term "police psychology" will be adopted in this chapter.

In this chapter, police psychology will encompass all law enforcement agencies and agents, with the caveat that they do much more than—and sometimes much less than—enforce the law. In the remainder of the chapter, we will sketch the development of police psychology, describe its current status, and try to predict its future. We will begin by describing its past. The past will be discussed within the context of four historical trends that characterize the expanding activities of police psychologists during the past 75 years.

## Historical Beginnings of Police Psychology

When did police psychology begin? Some have said that the profession was launched formally at the National Symposium on Police Psychological Ser-

Portions of this chapter (revised especially for *Critical Issues in Policing*, 3/E) appeared in the March, 1996, special issue of Criminal Justice and Behavior.

vices (NSPPS) held at the FBI Academy on September 17, 1984 (Chandler, 1990; McKenzie, 1984). The proceedings of this meeting were published in a monograph (Reese & Goldstein, 1986) titled, like Blau's (1994) work, *Psychological Services for Law Enforcement*. The NSPPS was antedated by a number of symposia, conferences, and workshops on police psychology, however. The Society of Police and Criminal Psychology, for example, has had annual conferences and symposia on topics pertaining to police psychology since 1971. To set 1984 as the benchmark for the origin of police psychology seems unjustified, given the amount of conference activity over a decade before that. Another important date in the history of police psychology was December, 1968, when Martin Reiser was hired by the Los Angeles Police Department as a full time psychologist. Soon afterward, in 1969, Reiser (1972) presented a paper at the Western Psychological Association Convention, Vancouver, titled "The Police Department Psychologist." Chandler (1990) referred to this presentation as the informal birth of the profession of police psychology.

There is no doubt that Reiser's contributions to the field have been invaluable. In the early 1970s, he was clearly the most prolific writer on police psychology. In 1972, in cooperation with the California School of Professional Psychology, he helped establish an internship in police psychology in the Los Angeles Police Department. To conclude, as Chandler did, that Reiser's paper marked the informal beginning of the profession is problematic, however. Psychologists were working in various capacities in law enforcement settings long before the 1970s. Reiser (1982) himself, in a collection of published papers, noted that he was not at all sure he was the first full-time police psychologist in the country. Reese (1986, 1987), a historian on psychological services to law enforcement, estimated that there were only six police agencies in the United States with full-time psychologists by 1977.

Before we become too myopic in our proclamations of historical firsts, we should realize our international colleagues may have been ahead of us. Viteles (1929) reported that police departments in Germany were using psychologists in a variety of capacities as early as 1919. Chandler (1990) noted that, in 1966, the Munich (Germany) police were employing a full-time, in-house psychologist to train officers to deal with various patrol problems, such as crowd control. The informal origin of police psychology probably goes back more than 50 years.

A review of the literature suggests that police psychologists have pursued four distinct, though overlapping, trends, beginning with an affinity for cognitive assessment and proceeding through personality assessment, a clinical focus, and an organizational approach.

## The Cognitive Trend in Police Psychology

The first trend was concerned with the cognitive functioning of police officers, specifically intelligence and aptitude. This track probably began in the United States with Louis Terman's (1917) testing (using the Stanford-Binet) of applicants for several fire fighter and police officer positions for the city of San Jose, California, in 1916. His results, which suggested police applicants were not a very intelligent lot, appeared in the first issue of the *Journal of Applied Psychology*. Five years after the Terman report, the intelligence level of police officers still was being debated, particularly in the work of Thurstone (1922, 1924) and Telford and Moss (1924).

Police officers were vindicated somewhat, however, when Maude Merrill (1927) administered the Army Alpha Intelligence Scale to a group of patrol officers and police applicants. These officers, as well as the applicants, scored solidly within the average intellectual range for the exam. The results of the Merrill study quieted the intelligence controversy, at least for awhile, until the debate heated up again during 1960s.

The cognitive approach, although never wholeheartedly subscribed to, had very little competition until the mid-1960s. Moreover, involving psychologists in policing seems to have been the exception rather than the rule. In a survey of 90 police departments (Oglesby, 1957), only 14 reported that they used some type of psychiatric or psychological input in their screening procedures. Only two departments said that they used a psychologist for the screening, with the rest preferring to use a psychiatrist. Interestingly, one department reported dropping the services of their psychiatrist because he rejected none of the 1,500 applicants. A subsequent survey by Narrol and Levitt (1963) to discover the extent of selection testing used by major police departments in the United States found an increase in the use of psychological testing. Specifically, they found that 100 percent of the departments used some kind of selection test, usually a standardized intelligence test (40 percent) or nonstandardized aptitude test (87 percent) that usually were developed by the department itself. Only 22 percent were using any kind of personality inventory or psychiatric interview. However, only 6 of the 55 cities surveyed indicated that they employed qualified psychologists in connection with their selection procedures.

## The Personality Assessment Trend

During the mid-1960s interest shifted to assessing the personality attributes of police officers. Some of the shift from cognitive appraisal to personality assessment was probably due to widespread concerns directed at "IQ tests" and the danger of adverse impact on minority groups. The major impetus, however, was the report by the President's Commission on Law Enforcement and the Administration of Justice (1967) recommending widespread use of psychological tests to determine the emotional stability of all potential officers. Specifically, the Commission asserted:

> [S]creening out candidates whose emotional stability makes them clearly unfit for police work—through psychological tests and psychiatric interviews—should also improve the capacity of police forces to improve community relations. . . . While there is no one psychological test which can reliably identify all candidates who are emotionally unfit for police service,

a combination of tests and oral psychiatric interviews can pinpoint many serious character defects. (pp. 164–65)

The Commission hoped that departments would reject police applicants who demonstrated racial and ethnic prejudice prior to being hired. Similarly, the 1968 National Advisory Commission on Civil Disorder called for screening methods that would improve the quality of the law enforcement officers hired (Scrivner, 1994).

In keeping with Commission recommendations, Congress provided LEAA funds for law enforcement agencies to retain the services of mental health professionals. Many psychologists currently working in some capacity in law enforcement started their professional involvement with the help of some aspect of LEAA funding. LEAA, which became President Johnson's centerpiece in his war on crime, also funded technical assistance, materials, training, college education (through LEEP, the Law Enforcement Education Program), and research, including searches for selection procedures that would identify emotionally suitable police officers. Because the funding was intended to identify the emotional stability and prejudices of law enforcement officers, psychologists would have to become more clinical and personality/psychopathology-based in their work with law enforcement organizations. In 1973, the Police Task Force Report of the National Commission on Criminal Justice Standards and Goals encouraged the establishment of a behavioral sciences resource unit or psychological consultants for all law enforcement agencies.

By the early 1970s, personality assessment had increased, but it certainly was not a universal screening procedure utilized by all law enforcement agencies. In a survey, Murphy (1972) found that only 44 percent of large municipal police departments used some kind of psychological test or inventory in evaluating applicants, most commonly the Minnesota Multiphasic Personality Inventory (MMPI). Murphy also found that only 13 percent of state agencies used psychological instruments for screening purposes.

Murphy (1972) concluded that general psychological testing for screening had not changed significantly over the 8 years since the Narrol and Levitt (1963) survey. However, he did notice an increase in the use of personality assessment. For example, the MMPI was the instrument of choice for nearly 50 percent of the agencies indicating that they used psychological testing in their screening and selection procedures. The MMPI is an extensive (566 questions) paper-and-pencil inventory that requires respondents to answer true or false to questions about themselves. The items delve into a wide range of behaviors, beliefs, and feelings, some of them very personal in nature.

The personality assessment trend had two research offshoots, the first being a search for the "police personality" (Lefkowitz, 1975). Agencies began to ask, "Does law enforcement draw a certain type of person?" Some psychologists obliged them by trying to answer. The question has yet to be answered satisfactorily, however, and researchers today have shifted their interests to other issues.

The second research offshoot involved an effort to identify instruments that could *select in* as well as *screen out*. Selecting-in procedures are intended to identify those attributes (almost invariably personality) that distinguish one candidate over another as being a potentially more effective officer. Implicit in this assessment is the ability to rank order applicants, allowing agencies to select the top candidates from a pool who passed the initial screening procedures. This approach assumes that there are traits, habits, reactions, and attitudes that distinguish an outstanding cop from a satisfactory one. There is precious little evidence, however, that psychologists can accomplish this goal in any satisfactory manner. For more than 20 years researchers have tried to develop an instrument or instruments that would help identify applicants who would become above-average or superior officers in the field. Up to now, this search for the elusive superior police personality has been very disappointing.

Screening-out procedures, on the other hand, try to eliminate those who demonstrate significant signs of psychopathology or emotional instability, or who lack the basic mental ability to perform the job in a safe and responsible manner (Meier, Farmer & Maxwell, 1987). On average, about 15 percent of candidates are screened out through personality assessment. Police psychologists have been far more successful in the screening-out than in the screening-in determinations. Research on officers who did not succeed in law enforcement, for example, has suggested that warning signs were present on MMPI measures (Bartol, 1991), rendering them "true negatives." That is, officers who were later found unsuitable for law enforcement often showed a discernible response pattern on psychological instruments used in the initial screening. The "false negative" picture (applicants evaluated as unsuitable at the time of testing but who do fine on the job) is much more difficult to obtain, however, because agencies generally heed the MMPI warning signs pointed out by the police psychologist. In other words, the agency does not usually hire those applicants evaluated as potential problems. Consequently, we never know how the weeded out group may have performed on the job.

## The Stress Trend

The third trend is best represented by the word "stress," which became the overriding theme from the mid 1970s to the early 1980s. More than ever before, psychologists were called upon to identify and dissipate stress, which presumably—if left unmanaged or untreated—would result in an array of psychological and physical health problems for the officer and potentially put the public at risk. "Stressors," "burnout," "post-traumatic stress disorder," and "critical incident trauma" became standard terms in the police psychologist's vocabulary. Whether police officers actually experienced more stress than members of other high-risk occupations (such as air traffic controller) remained highly debatable. Nevertheless, there was little doubt that stress played a major role in the lives of law enforcement officers at all levels within the organization. The focus on stress was significant because it propelled police psychologists away from their traditional testing functions and into a much larger realm of direct services to the law enforcement officers themselves. Consequently, psychologists began to offer not only stress management, but also crisis intervention training, hostage negotiation training, domestic violence workshops, and substance abuse treatment. Psychologists also began to offer counseling services to officers and their families at times the officer was undergoing high stress incidents, such as found in post-shooting stress reactions.

### The Industrial/Organizational Trend

The fourth trend reflects a discernible move into industrial/organizational kinds of issues and a drift away from exclusively clinical and mental health ones. During the mid-1970s, a trend developed toward looking more closely at the law enforcement organization rather than emphasizing—sometimes to the exclusion of other factors—the person. There were moves, of course, in that direction earlier. Bard's work (Bard, 1969; Bard & Berkowitz, 1969) promoted a closer look at training and the police organization from a psychological perspective, for example. We will examine this organizational trend in more detail later in the chapter, when the future of psychological services to law enforcement is discussed.

During the 1980s, the development of police psychology seemed to reach a plateau. Federal funding to state, municipal, and county agencies became limited, and law enforcement agencies were inclined not to require or seek additional psychological services unless absolutely necessary. Although psychologists continued to consult to law enforcement agencies, give workshops, provide screening services, and offer therapy and counseling, there is no indication that the decade of the 1980s was one of significant growth. However, police psychologists did continue to refine their profession through conferences, professional meetings, and publications.

## Current Trends in Police Psychology

Perhaps the best way to describe the present work of police psychologists is to ask police psychologists themselves what they are doing. The following data are taken from a nationwide survey of 152 police psychologists conducted by the author during the spring of 1994. Respondents were members of the police and public safety section of the American Psychological Association's Division of Psychologists in Public Service, the Council on Police Psychological Services (COPPS), the police psychology section of the International Association of Chiefs of Police, and the Society of Police and Criminal Psychology. The survey had a return rate of 74 percent, representing a good cross-section of the psychologists engaged in providing services to law enforcement. The respondents were asked to indicate whether they were a full-time in-house police psychologist, a full-time consultant to law enforcement, or a service provider to law enforcement as part of their professional activity. Therefore, much of the discussion will be based on these three major professional groupings. Forty respondents were full-time in-house psychologists, 36 were full-time consultants, and the remainder ($n = 76$) indicated that they worked with law enforcement as psychologists in some part-time capacity.

The respondents tended to be a rather senior group, with an average age of 48.7 ($SD = 5.5$) and an average experience of 11.8 years ($SD = 4.8$) in services to law enforcement. The age and experience data were highly similar to Scrivner's (1994) data on 65 psychologists employed in large-city police departments. No significant age differences were found by the survey between in-house psychologists and consultants, or between those employed full- and part-time. The average age of psychologists working in law enforcement underscores the point made above about the influence of LEAA funds on careers in police psychology.

Most (89 percent) of the respondents had Ph.D. degrees, followed by Ed.D. degrees (4.5 percent), master's degrees (3.6 percent), and Psy.D. degrees (2.7 percent). Most obtained their terminal degrees in clinical (60.7 percent), counseling (17 percent), or industrial/organizational (8 percent) psychology. Interestingly, the terminal degree-granting institution most frequently mentioned by the respondents was the California School of Professional Psychology (6.3 percent), probably reflecting the LAPD internship program started by Reiser. All but one of the CSPP graduates were working full time in providing psychological services to law enforcement.

The average salary for psychologists employed full-time in psychological services to law enforcement was $77,412 (median = $64,000). However, psychologists who considered themselves full-time consultants in law enforcement made considerably more than individuals employed as full-time in-house police psychologists (mean = $102,192, compared to $57,133; median = $80,000, compared to $53,000).

Approximately 25 percent of the respondents ($n = 36$) were women. However, only three were employed as in-house psychologists. On the other hand, 14 of the 36 full-time police consultants were women. There were no significant differences in salary or age between the men and women.

Participants in the nationwide survey were requested to indicate the type of services they provided specifically to law enforcement during a typical month, as well as the amount of time they usually spent on each activity (see table 1). As expected, the respondents, as a whole, indicated that preemployment screening consumed the largest percentage (34.3 percent) of their time. However, psychologists who engaged in full-time police services, particularly in-house psychologists, spent less time at this activity. In-house psychologists reported that only about 15 percent of their time involved preemployment screening. A greater portion (28.7 percent) of their time was occupied working directly with the officers, in such services as counseling

Table 1  **Average Monthly Activities (in Percentages) of Psychologists Who Provide Services to Law Enforcement**

| Activity | All[a] | Full-time In-house[b] | Full-time Consultant[c] | Part-time[d] |
|---|---|---|---|---|
| | | | Group | |
| Preemployment screening | 34.8 | 15.0 | 27.5 | 40.3 |
| Counseling/treatment—personnel | 19.8 | 28.7 | 23.2 | 17.0 |
| Counseling/treatment—family | 7.3 | 10.0 | 13.1 | 5.1 |
| Counseling/treatment—victims | 0.9 | 0.7 | 1.4 | 0.8 |
| Fitness for duty evaluations | 6.8 | 2.8 | 7.3 | 7.5 |
| Training of personnel | 6.9 | 8.1 | 5.3 | 7.1 |
| Profiling of offenders | 2.8 | 2.0 | 0.9 | 3.4 |
| Administration | 3.9 | 7.9 | 4.3 | 3.1 |
| Research and development | 3.0 | 3.9 | 2.6 | 2.9 |
| Consulting with management | 5.5 | 7.1 | 5.1 | 5.3 |
| Promotion evaluations | 2.0 | 4.0 | 0.7 | 1.9 |
| Direct services in field (e.g., hostage taking, post-shooting incidents) | 4.1 | 4.4 | 5.2 | 3.9 |
| Other (e.g., forensic hypnosis, handwriting analysis) | 2.6 | 4.8 | 3.3 | 1.8 |

[a]$n = 152$  [b]$n = 40$  [c]$n = 36$  [d]$n = 76$

and treatment. Full-time consultants, on the other hand, spent about 27.5 percent of their professional time in preemployment screening and 23.2 percent in the counseling of officers.

Interestingly, full-time consultants were more involved in providing various services to the family members of police personnel and were more engaged in fitness-for-duty evaluations. This pattern probably reflects a tendency for departments to contract out sensitive issues for more objective appraisals, thereby avoiding criticism about conflict of interest.

Unfortunately, very little time in a typical month was spent dealing with victims. It is interesting to note, however, that Delprino and Bahn (1988) reported that police departments saw a great need for this service. Apparently, few departments are able to provide it because of the more immediate, pressing demands of agency personnel.

One surprising finding of the survey was the amount of time consumed by criminal or psychological profiling of offenders. Criminal profiling refers to the process of identifying personality traits, behavioral tendencies, and demographic variables of an offender, based on characteristics of the crime (Bartol, 1995). On average, 2 percent of the total monthly work time of in-house psychologists and 3.4 percent of the monthly workload of part-time consulting psychologists were directed at criminal profiling. Although this may not seem to be a dramatically high percentage, the finding is surprising considering that a majority of the surveyed police psychologists (70 percent) did not feel comfortable profiling and seriously questioned its validity and usefulness. This skepticism was especially pronounced for the in-house psychologists (78 percent). One well-known police psychologist, with more than 20 years of experience in the field, considered criminal profiling "virtually useless and potentially dangerous." Many of the respondents wrote that much more research needs to be done before the process becomes a useful tool.

Several of the questions on the survey focused on the best way to prepare for police psychology as a career. Although 61 percent of the respondents had doctorates in clinical psychology, most indicated that, because of the rapid expansion of the psychological services requested by law enforcement agencies, a very broad graduate education in psychology with a strong research focus was critical. Nearly 20 percent of the respondents felt that course work or background in industrial/organizational psychology was highly desirable. Specific graduate course work most recommended by all respondents was assessment (38 percent), testing (37 percent), counseling (33 percent), and crisis intervention (23 percent).

The psychologists appeared to be extremely satisfied with their careers. Fifty-four percent indicated that they were extremely satisfied, and 39 percent were moderately satisfied; only 3 percent were neutral or dissatisfied. Women were especially satisfied with the profession, with all female respondents indicating they were either extremely (65 percent) or moderately satisfied (35 percent).

The police psychologists also were asked about their perceptions of the current, as well as the future, job market in police psychology. Full-time and part-time police psychologists perceived the market similarly, with about two-thirds of both groups seeing both the current and future job market as either *good* (defined as a balance between available positions and qualified psychologists), *very good* (more positions available than qualified psychologists), or *excellent* (many more positions than qualified psychologists). These data suggest that police psychologists, as a whole, perceive good opportunities in the field and see room for expansion in the future.

## The Future and All Its Promises

Predicting future trends in any professional field is risky business. In reality, the growth and future directions of police psychology in the United States depend greatly on political, economic, and social pressures, ultimately reflected in executive, legislative and, to a lesser extent, judicial decision making. The LEAA and a variety of presidential commissions had enormous influence on policing and police psychology during the late 1960s and 1970s. The media also have played a prominent role. Media-televised events focus public attention on police behavior, as they did during the 1968 Democratic Convention in Chicago. More recently, the videotape documenting Rodney King's beating by Los Angeles police officers, as well as the conviction of two officers by a federal jury, created a nationwide concern about the use of excessive force. As a result, police psychologist Ellen Scrivner (1994) was encouraged to conduct an extremely useful study examining the many psychological factors involved in excessive force and suggesting strategies for monitoring and preventing it. The Mollen Commission Report (July, 1994), detailing widespread police corruption in New York City, prompted police psychologists to address this disturbing behavior. And, in the relationship among crime, fear of crime, and the public perceptions of policing, the media are exerting a more powerful influence than ever before (Manning, 1994).

In an attempt to control police deviance, preemployment screening (of the screening-out variety) will continue to be an important service provided by police psychologists. Although organizational factors are relevant to explaining police behavior, the effort to identify potentially problematic officers should and will continue. Preemployment screening, though, increasingly will be affected by legislation and judicial decision making. It is quite clear, for example, that police psychologists who continue to resist using the MMPI-2 in favor of the MMPI do so at their own risk, in light of *Soroka et al. v. Dayton Hudson Corporation* (1991).

Target Stores (owned and operated by the Dayton Hudson Corporation) administered a battery of psychological tests to candidates for security officer positions. The battery, called "Psychscreen," was a combination of the MMPI and the California Psychological Inventory (CPI). Plaintiff Soroka argued, among other things, that MMPI questions probing religious attitudes and sexual orientation were invasive and offensive. The California Court of Appeals ultimately ruled that invasive psychological tests violated both the constitutional right to privacy and statutory prohibitions against improper inquiries into a person's sexual orientation and religious beliefs. Although the defendants could have attempted to justify continued use of the test, they chose instead to settle out of court and to stop using the test.

The *Soroka* case is probably just the beginning of legal challenges to the use of personality inventories in the screening and selection of law enforcement personnel. In the future, police psychologists will be asked to make very certain that any psychological test or inventory being used for screening and selection purposes be job validated. That is, test results must be shown to predict job performance in statistically, legally, and socially meaningful ways. Otherwise, legal challenges will seriously curtail the use of psychological tests in screening and selection procedures in the future.

The MMPI-2 was published in 1989 after seven years of research and development. The MMPI-2 differs in two important ways from the MMPI. First, the designers of the MMPI-2 eliminated outmoded words or idiomatic expressions. They also improved the grammar, punctuation and general readability of the scale. In addition, the new questions are less intrusive into the personal lives of the respondents. Questions about religious beliefs, sexual behavior, sexual orientation, and scatological habits are gone. Second, the normative sample for the MMPI-2 is more respresentative of the general population in the United States. In the first version, the sample was white, around age 35, married, high school education at best, and living in rural areas. The new sample represents all walks of life, an improved geographical distribution, and a much better distribution of ethnic and minority groups.

The MMPI-2 is a vast improvement over its predecessor and addresses many of the legal concerns about standardization and item content. Those psychologists who wish to reduce their potential time in court, however, should use the MMPI-2 in place of the MMPI and validate it the best way possible on the population being evaluated. Screening instruments—including the MMPI-2—will continue to be tested in the courts on validation issues. Just as surely will they be tested on offensive item content, however.

One piece of recent legislation which will affect the work police psychologists do is the Americans with Disabilities Act (ADA), which became fully effective in July, 1992. The ADA is the most far-reaching public law since the Civil Rights Act of 1964, affecting all levels of state and local governments, about 5 million private businesses, and some 43 million persons defined by law as physically or mentally disabled (Bartol & Bartol, 1994). The law prohibits employers from discriminating against any disabled persons who can perform the essential functions of the jobs they hold or desire to hold. It specifically prohibits oral questions or questionnaire items pertaining to past medical history or otherwise eliciting information about disabilities. It is unclear at this time how the law will affect screening and selection procedures, but if police psychologists validate their methods in relation to effective performance measures, the overall effect of the ADA on police psychology is apt to be minimal.

Psychologists seeking to expand their contributions beyond the traditional screening, therapy, training, and crisis-intervention areas may be drawn to the current zeitgeist of community policing. Its primary philosophy is straightforward: It attempts to form a coalition between the community and the police to solve community problems. In application, the concept is not that clear, however. "[C]ommunity policing provokes endless debate about its format, its operations, its utility and whether it includes problem oriented policing, location oriented policing, neighborhood oriented policing, known offender oriented policing, or is, conversely, an element in one of the others" (Strecher, 1991, p. 7). Moreover, proponents of community policing sometimes ignore segments of communities who do not feel that the police represent them. This current interest in community policing, then, challenges social and community psychology to give valuable input concerning attitudes and attitude change, as well as neighborhood and group dynamics. It should be an exciting area for police psychologists, especially those trained in research methods designed to evaluate programs and strategies used by the law enforcement community.

One area needing far more attention, by both practitioners and researchers, is the rural and semi-rural community. Police psychologists—at least those with high visibility—have studied and consulted with large, metropolitan police departments or statewide state police agencies, to the neglect of small town and rural law enforcement. Approximately 80 percent of the 17,000 local police agencies in this country are located in small towns (that is, having less than 50,000 people) and rural communities. The current interest in community policing may shift some attention to small-town and rural policing, but it would be optimistic to think that they ever will be the center of research focus. Nevertheless, the need for psychological services is great: Small-town policing generates its own unique stress, for example, and some crimes, such as domestic violence, are believed to be more hidden. Therefore, psychologists involved in police training programs in small towns and rural areas are faced with challenging tasks.

The composition of police forces will continue to change significantly in the future, which, in turn, will affect the nature of police psychology. The two decades ahead will see greater attention to gender issues in policing, an important trend which already is beginning to emerge. Research demonstrates that women and men are equally capable—cognitively, emotionally, and behaviorally—of doing law enforcement work (Bartol, Bergen, Volckens, & Knoras, 1992). There are some indications that women may have a more "gentling effect" on law enforcement, using communication and interpersonal skills more effectively. This may be a very crucial variable for policing in the future, especially as policing evolves into increased community involvement.

Women going into law enforcement still encounter sexual harassment and attitudinal resistance, primarily from their male supervisors. However, I anticipate a growing and substantial influx of women into both law enforcement and police psychology in the near future. In 1972, for instance, women constituted 4.2 percent of police officers employed in urban departments. By 1988, the figure had more than doubled to 8.8 percent (Manning, 1994; Martin, 1990). It is possible women will comprise at least 25 percent of the police forces within the next two decades. If these predictions are borne out, they will produce significant changes in police training and the prioritization of services. The needs of victims, for example, are more likely to be attended to with a better gender balance, both on police forces and among police psychologists.

The percentages of African Americans and members of other minorities will continue to increase, especially in the large metropolitan departments. At this writing, 58 percent of the officers in the Detroit Police Department are African American, and it is anticipated that the percentages in other major cities will begin to approximate that of the minorities within their community. It also is highly likely that the composition of police psychology will change. One glaring aspect of the police psychology survey described above is that only 3 of the 152 respondents were from minority groups.

The future also should see a shift from the counseling/clinical orientation to more non-mental health-oriented psychological services. This shift will be consistent with and accompany the overall changes occurring in policing. For example, there are clear indications that policing is moving away from the "professional crime fighting" model to a more "corporate strategy" model, where policing resembles a corporate business rather than a public service agency (Moore & Trojanowicz, 1988; Manning, 1994). Manning (1994) observed: "The currently fashionable language of economics and management used by command personnel to describe police functions, command obligations, and planning creates a picture of policing as a business" (p. 2). Problem-solving strategies and strategic decision-making models are likely to predominate in the very near future. Industrial/ organizational, community, and social psychology will be called upon to make many major theoretical and practical contributions to police psychology. These contributions will be especially notable in human resource management, police management skills, mediation, organizational psychology, community policing, human factors, and operations research. Psychological research on how to deal effectively with turnover rates, personnel dissatisfaction, and lowered morale in reactions to budget cuts and cycles of hiring blitzes and freezes will become critical.

During the personality assessment trend of police psychology, a group of political and social scientists were arguing that police behavior was not the result of some personality characteristic that existed prior to entry into law enforcement, but rather of the culture found within each department. Presumably, the rough edges of individual differences were sanded and polished by the social and political forces of the organization. Wilson (1968), for example, developed a departmental typology, consisting of various policing styles. He argued that the pre-existing personality of the individual really did not matter. The department promoted specific policing styles, with differences in policing being explainable by differences among organizations. Wilson's perspective has merit. For example, it is not uncommon for an individual to be regarded as a failure in one agency but a success in another. Nevertheless, individual attributes of some officers preclude them from being a success in any law enforcement setting. It is becoming increasingly apparent, therefore, that the study of police behavior requires a careful examination of all the systems involved, such as the individual or infra system, the organization, the family, the culture, and the community. Police psychologists need to be more sensitive to the interactions among these systems rather than to assume that one law enforcement organization is like any other.

Police psychology increasingly will become international in scope, with psychologists across the globe sharing ideas, research, and programs. Although this exchange takes place now, it will increase substantially within the next decade.

Traditionally, law enforcement has used psychologists on an "as needed" basis rather than for systematic human resource development and prevention (Scrivner, 1994). The growing array of available psychological services therefore has not been integrated systematically into law enforcement. For this to be accomplished, psychologists themselves must articulate what it is they have to offer; they cannot expect the police community to know intuitively how they can help. Psychological services directed toward prevention and proaction will, in the long run, bring more benefit to policing than the reactive activity that has been expected in the past.

More than anything else, police psychologists need to become better and more skillful researchers and evaluators of programs, including their own. One of the things that was most emphasized by practicing police psychologists in our survey was that aspiring police psychologists must be better equipped with research skills. In her survey, Gettys (1990) also found an unfortunate lack of research involvement by police psychologists. Chandler (1990) strongly recommended that future police psychologists become well versed and much more active in conducting research. He said this within the context of acknowledging that law enforcement agencies are highly prone to act on "hot" issues without the benefit of good research and evaluation. These "hot" issues have included missing children campaigns, voice stress analysis, use of psychics, ritualistic crimes, and satanic cults. Good research, he stated, eventually brings fad-like behavior in check. Chandler (1990) concluded:

> We have our work cut out for us. While specific research in police psychology has been too often flawed by poor technique, such as a failure to use control groups, we know we can do better. We can and should provide proof of the efficiency and effectiveness of police psychology programs. We can and should make use of research and evaluation to help us combat misinformation in law enforcement with valid fact. We can and should forge productive understanding and communication between law enforcement and professional research communities. We can and must do better. (p. 258)

Finally, we need a broad-based graduate program in police psychology that will encompass not only clinical areas but also will prepare aspiring police psychologists in the many areas described here, including industrial/organizational psychology, social psychology, psychology and law, the judicial process, policing, and a very solid foundation in research methods. With the exception of a master's degree in forensic psychology offered by the John Jay College of Criminal Justice and various internships sponsored by some universities, there are no academic graduate programs in the United States that specifically prepare future police psychologists for the enormously diverse demands that they will encounter in the future, although several programs are apparently in the planning. A majority of the respondents in the police psychology survey thought that a graduate program in police psychology was an excellent idea, but they also strongly recommended that the program be diverse and academically very broad. Several of the respondents believed that most traditional graduate programs are too narrow and circumscribed for training police psychologists. Therefore, it is highly likely police psychology will have several graduate programs exclusively devoted to the field within the next decade.

In conclusion, police psychology has an extremely promising future. Professions rarely develop along a continuum of steady growth, but usually expand and contract in a cyclical fashion. Police psychology is about to experience another upward swing, perhaps equal to the growth seen during the 1970s. Legislatures and much of the public continue to be convinced that the best way to deal with the crime problem is by improved and expanded policing, as demonstrated by the Anti-Crime Law of 1994. Although the law provides for preventive programs, it gives more support to law enforcement efforts, particularly those of the community policing variety. It is highly likely that this prioritization of policing will welcome the skills and knowledge of police psychologists. This anticipated growth in police psychology will be sustained, however, only if we engage in high-quality research designed to test the effectiveness of various programs, policies, methods, and innovations.

# References

Bard, M. (1969). Family intervention police teams as a community mental health resource. *Journal of Criminal Law, Criminology and Police Science*, 60, 247–50.

Bard, M., & Berkowitz, B. (1969). A community psychology consultation program in police family crisis intervention: Preliminary impressions. *International Journal of Social Psychiatry*, 15, 209–15.

Bartol, C. R. (1991). Predictive validation of the MMPI for small-town police officers who fail. *Professional Psychology: Research and Practice*, 22, 127–32.

Bartol, C. R. (1995). *Criminal behavior: A psychosocial approach* (4th ed.). Englewood Cliffs, NJ: Prentice-Hall.

Bartol, C. R., & Bartol, A. M. (1994). *Psychology and law: Research and application* (2nd ed.). Pacific Grove, CA: Brooks/Cole.

Bartol, C. R., Bergen, G. T., Volckens, J. S., & Knoras, K. M. (1992). Women in small-town policing: Job performance and stress. *Criminal Justice and Behavior*, 19, 240–59.

Bergen, G. T., Aceto, R. T., & Chadziewicz, M. M. (1992). Job satisfaction of police psychologist. *Criminal Justice and Behavior*, 19, 314–29.

Blau, T. H. (1994). *Psychological services for law enforcement*. New York: Wiley.

Chandler, J. T. (1990). *Modern police psychology: For law enforcement and human behavior professionals*. Springfield, IL: Charles C. Thomas.

Delprino, R. P., & Bahn, C. (1988). National survey of the extent and nature of psychological services in police departments. *Professional Psychology: Research and Practice*, 19, 421–25.

Gettys, V. S. (1990, August). *Police and public safety psychologists: Survey of fields of study, activities and training opportunities*. Paper presented at the annual convention of the American Psychological Association, Boston, MA.

Lefkowitz, J. (1975). Psychological attributes of policemen: A review of research and opinion. *Journal of Social Issues*, 31, 3–26.

Manning, P. K. (1994). Economic rhetoric and policing reform. *Police Forum*, 4, 1–8.

Martin, S. (1990). *Progress in policing*. Washington, DC: Police Foundation.

McKenzie, J. D. (1986). Preface. In J. T. Reese & H. A. Goldstein (Eds.), *Psychological services for law enforcement* (p. iii). Washington, DC: U.S. Government Printing Office.

Meier, R. D., Farmer, R. E., & Maxwell, D. (1987). Psychological screening of police candidates: Current perspectives. *Journal of Police Science and Administration*, 15, 210–16.

Merrill, M. A. (1927). Intelligence of policemen. *Journal of Personnel Research*, 5, 511–15.

Mollen Commission (1994). *Commission Report*. New York: Mollen Commission.

Moore, M., & Trojanowicz, R. (1988). *Corporate strategies for policing: Perspectives on policing*. Washington, DC: U.S. Government Printing Office.

Narrol, H. G., & Levitt, E. E. (1963). Formal assessment procedures in police selection. *Psychological Reports*, 12, 691–94.

Oglesby, T. M. (1957). Use of emotional screening in the selection of police applicants. *Public Personnel Review*, 18, 228–31.

Ostrove, E. (1986). Police/law enforcement and psychology. *Behavioral Sciences and the Law*, 4, 353–70.

President's Commission on Law Enforcement and Administration of Justice. (1967). *Task force report: The police*. Washington, DC: U.S. Government Printing Office.

Reese, J. T. (1986). Foreword. In J. T. Reese & H. A. Goldstein (Eds.), *Psychological services for law enforcement* (p. v). Washington, DC: U.S. Government Printing Office.

Reese, J. T. (1987). *A history of police psychological services*. Washington, DC: U.S. Government Printing Office.

Reese, J. T., & Goldstein, H. A. (Eds). (1986). *Psychological services for law enforcement*. Washington, DC: U.S. Government Printing Office.

Reiser, M. (1972). *The police psychologist*. Springfield, IL: Charles C. Thomas.

Reiser, M. (1982). *Police psychology: Collected papers*. Los Angeles: LEHI Publishing.

Scrivner, E. M. (1994). *The role of police psychology in controlling excessive force*. Washington, DC: National Institute of Justice.

*Soroka et al. v. Dayton Hudson Corporation*, 91 *Daily Journal D.A.R.* 13204 (1991).

Strecher, V. G. (1991). Histories and futures of policing: Readings and misreadings of a pivotal present. *Police Forum*, 1, 1–9.

Telford, F., & Moss, F. A. (1924). Suggested tests for patrolmen. *Public Personnel Studies*, 2, 112–44.

Terman, L. M. (1917). A trial of mental and pedagogical tests in a civil service examination for policemen and firemen. *Journal of Applied Psychology*, 1, 17–29.

Thurstone, L. L. (1922). The intelligence of policemen. *Journal of Personnel Research*, 2, 64–74.

Thurstone, L. L. (1924). The civil service tests for patrolmen in Philadelphia. *Public Personnel Studies*, 2, 1–5.

Viteles, M. S. (1929). Psychological methods in the selection of patrolmen in Europe. *Annals of the American Academy*, 146, 160–65.

Wilson, J. Q. (1968). *Varieties of police behavior*. Cambridge: Harvard University Press.

(6)

# Learning the Skills of Policing

*David H. Bayley*
*Egon Bittner*

## I. Introduction

How important is experience in learning to become an effective police officer? Police officers say vehemently that there is no substitute. The training given in police academies is universally regarded as irrelevant to "real" police work. Policing, it is argued, cannot be learned scientifically, in the sense that if A is done in Y situation and B is done in X situation, then Z will result. The life police officers confront is too diverse and complicated to be reduced to simple principles. As police officers continually say, every situation is different. What is needed, then, is not learning in the book sense but skills derived from handling a multitude of what seem like unique situations over and over again.

If this view of policing is correct, then it follows that the best officers are likely to be the most experienced, those who are older and have been in service longer. By extension, the only people fit to judge police activity in encounters with the public are other experienced officers. Certainly civilians could not make fair judgments, but neither could supervisors who had not experienced the peculiarities of a specific situation. In effect, the mysteries of the occupation are so profound that one not immersed repeatedly in police operations could not possibly understand the constraints as well as the possibilities of particular circumstances. Few officers would state the case as baldly as this, but these implications are fairly plain.

That this view of policing is self-serving is obvious. More troubling, however, is that it suggests that policing is not amenable to rational analysis and, by extension, to formal learning. Contrary to the pretensions of police "professionalism," officers commonly portray policing as being essentially a craft in which learning comes exclusively through experience intuitively processed by individual officers. Admittedly, policing is not yet

*Law and Contemporary Problems* 47: 35–59 (1984). Reprinted with permission of the publisher.

a science in the sense that a body of principles has been generated that officers may follow with a reasonable probability of achieving successful outcomes. Officers correctly perceive that there is a gap between the operational world and the classroom, between the lore of policing as it is practiced and principles of human behavior discovered by social scientists. It should not be forgotten that people who teach, such as the many academic observers of policing, have as large a vested interest in portraying policing as amenable to science and classroom learning as police officers do in rejecting it.

The purpose of this article is to show that the antinomy between policing as a craft and policing as a science is false. What police say about how policing is learned is not incompatible with attempts to make instruction in the skills of policing more self-critical and systematic. Progress in police training will come by focusing on the particularities of police work as it is experienced by serving officers and by analyzing that experience and making it available to future police officers. In order to achieve this, this article examines the work that patrol officers do, recognizing that while skills are required to carry out more specialized police duties such as criminal investigation, patrol work is the centerpiece of policing, occupying the majority of all police personnel, accounting for most of the contacts with the public, and generally initiating the mobilization of police resources.

## II. The Need for Learning

If patrolmen acted like automats most of the time, then there would be little scope for learning. This, of course, is far from the case. A vast amount of research has shown that patrol work is fraught with decision: patrol officers exercise choice constantly.[1] It should be noted in passing, however, that the importance of choice in patrol work is a variable, especially when viewed on a worldwide basis. In the United States, Britain, and Canada, responsibility for tactical decisionmaking is delegated to the lowest ranks. But in many countries of Africa, Asia, and Latin America, regulations expressly prohibit lower-ranking officers from making particular decisions. In such systems, patrolmen and constables are hardly more than spear-carriers in the police drama, mechanically patrolling according to fixed schedules and calling superior officers to handle almost any interaction with the public beyond detaining suspects in crimes personally witnessed.[2] Even in countries where legal authorization is not truncated, organizational practice may require higher-ranking officers to be summoned in specific circumstances.

In addition to command direction, the scope for learning in patrol work varies with the nature of situations encountered. Situations can be ranked along a continuum from the cut-and-dried to the problematic. For example, American officers have few doubts about what to do when a man is found drunk lying on the ground in the winter. He must be picked up and taken to a shelter. The choices are also fairly limited in serious traffic accidents, alleged housebreaking, and assault with a deadly weapon witnessed by an officer. This is not to argue that some choices are not involved in such cases—officers can turn a blind eye or overreact—but rather that the appropriate responses are clearly recognized by everyone involved—patrolman, public, and command officers. The appropriate action may not be easy to take, but it is obvious. A robbery in progress is dangerous, but the patrolman's appropriate response is straightforward. Investigating a young person on a street late at night after curfew is rarely dangerous, but the decision as to what corrective action should be taken is often perplexing.

American patrol officers recognize these variable features of the work they do and can talk about them with discernment. They have an acute sense of where danger lies and what kinds of situations cause them the greatest difficulty in deciding what to do. In fact, they are so accustomed to thinking about the place of discretion in policing that a favorite in-house joke is that their most problematic situation during each shift is deciding where to go for lunch. In our experience, patrol officers single out disturbances as the most problematic calls they receive, especially domestic disputes, meaning quarrels among people who are living in the same household. These include wife beatings, child abuse, fights between gay roommates, disputes over property by people living in a common-law relationship, violations of restraining orders, and unruly children. The next most problematic activities that police officers mention are proactive traffic stops, in which they choose to stop a moving vehicle for some reason, and maintaining order among teenagers congregating in public places. Observers of police work have also chosen these situations when illustrating the complexity of police work.[3] Survey data supports these impressionistic conclusions. Domestic disputes were by far the situation most commonly cited in 1966–67 by Denver police officers as requiring street decisionmaking, followed somewhat distantly by traffic violations.[4] In 1981, police officers in Battle Creek, Michigan also mentioned domestic disputes most frequently as their most problematic encounter.[5] Traffic violations were largely ignored. It seems likely that perceptions of the problematic nature of situations are related to the frequency of their occurrence in the working life of police officers. That is, if a particular kind of situation is rarely encountered, officers may not be sensitized to its complexity. Proactive traffic stops, for example, allow considerable scope for choice, but officers may not know this unless departmental policy encourages such activity.

Although some work that patrolmen do is clearly discretionary, it is uncertain precisely how much of it is. If situations calling for the use of discretion occur frequently, then the ability to make decisions becomes central to patrol work. On the other hand, if they occur infrequently, then the kinds of skills that experience teaches are less helpful. The uncomfortable fact is that despite the enormous attention given to studying patrol work, especially to charting the nature of calls for service, little is known about the degree to which police exercise discretion. Information has not been collected about how problematical the different kinds of encounters are.[6]

Specifying the scope for decision is not a necessary part of a description of situations. It is a conclusion requiring information about what officers *could* do. Nor can inferences about the scope for choice be drawn from typical outcomes that situations generate. "Service" situations, occasions in which law enforcement action is unlikely or inappropriate, are not necessarily less complex than "enforcement" situations.[7] The designation "order-maintenance" covers situations in which enforcement is appropriate but not automatically utilized. Although the decision is implied by definition, the choice may not be particularly difficult.

Unless studies are undertaken of the problematical nature of particular situations, even data from very detailed studies of the composition of police work will not reveal how much police work actually involves decision. However, information is available about the relative frequency of domestic disputes, which have been identified by patrolmen as being especially problematic. Eric Scott, for example, reported a breakdown of 26,000 calls for service in twenty-four metropolitan police forces in 1977 according to seventy-two categories.[8] He found that domestic conflict accounted for 2.7 percent of calls for service. Moving violations accounted for 1 percent, but this statistic is not informative because the study was of citizen calls for service, not of all observed policy mobilizations.[9] In another study, "domestic trouble" also accounted for 2.7 percent of all calls for service.[10]

These fragments of information suggest that the situations police consider most problematic are not encountered often. If these are the best examples police have of heavily discretionary situations, then making choices may not be the quintessence of patrol work, apart from the need to decide whether to act at all. Police officers may be exaggerating the proportion of problematic work, in part perhaps to enhance their own self-esteem and in part because such situations are especially disconcerting to officers. What is needed before firm conclusions can be drawn about how important experience might be in policing is a systematic mapping of the range of responses actually employed by patrol officers in the situations that occur most frequently.

Interestingly, the situations officers believe provide the greatest scope for decision are among the most dangerous police face. Federal Bureau of Investigation statistics show that, between 1975 and 1979, disturbances (including family fights, quarrels, and "man-with-a-gun") accounted for the largest proportion of police officers killed (17 percent). Robberies in progress, which are not particularly problematic, were next (16 percent), and traffic stops and pursuit were third (12 percent).[11] Although dangerousness and "problematicalness" are conceptually distinct, they appear to be associated to some extent. Because officers know these figures, it may be that their evaluations of the problematical nature of situations reflect their fears.

## III. What Experience Teaches Patrol Officers

Recognizing that focusing on domestic disputes and proactive traffic stops may overemphasize the problematic character of police work, we find that experience on the job contributes to learning about (1) goals, (2) tactics, and (3) presence. That is, when officers talk about what is informative in practical experience, these are the matters most frequently mentioned.

### A. Goals

Decisions about goals are antecedent to choices about tactics, which is not to imply that officers are always purposive. Some officers are essentially aimless, in that they do not try to align tactics and objectives. Any attempt to do so occurs after the fact, involving the false attribution of a rational purpose. Nonetheless, in explaining what they seek to achieve, whether truly or spuriously, patrol officers describe their operating goals as (a) meeting departmental norms, (b) containing violence and controlling disorder, (c) preventing crime, (d) avoiding physical injury to themselves, and (e) avoiding provoking the public into angry retaliation that threatens their careers. No priority can be given to these items; they are simply objectives that patrol officers try to achieve in varying combinations from situation to situation as they work. Each will now be explored in turn.

Departmental norms about what actions are to be undertaken are conveyed in many ways. Officers complain most about the "numbers game," numerical quotas that must be met by each officer. For example, commanders sometimes unfavorably compare the number of felony arrests made by one shift with those made by another, or the number of traffic tickets issued, or the amount of time spent "out of service" as opposed to patrolling. If the quotas are not met, officers are told to "earn their pay." Generally announced policies also constrain tactics, for example, with respect to using firearms against fleeing felons, arresting for minor offenses, or arresting without signed complaints in domestic disputes. The problem is that departmental policy is often not clearly expressed or understood. Supervisors indicate—sometimes subtly, sometimes directly—what they prefer by way of action. Officers are aware that what they normally do is not what "the sergeant" or "the lieutenant" would do. Officers cynically remark that calling a supervisor for assistance in a domestic fight usually produces "two domestics," one among civilians, another among police. Finally, tactical decisions are powerfully shaped by departmental procedures for reporting action. Many contacts with the public require filling out forms that are filed with the department. Often these forms present blocks to check, enumerating the actions taken. These forms structure choice, because officers know that if they take an action not specified, they will be required to provide an explanation. Explicit and detailed forms not only simplify reporting, they raise the cost of exercising initiative. They may also encourage specious reporting.

All of these cues as to what departments consider to be acceptable action are noticed by patrol officers, even when they are not followed. The expectations of departments are so constraining that officers, like youths walking through a graveyard at night, frequently strike brave postures privately about what is required. An officer may say proudly that, "When I'm on patrol I forget about all the higher-ups, I'm my own little police force." He may be, but the department has made him anxious nonetheless.

One of the great imperatives of a patrolman's life is the need to "reproduce order," in Richard Ericson's apt phrase.[12] It has been observed that police characteristically are called to deal with "something-that-ought-not-be-happening-and-about-which-someone-had-better-do-something-now."[13] An essential part of police work is taking charge. The means used to accomplish this end depend on the circumstances. They can involve hitting, shooting, referring, rescuing, tending, separating, handcuffing, humoring, threatening, placating, and discussing. The objective is to minimize the disruptions of normal life. As one officer said, "We keep the peace, we don't settle problems." Police recognize the superficiality of what they do, often blaming this on the pressure of work. The fact is that the police frequently seem to have too much time on their hands and they are forever apologizing for how slow a particular tour of duty is. Actually, officers may be right: they *are* too busy to give the kind of attention that would make any permanent difference to the circumstances encountered. The requirements for dealing with deeper levels of problems are too exorbitant for police to meet. Doing whatever is necessary to restore order is all that can reasonably be expected of the police.

Not only do police want to restore order, they want to lower the likelihood that future disorder, particularly crime, will occur. Though they tend to deny it, police officers are future oriented. The test of success in domestic fights, for example, is "no call-backs." Even while they deprecate the effect that their actions can have on the root causes of problems, they accept uncritically that they should work to deter future criminality. They do not view law enforcement as an end in itself but as a tool for convincing people not to do wrong.[14] Faced with the threat of disorder, officers use laws to get leverage over people, to threaten that if police orders are not followed, the people will go to jail.[15] This is one reason police condemn the decriminalization of nonconforming behavior in public places, such as drinking alcoholic beverages, being drunk, and loitering, that has taken place over the last generation. Such laws are needed, the police argue, to help them gain control before more serious incidents occur. But the police employ even longer time perspectives. This perspective shows up when they explain why they do not enforce the law in certain situations. Time and again they argue that an arrest or a citation would do more harm than good. Why give a traffic ticket, for instance, to an elderly woman who has run a red light and whose hands are shaking with fear as the officer comes up to the car window? A ticket is gratuitous in such circumstances. Why encourage a woman to sign a complaint against the drunken husband who has just blackened her eye when she admits she does not want a divorce, it is apparent the family cannot make bail, and even a short detention in jail may jeopardize the family's income? Whether the public approves or not, patrol officers continually make judicial types of decisions, deciding whether the imposition of the law will achieve what the spirit of the law seems to call for. Police officers are convinced that they know more about the deterrent utility of law than does anyone else. This attitude probably explains why they become so angry at prosecutors and courts that are more lenient than the police expected. They view prosecutors and courts as second-guessing the evaluations made by officers who are more immediately in touch with the practical reality of the situation.[16]

Patrol officers are continually alert to the danger of physical injury to themselves. They take great care with protective equipment such as guns, nightsticks, and sturdy multi-celled flashlights. Many officers now routinely wear light-weight protective vests under their uniform shirts. Sometimes vests are provided by police departments, but they are often purchased out of the officer's own pocket. Police conversation is thick with stratagems for avoiding injury, an urgency stressed from their earliest days in training: when knocking at residences where violence is suspected, do not stand in front of doors; when making traffic stops at night, blind the eyes of the driver with cruiser spotlights or a flashlight; when approaching a vehicle, one officer should linger slightly behind the vehicle on the right side, hand on weapon, while the other interrogates the driver; when questioning a driver, do not stand in front of the door so that its sudden opening could harm you; carry a small blackjack in the rear pocket in order to provide protection less provocatively than with a nightstick; unbutton holsters when responding to calls in particular areas; always keep your head covered in certain tenement neighborhoods; and never turn your back on particular types of people. Police work, according to officers, is fraught with unpredictable and frequently deadly violence. Getting home safely is a primary concern.

Police concern with deadly force is to some extent exaggerated. The death rate for police is well below that of several other occupations. In 1980, for example, the death rate per 100,000 police officers was 32.4, while it was 61 per 100,000 workers in agriculture, 50 per 100,000 workers in mining and quarrying, and 43 per 100,000 construction workers.[17] Police deaths, however, unlike those in other occupations, are not acts of God; they are generally the result of willful, deliberate attacks. They are personal, human-to-human, and imbued with malice in the same way that crime is generally. Just as the public finds small comfort in statistics showing that they are safer on the streets than in their bathtubs, police are more anxious in their work than construction workers are in theirs.

There is another aspect to policing, however, that accounts for officers' pervasive concern with personal injury. Police continually deal with situations in which physical constraint may have to be applied against people who are willing to fight, struggle, hit, stab, spit, bite, tear, hurl, hide, and run. People continually use their bodies against the police, forcing the police to deal with them in a physical way. While police seem to be preoccupied with deadly force, the more common reality in their lives is the possibility of a broken nose, lost teeth, black eyes, broken ribs, and twisted arms. Few officers are ever shot or even shot at, but all except the rawest rookie can show scars on their bodies from continual encounters with low-level violence.

As a result, officers develop an instinctive wariness, what one officer called "well-planned lay-back." While they never want to give the impression of being afraid, especially to their peers, they try to avoid having to struggle with people. Since they are obliged at the same time to establish control, they feel justified in acting with preemptive force. In effect, they learn to act with a margin of force just beyond what their would-be opponents might use. One officer likened it to taking a five-foot jump over a four-foot ditch. Never cut things too closely; if personal injury is likely, strike first with just enough force to nullify the threat. When guns are believed to be present, this margin can be deadly. Sometimes police concern with avoiding injury comes across as a peculiar fastidiousness, not simply anxiety, but distaste for having to soil themselves. Officers complain continually about having gotten blood on their shirts, rips in their down jackets, dirt on their trousers, and vomit in their cars. Many officers carry soft leather gloves for manhandling dirty people. In many residences officers will not sit down for fear of bugs. Police officers often act like people who have gotten dressed up to go to a party only to be confronted with having to wipe up spilled food or change a tire. The point is that police life is rough-and-tumble. Through preemption, overreaction, and simple avoidance, officers try to minimize the unpleasant, sometimes deadly, physical contact that is part of their job.

According to patrol officers, experience sharpens the ability to read potential violence in an encounter. The experienced officer avoids the use of unnecessary physical force, as the "hot dog" does not, but at the same time he is fully prepared to meet such force when necessary, especially by preempting it. The experienced officer has learned when to relax and when to attack. Competence involves the ability to do both and get away with it.

Finally, police worry a lot about repercussions from the actions they take that may affect their careers. They have in mind, in particular, complaints and civil suits. Police, unlike workers in most other jobs, are constantly being reminded of the fatefulness of their actions to themselves as well as to the public. They believe their jobs are on the line daily. So for police to avoid what would be viewed as a mistake by the department or the courts is an imperative.[18] One aspect of what police learn on the job, then, is what *not* to do. As an oficer remarked, "In policing, don'ts are often more important than do's."[19]

In sum, experience has a great deal to teach police about goals. Essentially, it teaches an instinct for priorities. What kind of goals can reasonably be achieved at the least cost to the officer? In Peter Manning's words:

> The central problem of [policing], from the agent's perspective, is not moral but distinctly practical. The aim is to define the work in ways that will allow the occupational members involved to manage it, to make reasonable decisions, control it, parcel it out into meaningful, solvable, and understandable units and episodes, and make this accomplishment somewhat satisfying day after day.[20]

This task involves juggling disparate goals that operate in varying time frames. By and large, police goals are short-range in that their achievement can be determined almost immediately. This observation is true with respect to departmental expectations, the establishment of control, the avoidance of injury, and the protection of the officer's career. The only exception is the objective of preventing future crime and disorder. It seems reasonable to suppose that short-run imperatives prevail in most cases because the information needed to judge whether preventive actions have worked are beyond the ken of the serving police officer. Learning to subordinate long-range to short-range goals makes police officers appear uncaring and hard-bitten. Their own awareness that they are dominated by short-run concerns tends to make them cynical. But this deprecation of their own efforts is not unique to police officers: it is an attitude developed by people in many occupations who learn to substitute practical, instrumental goals for larger visions of social effectiveness. It is found among teachers, doctors, lawyers, social workers, and businessmen. To some extent, then, what experience teaches the police is an acceptance of social impotency.

If experience teaches policemen how to juggle complex priorities in action, one can understand why civilian review is so threatening to them. Police officers say civilian review is unfair because outsiders do not have the experience to judge which actions are required in real-life situations. This view is plausible, but it ignores the fact that choices among tactics are only one part of the problem. Indeed, impressionistic evidence suggests that civilian review boards are frequently willing to accept police expertise. A greater danger, from the police point of view, is that civilian reviewers will insist on a different ordering of objectives, especially ones that ignore altogether the policeman and his career. This concern explains, perhaps, why hostility to civilian review seems to go with the job. It follows naturally from learning that goals have to be set in chaotic moments of action.

## B.  Tactics

Tactical choices are the second area in which the police claim that experience is essential to learning. It is no longer informative to point out that patrol officers do much more than enforce the law. This fact has been thoroughly established by research. But the range of options employed by patrol officers is much greater than this observation conveys. Patrol officers can discern as well as discuss an array of tactical alternatives. Moreover, they can distinguish actions that are appropriate at different stages of an intervention. What patrol officers do has commonly been described according to their culminating actions—arrest, referral, friendly advice, threats, and so forth.[21] But officers have done many things already before they decide how they will leave an encounter. Adequate description of police tactics requires paying attention to different stages in the evolution of police-public interactions.[22] An exploration of the tactics police use must distinguish at least three different stages: contact, processing, and exit. Each stage offers distinctly different choices to patrol officers. These choices will be explored in the cases of domestic disputes and proactive traffic stops, recognizing that these may be the most problematic situations for police officers.

At contact in domestic disputes, police may choose from at least nine different courses of action. As one would expect, these serve by and large to establish immediate control over events, to shift the axis of interaction from the disputants to the officers. The possible courses of action are: to listen passively to disputant(s), verbally restrain disputant(s), threaten physical restraint, apply physical restraint, request separation of disputants, impose separation on disputants, physically force separation, divert attention of disputants, or question to elicit the nature of the problem.

As officers settle into an encounter, having established control on their own terms, they may choose from among eleven tactics: let each disputant have his say in turn, listen in a nondirective way, actively seek to uncover the nature of the problem, accept the situation as defined by the complainant, reject the view of the complainant, follow the request made by the complainant, physically restrain someone, urge someone to sign a complaint, talk someone out of signing a complaint, investigate the incident further without indicating likely action, and indicate that there is nothing the police can do.

Finally, police need to terminate the encounter and make themselves available for other business. Their exiting actions may again be substantially different from anything done before; they may fail to find the other disputant, find the other disputant and warn or advise, arrest someone, separate disputants temporarily by observing one off the premises, by transporting one from the scene or by arranging a pickup by someone else, explicitly warn disputants about the consequences of future trouble, give friendly advice about how to avoid a repetition, provide pointed advice to disputant(s) about how to resolve the issue, suggest referral to third parties, promise future police assistance, transport injured persons to a medical facility, issue a notice of police contact, or simply leave.[23]

Even if these lists of tactics are not exhaustive, the number of alternatives open to officers is already formidable—nine at contact, eleven at processing, and eleven at exit. Experienced patrol officers have strong opinions about which of these courses of action to pursue under different circumstances. Moreover, they criticize one another for choosing the wrong one. For example, police academies often teach that officers should separate disputants immediately and never let them continue to argue. Officers say, however, that the ventilation of grievances is sometimes all that both parties want. The best defusing tactic, therefore, is to let them get things off their chests, with police playing the role of friendly referee. For wives, particularly, calling the police is an act of assertion in itself and they are satisfied when they have made their point. Rather than arresting the husband, the police are better advised to provide her with a safe opportunity to make a statement. When neighbors dispute, arrival of the police may actually exacerbate the argument as both parties feel they need not worry about things getting out of hand. So some officers covertly restrain the growing altercation by turning their backs or pulling away, indicating that they really do not care what happens. Frequently this action causes the dispute to lose some of its steam.

Officers are especially sensitive to actions they take that may make situations more explosive. They are particularly careful, for example, to avoid laying hands on people unless they absolutely must. Touching connotes restraint and it is apt to be resented. Officers say that people of a minority group are especially quick to anger when police touch them. So police learn to move people about verbally or by imposing their bodies without actually reaching out. This tactic is related to the need to save "face," something most officers recognize as being important. Police must be careful not to inflict humiliation gratuitously. For this reason, patrol officers think twice before writing out traffic tickets to fathers in front of their children, unless the violation is serious or the man uncivil.[24] Officers believe that older people get angry at traffic stops because they are accustomed to disciplining rather than being disciplined. They feel belittled. Thus, officers tread warily so as not to make acquiescence difficult. Similarly, many officers testify to thanks earned by not handcuffing men in front of their children but doing so outside the residence or in the patrol car. It also seems that men submit to handcuffs more tractably than do women, who frequently become hysterical and sometimes violent.

Demonstrating the importance of obtaining control without physical injury in the hierarchy of operating values, patrol officers have a great fund of stories about how violent situations were defused through cunning verbal ploys. For example, an officer who was a born-again Christian spotted religious decor in the home of a couple who had had a violent argument. He asked them what they thought the Lord would want them to do and ten minutes later they were reconciled. One tactic is to divert the attention of disputants, thus allowing emotions to cool. Noting what appears to be handmade furniture, an officer may say, "Do you make furniture? So do I." Others ask if they may use the bathroom, obliging the residents to point it out, or inquire what the score is of the baseball game on TV, or request a cup of coffee or a soft drink. One officer gained control in a domestic dispute by sitting down indifferently in front of the television set and calmly taking off his hat. The husband and wife were so nonplussed at this lack of concern for their fight that shortly they, too, lost interest. Stories like these are so common among officers that they should probably be taken with a grain of salt. The same stories crop up too often, suggesting that they have become part of the mythology of policing, passed on uncritically from officer to officer. Told always with pride, they are used to illustrate the subtlety of police officers. Most of the ploys so lovingly described are also clearly not in general use,[25] as most officers admit that while they try to defuse violence without using physical restraint, their own stratagems are more direct.

Officers also tend to agree on what actions are to be avoided, such as failing to gain control quickly enough when injury is likely, making threats that cause people to lose face, taking sides in an argument, leaving a dispute with a threat about what the police will do when they return, and making take-it-or-leave-it statements that the police cannot honor. These are the mistakes rookies make. Only experienced officers are presumed to have the diagnostic skills to know when these tactics can be used safely.

It is precisely with respect to the choice of tactics that the separation between the craft of policing and the science of policing is most destructive. Officers say experience teaches them what works. But does it? They manage to get along, which means avoiding affronting the department or getting seriously hurt or sued, but are they intelligently discriminating in their tactical choices so that they are raising the probability of achieving stated goals? Perhaps almost anything "works" most of the time, largely because the police are so authoritative in relation to the people with whom they have to deal. The questions that need to be answered scientifically are: (1) can the tactics and the circumstances of encounters be better matched so that patrol officers can more certainly avoid failures according to their own criteria; (2) are the long-run, post-encounter effects that officers want to accomplish truly achieved through the actions they choose; and (3) do the tactics they choose produce unintended consequences that deserve to be considered? At the moment, this kind of factual knowledge is not being provided to officers. The fault is not that of the serving police officer. By necessity, he must fall back on the lore that experience generates. The problem is that science has not illuminated the operational imperatives of the work that patrol officers do. Nor have police departments acknowledged that guidance could be useful. Crouched behind the statement that "every situation is different," they have failed to pay attention to what their own rank and file are telling them: namely, that learning about what "works" is possible and that it is taking place already through the haphazard mechanism of individual experience. While the partisans of science have failed to focus on the tactical world of the serving officer, police officers have not seen that it is contradictory to say that, although every situation is different, experience is crucial.

Turning to traffic stops, we have identified ten actions considered appropriate at contact, seven at processing, and eleven at exit. At contact, officers may leave the driver in the car, order him out, leave passengers in the car, order passengers out, ask the driver for documents, ask passengers for documents, order the driver to remain in the car, order passengers to remain in the car, point out the violation that prompted the stop, and ask the driver if he knew why the stop was made. At processing, officers may check whether the car and the driver are "clear," give a roadside sobriety test, make a body search of the driver, make a body search of the passengers, search the vehicle from outside, search the vehicle from inside, and discuss the alleged traffic violation. At exit, officers may release the car and the driver, release with a warning, release with a traffic citation, release with both a citation and an admonishment, arrest the driver for a prior offense, arrest for being drunk, arrest for crimes associated with evidence found during the stop, arrest for actions during the encounter, impound the car, insist that the driver proceed on foot, help the driver to arrange for other transportation, arrest the passengers for the same reasons as the driver, transport the driver someplace without making an arrest, and admonish the passengers.

Officers have different opinions about what tactics to apply at each stage, recognizing, of course, that some situations permit little latitude. On initial contact, for example, officers favor different gambits. Some tell the driver why he was stopped before asking for his license and registration. This settles the driver's natural curiosity and puts him on the defensive. Others first ask for documents, thus ensuring that the driver will not escape and demonstrating that information will be given only when the officer chooses. Still others like to begin with the question "Do you know why I stopped you?" hoping that the drivers, most of whom drive on the edge of the law, will admit an infraction even more serious than the one that led to the stop. The officer can then be magnanimous, agreeing to forgive the more serious offense in favor of the lesser that the officer was going to ticket anyhow. Not all these gambits can, of course, be tried in every situation; they depend on particular circumstances. But it is easy to see that each gives a distinctive impetus to the police-citizen interaction. At least police believe so, making choice of action on their part a test of professional savvy.

The crucial stage, from the public's point of view, is exit, where there are eleven different possibilities that are used singly or in combination. Most officers disagree strongly with the teaching that they should make up their minds whether or not to issue a ticket before approaching a stopped vehicle. Although some officers will ticket anyone—even their grandmothers, as other officers contemptuously say—most believe that individuation is essential to justice. It is unnecessary, for example, to give tickets for driving without a license to responsible people who admit their offense but can't produce their licenses. Officers, too, have left their wallets at home while running to do an errand or have forgotten to take their licenses out of their checkbooks after going to the bank. Drivers have been "cleared" on the basis of all sorts of identification, including credit cards and fishing licenses.

The key ingredient in exit decisions, apart from the seriousness of the offense, is the attitude of the driver. If the violation is minor, drivers who admit error and do not challenge the authority of the officer are likely to be treated leniently, unless departmental policy decrees otherwise. On the other hand, drivers who dispute the offense, question the value of what the officer is doing, use disrespectful language, and threaten to complain will virtually write themselves a citation. Officers are especially resentful of well-to-do people driving expensive late-model cars who threaten to complain to "the chief" or "the mayor." Officers are proud of their one-line put-downs of such people, such as, "Do you know the chief too? When you see him tell him Officer Jones gave you a ticket today." While much of this bravado is probably indulged only off the street, it accurately reflects what officers may consider in making exit choices. At the same time, officers often take amazing amounts of verbal abuse from people for whom profanity is as natural as breathing. The same is true for racial put-downs by blacks of white officers, such as studied, face-saving condescension and mutterings about "honky cops." Officers also know the importance that their own demeanor has in shaping the results of a stop. If they do decide to give a ticket, they try to be matter-of-fact, unless provoked, and to avoid verbal humiliation. The choice is between ticketing or lecturing and releasing. In the words of one officer, "chew or cite, but not both."

It would appear that the tactical choices patrol officers make, at least for domestic disputes and traffic stops, are much more extensive than is generally recognized. They have to learn what "works" in terms of objectives that they can reasonably judge in circumstances that vary enormously. They are anxious about the fatefulness of their actions for themselves as well as for others, fearful that the instant diagnoses they make will be incorrect. This is undoubtedly what prompts the often repeated assertion that every situation is different, which according to the officers' own testimony about the utility of experience, is not true. Donald Black has shown that tactical choices with respect to exiting actions in domestic disputes are affected by a small number of structural features in each encounter—race, class, age, status of complainant in the household, intimacy between the people involved, institutional affiliation of complainants, and attacks on police legitimacy.[26] However, the effect of these factors does not appear large, accounting for between ten and twenty-five percent of the variance.[27] As has been noted, officers want to emphasize the difficulty of their work. Confronted by social scientists probing to uncover choices, they may even exaggerate small differences in procedural detail, falsely attributing forethought to automatic decisions. None of this, however, contradicts the fact that choices *are* made, sometimes among a bewildering number of alternatives, and that officers cannot readily state the principles that they use to simplify the situational complexities faced. The best they can do is to tell anecdotes. That they do simplify, as Black points out, in no way diminishes the uncertainty they feel in making tactical choices. Having implicit operating principles does not lessen anxiety. Nor does it follow that experience is not important in learning to apply them. Moreover, officers are often genuinely trying to forecast the effects of their actions on a recurrence of the situation. Unfortunately, they have only rough-and-ready rules for doing so, probably involving the factors Black has noted. Here is where the lore of policing with respect to tactics is probably the least well-informed and the chances for bias to intrude the greatest.

What officers need, of course, is information that shows what the likely results will be from the use of tactics of different sorts in various situations. As Herman Goldstein has said:

> [S]ystematic analysis and planning have rarely been applied to specific behavior and social problems that constitute the agency's routine business. The situation is somewhat analogous to a private industry that studies the speed of its assembly line, the productivity of its employees, and the nature of its public relations program, but does not examine the quality of the product being produced.[28]

Such testing will not be easy to carry out, although the principles for doing so are clear.[29] This is scant comfort to patrolmen. In the absence of tested knowledge about what works, patrol officers have no resource to call on except their own collective experience. From their perspective, choice is an operational necessity, and they see trial and error as the only way to learn about it.[30]

### C. Presence

The third important feature that experience teaches is "presence." Effective policing is more than simply doing things, it involves *being* something. The key elements of effective presence are external calm and internal alertness. Police say repeatedly that it is essential to be nonprovocative in contacts with the public—to adopt a demeanor that pacifies, placates, and mollifies. "Always act," said an experienced officer, "as if you were on vacation." In effect, be careful not to heighten the tension already present. At the same time, officers must never relax. They must be constantly watchful and alert because danger can arise in an instant. Danger, however, is not the only threat. All officers with any seniority speak bitterly of the times they were "conned," accepting uncritically a story told to them on which they then acted. Police learn quickly that appearance and reality are often sharply different. People will use the police for their own purposes if they can, even if it means telling elaborate lies. Some people, police know, really are evil. As a result, police officers often appear indifferent, cynical, and unsympathetic in the most heart-rending situations. The presence that police officers cultivate is much like that of professional athletes, who talk, too, about the importance of balancing concentration and relaxation. One must be keyed up but not "choke." In policing, this means that officers must protect without provoking. The inward equanimity that leads to outward poise is not something people are born with, nor can it be taught. As in sports, it is learned through practice.

In summary, then, from the point of view of the patrol officer, policing is more like a craft than a science, in that officers believe that they have important lessons to learn that are not reducible to principle and are not being taught through formal education. These lessons concern goals—which ones are reasonable; tactics—which ones ensure achievement of different goals in varying circumstances; and presence—how to cultivate a career-sustaining personality. "Experience-tested good sense," as one officer said, is what police must learn over the years.

What has not been grasped, however, is that even as policing at the present time is more craft than science, learning *can* take place, skills *can* be increased, and levels of expertise *can* be discerned. Officers themselves recognize this point when they talk about how they "learned" to become effective. They also continually complain that standards of performance should distinguish degrees of coping ability, not mechanical conformity to specific do's and don'ts—excluding horrendous errors, of course.

Although seldom admitted, learning in policing involves discovering how each officer can achieve stated goals within his own personal limitations. If tactics are as varied as has been shown, then different styles may be equally effective. Some officers have a gift of gab, others do not. Some officers are so physically imposing they can reduce violence simply by "blotting out the sun"; others have to raise their voices, threaten retaliation, or spin a yarn. Being skilled in policing, as in carpentry, is a matter of learning to be effective with the materials and tools at hand.

The police community is very judgmental about skills displayed on the job, quite apart from formal systems of performance appraisal. Policemen judge the work of colleagues all the time. To begin with, patrol work is often performed before an audience of other officers. In domestic disputes, for example, several cars frequently respond when violence has been reported. As the premises suddenly fill up with large men in blue uniforms, the first officer on the scene has to give a lead as to how the situation will be handled. Whether comfortable or not, he dare not back away. He has to perform on-view. Rookies particularly feel the presence of this attentive audience. Remembering his own days as a rookie, one officer said, "It's like your ears are on stalks." Rookies cannot help notice when an experienced officer gives a snort of laughter or contemptuously turns his back.

And well they should be concerned, because police officers make judgments about the strengths and weaknesses of colleagues all the time which they do not hesitate to express. Reputations are made in a twinkling, especially for recruits or newly transferred personnel. Every unit has its known hotheads, deadbeats, unreliables, and head-knockers. They also have respected master craftsmen, although this designation is not used. These officers are cool, poised, inventive, careful, active, and nonviolent—officers who can cope without jeopardizing themselves or others. Appraisals of colleagues are a staple of police conversation, often taking place between partners in patrol cars and prompted only by hearing an officer speak over the radio: "Go get 'em, hot dog"; "Surprised he's not taking his fifth coffee break"; "Uh, oh, we'll have to cover that screw-up for sure"; and "Smith has got a rookie tonight." Judgments are also conveyed through preferences officers express for partners. Some are shunned, others are sought out. Occasionally, doubts about performance will be so serious that officers will indicate privately to supervisors that they will not work with a particular officer. Only the most insensitive policeman could fail to appreciate that if people are talking about others as openly as they do, they must be talking about him too. Officers know that reputations are on the line whenever they work. Among their own kind, they want to be known as master craftsmen, hoping to escape from the stigma of apprentice as soon as possible.

In policing, then, it is legitimate to talk about skills and to make judgments about performance. The critical question is whether there is a consensus about craftsmanship. That is, although officers recognize differences in performance, do they agree on what constitutes better as opposed to worse activity? Police officers could be in the tragic situation of wanting desperately to learn from experience yet receiving conflicting signals from their peers. Approval of skills may be given for nothing more profound than doing things "my way." In these circumstances, learning would consist of developing a mode of operation that bore little relation either to objective measures of effectiveness or approval by peers. The situation may not, however, be so dismal. Like teaching, good policing may be easier to recognize in practice than to define abstractly. Perhaps officers really do agree on who is especially skilled, raising the possibility that learning through emulation is possible. The truth of this matter would be important to test. It would also be easy to do. Officers would be asked to identify by name others whom they consider to be particularly skilled. If there was reasonable agreement, observers would then determine whether these individuals acted in terms of similar goals, chose similar tactics, and displayed the same presence. Observation would be better than asking officers about the qualities that caused them to identify others as being skilled, because officers might simply project onto others what they thought should be valued in themselves. Since patrol officers believe, almost as an article of faith, that supervisors evaluate performance superficially, ignoring displays of skill that do not show up in numbers, it would be important to solicit opinions about skilled officers from all ranks. Supervisors may not be quite as out of touch as they are portrayed to be. Alternatively, they may be emphasizing norms that increase the uncertainty patrol officers feel as they go about their daily work.

The final and indispensable step would be to determine whether the tactics chosen by master craftsmen really worked as intended. As in medicine, a proper bedside manner does not guarantee correct diagnosis or treatment. Only rigorous testing of the efficacy of tactical choices can at last transform police lore into the wisdom its practitioners think it to be.

## IV.  Can the Craft be Taught?

If learning to make correct choices takes place by and large in the crucible of experience, rather than through formal training, then the development of occupational skills is likely to be a lengthy process whose outcome is far from certain. It does not follow, however, that learning could not be accelerated and made more systematic. We would like to make four suggestions for making the transition from apprentice to master craftsman both faster and more assured.[31]

First, formal training programs must give more attention to the problematic nature of police work. Oddly, police keep talking as if policing were a craft, but recruits are instructed as if it were a science. As Manning remarked, "The striking thing about order-maintenance methods is how little they are taught, how cynically they are viewed, and how irrelevant they are thought to be in most police departments."[32] The reason is probably that training staffs do not know how to instruct in craftsmanship. As in colleges, teaching mainly consists of lecturing and listening. What is needed in police training, instead, is frank discussion, with case studies of the realities of field decision. Training in police academies is too much like introductory courses on anatomy in medical schools and not enough like internships. The problem, however, is that this kind of training would require admitting what command staffs would rather hide, namely, that in many situations no one is really quite sure what is the best thing to do.

Training must focus on the need for choice in specific, clearly delineated situations. The reality of police work must be brought into the classroom so that students and staff can discuss appropriate goals and tactics. They should also be encouraged to think reflectively about the cues that should be used to shape decisions and those that should not. These training objectives can be accomplished in several ways. Students and staff can simulate "street" encounters, taking the roles of citizens and police. Students can be asked to discuss how they would respond to a variety of written scenarios. Discrepancies among students should be highlighted, with an analysis made of what the likely results of responding in each way would be. Films and videotapes, now being developed fairly widely, could be used to portray the hurly-burly of real life. In all of these cases, master craftsmen, if they can be identified, should be used to help train recruits. This does not mean that they should have classes turned over to them, since they are generally not trained in instruction, nor should they be brought in primarily to excite the recruits with "war stories."[33] Rather, they should be used as authentic exhibits to help instructors explore the uncertainties of choice that police face on the street. It is their experience that should be deliberately and systematically tapped. Finally, academic discussion must alternate with observation of patrol operations. This practice is followed now in many departments. Unfortunately, debriefing is rarely systematic; field experiences are not used to prompt discussion about the range of goals and the probable effectiveness of various tactics.

Second, master craftsmen should be used as field instructors for rookies. This is the rationale behind programs in many departments in which probationary officers are assigned to experienced patrolmen for periods of time. Though field instruction programs are a considerable advance over training wholly in classroom settings, the full potential for uncovering significant craft skills is not being developed. Too often, appointment as a field instructor is a reward for having an unblemished record, not for recognition of superior skills, or it is a reward for meeting departmental criteria of performance, which are not necessarily those of craft operatives. The importance of discovering whether this gap in performance norms really exists has already been explored. Furthermore, field instructors are rarely trained to draw lessons from their own experience. They have no more insight into what they are doing than do other officers. In particular, they may be totally blind to alternative ways of accomplishing the same objective. They may be especially confident, which makes their advice particularly persuasive, but they are not necessarily more informed. Finally, because field instructors are often responsible for evaluating the performance of trainees, they are viewed as judges rather than as mentors. They intimidate the recruit rather than draw out his perplexity about police work. Training and evaluation should be more carefully separated, even though that may lengthen the probationary period.

Third, if policing does encompass varying levels of skill related to experience, it follows that learning can be continual and cumulative. The shape of the learning curve would need to be determined through research. It may be found that diminished returns set in relatively soon after an officer leaves the academy, or that learning continues fairly steadily throughout most of an officer's career. If learning tapered off rapidly, it would be necessary to find out whether this was due to the unexpected simplicity of the work or to the lack of encouragement for continued growth in skills. On the testimony of police themselves, learning should not be viewed as a short-run matter. It needs to be built into policing throughout an officer's career. This need is generally recognized under the rubric of in-service training. Unfortunately, in-service training relies primarily on sending people back to classrooms for traditional lectures and note-taking. If skills are to be further developed, what is needed are seminars among patrol personnel in which they share their understanding of appropriate goals and useful tactics. Officers must be helped to learn from one another less haphazardly than they do in the front seats of patrol cars. Such seminars should not be bull sessions, where people talk in a nondirective way. Seminars must be carefully led by people who are trained in maintaining focus, imposing discipline, and drawing out participants. In our own seminars with officers, we found that patrolmen frequently disagree about elementary facts concerning law, departmental policy, and the functioning of the criminal justice system. Opportunities for relevant instruction emerge out of the perplexity of officers themselves. Furthermore, although officers recognize that there are different ways for handling situations, they have never had an opportunity to share insights about the relative utility of these approaches. They do what comes naturally, which may be good or may be bad. The final benefit from forthright discussion is that it may resensitize jaded officers to the problems and potentialities of the job. Experience may teach, but it also rigidifies. Being comfortable in one's work is not the same as being effective in it.

In-service seminars may contribute to raising performance levels even though immediate skill development does not occur. Because they are a visible sign that departments take seriously the complexity of patrol work and value the learning that experience engenders, in-service seminars may raise the standing of patrol work. Officers are proud of what they have learned, not always with reason, and interested in demonstrating their skill. As in the famous Hawthorne study of industrial productivity, institutional attention to their workday life may rekindle the enthusiasm of officers for their work.

Fourth, assuming that experience is valuable in learning about police work, departments should reward advancement in skill development. Presently, police departments reward superior achievement by promoting people into supervisory positions or transferring them to non-patrol duties. Thus, they lose skills in patrol without assuredly gaining talent for other pursuits. Good patrolmen are not necessarily good supervisors, any more than they are good detectives, planners, or juvenile counselors. Police departments must find ways to encourage continued growth in patrol skills among the people who remain in patrol work.

Identifying and using master craftsmen in departmental training is an important first step. It demonstrates to the rank and file that skills are recognized, that what is learned on the street is valued. But there are other possibilities that should be explored as well. Pay raises might be given to people recognized by their peers as master craftsmen. Departments might also establish a special title, rank, or insignia for officers who are especially skilled in patrol work. The point is to convince patrol officers that the creative use of experience in learning to perform more effectively is appreciated.

## V. The Bottom Line

Experience teaches lessons to patrol officers that they consider crucial to effective performance and career longevity. Complicated decisions are being made on the street about goals and tactics in the face of enormously varied social circumstances. This being the case, obvious benefits would result from ensuring that what is being learned bears a close relation to approved goals, that correct tactical lessons are being reinforced, and that learning takes place as quickly as possible. In order to accomplish this, it is important to study the coherence among what pass as craft skills in departments and the connection between tactics and both short-range and long-range outcomes. Most important of all, police departments must face up to the implications for training or their own argument that policing is learned by experience.

The benefits of doing all this are obvious. First, giving institutional attention to the skills that experience teaches will raise morale and self-esteem among the most numerous police rank, the patrolmen, who bear the major responsibility for police performance. Emphasizing the subtlety of patrol work also redresses the overemphasis on criminal investigation, so often deplored by policemen and observers alike.[34] Patrol work would begin to be perceived as a disciplined activity, no less demanding than the work of detectives.

Second, police departments would be forced to develop techniques for measuring degrees of skill. It is a matter for fierce debate in police circles whether existing measures do so. Most patrolmen think they do not, arguing that evaluation is based on quantitative indicators which measure activity rather than effectiveness. As we have suggested, a careful study of the performance traits of officers recognized by their peers as being especially good at patrol work would help to clarify this matter. It does not follow, of course, that patrolmen are right. If a discrepancy exists between what officers and the organization think is good patrol work, it should be eliminated. If, on the other hand, the discrepancy exists only in the minds of the rank and file, steps should be taken to correct this impression.

Third, only by developing canons for better/worse, proper/improper, more/less useful patrol action can policing become truly professional. Professionalism—meaning the development and imposition of operating principles out of an ongoing cooperative analysis—is essential in both scientific and craft domains of work. Indeed, it is precisely when operating principles are unclear that responsible learning requires the systematic and sensitive pooling of experience. Paradoxically, policing has not developed the self-consciousness that claims about the craft nature of policing would entail. For all the talk, the police community has not acted as if it really believes that there is utility in studying experience. Policemen have wanted the autonomy of professionals without accepting the counterbalancing responsibility for regulating the work of practitioners in operational terms. It is not being argued that policemen are more duplicitous than other claimants to professional status, but police have not successfully convinced either themselves or the public that their work is highly skilled. Until they do, their talk about professionalism will seem presumptuous.

Here is the rub: Substantial risks are involved for the police in openly admitting that goals are not fixed, that law enforcement is often uncertain, and that tactical choices are matters of opinion. They become politically more vulnerable if they say outright that patrol work requires the development of skills over time, for it implies that the great mass of police officers are flying by the seat of their pants. Police officers may chafe at the fact that their work is undervalued because its subtlety is not understood, but the fiction of automatic decisionmaking protects them from being second-guessed.

Little imagination is required to foresee what would happen to public confidence in the police if they admitted that age, education, class, race, and sex were considered when they decide what to do. These factors *are* considered, however, and the police believe, on the basis of hard-won experience, that they must be considered. Here are some examples. A white man and a black man, each well-dressed, each carrying a television set from a retail store to the trunk of a car at 5:30 P.M., will probably be treated differently by the police. Officers will not only be more suspicious of the black man and more likely to stop and question him, they will also be more circumspect in their approach if they decide to confront him. They know that black men have had a belly full of "hassling" and are much more likely than white men to get angry. Another example deals with spouse assault reports made by Hispanic, as opposed to black, women. Because Hispanic women have been found to be less willing than black women to file complaints against husbands who beat them, police officers have to work harder to provide equal protection. Their approach to marital discord has to follow different lines from the beginning. Antagonism toward the police is often more intense in some places in a community than in others. Officers, therefore, take more precautions in those areas. From their point of view, this behavior is reasonable; from the public's, it is hostile, provocative, and demeaning. On a warm Friday night, shortly after dark, cruising patrol officers saw a small car pull away from the side door of a public school. As the car went past them, they saw that the driver was a white middle-aged man who hardly gave the police a passing glance. "Your basic pillar?" said one officer. "Yep," replied the other, "your basic pillar." The car was not stopped for investigation. Can such a decision be explained to the public without controversy?

A real distinction does exist between useful operational intelligence and prejudice, but because both utilize the same cues, they are difficult to separate in practice.[35] It would certainly be unrealistic, as well as unreasonable, to expect patrolmen not to make decisions about goals and tactics on the basis of situational circumstances such as the visible appearance of the people involved. Unless choice is precluded altogether in police work, officers cannot avoid developing stereotypes. To achieve the goals of control, crime prevention, personal safety, and career protection, patrol officers must adapt what they do to what they see.[36] In order to protect such decisions from prejudice, however, more examination of the link between visible cues and the results of particular tactics must be made. In particular, research must be undertaken to determine what really does work both tactically and strategically. Is it true, for example, that disproportionate attention to black teenager activity on the streets produces more criminal arrests than arrests of teenagers indiscriminately; that a criminal complaint pressed by the police with a wife's approval is not as effective in providing protection for the battered spouse who is Hispanic, even if the complaint is eventually withdrawn, as for the spouse who is black and prosecutes to the end; or that preemptive force against strapping black males controls violence and avoids injuries to police more surely than less provocative tactics? Addressing such questions is essential if prejudice and operational intelligence are to be distinguished. However, the point remains that if different approaches are found efficacious based on ascriptive stereotypes, as police officers certainly believe, imparting these lessons will look very much to nonpolice observers like legitimating discrimination.

In point of fact, the public may not disagree with police decisions as much as the police fear it does. John Clark compared what the police and public respectively thought were appropriate police actions in six hypothetical situations.[37] He found that the police tended to recommend arrest more and that they thought the public wanted more arrests than they really did. This evidence would suggest that the public would welcome more individuation, but that it is the police who are reluctant. In an international testing of what the public would approve in four criminal situations, the public agreed that police decisions should be affected both by the nature of the crime and the class of the perpetrator.[38] The public appeared to believe, as the police do, that actions should be bent to considerations of natural justice.

Undoubtedly, there are serious potential costs to the police in responding to the challenge of improving skills by forthrightly addressing how policing is learned. This is not the last word, however, about the public's likely reaction. Failure to confront the learning requirements of patrol work not only affects police performance and morale, but also does not solve the problem of public perception. Police are fooling themselves if they think so. If choice is unavoidable in police work, because goals and tactics must be determined situationally, pretending otherwise becomes a living lie that the public soon detects. Although facing the training implications of patrol work will be controversial, not doing so is also controversial. The police lose the opportunity for developing public acceptance of their professional status that would not only be gratifying but that they believe would enhance effectiveness. Part of the reason the public questions the use of discretion is that the police have always tried to appear exclusively as technical agents of law rather than instruments of public morality. A vicious circle has arisen. If police improved performance by testing the "lessons of experience" for efficacy, both through controlled observation and the sharing of collective police experience, and then imparted those lessons more systematically to police officers, the public might have more confidence in the police as moral arbiters. Unfortunately, at the present, the public's distrust of the police impels officers to hide the problematic nature of their work, causing departments to undervalue what the rank and file believe is critical to their work, to neglect intelligent appraisal of collective experience, and to pass up the opportunity to reward those who do patrol work particularly well.

## Footnotes

[1] *See generally* D. Black, The Manners and Customs of the Police (1980); K. Davis, Discretionary Justice (1969); W. LaFave, Arrest (1965); P. Manning, Police Work (1977); W. Muir, Police-Street Corner Politicians (1977); A. Reiss, Police and the Public (1971); J. Rubinstein, City Police (1973); B. Smith, Police Systems in the United States (1940); J. Wilson, Varieties of Police Behavior (1968).

[2] D. Bayley, The Police and Political Development in India (1969); D. Bayley, Patterns of Policing (forthcoming).

3 *See* D. Black, *supra* note 1, at 188-89; W. Muir, *supra* note 1, ch. 6; J. Rubinstein, *supra* note 1, at 153.

4 D. Bayley & H. Mendelsohn, Minorities and the Police 72 (1969). The authors cite figures of 38 percent and 14 percent, respectively.

5 Domestic disputes were mentioned by 29.3 percent of the officers surveyed. D. Bayley, Police and Community Attitudes in Battle Creek, Michigan: An Interim Report on the Evaluation of the Police Improvement Project (September, 1981) (unpublished report by the Police Foundation).

6 M. Farmer & M. Furstenberg, Alternative Strategies for Responding to Police Calls for Service 2 (1979).

7 M. Banton, The Policeman in the Community (1964); W. LaFave, *supra* note 1; P. Shane, Police and People (1980); J. Wilson, *supra* note 1; LaFave, *The Police and Nonenforcement of the Law*, 1962 Wis. L. Rev. 104.

8 E. Scott, Calls for Service: Citizen Demand and Initial Response, 28–30 (1980) (Bloomington, Indiana: Workshop in Political Theory and Policy Analysis, University of Indiana) (unpublished paper).

9 J. McIver & R. Parks, Identification of Effective and Ineffective Police Actions 13 (March 1982) (paper for the annual meeting of the Academy of Criminal Justice Sciences). Five percent of all calls for police service involved domestic and nondomestic conflict.

10 Lilly, *What Are the Police Now Doing* 6 J. Police Sci. & Ad. 51, 56 (1978).

11 U.S. Department of Justice, Sourcebook on Criminal Justice Statistics 326, table 3.81 (1981).

12 R. Ericson, Reproducing Order: A Study of Police Patrol Work 4 (1982).

13 Bittner, *Florence Nightingale in Pursuit of Willie Sutton: A Theory of the Police*, in The Potential for Reform in the Criminal Justice System 30 (1974).

14 A. Reiss, *supra* note 1, at 134–38.

15 Bittner, *supra* note 13, at 22–29; W. LaFave, *supra* note 1, at 138; C. Silberman, Criminal Violence, Criminal Justice 136 (1978).

16 Reiss argues that anger against the courts also arises from the fact that police arrest only when they feel it is morally justified. When courts are lenient, the policeman's sense of justice is affronted. A. Reiss, *supra* note 1, at 134–38.

17 Bureau of the Census, U.S. Department of Commerce, Statistical Abstract of the U.S. 179, 403, 415 (1981).

18 F. Ianni & E. Reuss-Ianni, Street Cops vs. Management Cops: The Two Cultures of Policing 24–28 (December 1980) (paper prepared for the seminar on policing at Nijenrode, The Netherlands).

19 This remark fits the dominant management strategy of police departments, which James Q. Wilson characterizes as constraint-oriented rather than task-oriented. J. Wilson, *The Investigators* 197–98 (1978).

20 P. Manning, The Narcs' Game 17 (1980).

21 Black uses categories of this kind: penal, compensatory, therapeutic, and conciliatory. D. Black, The Behavior of Law 6 (1976); Black *supra* note 1, ch. 5.

22 R. Sykes & E. Brent, *Policing: A Social Behaviorist Perspective* (1984). This sophisticated work tried to determine how antecedent stages shaped later ones.

23 Parnas, *The Police Response to the Domestic Disturbance*, 1967 Wis. L. Rev. 914-60; M. Haist & R. Daniel, Draft of a Report on Structure and Process of Disturbance Transactions (January, 1975) (unpublished draft at the Police Foundation), and J. McIver & R. Parks, *supra* note 9, are the only attempts to map tactics in domestic disputes known to the authors.

24 *See also* D. Black, *supra* note 1, at 34.

25 M. Brown, Working the Street ch. 9 (1981), found significant differences in the tactics officers said they would use in four scenarios presented to them. The scenarios

involved drunken driving, quarreling neighbors, assault between husband and wife, and disorderly juveniles in a public place.

[26] D. Black, *supra* note 1, at 75-80. Black's analysis applies to his four categories of action, which are termed exit actions in this article. He does not try to explain the structural determinants of the tactics police use at earlier stages of disputes.

[27] R. Friedrich, The Impact of Organization, Individual, and Situational Factors on Police Behavior (1977) (unpublished Ph.D. dissertation, available at University of Michigan, Ann Arbor, Dept. of Political Science).

[28] Goldstein, *Improving Policing: A Problem-Oriented Approach*, 25 J. Crime & Delinq. 236, 243 (1979).

[29] The authors will explore this problem and suggest specific research projects in a forthcoming paper.

[30] On the absence of research on this topic, see M. Wycoff, Reconceptualizing the Police Role (November 1980) (draft report from the Police Foundation for the National Institute of Justice). The Police Division of the National Institute of Justice has recognized the importance of this problem; their grant supported the work that led to this article.

[31] In putting forward these four recommendations, this article does not mean to imply that all police departments in the United States are remiss in these respects. There are departments in which these proposals have already been substantially incorporated. Nonetheless, many departments have not done so and should give these ideas serious consideration.

[32] P. Manning, Police Work 289 (1977).

[33] Van Maanen, *Working the Street: A Developmental View of Police Behavior,* in The Potential for Reform in Criminal Justice 88-91 (H. Jacob ed. 1974).

[34] P. Manning, *supra* note 32, at 372.

[35] M. Puch, Policing the Inner City 124 (1979), and C. Shearing, Cops Don't Always See It That Way (1977) (unpublished paper), show how police distinguish good people from bad people on the basis of ostensible features.

[36] Clark & Sykes, *Some Determinants* in Handbook of Criminology 467 (D. Glazer ed. 1974).

[37] Clark, *Isolation of the Police: A Comparison of the British and American Situations,* 56 J. Crim. L. Criminology & Police Sci. 327 (1965).

[38] Criminal Education and Research Center, Perception of Police Power: A Study in Four Cities 63–64 (1973).

# Field Training for Police Officers
## State of the Art

*Michael S. McCampbell*

Newly hired police recruits traditionally have received most of their basic training in the classroom. This training, which is one of the most important functions any police agency undertakes, tries to give recruits basic competency to perform as patrol officers.

Most academy training programs, however, leave a wide gap between the classroom and the "real world" of police work. Field training programs therefore play a significant role in teaching new officers to handle themselves effectively on the job. Exposure to actual street experience and accompanying patrol situations helps recruits apply principles they have learned in the classroom to live situations.

The earliest formal field training program appears to have been established in the San Jose, California, Police Department in 1972. The San Jose program originated as a result of a 1970 traffic accident involving an on-duty San Jose police recruit who was negligently operating a police vehicle. A passenger in the other vehicle was killed, and the officer was seriously injured. The city subsequently dismissed the officer, and a review of the personnel records revealed serious inadequacies in the department's recruit training and evaluation procedures.

Today, the "typical" field training program consists of *formalized*, on-the-job instruction by specially selected and trained personnel called Field Training Officers (FTO's). Field training (generally combined with periodic evaluation of the recruit's performance) usually occurs immediately after the recruit completes the classroom portion of basic training.

Field training programs often are divided into three or more phases. Although agencies may vary the length of the phases, each program normally consists of an introductory phase and several training and evaluation phases. During the introductory phase, the recruit becomes familiar with agency policies and local laws; during the training and evaluation phases, the recruit is gradually introduced to the more complicated tasks patrol officers confront.

National Institute of Justice. *Research in Brief*. November, 1986.

A final phase, consisting solely of evaluation of the recruit's performance, also may occur. During this phase, the FTO may act strictly as an observer and evaluator while the recruit performs all the functions of a patrol officer. This final test determines if the recruit is able to work alone.

This *Research in Brief* presents the results and recommendations of a national survey of field training programs in police departments across the country. The survey was augmented with case studies in four police departments.

## The Need for Field Training

Although field training programs are relatively new to American policing, various authors and commissions have long recognized the need for such programs.

In 1965, the President's Commission on Law Enforcement and Administration made numerous recommendations to improve the management of police departments, including a recommendation that agencies implement supervised field training programs.

In 1973, the National Advisory Commission on Criminal Justice Standards and Goals recommended that a minimum of four months of coached field training be included as a regular part of the recruit training process. The commission recommended that coaches (i.e., FTO's) receive 40 hours of specialized training and encouraged coaches to evaluate recruits.

Criminal justice scholars, including Wilson and McLaren (1972), Goldstein (1977), and Territo et al. (1977), have suggested that field training programs are important tools in developing effective police officers.

The concept of field training received its most important support from the Commission on Accreditation for Law Enforcement Agencies, Inc. (CALEA) in 1983. This organization, the nation's only police accrediting agency, devoted an entire chapter of *Standards for Law Enforcement Agencies* exclusively to training. The chapter contains 45 standards for training, one of which *requires* all agencies seeking accreditation to conduct formal field training for their recruits. This standard, along with the nearly 1,000 other standards associated with CALEA accreditation, was approved by the four major law enforcement associations in the United States: the Police Executive Research Forum, the International Association of Chiefs of Police, the National Sheriffs' Association, and the National Association of Black Law Enforcement Executives.

## The Goals of the Field Training Research Project

In response to the continuing emphasis on field training programs, the National Institute of Justice sponsored research to examine the following questions and to make recommendations:

- How many agencies in the United States conduct field training programs?
- What characteristics are common to all field training programs?
- What impact, if any, have field training programs had on civil liability suits or EEO complaints filed against user agencies?
- What are the costs of field training programs?
- In what ways can field training programs be improved?

## The Survey

The research project consisted of two major parts—a survey questionnaire and site visits to four agencies with well developed field training programs. The survey questionnaire, which consisted of 33 multiple response questions, was designed both to identify law enforcement agencies that use field training programs and to describe various aspects of those programs.

Questionnaires were sent to 588 randomly selected state and local agencies. The agencies were selected with the assistance of the National Criminal Justice Reference Service (NCJRS), which maintains a computerized data base of criminal justice agencies. Table 1 presents the sample of agencies that received a questionnaire and the agencies that responded.

**Table 1.**
**Samples of agencies**

| Agency size (number of sworn officers) | Agencies that received a questionnaire | | Respondents | | Respondents with programs | |
|---|---|---|---|---|---|---|
| | N | % | N | % | N | % |
| 300 plus | 277 | 100 | 142 | 51 | 107 | 75 |
| 200-299 | 109 | 100 | 40 | 37 | 29 | 73 |
| 100-199 | 35 | 10 | 27 | 77 | 14 | 52 |
| 50-99 | 84 | 10 | 34 | 41 | 18 | 53 |
| 25-49 | 83 | 5 | 45 | 54 | 15 | 33 |
| Total | 588 | | 288 | 49% | 183 | 64% |

## The Findings

The most important findings from the survey questionnaire have implications far beyond the scope of the initial research questionnaire.

- The trend in law enforcement training is toward the use of field-training programs, and the trend is relatively recent: 67 percent

(122 agencies) reported that their programs are less than 10 years old. Agencies of every size and in all sections of the country have some form of a program. Sixty-four percent (183) of all respondents reported that they have a field training program.

However, a substantial portion (105 or 36 percent) reported that they do not use field training programs. Of these agencies, 49 percent reported that they provide on-the-job training with a senior officer combined with additional classroom instruction in lieu of field training; 46 percent reported using only on-the-job training with a senior officer. The remaining 4 percent either use no additional training or failed to answer the question.

*In the discussion that follows, all percentages pertain only to the 183 agencies (64 percent of all respondents) that reported using field training programs.*

- The San Jose Police Department field training program is the model for a large percentage of programs; 57 percent (105 agencies) attribute their program directly to the San Jose model.
- Field training programs appear to have been implemented in response to perceived personnel problems and the need to improve the recruit training process. These reasons were reported by 95 percent (173 agencies).
- Field training programs appear to have reduced the number of civil liability complaints filed against law enforcement agencies. Of the agencies with programs, 30 percent (54 agencies) reported fewer of these complaints as a result of their programs.
- Field training programs also may be associated with a decrease in EEO complaints. Twenty-one percent (38 agencies) reported that they observed a decrease in these complaints since implementing their programs.
- Recruit evaluation is an important part of most field training programs. The majority of respondents (65 percent) reported using daily evaluation of recruits. Additionally, more than 95 percent reported using standardized evaluation guidelines and indicated that they could dismiss recruits based on poor performance.
- The Field Training Officer (FTO) is the single most critical position in field training programs. Agencies reported devoting considerable time and resources to selecting, training, and retaining FTO's. Eighty-two percent (150 agencies) reported that their FTO's received special training prior to assuming their duties. However, only 40 percent (74 agencies) reported that their FTO's receive extra pay.
- The costs associated with field training programs appear to depend mainly upon whether FTO's receive extra compensation, either as salary supplements or overtime pay. The San Jose Police Depart-

ment reported that its major costs are incurred by paying FTO's an extra 5 percent above a patrol officer's salary. San Jose keeps these costs to a minimum by paying the extra salary *only* when the FTO is actually assigned to train a recruit.

- Respondents identified the major benefits of field training programs as standardization of the training process and better documentation of recruit performance. Better documentation improves the agency's ability to make informed decisions about recruit retention.
- Field training programs have several characteristics in common: training is divided into identifiable phases; the personnel who train recruits are specially selected and trained; training and evaluation techniques are standardized and evaluation by FTO's occurs regularly; and programs are used to continue the personnel selection process.
- Generally, respondents suggested that field training programs could be enhanced by upgrading the quality of the FTO, primarily through improved FTO selection, training, and compensation.

## Detailed Descriptions of Programs Through Site Visits

In addition to the questionnaire responses, the research findings were based on indepth examination of field training programs in four police departments: San Jose, California (1,000 sworn officers); Newport News, Virginia (236 sworn officers); Flagstaff, Arizona (59 sworn officers); and Largo, Florida (99 sworn officers). The site visits contributed better understanding of the "real world" application of field training programs. Chiefs, managers, field training supervisors, FTO's, and recruits were interviewed at each site, and the documentation (manuals, records, policies, etc.) of each site's program was reviewed and analyzed thoroughly.

The programs differ in many ways, but they also have many things in common: Each program has distinct phases of training with specific types of training that occur in each phase; the FTO's evaluate each recruit officer's performance and are responsible for determining the recruit's suitability for the position; FTO's are carefully selected and trained before they assume their duties; and the agency's chief executives are committed to the concept of field training.

### San Jose, California

As the questionnaire responses showed, the San Jose Police Department's field training program has become a model for law enforcement agencies across the country. The San Jose program is highly structured and goes far beyond the usual field training process.

Control is the one word that best describes San Jose's program. The department controls the entire 14-week process very tightly by using standardized lesson plans, training guides, and departmental policies. Every effort is made to ensure that all recruits receive the same opportunity to succeed.

The Patrol Division administers the field training program; six-officer teams consisting entirely of FTO's and their sergeants conduct the training. These teams work only in specific sections of the city that have been identified as areas that provide the best opportunity to introduce the recruits to a cross section of police work. The recruit normally spends four weeks with three different FTO's. As in other field training programs, the FTO's must train recruits in addition to performing their normal patrol duties.

Recruits receive a combination of classroom and practical skills instruction in addition to on-the-job training with the FTO. FTO's evaluate recruits daily; sergeants evaluate them weekly. In the final two weeks of training, an FTO rides in plain clothes with the recruit and if performance is satisfactory, the recruit is then allowed to work a beat in a solo capacity. If not, the recruit is given remedial training in weak areas and reevaluated at a later date.

### Newport News, Virginia

The Newport News Police Department began its field training program three years ago when a progressive chief (who has since left) was hired from outside the agency. He recognized that the practice of using untrained, possibly unqualified senior officers to train recruits was inadequate.

Newport News has a "basic" field training program. It is representative of many programs across the country in that it is loosely based on the San Jose model but lacks the depth of that program. It has neither the heavy emphasis on evaluation nor the strict reporting requirements of the San Jose program.

FTO's are assigned to all patrol squads throughout the city and are supervised by patrol sergeants. However, primary responsibility for operation of the program rests with a staff unit, the Administrative Services Bureau.

As in San Jose, each recruit normally works with three different FTO's over a period of 12 weeks. The FTO's evaluate their recruits every two weeks; the sergeants evaluate the recruits monthly. At the end of 12 weeks, an FTO rides with the recruit an additional four weeks to determine if the recruit is capable of working alone.

Like San Jose, Newport News follows a training guide that defines all subject areas. However, this guide has much less detail than San Jose's program material.

### Flagstaff, Arizona

Flagstaff's program is seven years old and has many elements in common with the other models, i.e., training phases, daily evaluation, standardization of training, and evaluation. Flagstaff's program demonstrates how the concepts found in large-scale field training programs can be successfully integrated in a small agency with only 59 sworn officers.

FTO's are assigned to all patrol squads and work all areas of the city. The patrol sergeants are expected to assume the role of field training supervisors when recruits are assigned to their squads for training. Each recruit works with three FTO's during a 9-week period in which the recruit is evaluated daily by the FTO's and weekly by the sergeants. At the end of 9 weeks, a corporal evaluates the recruit for two weeks.

One segment of the Flagstaff program is unique. During the final week of training, the recruit is assigned to the Criminal Investigations Section to become familiar with investigative procedures including case preparation, use of evidence, grand jury procedures, and other aspects of investigation. Following this week, the recruit is assigned to a patrol squad for regular duty.

### Largo, Florida

Largo's field training program differs considerably from the others. The first part of most field training programs introduces recruits to patrol duties, but in Largo the process begins by assigning recruits to the investigative, administrative, and traffic functions. Patrol skills are the last subject area the recruit learns. The philosophy behind this five-year-old approach is that recruits are better qualified to operate in the patrol environment if they learn these other skills first.

During the first six weeks of the field training program, the recruits learn departmental policies, report writing, and state and local laws; skills training in firearms and baton; and on-the-job training in crime prevention, communications, investigations, property control, and accident investigations. During this period, recruits are evaluated weekly by specially designated personnel within each specialized unit.

For the next six weeks, recruits are assigned to patrol field training. This phase has many things in common with the San Jose program, including daily evaluation by the FTO and training program guides. However, in Largo, the recruit is assigned to one FTO only and works only one shift.

The final segment of the Largo program is called the "shadow phase." In this phase, which usually lasts one week, the recruit patrols an area alone while an FTO patrols an adjacent area. The FTO evaluates the recruit's performance by observing how he or she handles the day-to-day assignments of a patrol officer.

Another unique feature of the Largo field training program is the use of an oral review board to determine recruit proficiency. Although other agencies use oral boards to review a recruit's progress, Largo requires the recruit to appear before this board at the end of each phase and to pass an examination. The first three appearances before the board consist of a structured interview combined with proficiency examinations in skills such as baton use and handcuffing. The final appearance employs role playing in various scenarios in which knowledge, skills, and abilities necessary to be an effective patrol officer are used. The board consists of management and nonmanagement personnel who determine whether the recruit will be retained or dismissed.

## Recommendations for Field Training Programs

Findings from both the survey and the site visits indicate that field training programs offer effective ways for agencies to improve their selection and training processes. The savings in money and resources that result from quality field training programs can be better used to accomplish the agency's primary mission—protection of life and property.

Law enforcement agencies that do not already have a field training program should seriously consider implementing one; those that do have programs should seek ways to improve them. Agencies will find that the following recommendations require a commitment of agency time and resources, but the results are well worth the effort.

**Chief executives should view the field training program as a normal part of the recruit selection process.**

Commitment by the agency head is of paramount importance to success of the program, and all policy statements that describe program goals should reflect this commitment.

**Administrative control of the field training program in larger agencies should be assigned to the patrol function.**

Field training is so closely related to patrol that it should not be organizationally far removed from it. Assigning the program to patrol will reduce the administrative problems that inevitably occur when program policy formulation and decision making is split between two functional areas of the agency. For example, assigning FTO's to patrol, but requiring them to answer administratively to another unit may increase the paperwork flow and decisionmaking process.

**All training in the field program should occur in a planned, organized sequence and be identified by clearly written policies.**

A well-structured field training program increases the possibility that all recruits will receive the same quality and quantity of training. The chances are reduced that critical subject areas will be overlooked. Individual FTO's or first line supervisors should not be left to decide what training occurs in what sequence.

**Agencies should perform a task analysis for the job of patrol officer and use the analysis as the basis for evaluating recruits.**

Whether the evaluation takes the form of numerical scales or short descriptors, the evaluation should be based on a task analysis of the patrol officer's job. If evaluation is not based on validated, job-related criteria, the agency becomes vulnerable to lawsuits within the department as well as from the public.

**Agencies should use standardized evaluation guidelines to reduce FTO discretion.**

Standardized guidelines that clearly define acceptable and unacceptable performance will ensure that FTO's use the same criteria for evaluating every recruit. Standardization is one of the keys to fair, impartial evaluation.

**FTO's should give recruits a written evaluation every day.**

First, and most important, this procedure ensures that the recruit receives immediate feedback and thus learns more quickly. Second, daily evaluation ensures that the FTO remembers how the recruit performed in a specific situation. Weekly evaluation may tend to dilute the evaluation into generalized statements that are less effective in documenting poor performance.

Daily evaluation also ensures that poor performance trends are more quickly identified, documented, and remedied. This job-related standardized documentation is especially critical in reducing the number of successful appeals of personnel decisions resulting from poor performance.

**Each recruit should be assigned to several FTO's.**

This will allow different experienced trainers to observe and evaluate the recruit. It will also prevent the possibility of bias and personality conflicts that could interfere with the training process.

**The FTO's role as a trainer and patrol officer should be well defined.**

Particular attention should be given to avoiding conflict between the two roles. The FTO's duties should be clearly defined in a manual that completely describes the field training program.

**Agencies should conduct a job task analysis for the position of FTO.**

This will ensure that the most qualified person is selected for this critical task. It will also assist in tailoring effective training programs for FTO's.

**FTO's should receive at least 40 hours of training before they are allowed to assume their duties.**

The emphasis on FTO training should be on building skills in leadership, motivation, evaluation, and teaching. FTO's should receive additional annual training to sharpen their skills in these critical areas. The use of carefully selected and trained FTO's is a significant improvement over the use of senior officers whose aptitude, motivation, and abilities to train recruits is often left to chance.

**Agencies should consider offering extra compensation to ensure that the most qualified personnel are attracted to and retained in the position of FTO.**

Costs may be kept to a minimum by compensating the FTO only when he or she is actually training a recruit.

**Field training programs should be evaluated at least annually.**

Annual program review will help agencies identify problems as they arise. The evaluation should include a review of program length, FTO selection and training, the recruit evaluation process, and all training manuals. It also should contain a review of statistics generated by the program including at least the following information:

- Number of recruits entering the program;
- Number of recruits voluntarily resigning;
- Number of recruits dismissed as a result of the program;
- Number of successful recruits.

It is best if this information is collected quarterly and maintained by race, sex, and age of participants. The quarterly report also should contain specific data on program staffing levels, changes, and highlights, as well as program costs and other fiscal data to help administrators justify the program in budgetary terms. Such information will ensure that the program meets its goals and objectives and that selection and retention problems are identified.

In summary, properly administered field training programs can result in  improved service to the community. The programs are relatively inexpensive to operate, particularly when compared with the tax dollars that may be saved by reducing civil liability and EEO lawsuits. Better trained and qualified officers who are the products of these programs can increase the department's overall effectiveness.The direct long-term result will be an improvement in the department's relationship with the community.

# References

Commission on Accreditation for Law Enforcement Agencies, Inc., *The Standards for Law Enforcement Agencies*. Fairfax, VA: CALEA, 1983.

Goldstein, Herman. *Policing in a Free Society*. Cambridge, MA: Ballinger Publishing,1977.

National Advisory Commission on Standards and Goals, *Report of the Commission, Report on the Police*. Washington, DC: Government Printing Office, 1973.

Territo, Leonard; Swanson, C. R., Jr.; and Chamelin, Neil C. *The Police Personnel Process*. Indianapolis: Bobbs-Merrill Company, 1977.

The President's Commission on Law Enforcement and Administration of Justice, *Task Force Report: The Police*. Washington, DC: Government Printing Office, 1967.

Wilson, O. W., and McLaren, Roy C. *Police Administration*, 3d ed. New York: McGraw-Hill, Inc., 1972.

# 8

# Police Discretionary Behavior
## A Study of Style

*Laure Weber Brooks*

## Introduction

The exercise of discretion by police has been the focus of an enormous amount of research. These issues of how police spend uncommitted time, how quickly they respond to calls for assistance, and what police do when handling a call for service have all received attention. While all police officers exercise some discretion, not all exercise the same levels of discretion. There are many factors which affect the degree of leeway an officer has in determining outcomes. Officers may develop response styles and these styles may not only affect police perceptions, but they may also predispose the officer to act in certain ways. Additionally, levels of discretion are contingent on the flexibility that police departments allow their officers in handling day-to-day calls for service. When organizational rules are strict, less discretion is afforded to police. Conversely, when rules are vague or lax, officers are allowed, or perhaps forced, to make their own decisions on how to conduct themselves.

Much research attention has been paid to the examination of what factors affect police discretionary behavior. To explain this behavior, research has focused primarily on the characteristics of the situation in which police act (Riksheim and Chermak, 1993; Klinger, 1994; Lundman, 1994; Klinger, 1996; Worden and Shepard, 1996; Worden, 1989; Black and Reiss, 1970; Black, 1971; Piliavin and Briar, 1964; Friedrich, 1977; Smith and Visher, 1981; Ericson, 1982; Reiss, 1971; Black, 1980). Other discretionary factors which have received scholarly attention include: characteristics of the police organization (Mastrofski, Ritti, and Hoffmaster, 1987; Crank, 1993; Riksheim and Chermak, 1993; Wilson, 1968; Smith, 1984; Brown, 1981; Guyot, 1979; Ericson, 1982; Mastrofski, 1981; Swanson, 1978; Chatterton, 1983; Sherman, 1983); characteristics of the environment or neighborhood in which the police work (Crank, 1993; Riksheim and Chermak, 1993; Rossi, et al., 1974; Smith, 1986; Nardulli

Prepared especially for *Critical Issues in Policing*, 3/E by Laure Weber Brooks.

and Stonecash, 1981; Bayley and Mendelsohn, 1969; Wilson, 1968; Ostrom et al., 1977; Brown, 1981; Mastrofski, 1981; Reiss, 1971; Smith and Klein, 1984); and characteristics of the officer involved in the encounter (Crank, 1993; Brooks, Piquero, and Cronin, 1993; Riksheim and Chermak, 1993; Friedrich, 1977; Finckenauer, 1976; Bloch and Anderson, 1974; Banton, 1964; Fyfe, 1978; Rossi, et al., 1974; Worden, 1989; Brown, 1981; Westley, 1970; Brooks, 1986). Taken together, the research concerning these four dimensions (situational, organizational, environmental, and officer) provide us with information on the determinants of police behavior.

With the advent of community policing, which has as a basic tenet the recognition that law enforcement behavior is not always the best way to handle social problems (Mastrofski, Worden, and Snipes, 1995), scholars have speculated about how police discretion may be influenced by this movement. Mastrofski, Worden, and Snipes studied the determinants of police discretion in a police department which had implemented community policing. They explored the possibility that, due to the focus on community preferences and less focus on legal requirements that community policing encourages, officers might tend to rely less on legal variables (strength of evidence, seriousness of offense, the preference of the victim, etc.) and more on extralegal variables (suspect and victim characteristics). They found, though, that legal variables actually showed a much stronger effect on the arrest decision than did the extralegal ones; however, this depended on the officer's attitude about community policing. Officers who were supportive of community policing were more selective in making arrests and tended to rely less on legal variables, than were officers who were not supportive of community policing. Overall, the more positive officers were toward community policing, the less likely they were to effect an arrest (Mastrofski, Worden, and Snipes, 1995). These researchers concluded that pro-community policing officers do arrest more selectively and do rely less on legal variables, but show no greater reliance on extralegal variables to guide their arrest decision (Mastrofski, Worden, and Snipes, 1995).

This chapter will commence with a discussion of the definition of police discretion in order to present a clear picture of the focus of this research, while discussing both the benefits and the problems associated with police discretion. Next, attention will turn to the role of police in society. Third, a discussion of police orientations or styles of policing is presented. Finally, this chapter will conclude with a discussion of research findings concerning the determinants of police behavior.

## Police Discretion

At least some discretion is exercised in every aspect of the police task. Some discretionary actions involve very subtle and perhaps minor decisions, while others involve blatant and important ones. Police discretion exists when officers have some leeway or choice in how to respond to a situation.

The fewer the rules about handling incidents and situations, the more discretion officers have. Discretion involves both action and inaction (Ericson, 1982). Not doing something may be equally as important as doing something. Discretion involves both having the power to decide which rules apply to a given situation and whether or not to apply these rules (Ericson, 1982). Both of these decisions have potentially important implications for the community and for the police department.

The myth that police officers enforce all of the rules all of the time, known as full enforcement, has fortunately been questioned. Perpetrators of this myth may have falsely believed that the myth would protect officers from public scrutiny and accusations of unequal treatment. However, it accomplished just the opposite. It is apparent that officers cannot and do not practice full enforcement, and the community would not be likely to desire this anyway. Rather, the current strategy is to admit that officers exercise discretion and to convince the community that the officers use their discretion fairly and appropriately.

Police discretion has been justified on many grounds, such as: (1) vague laws which require officers to use their judgment; (2) limited resources of the police department and the criminal justice system; (3) the possibility of community alienation if police truly engaged in a full enforcement approach; (4) the idea that police need to be able to exercise discretion in order to individualize the law; and (5) that discretion is necessary to deal with law violations which are either minor or involve moral offenses. On the other hand, the exercise of police discretion poses some difficulties. The results of an exercise of discretion on the part of police may include: (1) unequal treatment of citizens; (2) an interference with due process; and (3) a reduction of deterrent effect which may come with police sanctioning. Police discretion has also been criticized due to the fact that many police discretionary decisions are unreviewable.

Police discretion exists at both the individual level and at the administrative or departmental level. The former type of police discretion generally involves the day-to-day choices of the patrol officer and includes such decisions as how to patrol, whom to arrest, whom to stop and frisk, whether to stop a vehicle and whether to ticket or issue a citation, etc. Some of these individual discretionary judgments may be influenced by the second major type of police discretion—departmental policy.

Administrative or departmental police discretion involves such decisions as manpower levels, allocation of personnel, allocation of resources, the development and support of departmental programs, training, rotation, enforcement priorities, and also includes departmental policy governing officer behavior. Police departments are being both encouraged and perhaps compelled to enact clear policies regulating officer actions. As Alpert and Fridell (1992) aptly point out, the purpose of departmental policy is to reduce officer or individual discretion, as well as to help officers prepare for situations they may confront. Clearly, some officer decisions, such as the decision to arrest, how to patrol, and to stop and frisk, should be made with a significant amount of individual discretion while others, such as the use of deadly force and continuing a police pursuit, are certain candidates for a reduced amount of discretion. Not only does departmental policy limiting officer discretion protect the community, it also protects the officer and makes the officer's job easier. In order for this to occur, police departments need to enact well-thought-out and very clear policies, provide training and supervision, and ensure that officers are aware of these policies and are able to follow them without confusion.

## The Police Role

To understand the behavior of police, we need to first clarify the functions of police or the police role in society. This is necessary in order to understand fully the demands and expectations placed on police by the public and the police organization.

The appropriate role of police is an area where there is some dissension among scholars. Most agree that in practice police have multiple functions, many of which involve situations where no crime has occurred (e.g., dispute settlement, providing transportation, giving directions, investigating suicide threats, rescuing sick or injured animals, and providing medical treatment). While some scholars disagree that police response to such matters should be an appropriate police function, most would concur that they do represent a substantial portion of police activity (Goldstein, 1977; Nardulli and Stonecash, 1981; Scott, 1981; Reiss, 1971; Mastrofski, 1983).

In defining what the police role is, some scholars focus on the coercive nature of police work or use of legitimate force (Brown, 1981; Bittner, 1970; Reiss, 1971; Packer, 1968). Bittner (1970) argues that the capacity to use force is the core of police work. Specifically, police are the ". . . mechanism for the distribution of nonnegotiable coercive force employed in accordance with the dictates of an intuitive grasp of situational exigencies" (p. 46). In other words, we need to examine the police role in terms of the ultimate authority to use situationally justified force. Even though relatively few encounters actually involve the use of force, the ability of police to invoke force is the crux of their authority and is central to obtaining the control of citizens.

Some scholars claim that police have a virtual monopoly on the legitimate use of force, and this is critical to an understanding of their role (Reiss, 1971; Packer, 1968). Police are one of the few occupational groups permitted, and in certain situations, required, to use force. It has been argued that the role of police is based on the legitimate use of coercion (Brown, 1981). This coercion defines the role of police and is instrumental in the performance of most activities. In other words, police are permitted to "handle" situations because they are granted the authority to use force.

Other scholars, in defining the police role, stress the multiple functions inherent in police work (Wilson, 1968; Goldstein, 1977; Banton,

1964). They recognize not only the law enforcement role of police (involving activities such as crime detection, taking criminal complaints, writing reports, making arrests, investigating, protecting crime scenes, questioning, and frisking persons), but also the noncriminal component of policing. While this noncriminal component is referred to in different terms in the police literature (e.g., keeping the peace, order maintenance, service, etc.), and all do not agree on the exact nature of these noncriminal activities, most recognize there is a distinction between traditional law enforcement response and this noncriminal dimension. However, for certain situations (such as arrest for domestic violence), the distinction between law enforcement and order maintenance behavior is less clear. Of major importance is the recognition that the police task is one most accurately described as dealing with many different types of problems (Goldstein, 1979).

The degree of discretion exercised by police may vary depending on the nature of the call for service. Wilson (1968:85) contends that in law enforcement situations where serious law breaking occurs, guilt is the only necessary element to be assessed by the police officer. This is not the case in order maintenance situations (where less serious or no lawbreaking occurs) in which discretion plays a greater role. In the latter type of encounter, laws must be interpreted, standards of appropriate conduct must be determined, and blame must be assigned. Wilson further contends that individual police departments have differing emphases on law enforcement and order maintenance roles. He identifies three types of police departments: "watchman," "legalistic," and "service," each of which is organized differently among these dimensions.

It is clear then, that police in our society have multiple functions to perform. Additionally, the exercise of discretion depends on many factors. One important factor concerns the development of styles or orientations. This issue is discussed in the following section.

## Orientations of Police or Styles of Policing

Given the wide discretion of police and their multiple functions, many of which are noncriminal, it is interesting to consider how these discretionary judgments are made. In view of suggestions made in previous research, we can no longer ignore the role that attitudes, orientations, or styles of policing play (Brown, 1981; Smith and Klein, 1984; Berk and Loseke, 1981; Brooks, 1986). Wilson (1968:38) contends that police make judgments about situations and individuals, and practice distributive justice. They evaluate the moral character of victims and suspects, and these judgments determine action. Worden (1995:50) argues that a police officer's belief system is "comprised of beliefs, attitudes, values, and other 'subjective outlooks'."

The role that police attitudes play in determining police behavior has received much attention in the domestic assault area. For example, it has long been contended that the attitudes police have toward women in general may explain the low rate of arrest in these incidents. Arrests have been rare for domestic assaults, and many argue that this is a direct result of negative attitudes or proprietary beliefs of police toward women (Dobash and Dobash, 1977; Martin, 1976; Roy, 1979). It has been argued that, in research on police response to domestic disturbances, the police decision of how to respond involves predispositions (Berk and Loseke, 1981). Police response is a judgmental process involving the knowledge of past experiences and past outcomes, as well as normal beliefs. It is argued that police attitudes toward family violence, women as victims, and their perceptions of situational exigencies strongly determine their actual response (Berk and Loseke, 1981).

Others have also suggested that the exercise of police discretion is structured by the officer's belief system. Police develop indicators which are used to determine behavior. Past experience leads police to make conclusions concerning suspiciousness, crime proneness, and the moral character of certain types of individuals. They may make assumptions that blacks and poor individuals are more likely to commit crime and are likely to be lacking in morality. It is contended that police officer behavior is directly affected by predispositions (Werthman and Piliavin, 1967).

Police develop styles of policing which affect their discretionary behavior (Chatterton, 1983; Wilson, 1968; Brown, 1981). Some have argued that certain types of police departments encourage different styles of policing. For example, in a "legalistic" police department, law enforcement activities are emphasized over order maintenance behavior (Wilson, 1968). In the same vein, Chatterton (1983) argues that an individual officer's style of policing affects the outcome of encounters. He argues that "snatchers" are overzealous officers who are preoccupied with arrest and are unlikely to consider moral justice or fairness as important determinants of arrest. Conversely, the "good bobby" operates on the premise that "doing justice" is the underlying goal of policing and is likely to consider not only the legal dictates that make arrest a viable disposition, but also the moral desert of the arrest sanction.

Brown (1981:24–31) has perhaps been the strongest advocate of the need to consider police attitudes or orientations in our understanding of police discretionary behavior. Brown argues that to understand what determines the routine choices that patrol officers make, we need to examine the beliefs that officers hold toward their job, the law, and the events and people they confront in the daily course of their occupation. Police do not react to each incident as though it were unique; rather, they generalize. They fashion a coherent set of beliefs or orientations which guide their behavior. The belief system they develop structures their perceptions and definitions of order, and thereby provides the norms and standards that influence their discretionary behavior. Brown contends that the exercise of discretion requires the use of beliefs and values or an "operational style" (p. 26). According to Brown, the decision to act is partly the result of a succession of choices that the patrol officer has made prior to the actual encounter (such as decisions on the appropriateness of service or order maintenance activities, crime control preoccupation, utilization of time, etc.). These decisions or attitudes shape discretionary choices, although Brown argues that action is not totally based on beliefs but also on other factors such as organizational and environmental characteristics. He argues that the operational style is made up of two characteristics: aggressivity (how much initiative the officer shows and how preoccupied the officer is with order) and selectivity (whether the officer prioritizes). He cross-classifies these two characteristics, which results in four operational styles: the clean beat crime fighter, the old style crime fighter, the service officer, and the professional (Brown, 1981). Brown contends that the overall style the officer has will influence the decisions that he/she makes.

Muir (1977), like Brown, argues that two characteristics make up an officer's overall style. For Muir, an officer's style is determined by whether or not the officer possesses passion ("the ability to integrate coercion into one's morals") and perspective ("intellectual objectivity"). He develops four types of officers: professionals, reciprocators, enforcers, and avoiders.

Ericson (1982:25) contends that officers develop a "recipe of rules" which guide their behavior. This recipe of rules is essentially a collection of rules-of-thumb learned on the job which mediate actual events, police departmental rules, and legal codes. The community, the law, and the policing organization provide the officer with rules, and these rules provide the officer with a sense of order—what the officer perceives as appropriate conduct. This sense of order may affect not only the ultimate outcome of encounters, but also the process by which police achieve their outcome. This process involves the interaction between police and citizens, both as complainants and suspects.

It is clear from this review of the literature that many scholars believe that attitudes can play a role in police discretionary behavior. Many suggest that police officers act on the basis of predispositions or overall orientations and that these predispositions provide an interpretive framework in which the situational cues are evaluated. Predispositions supply the officer with a repertoire of possible behavior and, from this collection, the officer selects an appropriate response to a specific situation. While there exists intuitive support for the connection between police attitudes and behavior, little empirical research has been conducted to examine this issue, and the few studies which have addressed this have found disappointing results (Crank, 1993; Worden, 1989). The next section reviews previous research to identify what factors affect police discretionary behavior.

## Predictors of Police Behavior

Much research has focused on determining what factors predict police behavior. While most of the attention has been paid to situational characteristics, however, research has also examined the neighborhood, the police organization, and the officer. Each level will be discussed in turn.

## Organizational Variables

Organizational variables deal with characteristics of the police department in which the officer works and would include such factors as how bureaucratic and/or professional a police agency is, the size of the police department, whether the department rotates its officers among different areas, and supervision levels. Research examining organizational variables and their effect on police behavior has been minimal in recent years. A recent review of the literature has concluded that: organizational variables have largely been ignored in the study of police service behavior; organizational variables do appear to influence police use of force; and the effect of organizational variables on police arrest behavior is unresolved (Riksheim and Chermak, 1993).

The word "bureaucracy" has been used rather loosely in the police literature, but there does appear to be some consensus of the characteristics that bureaucratic police departments share. Bureaucratic police departments are thought to have a high degree of vertical differentiation (a tall rank structure), in which efficiency, discipline, and productivity are stressed (Bittner, 1970:52–62; Manning, 1977:193–97).

Skolnick (1966:11), in his case study of two police departments, contends that the degree to which a police department is organized around the military model with its stress on regulations, hierarchy, and obedience, determines an officer's "conception of order." This conception of order may be thought of as what police view as acceptable or appropriate conduct. He argues that in militaristic police departments, police members will have a rigid conception of order and routinism. Officers from these departments will be so concerned with following the rules and regulations that they will feel compelled to follow them to the letter in order to avoid punishment. This rigid conception of order (or low tolerance for rule violators) may result in an emphasis on crime control behavior (arrest, investigation, etc.). Aggressive police work may be seen by police as a way to accomplish goals but may result in police-community relations problems.

Police departments may also be classified on the basis of professionalism. Professional police organizations have been characterized in many different ways, but are thought to be agencies in which education, service, and citizen respect are central (Goldstein, 1977:2 3). Professional departments may have tall or shallow rank structure but generally have wide ranges of specialty units. These specialty units (such as crime prevention or police-community relations units) are thought to express the department's commitment to service and positive police-community relations. Professional police departments may be identified by various factors such as college incentive pay, community-relations training, and high percentage of officers who are college educated (Smith and Klein, 1984; Swanson, 1978).

Smith's (1984) research is one of the few attempts to clarify the issues of bureaucracy and professionalism in police departments. Smith finds, when examining discretionary decisions by type of police organization, that there are differences in factors that affect the decision to arrest. He finds that increasing the degree of bureaucracy in professional departments results in a shift from conciliatory to punitive responses by police, at least in settling interpersonal disputes. Smith and Klein (1984) find that the probability of arrest increased as departments became more bureaucratic and more professional.

The size of a police department relates to how bureaucratic it is and some research has examined the effect of an agency's size on police discretionary behavior. Mastrofski, Ritti, and Hoffmaster (1987) found that officers in the larger, more bureaucratic police agencies were much less likely to arrest than were officers from the smaller departments. Contrary to Brown's (1981) findings, Mastrofski, Ritti, and Hoffmaster (1987) found that as department size and level of bureaucracy increased, the willingness of officers to make DUI arrests decreased. They argue that this may be the result of the fact that small police departments may be easier to control by supervisors and that discretion in large police agencies is less accountable (Mastrofski, Ritti, and Hoffmaster, 1987). It may be that large police departments are expected to have less effective controls on their members (due to the numerous members in the department), less group stability, and fewer and less effective links to the community—all of which detract from a service style of policing (Mastrofski, 1981).

The size of a police agency affects the social distance between supervisors and subordinates (Banton, 1964). The ratio of supervisors to subordinates (span of control) may give some indication as to the level of supervision in a police department. It appears that the quality of supervision is related to rule infraction (Reiss, 1971). In departments where supervision is close, officers have less of an opportunity to violate the rules of an organization.

How frequently police departments rotate their officers may also influence how officers behave. Departments which frequently rotate their personnel into different beats, shifts, or units inhibit close relations with community members (Brown, 1981:58, Murphy and Pate, 1977:39). Mastrofski (1981) argues that an officer's continued presence in a neighborhood increases the likelihood of repeated contact with citizens and helps officers develop empathy through an understanding of problems. He argues that this understanding will result in fewer instances of force and arrest. Murphy and Pate (1977:39, 225) use the phrase "stranger policing" to refer to jurisdictions which frequently rotate their officers. Davis (1978:135) discusses the "territorial imperative" which occurs when officers become protective of their area and their residents. This theme is central to the concept of community policing.

### Neighborhood Variables

Prior research has identified several neighborhood or environmental variables which appear to be related to police discretionary behavior. They include: racial composition of a neighborhood; socio-economic status of an area; and the neighborhood crime rate.

Rossi et al. (1974:151) conclude that in the poor neighborhoods they studied, the black population experienced high levels of what they considered to be abusive practices by the police. This perception could lead to a mutual hostility between the police and the public. Research has found that in poor neighborhoods and neighborhoods where the proportion of black residents was high, there was more of a demand for police intervention (Walker, 1991; Nardulli and Stonecash, 1981). This was due to the increased number of "happenings" in these areas, as well as a belief in the appropriateness of calling the police in these areas (Nardulli and Stonecash, 1981:86–88). Similar results were found with respect to low socio-economic status neighborhoods.

Research examining the relationship between neighborhood socio-economic status and arrest finds that these variables are significant predictors of this discretionary decision (Riksheim and Chermak, 1993; Smith, 1984; Smith and Klein, 1984; Smith, 1986). Bayley and Mendelsohn (1969:89) contend that most discretionary situations occur in poor or minority areas. They argue this is due to the belief by police that property crimes (those which require little discretion by police) are most common in middle- and upper-class areas and that violent crimes (which involve a great deal of discretion by police) are most common in poorer areas. They argue that due to the danger to police associated with violent crimes, police are more alert and suspicious in minority neighborhoods (Bayley and Mendelsohn, 1969:89–90).

It has been argued that police are more likely to listen to a complainant's preference for arrest in a high socio-economic status neighborhood than in a poorer one (Smith and Klein, 1984). Additionally, police respond differently to the settlement of disputes depending on the socio-economic status of a neighborhood. Regardless of whether or not a preference for arrest was expressed, as the percentage of households below the poverty level increased, so did the probability of arrest (Smith and Klein, 1984).

Research examining how the crime rate of a neighborhood affects police discretionary behavior has resulted in mixed findings (Riksheim and Chermak, 1993). Perceptions of crime risk and the potential for danger to police may affect how police behave, and may appear to justify a coercive or aggressive police response in the minds of police (Mastrofski, 1981; Bayley and Mendelsohn, 1969). Some research has indicated that the neighborhood crime rate may influence officer attitudes (Brooks, Piquero, and Cronin, 1994).

## Situational Variables

Situational variables have received most of the research attention in terms of their effect on police discretionary behavior and involve characteristics of the encounter between the citizen(s) and the police. They include such variables as the characteristics of both the suspect and the complainant, the type of call for service or crime involved, and how visible the encounter is.

One of the most frequently examined situational variables has been the race of the suspect and the results found in research are mixed. Some fairly recent research has found that black suspects are more likely to be arrested and/or to be treated more punitively by police (Powell, 1990; Smith and Visher, 1981; Smith and Davidson, 1984; Brooks, 1986), but other studies report no effect (Klinger, 1996; Smith and Klein, 1983; Smith, 1984). Some research on deadly force finds that blacks are disproportionately shot more often than are whites, however this may be due to an overrepresentation in serious crime (Geller and Karales, 1981; Fyfe, 1980), while other research reports no racial effect on deadly force decisions (Blumberg, 1981).

Early research found gender differences in police treatment of suspects and complainants, but recent research has found that either no gender differences occur or that they are less prominent than previously thought (Klinger, 1996; Smith and Visher, 1980; Smith and Visher, 1981; Krohn et al., 1983; Visher, 1983; Smith and Klein, 1983; Smith, 1984).

It is generally supported in the literature that individuals in the lower socio-economic strata receive harsher treatment by police (Black 1971; Reiss, 1971; Black and Reiss, 1967; Friedrich, 1977; Black, 1980; Riksheim and Chermak, 1993). It is important to note that these general findings may be related to the race and demeanor of the suspect and the complainant.

Research is also somewhat mixed regarding the effect of a citizen's age on police discretionary behavior. Some research finds that young suspects are more likely to be arrested, to be the recipients of deadly force by police, and/or that older complainants were more likely to be taken seriously (Sherman, 1980; Friedrich, 1977), while other research indicates that suspect age is not an important predictor of police behavior (Klinger, 1996; Smith and Visher, 1981; Smith and Davidson, 1983; Smith, 1984; Visher, 1983).

The demeanor, or attitude, of the suspect and the complainant have received considerable attention, especially recently, in the research literature. The general finding has been that disrespectful or uncooperative citizens are more likely to be treated punitively—in other words: arrested, targets of force, less often accommodated as complainants (Black and Reiss, 1970; Black, 1971; Brooks, 1986; Piliavin and Briar, 1964; Friedrich, 1977; Smith and Visher, 1981; Ericson, 1982; Sherman, 1980; Visher, 1983; Smith, 1986; Smith, 1987). A hostile attitude may signify a threat to an officer's control or a challenge to their authority. However, questions concerning the measurement of demeanor have been raised (Klinger, 1994). Klinger argues that previous studies examining the effect of suspect demeanor on police behavior have been flawed due to the failure to properly measure demeanor. Specially, he argues that previous research may have included illegal conduct by the suspect in the measure of demeanor and that previous research does not control adequately for the suspect's behavior during the entire encounter (before police arrive, toward police during the encounter, and toward others during the encounter). He finds that when these two problems are corrected, demeanor does not significantly effect arrest, except in the case of extreme hostility (Klinger, 1994, 1996) and suggests that there may be implications for findings concerning other extralegal variables as well. Several scholars responded to this argument and reanalyzed data sets with new measures of demeanor. Lundman (1994) did find that the effects of demeanor depended on how demeanor was measured, while Worden and Shepard (1996) concluded that their research provides no evidence that previous research findings were flawed due to an improper measurement of demeanor.

Research has been fairly consistent in the finding that when a complainant expresses a preference for arrest, an arrest is more likely to occur (Black, 1971; Friedrich, 1977; Smith and Visher, 1981; Visher, 1983; Smith, 1987; Worden, 1989; Brooks, 1986). The degree of relational distance or the degree of intimacy between suspects and complainants seems to be related to police behavior as well. Research indicates that as relational distance decreases or intimacy increases, police are less likely to take official action (Black, 1971, 1970; Friedrich, 1977; Smith and Visher, 1981). It may be that police believe that taking official action against a suspect who is in a relationship with the complainant may cause future problems, or they may feel that it is not part of police responsibility.

Characteristics of the encounter itself have received attention in the study of police discretionary behavior. Generally, research indicates that the more serious the offense police encounter, the more likely a harsher disposition will be the result (Wilson, 1968; Ericson, 1982; Black, 1971; Piliavin and Briar, 1964; Smith and Visher, 1981; Brooks, 1986; Visher, 1983; Sherman, 1980; Smith and Klein, 1983; Smith, 1984).

Police, with the many demands on their time, may have to prioritize and choose to take action when dealing with serious crimes. However, most research has found that the presence of injuries was not an important determinant of arrest (Smith and Klein, 1984; Worden and Pollitz, 1984). Some research has found that when an encounter is visible (public) or when others were present (including supervisors), police would be more likely to either write a report, make an arrest, or use force (Friedrich, 1977; Brooks, 1986; Reiss, 1971; Smith and Visher, 1981; Smith and Klein, 1983; Smith, 1984). Police may behave aggressively or officially when encounters are visible to others due to a belief that they must appear in control.

## Officer Characteristics

Researchers have examined characteristics of the police officer (i.e. experience, race, gender, attitudes, etc.) to determine how they may influence what police do. Overall, these characteristics have not been found to exert strong influences on police discretionary behavior (Riksheim and Chermak, 1993); however, some significant findings do emerge.

Some research has shown that less experienced officers perform more "work" (are more aggressive, stop and frisk more often, arrest more often) but more experienced officers engage in higher quality work and/or are less likely to engage in a legalistic manner (Friedrich, 1977; Sherman, 1980; Crank, 1993), while other research has found no relationship between individual officer experience and arrest behavior (Smith and Klein, 1983; Worden, 1989). Some research has suggested a connection between officer experience and certain officer attitudes (i.e. cynicism, role definition, perception of the public, perception of support by the criminal justice system) which may relate to discretionary behavior (Brooks, Piquero, and Cronin, 1993; Canter and Martensen, 1990; Hayeslip and Cordner, 1987).

It has been assumed that the level of education of an officer affects police behavior (Goldstein, 1977), and the advent of police professionalism has definitely incorporated this premise. The research, however, has resulted in findings which suggest that there is no measurable effect of post-secondary education on police behavior (Worden, 1989, 1990; Smith and Klein, 1983; Crank, 1993), but there may be a negative effect on arrest if officer education is measured at the departmental level (Smith and Klein, 1983). Some research has also suggested a link between officer education and certain attitudes (attitudes toward legal restrictions, attitudes toward discretion, perceptions of ethical conduct, cynicism, attitudes toward the community, solidarity, use of force, role) which may in turn influence police behavior (Shernock, 1992; Worden, 1990; Canter and Martensen, 1990; Hayeslip and Cordner, 1987; Brooks, Piquero, and Cronin, 1993).

The race of an officer has been examined in terms of its effect on police behavior. Early research reported a link between officer race and arrest behavior (Sherman, 1980), however more recent research finds no such effect (Worden, 1989; Smith and Klein, 1983). Some research concerning race and the use of force have reported racial differences. In general, the deadly force literature concludes that black officers are overrepresented in police shootings of citizens, although most researchers note that this relationship is most likely due to differential deployment of black officers in high crime areas and to the higher rate of black officers residing in these areas (Geller and Karales, 1981; Fyfe, 1978). There is some evidence that race may play a role in officer attitudes, which may influence their behavior (Brooks, Piquero, and Cronin, 1993).

Generally, recent research has indicated that the gender of an officer exerts no influence on police behavior (Worden, 1989) while some earlier research found that females were less likely to make arrests, use deadly force, and be involved in deadly force situations (Sherman, 1980; Horvath, 1987; Grennan, 1987). Research has also suggested that officer attitudes may be related to gender (Dorsey and Giacopassi, 1986; Brooks, Piquero, and Cronin, 1993).

Unfortunately, there has been little empirical work examining police attitudes and their influence on police discretionary behavior, and the research which has been done on this issue has yielded disappointing results. As indicated previously, many scholars have speculated that attitudes influence behavior; however, few researchers have been able to actually demonstrate this link. Job dissatisfaction has been found to be related to police behavior, with high levels of job dissatisfaction associated with less legalistic and order maintenance behaviors, and police professionalism and attitudes toward street justice being unrelated to either behaviors (Crank, 1993). Some research has found that crime-control oriented officers are more likely to use force, but less likely to use the arrest sanction, than are officers who did not espouse this philosophy (Brooks, 1986). There has been some indication that attitudes may influence proactivity in traffic enforcement, but these attitudes play a very small role (Worden, 1989). Overall, it seems apparent that attitudes contribute little to our understanding of police behavior (Worden, 1989; Smith and Klein, 1983; Riksheim and Chermak, 1993); however, it has been suggested that maybe the more fundamental attitudes held by police officers would do better in explaining police discretionary behavior than would the specific occupational attitudes typically examined in research (Worden, 1989). Certain police officer attitudes have been found to relate to other officer attitudes (Worden, 1995; Brooks, 1986), but additional research needs to clarify the presumed attitude-behavior link.

## Conclusions

Since police exercise so much discretion, it is important to understand the factors which affect their discretionary choices. It appears as though organizational, situational, neighborhood, and officer characteristics all may play some part in the decisions that police make. While much research has focused on the determinants of police behavior and much has been learned in the process, there is still a great deal that is unexplained. As researchers use more sophisticated designs and methods, it becomes apparent that the study of police discretionary behavior is a complicated endeavor. Adopting a community policing philosophy in police departments would seem to influence the discretionary choices that police officers make and future research might do well to explore this issue. Additionally, while attitudes of police officers appear to contribute little to our understanding of police behavior, more attention should be paid to this area.

## References

Alpert, G. and L. Fridell. 1992. *Police Vehicle and Firearms: Instruments of Deadly Force*. Prospect Heights, IL: Waveland Press.

Banton, M. 1964. *The Policeman in the Community*. New York: Basic Books.

Bayley, D. H. and H. Mendelsohn. 1969. *Minorities and the Police*. New York: Free Press.

Berk, S. F. and D. Loseke. 1981. "Handling Family Violence: Situational Determinants of Police Arrest in Domestic Disturbances." *Law and Society Review* 15 (2).

Bittner, E. 1970. *The Functions of Police in Modern Society*. Rockville: National Institute of Mental Health.

Black, D. 1971. "The Social Organization of Arrest." *Stanford Law Review* 23:1087–111.

_____. 1980. *The Manners and Customs of Police*. New York: Academic Press.

Black, D. and A. Reiss. 1967. *Studies of Crime and Law Enforcement in Major Metropolitan Areas Vol. 2 , Field Surveys III*. Section I: "Patterns of Behavior in Police and Citizen Transactions." Washington, DC: Government Printing Office.

_____. 1970. "Police Control of Juveniles." *American Sociological Review* 35:63–77.

Bloch, P. and D. Anderson. 1974. *Policewomen on Patrol: Final Report*. Washington, DC: Police Foundation.

Blumberg, M. 1981. "Race and Police Shootings: An Analysis in Two Cities," in *Contemporary Issues in Law Enforcement*. J. J. Fyfe (ed). Beverly Hills: Sage.

Brooks, L. W. 1986. "Determinants of Police Officer Orientations and Their Impact on Police Discretionary Behavior." Unpublished Ph.D. Dissertation. Institute of Criminal Justice and Criminology, University of Maryland.

Brooks, L. W., A. Piquero, and J. Cronin. 1993. "Police Officer Attitudes Concerning Their Communities and Their Roles: A Comparison of Two Suburban Police Departments." *American Journal of Police* 12:115–39.

_____. 1994. "'Workload' Rates and Police Officer Attitudes: An Examination of 'Busy' and 'Slow' Precincts." *Journal of Criminal Justice* 22.

Brown, M. K. 1981. *Working the Street: Police Discretion and the Dilemmas of Reform*. New York: Russell Sage Foundation.

Canter, P. and K. Martensen. "Neiderhoffer Revisited—Comparison of Selected Police Cynicism Hypotheses." Paper Presented to the 1990 American Society of Criminology Annual Meeting in Baltimore, Maryland.

Chatterton, M. 1983. "Police Work and Assault Charges." In *The Police Organization*. M. Punch (ed), 194–221. Cambridge: The MIT Press.

Crank, J. P. 1993. "Legalistic and Order-Maintenance Behavior Among Police Patrol Officers: A Survey of Eight Municipal Police Agencies." *American Journal of Police* 7:103–26.

Davis, E. M. 1978. *Staff One: A Perspective on Effective Police Management*. Englewood Cliffs, New Jersey: Prentice-Hall.

Dobash, R. E. and R. P. Dobash. 1977. "Wives—The Appropriate Victims of Marital Violence." *Victimology*. 2(34): 426–42.

Dorsey, R. and D. Giacopassi. 1986. "Assessing Gender Differences in the Levels of Cynicism Among Police Officers." *American Journal of Police* 5:91–112.

Ericson, R. 1982. *Reproducing Order: A Study of Police Patrol Work*. Toronto: University of Toronto Press.

Finckenauer, J. 1976. "Some Factors in Police Discretion and Decision-Making." *Journal of Criminal Justice* 4.

Friedrich, R. J. 1977. "The Impact of Organizational, Individual, and Situational Factors on Police Behavior." Ph.D. Dissertation. Department of Political Science, University of Michigan.

Fyfe, J. J. 1978. "Shots Fired: An Examination of New York City Police Firearms Discharges." Ph.D. Dissertation. School of Criminal Justice: State University of New York at Albany.

Fyfe, J. J. 1980. "Geographic Correlates of Police Shootings: A Microanalysis." *Crime and Delinquency* 17:101–13.

Geller, R. and K. Karales. 1981. *Split Second Decisions: Shootings of and by the Chicago Police*. Chicago Law Enforcement Study Group.

Goldstein, H. 1977. *Policing a Free Society*. Cambridge: Harvard University Press.

_____. 1979. "Improving Policing: A Problem Oriented Approach." *Crime and Delinquency* 25:236–58.

Grennan, S. 1987. "Findings on the Role of Officer Gender in Violent Encounters With Citizens." *Journal of Police Science and Administration* 15:78–85.

Guyot, D. 1979. "Bending Granite: Attempts to Change the Rank Structure of American Police Departments." *Journal of Police Science and Administration* 7:253–84.

Hayeslip, D. and G. Cordner. 1987. "The Effects of Community-Oriented Patrol on Officer Attitudes." *American Journal of Police* 6.

Horvath, F. 1987. "The Police Use of Deadly Force: A Description of Selected Characteristics of Intrastate Incidents." *Journal of Police Science and Administration* 15:226–38.

Klinger, D. A. 1994. "Demeanor or Crime? Why 'Hostile' Citizens Are More Likely To Be Arrested." *Criminology* 32:475–93.

_____. 1996. "More on Demeanor and Arrest in Dade County." *Criminology* 34: 61–82.

Krohn, M., J. Curry, and S. Nelson-Krueger. 1983. "Is Chivalry Dead? An Analysis of Changes in Police Dispositions of Males and Females." *Criminology* 21: 395–416.

Lundman, R. J. 1994. "Demeanor or Crime? The Midwest City Police-Citizen Encounter." *Criminology* 32:631–56.

Manning, P. 1977. *Police Work: The Social Organization of Policing*. Cambridge: The MIT Press.

Martin, D. 1976. *Battered Wives*. San Francisco: Glide Publications.

Mastrofski, S. 1981. "Policing the Beat: The Impact of Organizational Scale on Patrol Officer Behavior in Urban Residential Neighborhoods." *Journal of Criminal Justice* 9:343–58.

_____. 1983. "The Police and Noncrime Services." In *Evaluating Performance of Criminal Justice Agencies*, G. Whitaker and C. D. Phillips (eds). Beverly Hills: Sage.

Mastrofski, S. D., R. Ritti, and D. Hoffmaster. 1987. "Organizational Determinants of Police Discretion: The Case of Drinking-Driving." *Journal of Criminal Justice* 15:387–402.

Mastrofski, S. D., R. E. Worden, and J. B. Snipes. 1995. "Law Enforcement in a Time of Community Policing." *Criminology* 33:539–63.

Muir, W. K. 1977. *Police: Streetcorner Politicians*. Chicago: University of Chicago Press.

Murphy, P. V. and T. Pate. 1977. *Commissioner*. New York: Simon and Schuster.

Nardulli, P. F. and J. M. Stonecash. 1981. *Politics, Professionalism, and Urban Services: The Police*. Cambridge: Oelgeschlager, Gunn, and Hain.

Ostrom, E., R. B. Parks, and G. Whitaker. 1977. *The Police Services Study*. Bloomington: Workshop in Political Theory and Policy Analysis, Indiana University.

Packer, H. 1968. *The Limits of the Criminal Sanction*. Stanford: Stanford University Press.

Piliavin, J. and S. Briar. 1964. "Police Encounters With Juveniles." *American Journal of Sociology* 70:206–14.

Powell, D. D. 1990. "A Study of Police Discretion in Six Southern Cities." *Journal of Police Science and Administration* 17:1–7.

Reiss, A. 1971. *The Police and the Public*. New Haven: Yale University Press., E. C. and S. M. Chermak. 1993. "Causes of Police Behavior Revisited." *Journal of Criminal Justice* 21:353–82.

Rossi, P., R. Berk, and B. Eidson. 1974. *The Roots of Urban Discontent: Public Policy, Municipal Institutions, and the Ghetto*. New York: John Wiley and Sons.

Roy, M. 1979. *Battered Women: A Psychosociological Study of Domestic Violence*. New York: Van Nostrand.

Scott, E. J. 1981. *Calls For Service: Citizen Demand and Initial Police Response*. Washington, DC: National Institute of Justice.

Sherman, L. 1980. "Causes of Police Behavior: The Current State of Quantitative Research." *Journal of Research in Crime and Delinquency* 17:69–100.

_____. 1983. "Reducing Police Gun Use: Critical Events, Administrative Policy, and Organizational Change." In *Control in the Police Organization*. M. Punch (ed) Cambridge: The MIT Press.

Shernock, S. 1992. "The Effects of College Education on Professional Attitudes Among Police." *Journal of Criminal Justice Education* 3:71–92.

Skolnick, J. 1966. *Justice Without Trial: Law Enforcement in a Democratic Society*. New York: John Wiley & Sons.

Smith, D. A. 1984. "The Organizational Aspects of Legal Control." *Criminology* 22:19–38.

_____. 1986. "The Neighborhood Context of Police Behavior," In *Crime and Justice: An Annual Review of Research Vol. 8*. A. J. Reiss and M. Tonry (eds).

_____.1987. "Police Response to Interpersonal Violence: Defining the Parameters of Legal Control." *Social Forces* 65:767–82.

Smith, D. A. and L. A. Davidson. 1984. "Equity and Discretionary Justice: The Influence of Race on Police Arrest Decisions." *Journal of Criminal Law* 75:234–49.

Smith, D. A. and C. Visher. 1980. "Sex and Involvement in Deviance/Crime: A Quantitative Review of the Empirical Literature." *American Sociological Review* 45.

_____. 1981. "Street Level Justice: Situational Determinants of Police Arrest Decisions." *Social Problems* 29:167–78.

Smith, D. A. and J. R. Klein. 1983. "Police Agency Characteristics and Arrest Decisions." In *Evaluating Performance of Criminal Justice Agencies*. G. D. Whitaker and C. D. Phillips (eds.). Beverly Hills: Sage.

Smith, D. A. and J. Klein. 1984. "Police Control of Interpersonal Disputes." *Social Problems* 31:468–81.

Swanson, C. 1978. "The Influence of Organization and Environment on Arrest Policies in Major U.S. Cities." *Policy Studies Journal* 7:390–418.

Visher, C. A. 1983. "Gender, Police Arrest Decisions, and Notions of Chivalry." *Criminology* 21:5–28.

Walker, S. 1991. *The Police in America*, 2nd ed. New York: McGraw-Hill.

Werthman, C. and I. Piliavin. 1967. "Gang Members and the Police." In *The Police: Six Sociological Essays*. David Bordua (ed). New York: John Wiley & Sons.

Westley, W. A. 1970. *Violence and the Police: A Sociological Study of Law, Custom, and Morality*. Cambridge: The MIT Press.

Wilson, J. Q. 1968. *Varieties of Police Behavior*. Cambridge: Harvard University Press.

Worden, R. E. 1989. "Situational and Attitudinal Explanations of Police Behavior: A Theoretical Reappraisal and Empirical Assessment." *Law and Society Review* 23:667–711.

Worden, R. E. 1990. "A Badge and a Baccalaureate: Policies, Hypotheses, and Further Evidence." *Justice Quarterly* 1990:565–92.

_____. 1995. "Police Officers' Belief Systems: A Framework for Analysis." *American Journal of Police* 14:49–81.

Worden, R. E. and A. A. Pollitz. 1984. "Police Arrests in Domestic Disturbances: A Further Look." *Law and Society Review* 18:105–19.

Worden, R. E. and R. L. Shepard. 1996. "Demeanor, Crime, and Police Behavior: A Reexamination of the Police Services Study Data."*Criminology* 34:83–105.

# Making Rank
## Becoming an American Police Sergeant

*John Van Maanen*

One of the most distinctive characteristics of American police agencies is that virtually everyone in the organization, from station house broom to chief, shares the common experience of having worked the street as a patrol officer. Lateral entry is a feature of only the highest departmental positions, and even here it is quite rare to appoint a "citizen" or, in police argot, "civilian" who has not had extensive police experience at all levels. As one moves down the hierarchical ladder, lateral entry is unknown and supervisory positions are filled only from the pool of applicants directly below the vacant slot. The opportunity structure is such that, as people move up, openings move down.

This bottom-up, closed promotion system assures that applicants to the supervisory ranks, including that of sergeant, have been exposed to the so-called "street culture" of policing.[1] Although there are certainly local variations in this culture, general elements include the deeply held beliefs among police officers who work the street that one can't police by the book; that most publics served by the police are, in the main, ungrateful, uncooperative, and uncaring; that real police work centers on crook catching; that any action is better than none (the police are always expected to do something); that the unexpected is to be expected in police work; and that there are few things police officers have not seen, heard, or dealt with. More generally, the cultural knowledge carried by street-level police officers holds that there can be no practical theory for accomplishing police tasks because each task is different and its performance highly contingent on the information any officer has in hand or is developing. One may second-guess what another officer has done, but such second-guessing cannot be pursued very far.[2]

The street is not, however, the only working context for departmental employees of the police officer rank. Although the patrol division is by far the largest administrative unit in American police agencies (comprising roughly 60 percent of the membership), other units also make use of such lower-level officers as detectives, crime scene investigators, dispatchers, administrative aides, juvenile officers, public relations officers, traffic officers, computer programmers, jailers, video technicians, K–9 (dog) officers, statisticians, training instructors, records and property clerks, alarm experts, chauffeurs for public officials, and on and on. The American police organization examined in this article (Union City, a pseudonym) has over 50 separate positions available to employees, carrying the police officer rank beyond that of patrolman or patrolwoman.[3] More to the point, when officers move by choice or command from the patrol division and the beats that comprises the division, the much analyzed street culture of policing becomes less apparent, and, as I will argue, its usefulness as a blueprint for an officer's action less clear.

To avoid rushing the story, let me outline it first. In the following section, I describe the promotional system of the Union City Police Department from the perspective of those officers who are concerned about making the sergeant's rank. Although there are departmental peculiarities in this description, I believe most of the material is familiar to police officers in virtually all good-sized departments. The next section moves longitudinally to consider the organizational socialization practices common at the sergeant level. Such practices are more notable for their informal, tacit character than for their formal, explicit nature. This point is very much pertinent to the third section of this article which examines some of the visible contrasts between those first-line supervisors whom the police regard as "street sergeants" and those whom they regard as "station house sergeants." It is my view that this distinction rests not on the nature of police work per se, nor on the personal predispositions of those performing the sergeant's role, but rather it rests on the way organizational careers are fashioned in police agencies.

## Making the List

Becoming a sergeant in good-sized American police agencies is governed by departmental and civil service procedures designed (at least in part) to legitimize the impartiality and rationality of the selection process. The rules an agency adopts provide the framework within which candidates compete for promotion. But, like all rule systems, the rules governing police promotional practices do not specify their own application, and observers of and participants in the promotion process must therefore exercise an interpretive turn if they are to judge how the system "really works."

To those occupying the entry-level rungs of police agencies, the sergeant selection process is seen to favor those candidates who are assigned outside the patrol division where, historically, some 55 percent to 65 percent of departmental personnel are assigned. Of importance, senior police officials believe these candidates are less likely to bring the "patrolman's mentality" to the sergeant role than candidates whose police experience consists primarily of street duties. From the perspective of those who are supervised, sergeants who have lost (or, perhaps, never acquired) the "patrolman's mentality" are the station house sergeants of the police world; those who have it are the street sergeants. If the logic that lies behind the activities of a police sergeant is to be understood, this distinction is crucial. First, however, a description of the selection and socialization processes associated with the sergeant role is required, for it is from such processes that the station house and street sergeant contrast derives.

Most police agencies require a minimum number of years on the force before a member is allowed to apply for a sergeant position. In Union City, a three-year "waiting period" is officially the standard, although the average time before an officer is appointed sergeant exceeds 12 years (Van Maanen, 1983). The official basis for promotion is provided by the local civil service agency and consists of a ranked list of all eligible candidates (i.e., all those who choose to take the most recently administered sergeant's examination). Sixty to sixty-five percent of those eligible take the test. The final ranked list is based upon scores given for both the written and oral portions of the exam, plus a shifting formula that may add points for years of experience, minority status, supervisory ratings, peer ratings (on occasion), military experience, and departmental commendations.[4] A high score on the written exam (multiple choice and essay questions) assures a candidate an oral interview before a panel of departmental and community representatives. A high score on the oral examination makes relevant other particularistic criteria such as years of experience and performance ratings. The quantitative differences among candidates are often ridiculously small:

> The last time I took the exam I pulled a 94 on the written which put me 156th on the list. If I'd of gotten a 95 I'd of been about the 50th on the list, which would have put me in the oral boards where I know I could of come out well.

Despite elaborate civil service codification and official departmental disclaimers, the sergeant selection process in most, if not all, American police agencies provides more than a little room for sponsorship to work its effects. In particular, visibility of an officer to senior and ranking officers in a department is considered important by all, and my own observations strongly support this contention. Although it is not the outright favoritism of the sort associated with the legendary "hook" or "rabbi" systems (Radano, 1969; Niederhoffer, 1969), it does give some slight advantage to those officers who carry demographic characteristics currently fashionable among those who assess the legality of selection procedures and, more crucially, gives advantage to those officers who have moved appropriately around the departmental division structure. Experience counts, but it counts only in particular ways.

In Union City, for example, additional points for an aspiring sergeant can be accrued from taking on different assignments. High supervisory assessments on a variety of jobs are explicitly taken into account (and converted to points) by the oral review board. Officers are told (no doubt for mixed reasons) of the advantages of rotating across divisions and, in the process, becoming familiar with more supervisors in the organization, more duties performed by the agency, and, significant because of their testable relevance, more departmental rules and regulations. "The more you've seen outside of patrol," claimed one high-ranking Union City officer, "the more attractive you are to the brass."

The promotional system, then, favors not only those officers skilled at test-taking but also those willing and able to cultivate relationships that lead them outside the patrol division. Although there is no fixed or certain route to the sergeant's post in most departments, some sort of what Roth (1963: 14) calls a "sentimental order" will undoubtedly exist. In Union City, for example, patrolmen commonly held that the administrative aide jobs were most helpful if one desired advancement.

> If you want to make sergeant in a hurry, you've gotta get yourself assigned to the Chief's office (Administrative Services Bureau). If you get there, you'll meet all the honchos and, when it comes to taking the orals, what those guys say gets listened to.

It should be emphasized that the path to sergeant is, nonetheless, varied. Even though the promotional system does allow for commonsensical theorizing on the part of the concerned officers, such accounts are often wrong.

> I was 265th on the last exam. I expected with the extra time on, more course units, and now being a detective, to move up the list to at least inside 100. But when the list came out I was below 300, worse than before. You can never tell.

The particular examination process this officer describes represented a change in Union City from previous tests. Formerly, the testing process consisted of lengthy multiple choice and essay questions judged against so-called objective standards. In 1978, however, the local Civil Service Agency in charge of promotional exams adopted a new format that covered about half the written test. The effect of this change was to disrupt radically an officer's ability to predict how well he would do on the written portion of the exam, and, hence, where he would fall when cuts were made for the oral examination. The point here is, of course, not related to the exam itself, but to the fact that such exams change over time, and with such changes often go an officer's sense of knowing where he stands on the road to promotion.

The critical "first-cut" function of the written exam is a source of considerable grumbling for many officers. They regard such formal questioning as inappropriate and as having little or nothing to do with a sergeant's proper role. Promotional exams stress study and recall, official policy, knowledge of the law, and "going by the book." To many policemen, such matters are altogether peripheral and unimportant.

Most sergeants wouldn't make a pimple on a street cop's ass. They fucking hide for three months before the exam and hit the books as if knowing the state and muni codes were the most important things in the world. And, when they finally make it, they still think so.

This officer is speaking of station house sergeants. He is, however, careful to imply that there are exceptions to the rule. Exceptions are the street sergeants of the police world who are thought to make rank without "playing the game" of cultivating relationships with higher-ups, seeking intraorganizational transfers out of patrol, or devoting themselves to lengthy and intensive study. Street sergeants make rank, it is claimed, by virtue of experience, savvy, or accident. Experience counts because seniority points based on the length of an officer's service in the agency are added to exam scores. Experience also counts because it can confer a test-taking advantage to those who have sat for previous exams. Savvy or raw intelligence explains how some officers do well on the exam without "hitting the books," a rather neat account because it suggests that such officers owe their success to exceptional commonsense and not to exceptional efforts at learning legal and departmental rules. Accident in promotional matters accounts for those officers who have somehow "slipped through" the selection screens by pure fortune or happenstance. A belief in fate, of course, may be one reason why many would-be street sergeants continue to participate in the promotion process over and over again despite repeated failure.

In any event, the competition for sergeant in most police agencies is keen, the results uncertain, and the material rewards to be gained slight. The pay differential between patrol officers and sergeants in Union City is less than 200 dollars per month, and a sergeant's opportunity for overtime, court-time, and off-duty work are quite restricted. Among patrol officers, conventional wisdom has it that sergeants take home less pay than they do. Yet, when the sergeant's exam comes around every three years or so, some 450 of the 800 eligible officers sign up and go through the testing and labeling routines. As suggested, however, advancement may be only one of several reasons for participating in the selection process. Practice for future tests, pressure from others, curiosity, a day off the streets, and interest in how well one stacks up next to colleagues are all motives heard in police agencies. Indeed, relative standings on the exam ladder become part of the patrolman's world, and can be put to inventive uses:

Last time I was 412 on the list and Joey, my partner, was 380. That bastard used to kid me all the time about his 32 more gray cells. It was actually pretty funny. One time we had this lady stopped for criminal trespass and she started wising off about knowing the law and all, so I told her that she better not talk to me no more 'cause I was only 412th on the sergeant's list, but my partner was 380th. She shut up after that one. I think she figured we were crazy.

In the eyes of most would-be sergeants or, as the police might say, "wannabees," the most discussed feature of the promotional process is its perceived capricious character. The process, in all its many parts, is seen as a gauntlet, and those who do well, despite their good or bad reputations within the department, are regarded as lucky. They may still be seen as qualified for the sergeant's role, but feelings about the arbitrary nature of the selection process itself persist, separate from judgments about particular individuals so selected. The process is regarded as testing inappropriate skills and knowledge, giving unfair advantage to certain officers distinguished only by their demographic status (minorities, college graduates, veterans, women, senior citizens, etc.), and emphasizing "tricks" or all too subtle questioning (certain test items become part of the departmental folklore on the basis of their slippery intent or multiple meanings). In general, the process is seen by most who submit to it as mildly embarrassing, a process that dishonors far more than it honors.

One could hardly expect a favorable impression of a testing procedure that regularly screens out over 95 percent of its takers. Yet promotion to the rank of sergeant by a screening process viewed as capricious does not in itself enhance the new officer's authority over his subordinates. Rather, the respect a sergeant is able to command from subordinates ultimately depends on what he is able to accomplish after selection. If anything, his credibility among subordinates is probably harmed more than helped by the promotion process in effect in most American police agencies. At the very least, the selection of sergeants for most police officers seems to be a process that is, if not indecipherable, both biased and without obvious logic.

## Sergeant Socialization[5]

The actual placement of a sergeant in an organizational slot can occur any time during a given list's run of eligibility (i.e., before the next test is given). That is, a person may be number one on the list, but if no slots open up during this period, the candidate may, as the police say, "die number one on the list." When slots become available through vacancy chains begun with retirements, exits, deaths, or the addition of a position, appointments are made on a one-by-one basis from among the cluster of top ranked names on the list. The process can occur overnight, and though those selected may have been thinking about this forthcoming change of status for some time, wondering and hypothesizing about how to approach the new role, the promotion itself comes on a demand-only basis. Consider the experience of one newly promoted sergeant:

> I'd been working in the communications center for about 18 months. I was number three on the list and right after the test I transferred in. I didn't want to stay in patrol 'cause I knew I'd be moving up soon and didn't want to have to work with some guy one night and turn around and be his boss the next. Captain Oliver comes down one night and gives me the word that I'm going relief in Central next Tuesday, which is pretty much where I fig-

ured I'd be. Even though I knew I was going, I was a little shook. It took so long to happen so fast.

These remarks convey how becoming a sergeant is anything but an orderly, well-defined passage. The process is personalized, sudden, disjointed, and difficult to categorize. But despite these seemingly particularistic features, there are at least five characteristics common to sergeant socialization in Union City. Moreover, the import of these characteristics considered as a whole is to suggest that the work-related interests and identities a sergeant brings to the new role are more likely to be confirmed than altered by the passage. In this sense, street and station house sergeants are not so much made by the rank as imported to it.

First, making rank of sergeant is a most uncertain process. Officers who successfully complete the passage consider themselves as survivors more than winners. Not only must officers do well on the set of sergeant examinations, they must also endure a lengthy waiting period during which their actual promotions remain problematic. The time between the announcement certifying high position on the list and actual placement in the sergeant's ranks is full of danger. Most men high on the list quickly try to locate themselves in positions where there is little risk of making serious mistakes or of angering any of the brass who will draw from the top names on the list or who may influence such a draw.[6] Yet such precautions may be in vain because there is no guarantee that even if a man is number one on the list, his name will be called. Indeed, I suspect most police agencies contain a few officers who become living legends for existing endlessly on the short list for sergeant but never make the grade.

For those officers who are called up, the understandably risk-adverse strategies they adopt while seeking promotion, coupled with the agency's penchant for promoting those who are assigned to police duties outside the patrol division, tend to amplify whatever experiential gaps already exist between a newly appointed sergeant and his subordinates. In Union City, virtually all novice sergeants go to the patrol division, the largest in the department. It is, for many, a division they may have been away from for quite some time. A chronic complaint among patrol officers in Union City was that their sergeants have forgotten "what it's like on the streets."

There is some truth to such grumbling. For example, of the twenty-six sergeants who were selected in Union City between 1975 and 1978, only six came directly from the patrol division. Of the twenty who did not, sixteen of them had been out of patrol (and most out of the "bag" or uniform) for over three years. Patrol may be the core mission emphasized by a police department, but its centrality and importance seem not to be reflected, at least in Union City, in the workings of its promotional reward system.

In police agencies, especially in the patrol division, territory and team-based loyalties are crucial (Van Maanen, 1974: 113–16). Officers are distrustful of anyone they do not know well. If outside colleagues are treated with caution when transferred into a squad, this caution and restraint is only magnified when a new sergeant enters from outside the division and the squad. A new sergeant can count on prelusive courtesies, but little more. As others have noted, authority in police agencies is based primarily upon personal relations with subordinates and is not easily transferred across segments (or ranks) in the organization (Bittner, 1970; Rubinstein, 1973; Muir, 1977).[7] Though newly appointed sergeants are quite aware of this aspect of police life, they are still rankled by the behavior of officers who are reluctant to grant them at least some authority and credence based on the clinical and practical expertise that even the greenest of sergeants believe they possess.

> When I came into this unit, I'd worked 11 years in patrol and 3 years upstairs. I was about 15 years older than the oldest guy in the squad. You'd think that would count for something. Not among these guys. I was here for almost six months before they started asking me for anything other than a day off. Cops are a strange breed. They don't think it's possible for someone who hasn't worked their little patch to know anything about what they do. I had to actually get out there and start answering calls before they started to take me seriously.

Second, the passage from police officer to sergeant is an individual, solitary process. Unlike the police academy where initiates are introduced to the organization in a collective fashion surrounded by peers, there is no formal training period or cohort group of rookie sergeants to ease the passage. Several officers may be promoted together, and a ceremony of sorts may attend to this passage, but each sergeant is almost sure to be given different and interactionally distant assignments. An officer may be coached informally by another, more experienced sergeant before and upon assuming the role, but there is no guarantee that this will occur. The rookie sergeant must seek out advice and counsel on his own, and his adjustment to the role will depend very much on the network of personal ties he maintains in the agency (itself a function of assignments, past and present).

Third, the usual assignments given to new sergeants are relief assignments. They are not provided permanent supervisory responsibilities in a given squad, in part because such assignments are thought by the captains who pass them out to require more experienced supervisors and in part because such assignments are used by captains (and higher officials) as rewards for sergeants who have already demonstrated their abilities. Permanent positions, unless they are in the least desirable segments of the organization (the jail, property room, community service division, etc.), are typically filled by veteran sergeants. Thus, new sergeants, as they learned when they first joined the patrol division as rookie officers, must rely on their developed or developing ties with influential others in the department if they are to shed an undesirable assignment for a more desirable one.

Being assigned a relief role in the patrol division means, among other things, that a novice sergeant will find himself supervising different squads on each shift. Within each squad there is little incentive for members to go out of their way to produce for the relief man or to develop more than a passing regard for him. They will be civil and accord him proper respect, of course, but they will do little more. If a given squad is tightly organized, intimately familiar with one another, and beholden to their regular sergeant for whatever work routines they have established, the new sergeant will have only a caretaking role to perform.

Fourth and relatedly, part of a sergeant's authority rests on the desirability of the assignment he supervises. A rookie sergeant is likely to be "broken in" on the least desirable assignments, such as those in the "cow precincts" where nothing much of police interest happens—for this is where supervisory turnover is likely to be highest. Such assignments are also the most difficult to manage because few people are in these segments of the organization by choice. The men for whom a new sergeant is responsible may well be the most troublesome in the department with lengthy histories of reassignment and transfer. From this perspective, the first assignment a sergeant is provided is likely to be the most difficult, for reasons that go beyond the fact that he is inexperienced.

Finally, in large departments the initial posting of a sergeant is likely to be one in which the sergeant knows few if any of his new charges. By and large, few officers have reputations (or contacts) that are widespread within the organizations. Policing for most men is a rather contained occupation where one comes to know well only those with whom one works closely—those working the same division, precinct, sector, shift, and squad. Lacking knowledge of the character, predilections, and tastes of the new sergeant, squad members will prefer to sit back and observe the new man in action before making judgments about how they will respond to his command. Moreover, if an officer does have a reputation throughout the department, it is probable his notoriety rests on endeavors that make him less likely to become a sergeant rather than those that do.

Assignment to a given squad, then, most often puts a sergeant in the midst of strangers where establishing personal contact and comfortable working relations with others will be a primary task. Because he does not often witness the actual work performed by the men of his squad, he must become familiar with their working styles indirectly by determining their normal radio voices, backup practices, inclinations to share in the risks of policework, and work avoidance strategies. But, more important, he must learn how to get along with these officers by discovering their idiosyncrasies, street interests, family concerns, temperaments, leisure pursuits, and so on. The tone of the early interactions between sergeants and their officers is, therefore, likely to be both solicitous and social in nature; for, as most sergeants know only too well, they must have the affaction of their men before they can expect much out of them. In this respect, the new sergeant must come to know his men before he can find and command them. This initial requirement puts a stamp on further dealings, for it effectively puts persons and personalities at the center of the working relations between sergeants and subordinates.

I have described selected aspects of the passage from police officer to sergeant in some detail for I consider it to be a neglicted topic of study. In contrast to the intense and deliberate socialization of new recruits to the police career, sergeant socialization is relatively mild. The passage to sergeant is unpredictable and uncertain in timing, individual, informal, based on a contest, and disjunctive. This suggests that its effects will be largely confirmatory or celebrative of the beliefs and action patterns already possessed by those undergoing the casual rites of passage (Van Maanen and Schein, 1979). The liminal, betwixt-and-between period associated with making the rank of sergeant officially provides the newcomer with precious little in the way of new skills or ways of thinking about the assumed job. The rookie sergeant, then, is left more or less to his own devices in coming to terms with the new role. It is to these matters I now turn.

## Strategies of Adaptation[8]

Given the socialization features set forth above, the sociologically inclined might suppose the new sergeants will enact their respective roles in divergent, creative, situationally responsive, and particularistic ways. Police officers also believe this to be the case. Patrol officers, in particular, talk about and personify their sergeants in highly individualistic terms, taking care to point out to an interested listener the wide variety of sergeant proclivities.

> Now you take Sergeant Johnson. He was a drunk hunter. That guy wanted all the drunks off the street, and you knew that if you brought in a couple of drunks a week, you and he would get along just fine. Sergeant Moss, now, is a different cat. He don't give a rat's ass about drunks. What he wants are those vice pinches. Sergeant Gorden wanted tickets, and he's hound your ass for a ticket a night. So you see, it all depends on who you're working for. Each guy's a little different.

Such views, however, have their limitations. Claims of idiosyncrasies run only on the surface, representing something of a collective rationale patrol officers whistle to one another as they go about various tasks they consider merely the peculiar preferences of a given sergeant. But, there is also another tune they whistle, and this tune corresponds to a recognized, deeper structure associated with the performance styles and standards of sergeants. It is this latter structure that brings forth the labels "street" and "station house sergeant," for they are tags related intimately to the path a given patrol sergeant has followed toward promotion.

There are, as noted earlier, two basic paths open to police officers who aspire to the three-striped rank of sergeant. The path more frequently followed (in Union City, at least) is interdivisional and experientially diverse, involving an officer in various functional areas of the department. The other, less frequently followed path is intradivisional and experientially singular, involving an officer in assignments limited to the patrol division. The former path is associated with station house sergeants and brings officers into everyday contact with matters of administrative concern in the department. Paperwork, planning, recordkeeping, public relations, investigatory procedures, fine points of the law, statistics, press relations, data banks and files, clerical responsibilities, interorganizational relations, case loads, cost accounting, report generation, budget preparation, program development, image-making, grant-getting, and project monitoring are all examples of matters of some importance to many police officers who, without benefit of promotion, have nevertheless moved away from the patrol division and become embedded in what Reuss-Ianni (1983) calls the managerial culture of police organizations. The latter path is associated with street sergeants and is marked solely by membership in the field or street culture of policing, a culture distinguished by its disdain for administrative concerns and its emphasis on action, crook-catching, independence, and street smarts. This culture also promotes intense peer relations and an emphasis on the importance of supporting one's mates, both occupationally vis-á-vis the villains of the street and organizationally vis-á-vis the brass of the department. Although all new sergeants have at least modest exposure to and involvement with the street culture of policing, not all new sergeants have exposure to and involvement with the administrative culture. And, herein lies at least a partial explanation for the diversity of role performances among sergeants.

As the generic label implies, station house sergeants (alternatively, "precinct" or "desk" sergeants) are those supervisors seemingly always at or near their office work stations when on duty. Nicknames are revealing here. Station house sergeants are known to patrol officers by such titles as "Hats-on Harry," "Sitting Bill," "By-the-Book Brubaker," "Nine-to-Five George," "Fixed-Post Porter," and my favorite, drawn from Chatterton (1975), "Edward, the-Olympic-Torch-Who-Never-Goes-Out." What these sometimes endearing, sometimes cutting monickers suggest is a work style well understood by those subject to its whims. These sergeants become obvious to patrol officers by their avoidance of specific entanglements outside the "office" in the often messy world of hands-on policing.

In line with such avoidance tactics, station house sergeants define their roles in terms of standing behind the men assigned to them and being responsible for their conduct on the beat. This is a managerially approved definition, and station house sergeants are quick to point out the importance of such a charge by noting just how difficult it is for them to motivate their men to fulfill their quotas, properly fill out their reports, stay in line with departmental rules and regulations, and answer their calls within tolerable time limits. It is a fairly formal, relatively distant supervisory style that is enacted by station house sergeants and is a style best seen in contrast to their counterparts—the "street sergeants."

If station house sergeants are believed to stand behind their men, street sergeants are believed to stand alongside them. It is a collegial role that is enacted, not behind a desk or in departmental offices, but on the streets where calls are taken, arrests produced, coffee inhaled, and the mundane to dramatic rituals of policing acted out. Street sergeants also have their share of revealing titles: "I'LL Take-It Sam," "Billyjack," "E.T.

(phone Rome)," "Shooter McGee," "Mr. Smith and Wesson," "Peeping Tom," "Radio-Free Lebaron," and "Walker the Stalker." These sobriquets reflect the behavioral predilections of street sergeants, such as their presumed preference for live (or in police parlance, "on-view") action, their tendency to override or otherwise horn-in on calls originally assigned to a particular patrol unit, their distaste for official departmental procedures, and so on. Street sergeants define their mission in terms of their responsibility not for the men of their command, but for the beat or territory they command. When asked about the objectives of their jobs, they are likely to respond in ways quite similar to those whom they supervise—"keeping a clean patch," "getting the bad guys,'" "holding the line," or, more generally, "not letting the assholes take over the city."

Street sergeants typically come to their new roles directly from field locations where police administrators rarely penetrate (Van Maanen, 1974). Moreover, when assuming the new role, many parts of the old role remain both present and relevant. Cognitive similarities between the roles are apparent: a car and dispatch code are still assigned to a sergeant; personally assigned turf is again provided (albeit, a large one, encompassing several beats); the same uniform is still worn, even if there are extra stripes on the sleeve; and, from the street cop's perspective, the assholes are still out there roaming about uncaught and untaught. It is hardly surprising that without much exposure to differing kinds of police roles, the new sergeanting role is adopted in a fashion so similar to the way the old patrol officer role is played.

Station house sergeants, however, have often been out of the patrol division and uniform ("out of the bag") for some time and have become more or less accustomed to and, critically, come to value certain managerial or bureaucratic dimensions of police agencies (e.g., budgets, plans, reports, standard operating procedures, targets, etc.). They have worked more closely with those occupying the higher ranks of the agency than is possible for those in patrol and, in general, they have begun to appreciate the logic embedded within the administrative tasks they have been assigned (i.e., rationality, efficiency, predictability, accountability, discipline, etc.). It appears also that those officers outside the patrol division who claim serious aspirations to the sergeant's role develop a rather deep suspicion of their all-too-canny former colleagues in the patrol division who are "out there" on the street, out of view, and, perhaps, out of control.

Obviously, the whole story is not woven by using only these two yarns. Individual personalities are involved; extracurricular interests play a part; family and educational background matter; and, for some sergeants, the paths taken into the role are circuitous, moving in and out of the patrol division, and not nearly so pat as my examples suggest. Nonetheless, it is true that the administrative and street cultures of police organizations are recognized by sergeants and their men alike. Not only are they recognized, but sergeants typically perform their roles in ways more or less consistent with the dictates of one culture and, hence, opposed to the other.

As Chatterton (1975) makes clear, however, it is not the case that patrol officers necessarily prefer one role to the other. Both orientations have their shortcomings. Street sergeants, for example, are often seen to poach and to undersupervise while intruding too frequently and competitively into the vaunted autonomy patrol officers believe is their due in the field. At the same time, station house sergeants are thought to be preoccupied by the rule book and, thus, unappreciative of the situational particulars which, to patrol officers, render rules and regulations irrelevant and sometimes downright dangerous as guides to practical action. Patrol officers may take exception to both the on-view judgments of street sergeants and the retrospective counts of activity made by station house sergeants.

On the other hand, street sergeants are thought to know the score, to know what is "coming down" on particular beats and, hence, not to be too persnickety about the legal niceties surrounding police work. Station house sergeants have their good points too. They can almost always be located when questions arise and reports need adjustments or signatures; they typically have more intradepartmental clout, they are useful when a patrol officer would like a change of shift, precinct, or partner; and they tend, on average, to have more small favors than street sergeants to dispense to those officers they believe more deserving than others. For those on patrol, station house sergeants are, therefore, somewhat easier to work for because their behavior is more predictable, although the grounds for such predictability may strike many officers as patently ridiculous (e.g., writing misdemeanor drinking-in-public tickets as a way of staying on good terms with a given sergeant). However, no matter what a particular, and always peculiar, patrol officer's feelings are about a given sergeant, all would agree, whatever a station house sergeant is, a street sergeant is not.

## Comment

A central point of this quick look at the making of police sergeants is to call attention to the relevance of a sergeant's work history as a way of understanding how the supervisory role comes to be defined and carried out. A sergeant comes to the new role with the lessons learned in the old role(s). New things, in the absence of great surprise or compulsion, will be learned in old ways.

If a sergeant spends his first duty day behind the wheel of a prowl car getting the feel for the sector he is now at least nominally in charge of, instead of schmoozing in the precinct and staking out his office territory, it is not difficult to guess from where in the agency he came. To understand how a new sergeant is made is to also understand the orientation the man brings with him to the bundle of tasks he is to perform as a sergeant; a bundle which, for many, turns out not to be so very new at all. In most police agencies, little or no effort is made to correct whatever supervisory task, or value or performance perspectives and standards the previous role(s) may have engendered.

This is not a particularly novel or sharp observation. Yet it is too often overlooked when calls are put forth by public officials, reform-minded researchers, or high-ranking police administrators for "better quality management," "closer supervision," or "greater accountability among the troops." The facts of the matter seem to be that selection procedures favor administratively inclined candidates, and those candidates, when bestowed with the sergeant rank, tend to take a relatively remote supervisory stance toward the supervised. Matters of subordinate craft and competence in the field are not of great interest to station house sergeants. More often than not, these sergeants direct and evaluate the performance of their men on the basis of official, albeit indirect, productivity measures (e.g., calls answered, tardiness, tickets amassed, arrests logged, citizen complaints filed, street stops, miles logged, sick or vacation days taken, etc.).

A pogo-like aphorism seems to be at work in many police agencies wherein police administrators can say with some confidence: "We have met the new sergeants and they are us." This is certainly not unique to police agencies, for all organizations, large and small, appear to select for promotion those recruits who are more similar to incumbents than those who are dissimilar (Dalton, 1959; Kanter, 1977). It is a problem, however, when the promotional machinery begins to consistently crank out the more peripheral members of one rank for insertion into the rank above. Organizations are bifurcated, goals are thwarted by design, standards and morale decay, distrust multiplies, information is withheld, cliques, cabals, and little conspiracies abound, and so on.

This situation, I believe, now characterizes a good many American police agencies (Van Maanen, 1983: 308–12). In some, the admission of promotion-seeking by an officer in the patrol division is enough to invite ridicule from his colleagues. Part of this, of course, flows from the difficulties of obtaining promotion in the first place, and, consequently, reflects the dead-end nature of many police careers ("once a patrolman, always a patrolman"). But another part of it reflects what patrol officers regard as the insensitivity, the aloofness, the detachment, the hyper-concern for appearances, and the blatant currying of favor by sergeants with those above them in the police hierarchy.

No doubt, as a class, all bosses suffer a certain amount of resentment from their subordinates. Police bosses, however, do not have the relative luxury of being able to see much of what it is their respective subordinates do. Worse, they don't seem to mind. Station house sergeants see nothing untoward about their unobtrusive, distant, and literally seat-of-the-pants supervisory style. They are also amused more than threatened by energetic colleagues who seem always to be on the street, jumping from one call to the next. They are amused, perhaps, because in the long run they know these colleagues will not get very far unless they begin to see things their way and shed their ludicrous "patrolman's mentality." Station house sergeants are in the majority. Moreover, if they are relatively young, they know that the same tactics that brought them three stripes are likely to bring them more. If the patrolman's mentality is seldom encountered at the sergeant's level, it is even more rare further up the chain of command.

I will close, then, with the somewhat gratuitous suggestion that police officials might begin thinking of ways to preserve, not obliterate, the so-called patrolman's mentality throughout the ranks. In management circles of police agencies, this suggestion is something of a heresy, but I think it at least worth considering what the consequences might be were there more, not less, street sergeants on the beat. As it stands now, the care and close oversight of police work is a small, but regrettably undervalued part of what sergeants might do. Of course, most sergeants do see to it that at least some police work gets done and documented. But, as Bittner (1983) recently pointed out, few sergeants show much interest in whether or not such work is done well. This, perhaps more than anything else, is the central problem facing police command.

## Footnotes

[1] I use the phrase "street culture" rather than the more familiar "occupational culture" to draw attention to the distinctions police officers themselves often make within their organizations. The street culture of patrol work is widely known in police circles by virtue of the fact that practically all members work the street early in their respective careers. Yet it is equally true that this culture is less relevant as a problem-solving device as officers move beyond its reach and application. Reuss-Ianni (1983) makes this point as does Manning (1980).

[2] There are many converging descriptions of this cultural knowledge. Some of the better ones are found in Bittner (1970), Westley (1970), Rubinstein (1973), Manning (1977), Muir (1977), Punch (1979), and Holdaway (1983).

[3] I regard "Union City" as a large, ordinary, municipal police agency. There are more than one thousand uniformed officers in this department and the community policed is reasonably representative of urban areas in the United States. The data on which I draw in this article comes from my own participant-observation work in Union City. I have discussed my mostly ethnographic methods (conducted largely at the street levels of policing) at some length elsewhere (Van Maanen, 1982). The male pronoun is used throughout this article to depict individuals within the organization because, at the moment, gender is hardly a variable in police organizations. Changes are numerically afoot here, and there are large variations across departments, but most of what is said in this article about police sergeants and officers applies equally well, I think, to both men and women.

[4] There is more than a little mystery associated with the methods used to develop the final rankings. Most of the mystery lies in the always obscure and unarticulated reasoning by which the oral boards convert interview performances into points.

[5] Socialization, as I use the term here, is of the organizational sort. The term is meant to convey in shorthand fashion the way an individual learns to perform a newly assigned (work) role. In this section, the structural side of the socialization process is given more weight than the phenomenological, although, as I try to illustrate, the two are closely connected. For a detailed theoretical statement of the perspective alluded to here, see Van Maanen and Schein (1979).

[6] Those designated as selectors of sergeants in Union City and blessed with the Chief's approval do their selecting from a pool of names. They are not forced to work their way down the list of eligibles serially, although they are allowed to go

only so far down the list to pluck a name. It is possible (yet not likely) that one could place in the top five on the list and not be selected, even though as many as ten or more people were chosen from the list. In recent years, however, Union City selectors have gone straight down the list, perhaps as an attempt to reduce their legal vulnerability on promotional issues.

[7] Authority is also tied to knowing the territory over which one is responsible (Van Maanen, 1974). The territorial or turf basis of policing is a prominent theme in the patrol division where much police wisdom rests on coming to know the typical ways in which social space and time are used by citizens within one's district. Such wisdom does not transfer to other districts, however. If the clinical expertise of a sergeant is a possible source of influence beyond the positional and personal sources, sergeants new to a district will possess precious little of it. In this sense, they are quite dependent on their subordinates for police wisdom regardless of the experience they may have had in other districts.

[8] The data presented in this section are quite consistent, I think, with the observational reports of other fieldworkers who have spent time with the police in social and geographical regions far distant from Union City. Compare, for example, the research reports of Manning (1977, 1979), Chatterton (1975, 1979), Punch (1979), Holdaway (1980), and Reuss-Ianni (1983). Chatterton's work, in particular, has been influential in the writing of this article, not only because of its analytic bite, but because he comes as close as I think is possible to describing everyday life in the precinct and on the beat. That sergeants are a part of this scene and would be sorely missed by all were they to suddenly vanish is a point about which not all police observers have been so very careful.

## References

Bittner, E. (1983) "Introduction," pp. 11–26 in M. Punch (ed.) *Control in Police Organizations.* Cambridge: MIT Press.

_____. (1970) *The Functions of the Police in Modern Society.* Washington, DC: U.S. Government Printing Office.

Chatterton, M. (1979) "The supervision of patrol work under the fixed points system," pp. 83–101 in S. Holdaway (ed.) *The British Police.* London: Arnold.

_____. (1975) "Organizational relationships and processes in police work." Unpublished Ph.D. Thesis, University of Manchester.

Dalton, M. (1959) *Men Who Manage.* New York: John Wiley.

Holdaway, S. (1983) *Inside the British Police.* Oxford: Basil Blackwell.

Kanter, R. (1980) *The Police Station. Urban Life* 9(2): 79–100.

_____. (1977) *Men and Women of the Corporation.* New York: Basic Books.

Manning, P. K. (1980) *The Narc's Game.* Cambridge: MIT Press.

_____. (1979) "The social control of police work," pp. 41–65 in S. Holdaway (ed.) *The British Police.* London: Arnold.

_____. (1977) *Police Work.* Cambridge: MIT Press.

Muir, W. K. (1977) *Police: Streetcorner Politicians.* Chicago: Univ. of Chicago Press.

Niederhoffer, A. (1967) *Behind the Shield.* New York: Doubleday.

Punch, M. (1979) *Policing the Inner City.* London: Macmillan.

Radano, G. (1969) *On the Beat.* New York: Collier.

Reuss-Ianni, E. (1983) *Street Cops and Management Cops.* New Brunswick, NJ: Transaction.

Roth, J. (1963) *Timetables.* Indianapolis: Bobbs-Merrill.

Rubinstein, J. (1973) *City Police.* New York: Farrar, Straus, and Giroux.

Van Maanen, J. (1983) "The boss: a portrait of the American police sergeant," pp. 275–317 in M. Punch (ed.) *The Control of the Police.* Cambridge: MIT Press.

_____. (1982) "Fieldwork on the beat," pp. 103–51 in J. Van Maanen et al. (eds.) *Varieties of Qualitative Research.* Beverly Hills: Sage.

_____. (1974) "Working the street," pp. 83–130 in H. Jacob (ed.) *The Potential for Reform of Criminal Justice.* Beverly Hills: Sage.

_____. and E. H. Schein (1979) "Toward a theory of organizational socialization," pp. 209–69 in B. Staw (ed.) *Research in Organization Behavior*, Vol. 1. Greenwich, CT: JAI Press.

Westley, W. (1970) *Violence and the Police.* Cambridge: MIT Press.

# 10

# Policing and Reflection

*Peter K. Manning*

This article explores the consequences of reflexivity on policing.[1] Reflexivity is defined as the anticipatory shaping of action choices by imagining the response of the other. This "imagining" is shaped by the self's beliefs about others' anticipated reactions (Cullum-Swan, personal communication). Although reflexivity can be considered at the role level, it is also a correlate of framing (Goffman, 1974: 76) in the sense that once framed, an activity orchestrates expectations, but reflecting on action is also a structural property of modern societies (Giddens, 1991). Here, I explore television's role in reflexivity to suggest the importance of reflexivity to theorizing police.

## Master Trends

Modern society is both reflective and reflecting. It is shaped by consideration and modification of decisions in light of their anticipated consequences. This process of reflection and consideration is central to social organization when social integration is partially determined by negotiation and social construction of meanings, and where stranger-stranger interaction is the mode. Clearly, the mass media play a central role in modern consciousness and should significantly shape systematic interpretive social theory. Unfortunately, current models of interaction and communication are derived from the assumptions of early twentieth century social psychology—the ideas of William James, G. H. Mead, and Charles Cooley.

Mass media, especially television, must be dragged into modern theorizing because our sources of information and sensibilities are increasingly mediated. The media amplify the relevance of imagery, heighten reflexivity and create seductive, alternative, often layered or laminated, social realities. Mass media create and authoritatively reify social forms, alter and reshape boundaries between the private and the public, personal and impersonal, and modify and mix communicational genres. Media events (those either created wholly by the media, or amplified and dissem-

Reprinted with permission from the *Police Forum*, Vol. 6, No. 4, Oct. 1996, pp. 1–5.

inated by them) compete profoundly with socialization and personal experience for salience in shaping world views. Media present mini-realities fabricated from fragments of actual events, fantasies, gossip, recreations, simulations, infotainments, altered and distorted imagery and self-conceptions, combining at times, cartoons, graphics and human figures. Importantly, forms of electronically created reality, virtual reality, cyber- and hyper-space, and hypertexts, that simulate interpersonal relations by facilitating visual, computer-based, media connections between people, compete for relevance, time and intimacy, with embodied interpersonal relations. Electronically mediated communication via bulletin boards, e-mail, hypertexts, and FAXs, *simulates* the intimacy of personal private communication but does not require the use of a personal identity, real address, or even a socially legitimated self. Internet transactions are communications between electronically activated addresses, some of which may be false, mere numbers, or misrepresentations. This depersonalizes communication and mitigates authorship and obligation.

As this litany suggests, social control, whether by third parties, formal agencies of social control or informal sanctions, is matter of symbolizing consequences of behavior. When the imagery of control is conveyed electronically, social control works through distant surveillance and society resembles Bentham's panopticon, social control takes new forms and varieties.

In short, the self and other, ideas spawned nearly 100 years ago by philosophers, are now bound together in a symbolic threesome that includes the media. Given these changes in society and social control processes, re-thinking policing and other forms of social control is imperative. Television holds preeminent place in mediating experience. First, a quick overview of the sources of television's power (Manning, 1996).

## Some Consequences of Television's Perspective

Television's power comes from its counterintuitive presentation of time and space unfolding before the viewer's eyes. Violating the logic of causality, it represents itself as presenting the present, or the now, immediately. Watching television is an engaging experience that combines the real, the might be real, the surreal and the fantastic. Because it is a frame, it connects domestic life and the external world in marvelous complexity.

Its affect on personal relations is most striking when it seeks the immediate and thrusts itself into personal space, showing reactions to disasters, serial murders, or grand accomplishments. It also mimics the immediate, showing people's reactions to the aggressive intrusion of cameras, video crews, lights, microphones and the interviewer.

The immediate fabrication of realities is television's forte. Television is a commercial industry which seeks to commodify visual pleasures. Interaction results between television's institutional biases, program structure and content and viewers' perceptions, producing reflexivity (seeing self seeing self as media sees self and others) in terms of television's perspective and a selectively induced blindness to other aspects of social structure. Here are some generalizations about the effects of television on the shape of experience.

Television provides a kind of meta-reading, or interpretations of interpretations, of experience. While local experience is both shaped by television and reduced in importance by it (Meyrowitz, 1986: Ch.6), overall local knowledge and experience are declining in importance in socialization. Television's eye and perspective compete with other knowledge. Recall that television produces and reproduces a special kind of distant and ironic perspective on much of social life. Television displays image assemblages or a pastiche that is often ironic and anti-authoritarian. Recycling views of the police on sit-coms, excessive parodies of violence in films; police knowledge and taste on *Cops*; *Hard Copy* and *America's Most Wanted* and on cartoons, it both caricatures authority and exaggerates its importance. Television "re-enacts" police-public scenes, conflating hypothetical dialogue, possible scenarios, real people and actors, tapes of actual voices and re-created dialogues, calling these "reality shows" (*Detroit Free Press* 14 July, 1991).

Television amplifies some emotions, and is lodged in the self. Television is framed apart from everyday life yet is deeply grounded in it. Television is rooted in the emotional preconditions and predispositions of modern life, and reproduces experiences meaningful to the viewer's self. Television is a powerful projective source from which emotions are read and read-off (Goffman, 1959: Ch 1). Television seems to produce a seductive electronic place, not exclusively the world of the floating *simulacra* (symbols without clear referents), or even Baudrillard's hyperreality (1990), but an active source of experience. Television, in some dialogue with viewers' readings, produces redundant, cybernetic, emotional, and expressive communication that provides a kind of "back channel" self-affirmation.[2]

## Policing and Media

The dominant explanation for the behavior of the police is a socio-cultural theory. Assuming that policing is shaped by a single subculture arising from the interaction of a risky and dangerous working environment, the need to assert authority and apply violence, and the social isolation of officers (Skolnick, 1967), the experience of the urban patrolman is thus caricatured. Modifications of this view, and theories of policing based on the centrality of violence (Bittner, 1992), omit the effects of police views of themselves as an aspect of their conduct and decisions (Kappeler, Sluder and Alpert, 1994). The conflict between internal rules, regulations, policies and procedures and external audiences' expectations is a powerful source of police dilemmas that puts segments of police at risk differentially. Information technology has segmented policing and given rise to a middle management cadre. The high politics of policing, relations with the power elites in a community, elected officials, and significant minority groups, is made more salient by the community policing reform movement.

Unfortunately, theories of policing heretofore discuss the media only in the context of managing them or their role in amplifying scandals. Mass media, especially television, sets public expectations, amplifying scandal and police crimes, misconduct, and rule-violation, as well as amplifying the symbolic connection of the police to the law and the moral structure of society.

Real policing appears on the news, recreations of policing on *Emergency 911*, dramatizations of policing on *Cops*, fantasies surround police in feature films, and officers discuss and reflect on policing in talk shows, features and interview programs. The media eyes policing dramatically, as news, as feature material, and as an exciting source of probative "investigative journalism" and scandalous misconduct. Media reshow and reshow police-dominated scenes, looping them back into consciousness. The O.J. Simpson trial saturated even the most avid viewer with repeated film snippets. These salient amplification loops serve to punctuate and encourage police focus on *symbolic violence*, that is, maintaining the imagery of vertical and horizontal ordering consistent with the conventional wisdom (Manning, 1997), and to give credence to their role in communications work generally (Ericson, forthcoming). The police see themselves as we do: as at least in part a product of mass media imagery. Let us now rehearse the logic of police reflexivity.

## The Logic of Police Reflexivity

*Police Work* (1977) argued, following Hughes (1958), that metaphorically the police claim a mandate to assert binding moral definitions of the nature of the risks they are permitted to take. An occupational culture grows up around the routine risks and mistakes (Hughes, 1958). Given this mandate, that is if a negotiated legitimacy is granted, they will seek a license to practice, to be paid and rewarded for their social role. The mandate and license are thus matters negotiated in the arena of public opinion, and reflect transactions between significant and powerful audiences and the police. The mandate expands and contracts reflecting the tasks society expects and rewards, and in connection with similar dynamics of other competing occupations. Critical in this expansion and contraction process are scandals and public events that display for public scrutiny practices normally concealed and kept well backstage.

Risk plays a central role in policing, but "risk" is in part objective and in part a social construction. The work involves periodic high risk situations in which the probability of making an error is high, and police in the past were well-protected by common-law tradition (in liability and torts), case law, and criminal law, against prosecution for their judgments. The police culture reflects, responds to, and incorporates routine risks and solutions thereto. The occupational culture is a social creation that mystifies, dramatizes and elevates the ideological notion that policing is essentially risky, violent crime control. Risk is also avoided by officers; both risk avoidance and risk-seeking are commonly seen. Consider the viability of the advice: "keep low, don't rock the boat;" emphasis upon "covering your ass" (having a ready excuse or account for any detected error or lying about it) and the fear of capricious discipline. Patrol officers find risk in not only in citizen encounters, but in the possible consequences of errors, given the punitive and rule-focused character of the police-bureaucracy, and the inherent conservatism of senior officers. Evidence from our recent COPS-funded research suggests that many patrol officers resist "community policing" because it alters their role repertoires and significant audiences, and seek job protection in union contracts.

The media add a new and growing level of risk because of their access to police records (through the Freedom of Information Law). Television's (since 1974 with the introduction of hand-held video cameras) ability to respond quickly to events is awesome. The combination of mobile units for monitoring images and sound, satellites for world-wide transmission, small hand-held television cameras, citizen access to 911 and emergency numbers via cellular phones, the commonality of citizen-owned video cameras, and computers and faxes that send and receive images digitally all reduce the lag between event and coverage, even world-wide coverage, to minutes. Local news formats including routine on the scene reporting, the emphasis on the banal, titillating and commercial, and emergent journalistic ethics which emphasize, especially since Watergate, anti-authoritarian and anti-institutional biases, all contribute to the police as a cynosure. Police, in turn, employ media officers, attending training schools and Management Institutes on media management, issue press releases and videos, and use the media to convey their accomplishments. These structural conditions tend to both amplify and reduce protection for police risk-taking.

## Police Events and Reflections

Television has subtle effects on policing and vice-versa, but these effects are not well-known. I speculate here on the kinds of events that shape policing and those relevant to a communicational theory of policing. The number of media-amplified incidents involving the police since the wide-spread dissemination of the video of the Rodney King beating is remarkable. Here are some observations:

1. The police self is shaped by mass media, pop culture versions of the self, particularly those televised, while television's police reflect partially and in a systematically distorted fashion police views of themselves policing.

2. Media revelations of scandal and malfeasance create media issues arising from the media, sustained by the media, and amplified by the media. These revelations are looped, and stimulate a media-reaction cycle. The first indications are responded to by "containment moves" by police, attempts to maintain the original police

framing of an event (Goffman, 1974). Police actions are seen as "damage control," rather than response to the problem (Chan, 1996), and the media continue to make counter-counter-containment moves.

3. The significant others of police are not only embodied others in co-presence, but may be television figures, celebrities, and media heroes: Clint Eastwood as Harry Callahan, Jack Lord as Steve McGarrett of *Hawaii 5-0*, figures on *Adam 12*, and *Dragnet* (sanitized renditions of the LAPD) as well as the anti-heroes on *Hill Street Blues*, *NYPD Blue* and *Homicide*. These figures are evoked by cliché, shorthand phrases, such as "Make my day," and "Just the facts, Ma'am."

4. Police life choices and selves are shaped by abstracted typifications and stereotypes seen on "Infotainment" programs (combining "information" and "entertainment") such as *True Stories of the Highway Patrol*, *Cops* and *America's Most Wanted*. These programs, like *Rescue 911*, are *simulations* of policing, combining written scripts, commentary, reflections, and interviews with film of working police. These shows contain scenes stylishly edited by skilled television producers, cut from hours of film and censored by officers and administrators in the host police departments (Hallett and Powell, 1995).

5. Police see themselves as international figures. Both the relative salience and number of mass media figures shaping experience are expanded by cable, mass satellite distribution of television and movies, and international cable channels that broadcast in indigenous languages. The beating of Rodney King was shown internationally within hours of its appearance on a Los Angeles television station.

6. The police are active in live scenes, nightly news and in emergency situations, now frequently covered quickly by television. The media are also "on the scene," televising brutal and tragic events live—suicides, murders and violent assaults, natural and human-caused disasters (hurricanes, floods, tornadoes, earthquakes and explosions) and human-caused tragedies such as terrorist bombings and hostage situations. Police and other agents of control (soldiers, firefighters, EMS technicians and ambulance drivers), are typically asked to explain what happened, what is happening, or what will happen.

7. Media cover assiduously axial media events, events created by their actions, such as showing the Rodney King beating, the sequel of the Rodney King beating, the riots after the acquittal of LAPD officers Koon and Powell (convicted later of beating Rodney King), and the O.J. Simpson trial of February-September, 1995 (Manning, 1996, Goodwin, 1995). Axial media events are real world events transformed using television's code so that the line between personal experience, audience experience, and politics is blurred and reduced. Political, moral and personal meanings are conflated in a

series of brief repeated images.

8. Axial media events become interwoven tightly with actual events and shape policing. This is almost the essential feature of a media "scandal." For example, an LAPD detective, Mark Fuhrman, testifies in the Simpson trial, says he has not used "nigger" in ten years, and subsequently is found to be a liar. This raises questions about the credibility of other evidence he has presented. The media publicize his perjury. Chief Willie Williams of the LAPD, interviewed on *Good Morning America*, minimizes racism in the force, says it is being dealt with, and announces that the LAPD are investigating Fuhrman's previous cases (*GMA* Aug. 30, 1995). Two LAPD detectives appear on *GMA* (March 1, 1996) and *Geraldo* on CNBC (April 22, 1996) defending their actions.

9. One media makes "news" of other media's stories. These media loops are often highly embedded. The Fuhrman story is written about in the newspapers and news magazines. Television reporters interview officers in the LAPD and elsewhere about their reactions to the media reactions to Fuhrman's televised remarks. These were played from a tape and shown on graphics on the screen before the interviews. The media promote complex intertextuality (using one text within another) and stimulate reflexivity. The *Washington Observer* (August, 31 1995) claimed that "The Fuhrman tapes are the missing sound track for the Rodney King beating."

10. Real events, e.g., the AFT-FBI raid on the Waco compound of Koresh and his followers in April, 1993, become the basis for television movies in matter of months. Media sitcoms and action stories are converted into TV shows and movies; movies are converted into TV shows, movies scripts made into books. LAPD officers see themselves portrayed in re-runs of Jack Webb Productions (*Adam 12* and *Dragnet*). Webb had been advised by LAPD Chiefs Davis and Parker and sought to portray the LAPD as they urged (Gates, 1993). Chief Gates played himself and another chief in two televised dramas.

11. The justice system uses videos to prove and prosecute. Videos were used in the prosecution of Marion Barry for drug use; the FBI's ABSCAM operation to trap corrupt politicians, and in the Simpson trial. They are used to improve efficiency e.g., faxing accident reports to citizens, videoing bookings for transmission to the jail to reduce paperwork (in Lansing, Michigan).

12. Media is claimed by media to shape police behavior. A reduction in baton beatings, and the use of taser guns, is reported after the Rodney King events (*Newsweek* September 4, 1995). William Bratton resigns or is fired by the mayor as police commissioner, according to *Newsweek* (April 7, 1996), because he was taking too much media attention away from Mayor Giuliani.

13. Videos of police misconduct become the basis for national news, e.g., the high speed chase and beating of fleeing immigrants by the Riverside County, California Sheriff's Department (March, 1996); the videoed brutalizing of a black women by a state patrolman in South Carolina after she had not stopped when he had signaled to stop (from an unmarked car) (April, 1996).

14. Police engage in media-publicity contests. A few days after the videos of the South Carolina State Trooper screaming at and dragging the black motorist out of her car appeared, the Director of Public Safety in South Carolina appeared on *Good Morning America* (April 23, 1996). He provided a video that he narrated showing a state patrol officer standing beside a car talking to a stopped motorist. He was suddenly grazed by the rear view mirror of a passing truck. The director praised the officer, citing him as an example of the high quality of police in South Carolina: "The officer showed courage and determination, got in his car, pursued the motorist, was verbally assaulted but arrested him with the help of citizens. He followed proper procedures . . . . did not lose his cool."

15. Videos in turn are used to protect and defend police actions. The Lansing, Michigan Police Department filmed a raid of an illegal drinking establishment that consisted of shadowy scenes of officers booking suspects, because a woman present claimed harassment. Lansing police released to the press a video of the jailing of a man who subsequently died in custody (MSU State News 14 March 1996).

In these ways, media create and sustain police selves, reflect on those selves and interweave the real and imaginary in their renditions of police work. Police find the media monitoring their behavior, e.g., news helicopters filmed the chase of immigrants in Riverside County, and supervisors review film from car-mounted cameras. Police selectively use electronic and visual technology for defense and containment of media scrutiny. Police counter media definitions with their own media technology. Visual forms of social control shape policing internally and externally. This means at the very least that media working and effects, their simulacra (and its commodification), are relevant to constructing theories of police behavior in the late nineties.

## Notes

[1] The concept of reflexivity is widely used and cited in the social sciences. e.g., Sewell, 1992, Luhman 1990, Giddens 1991, and G. H. Mead, 1934.

[2] Television is not all of a piece. It shows films of ballet, classical theatre and concerts; "live" coverage of games, news conferences and disasters, live on film debates in the British Parliament, the U.S. Senate and House, highly stylized news, religious ceremonies, and advertising and promotional programs for real-estate selling, fortune hunting, etc., created genres such as "rockumentaries," "docudramas," and "fact-based dramas," and reshown (films of) all of the above. It combines genres,

innovatively shaping them, and embedding one within the other, e.g., showing news clips of past sports events at the half-time of a televised game and employing a round-table talk-show format to discuss them. As a result, it is laminated "internally" with meaning.

## References

Baudrillard, Jean. 1990. *Selected Writings* edited by Mark Poster. Palo Alto: Stanford University Press.

Bittner, E. 1992. *Aspects of Police Work.* Boston: Northeastern University Press.

Chan, J. 1996. "Changing Police Culture." *British Journal of Criminology* 36:109–34.

Ericson, Richard. Forthcoming. *Policing the Risk Society.* University of Toronto Press. forthcoming.

Gibbs, Jack. 1989. *Control.* Urbana: University of Illinois Press.

Giddens, A. 1991. *Modernity and Self-Identity.* Palo Alto: Stanford University Press.

Goffman, E. 1974. *Frame Analysis.* New York: Basic Books.

Goffman, E. 1959. *The Presentation of Self in Everyday Life.* Garden City: Doubleday Anchor.

Goodwin, C. 1995. "Professional Vision." *American Anthropologist* 96:606–33.

Hallett, M. and D. Powell. 1995. "Backstage with 'Cops': The Dramaturgical Reification of Police Subculture in American Infotainment." *American Journal of the Police.*

Hughes, E. C. 1958. Men and Their Work. Glencoe, IL: Free Press.

Kappeler, V., R. Sluder and G. Alpert. 1994. *Forces of Deviance.* Prospect Heights, IL: Waveland Press.

Luhmann, N. 1990. *The Risk Society.* Berlin: deGruyter/Aldine.

Lyon, D. 1995. *The Surveillance Society.* Minneapolis: University of Minnesota Press.

Manning, Peter K. 1977. *Police Work.* Cambridge, MA: MIT Press.

Manning, Peter K. 1996. "Dramaturgy, Politics, and the Axial Event." *The Sociological Quarterly* 37: 261–78.

Manning, Peter K. Forthcoming, 1997. "Media Loops." In Donna Hale and Frankie Bailey, eds., *Popular Culture, Crime and Justice.* Belmont, CA: Wadsworth.

Mead, G. H. 1934. *Mind, Self and Society.* Chicago: University of Chicago Press.

Meyrowitz, J. 1986. *No Sense of Place.* New York: OUP.

Sewell, William, Jr. 1992. "A Theory of Structure: Duality, Agency and Transformation." *American Journal of Sociology* 98: 1–29.

Skolnick, J. 1967. *Justice Without Trial.* New York: Wiley.

# Section III

## Management and Organization

The purpose of policing, beyond protecting life, is to control crime and maintain order, which involves the unique ability to use force to conduct daily activities. As a result of this, several methods have been developed by which administrators can organize and manage police departments. The articles chosen for this section describe potential conflicts which must be controlled in a fair and impartial manner. Unlike conflicts in other organizations, those faced by the police can result in violence or injury.

In the first selection, "Good Policing," James Fyfe examines the history of police as crime fighters and the consequences of vague definitions of the police role. Fyfe advises asking street cops to define good policing as they see it in their everyday work. He suggests management set priorities and define police effectiveness so that both management and police on patrol know what their goals are.

Unlike violence, which has been an integral part of police work since the beginning, the problem of AIDS for the police has only recently been an issue. In "The AIDS Epidemic and the Police: An Examination of the Issues," Professor Mark Blumberg raises some serious concerns faced by the police when dealing with AIDS. He focuses on the dual issues of police officers with AIDS and citizens with AIDS.

Another major concern for the police is addressed by the next article, "Police, Civil Liability and the Law." Rolondo V. del Carmen and Michael R. Smith discuss the liability of law enforcement officers under federal and state laws. There are many types of conduct that may trigger a lawsuit; police officers and administrators need to be aware of this and follow the legal standards that can prevent liability.

In the next selection, Eve and Carl Buzawa describe the historical and current trends in police response to domestic violence. They trace the changes that have occurred in how the police respond to and perceive calls for domestic violence. Their article provides an excellent overview of the problems relating to domestic violence.

The final article covers the need for police performance measures that focus on the new model of community policing. Geoffrey P. Alpert and Mark H. Moore argue that administrators need to acquire adequate information on specific neighborhoods in order to provide effective neighborhood policing.

# 11

# Good Policing

*James J. Fyfe*

According to Peter K. Manning (1977), the social mandate of the American police is a hodge-podge of conflicting duties and responsibilities that has developed with little input from the police themselves. He is correct. Firefighting, the uniformed public service frequently compared to policing, has a clear mandate that firefighters have helped to fashion: the fire service exists to prevent fires and to extinguish as quickly and as safely as possible all those it did not prevent. It is virtually impossible to derive a similarly succinct and comprehensive statement of the police role. Instead, it is safe to say only that police perform a variety of services that must be available seven days a week, 24 hours a day, that may require the use or threat of force, and that are not readily available from any other public agency or private institution.[1]

## Doing What Nobody Else Does

Police responsibility for these tasks not handled by others has meant that the police sometimes are called upon to do the impossible or to attempt to provide services they have not been adequately prepared to perform. The historic reluctance of police to intervene in domestic disputes,[2] for example, probably has more to do with the difficulty of straightening out other peoples' arguments in the middle of the night than with the purported danger to police of such assignments. A line of research has recently demonstrated that *domestics* are not nearly the police job hazard they were assumed to be (see, e.g., Margarita, 1980; Konstantin, 1984; Garner and Clemmer, 1986). The difficulty of resolving these arguments while they are at flashpoint, however, has long been clear, and is a task that might better be handled by social workers provided with protective police escorts. Social workers understandably have not volunteered to play such a role. Consequently, the police have been stuck with it on grounds that they are available and that their duties include order maintenance.

James J. Fyfe, "Good Policing," in Brian Forst, Ed., *The Socioeconomics of Crime and Justice*. Reprinted by permission of M. E. Sharpe, Inc., Armonk, New York 10504.

In the past, the ready, round-the-clock availability of the police has caused them to be assigned to many duties that fit under this *order maintenance* rubric only by the most liberal definition. In the late Nineteenth Century, Philadelphia police provided lodging for more than 100,000 people every year. Early in the Twentieth Century, New York police stations were the distribution points for food and coal doled out to the poor under "home relief" programs (Monkonnen, 1981:81–106).

In addition, the close ties of the police to the powerful have, in many places, made police departments a major vehicle of job patronage. A major factor in historic analyses of policing is the great extent to which attainment of formally stated police goals has continually been affected by use of police departments as means of politically dispensed upward mobility for newly arrived ethnic groups and recently empowered racial minorities (Fogelson, 1977; Walker, 1977; Wilson, 1964).

The closeness of the police to communities and to politicians has also led to corruption, especially in inner-cities where police have been charged with enforcing laws that had been enacted by conservative rural-dominated legislatures, but that found little support in the hurly-burly of urban life. In such places, it became the job of locally controlled police to protect illegal businesses—most notably, gambling and prostitution—from disruptions caused by both other law enforcement agencies and by unruly clientele who might scare off paying customers.[3]

This trend reached a peak during Prohibition, when official corruption became the standard operating procedure of many American police departments (Citizens' Police Committee, 1969). By the time Prohibition ended, however, the United States was deep in the Great Depression, and a constricted job market made policing an attractive career option to well-educated people who in better times would have gone into more traditional white collar and professional work. In many cases, this new breed was repulsed by old school corruption and sought to turn policing into a respectable undertaking.

## Police as Crime Fighters

Two icons of these new professionals were J. Edgar Hoover, whose FBI waged a bloody and successful war against the gangsters of the early 1930s, and August Vollmer, who had earlier made the Berkeley Police Department an exemplar of efficiency and technological excellence (Carte and Carte, 1975). These two role models led many local police to attempt to do away with the ambiguity of their mandate by redefining themselves first and foremost as professional crime fighters. These new professionals among police believed that, like FBI agents, local police would win their war by adopting the selective personnel standards and high technology employed with such apparent success by both Hoover and Vollmer. Unfortunately, the police were to find over the long run that the experiences of Hoover and Vollmer were not readily generalizable to other times and places.

## J. Edgar Hoover

Hoover's Depression-era successes came not in a broad-fronted war, but in a series of skirmishes against a small number of spectacular outlaws. When local police attempted to apply this same model of *the resolute and professional lawman on the track of bad guys*, however, they eventually became stymied. Police used this strategy over three decades and took great credit for the comparative domestic tranquility that then prevailed. Then, in the 1960s, American crime exploded. Since that watershed decade, the police have learned that the techniques that had been so useful to the FBI in its war against a few colorful characters meant little when a huge baby-boomer generation entered its crime-prone adolescent years, or in inner-city crime factories that systematically turn out criminals in overwhelming numbers. Hoover could declare victory when his agents had rounded up or killed the likes of John Dillinger, "Pretty Boy" Floyd, "Babyface" Nelson, and other legendary bandits of the era. But no such easy victory is possible over the rampant and ubiquitous street crime that has literally consumed many inner-cities.

## August Vollmer

In the same way that police were misled by Hoover's victories, police attempts to emulate Vollmer's example generally have been based on an inexact analogy. Without question, Vollmer turned the Berkeley Police Department into the early Twentieth Century American ideal. The Berkeley department was extremely selective, allowing only the very best young men to wear its uniforms. Under Vollmer, the department's apparent success in stifling crime, combined with its great responsiveness to the needs of the *good people* of the community, won it universal admiration at home (Carte and Carte, 1975). But history suggests that, like the "service" style police departments studied by James Q. Wilson during the 1960s (Wilson, 1968)—the Nassau County (NY) Police Department, for example—the Berkeley Police Department enjoyed such apparent success and exalted status largely because it was serving an ideal community that didn't need much from it.

When Vollmer was the police chief of Berkeley, the city was the fast-growing, prosperous, homogenous, and well-educated home to wealthy families who had been scared out of San Francisco by the crime, disorder, bawdiness, earthquake, and fire for which that bigger city on the Bay was best known at the time. Berkeley also was home to the first campus of the University of California, an industry of the type that did not draw employees or clients likely to cause the police much trouble. Indeed, if early Twentieth Century Berkeley undergraduates sought to raise hell, it was easy enough for them to ferry across the Bay to the more exciting Sodom of San Francisco or to simply walk across the city line to the Gomorrah of Jack London's Oakland waterfront.

Wilson studied Nassau County, the Long Island suburb adjacent to New York City, when policing there was the same sort of cakewalk that

Vollmer's staff had enjoyed a half-century earlier in Berkeley. Until World War II, Nassau County consisted largely of farms, a few small towns, and estates like those occupied by Fitzgerald's Jay Gatsby and friends. During the War, Long Island's expansion began with the growth of its defense industries and aircraft manufacturers. In the years immediately after the War, Nassau County became a booming suburb that, except for its larger population, was much like those that sprouted around Los Angeles at the same time. Generous GI financing, a new highway system, and quick construction methods combined with the desire for the good life—a patch of green away from mean city streets—overnight turned potato fields into tract housing. By the time Wilson observed its police department, the population of Nassau County had nearly doubled during the 1950s—to 1.3 million by 1960—and the county boasted a tax base larger than all but a small handful of U.S. cities. The non-white population in areas served by the County police (as opposed to the generally more exclusive towns policed by a few small independent departments) was 2.5%, and was located largely in a few small and long-established enclaves that had started as the homes for domestic help to the wealthy (Wilson, 1968:224). The county's homicide rate was less than one-sixth the national average and, despite the fact that its ratio of cars:population was far higher than the national norm, Nassau's vehicle theft rate was only one-third the national average (see Wilson 1968:86–93). Like Vollmer's Berkeley Police Department, Nassau selected its officers carefully, paid and equipped them well, and asked them to give friendly service to a homogenous populace who sought to share peace, quiet, and stability with their neighbors.

Wilson's Nassau differed from Vollmer's Berkeley chiefly in size and by virtue of the high percentage of its population that wore blue collars at work. Both places enjoyed freedom from poverty, inequity, class and ethnic conflict, or social discord of any other type. Both had ideal police departments because both were populated by people of means who had chosen to move there from elsewhere in order to be part of an idyllic community.

In the years since Vollmer's tenure and Wilson's studies, both Berkeley and Nassau have changed. Neither has remained homogenous, uniformly prosperous, or untroubled by decay, conflict, social discord, homelessness, unemployment. Regardless of the quality and competence of its chief executives or what they may have accomplished since Vollmer's halcyon days, nobody in policing regards the Berkeley Police Department as *the* local American law enforcement agency that stands in a class by itself, *the* role model for professional policing. Nobody studies policing in Berkeley[4] and nobody in policing knows much about what may be going on there. Nor has any scholar recently studied police in Nassau County. There, while the number of residents has declined slightly over the last three decades, the population has grown much more heterogenous. The percentage of non-white residents has increased five-fold to 13.3 percent, and Hispanics—virtually unknown in the County at the time of Wilson's work—comprise another 3.3 percent (U.S. Department of Commerce,

p. 72). In addition, crime rates have increased, closings of defense and air-craft manufacturers have severely hurt the economy, and even the most casual observer would not expect a replication of Wilson's work to come up with the same rosy picture he found a quarter-century ago.[5]

## Lessons Learned?

The two lessons of these experiences have not been easily digested by either the police or the public. The first of these lessons is that *neither the low crime rates during the golden years of J. Edgar Hoover and August Vollmer nor the great increases since then have had much to do with the police or law enforcement.* Despite Vollmer's good efforts, Berkeley boasted low crime rates during his years because it was a fast-growing, prosperous, homogenous, and highly-educated town in which the major employer was the state's flagship university. Around the country during the Depression years of Hoover's climb to fame, most people were concerned with putting bread on the table and were too beaten down to be aggressive. Thus, minor property crime was common but—except for a rash of well publicized kidnapings and one-man crime waves of the type he vigorously stifled—violent crime generally was not much of a concern.

With the exceptions of a few defense industry boomtowns, the home front remained quiet during World War II because most young men of crime-prone age were either in the military or busy working overtime to supply or fill in for the boys overseas. Crime remained low throughout the Fifties, probably because the generation then at peak crime age (roughly 16–24) was small in number: it had been born in the Depression, when birth rates had dropped.

The Sixties changed all this. Urban crime rates soared virtually every-where regardless of whether police conformed to the ideal of professional-warrior-against-crime. The increase in crime was attributable to several converging forces, but two probably are most important. The huge baby-boom generation entered adolescence, so that an unusually large percent-age of the population was in its most crime-prone years. In addition, cities changed. For years, blacks and Hispanics had steadily been replacing white city dwellers who had fled to suburbs like Nassau County, taking businesses, jobs, and the cohesiveness of their former neighborhoods with them. This pattern came to a head in the Sixties: old communities broke up to be replaced by impersonal and densely populated projects. Racial, cultural, and class conflicts arose. Urban tax bases eroded, municipal ser-vices declined, and all the ills of the inner-city flourished as they had not since the great waves of European immigration a half-century earlier. Since the Sixties, the death of Jim Crow, the increased mobility of the black mid-dle-class, and cutbacks in social programs have aggravated these condi-tions. With few strong community institutions or positive role models for young people, inner-cities have grown even more desolate and hopeless.

Thus, it is unrealistic to model the police on Hoover's FBI or, even, to think of the police as our first line of defense against crime. In large measure, the presence or absence of crime has nothing to do with the police. Indeed, even though many people continue to think of *police* and *law enforcement* almost interchangeably, the boom in scholarly studies of policing that began in the 1960s has shown with some consistency that only a small proportion of street police officers' time—in the neighborhood of a quarter—involves law enforcement or investigation of crime. Eric Scott, for example, studied more than 26,000 calls for police service in three urban areas. Two percent of these involved reports of violent crime; seventeen percent involved reports of nonviolent crime, and five percent concerned people or circumstances that had aroused citizens' suspicions. The remaining 76 percent concerned interpersonal conflict (seven percent); requests for medical assistance (three percent); traffic problems (nine percent); dependent persons in need of police care (three percent); noise and other public nuisances (11 percent); calls for miscellaneous assistance (12 percent); requests for information (21 percent); provision of non-crime related information (eight percent); and various police internal matters (two percent) (Scott, 1981:28–30; see also, Reiss, 1971; Webster, 1970; Wilson, 1968). In short, the clientele of the FBI consists almost exclusively of criminal suspects and victims and witnesses to crime, but most of the people with whom the police interact need help with problems not related to crime.

The second lesson is that *policing can probably be regarded as ideal only in places that are themselves idyllic and untroubled.* This is a message with important implications for police reformers, many of whom currently urge adoption of new *community-oriented* and *community-based* policing models. According to the first of Trojanowicz and Bucqueroux's three paragraph definition (1990:5–6):

> Community Policing is a new philosophy of policing, based on the concept that police officers and private citizens working together in creative ways can help solve contemporary problems related to crime, fear of crime, social and physical disorder, and neighborhood decay. The philosophy is predicated in the belief that achieving these goals requires that police departments develop a new relationship with the law-abiding people in the community, allowing them a greater voice in setting local police priorities and involving them in efforts to improve the overall quality of life in their neighborhoods. It shifts the focus of police work from handling random calls to solving community problems.

Trojanowicz and Bucqueroux go on to say that this new model requires the designation of some patrol officers as "Community Policing Officers." Each of these CPOs should be assigned on a continuing basis to the same small geographic area. There, from their patrol cars and the responsibility of responding to radio calls, CPOs can then develop collaborative relationships with community members. These relationships, in turn, will allow "people direct input in setting day-to-day, local police priorities, in exchange for their cooperation and participation in efforts to police themselves" (Trojanowicz and Bucqueroux, 1990:5).

While there certainly is room for greater and more imaginative police interaction with the communities they serve, it often is difficult to distinguish these new community-oriented models from Wilson's *service* style of policing and from such police arrangements as the democratic team policing alternative of John E. Angell (1971) and neighborhood team policing (see Sherman, et al., 1973). Indeed, I can find virtually nothing in descriptions of recent community policing models that differs from my own experience in two New York City police precincts that included Neighborhood Police Teams more than two decades ago.

But these prior attempts to rearrange police departments and their relationships with communities have either been discarded or, as in the case of Wilson's service style, apparently have been feasible only so long as there exists a monolithic community to which the police can become oriented.[6] Unfortunately, in the areas most in need of high quality police services—however such quality be defined—the *community* and its needs are neither readily identifiable nor monolithic.[7] Instead, as Wilson suggested, such neighborhoods are marked by great social, racial, and political cleavages, and by divergent views about law enforcement and order maintenance policies and practices (Wilson, 1968:288-89; see also, Greenberg and Rohe, 1986). As long as this is so, virtually every police policy or action will offend some interests in the community and near unanimous approval of the police, as in Vollmer's Berkeley or 1960s Nassau County, will remain unattainable. Further, as long as communities define the police role in the expectation that police will merely respond unquestioningly to their wishes, the police mandate will continue to be amorphous and unclear.

## Consequences of Unclear Direction

### Priority Setting

The consequences of vague definition of the police role and minimal police participation in specifying it are widespread. Police have not been given much direction for setting priorities among the melange of duties and responsibilities they have been assigned. The police are expected both to maintain order and to enforce the law but, in important instances, these two obligations may conflict. Uniformed officers assigned in response to citizens' complaints that specific streets have become open air drug markets, for example, usually are instructed by their superiors to enforce the law aggressively. But officers who follow such instructions by arresting the first minor offender they see may find themselves off the street and caught up in the booking and court processes for hours. While these officers are gone, their beats remain open territory, dealers do uninterrupted land-office business, and law-abiding citizens wonder what happened to the cops they had asked for. The final frustration in such cases usually comes when arrestees are slapped on the wrist by the courts, treated like public nuisances rather than as the purveyors of poison that officers and residents see.

A better alternative might be to direct officers to avoid making arrests except in major cases and, instead, to attempt to drive dealers off the street by maintaining as high a degree of presence as possible. If this were done, police officers might rid their beats of drug trafficking and restore order to lawless streets, just as they routinely have done in neighborhoods marred by street prostitution and other annoying public order offenses. Importantly, however, such a strategy would generate little of the enforcement "activity" so often used to justify police budget requests (Rubinstein, 1973)

## Trying to Quantify Quality

Quantitative measures of police activity—numbers of tickets, arrests, calls for service, minutes and seconds required to respond to calls—often mislead. They say nothing about the vigor or quality of police service or, as in this street drug dealing example, about whether the numbers presented have had any substantial effect on the problem the police were marshalled to address (see, e.g., Rubinstein, 1973). But, regardless of their limited usefulness as a measure of police effectiveness—or their questionable accuracy—numbers are part and parcel of American policing. From the annual figures of the FBI's Uniform Crime Reports through the flashy charts and bar graphs that characterize police departmental annual reports to the monthly activity reports of patrol officers and traffic cops, policing revolves around numbers.

Herman Goldstein (1979) called this tendency to measure police performance in quantitative terms a "means-ends syndrome." It exists, he suggests, because of the ease of toting up the frequency and rapidity with which police use the tools available to them—arrests, tickets, response time—and the difficulty of sitting down and resolving Manning's dilemma by clearly defining police goals, measures of the extent to which they have been achieved, and some notion of whether the police actions involved in doing so may have created or aggravated other problems. From a desk in police headquarters, it is very easy and often very convincing to report to a concerned city councilperson that the police response to complaints about drug dealing on 25th Street has resulted in *n* arrests. It is not so easy to go out and measure the level of apparent drug activity on 25th Street, or to determine whether police presence has displaced it to 24th Street. Even when such measures are attempted, the absence of impressive arrest numbers often makes them less than convincing.

## Prevention and Apprehension

This situation is a conundrum and a contradiction of the principles enunciated by Sir Robert Peel when he established the first modern urban police in Dublin and in London (Palmer, 1988). Before Peel's "Bobbies," police forces existed in continental Europe, but these generally focused their activities on political criminals and on after-the-fact investigations of crime; the notoriously persistent Javert of Hugo's *Les Miserables* is a case in point. But Peel, inspired by the Enlightenment view of man as a rational and ultimately redeemable creature, designed the London Metropolitan Police to be *preventive* rather than punitive. The widespread presence on the streets of police in distinctive but purposely non-military uniforms, Peel reasoned, would convince potential criminals that successful crime was impossible. Accordingly, Peel also reasoned, the best measure of police success in crimefighting would be the *absence* of crime, disorder, and related police business, rather than the measures of law enforcement activity currently in vogue in the United States.

Certainly, police today also are expected to prevent crime. A considerable amount of research, however, suggests that their ability to do so, especially in sprawling, multicultural American cities, is more limited than Peel, Hoover, or Vollmer believed (Kelling, et al., 1974; Police Foundation, 1981). Further, the incentive to develop more sophisticated prevention strategies is diminished by news and entertainment media that grant police their greatest glory for arresting those whom they have failed to deter in the first place. *Cops 'n' robbers* make for spectacular headlines and sensational docudrama, but the work of police crime prevention officers has never been the focus of any movie or TV series. This emphasis and glorification of apprehension over prevention spills down to the lowest level of policing, where the greenest beat cops learn early in their careers that "important arrests" are enthusiastically counted and rewarded, while nobody knows—or seems to care—how many crimes did not occur because of officers' vigilance.

On occasion, the consequences of this apprehension-oriented incentive system are bizarre and certainly not what Peel intended. In some departments, instead of cruising by bars at closing time to make sure that drunks do not attempt to drive home, officers hide in darkened cars a block or two away to catch them after they have gotten into their cars and driven off. In using this technique to gain credit for arrests, these officers allow drunks to commit the very same life-endangering acts one might expect the police to prevent. In Los Angeles, an elite squad has for years refrained from intervening while, as its officers anticipated, armed burglars and robbers have victimized unsuspecting citizens. Instead of preventing these victimizations, officers have stood by and watched in order to confront their quarry—often with bloody results—after all doubt about their intentions has been removed. "Public safety is certainly a concern," the unit's commander told the *Los Angeles Times*, "but we have to look beyond that because if we arrest someone for attempt, the likelihood of a conviction is not as great" (Freed, 1988; Skolnick and Fyfe, 1993).

### Accusations of Discrimination

At the same time that police are charged to enforce the law firmly and fairly, they also are expected to be judicious and selective in their enforcement efforts. Unfortunately, the police have received little guidance in establishment of criteria to distinguish between unfair discrimination and discretion that serves some legitimate social end. Consequently, "selective enforcement" often is little more than individual officers' *ad hoc* decisions about which driver should receive a ticket and which should not; which loudmouthed kid should be arrested, which taken home to his parents.

Regardless of how judicious a police department may be, the absence of meaningful decision-making standards dictates that any agency that polices a pluralistic constituency will be the subject of regular criticism and dissatisfaction on the part of one or more subpopulations. Further, the absence of such standards means that the best-intended police officers in such a department will be left confused and vulnerable to accusations of arbitrariness. Motorists know that cops do not issue tickets for all the traffic violations they witness. Consequently, every experienced cop has heard bitter motorists allege that the tickets they have just been handed were motivated by questions of race or class rather than by the need to enforce laws against traffic violations that so many others commit without punishment.[8]

Further, in a society in which race and class are as closely related as ours, it often is hard to draw a line between discretion and discrimination. The fundamental precept of the juvenile justice system—to *help and reform*, rather than to *punish*—generally dictates that police interventions into kids' minor delinquencies should be no more intrusive and formal than whatever may be necessary to accomplish two goals. First, the action selected—ranging anywhere from warning through arrest and booking—should give officers some sense that the youngsters involved have learned the errors of their ways. Second, officers should be assured that, after they leave the scene, responsible parties will carefully supervise the miscreants and keep them on the straight and narrow. But when cops act on these precepts, their dispositions of juveniles who have been involved in minor delinquencies result in numbers heavily skewed by class and, therefore, by race. Middle-class kids are skilled at ingratiating themselves to people who can affect their futures. When the police bring them home or to police stations after such kids have done wrong, the police meet concerned, stable families from nice neighborhoods. Most important, the police get convincing assurances from Moms and Dads that it will be a long time before Junior—who is by now teary-eyed and apologetic—has another opportunity to misbehave. Consequently, the police typically take no formal action, but leave such kids to the care of their parents.

Street kids learn early to challenge authority. In the ghetto, where life often includes no thoughts of the future beyond tomorrow, the middle-class skill of ingratiating oneself to people who can affect one's future is meaningless and denigrated. Often, ghetto kids come from home environments in which no meaningful control is exercised over their conduct. In such circumstances, cops are likely to conclude that helping kids to find the straight and narrow can only be accomplished by invoking the formal juvenile justice system. This, of course, has two effects. First, it punishes these youngsters by attaching formal delinquent labels to them. Second, it generates statistics that can be used to put police on the defensive by those who claim that cops' decisions routinely are racist. In fact, the statistics may hide well-intended decisions to arrest or release juveniles that, like police and judicial decisions related to adults' bail and pre-trial release, appropriately are driven by variables independent of the instant offense. Judges' bail decisions and police releases on adult suspects' own recognizance are based on assessments of the probability that defendants will be back in court on schedule. Cops' decisions about what to do with young violators often are based on officers' assessments of the probability that police will have no further contact with the youngsters involved. Thus, the goals of these decisions—to achieve the hope of seeing subjects again in the first case; to achieve the hope of never seeing them again in the second—are different, but the criteria used in making them should be similar. Unlike police and court discretion related to adult criminal defendants (see, e.g., Thomas, 1976; Institute for Law and Social Research, 1980), however, police decisions concerning juvenile offenders generally are unbounded by rules or guidelines and, therefore, remain subject to criticism.

## Defining Good Policing

The discussion to this point suggests the overarching dilemma caused by the absence of a clear police mandate: beyond some prescriptions for specific field situations in which closure is rapid and clearly identifiable, we have yet to derive a widely accepted definition of police effectiveness. Within policing, the absence of such a definition reverberates at every level. The requirements for entry into an occupation, for example, should be those that best predict satisfactory job performance. But the absence of clearly articulated standards for assessing police effectiveness means that police entry requirements can be no more than guesses about which candidates are likely to be abusive, to beget scandals, or, through physical disability or acts that create legal liability, to impose great financial losses on those to whom they have applied for employment. Some police candidates are screened out on the basis of bizarre personal histories or criminal records. Others, however, survive this screening and demonstrate their lack of suitability for policing only after they have been locked into it by civil service tenure. Equally important, the imprecision inherent in searches to fill jobs that are not clearly defined undoubtedly results in the loss of fine candidates whose membership in policing would undoubtedly increase its representativeness of the population.

### The Absence of the Satisfaction of a Job Well Done

Those who make it through this screening find that police work carries many rewards. Although no honest police officer ever becomes rich, policing in most parts of the United States pays a decent wage which, despite the last couple of decades' police layoffs in financially strapped cities, also is very dependable. In the busiest jurisdictions, the police workday goes very quickly and, in the words of a recruiting poster in use when I began my police career, often includes "a view of life your deskbound friends will never see." Certainly, this view is not always pleasant or fulfilling: the things police see cause some to become chronically distrustful and hardened, ultimately leading to great problems in their private lives. Other officers, however, draw from their work greater appreciation of their own comparative good fortune. However trying, regular exposure to violence, exploitation, greed, madness, cruelty, poverty, hopelessness, addiction, and the rest of humankind's most serious ills puts into perspective and makes less insurmountable the annoyances of middle-class life.

Specific police actions—cracking a big case, pulling a driver from a burning car, talking an emotionally disturbed person out of a suicide attempt—also provide a great deal of satisfaction and official praise for police officers. But, absent the opportunity to engage in such heroics, cops may try their hardest to earn their salaries without ever knowing whether they are doing well or whether their work has made a difference, and without ever receiving formal acknowledgment of their efforts.

This issue involves much more than the salving of cops' tender egos. A quarter-century ago, Arthur Neiderhoffer (1969:95–108) reported that New York City police patrol officers, the street cops who performed the most familiar but most ill-defined and least prestigious work in their department, had higher levels of cynicism than any other officers he studied. Over time, Neiderhoffer suggested, the intractability of patrol officers' work and their inability to get out of it and into more glamorous assignments may lead to a sense of frustration and victimization. These, in turn, may alienate officers—and, indeed, whole police departments—from the community, causing the dysfunctional *us and them* relationship between police and citizens found in many jurisdictions and manifested by incidents like the beating of Rodney King. It was no accident that the King incident involved the Los Angeles Police Department, the agency that, more than any other big city U.S. police department, had come to define itself as a beleaguered thin blue line that protects ungrateful and undeserving citizens from themselves (see, e.g., Gates, 1992).

Indeed, Carl Klockars (1980) suggests that the gap between what police are expected to achieve and what they can achieve encourages them to brutality, perjury, and other fabrications of evidence against guilty people who would otherwise go free. Anxious to achieve the noble end of seeing that offenders receive deserved punishment, good cops, asserts Klockars, become very frustrated by a criminal justice system that too often seems to dismiss cases for reasons that have nothing to do with whether arrestees actually committed the offenses of which they were accused. Then, like Clint Eastwood's movie character, "Dirty Harry" Callahan, some of these officers render a violent brand of street justice and/or lie from the witness stand in order to assure that the guilty get what they deserve. The now famous videotape showing Los Angeles police beating Rodney King while he is on his hands and knees memorialized the first half of such an episode. Absent George Holliday and his videocam, the episode's second half would have been the prosecution the police had initiated against Mr. King before they knew they had been caught by George Holliday and his videocam. At this court proceeding, the police who arrested and beat King would undoubtedly have offered perjured testimony to the effect that King was standing upright and physically attacking them when they used no more than necessary force to subdue him.

## Cops' Rules

Elizabeth Reuss-Ianni (1984) has written that police estrangement may extend to conflicting "street cop" and "management cop" subcultures within police departments. Where these exist, street cops see themselves as excluded from a management system that espouses lofty ideals and that employs meaningless statistics and other forms of smoke and mirrors in order to give the illusion that these ideals are being achieved. Consequently, street cops see their leadership as an illegitimate and naive obstacle that must be surmounted if *real* police work is to be accomplished.[9]

Like the values constructed and honored by lower class delinquent boys in response to rejection by middle-class teachers (Cohen, 1955), however, street cops' definitions of admirable behavior are developed without input from above and, in addition to serving as guideposts to survival in a harsh world, often are antithetical to those publicly espoused by official police spokespersons. Reuss-Ianni's astute observations of New York City police led her to formulate a list of the rules that govern street cops' interactions with each other and with their supervisors and administrators:

Watch out for your partner first and then the rest of the guys working the tour [shift];

Don't give up another cop;

Show balls [physical courage];

Be aggressive when you have to, but don't be too eager;

Don't get involved in anything in another guy's sector [car beat];

Hold up your end of the work;

If you get caught off base, don't implicate anybody else;

Make sure the other guys [officers, but not supervisors or administrators] know if another cop is dangerous or "crazy";

Don't trust a new guy until you have checked him out;

Don't tell anybody else more than they have to know, it could be bad for you and it could be bad for them;

Don't talk too much or too little;

Don't leave work for the next tour;

Protect your ass;

Don't make waves;

Don't give [supervisors] too much activity;

Keep out of the way of any boss from outside your precinct;

Don't look for favors just for yourself;

Don't take on the patrol sergeant by yourself;

Know your bosses;

Don't do the bosses' work for them [e.g., let them discover miscreant officers without assistance];

Don't trust bosses to look out for your interest (Reuss-Ianni, 1984:14-16).

The adversarial relationship between "street cops" and "management
cops" suggested by many of these rules has its roots in the pyramidal, military style of police organization that so sharply distinguishes between
administrators and those on the frontlines.[10] Thus, as we see over and
over again in both examples of great heroism and officers' reluctance to
expose the wrongdoing of colleagues (Christopher, et al., 1992; Daley,
1978; Maas, 1973), street cops' primary loyalties are to each other rather
than to the bureaucracies in which they work or to the taxpayers who pay
their salaries. In the absence of formal recognition of what street cops justifiably regard as good work, street cops' reward systems consist primarily
of their peer groups' status rankings of their members, and the highest status in this system is the recognition that one is *a cop's cop*. The irony that
those who win this high accolade from their peers often are regarded with
antagonism and suspicion by police administrators is evidence of the
depth of the cleavage between management and street cops.

## What To Do

Several scholars have suggested solutions to all or part of this dilemma of
the vague police mandate. Manning (1977:374) argues that police should
focus on enhancing their ability as crime-fighters and on delegating to other
agencies as many of their traffic control and other non-crime related service
tasks as possible. However easy this proposal might appear to make police
lives and evaluation of police performance, it is unrealistic. There is no evidence that any other agencies are anxious to fill the police role as round-
the-clock-first-responders to the wide variety of non-enforcement tasks currently handled by police. Further, it is not easy to distinguish in advance
between crime-fighting and police non-crime service tasks. Most police services are rendered in response to citizens' telephone calls for help of some
kind or other. In some cases, 911 operators can determine very quickly that
those who respond to assist must be authorized and equipped to use force
and to enforce laws. In most cases, however, this is not possible, and officials must actually arrive at the scene to determine whether calls for services of the types currently handled by police require use of force, law
enforcement, or both. Hence, it probably is wishful thinking to plan for
police delegation to other authorities of such non-enforcement tasks as
handling domestic calls, resolving neighbors' disputes, chasing noisy
streetcorner groups, dealing with emotionally disturbed street people, and
responding to vehicle accidents.

Klockars sees severe punishment of officers who use dirty means to
achieve noble ends as the appropriate approach to the "Dirty Harry Problem." But, paradoxically, even he recognizes that this solution is unsatisfactory:

> In urging the punishment of policemen who resort to dirty means to achieve some unquestionably good and morally compelling end, we recognize that we create a Dirty Harry problem for ourselves and for those we urge to effect such punishments. It is a fitting end, one which teaches once again that the danger in Dirty Harry problems is never in their resolution, but in thinking that one has found a resolution with which one can truly live in peace (Klockars, 1980:47).

Klockars' realization that it would be difficult to live in peace with this resolution is correct, but for reasons he seems not to take into account. Punishment achieved by end runs around due process is no more an "unquestionably good and morally compelling end" than is family prosperity obtained by a breadwinner's thefts from his or her employer. In both cases, the most peaceful and satisfying resolution might be achieved not by punishing the wrongdoer, but by preventing the wrongdoing in the first place. This might be accomplished by demonstrating to the people on whose behalf the wrongdoing is likely to be conducted—the public in Klockars' case; the family in my analogy—that their desires are unrealistic and likely to impose other, unquestionably bad, costs.

Breadwinners usually can bring the desires of overly demanding families into line with reality by pointing out the limits of family resources and that the immorality and costs of stealing apply regardless of whether one is caught with a hand in the till. Public officials should make sure that their constituents know that the widespread desire to ignore constitutional limits so that *justice may be done* is oxymoronic and equally immoral and costly. Punishing wrongdoers without regard to the process that has been prescribed by 200 years of American experience weakens the entire society, perpetuates the myth that society can rely on the police as its primary defense against crime, and encourages society's policy makers to allow the continued festering of the social conditions that have turned our inner-cities into crime factories. Unfortunately, in this era of concern over law and order and apparent resolve to address the crime problem by harshness alone, few public officials seem willing to bring forth this message.

Mastrofski's suggestions seem closer to the mark and are more strongly supported by the work and experiences of other scholars. He suggests that the broad and vague mandate of the police is here to stay. He indicates also that the extent to which it is accomplished is best assessed at close range, at the micro-level of the quality of police officers' daily encounters with citizens:

> . . . what police officers themselves know about good policing has to do with how officers respond to the particular circumstances they are called to handle. This is the craft of policing, about which a great deal is known, yet uncodified: making good arrests, deescalating crises, investigating crimes, using coercion and language effectively, abiding by the law and protecting individual rights, developing knowledge of the community, and imparting a sense of fairness by one's actions (1988:63).

There is reason to believe that this is a feasible approach to the eventual derivation of a definition of *good policing*. As Bayley and Garofalo (1985) have reported, line police officers are excellent assessors of their peers' talents. These two researchers asked groups of street officers to identify the most outstanding of their number. Subsequently, Bayley and Garofalo observed both officers identified as outstanding and their colleagues at one of their most difficult police tasks, intervention in disputes. They report finding quantifiable differences between the manners and techniques employed by the *cops' cops* and the rest, most notably that the officers who had been identified as outstanding were less judgmental and more helpful than their peers in their dealings with disputants. Thus, even though the officers Bayley and Garofalo had asked to rate their peers had not been requested to specify *why* they thought some officers better than others, it appears that these officers had observed something different about the work of *cops' cops* that could subsequently be documented empirically.

Hans Toch and his colleagues (Toch, et al., 1975) had earlier approached much the same problem from a different angle. They identified a group of Oakland police officers who frequently were involved in on-the-job violence they seemed to provoke or manufacture. These violence-prone officers were themselves asked to analyze the problem of violence between police and citizens,[11] and to develop solutions to it. The most intriguing result of this work was the creation by these officers of an officially approved Peer Review Panel, consisting mostly of violence-prone officers. This panel met regularly with officers whose apparent violent activities had been brought to light in incident reports or by supervisory referral, and was

designed (1) to stimulate the subject to study his violence-related arrests over time and to help him tease out cues to his contributions to violent incidents and (2) to assist the subject to define and formulate alternative strategies for coping with violence-precipitating incidents (Toch, 1980:60).

This program was, by all measures, a success. It allowed these most violent-prone street cops to diagnose their own problems, to analyze the more generic problem of police-citizen violence, and to devise solutions to it. It enhanced their analytic sophistication and helped to break down the adversarial relationship between street cops and management. Involvement in violent incidents by officers who participated in the program declined vis-á-vis that of other officers. Further, and just as important as substantive results, the Oakland work showed that:

[p]rograms that are usually resisted as arbitrary interferences with the officers' autonomy can become experiments in whose outcome the officers have a proprietary interest and a substantial stake (Toch, 1980:61).

This early exercise in what has since come to be known as *Problem-Oriented Policing*—identifying a problem and the most desirable outcome of attempts to resolve it; carefully analyzing the problem and devising appropriate means of resolving it (see, e.g., Goldstein, 1990)—was the basis for a project I subsequently directed in Dade County, Florida (Fyfe, 1988). There, a task force consisting of Metro-Dade Police Department street officers, trainers, investigators, and field supervisors was assembled and asked to analyze a random sample of reports of police-citizen encounters that had *gone wrong*, in the sense that they had resulted in citizens' complaints against officers, use of force by officers, or injuries to officers. The analysis required task force members to identify every decision and action of the officers in each encounter; to describe its effects (in terms of increasing or decreasing whatever potential for violence may have existed); and, where appropriate, to prescribe alternative decisions or actions that may have better served to defuse potential violence. The goals of this analysis were to identify the most satisfactory resolutions of several types of frequently encountered potentially violent encounters between police and citizens,[11] and to construct a detailed list of "Do's and Don't's" that would help officers to achieve these resolutions.

In other words, the project enlisted officers to define *jobs well done* in street cops' most challenging work, and to identify the steps most likely to help officers to do such jobs well. This project, conducted under rigid social science experimental conditions, eventually resulted in a five-day "violence reduction training program" that was delivered to all Dade County officers between February 1988 and February 1989. In the three years since then, Metro-Dade police records show that complaints against officers, use of force by officers, and injuries to officers all have declined between 30 and 50 percent.

All of this signals that street cops know more than anybody about what is *good policing* and who are the *cop's cops*. But, until the groundbreaking work of Toch, Grant, and Galvin, nobody had asked them. When they have been asked, street officers have responded with remarkable accuracy. In Oakland, street cops—notably, the *most violent* street cops—were empowered to address the problem of which they were the major part, and came up with solutions. Bayley and Garofalo asked street cops to identify the stars among themselves, and the answers appear to have been substantiated by observations of cops at work. I asked street cops, trainers, and supervisors below the policy making level to define *good policing* in a variety of challenging situations. The answers resulted in a course of training that has been followed by remarkable reductions in police-citizen violence in one of the country's most volatile policing environments.[12]

The implications seem clear. As Manning (1977) has noted, the police mandate is vague, internally inconsistent, and generally uninformed by the police themselves. If we are to derive a clear statement of the police mandate and how well it is accomplished, we should start by asking street cops to define *good policing* at the micro-level of their one-on-one interactions with citizens. Then, brick-by-brick, we will build meaningful macro-level definitions of the police mandate, good policing, good police department, and good cops.

## Footnotes

[1] This definition owes much to the work of Egon Bittner and Herman Goldstein.

[2] Here, I distinguish between domestic disputes and domestic *violence*. In my view, the role of the police in situations involving violence of any kind is clearcut: to see that no violence occurs after the police have arrived on the scene, and to arrest those who have engaged in criminal violence before the arrival of the police.

[3] See, e.g., James Q. Wilson's description of "watchman" police agencies in *Varieties of Police Behavior* (Cambridge, MA: Harvard University Press, 1968).

[4] The most recent exception to my assertion apparently is a 1978 doctoral dissertation which compares dispositions of citizens' complaints in Berkeley, Contra Costa County (CA), Kansas City, Oakland, and San Jose (Perez, 1978).

[5] In addition to changes in Nassau County specifically, a more general trend to increased accountability for police actions has meant that activities regarded as acceptable at the time of Wilson's study would today be condemned as both indiscriminate and wasteful. Of Nassau County's special "burglary patrol," for example, Wilson noted:

> During 1965 this patrol, operating in high-risk areas of the county, stopped and searched over twelve thousand vehicles and questioned over fourteen thousand "suspicious persons." Eighty-six arrests resulted, but only nine were for burglary (Wilson, 1968:204).

[6] The more successful of the two Neighborhood Police Teams in precincts where I worked was in Brooklyn Heights, a highly organized brownstone neighborhood populated largely by upper middle-class residents who were very anxious to see that their community remained fashionable and expensive. The second NPT, in the tough Hell's Kitchen area of Manhattan's West Side, engendered considerably less interest and enthusiasm among residents.

[7] Monolithic community norms related to the police and their role in the community are not necessarily a good thing. In ethnically or racially changing neighborhoods, for example, the most powerful sentiment regarding the police may be a bigoted desire for their assistance in harassing the newcomers back to whence they came (Mastrofski, 1988).

[8] In my own 16 years of police experience, the specific race or class of the ticketed violator did not matter as much as the perception that police treated *others* with great leniency. I have heard whites claim that "you wouldn't give me this ticket if I were black" because, e.g., "you know they run this city," as often as I heard the converse claim from black violators. Similarly, obviously well-heeled violators bemoaned their tickets with claims that police enforcement efforts would be better directed at people driving dangerous "clunkers"; people in clunkers argued that enforcement should focus more heavily on luxury car drivers who "thought they owned the road" and could better afford tickets.

[9] Former Los Angeles police officer Mike Rothmiller has painted a similar picture of his department, where street officers used the pejorative term "pogues" to refer to their naive, and often venal, police supervisors and administrators (Rothmiller and Goldman, 1992).

[10] I have argued elsewhere that the military organizational model is a historical accident that probably is the single most inappropriate way to structure police organizations (Fyfe, 1992; Skolnick and Fyfe, 1993).

[11] The research showed that, the most frequently encountered potentially violent encounters between Dade County police and citizens were routine traffic stops; responses to reports of crimes in progress or police investigations of suspicious persons; disputes; and "high risk vehicle stops" of cars occupied by persons suspected of criminal activity (Fyfe, 1988).

[12] It is more than modesty that causes me to refrain from attributing this decline in police-citizen violence and tension exclusively to the project I directed. The training was part of a wide variety of personnel, training, and administrative changes that began in the

early 1980s and that have resulted in a major philosophical shift in the Metro-Dade
Police Department. It is today a much more community oriented and representative
police department than was true a decade ago.

## References

Angell, John E., "Toward an Alternative to the Classic Police Organizational
Arrangements: A Democratic Model," *Criminology* 9:185–206 (1971).

Bayley, David H., and James Garofalo, "The Management of Violence by Police
Patrol Officers," *Criminology* 27:1–25 (February 1989).

Carte, Gene E., and Elaine H. Carte, *Police Reform in the United States: The Era
of August Vollmer, 1905–1932*. Berkeley: University of California Press, 1975.

Christopher, Warren, et al., *Report of the Independent Commission on the Los
Angeles Police Department*. City of Los Angeles: 1991.

Citizens' Police Committee, *Chicago Police Problems*. Montclair, NJ: 1969 Patterson Smith reprint of 1931 original.

Cohen, Albert K., *Delinquent Boys: The Culture of the Gang*. New York: The Free
Press, 1955.

Daley, Robert, *Prince of the City: The True Story of a Cop Who Knew Too Much*.
Boston: Houghton-Mifflin, 1978.

Fogelson, Robert M., *Big-City Police*. Cambridge: Harvard University Press, 1977.

Freed, David, "Citizens Terrorized as Police Look On," *Los Angeles Times*, September 25, 1988, pp.1, 3–5.

Fyfe, James J., "Lessons of Los Angeles," *Focus*. Washington, DC: Joint Center for
Political and Economic Studies, August 1992.

_____, *The Metro-Dade Police Citizen Violence Reduction Project: Final Report*.
Washington, DC: Police Foundation, 1988.

Fyfe, James J., and Jeanne Flavin, "Differential Police Processing of Assault Complaints," paper presented at Annual Meeting of Law and Society Association,
Amsterdam, June 1991.

Garner, Joel, and E. Clemmer, *Danger to Police in Domestic Disturbances: A New
Look*. Washington, DC: National Institute of Justice, 1986.

Gates, Daryl F., *Chief: My Life in the LAPD*. New York: Bantam Books, 1992.

Goldstein, Herman, "Improving Policing: A Problem Oriented Approach," *Crime
and Delinquency* 25:236–58 (April 1979).

_____, *Problem-Oriented Policing*. New York: McGraw-Hill, 1990.

Greenberg, Stephanie W., and William M. Rohe, "Informal Social Control and Crime
Prevention in Modern Urban Neighborhoods," pp. 79–118 in R. B. Taylor, ed.,
*Urban Neighborhoods: Research and Policy*. New York: Praeger, 1986.

Institute for Law and Social Research, *Pretrial Release and Misconduct in the District of Columbia*. Washington, DC: Institute for Law and Social Research,
1980.

Kelling, George L., Tony Pate, Duane Dieckman, and Charles E. Brown, *The Kansas
City Preventive Patrol Experiment: Summary Report*. Washington, DC: Police
Foundation, 1974.

Klockars, Carl, "The Dirty Harry Problem," *Annals of the American Academy of
Political and Social Science* 452:52 (November 1980).

Konstantin, David, "Homicides of American Law Enforcement Officers," *Justice
Quarterly*, 1:29–37 (March 1984).

Maas, Peter, *Serpico*. New York: The Viking Press, 1973.

Manning, Peter K., *Police Work: The Social Organization of Policing*. Cambridge:
MIT Press, 1977.

Margarita, Mona, "Killing the Police: Myths and Motives," *Annals of the American Academy of Political and Social Science* 452:72–81 (November 1980).

Mastrofski, Stephen D., "Community Policing as Reform: A Cautionary Tale," pp. 47–68 in Jack R. Greene and Stephen D. Mastrofski, eds., *Community Policing: Rhetoric or Reality.* New York: Praeger, 1988.

Monkonnen, Erik, *Police in Urban America, 1860–1920.* Cambridge: Cambridge University Press, 1981.

Neiderhoffer, Arthur, *Behind the Shield.* Garden City, NY: Doubleday, 1967.

Palmer, Stanley H., *Police and Protest in England and Ireland 1780–1850.* Cambridge: Cambridge University Press, 1988.

Perez, Douglas, "Police Accountability: A Question of Balance." Ph.D. dissertation, University of California, Berkeley, 1978.

Police Foundation, *The Newark Foot Patrol Experiment.* Washington, DC: Police Foundation, 1981.

Reiss, Albert J., Jr., *The Police and the Public.* New Haven: Yale University Press, 1971.

Reuss-Ianni, Elizabeth, *Two Cultures of Policing: Street Cops and Management Cops.* New Brunswick, NJ: Transaction Books, 1983.

Rothmiller, Mike, and Ivan G. Goldman, *L.A. Secret Police.* New York: Pocket Books, 1992.

Rubinstein, Jonathan, *City Police.* New York: Farrar, Straus and Giroux, 1973.

Scott, Eric J., *Calls for Service: Citizen Demand and Initial Police Response.* Washington, DC: U.S. Government Printing Office, 1981.

Sherman, Lawrence W., Catherine H. Milton, and Thomas V. Kelly, *Team Policing: Seven Case Studies.* Washington, DC: Police Foundation, 1973.

Skolnick, Jerome H., and James J. Fyfe, *Above the Law: Police and the Excessive Use of Force.* New York: Free Press, 1993.

Thomas, Wayne H., *Bail Reform in America.* Berkeley: University of California Press, 1976.

Toch, Hans, "Mobilizing Police Expertise," *Annals of the American Academy of Political and Social Science* 452:53–62 (November 1980).

Toch, Hans, and J. Douglas Grant, *Police as Problem Solvers.* New York: Plenum Press, 1991.

Toch, Hans, J. Douglas Grant, and Raymond T. Galvin, *Agents of Change: A Study in Police Reform.* Cambridge: Schenkman, 1975.

Trojanowicz, Robert, and Bonnie Bucqueroux, *Community Policing: A Contemporary Perspective.* Cincinnati: Anderson Publishing, 1990.

United States Department of Commerce, *1990 Census of Population and Housing, Summary of Population and Housing Characteristics,* New York, CPH-1-34. Washington, DC: United States Government Printing Office, 1991.

Walker, Samuel, *A Critical History of Police Reform: The Emergence of Professionalism.* Lexington, MA: Lexington Books, 1977.

Webster, John, "Police Time and Task Study," *Journal of Criminal Law, Criminology and Police Science* 61:94–100 (1970).

Wilson, James Q., "Generational and Ethnic Differences among Career Police Officers," *American Journal of Sociology* 69:522–28 (March 1964).

_____. *Varieties of Police Behavior.* Cambridge: Harvard University Press, 1968.

# The AIDS Epidemic and the Police
## An Examination of the Issues

*Mark Blumberg*

## Introduction

Police work has always been characterized by potential danger. Not only must law enforcement officers be concerned about the harm that may result from confrontations with offenders, but there are other risks as well, such as traffic accidents and injuries that occur in the course of performing routine duties. However, the AIDS epidemic has created new uncertainties for law enforcement personnel. For the first time in memory, some police officers fear that in addition to injury, they now face the risk of contracting a fatal disease as a result of their occupation. This article examines whether this concern is warranted and other AIDS-related issues that affect law enforcement.

## History and Nature of the AIDS Epidemic

The first cases of acquired immunodeficiency syndrome (AIDS) in the United States were diagnosed among gay males in 1981 (Friedman and Klein, 1987). It was not long before this illness was also reported among intravenous drug users. When additional cases began appearing among both hemophiliacs and blood transfusion recipients, there was a strong suspicion that the ailment was being transmitted through a pathogen in the blood. In 1983, scientists discovered the cause of this disease, the human immunodeficiency virus (HIV). Two years later, the Food and Drug Administration licensed a blood test to determine whether a person had become infected with HIV (Altman, 1987:56).

Scientists estimate that as many as 800,000 Americans may be infected with the AIDS virus (Ho, 1996). Because the incubation period between infection with HIV and the manifestation of illness is many years (Institute of Medicine, 1988), individuals generally appear healthy but are

Prepared especially for *Critical Issues in Policing*, 3/E, by Mark Blumberg.

able to transmit the virus to others. Although there is no cure for AIDS, physicians are able to treat this disease through a combination of drugs. Unfortunately, this therapy is very expensive and requires that patients follow a rigid schedule and take between 14 and 20 pills each day (Waldholz, 1996). Furthermore, it is not known whether the medical benefits of this treatment continue over the long term. However, this regimen offers hope that AIDS may eventually become similar to other chronic diseases which patients are able to manage (e.g., diabetes).

It is important to recognize that the human immunodeficiency virus is difficult to transmit. In fact, the only known modes of transmission are sexual activity, blood-to-blood contact (primarily through needle sharing), and transmission from an infected mother to a newborn infant (Friedland and Klein, 1987). Scientists have clearly established that the virus is not spread as a result of everyday casual contact nor is it transmitted through insect bites, the sharing of food or by using toilet facilities (Lifson, 1988). Transmission through casual contact has been ruled out as a result of studies that examined hundreds of persons who lived in households or boarding schools where an HIV infected individual also resided. Not a single case was discovered in which any person had become infected except through perinatal events (i.e., transmission that occurs in the birthing process), sexual activity, or contact with blood (Lifson, 1988; Friedland and Klein, 1987). This finding is even more striking because many of these individuals, not knowing that they were living with a seropositive[1] individual, routinely shared eating utensils, toothbrushes, plates and many other household items.

In most Western nations, the overwhelming majority of persons with AIDS are either gay/bisexual males or intravenous drug users. To date, these groups account for 83 percent of the diagnosed cases of "full-blown" adult/adolescent AIDS in the United States. At the present time, heterosexual transmission accounts for 8 percent of the total (Centers For Disease Control and Prevention, 1995:10). The latter is composed primarily of females who have become infected as a result of sexual contact with intravenous drug users.

The AIDS epidemic has engendered much fear, and persons infected with the virus have often been subjected to various forms of discrimination (Gostin, 1990; Blendon and Donelan, 1988; Altman, 1987). Although public passions have cooled somewhat in recent years, a number of disturbing incidents occurred during the 1980s including parental boycotts of schools in various communities that granted admission to seropositive children and the burning of a home in Arcadia, Florida, where three infected hemophiliac brothers lived (*New York Times*, 1987). There have also been cases in which law enforcement officers responded inappropriately to situations involving HIV infected citizens. Perhaps it was inevitable that this epidemic would elicit a strong emotional response in some persons. After all, AIDS appeared many years after medical science was thought to have conquered all the major threats to public health. In addition, the disease evoked fears of the unknown and forced society to confront such highly charged issues as death, sexual morality and illicit drug use.

## Law Enforcement Officers with HIV/AIDS

In the early days of the epidemic, many police administrators believed that AIDS was a problem that was unlikely to affect many law enforcement officers. The perception was that this was a virus confined mainly to "high-risk" individuals unlikely to seek employment in policing. However, that view may not be correct. Not only is the number of HIV infected persons in the general population quite substantial, but law enforcement agencies may contain more persons drawn from "high-risk" backgrounds (i.e., homosexual/bisexual males and individuals with a history of intravenous drug use) than is commonly believed. For these reasons, police agencies are likely to confront an increasing number of situations in which personnel issues related to HIV arise.

Historically, police departments have not been friendly places for gay applicants. Although few, if any, organizations had explicit bans that prohibited the hiring of homosexuals, these applicants were often screened out in the recruitment process. This occurred for several reasons. For one thing, many administrators believed that homosexuality was not compatible with the conduct expected of a police officer. Second, Burke (1992) has noted that the police culture is characterized by a number of features which are not hospitable to gay people (e.g., machismo). Third, sodomy statutes which exist in a number of jurisdictions were sometimes cited as a justification for excluding homosexuals. Finally, the paramilitary image of law enforcement discouraged some gay people from applying.

In recent years, much has changed. Not only have gays achieved greater societal acceptance, but there is growing political support for the idea that sexual orientation should not be a barrier to employment. As a consequence, some police departments (mostly in cities with substantial gay populations) are openly recruiting gay officers (Berrill and Herek, 1992). In other cases, the screening process is no longer being used to exclude qualified gay applicants. While there have always been gay people working in law enforcement (usually closeted), the number is likely to increase as this type of job discrimination becomes less socially acceptable.

The other major risk group for HIV infection is intravenous drug users. Obviously, this practice violates the law, and police departments do not and should not hire applicants who use illicit substances. However, the Americans with Disabilities Act (ADA), enacted by Congress in 1990, may prohibit police departments from discriminating against otherwise qualified applicants who have successfully completed a drug rehabilitation program (Schneid and Gaines, 1991). If this is the case, it is likely that the number of seropositive individuals who apply for police work will increase.

As more individuals from "high-risk" groups seek to enter law enforcement, police administrators will be forced to confront such questions as: (1) whether departments should test potential recruits for the virus; (2) whether seropositive applicants should be allowed to enter law enforcement and; (3) whether officers who become infected with HIV or develop symptoms of AIDS should be permitted to continue working. Unfortunately, a recent survey of state police departments found that most of these agencies have not formulated any policy with respect to the employment of persons with HIV/AIDS (Edwards and Tewksbury, 1996).

There are many reasons why police departments should not test applicants for HIV. First, this practice would violate state statutes in many jurisdictions, which prohibit the testing of persons without their informed consent (Hammett, 1987a:29). Second, HIV testing may also violate the Americans with Disabilities Act which forbids employers from conducting pre-employment physical examinations (Schneid and Gaines, 1991). Third, because employers may not legally base a hiring decision on an applicant's HIV status, the results of this test are irrelevant. Fourth, the test is not able to determine the length of time before an infected individual will manifest symptoms of illness. Finally, HIV testing by employers may subject applicants to future discrimination. For these reasons, the testing of potential recruits is a totally unjustified expenditure of scarce law enforcement dollars.

Basically, testing is inappropriate because police agencies have no legitimate need for this information. There is no rational basis for excluding otherwise qualified seropositive applicants from law enforcement. Because the AIDS virus is not transmitted through the kinds of duties that police officers generally perform, it is highly unlikely that an infected individual would pose any danger either to his/her colleagues or to the community.

It is possible to speculate regarding scenarios that might pose some theoretical risk. For example, it could be asserted that a seropositive police officer with an open sore might transmit the virus while attempting to restrain a violent suspect. Conceivably, this could occur if the suspect received a cut during the altercation and was exposed to blood from the officer.[2] However, almost two decades have passed since AIDS first appeared in the United States, and there is not a single report in the literature of a police officer infecting a citizen in the course of his/her occupational activities. Therefore, it must be concluded that this risk is more theoretical than real and that any danger is so minimal as to make a policy of exclusion totally unwarranted.

In order to assess the risk that infected officers pose, it is helpful to examine the situation with respect to health-care workers. To date, except for a Florida dentist who may have intentionally infected several patients (Altman, 1991), there is not a single documented case of any person who became infected as a result of contact with a surgeon (*New York Times*, 1991b) or other health-care provider in a medical setting (Altman, 1992). This finding is quite reassuring given the fact that physicians perform invasive procedures whereas law enforcement personnel do not have this type of contact with citizens.

There are other reasons why police agencies should not bar otherwise qualified seropositive applicants. Discrimination of this type is prohibited by the Americans with Disabilities Act as well as by various state statutes (Gostin, 1990) which make it illegal to discriminate against disabled individuals. Also, the wholesale exclusion of persons infected with HIV would deny agencies the services of many qualified applicants who might make excellent police officers and who, in many cases, will remain healthy for a long period of time.

Another question that administrators must confront is: How should departments respond in cases where personnel become ill and develop "full-blown" AIDS? Although this may seem like a complex issue, the critical variable is whether the individual can still perform his or her job. Because AIDS qualifies as a disability under the ADA, departments must make reasonable accommodations for their employees in these cases (Schneid and Gaines, 1991). Therefore, it will become necessary to determine if the officer can continue to work and whether certain reasonable accommodations are needed. The Act does not require employers to go to extraordinary lengths, and police officers who no longer can fulfill their responsibilities may be placed on disability. Likewise, officers who develop a condition that places others at risk (e.g., tuberculosis) as a result of their impaired immune system should not be allowed to work while they are infectious.

## The Risk of Occupational HIV Infection

In the early days of the AIDS epidemic, some police officers suggested that they should be permitted to refuse assignments that brought them into contact with seropositive citizens. In a few departments, police officers refused to transport prisoners or handle evidence at crime scenes because they were fearful of contracting the virus (Hammett, 1987a:31). However, incidents of this nature have become infrequent in recent years as more knowledge has been gained regarding how AIDS is transmitted and as departments increasingly make this information available to their personnel. In fact, a recent survey indicates that a majority of state police organizations are now offering HIV/AIDS training to both recruits and in-service personnel (Edwards and Tewksbury, 1996).

As previously noted, medical researchers have conclusively demonstrated that HIV is not transmitted through casual contact. For this reason, the overwhelming majority of police activities present absolutely no risk of viral infection. Included in this category are such routine duties as taking reports from citizens, making arrests, transporting prisoners, and responding to a variety of requests from the public for police service. Nonetheless, some officers continue to express anxiety that certain types of interactions with offenders and/or citizens may place them at risk of infection (Sheridan, et al., 1989). A number of these concerns are examined below in order to determine whether this apprehension is indeed warranted.

## Biting/Spitting Incidents

Part of the responsibility that police officers have been given by society is the arrest of persons who have violated the law. It is no surprise that suspects do not always willingly submit to police authority. In some cases, offenders engage in assaultive behavior in an attempt to escape, to inflict harm upon the officer or to express their anger. These attacks can include such things as spitting on the officer, biting, or stabbing with a needle that was used to inject intravenous drugs. In the past, the police generally were resigned to the fact that this type of behavior on the part of suspects was an inevitable, although unfortunate, aspect of their job. However, the AIDS epidemic has made some officers fearful that these attacks could result in infection with a lethal virus. This concern is heightened because unlike other risks associated with police work, HIV can be passed on to spouses or lovers through sexual contact.

Fortunately, these assaults pose little risk. In fact, being spat on by a seropositive individual poses almost no danger of HIV infection. There are several reasons why this is the case. For one thing, the virus does not pass through intact skin, and even if a seropositive assailant were to spit directly on an open sore, there is not enough virus in saliva to actually transmit HIV. Hammett (1988:16) notes that one quart of saliva would have to enter the bloodstream for infection to occur. For this reason, the Centers For Disease Control no longer recommend that "universal precautions" be taken in situations involving contact with saliva unless this body fluid contains visible blood (Hammett, 1989:2–3). As a consequence, the only conceivable risk to an officer from this type of assault would be in cases where the assailant was bleeding from the mouth. However, this danger can be negated by keeping all open sores properly bandaged.

Intuitively, one might think that bites pose a serious risk of HIV infection. However, this is not the case due to the fact that it is the perpetrator who comes into contact with blood as a result of the assault and not the victim. The latter only comes into contact with saliva from the offender. Again, the only conceivable risk would be in situations where the assailant had blood in his or her mouth. However, this is a negligible risk. Medical researchers who have examined numerous cases in which health-care workers and others received bites from seropositive individuals have concluded that the potential for the transmission of HIV in this manner is negligible, but biologically possible (Richman and Richman, 1993).

## Needle Sticks

Needle-stick injuries pose a slightly greater risk. Police officers may be cut with a needle that is contaminated with the blood of a seropositive individual either through a deliberate attack or as the result of an accidental injury that occurs in the course of conducting a search. In either case, there is a small risk of infection. Studies of health-care workers who were inadvertently pricked with needles used on seropositive patients indicate that 0.4 percent (approximately 1 out of 250) became infected with HIV

(Peterman and Petersen, 1990:401). Although this is a relatively small risk, it is one that police officers must minimize. Agencies must include as part of their AIDS education and training program information that helps officers to conduct searches in a manner designed to avoid this type of injury. For example, employees should be instructed to have suspects empty their own pockets instead of reaching in and taking a chance of contacting a contaminated needle (Hammett, 1987b).

Training must also focus on violent offenders who attempt to assault officers with contaminated needles. Police departments should examine various strategies that aim to protect personnel from these individuals. One question that may arise is how far officers may go to avoid needle-stick wounds. For example, is it permissible to use deadly force as a last resort to defend against this type of injury? As a general rule, firearms can be used to protect the officer from death or serious bodily injury. Does a small risk of becoming infected with a lethal virus meet this test? Administrators must formulate policies which provide guidance to police officers with respect to these issues.

### Crime/Accident Victims

Another source of anxiety for police officers is the fear that they will become infected with HIV as a result of contact with blood in the course of rendering first-aid to automobile accident or crime victims. This is not an implausible concern because the virus is transmitted through exposure to contaminated blood. Indeed, there have been a small number of cases in which health-care workers became infected in this manner (Ippolito, Puro and DeCarli, 1993). However, with proper training and by taking a few reasonable precautions, police officers can protect themselves from this risk.

One of the most important aspects of AIDS prevention is the adoption of "universal precautions" which have been prescribed for public safety personnel by the Centers For Disease Control and Prevention. This means that officers presume any blood they encounter is infected with HIV and precautions are automatically taken in all such cases. It is not sufficient to follow these procedures only in situations that involve persons who are perceived to be at "high-risk." Among the necessary steps that should be followed are the use of protective gloves whenever "contact with blood, other body fluids containing visible blood, tissues, semen, and vaginal secretions is likely" (Hammett, 1989:2) and keeping all open sores properly bandaged. In addition, personnel must thoroughly cleanse all objects that become contaminated with blood or other body fluids that may contain HIV.

## Education and Training

The only effective weapon that is currently available to stem the spread of HIV is proper education. For this reason, it is imperative that police departments provide their personnel with comprehensive and accurate information regarding AIDS. Yearwood (1992:76) reports that "officers who have a greater understanding of how the virus is, and is not transmitted, are less likely to exhibit inappropriate fears about contracting the virus during the course of their occupational duties." In addition, he notes that officers who are well informed hold less negative attitudes toward persons with AIDS and are less likely to fail to perform required duties.

AIDS education and training are designed to minimize the risk of viral infection. However, it is important that departments do not take an unduly alarmist tone. The threat of HIV must be placed in perspective. Although there are several police officers who allege that they became infected with HIV as a result of their employment (Bigbee, 1993), the Centers for Disease Control and Prevention have not documented a single case of this type anywhere in the United States since the beginning of the epidemic (Hammett, Harrold, Gross and Epstein, 1994). In fact, AIDS poses far less risk to officers than do traffic accidents, criminal assaults and other injuries that police routinely encounter as a part of their job. These facts must be succinctly communicated to the rank-and-file.

Proper education and training are important for other reasons as well. First, there are many officers who are misinformed regarding HIV (Yearwood, 1992). Second, accurate information can teach the police how to avoid the types of "high-risk" behavior in their personal lives that could transmit the virus. Third, educated officers will understand that casual contact with infected individuals poses absolutely no danger. Therefore, they will be in a position to offer compassion toward persons who are suffering from this disease. Fourth, a clear understanding of HIV should result in fewer incidents where police feel compelled to take inappropriate precautions, such as wearing yellow gloves at a gay rights demonstration to avoid infection (*Newsweek*, 1987). Fifth, police who receive proper training are less likely to engage in activities that result in civil liability. This is an important concern in light of a recent appellate court decision that an arrestee could sue an officer who told others that the suspect was seropositive (AELE, 1995:51). Finally, personnel who are knowledgeable about AIDS can serve as an invaluable public health resource in educating others about this danger (Sheridan et al., 1989).

The police are especially well suited to the role of AIDS educator because much of their work involves contact with persons who engage in "high-risk" behavior, such as intravenous drug users. Although AIDS has been associated in the public mind with homosexuality (Altman, 1987), 32 percent of "full-blown" AIDS cases reported to date have been among persons who have a history of injecting drugs (Centers for Disease Control and Prevention, 1995:10). In addition, the majority of cases linked to heterosexual transmission have been diagnosed among individuals who are the sex partners of intravenous drug users. Clearly, there is little hope of slowing the spread of this epidemic unless IV drug users are encouraged to alter their behavior.[3] Because the police have considerable contact with these individuals, they are in a unique position to provide them with accurate information regarding viral transmission.

## AIDS and Anti-Gay Violence

In recent years, there has been a disturbing rise in the reported number of hate crimes directed at gay men and lesbians (Berrill, 1992). Although it is difficult to determine how much of this increase is due to changes in reporting practices, the available data suggest that these attacks have become more common. Approximately two-thirds of the groups who reported incidents to the National Gay and Lesbian Task Force in 1989 responded in the affirmative when asked whether fear and hatred associated with AIDS had fostered anti-gay harassment and violence in their communities (Berrill, 1992:38). On the other hand, it is possible that the upsurge in violence may have less to do with fear of AIDS than the unprecedented visibility that the media has given to gay and lesbian issues since the beginning of the epidemic. Regardless of motivation, police departments must respond aggressively to this problem. AIDS cannot be used as an excuse to break the law and harm others.

Unfortunately, many of these incidents go unreported either because victims fear that the police are anti-gay, that their complaints will not be handled in a professional manner, or that their sexual orientation will be publicly disclosed (Berrill and Herek, 1992). For this reason, agencies must implement policies and procedures to ensure that these matters are dealt with in a conscientious manner. Administrators must stress that the police department exists to protect all citizens, regardless of sexual orientation. Officers should be trained to recognize all types of hate crimes, including acts of anti-gay violence. Appropriate administrative action must be taken in situations where personnel fail to respond properly.

Some police departments have taken an important step to combat this problem. Boston, Chicago, New York and San Francisco have each established special units that are trained to investigate and respond to hate crimes (Berrill and Herek, 1992). This action should be taken in all jurisdictions where the level of violence is such that it constitutes a serious law enforcement problem. The creation of a special unit not only ensures that the agency has the necessary expertise to deal with these offenses, it also sends a strong signal to the community that this type of criminal behavior will not be tolerated.

## Conclusion

This article has examined three important concerns that the AIDS crisis has raised for police administrators: (1) how departments should respond to HIV infected officers; (2) the actual risk of occupational HIV transmission that law enforcement personnel confront and; (3) how departments should respond to the reported increase in the level of anti-gay violence that has accompanied the AIDS epidemic.

Implementing satisfactory policies in these areas should not be difficult. In fact, the challenges posed by the AIDS epidemic are no greater than many other responsibilities that the police are routinely called upon to perform. After all, the danger of occupational HIV transmission is far less than the risk an officer faces when driving a patrol car or attempting to arrest a suspect who has violated the law. Likewise, the task of protecting the public from bias-related offenses is not much different from the usual police role of protecting the public from other types of crime.

## Notes

[1] The term "seropositive" refers to persons infected with the human immunodeficiency virus (HIV), regardless of whether they exhibit symptoms of illness.

[2] *The New York Times* (1991a) reports the case of a seropositive male who may have become infected as a result of repeatedly seeking out and beating gay men. Obviously, a law enforcement officer who engaged in this type of assaultive behavior should be fired regardless of his/her HIV status.

[3] There is considerable evidence that intravenous drug users are willing to change their behavior in order to reduce the risk of HIV infection (Treaster, 1991; Blumberg, 1990; Becker and Joseph, 1988).

## References

AELE (1995). "Arrestee Could Sue Arresting Officer for Releasing to Others Information that He Was HIV Positive, Even Though Test Results Later Turned Out to be False." *Liability Reporter* 268:51 (April).

Altman, Dennis (1987). *AIDS in the Mind of America: The Social, Political, and Psychological Impact of a New Epidemic.* Garden City, NY: Anchor Books.

Altman, Lawrence K. (1991). "An AIDS Puzzle: What Went Wrong in Dentist's Office?" *New York Times,* July 30, p. 3.

Altman, Lawrence K. (1992). "U.S. to Let States Set Rules on AIDS-Infected Health Workers," *New York Times,* June 16, p. C7.

Becker, Marshall H. and Jill G. Joseph (1988). "AIDS and Behavioral Change to Reduce Risk: A Review," *American Journal of Public Health* 78(4): 394–410.

Berrill, Kevin T. (1992). "Anti-Gay Violence and Victimization in the United States: An Overview." In Gregory M. Herek and Kevin T. Berrill (eds.), *Hate Crimes: Confronting Violence Against Lesbians and Gay Men.* Newbury Park, CA: Sage Publications.

Berrill, Kevin T. and Gregory M. Herek (1992). "Primary and Secondary Victimization in Anti-Gay Hate Crimes: Official Response and Public Policy." In Gregory M. Herek and Kevin T. Berrill (eds.), *Hate Crimes: Confronting Violence Against Lesbians and Gay Men.* Newbury Park, CA: Sage Publications.

Bigbee, David (1993). "Pathogenic Microorganisms: Law Enforcement's Silent Enemies." *FBI Law Enforcement Bulletin* 62(5): 1–5.

Blendon, Robert J. and Karen Donelan (1988). "Discrimination Against People With AIDS," *New England Journal of Medicine* 319(15): 1022–26.

Blumberg, Mark (1990). "The Transmission of HIV: Exploring Some Misconceptions Related to Criminal Justice," *Criminal Justice Policy Review* 4(4): 288–305.

Burke, Marc (1992). "Cop Culture and Homosexuality." *The Police Journal* (January): 30–39.

Centers for Disease Control and Prevention (1995). *HIV/AIDS Surveillance Report* 7(2).

Edwards, Terry D. and Richard Tewksbury (1996). "HIV/AIDS: State Police Training Practices and Personnel Policies." *American Journal of Police* 15(1): 45–62.

Friedland, Gerald H. and Robert S. Klein (1987). "Transmission of the Human Immunodeficiency Virus, " *The New England Journal of Medicine* 317(18): 1125–35.

Gostin, Lawrence O. (1990). "The AIDS Litigation Project: A Review of Court and Human Rights Decisions, Part II: Discrimination," *JAMA* 263(15): 2086–93.

Hammett, Theodore M. (1989). *AIDS and HIV Training and Education in Criminal Justice Agencies.* Washington, DC: National Institute of Justice, August.

Hammett, Theodore M. (1988). *AIDS in Correctional Facilities: Issues and Options,* 3rd ed. Washington, DC: National Institute of Justice.

Hammett, Theodore M. (1987a). *AIDS and the Law Enforcement Officer: Concerns and Policy Responses.* Washington, DC: National Institute of Justice, June.

Hammett, Theodore M. and Walter Bond (1987b). *Risk of Infection with the AIDS Virus through Exposure to Blood.* Washington, DC: National Institute of Justice, October.

Hammett, Theodore M., Lynne Harrold, Michael Gross and Joel Epstein (1994). *1992 Update: HIV/AIDS in Correctional Facilities.* National Institute of Justice and Centers for Disease Control and Prevention (January).

Ho, David (1996). "AIDS Conferees Debate How Early to Offer New Drugs." *Wall Street Journal,* July 12, p. B1.

Institute of Medicine (1988). *Confronting AIDS: Update 1988.* Washington, DC: National Academy Press.

Ippolito, Giuseppe, Vincenzo Puro, and Gabriella De Carli (1993). "The Risk of Occupational Human Immunodeficiency Virus Infection in Health Care Workers." *Archives of Internal Medicine* 153:1451–58.

Lifson, Alan R. (1988). "Do Alternate Modes for Transmission of Human Immunodeficiency Virus Exist?" *JAMA* 259(9): 1353–56.

*Newsweek* (1987). "The Problem With Testing," June 15, p. 60.

*New York Times* (1991a). "Man Who Beat Gay Men Has the AIDS Virus," March 22, p. A19.

*New York Times* (1991b). "Surgeons Rebuff U.S. AIDS Request," October 25, p. A21.

*New York Times* (1987). "Family in AIDS case Quits Florida Town after House Burns," August 30, p. 1.

Peterman, Thomas A. and Lyle R. Petersen (1990). "Stalking the HIV Epidemic: Which Tracks to Follow and How Far," *American Journal of Public Health* 80(4): 401–2.

Richman, Katherine M. and Leland S. Richman (1993). "The Potential for Transmission of Human Immunodeficiency Virus through Human Bites." *Journal of Acquired Immune Deficiency Syndrome* 6(4): 402–6.

Schneid, Thomas D. and Larry K. Gaines (1991). "The Americans With Disabilities Act: Implications For Police Administrators," *American Journal of Police* 10(1): 47–58.

Sheridan, Kathleen, John S. Lyons, Marian Fitzgibbon, Edward P. Sheridan and Martin J. McCarthy (1989). "Effects of AIDS Education on Police Officers' Perceptions of Risk." *Public Health Reports* 104(5): 521–22.

Treaster, Joseph B. (1991). "Fearing AIDS, Users of Heroin Shift to Inhaling Drug," *New York Times,* November 17, Metro, p. 34.

Waldholz, Michael (1966). "New AIDS Treatment Raises Tough Question of Who Will Get It." *Wall Street Journal,* July 3, p. A1.

Yearwood, Douglas L. (1992). "Law Enforcement and AIDS: Knowledge, Attitudes, and Fears in the Workplace," *American Journal of Police* 11(2): 65–80.

# 13

# Police, Civil Liability, and the Law

*Rolando V. del Carmen*
*Michael R. Smith*

Not since the riotous times of the 1960s have police officers operated under closer public scrutiny. The infamous beating of Rodney King by Los Angeles police officers and a host of similar incidents captured on videotape have served to heighten public awareness and concern over police arrest practices. Lawsuits filed against the police are an increasing concern of both individual officers and of the agencies for which they work. Today, more than ever, concern over civil liability drives police training and rule-making. For many law enforcement agencies, the danger of losing a multimillion-dollar lawsuit is a reality they can no longer ignore.

The purpose of this chapter is to provide an overview of the law governing police civil liability. It begins with a discussion of law enforcement officers' liability under state law. Next, the chapter takes up federal civil liability arising under Title 42, Section 1983 of the United States Code. Finally, this chapter discusses the potential liability of law enforcement agencies and police supervisors for the actions of their employees.

## Liability of Law Enforcement Officers under State Law

Law enforcement officers can be sued under state law for a variety of torts. A *tort* is a civil wrong, other than a breach of contract, for which a person can recover damages. In the typical civil suit brought against a police officer under state law, a plaintiff alleges that the officer owed him or her a legal duty, that the officer breached that duty, and that the breach caused the citizen to suffer some kind of harm, either physical or emotional. By suing the officer in civil court, the plaintiff usually hopes to recover monetary damages to compensate for the harm suffered (compensatory damages) or to punish the officer for his wrongdoing (punitive damages). Although the ele-

Prepared especially for *Critical Issues in Policing*, 3/E by Rolando V. del Carmen and Michael R. Smith.

ments of a tort may vary from state to state, almost all states recognize some version of the following torts.

### Assault and Battery

A police officer commits the tort of *assault* when he or she intentionally, and without legal justification, places someone in fear of bodily harm. In addition, the threat must usually be immediate and the officer must have the apparent means to carry out the threat. *Battery*, on the other hand, is the intentional and unlawful touching of one person by another without legal justification. Although assault and battery frequently occur together, they are separate torts. Thus, an officer can commit an assault without also committing a battery and vice versa.

State law, either by statute or judicial decision, permits a police officer to use force or the threat of force to carry out his or her lawful duties. It is only when an officer threatens someone inappropriately or uses too much force that the officer may commit the torts of assault or battery. Under the law of most states, the burden is placed on the officer to prove that the act was reasonable under the circumstances. If an officer can show that he or she used *only* the amount of force necessary to carry out the officer's duties (such as making an arrest), then the officer will usually prevail in the lawsuit.

### False Arrest or Imprisonment

*False arrest* and *false imprisonment* are torts that usually arise when an officer arrests someone without a sufficient legal basis. For example, a warrantless arrest without probable cause may lead to a charge of false arrest, as may arresting the wrong person named in an arrest warrant. False imprisonment, on the other hand, refers to the act of illegally confining a person or restricting his or her freedom of movement. Usually, false imprisonment follows a false arrest because if the arrest itself is illegal, then the resulting confinement of the arrestee is also illegal.

### Malicious Prosecution and Abuse of Process

These two related torts provide citizens with a legal cause of action against an officer who misuses the legal process. A citizen has a legal basis for malicious prosecution if he or she can prove that a police officer initiated a criminal prosecution against the citizen, that the case terminated in the citizen's favor (either by a judicial dismissal or a not guilty verdict), that the officer did not have probable cause to initiate the prosecution, and that the officer was motivated by malice or bad faith. Abuse of process is similar to malicious prosecution, except that it typically involves an allegation that a police officer has used some aspect of the legal process, such as the filing of criminal charges, to harass or cause harm to the complaining citizen.

## Negligence

Unlike the torts discussed above, the tort of negligence does not require that the officer intentionally cause harm to someone. Rather, it merely requires a citizen to show that a police officer owed the citizen a legal duty, that the officer acted unreasonably in discharging the duty, and that the breach of the duty resulted in damage to the citizen. Negligence is the most commonly used tort theory in lawsuits brought against the police. Suits for negligence range from car accidents, to allegations that police failed to protect a citizen, to charges that officers did not respond promptly to a request for help.

## Wrongful Death

The tort of wrongful death is most commonly created by state statute. It allows family members of persons allegedly killed by police misconduct to recover damages for the pain and suffering of the person killed, medical and funeral expenses, loss of potential lifetime income, and their own emotional suffering. A person seeking to recover damages for the wrongful death of a family member must allege and prove liability under an existing tort theory. For example, the spouse of a person killed by a stray police bullet must prove that the officer who fired the bullet acted negligently or recklessly. Thus, the family member must prove the tort of negligence as a means to recover damages for wrongful death.

The torts listed above are the most common of those alleged against the police. The list is not exhaustive, however, and there are other torts that those injured by police occasionally use as a basis for bringing lawsuits. State tort suits generally make up the majority of civil lawsuits filed against police officers. Unlike a criminal case, which can be filed only by the prosecutor, any licensed attorney can file a tort suit, and most are heard in local county or municipal courts.

# Liability of Law Enforcement
# Officers under Federal Law

Title 42 of the United States Code, Section 1983 provides that:

> Every person who, under color of any statute, ordinance, regulation, custom, or usage, or any State or Territory or the District of Columbia, subjects, or causes to be subjected, any citizen of the United States or any other person within the jurisdiction thereof to the deprivation of any rights, privileges, or immunities secured by the Constitution and laws, shall be liable to the party injured in an action at law, suit in equity, or other proper proceeding for redress . . .

This statute is part of the Civil Rights Act of 1871. It was originally enacted to provide a means of redress for victims of government inaction in the face of Ku Klux Klan activity. In the period following the Civil War, local officials in the South frequently refused to prosecute Klansmen who terrorized African Americans. By enacting Section 1983, Congress attempted to give these victims a means of recovering damages from law enforcement officials who failed to do their jobs (Fontana, 1990).

Section 1983 creates no substantive rights, meaning it is not a statute that makes conduct illegal that otherwise would not have been. Rather, it is a vehicle for bringing suit against government officials acting under color of state law for violating a person's federal rights.

Section 1983 applies only to persons acting under color of *state* law. Thus, it applies only to state and local law enforcement officers who exert authority derived from state law. In contrast, federal law enforcement officers, such as FBI agents, act pursuant to federal law and thus are exempt from liability under Section 1983. However, in *Bivens v. Six Unknown Agents of the Federal Bureau of Narcotics* (1971), the Supreme Court recognized a private right of action for damages against federal officers who violated the Fourth Amendment. While federal agents are beyond the reach of Section 1983, they can be held directly liable under the Constitution for violating a person's constitutional rights.

## Two Requirements

In order to state a claim under Section 1983, a citizen must allege that (1) a law enforcement officer deprived the citizen of a federal right, and (2) the officer who deprived the citizen of the right acted under color of state law. The citizen also must show that the officer's actions caused physical suffering or emotional harm. Although virtually any constitutional or federal statutory violation can serve as the basis for a Section 1983 claim, the most frequent violations alleged against law enforcement officers involve the Fourth, Eighth, and Fourteenth Amendments to the Constitution.

Typical Fourth Amendment claims allege excessive use of force (*Graham v. Conner*, 1989; *Jenkins v. Averett*, 1970), unreasonable searches (*Ward v. San Diego County*, 1986), or false arrest or imprisonment (*Pierson v. Ray*, 1967; *McIntosh v. Arkansas Republican Party-Frank White Election Commission*, 1987). Common Eighth Amendment claims also involve excessive force (*Hudson v. McMillian*, 1992), but include allegations of failure to provide services to incarcerated persons (*Estelle v. Gamble*, 1976) and failure to protect such persons from others (*Stubbs v. Dudley*, 1988). The Fourteenth Amendment has been used in various cases alleging gross negligence by police officers (*Fargo v. San Juan Bautista*, 1988; *Nishiyama v. Dickson County*, 1987) and has also been used as the basis for allegations of failure to properly train law enforcement personnel (*City of Canton v. Harris*, 1989).

## Official or Individual Capacity

A law enforcement officer can be sued under Section 1983 in either his or her official or individual capacity. A suit against an officer in the officer's official capacity is really just another way of suing the agency for which the officer works (*Kentucky v. Graham*, 1985). How law enforcement agencies and supervisors can be held liable for the actions of their employees is discussed below. An officer also can be sued in his or her individual capacity, which means that the complainant seeks to recover damages from the officer, not from the agency. Thus, state and local law enforcement officers may be subject to full, personal liability for actions taken while carrying out their official duties (*Monroe v. Pape*, 1961). For example, if a police officer uses excessive force when making an arrest, the suspect can sue the officer in his or her individual capacity and recover damages from the officer personally.

Law enforcement officers employed by a state, such as state police officers or highway patrol officers, cannot be sued in their *official* capacities, however. As noted previously, such suits are just another way of suing the state itself. In *Will v. Michigan Department of State Police* (1989) the Supreme Court held that states are not "persons" as that term is used in Section 1983. Thus, lawsuits against states and against state officers in their *official* capacities are no longer permitted under Section 1983. Remember, though, that state law enforcement officers can be sued under Section 1983 in their *individual* capacities.

Since 1967, the Supreme Court has recognized that police officers have qualified immunity if they are sued under Section 1983 (*Pierson v. Ray*, 1967). This means that if a reasonable police officer believes that a certain course of action is permissible under existing law, then an officer who engages in that course of action will be immune from liability (*Anderson v. Creighton*, 1987). Thus, if a reasonable police officer believes that probable cause exists to make an arrest, then the officer making the arrest will not be liable for damages under Section 1983, even if a court later determines that probable cause did not exist. However, any officer seeking to raise the "good faith" or qualified immunity defense in a Section 1983 lawsuit has the burden of persuading the judge or jury that he or she acted reasonably under the circumstances.

## Liability of Law Enforcement Agencies

Civil lawsuits against police officers used to be filed only against the officers themselves. The current tendency among plaintiffs is to sue the officer and anybody else who allegedly had anything to do with the act, such as the immediate supervisor, the police chief, the agency, or the municipality itself. This strategy is based on the "deep pockets" theory: while the officer may have a "shallow pocket" (his or her resources are limited), the supervisor and department have a "deep pocket" (the supervisor or agency have much greater resources with which to satisfy a judgment).

Law enforcement agencies may be sued and held liable under state tort law or Section 1983. In a typical Section 1983 action against a city or agency, the plaintiff makes the following allegations: (1) that there is or was *policy* promulgated by a city or agency policymaker, or, in the absence of a policy, a custom existed; (2) that the policy or custom caused the *injury* to the plaintiff; and (3) that the injury constituted a *violation* of the plaintiff's constitutional rights.

In *Monell v. Department of Social Services* (1978), the Supreme Court held that municipal liability may be imposed for conduct that "implements or executes a policy statement, ordinance, regulation, or decision officially adopted and promulgated by municipal officers" or if such conduct results from "custom" even though such custom has not received formal approval through official decision-making channels. What constitutes official policy or custom and who is a *policymaker* are questions that have troubled the courts. First, what is official policy or custom?

For a policy to be official, it must be officially adopted and promulgated by the municipality's lawmaking officers or by an official to whom lawmakers have delegated policy-making authority. It may be in the form of law, written regulations, directives, or policy statements by high executive officials (*Grandstaff v. City of Borger*, 1985). Custom, although unwritten, may also constitute official policy. By definition, a custom is not something that has been officially adopted or promulgated by policymakers, but it may be so common and well settled that it can be said to represent official policy.

The terms "official policy" and "custom" have been given various meanings by different courts. One court, for instance, has decided that a county policy established in the sheriff's handbook requiring indiscriminate strip searching of all pretrial detainees was an "official policy" that led to municipal liability (*John Does 1–100 v. Boyd, 1985*). On the other hand, the Supreme Court has ruled that a single act of excessive force by a police officer is insufficient to establish a city policy of failing to adequately train its officers (*Oklahoma City v. Tuttle*, 1985). With regard to custom, the Eighth Circuit Court of Appeals found that a city custom existed of failing to investigate or act on citizen complaints of physical and sexual misconduct by police officers (*Harris v. City of Pagedale*, 1987). In that case, the plaintiff was able to establish the existence of the custom by presenting evidence of several incidents of sexual misconduct by various officers.

Who qualifies as an official policymaker is a question of state law that must be determined by the court *before* the case is submitted to the jury (*Jett v. Dallas Independent School District*, 1989). In *Pembauer v. City of Cincinnati* (1986) four members of United States Supreme Court provided some guidance on who may be considered an official policymaker. In that case, the justices stated that "municipal liability attaches only where the decision maker possesses final authority to establish municipal policy with respect to the action ordered." Justice Brennan gave the example of a county sheriff who has the authority to hire and fire employees but is not the county official responsible for setting employment policy. In that case, the county or sheriff's department would not be liable under Section 1983 if the sheriff improperly fired an employee in violation of the employee's constitutional rights. However, any unconstitutional decision by the sheriff regarding law enforcement matters would give rise to liability because the sheriff possesses final authority over law enforcement activities in the county.

Not every police supervisor falls into the category of policymaker, although the police chief or sheriff probably would. The further down the supervisory chain a police official falls, the less likely it is that the supervisor will be considered an official policymaker. Furthermore, it would be rare for a court to find that a line-level police officer is a policymaker whose actions express official policy.

In addition to agency liability under Section 1983 for official policy, local governments and their law enforcement agencies can also be held liable for failing to adequately train their officers. In *City of Canton v. Harris* (1989) the Supreme Court said that failure to train can be the basis of liability under Section 1983 for cities or municipalities if such failure to train amounts to deliberate indifference. While the Court unanimously agreed that deliberate indifference should be the standard for liability, it did not define with precision what "deliberate indifference" means. However, in 1992 the Court came closer to defining what it meant by deliberate indifference. The Court held that the family of a city worker killed while working in a sewer did not prove that the city failed to properly train its employees because the family members were unable to show that the training standards maintained by the city were "arbitrary" or "conscience-shocking" so as to deprive the deceased city worker of his due process rights under the Fourteenth Amendment (*Collins v. City of Harker Heights*, 1992).

These cases suggests that failure to train claims brought under the Fourteenth Amendment must be particularly egregious before courts will recognize them. For example, in a recent case from Texas, the Fifth Circuit Court of Appeals held that the alleged failure to train must amount to gross negligence before it can be submitted to a jury (*Baker v. Putnal*, 1996). Applying that standard, the court found that the city of Galveston was not grossly negligent in training an officer to use a firearm when the city trained the officer according to written guidelines maintained by the state of Texas and by the Galveston Police Department. In another case, the Eleventh Circuit Court of Appeals ruled that deputies were not improperly trained when they checked a potentially suicidal jail inmate every 15–20 minutes, even though the inmate killed himself between cell checks (*Williams v. Lee County, Alabama*, 1996). The court noted that the deputies had been trained on how to deal with suicidal inmates by a staff training manual and by a video produced by the National Sheriff's Association. The court found that this training did not amount to deliberate indifference and ruled in favor of the county.

Unlike officers who are sued under Section 1983 in their individual capacities, municipalities and local law enforcement agencies cannot assert the defense of "good faith" or qualified immunity. In *Owen v. City of Independence* (1980) the Supreme Court ruled that municipalities have no immunity from damages under Section 1983. Thus, if a plaintiff seeks to hold a law enforcement agency liable for an official policy or custom, the agency cannot claim that it adopted the policy with the reasonable belief that it did not violate existing law. States and state officers sued in their official capacities are not "persons" within the meaning of Section 1983; thus, state police departments and highway patrol agencies cannot be sued under Section 1983.

## Liability of Police Supervisors

There are advantages to including supervisors and departments in a liability lawsuit. First, lower-level officers may not have the financial resources to satisfy a judgment, nor are they in a position to prevent similar future violations by other officers. Second, the chances of financial recovery are enhanced if supervisory personnel are included in the lawsuit. The higher the position of the employee, the closer the plaintiff gets to the deep pockets of the county or state agency. Third, inclusion of the supervisor and agency may create inconsistencies in the legal strategy of the defense, thereby strengthening a plaintiff's claim against one or more of the defendants.

A supervisor may be sued in his or her individual capacity. When a supervisor is sued in an individual capacity, the plaintiff implies that only the supervisor, not the agency, is responsible for what happened. Most plaintiffs prefer to sue the supervisor in his or her official capacity because of the deep pockets theory. In general, a supervisor cannot be held personally liable if the violation was not random or unauthorized but rather resulted from agency or state policy (*James v. Smith*, 1986). If a supervisor is held liable in an official capacity, liability is generally paid by the agency. Conversely, if the agency was not at all at fault or in any way involved in what a supervisor did, then liability belongs to the supervisor alone.

Supervisors in the private sector are often sued based on the legal theory of *respondeat superior*, which literally means "let the master answer." Under this doctrine, the master is responsible for the lack of care by the servant toward those to whom the master owes a duty to use care. Liability attaches if the failure of the servant to use such care occurred in the course of employment. This common-law doctrine does not, however, apply to public employment, because public officials, police supervisors, for example, are not "masters" of their subordinates; instead they are employees who, like their subordinates, serve a common master: the government agency.

Although the respondeat superior doctrine does not apply to public employment, it does apply to sheriffs. This is because, under traditional practice and common law, deputies serve at the discretion of the sheriff and therefore act in the sheriff's name and on his or her behalf. The only exception is when state law modifies this traditional relationship. In some states, such as Mississippi, state law specifically provides for the liability of sheriffs for acts of their deputies. In most counties or local governments, sheriffs are elected directly by the public and are answerable directly to the voters rather than to a council, a board, or an elected official. This is not the case with police chiefs, who obtain their position by appointment.

## Liability to the Public For What Subordinates Do

A supervisor is liable to the public for what he or she does if the supervisor: (1) authorized the act, as when a police chief authorizes the arrest of a suspect without probable cause and without a warrant; (2) participated in the act, as when a police chief takes part in the illegal arrest of a suspect; (3) directed the act, as when a police chief directs his officers to search an apartment without probable cause and without a warrant; (4) ratified the act, as when a police chief later learns of an illegal act committed by a subordinate and approves of it; (5) was present at the time the act was committed and could have prevented but failed to do so, as when a police chief fails to stop the beating of a suspect in his or her presence; and/or (6) created the policy of custom under which the unconstitutional practices occurred, as when a police chief issues an unconstitutional policy directive. In all of these instances, however, the supervisor has some direct participation in the act. There are instances, however, when the supervisor may not be directly involved in the act but can be sued anyway because of what his or her subordinates do. An example would be if a supervisor was grossly negligent in managing the subordinates who engaged in the unlawful conduct, as when a sergeant fails to supervise the line-level officers handling a major incident.

In general, supervisors may be liable in Section 1983 cases only if there is an "affirmative link" between the plaintiff's injury and the action or inaction of the supervisor. For instance, a supervisor may be liable for negligent failure to train if there an affirmative link between the injury caused by the subordinate and the lack of training. If an innocent bystander, for example, is seriously wounded because of the negligent shooting by the police of a crime suspect, the bystander can possibly recover damages if he or she proved that the officer who fired the shot had not been properly trained by the officer's supervisor.

Supervisory liability stemming from negligence is one of the most frequently litigated areas of liability and therefore merits extended discussion. Negligence, for purposes of tort liability, may be simple or gross. Simple negligence generally means an absence of that degree of care and vigilance that persons of extraordinary prudence and foresight are accustomed to using. Stated differently, simple negligence is a failure to exercise great care. In contrast, gross negligence means failure to exercise ordinary care or that care which a careless person would use under the circumstances. For example, driving 60 miles an hour on a 55-mile-an-hour highway may be simple negligence, but driving 100 miles an hour may come under the category of gross negligence. Most courts require at least gross negligence or deliberate indifference to establish supervisory liability (Nahmod, 1986). The problem, however, is that the difference between simple negligence and gross negligence is one of degree and is not always easy to ascertain. What is simple negligence to one judge or jury might be gross negligence to another.

Current case law indicates that there are seven general areas from which supervisory liability based on negligence may arise: (1) negligent failure to train; (2) negligent hiring; (3) negligent assignment; (4) negligent failure to supervise; (5) negligent failure to direct; (6) negligent entrustment; and (7) negligent failure to investigate or discipline. These areas of supervisory liability are not mutually exclusive, meaning that they overlap. In fact, plaintiffs often allege two or more areas in the same complaint and leave it to the court or judge to determine the grounds for liability. For example, it is not unusual for a plaintiff who files a case based on police use of deadly force to allege that the supervisor should also be held liable for negligent failure to train, supervise, direct, hire, or entrust. In many cases, plaintiffs allege negligence in all seven areas in the hope that some, if not all, can be proven by the facts presented during the trial.

As stated previously, civil liability cases may be brought under state tort law and/or Section 1983. It is clear that a lawsuit for supervisory negligence may be brought under state tort law, negligence being a category of state tort. Controversy, however, surrounds the issue of whether supervisory liability for negligence can be brought under Section 1983. Some lower courts say that liability exists, others say it does not. The United States Supreme Court has said that inadequate police training may serve as the basis for municipal liability under Section 1983, but only if the failure to train amounts to deliberate indifference to the rights of persons with whom the police come in contact and the deficiency in the training program is closely related to the injury suffered (*City of Canton v. Harris*, 1989). Lower courts interpreting the *Harris* decision seem to require a showing of gross negligence on the part of the police before allowing the case to be heard by a jury.

**Negligent failure to train.** Negligent failure to train has generated a spate of lawsuits under state tort law and Section 1983. As early as 1955, a state court entertained tort action for monetary damages resulting from improper or negligent training (*Meistinsky v. City of New York*, 1955). The actual allegation in these cases is that the employee has not been inducted or trained properly by the supervisor or agency and thus lacks the skills, knowledge, or competence required of him or her in the job. The administrative agency and the supervisor share a responsibility to train employees, and failure to discharge this obligation subjects the supervisor and agency to liability if it can be proved that the violation at issue was the result of failure to train or improper training (*Owens v. Haas*, 1979).

In *Rymer v. Davis* (1985), the Sixth Circuit Court of Appeals upheld a judgment of $82,000 against the police officer and $25,000 against the city for deprivation of rights arising from injuries sustained during an arrest. In this case, the police officer beat and kicked the plaintiff violently during the arrest. The arrestee was treated by an emergency medical technician, who recommended that he be taken to a hospital. The officer rejected this recommendation and instead jailed the arrestee for the night. Liability was imposed on the city because the court found the following at the time of the incident:

> The City has no rules or regulations governing its police force. Nor did the City require any pre-employment training. The initial training received by the officers was on-the-job training. Although the City required the officers to complete forty hours of training each year after being hired, none of the training received by Officer Stillwell instructed him on arrest procedures of treatment of injured persons. The City's police officers used their own discretion in the arrest and treatment of persons suspected of criminal activity.

The decision is significant because it suggests the following courses of action police departments must take: (1) A pre-employment training program must be in place; and (2) the training program must focus on the skills needed in policing, including arrest procedures and the treatment of injured persons.

As stated earlier, the United States Supreme Court held in *City of Canton v. Harris* (1989) that failure to train can be the basis of municipal liability under Section 1983. The Court held that cities and municipalities may be held liable for damages if the failure to train is based on deliberate indifference to the rights of those with whom the police come into contact. The court then said that "it may happen that in light of the duties assigned to specific officers or employees the need for more or different training is so obvious, and the inadequacy so likely to result in violation of constitutional rights, that the policymakers of the city can reasonably be said to have been deliberately indifferent to the deed." It would seem to follow that if a municipality can be held liable for failure to train based on deliberate indifference, supervisors could also likely be held liable based on the same standard.

The question supervisors often ask is: Will a single act by a subordinate suffice to make the supervisor liable for failure to train? Although there in no unanimity, most lower courts hold that a pattern must be proved and established for liability to ensue. A single act, therefore, usually does not suffice. The exception is if the act is the result of an agency policy or custom.

To summarize, negligent failure to train has resulted in judgments against supervisors and is perhaps currently the most frequently litigated area in the field of supervisory liability. Supervisors must be aware of the need for proper training. Furthermore, this need must be brought to the attention of policymakers who may also be liable for damages if injury results.

***Negligent hiring.*** The risk of negligent hiring liability increases the importance of proper background investigation prior to employment. Liability ensues when: (1) an employee is unfit for appointment; (2) such unfitness was known to the employer or should have been known through a background investigation; and (3) the employee's act was foreseeable. In *Moon v. Winfield* (1974), the department hired a police officer despite a record of a pre-employment assault conviction, a negative recommendation from a previous employer, and a falsified police application. The officer later assaulted a number of individuals in separate incidents. He and the supervisor were sued and held liable. In *Peters v. Bellinger* (1959), an Illinois court held a city liable for the actions of a police officer who was hired despite a felony record and who appeared to have been involved in many street brawls. Liability was based on the complete failure of the agency to conduct a background check prior to the hiring of the applicant.

A case recently decided by the Fifth Circuit sheds light on some aspects of liability for negligent hiring (*Wassum v. City of Bellaire*, 1988). In Wassum, a city police officer who was raped by a fellow police officer brought a civil rights action against the officer, the police chief, and the mayor. The female officer alleged that the city and the police department were negligent in hiring her assailant, Casey, because they failed to verify his entire employment history, they did not require him to undergo a polygraph examination, and they did not subject him to an adequate psychological examination.

The district court held Casey liable in the amount of $1 million in actual damages and $3 million in punitive damages, but the city, the mayor, and the police chief were not held liable. The court conceded that these officials were arguably negligent in their pre-employment screening of Casey, but concluded that they did not act with gross negligence or deliberate indifference, the standard of culpability needed for liability in negligent hiring cases. The failure of the city to administer a polygraph test to screen the applicant was held not to constitute gross negligence. The court said, "While polygraph tests are used with greater frequency today, there is still some question of their efficacy. Some states have prohibited the practice of requiring submission to a polygraph test as a precondition of employment."

On appeal, the Fifth Circuit affirmed the decision of the district court. Regarding the agency's failure to verify Casey's employment record back to age sixteen, as suggested by the Texas Commission on Law Enforcement Officer Standards and Education guidelines, the court concluded that such failure amounted to no more than simple negligence, adding that "failure to follow this recommended screening guideline does not render the city consciously indifferent to the safety of its citizens."

Despite the Fifth Circuit's favorable decisions (for supervisors and agencies) in *Wassum* and *Bullins*, good background investigations are a must for protection against lawsuits in negligent hiring cases. Such investigations can be undertaken in a number of ways, depending on agency resources. Regardless of the method used, background investigations must follow adequate procedures whereby unfit applicants may be identified and rejected.

On April 22, 1996, the United States Supreme Court accepted a case on the issue of negligent hiring. That case involves a ruling by a federal district court, upheld by the Fifth Circuit Court of Appeals, that a county was liable under Section 1983 for a deputy sheriff's violent behavior (causing injury to a woman) when the county "disregarded the man's own police record and tendency toward violence when it hired him" (*New York Times*, p. A15). The narrow issue before the Court is "whether the county's hiring decision, an apparently isolated act that was not part of a larger pattern" and did not by itself violate state law, was sufficient to hold the county legally liable for the woman's injuries under Section 1983. That case will likely be decided soon and should shed further light on the issue of liability for negligent hiring.

***Negligent assignment.*** Negligent assignment is the assigning of an employee to a job without ascertaining employee competence or the keeping of an employee on the job after he or she is known to be unfit. An example would be assigning a reckless driver to drive a government motor vehicle or assigning an officer who has had a history of child molestation to run a weekend camp program for juveniles. A supervisor has an affirmative duty not to assign a subordinate to a position for which he or she in unfit and/or to leave a subordinate in such a position.

In *Moon v. Winfield* (1974), a case mentioned previously under negligent hiring, liability was imposed on the police superintendent for failure to suspend or transfer an errant police officer to a nonsensitive assignment after numerous disciplinary reports had been brought to the supervisor's attention. In *Moon*, the superintendent had five separate misconduct reports before him within a two-week period and also a warning that the officer had been involved in a series of incidents involving mental instability. The court held that supervisory liability ensued because the supervisor had authority to assign or suspend the officer but failed to do so. *Moon* is also a good example of a case where the plaintiffs allege several areas of supervisory negligence in their lawsuit.

In a 1989 case, the First Circuit Court of Appeals held a police supervisor liable under Section 1983 for negligently allowing a violence-prone officer to lead an anti-drug task force (*Gutierrez-Rodriguez v. Cartagena*, 1989). While conducting a drug sweep, plainclothes members of the task force approached a man seated in an automobile with their weapons drawn. When the man attempted to flee, the officers shot him. The court held the supervisor liable because, among other things, he knew of the squad leader's propensity for violence (based on a history of previous complaints) but allowed him to remain as the leader of the task force.

Negligent assignment cases collectively say that supervisors must be aware of the weaknesses and competencies of their subordinates and must not assign them to perform tasks for which they lack skill or competence. If they fail to do so, the supervisors themselves may be held liable for violating a person's constitutional rights.

***Negligent failure to supervise.*** Negligent failure to supervise is the abdication of the responsibility to properly oversee employee activity. An example would be tolerating a pattern of physical abuse of suspects, racial discrimination, or pervasive deprivation of suspects' rights and privileges.

In *Lenard v. Argento* (1983), the Seventh Circuit held that, at a minimum, a plaintiff must show that the supervisory official at least implicitly authorized, approved, or knowingly acquiesced in the unconstitutional conduct of the offending officer. The mere fact that the supervisor, long before attaining his position, had heard rumors that the subordinate officer had shot and injured another person while on duty was not sufficient, according to the court, to establish liability on the part of the supervisor (*Chestnut v. City of Quincy*, 1975).

Tolerating unlawful activities in an agency might constitute deliberate indifference, to which liability attaches. The essential question is: Did the supervisor know of a pattern of behavior but fail to act on it? Also, in Section 1983 cases, failure to supervise leads to liability only if there is a history of widespread abuse (*Brown v. Watkins*, 1982). A related question arises: What constitutes knowledge of a pattern of behavior? Some courts hold that actual knowledge is required, which may be difficult for the plaintiff to prove; others have ruled that knowledge is present if a history of violation is established and the official had direct and close supervisory control over the subordinates who committed the violations.

In one case, the Eleventh Circuit Court of Appeals decided that a supervisor can be held liable for the use of excessive force by a police officer "when a history of widespread abuse puts the responsible supervisor on notice of the need for improved training or supervision, and the official fails to take corrective action." In that case, the plaintiff alleged that the city's public safety director, who was responsible for disciplining police officers and setting departmental policy, was aware of a pattern of police use of excessive force but failed to correct the problem. Such failure resulted in the use of excessive force by a police officer against the plaintiff (*Fundiller v. City of Cooper*, 1985).

In another case, the court said, "A police officer chief who persistently fails to discipline or control subordinates in the face of knowledge of their propensity for improper use of force thereby creates an official custom or de facto policy actionable under Section 1983" (*Skevofilax v. Quigley*, 1984). Thus, the current law on liability for negligent failure to supervise is best summarized as follows:

> To be liable for a pattern of constitutional violations, the supervisor must have known of the pattern and failed to correct or end it . . . Courts hold that a supervisor must be "casually linked" to the pattern by showing that he had knowledge of it and his failure to act amounted to approval and hence tacit encouragement that the pattern continue. (Hardy & Weeks, 1980, p. 7)

Another writer notes, "The importance of this principle is that supervisors cannot shut their eyes and avoid responsibility for the acts of their associates if they are in a position to take remedial action and do nothing" (Palmer, 1980, p. 24).

**Negligent failure to direct.** Negligent failure to direct is the failure to inform employees of the specific requirements and proper limits on the job to be performed. An example would be the failure by a supervisor to inform an officer of the proper limits of the use of deadly force or the allowable scope of searches after arrest. In *Ford v. Brier* (1974), the district court held that the supervisor's failure to establish policies and guidelines concerning the procurement of search warrants and the execution of various departmental operations made him vicariously liable for the accidental shooting death of a young girl by a police officer. In another case, *Dewell v. Lawson* (1974), the failure to direct consisted in the chief's negligence in establishing procedures for the diabetic diagnosis and treatment of jail inmates. The suspect, detained for public drunkenness, experienced a diabetic reaction that resulted in a diabetic coma, a stroke, and brain damage. The jailer did not recognize this condition and therefore failed to provide for proper medical care; the result was death. Liability was assessed for negligent failure to direct.

**Negligent entrustment.** Negligent entrustment is failure of a supervisor to properly supervise or control an employee's custody, use, or supervision of equipment or facilities entrusted to him or her on the job. An example would be the failure to supervise the use of vehicles and firearms resulting in death or serious injury to a member of the public. Negligent entrustment differs from negligent assignment in that it concerns not overall employee competence, but specifically competence in the handling of hardware, equipment, or facilities, such as a gun or a motor vehicle.

In *Roberts v. Williams* (1971), an untrained but trustworthy guard was given a shotgun and the task of guarding a work crew by a convict farm superintendent. The shotgun discharged accidentally, seriously wounding an inmate. The court held the warden liable based on his negligence in permitting an untrained person to use a dangerous weapon.

In *McAndrews v. Mularchuck* (1960), a periodically employed reserve patrol officer was entrusted with a firearm without adequate training. He fired a warning shot that killed a boisterous youth who was not armed. The city was held liable in a wrongful death suit. Courts have also held that supervisors have a duty to supervise errant off-duty officers where the officers had property, guns, or nightsticks belonging to a government agency.

The test of liability for negligent entrustment is deliberate indifference. The plaintiff must be able to prove that the officer was incompetent, unexperienced, or reckless and that the supervisor knew or had reason to know of the officer's incompetence. The supervisor's best defense in these cases is to show that there had been proper supervision and training concerning use and custody of equipment and that the act occurred despite adequate precautions.

**Negligent failure to investigate or discipline.** Negligent failure to investigate or discipline is the failure on the part of the supervisor to look into complaints and take proper action when needed. In one case, the court said that when it can be shown that supervisors are aware of the dangerous tendencies of an officer but do nothing to correct the problem, the supervisors retain that officer in that job at their own risk (*Sims v. Adams*, 1976).

A supervisor has an affirmative duty to take all the necessary and proper steps to discipline and/or terminate a subordinate who is obviously unfit for service. Unfitness can be determined either from acts of prior gross misconduct or from a series of prior acts of lesser misconduct indicating a pattern. Knowledge of fitness may be actual or presumed.

In a recent case, the Fourth Circuit Court of Appeals held that a plaintiff in a Section 1983 lawsuit had presented sufficient evidence to allow the case to proceed to the jury on the question of whether a highway patrol sergeant should be held liable for failing to take corrective action against a state trooper (*Shaw v. Stroud*, 1994). In the *Shaw* case, a North Carolina state trooper shot and killed a man while attempting to arrest him for driving under the influence. The trooper had been the subject of numerous citizen complaints alleging that he had used excessive force. Although the trooper's sergeant was aware of these complaints, he did nothing to investigate the allegations or to ensure that the trooper did not commit acts of excessive force in the future. The court of appeals held that the evidence of the supervisor's negligence was sufficient to be submitted to the jury for a decision on whether the sergeant should be held liable for contributing to a man's death by failing to take disciplinary action against the trooper based on his past history of misconduct.

Supervisory liability also may be found if the agency's disciplinary system is inadequate. In the *Gutierrez-Rodriguez* case discussed previously under negligent assignment, the head of the police department disciplinary system was held personally liable as a supervisor because the court found the system to be grossly deficient as to reflect a reckless and callous indifference to the rights of the citizens (*Gutierrez-Rodriguez v. Cartagena*, 1989). Specifically, the court found the following procedures to be inadequate: (1) the officers investigated could refuse to testify or give a statement; (2) the complaining members of the public had to go to the police station if they were to give sworn written statements about police misconduct; (3) the agency did not have any provision for remedial training as one of the disciplinary options; (4) the withdrawal of a complaint closed the internal investigation without the agency doing anything about it; and (5) the immediate supervisors of the officers were not at all involved in the disciplinary process. This case indicates that a department must have clear disciplinary procedures and that these procedures must be adequate and proper, not just in terms of protecting the rights of the police officers involved, but also in terms of protecting the rights of the general public.

Proper investigation of any and all complaints against subordinates is needed if a supervisor is to successfully raise a defense. For example, in *Hogan v. Franco* (1995), a federal district court held a police chief liable for failing to thoroughly investigate a complaint by an arrestee that he had been physically abused. The court found that the internal investigative procedures instituted by the chief were biased in favor of the agency, and thus the chief allowed cursory investigations to occur. Although not all investigations need to be formal or time consuming, they must be thorough and accurate. The type of investigation required and the procedure to be followed should be defined by the agency policy or the agency manual. The result of the investigation must be properly documented by the supervisor. Documentation can range from a brief entry in the personal record of the officer to a more extensive record of the internal investigation entered in the subordinate's file.

## Conclusion

Civil liability of law enforcement officers and their agencies will continue to be a problem and a topic of debate into the foreseeable future. A 1986 survey of police chiefs from the 20 largest cities and dozens of other municipalities with populations over 100,000 revealed that most of the police chiefs, their officers, and their agencies have been sued in the past and expect to be sued in the future (McCoy, 1987). In Houston, Texas, the number of complaints alleging police misconduct soared by 245 percent between 1980 and 1985 (*Houston Chronicle*, 1986).

Nevertheless, despite the apparent increase in lawsuits against police, most are unsuccessful. Because of the Supreme Court's recent decision that states are not "persons" amenable to lawsuits under Section 1983, its rules relating to the deliberate indifference standard, and the doctrine of qualified immunity, police officers today enjoy a greater level of protection from federal civil liability than in the past. Furthermore, even in state tort suits, police often fare well with juries who have little sympathy for those who sue the police, many of whom are perceived to have engaged in criminal activity at the time the police allegedly violated their rights.

As the sheer number of lawsuits against the police increases, however, the number of successful lawsuits will likely increase as well. Despite the social costs of holding law enforcement officers civilly liable for their misdeeds, lawsuits against police serve the useful functions of helping to reduce incidents of misconduct and holding the police more accountable to the public. After all, accountability to the public is central to the practice of policing a free society. The bottom line is that police officers and administrators must be aware of the type of conduct that may trigger a lawsuit and what legal standards must be followed to avoid liability.

## References

*Anderson v. Creighton*, 483 U.S. 635 (1987).
*Baker v. Putnal*, 75 F. 3d 190 (5th Cir. 1996).
*Bivens v. Six Unknown Agents of the Federal Bureau of Narcotics*, 403 U.S. 388 (1971).
*Brown v. Watkins*, 669 F.2d 979 (5th Cir.. 1982).
*Chestnut v. City of Quincy*, 513 F.2d 91 (5th Cir. 1975).
*City of Canton v. Harris*, 489 U.S. 378 (1989).
*Collins v. City of Harker Heights*, 530 U.S. 115 (1992).

*Dewell v. Lawson*, 489 F.2d 877 (10th Cir. 1974).

*Estelle v. Gamble*, 429 U.S. 97 (1976).

*Fargo v. San Juan Bautista*, 857 F.2d 638 (9th Cir. 1988).

Fontana, V. (1990). *Municipal liability: Law and practice*. New York: Wiley.

*Ford v. Brier*, 383 F. Supp. 505 (E.D. Wis. 1974).

*Fundiller v. City of Cooper*, 777 F.2d 1436 (11th Cir.1985).

*Graham v. Connor*, 490 U.S. 386 (1989).

*Grandstaff v. City of Borger*, 767 F.2d 161 (5th Cir. 1985).

*Gutierrez-Rodriguez v. Cartagena*, 882 F.2d 553 (1st Cir. 1989).

Hardy, P. & Weeks, J. (1980). *Personal liability of public officials under federal law*. Unpublished manuscript.

*Harris v. City of Pagedale*, 821 F.2d 499 (8th Cir. 1987).

*Hogan v. Franco*, 896 F. Supp. 1313 (N.D.N.Y. 1995).

*Houston Chronicle*. (1986, August 8), p. 1.

*Hudson v. McMillian*, 112 S. Ct. 995 (1992).

*James v. Smith*, 784 F.2d 149 (2d Cir. 1986).

*Jenkins v. Averett*, 424 F.2d 1228 (4th Cir. 1970).

*Jett v. Dallas Independent School District*, 491 U.S. 701 (1989).

*John Does 1–100 v. Boyd*, 613 F. Supp. 1514 (D. Minn. 1985).

*Kentucky v. Graham*, 473 U.S. 159 (1985).

*Lenard v. Argento*, 699 2d 874 (7th Cir. 1983).

*McAndrews v. Mularchuck*, 162 A. 2d 820 (N.J. 1960).

McCoy, C. (1987, January 19). Police liability is not a crisis. *Crime Control Digest*, p. 1.

*McIntosh v. Arkansas Republican Party-Frank White Election Committee*, 856 F.2d 1185 (8th Cir. 1987).

*Meistinsky v. City of New York*, 140 N.Y.S. 2d 212 (1955).

*Monell v. Department of Social Services*, 436 U.S. 658 (1978).

*Monroe v. Pape*, 365 U.S. 167 (1961).

*Moon v. Winfield*, 383 F. Supp.31 (N.D. Ill. 1974).

Nahmod, S. (1986). *Civil rights and civil liberties litigation* (2d ed.). New York: Shephard's McGraw-Hill.

*New York Times*. (1996, April 23), p. A15.

*Nishiyama v. Dickson County*, 814 F.2d 277 (6th Cir. 1987).

*Oklahoma City v. Tuttle*, 471 U.S. 808 (1985).

*Owen v. City of Independence*, 445 U.S. 622 (1980).

*Owens v. Haas*, 601 F.2d 1242 (2nd Cir. 1979).

Palmer, J. (1980). *Civil liability of correctional workers*. Unpublished manuscript.

*Pembauer v. City of Cincinnati*, 475 U.S. 469 (1986).

*Peters v. Bellinger*, 159 N.E. 2d 528 (Ill.App. 1959).

*Pierson v. Ray*, 386 U.S. 547 (1967).

*Roberts v. Williams*, 356 F.2d 819 (5th Cir. 1971).

*Rymer v. Davis*, 754 F.2d 198 (6th Cir. 1985).

*Shaw v. Stroud*, 13 F. 3d 791 (4th Cir. 1994).

*Sims v. Adams*, 537 F. 2d 829 (5th Cir. 1976).

*Skevofilax v. Quigley*, 586 F. Supp. 532 (D.N.J. 1984).

*Stubbs v. Dudley*, 849 F.2d 83 (2d Cir. 1988).

*Ward v. San Diego County*, 791 F.2d 1329 (9th Cir. 1986), *cert. denied sub nom. Duffy v. Ward*, 483 U.S. 1020 (1987).

*Wassum v. City of Bellaire*, 861 F 2d 453 (5th Cir. 1988).

*Will v. Michigan Department of State Police*, 491 U.S. 58 (1989).

*Williams v. Lee County, Alabama*, 78 F. 3d 491 (11th Cir. 1996).

# 14

# Traditional and Innovative Police Responses to Domestic Violence

*Eve S. Buzawa*
*Carl G. Buzawa*

When we discuss the police response to domestic violence, we acknowledge that few areas of policing have exhibited as much change and remain as controversial as does the police response to domestic violence. Partially due to the process of change as well as to the controversies, the particular style of policing used by different officers within a department and certainly between departments varies to a far greater extent than before. "Model" pro-intervention policies and practices exist in uneasy juxtaposition with a traditional non-activist response even if "official" policies read similarly. In this article, we will explore both the continuing themes of police response and the dynamics of change.

## Traditional Policing

The traditional police response to domestic violence had several characteristics: few domestic violence cases were formally addressed by the criminal justice system, with the majority "screened out"; police avoided intervention in most cases resulting in a perfunctory job; and there was a strong, sometimes overwhelming, bias against arrests.

### Case Screening

Researchers know that historically only a minority of domestic assaults among intimates resulted in the dispatch of police officers due to screening by victims and bystanders (lowered demand) and due to explicit police decisions.

While estimates varied widely, research generally confirmed that historically less than 10 percent of domestic violence incidents were ever reported to the police. Even at present, most research finds calls to the police regarding domestic violence remain atypical in most communities.

Prepared especially for *Critical Issues in Policing*, 3/E by Eve S. Buzawa and Carl G. Buzawa.

Furthermore, the minority that chose to call the police did not truly reflect the widespread nature of domestic violence. For example, non-participants (witnesses) who called had their own motivations (i.e., quieting noisy altercations rather than stopping actual violence). As a result, violence among acquaintances or strangers, more likely to be committed in public, was far more likely to be observed than those involving married or currently cohabiting adults. Neighbors and other bystanders tended not to report such occurrences since family disputes were often viewed from the stigma of being a "problem family" and/or viewed as an expected and annoying, or at times even entertaining, neighborhood distraction. However, when it was reported, it was more likely in lower socioeconomic neighborhoods where the close proximity of living made these situations more observable to outsiders and where there was a tradition of calling the police.

Victims had their own bias; middle- and upper-income victims of spouse abuse reported a far lower percentage of domestic violence cases to the police, due in part to the social distance between the police and these communities, the shame at involving the police in family problems and the real factor of economic dependence of women without their own careers. Hence, while domestic violence appears to exist in all classes, even if more commonly in lower classes (Moore, 1996), violence in the higher economic groups was more likely to be handled by doctors, the clergy or other family members. The police were associated with crime control and the "lower" classes and were "known" to be organizationally unsympathetic to such complaints.

Reluctance to call the police occurred regardless of the severity of violence. One study reported that only 10 percent of cases involving serious injury were reported, not much different than among those with slight or no injuries. Another recent study of police and emergency room cases found that the most severe cases of violence resulted in demands for medical rather than police assistance. These "medical" cases were not customarily reported to the police. Clearly, the net effect was that traditionally police/citizen encounters were a rarity, being relegated to a small minority of potentially reportable incidents.

Of equal significance, police historically reduced their domestic assault caseloads even further. Cases were excluded by dispatcher call screening and the neutral technology of call prioritization. Thus, many assaults, even those constituting a felony by anyone's definition, were re-categorized as minor "family trouble calls." Consequently, the caller was discouraged from demanding a police response and instead diverted out of the system. They would be referred to social service agencies or incorrectly told that the police could not provide assistance for "marital" conflicts. If police intervention was still requested, dispatch would occur only when time permitted, often hours later. One study found, in a sample of cases, over two-thirds of domestic violence cases were "solved" without dispatch of officers. While formally condemned, this practice was unofficially accepted and well documented. While the police might be singled out for their failure to protect victims of crime, this inattention was a reflection of the then generally pervasive lack of societal concern. At that time domestic violence was "known" to be a problem of the "lower classes" and minority groups, so no one seemed to care. The police could—and did—short-change domestic violence victims without fear of adverse consequences.

## Police Avoided Intervention

Research exploring police attitudes has consistently shown that most police officers, regardless of individual or department characteristics, historically (and to a lesser extent to this date) strongly dislike responding to domestic violence incidents. Several reasons explain this reluctance: organizational impediments to adequate performance; lack of sufficient/sophisticated training; cynicism as to efficacy of the response, a belief that such calls are not "real" policing; and finally, somewhat excessive worries over officer safety.

***Organizational impediments.*** Until successive waves of reform legislation were enacted in the 1970s and early 1980s, virtually all states limited police arrest powers in cases of misdemeanor assaults, including domestic violence cases. Unless police actually witnessed the incident, they could not make a warrantless arrest. This single factor severely limited responses. Domestic violence assaults—absent homicide—are typically misdemeanors. This remains true regardless of extent of injury or use of weapons. Due to this restriction on responding to misdemeanor assaults, few arrests and little effective action could be taken since most offenders retained enough self-control to avoid continuing to batter the victim in the officer's presence. As a result, many police believed that their role was peripheral, being restricted to a perfunctory, service-oriented call (to separate the parties) rather than actual law enforcement with arrest as a realistic outcome.

Another major organizational impediment to effective action, at least for large police departments, was that information systems historically did not effectively inform responding officers of an offender's prior history of assault. Because record systems were not well organized nor computerized, large departments often had little ability to differentiate between first offenders and hard core recidivists—unlike the "rap sheets" distributed for repeat offenders for felonies and certain other offenses. As a result, police tended to treat all offenses as isolated occurrences.

Finally, the number and distribution of these calls posed a significant challenge to police resources. Apart from traffic and code enforcement actions, domestic violence calls typically constitute the single largest category of complaints in many cities. Domestic violence typically occurs during the weekend evenings when other calls—including substance abuse related offenses such as drunk driving, bar fights, gang incidents, loud parties, crimes including breaking and entering, robberies and certain other assaults—put major organizational demands on police time.

*Lack of training.* Independently of organizational and legal issues, police also have not been well trained to cope with domestic violence incidents. In many cases, police had profound ignorance of the proper methods of handling domestic violence cases. In fact, in one sample, over 50 percent of the officers did not even know probable cause requirements for domestic violence related assault (Ford, 1987).

*Police attitudes.* It has long been known that police are cynical toward the public and the impact of their intervention, particularly in social service type calls (Manning, 1977). This attitude is especially relevant to domestic violence cases. Responses to traditional law enforcement and even code violations demand certain fairly routinized behavior. In sharp contrast, the skills of handling a dynamic and potentially volatile intervention among intimates requires both specialized skills and a willingness to expend considerable effort. Neither are especially likely if the officer is cynical and believes no positive outcome is likely.

Officers quickly decide that, from their perspective, not all victims give a complete or honest account of the situation, thus reinforcing police tendencies to be wary and skeptical. This leads officers to define their role in domestic violence cases not in terms of "enforcing the law" but in terms of "handling the situation." Class issues reinforced such cynicism. Research has shown that when police confront members of the lower economic classes and/or minorities of any class, they often tend to act in a bureaucratic, impersonal, authoritarian fashion, and they are unlikely to show compassion toward victims. To some extent, this may be due to global racist and class assumptions about the lives and mores of those policed.

For example, many interviewed officers will readily state that violence is a "normal part of the lives of the lower class." The implication is that domestic problems are a logical outgrowth of this environment. Defining such behavior as "normal" in the participant's lives means that the officers become less willing to aggressively intervene in a cycle of violence and are more inclined to "manage" the dispute to avoid more "serious" public breaches of peace. From this perspective, it is far preferable to an officer to temporarily calm down a situation rather than to attempt to resolve underlying conflict or to treat violence as a criminal activity.

General cynicism is compounded by specific feelings of the police toward violence between intimates. Risking overgeneralization, they tended to believe that intervention in such affairs was not their proper responsibility nor even wholly appropriate. They tended to be uncomfortable with social-work tasks and greatly preferred law enforcement. An arrest of an offender for a domestic assault charge was simply a "garbage arrest" similar to "drunk and disorderly." It was even worse when no arrest resulted even if a potential crisis was diffused. This was of little value to an officer's self image as a "crime fighter" or, in fact, to his or her career where acts of heroism and/or "significant arrests" might distinguish the officer for promotion.

*Fear of Injury.* To this day, police view responding to "domestics" as being particularly dangerous. Many officer deaths and serious injuries have occurred during family violence calls. Anecdotal evidence of unprovoked attacks by offenders and "unappreciative" victims are legion among almost all departments.

This is explainable—almost no other source of injury is as unpredictable or as personally outrageous as being assaulted when responding to a call for help in a domestic case. Resistance might be expected from an offender; after all, "power" in what he may consider to be "his castle" is being externally challenged. However, officers say that when they try to interview the person they came to help, victims often "turn" against them or, at best, show no interest in pressing charges.

For many years, the FBI reinforced such beliefs by publishing annual reports to "show" that "disturbance calls" were among the most common sources of officer death. However, this has been seriously questioned. A 1988 report sponsored by the National Institute of Justice found rates of police injury were overstated by three times in prior FBI reports due to the then current practice of lumping together all "disturbance" calls (e.g., including "domestics" with gang fights, bar brawls, etc.). When this obvious disparity was removed, the rate of officer deaths declined markedly. Despite this report, police to this date emphatically believe that responding to domestic violence cases is very dangerous, especially if they have to make an arrest.

## Police Did Not Make Arrests

Viewed in isolation and without knowledge of past practices, one might suppose a high rate of arrest for cases of domestic assault. After all, there is a known victim, usually with an apparent, often severe, injury. Since the offender is known, apprehension is relatively straightforward. Historically, such activism did not occur. Instead, the closer the relationship between victim and offender, the less likely an arrest would be made.

There are varied reasons for reluctance to arrest. Police departments generally discourage arrests for certain offenses since they force a further diversion of scarce resources, including not only the extra time spent by the officer, but also by booking sergeants, lock-up personnel, and the time needed for court appearances. In the past, it was difficult to organizationally justify an arrest as it involved a low-status misdemeanor with relatively poor chances of conviction.

Many victim advocates have argued that the failure to arrest in domestic violence cases simply validates the claim that police do not care about female victims of violence (Lerman, 1981; Stanko, 1989; and Ferraro, 1989). Police researchers are generally less surprised. They note the inherent difficulties to face in making unpopular arrests, especially in the context of increasing demands on police with decreasing resources. Confronted with political pressure to handle an "epidemic" of drugs, drunk driving, street violence and other public disorder offenses, their role in less notorious crimes is defined by societal input and demand. Organization-ally, past societal and consequently legal definitions of domestic violence as a misdemeanor impacted on the police interpretation of appropriate priorities in making arrests.

The above analysis also assumes implicitly that police departments disproportionately fail to make domestic violence arrests. This assumption has itself been debated. On the other hand, in a review of past research, Elliott (1989) found that arrest rates for non-family assaults were not sig-nificantly greater than rates for domestic assaults. Before reaching the con-clusion that police are equally unlikely to arrest for stranger assault, a variety of other factors need to be considered such as seriousness of injury, and perhaps most importantly, whether the reason for failure to arrest in stranger assault (unlike domestic cases) is simply that in the majority of cases the assailant cannot be identified or located! Nonetheless, the result is that arrest is simply not an option exercised by the police with great fre-quency in *any* normal assault absent very serious injury. In any case, in many police departments, stranger assaults may led to arrests more often than violence among intimates. To justify this discrepancy, officers simply denigrated the extent of the injuries observed in a domestic case or the vic-tim attitude and/or termed the incident a misdemeanor disturbance instead of a felony.

In contrast, we believe that victim preferences for arrest were often ignored far more often in domestic assault than in stranger assaults. In several studies conducted by the authors, we found that some departments clearly differentiated between incidents involving strangers, acquaintan-ces, and intimates in their reporting and arrest practices. Using police reports (biased in their favor) and controlling for victim injury and victim preference for arrest, we found there was a far higher probability of making an arrest in stranger assaults (as much as 3.5 times more likely) with far fewer arrests in assaults between intimates. Not surprisingly, assault between acquaintances fell in the middle of this continuum, showing a clear inverse correlation between victim/offender relationships and the police decision to arrest. It is interesting that a content analysis of the reports confirmed that officers perceived domestic violence cases differ-ently, and less seriously, than other assaults. This result was found in recent years after reform legislation had been passed actually *favoring* or mandating arrest in domestic violence situations (Buzawa and Austin, 1993; Buzawa and Buzawa, 1996).

**When arrests have occurred.** Historically, when arrests were made, they were not the result of a reasoned application of textbook law and procedure. In fact, research shows only a weak correlation between the extent of victim injury and other factors usually relevant to police deci-sions to arrest. Instead, in common with other relatively minor offenses, specific factors predominate in the decision to arrest: how the police and offender interacted, how police perceived the victim's conduct and police "organizational" issues.

Most studies appear to show that the primary influence of the offender on the officer's decision to arrest is what he does *after* the officer arrives. If disrespectful or still violent in the officer's presence, this implies a threat to the officer's ability to control the situation. Arrest then becomes a vehicle to assert police authority rather than to protect a victim from future assaults or vindicate her rights. The victim also directly or indirectly strongly influences arrest decisions. Her preference was critical since she was in the best position to state her rights and her cooperation was essential to successful prosecution. As a result, some studies have shown that victim preference was a de facto prerequisite to arrest.[1]

Interaction with the victim also effects arrest rates in other, more troublesome ways. Police regularly judge the conduct of the citizens with whom they interact. This discretion is necessitated by their occupationally ambiguous and potentially dangerous environment. However, in the context of domestic violence, police may judge the victim's overall conduct inappropriate. For such cases, the officer may believe her injuries did not justify an arrest. When the victim lives with her assailant, arrests are less common because the police viewed the victim's conduct as "demonstrating" that she was not really seriously harmed while also limiting the probability that arrests would lead to successful prosecution. Similarly, arrests were unlikely if the victim acted in a manner which in some way offends the officers. Hence, if she was an "unfaithful spouse" or if she attacked the offender, officers seldom made arrests.

If the victim remained "rational," "undemanding" and very deferential to the police, in short a "good" woman, they awarded her preferences far more weight in the decision to arrest. Conversely, we found that when the victim was disruptive, intoxicated or verbally demanding or abusive toward the officers, she was virtually ignored. Finally, a few studies have reported the impact of organizational factors having no relationship to the offense itself and often unknown to the public. For example, arrests appear less likely to be made during particularly busy periods or at the end of an officer's shift.

## Why Has Change Occurred?

After the existence of relatively stable policies of police inaction, sudden and profound change has swept departments throughout the country. Commencing with pioneer legislation enacted in 1977 in Pennsylvania, all states and the District of Columbia have passed domestic violence reforms. Arrests are encouraged for domestic assaults (or even "mandated" in many recent laws), new statutory specific "domestic violence" offenses were incorporated into the criminal code and were passed, and protective or restraining orders (TROs) became available. While many provisions merely encouraged police action, real impediments were removed. For the first time, most statutes allowed warrantless arrests for domestic violence related assaults even though unwitnessed by police. In conformity with this statutory direction, most departments officially changed their policies.

It would be simplistic to assert that any particular factor itself accounted for the shift in official policies. In part, this change was a logical extension of an overall trend to criminalize deviance. While illegal for many years, domestic violence and many other inappropriate actions had been tacitly tolerated because of failure to rigorously enforce existing laws. As society has become more conservative and punitive toward offenders, efforts to rehabilitate have been discredited while punitive solutions are emphasized. For example, drug offenders and youthful offender programs have been dropped or not adequately funded in favor of trying addicts as criminals and juveniles as adult offenders. Drunk drivers are being prosecuted at unprecedented rates. In this context, battered women advocates, policymakers and researchers have emphasized the criminal context of a domestic assailant's actions and deride as wholly inappropriate or sexist any attempt to promote conflict mediation or other actions short of formal arrest and prosecution. In this climate, it is not surprising that an abortive reform movement of the 1970s emphasizing conflict resolution and offender rehabilitation using specialized "crisis intervention units" was quietly abandoned in favor of arrest-oriented policing.

The orientation toward punishment is also due to the theoretical assumption that arrests will somehow "deter" future assaults. Deterrence theory suggests that a police action such as arrest may be justified even if a subsequent conviction is unlikely, if it deters the offender (or other potential offenders) from future assaults. Hence, the ability of the police to "shame" the offender or hold him to public scorn by arrest is potentially useful to modify future behavior. The societal good therefore became in itself a valid justification for making domestic violence arrests (Sherman and Berk, 1984).

It is interesting that academics, often staunchly liberal in other contexts, and many feminists failed to find anything distressing about using the police in this manner. While the police as an institution are often deeply mistrusted by these same people, they largely endorsed changes that increased police involvement in intimate disputes and family violence without allocating additional resources for training or even demanding a commitment from other institutions to prosecute and then hopefully rehabilitate some offenders. Evidence was ignored that suggested such statutes were used far more frequently against minorities and disadvantaged males than other offenders, and largely not at all against the middle-class, "respectful" or "respectable" white males.

Pro-arrest policies also address administrative concerns regarding public reaction and legal repercussions for inaction. As a result of publicity, political pressure on the police has shifted from the previous model of "let the police decide" to an environment where police decisions are rigorously questioned as to their motivations and sufficiency. Political pressure has become a major factor speeding the adoption of pro-arrest practices. Lawsuits have also proliferated addressing the more egregious failure of the police to respond appropriately. In fact, the "clarity" of a mandatory arrest policy (where arrests must be made and police discretion is removed) and its resultant ability to be justified in court may, at least partially, explain why police officials have so eagerly embraced such policies.

While the increased criminalization of offenses, political pressure and fear of lawsuits undoubtedly set the stage for change, the rapidity of change has been startling. In our minds, the immediate catalyst for such action was the "Minneapolis study" (Sherman and Berk, 1984). This study used an experimental research design to "prove" that arrest was far more effective to deter future violence than merely separation of the parties or officer "mediation."

Despite the limited scope of this research and its lack of a theoretical analysis of its findings, it was vigorously promoted by its authors and was cited (often incorrectly) by hundreds of departments and subsequent research papers as justifying or even mandating arrests to "deter" violence. Despite intense publicity and official sponsorship, researchers began to note the incongruity of the Minneapolis results with findings from general criminology and juvenile delinquency studies that simply did not show such deterrent effects of arrest (Elliott, 1991).

While the first wave of pro-arrest policies was based on the MDVE's finding of a deterrent effect of arrest, subsequent research has tended to cast doubt on this relationship. The MDVE Replication Studies discussed in further detail in Zorza and Woods (1994), Bowman (1992), and Buzawa and Buzawa (1996) do appear to demonstrate that the role of arrest itself in treating domestic violence is problematic. Although deterrence may exist for some period of time for some groups (Berk, et al., 1992; Pate & Hamilton, 1992; Sherman, 1992), the results in several of the studies showed little or no reduction or prevention of continuing violence when arrest was isolated as a single variable (Dunford et al., 1989; Hirschel et al., 1991). Perhaps most disturbingly, in one study the group *most* likely to commit severe beatings in the future (the unemployed with a previous criminal history of violent crime) became even *more* likely to commit abuse five months after arrest than those not arrested (Sherman, 1992).

Sherman inferred from such data that arrest simply would be ineffective where the suspect had weak social bonds to the community. In such cases, he predicted that arrest would actually increase violence. We find his position to be as overstated as his earlier position in 1984 of favoring arrest. However, the research in general does continue to point out the necessity of anticipating how a varied group of offenders might respond to a particular sanction (e.g., some may respond as predicted, while others may display wholly different behavior).[2]

The replication studies' results are not surprising to many domestic violence researchers and practitioners. It has already been established that a victim is in greatest danger in the period immediately following separation from the batterer rather than while the victim is living with the batterer. Challenging a batterer who is accustomed to being the more powerful partner often results in immediate anger at having his control challenged. Arrest is perceived as a greater form of confrontation. A violent individual who resorts to abuse as part of a generally violent or criminal lifestyle will not be easily deterred by being locked up for a few hours and then released. Rather, he may become even further enraged, placing the victim in greater danger upon release. Similarly, contact with the criminal justice system may not be unfamiliar, and being arrested yet released after a short time becomes a relatively minor event.

For other offenders, the act of bringing the offender into the purview of the criminal justice system by whatever means (warrantless arrest by the police, arrest subsequent to a warrant or a summons to appear before a court official) may have some long-term effect in recidivism. The possible key may be the criminal justice system's ability to mandate rehabilitation. Hence, an arrested person's exposure to counseling to learn to control anger and substance abuse therapy may account for recidivism differences seen in some, but not all studies. At the same time, there does appear to be a population unresponsive to *any* type of intervention. This might necessitate incapacitation as it would for any other type of dangerous offender.

While the foregoing replication studies en masse and individually were subjected to a thorough methodological critique by Bowman (1992) and Zorza and Woods (1994), they do demonstrate the limited impact of one party's action taken out of context—the arrest made by the police. Clearly, arrest cannot be considered in isolation from other aspects of the criminal justice system or characteristics of the offender. Arrest without long-term involvement does not appear to work as intended. If arrested violators are released without prosecution, they often wrongly conclude that society simply does not care. If prosecutors do not assist victims, pressure ultimately develops for victims to "voluntarily" drop cases. Similarly, prosecutors may decide that they should not use scarce resources if judges fail to treat domestic violence as a serious crime or fail to sentence offenders. In any event, despite the frequent failure to examine the police effort in a systemic context and the lack of agreement as to the ideal police response, virtually all reform legislation and administrative directives have directed police to more aggressively use arrests. Many states now mandate arrest upon the occurrence of certain circumstances or upon violation of newly expanded protective orders (Hart, 1992; Buzawa and Buzawa, 1996).

## Changes in Training

Another area of profound change has been the training given to new officers and in-service personnel. In response to statutory mandates and in recognition that materials were seriously out of date, departments throughout the country have rapidly shifted from curricula that emphasized the futility and danger of intervention to those that stress the essential role of the police within a coordinated program to handle domestic violence.

There is some evidence that real attitudinal change is taking place among those exposed to modern training materials. One experiment simulated how trained officers versus an untrained control group handled domestic incidents. The trained officers performed far more competently in handling the incident and in diffusing its emotional intensity (Buchanan and Perry, 1985).

However, it is presently unclear as to the long-term effect of exposure to training. Many analysts continue to believe that the subculture of policing is highly cynical, maintaining a cohesive and stable (and largely negative) view of their mission and the public that they serve. They say that police tend to dismiss out of hand the results of research that contradicts preconceived attitudes and instead rely on "street" experience. If this is true, then despite training, officers may quickly revert to preconceived attitudes and practices that can successfully circumvent legal and organizational requirements. Training may be overshadowed by: the contradictory pressures of the police organization's paramilitary structure, coupled with an inability to control officer conduct on the street; inability to provide rewards for appropriate behavior; and the retrograde informal "training" that new officers receive from cynical, hardened peers. Finally, many victim advocates believe that the social structure within American society is patriarchal. Unless the criminal justice system is subjected to continuing pressure, it will revert to patriarchal norms that diminish crimes against women. The result is despair about affecting long-term attitudinal change, reinforcing the belief that the only way to effect change is through even more political pressure, restrictive laws, and the potential of lawsuits.

### Violence Against Women Act

Until relatively recently, it could reasonably be stated that the federal response to domestic violence was quite limited. While specific federal funding agencies such as the National Institute of Justice, Centers for Disease Control, and several others funded demonstration projects, experimental and evaluation research, there was little actual legislation that set forth what actions were expected by local law enforcement. This has markedly changed. In 1994, the Violence Against Women Act (VAWA), Title IV of the Violent Crime Control and Law Enforcement Act of 1994, provided extensive funds to local, state, and Indian tribal governments to develop and strengthen post-law enforcement and prosecution strategies to combat violence against women. In addition, moneys were expended for control of sexual assaults, with prime emphasis on enhancing the capabilities of local law enforcement.

Numerous direct grants were distributed to state and local agencies. In fiscal year 1995, $23.5 million were funded. Additional programs provided for enhancements to data collection between departments (e.g., setting up interjurisdictional files on offenders violating protective orders), toll-free hotlines for victims to more effectively seek assistance from police and shelters in rural areas, and direct funding of programs for victims and batterers.

## The Impact of Change

Clearly, there has been a broadening of the structural role of police in domestic violence cases. Increased support exists for formal organizational changes emphasizing proactive policing, especially the use of arrest. A more activist response in training is evident at the national, state and local levels.

What is more problematic is the actual change in "street-level" justice. Most research has examined either the classic patterns of police behavior or, if more recently conducted, the "new" policing. The latter, while having far greater potential to break a cycle of violence, has not reached its full potential. Many departments (and certainly individuals in almost all departments) still believe that the police role in the control of domestic violence should be quite limited. Unless trained, patrol officers remain equivocal about the proper police role in this field. While higher percentages than in the past may acknowledge that a crime has been committed, they remain deeply frustrated by the failure of intervention to lead to immediate change in a family. This often feeds cynicism and a desire to circumvent policies believed to be inappropriate.

Even without empirical data, a pattern may be emerging. Most high-level police officials now willingly embrace pro-arrest policies. However, this is met with various degrees of passive resistance from lower-level supervisors and line personnel. This is not surprising since police administrators historically have often tended to be more progressive (or at least politically responsive) than line personnel. The importance of this dichotomy is that the public often incorrectly assumes street-level behavior reflects the administrative goals and stated policies. In fact, substantial discretion is placed with the line officers. As such, they can be critical obstructions to implementing any new policy. Without attitudinal change, the imposition of new rules and laws sometimes leads to a subversion of policies.

Police literature suggests that in such cases, actual change may be problematic. Official rules, no matter how strict, are difficult to enforce when the usual measure of output—decisions to arrest/not arrest—depends upon an officer's judgment as to proof of injury, probable cause and defenses (such as self-defense). This makes implementation uncertain and fraught with unexpected consequences. For example, one study found that when the Phoenix Police Department first tried to enforce a new presumptive arrest policy (e.g., a policy in which arrest was favored unless other factors overrode this presumed cause of action), the polices were ignored, circumvented or changed almost beyond recognition (Ferraro, 1989).

The increased threat of arrest may also be used *against* the victim as in, "if we receive another call from this house, *both* of you will be arrested." This is not an idle threat. In fact, studies of mandatory arrest laws in both

Oregon and Connecticut found that, at least initially, dual arrest of both parties was very common.

It may be useful to look at what actually happened in one state when a new statute favoring arrest was enacted. Connecticut passed a new law mandating arrest for domestic violence in 1987. In 1989, the Connecticut State Police reported that over 10,000 family violence incidents led to arrests within a six-month period, a figure startlingly high—at least as compared to past practices. However, a study of the implementation of this new Connecticut statute reported that at that time, roughly 20 percent of arrests for family violence were "dual arrest" incidents and, if non-intimate family violence was omitted, about 35 percent of adult intimate violence involved dual arrest. This is especially troubling since for women it was usually the first arrest, even though 43 percent of the women arrested were previously identified in police reports as victims. Not surprisingly, a dual arrest significantly decreased chances of prosecution as victims were obviously effectively coerced to reconcile and mutually drop criminal complaints (Martin, 1994).

## Is Systemic Intervention the Answer?

As a result of the acknowledged problems of trying to change police behavior in a systemic vacuum, a recent trend has been the development of centralized units of police, prosecutors and probation departments to cope with the problems presented by domestic abuse. "Demonstration" or "model" programs have been created in some jurisdictions such as Quincy, Massachusetts; Duluth, Minnesota; and San Diego and Santa Barbara, California. They start with a commitment to organizational excellence by the administrative heads of the affected police, prosecutors' offices, the judiciary and probation departments. Insistence on following up cases is typically mandated by policy and by actual supervisory practices.

There is an attempt to change the attitudes of the officers and caseworkers as well. As such, an essential component is the development and use by both pre-service and in-service officers of modern training programs that emphasize actions required of officers and necessary coordination with other agencies such as shelters, victim advocates and prosecutors. Information systems are developed to directly link offender data, arrest warrants, and outstanding protective orders. Of perhaps equal importance, the phenomenon of victim attrition is directly addressed. Victim support personnel are assigned and/or coordinated by special assignment within prosecutors' offices and somewhat less formally by nongovernmental victim-rights advocates. Offenders are sentenced to intensive probation, often with requirements to attend treatment and/or substance abuse programs.

Evaluation of the effects of such programs is in its early inception. It appears that the programs do seem to lessen subsequent violence among many offenders that are arrested. They probably also deter many others who now believe they may not only be arrested but also prosecuted to conviction if they abuse their mates. Many women with whom we have spoken also feel for the first time that society cares about their problems. As a result, they are much less willing to tolerate abuse of themselves or their children. Even agency personnel feel better about their role because of a tangible output and enhanced prospects for a satisfactory outcome.

In any event, there is certainly little doubt that such efforts pay off in terms of a dramatic increase in arrest rates of offenders. These arrests occur not only at far higher rates after an initial act of abuse but also for violation of a subsequent restraining order forbidding future abuse or even contact. A recent study has documented that 15.4 percent of all restraining-order defendants in one such model jurisdiction were arrested for violating these orders within six months of their issuance (Isaac, 1994) while others presumably violate the orders but are not reported. Another recent study conducted in Quincy, Massachusetts reported that in 1990, out of 663 male restraining order defendants, almost 50 percent re-abused the same victim within two years (Klein, 1994). In all of Massachusetts in 1992, over 6,000 individuals were arrested for violating restraining orders alone. Of these offenders, almost 1,000 entered probation.

This is a message of mixed news. In one sense, the police operate in such jurisdictions in the context of a system that refuses to abandon responsibility when faced with a particularly recalcitrant abuser. In short, our implicit assumption is that criminal justice intervention will dramatically affect the cycle of abuse. On the other hand, there is a core of abusers that are not, and apparently will not, be deterred.

In addition, we are concerned that there may be unintended consequences to victims, offenders, families, and agencies of efforts to rigorously and proactively implement systemic policies of control. These concerns are bolstered both by empirical evidence and observations arising from the Quincy research. In Quincy it has become apparent, from even cursory conversation with key actors in the criminal justice system, that implementation of laws designed to prevent domestic violence has already had substantial consequences, both intended and unintended. Most publicity, as it should, has gone toward the impact that aggressive enforcement has had on certain victims who are far quicker now to engage the system to stop abuse, and on the larger numbers of violent offenders who have either voluntarily stopped abuse or have been incarcerated. By every indication, the community is becoming markedly less tolerant of abuse, and agencies now see their efforts being rewarded through highly visible impact on some victims and their families. Although we readily acknowledge that society should and must aggressively intervene in domestic violence cases, we also must explore whether such intervention efforts lead to tertiary problems which may result in unanticipated consequences to the victim, the offender, the intervening agencies, and society in general.

## Why Unanticipated Consequences Should Be Expected: A Profile of the Batterers

Along with Professors Hotaling and Byrne, and Andrew Klein of the Quincy district court, we are currently examining the process and outcomes of domestic violence abuse in the Quincy District Court (QDC). The QDC has been nationally recognized as a model in the Violence Against Women Act for its integrated response. Few jurisdictions have moved more aggressively to intervene in such cases. It has been featured on *60 Minutes* and in numerous other television and radio programs and newspaper articles and has won a Ford Foundation "Innovations in State and Local Government Award" for its model domestic abuse program. Courts nationwide are currently attempting to emulate QDC. Quincy police arrest 75 percent of abusers when called to the scene of an incidence of domestic abuse. Model police crime scene investigations help ensure successful prosecution without requiring excessive victim involvement. The court itself issues 2,000 restraining orders per year in a jurisdiction of only 250,000 inhabitants. In contrast, in all of New York State in 1987, only 25,000 such orders were issued.

Their district attorney's office has successfully prosecuted 70 percent of domestic violence arrestees. Most offenders are sentenced to probation which is strictly enforced. Each year, it sends about 100 abusers to the county's House of Correction when they re-abuse their victims and/or fail to fulfill their various conditions of probation. Examination of the data in such a "model" setting is informative of the fundamental limits of a system mandating an aggressive criminal justice response. While the research is presently ongoing, data examined to date is certainly suggestive that a certain subset of domestic violence batterers (represented by those that are actually arrested) are a serious group of offenders, not easily deterred from future assaults and prone to retaliate.

Of 277 domestic violence batterers on probation in 1994, 208 of these offenders have been charged with violating probation. Thirty have been sentenced to the House of Correction with an average sentence of three months or less. Excluding defendants held without bail or those unable to meet bail, this represents the majority of QDC domestic violence post-trial commitments. In other words, community-based supervision (probation) is the "going rate" for domestic violence offenses.

We found that domestic violence batterers are the category of offenders most likely to fail *scheduled* drug/alcohol testing, with a non-compliance rate exceeding that of drunk drivers. Clearly, this group does not worry about consequences of failure to comply with court requirements. On a more global basis the vast majority (80 percent) of male batterers had substantial prior criminal records for unrelated and related crimes.

The number of prior crimes charged against them positively correlated with re-abuse over two years. Almost 50 percent of the abusers re-abused their victims over two years as measured by new arrests or the issuance of new restraining orders. Re-abuse correlated with abuser characteristics, not incident or victim characteristics, including whether or not the victim maintained the restraining order or dropped it before its legal termination date. In fact, we believe that any strategy for intervention presents some threat of unanticipated consequences against victims:

1. *Increased violence and harassment.* In certain circumstances, intervention has actually provoked further violence against partners. In at least two reported cases, abusers sentenced to jail have subsequently been indicted for trying to hire hit men to harm the abusers' partners while they remained in jail (see *Commonwealth vs. Phillips*, 1994). Another case was reported where an abuser, held without bail in jail for contacting his partner in violation of a restraining order, used jail phones to call her 228 times over the course of his ten-day stay awaiting trial for the original charges (*Boston Globe*, July, 10, 1994).

2. *Judicial intervention has itself been seized upon as a weapon.* Deterred by criminal court and restraining orders from continuing *physical* abuse of their current partners, there seems to be a growing trend of abusers to seek new vehicles to continue abuse. Child protective agencies and probate courts report that abusers, who previously totally ignored their offspring, suddenly are suing for visitation and custody as a vehicle for abusing, harassing, punishing and even tracking down partners. Abusers are also reporting former partners to state protective agencies for allegations of child neglect and abuse, including ironically, the victim's failure to protect the child from his abuse.

   Similarly, as discussed earlier, the number of abusers seeking restraining orders has increased every year as abusers see judicial offense as the best defense. In the 1980s, there were at most only 10 percent males seeking restraining orders. This proportion has grown to 20 percent (Annual Reports, Mass Trial Court, Boston, 1985–1994). In many cases, they are getting *ex parte* orders even if permanent orders are denied after the woman refutes allegations. Although reversed after the initial ten-day period, the effects of temporary orders on the woman and children are unknown. In a recent homicide case in Lynn, Massachusetts, it was revealed that the alleged murderer had secured two temporary restraining orders against the woman. He eventually stalked and shot her, wounding her and killing both her brother and new boyfriend (*Boston Globe*, December 13, 1995).

3. *Use of batterer treatment programs to reinforce batterer's behavior.* Many treatment programs have reported that batterers form support groups among themselves and exchange ideas about new and more "effective" ways of victimizing the woman. There is some evidence that treatment could actually increase violence against victims (Harrell, 1991). Hence, clinical programs that might be expected to temper violent behavior might instead trigger new (often less sanctioned) forms of intimidation and harassment.

4. *Harassment and stalking of victims*. Harassment as a crime against domestic violence offenders who have left their abusive partners is becoming epidemic. One estimate is that up to 80 percent of offenses related to the new "anti-stalking offenses" arise out of domestic violence situations (Buzawa and Buzawa, 1996). In these cases, stalking becomes the best method of many offenders concerned about prosecution for actual violent episodes. Hence, in Quincy, a visitation center established so that abusive men could visit their children without endangering their children's mothers reported that one of the most common violations of visitation committed by these abusive men is that they illegally extract information from their children about their abused partner's location (Kelleher, 1995). As noted earlier, some abusers will even go so far as soliciting a friend to continue their abuse for them while in jail. Being incarcerated may be perceived by the inmate as insulating himself from further charges of abuse.

5. *Victims are stigmatized*. Victims have been subjected to differential treatment because of their battering. In several cases, women were fired from their jobs because they were endangering employee safety due to a restraining order they had in effect on batterers that stalked or harassed them at work.

6. *Displacement to new victims*. Frequently, when batterers are confronted with a victim willing to initiate criminal justice intervention, they may seek alternate victims who do not disclose abuse. Anger at criminal justice intervention may result in increased danger, not only to the victim but also to other family, friends, or co-workers. In fact, often batterers go to extraordinary efforts to track victims to shelters, friends' homes, or places of employment.

## Unanticipated Consequences for Agencies

1. *Displacement of Resources*. An unintended consequence of enhanced enforcement of policies is that agencies may develop various means to limit demands imposed by these well-meaning policies and statutory directives. As noted earlier, stated policies are always considered discretionary and open to interpretation. To understand the consequences, it is critical to know what the stated policy *is* and how it is carried out. In some cases, police may simply ignore pro-arrest policies. In other departments, police screening of calls may limit organizational demands, even if statutes specify differently.

Although difficult to quantify, strains on resources have inevitably led to a de-emphasis by the police, prosecutors, and courts on other crimes. It has been theorized that police may downgrade or increase call screening on other calls to avoid mandatory processing of an assault. Further, laws in certain jurisdictions have increased local jail population. In addition, the violent nature of these new inmates has created new problems for staff at detention centers and jails. Examining the impact of agency costs solely from the narrowness of an economic perspective parallels the error of focusing on arrest (Institute for Women's Policy Research, 1995). Diversion of resources from other priorities, dissipation of existing initiatives and demoralization of staff can be far more costly than economic costs. For example, mandatory arrest may raise concerns about contradictions with current community policing initiatives, especially in minority and low-income communities. In these communities efforts have been increased to improve citizen encounters, yet mandatory arrest policies have disproportionate impact there.

2. *Violence against police and court personnel.* Violence associated with domestic violence cases has seeped into the courthouse. Court officers now report increased violence inside the courtrooms. A graphic demonstration of this was recently filmed by PBS at a routine bail hearing on an alleged domestic assault in Quincy in order to obtain background tape for a documentary. They were astounded when the cameraman found himself filming the defendant assaulting a bevy of court officers while screaming to his girlfriend, the alleged victim, "I love you."

## Conclusions

We believe it is currently overly simplistic to state that the police do not care or are unresponsive to the needs of domestic violence victims. Many officers and departments now more actively attempt to intervene. They correctly perceive their job to protect the victim and maintain society's goal to prevent violence. However, it is also an overgeneralization to state that police currently do everything possible to handle this pervasive problem. There are clearly many instances where the police continue to respond, if at all, perfunctorily—with the goal of extracting themselves as quickly as possible.

Research instead should acknowledge and build upon the following observations. There has been an almost unprecedented rapid, profound change in policies on domestic violence. Only a decade or so earlier, most departments had explicit policies or guidelines directing officers to separate parties and exit the premises. Within a relatively short time span, official policies have recognized the official role of the police in stemming violence and have undertaken extensive efforts to change deeper, ingrained practices. Responding to prevailing social science research, federal pressure, lawsuits and political pressures from the battered women's movement, many departments have undergone at least two policy changes, including initially setting up crisis intervention/mediation-type efforts and now advancing a pro-arrest policy. These changes have also been reflected in official training materials that now more clearly define the police role in domestic violence intervention. Failure to acknowledge this sets up a "straw man" argument, allowing some writers to continue to critique the police for ideological or political reasons or out of ignorance of real changes.

Nevertheless, it is uncertain how extensive change has been on the street. Studies are contradictory. Some show major increases in rates of arrest and/or other indices of real change; others indicate an apparent resistance to change. We can understand that this may be very disheartening to advocates for battered women, who see the many failures of police intervention and are still on the firing line, helping victims cope with real crises. Being confronted with unresponsive, uncaring officers or departments not unexpectedly reinforces their negative image of the police.

However, those that study implementation of change will recognize that change occurs sporadically, often organization by organization and in some cases with wide gaps within an organization. Some officers readily change their attitudes and behavior immediately. Others are far more skeptical. Still others will never change their attitude but are forced by department pressure, or fear of liability, to begin to change. Finally, one might expect a residual category of officers who, until the day they retire, will always treat domestic violence as a low-priority item.

Street-level change appears sporadic, with some departments having "reformed" their policies to comply with legislative intent of revised statutes. We therefore strongly suggest that future research focus on those factors that have selectively led to change in some organizations while not in others.

The possibility of unintended, adverse consequences to the victim and her family, the police, other agencies, and even the abuser should be explored to determine the extent and depth of such consequences and what methods could be pursued to limit negative impacts while preserving the recognized benefits of a proactive response. From this effort, we would anticipate even further growth of integrated programs with a better understanding of the diverse needs of the population of victims and batterers.

Many questions still remain to be answered—particularly the policy issue of the proper role of arrest, especially in the context of integrated programs. Other questions include:

- What "costs," economic and otherwise, are incurred by departments that use arrest widely?
- Can the phenomena of "dual arrests" be alleviated?
- Can victim preferences in arrest decisions be further emphasized?
- Can aggressive arrest practices be successfully reconciled with competing initiatives of modern police administrators, including community policing (a policy that appears to deliberately make police *less* authoritative), which places an emphasis on responding to public disorder?

We also expect future research will address:

- How effective are recent initiatives focusing on an integrated criminal justice? Have we really found the best solution to domestic violence?

- What makes certain departments change? Is the most effective motive for agency change fear of adverse consequences (e.g., political pressure and/or lawsuits)? If so, are there other methods to effect the behavior of those agencies and officers who to date have refused to change? In such cases can a dynamic police executive implement rapid and profound organizational change simply through leadership? Is there a particular training scheme/orientation which is more effective than others at increasing the rate of change?
- Can measures of police accountability realistically be increased?
- Are particular characteristics of police organizations, or of the service population of their respective cities, conducive to rapid or slower rates of change?

We expect that few of these issues will be resolved conclusively in the near future.

## Notes

[1] Of course, the problem is that a victim's desire to arrest was itself usually *insufficient*. In fact, we found that while victim preferences were very important in Detroit, Michigan, in other departments this was not a factor. A study of Massachusetts departments found that approximately 75 percent of the responding officers could not even *report* what the victim's preferences were, let alone follow them.

[2] Preliminary research in Quincy, Massachusetts (Buzawa, Hotaling, Klein & Byrne, 1996) indicates that prior criminal record may be the critical variable (as with other offenses), rather than social class or employment. If proven, policy implications may be easier to implement.

## References

Bachman, R. and A. L. Coker. (1995). "Police Involvement in Domestic Violence: The Interactive Effects of Victim Injury, Offenders' History of Violence, and Race." *Violence and Victims* 10(2): 91–106.

Bayley, D. H. (1986). "The Tactical Choices of Police Patrol Officers." *Journal of Criminal Justice* 14: 329–48.

Berk, S. F., A. Campbell, R. Klap, and B. Western. (1992). "Beyesian Analysis of the Colorado Springs Spouse Assault Experiment." *Criminal Law and Criminology* 83:170–200.

*Boston Globe*, July 10, 1994.

*Boston Globe*, December 13, 1995.

Bowman, C. (1992). "The Arrest Experiments: A Feminist Critique." *Journal of Criminal Law and Criminology* 83(1): 201–8.

Buchanan, D. R. and P. A. Perry. (1985). "Attitudes of Police Recruits Towards Domestic Disturbances: An Evaluation of Training." *Journal of Criminal Justice* 13:561–72.

Buzawa, E. (1979). "Legislative Responses to the Problem of Domestic Violence in Michigan." *Wayne Law Review* 25(3): 859–81.

Buzawa, E. (1988). "Explaining Variations in Police Response to Domestic Violence: A Case Study in Detroit and New England." In G. Hotaling, D. Finkelhor, J.

Kirkpatrick and M. A. Straus (Eds.), *Coping with Family Violence: Research and Policy Perspectives* (pp. 169–82). Newbury Park, CA: Sage Publications.

Buzawa, E. and T. Austin. (1993). "Determining Police Response to Domestic Violence Victims." *American Behavioral Scientist* 36:610–23.

Buzawa, E. and C. Buzawa. (1996). *Domestic Violence: The Criminal Justice Response*, 2nd ed. Newbury Park: Sage Publications.

Buzawa, E., G. Hotaling, A. Klein and J. Byrne. (1996). *Understanding, Preventing and Controlling Domestic Violence Incidents: A Evaluation Of The Effectiveness of Formal and Informal Deterrence Mechanisms.* Research in Progress under a grant from the National Institute of Justice.

*Commonwealth v. Phillips*, Worcester Superior Court, April 19, 1994.

Dunford, F. W., D. Huizinga, and D. Elliot. (1989). *The Omaha Domestic Violence Police Experiment: Final Report to the National Institute of Justice and the City of Omaha.* Boulder, CO: Institute of Behavioral Science.

Dutton, D. G. (1986). "Wife Assaulters' Explanations for Assault: The Neutralization of Self Punishment." *Canadian Journal of Behavioral Science* 18(4): 381–90.

Elliott, D. S. (1989). "Criminal Justice Procedures in Family Violence Crimes." In L. Ohlin and M. Tonry (Eds.), *Crime and justice: A review of research* (pp. 427–80). London: University of Chicago Press.

Ferraro, K. (1989). "Policing Woman Battering." *Social Problems* 36: 61–74.

Ford, D. (1983). "Wife Battery and Criminal Justice: A Study of Victim Decision-making." *Family Relations* 32:463–75.

Harrell, A. (1991). *Evaluation of Court Ordered Treatment for Domestic Violence Offenders (Final Report).* Washington, DC: Urban Institute.

Hart, B. (1992). *State Codes on Domestic Violence: Analysis, Commentary and Recommendations.* Reno, NV: National Council of Juvenile and Family Court Judges.

Hart, B. (1995). "Coordinated community approaches to domestic violence." Paper presented at the Strategic Planning Workshop on Violence Against Women, National Institute of Justice, Washington, DC (March 31). Reading, PA: Battered Women's Justice Project, Pennsylvania Coalition Against Domestic Violence.

Hirschel, J. D., I. W. Hutchison, C. W. Dean, J. J. Kelley, and C. E. Pesackis. (1991). *Charlotte Spouse Assault Replication Project: Final Report.* Washington, DC: National Institute of Justice.

Institute for Women's Policy Research (1995). Measuring the Costs of Domestic Violence and the Cost Effectiveness of Interventions: An Initial Assessment of the State of the Art and Proposals for Further Research. Unpublished paper.

Isaac, N. (1994). "Men who Batter, Profile From a Restraining Order Database." *Archives of Family Medicine* 3(1): 50–54.

Klein, A. (1994). Recidivism in a Population of Court Restrained Batterers After Two Years. Unpublished dissertation. Northeastern University.

Langan, P. and Innes, C. (1986). *Preventing Domestic Violence Against Women.* Bureau of Justice Statistics. Washington, DC: Department of Justice.

Langley, R. and R. Levy. (1977). *Wife Beating: The Silent Crisis.* New York: Dutton.

Lanza-Kaduce, L., R. Greenleaf, and M. Donahue. (1995). "Trickle Up Report Writing: The Impact of a Pro-arrest Policy for Domestic Disturbances." *Justice Quarterly* (12)3: 525–42.

Lerman, L. (1981). *Prosecution of Spouse Abuse Innovations in Criminal Justice Response.* Washington, DC: Center for Women Policy Studies.

Loving, N. (1980). *Responding to Spouse Abuse and Wife Beating: A Guide for Police.* Washington, DC: Police Executive Research Forum.

Manning, P. (1977). *Police Work.* Cambridge: MIT Press.

Manning, P. (1988). *Symbolic Interaction: Signifying Calls and Police Response.* Cambridge: MIT Press.

Martin, M. E. (1994). "Mandatory Arrest for Domestic Violence: The Court's Response." *Criminal Justice Review* 19(2): 212–27.

Moore, A. (1997). "Intimate Violence: Does Socioeconomic Status Matter?" In Albert Cardarelli (Ed.), Violence Between Intimate Partners: Patterns, Causes and Effects. Needham Heights, MA: Allyn and Bacon.

Pate, A. and Hamilton, E. (1992). "Formal and Informal Deterrents to Domestic Violence: The Dade County Spouse Assault Experiment." *American Sociological Review* 57:691–97.

Pierce, G., S. Spaar, and B. Briggs. (1988). *Character of Calls for Police Work.* National Institute of Justice. Washington, DC: Department of Justice.

Sanders, D. (1988). "Personal Violence and Public Order: The Prosecution of 'Domestic' Violence in England and Wales." *International Journal of the Sociology of Law* 16:359–82.

Sheptycki, J. W. E. (1993). *Innovations in Policing Domestic Violence.* Newcastle upon Tyne: Athanaeum.

Sherman, L. (1992). "The Influence of Criminology on Criminal Law: Evaluating for Misdemeanor Domestic Violence." *Journal of Criminal Law and Criminology* 85(1): 901–45.

Sherman, L. W. and R. A. Berk. (1984). "The Specific Deterrent Effects of Arrest for Domestic Assault," *American Sociological Review* 49: 261–72.

Stanko, E. A. (1989). "Missing the Mark? Police Battering." In J. Hanmer, J. Radford, and B. Stanko (Eds.), *Women, Policing and Male Violence* (pp. 46–49). London: Routledge & Kegan Paul.

Straus, M. A. and R. G. Gelles. (1990). "How Violent are American families? Estimates from the National Family Violence Resurvey and Other Studies." M. A. Straus and R. J. Gelles (Eds.). *Physical Violence in American Families: Risk Factors and Adaptations to Violence in 8,145 Families* (pp. 49–73). New Brunswick, NJ: Transaction Publishers.

Urban Institute (1996, March 29). *The VAWA Act of 1994: Evaluation of the STOP Block Grants to Combat Violence Against Women.* Washington, DC: The Urban Institute.

Victim Services Agency (1988). *The Law Enforcement Response to Family Violence: A State by State Guide to Family Violence Legislation.* New York: Victim Services Agency.

Zorza, J. (1994). "Must We Stop Arresting Batterers? Analysis and Policy Implications of New Police Domestic Violence Studies." *New England Law Review* 28: 929–90.

Zorza, J. and L. Woods. (1994). *Analysis and Policy Implications of the New Police Domestic Violence Studies.* New York: National Center on Women and Family Law.

# 15

# Measuring Police Performance in the New Paradigm of Policing

*Geoffrey P. Alpert*
*Mark H. Moore*

## Introduction

During the 1980s and 1990s there has been a resurgence of interest in community policing. As an outgrowth of police-community relations, the concept of community policing has become the goal, method, and guiding principle for police. Unfortunately, community policing remains a concept and philosophy in search of a process, without proper ways to document or evaluate its efforts. This chapter focuses on community-oriented policing and takes a new approach to the measurement and evaluation of police performance. Before outlining our paradigm of police performance measures we will review the conventional measures and why we believe a new way of thinking must direct our attention to new performance measures.

Citizens and their elected representatives have long sought a bottom line to measure police performance. The goals have been to reassure the public that hard-earned tax dollars were being spent to achieve important results and to hold police managers accountable for improving organizational performance. As police agencies matured, four generally accepted accounting practices became enshrined as the key measures to evaluate police performance. These include—

1) reported crime rates
2) overall arrests
3) clearance rates
4) response rates.

As these measures became institutionalized over the years, investments were made in developing information systems to record police performance consistent with these measures. Statistical reports using these

Bureau of Justice Statistics–Princeton University Study Group on Criminal Justice Performance Measures, *Performance Measures for the Criminal Justice System*, 1994, pp. 109–42.

measures were routinely issued. Further, the media, overseers in city councils, and auditors in city managers' offices have all been primed to acknowledge and use these measures to compare police performance from year to year and to compare local accomplishments with those of other cities. For most practical purposes, these are the statistics by which police departments throughout the United States are now held accountable.

These measures remain critical as part of an overall system for measuring police performance. As currently used, however, these measures reflect an increasingly outmoded model of police tasks and fail to capture many important contributions that police make to the quality of life. More important, these measures may misguide police managers and lead them and their organizations towards purposes and activities that are less valuable than others that can be achieved with limited and diminishing resources.

Police performance measures should focus on a new model of policing that emphasizes their charge to do justice, promote secure communities, restore crime victims, and promote noncriminal options—the elements of an emerging paradigm of criminal justice (DiIulio, 1992: 10–12). The purpose of this chapter is to describe how policing fits in with this new paradigm, including implications for restructuring the overall objectives and measuring the accomplishments of policing through police agency performance measures (Kelling, 1992).

## The Evolving Strategy of Policing

Historically, policing in America has been inspired and guided by a vision of *professional* law enforcement. This vision is a coherent strategy of policing defining the principal ends, means, and legitimating principles of the police enterprise (Wilson and McLaren, 1977).

### Professional Law Enforcement:
### The Dominant Strategy of Policing

In this vision, the primary, perhaps exclusive goals of the police are to reduce crime and criminal victimization. Police seek to achieve this goal by arresting and threatening to arrest those who violate the criminal law. They organize themselves to produce this result by:

1) patrolling city streets hoping to detect and deter crime
2) responding rapidly to calls for service
3) conducting investigations after crimes have been committed
    to identify criminal offenders and develop evidence to be used
    in prosecutions.

In essence, in the vision of professional law enforcement, the police are seen as the all-important entry point to the criminal justice system—the gatekeeper managing the first step in bringing the force of the criminal law to bear on offenders.

To deal effectively with serious crime and dangerous criminal offenders, specialized skills are required. The police have had to learn how to use legitimate force with skill and confidence. They have had to improve their ability to investigate and solve crimes to reduce the chance that serious offenders could escape accountability. Thus, in search of increased effectiveness in dealing with an increasingly challenging and urgent problem, the police consciously narrowed their focus and refined their skills in responding to serious crime and dangerous offenders. By relying on the techniques of patrol, rapid response, and retrospective investigation, the police have been kept at the forefront of community life and have been made available to anyone who needed them when a crime occurred.

## Limitations of Professional Law Enforcement

Recently, enthusiasm for this strategy of professional policing has waned. The professional policing model has been ineffective in reducing crime, reducing citizens' fears, and satisfying victims that justice is being done. Indeed, recent research indicates that a majority of the population believes that the crime problem has become progressively worse during the past decade (Gallup, 1992, cited in Bureau of Justice Statistics, 1992: 185). Similarly, citizens have lost confidence in the criminal justice system to protect them (Cole, 1992: 23).

Such charges are, in many respects, unfair to the police. It is unreasonable to expect the police to reduce crime all by themselves. Crime rates are affected by vast social, economic, and political forces. No matter how professional, police cannot solve the "root causes" of crime. They cannot be blamed for increasing unemployment, increasing inequality, or eroding family structures (Bazelon, 1988). In addition, police are dependent on the rest of the criminal justice system to give significance to arrests.

## Toward a New Paradigm of Policing

Many police executives are beginning to think about and experiment with a strategy of policing that differs from the professional model and emphasizes the development of a strong relationship with the community. *The essence of this new paradigm is that police must engage in community-based processes related to the production and maintenance of local human and social capital. The means by which these lofty goals are to be achieved are through the development of strong relationships with institutions and individuals in the community.* While the specific elements of this new strategy of policing have not been agreed upon or clearly delineated, the broad characteristics are reasonably clear.

The major theme of *building a strong relationship with the community* has two justifications. First, it is an important way to make enforcement more effective. Second, it is a way to prevent crime and make the community co-producers of justice (Skogan and Antunes, 1979).

One excellent example comes from the Metro-Dade Police Department (MDPD) in Miami, Florida. In June 1992 the staff of the Northside

Station of the MDPD conducted a survey of local residents (mostly African American) to determine if any public personalities or activities could serve as common ground between the police and young males (Metro-Dade Police Department, 1992). What emerged was a fascinating finding. The young respondents identified local rap radio disc jockeys and rap music as personalities and activities that interested them.

In March 1993 the police turned these empirical findings into action. They created a series of "Jammin' with the Man" concerts. Local disc jockeys were invited to hold concerts in local parks sponsored by the police. While the youths enjoyed the music and festivities, the police were there, talking with the youths and encouraging them to talk and work with the police to understand each other. Although more than 5,000 people attended the first event, there were no negative incidents. The MDPD report concluded by noting:

> While *Jammin' with the Man* was originally intended to be a single step in a process to improve police-community relations, a step aimed particularly at young men, [it] seems to have become part or all of the answer. It has also become an educational experience for the community as they see police as agents of peace rather than enforcers of law. More importantly, it has demonstrated that the mere act of the police engaged in active listening has the effect of empowering them and perhaps alleviating some of their sense of alienation. (Metro-Dade Police Department, 1993: 6)

In other words, this project provided an excellent vehicle for the police to create and maintain positive contacts with members of the community they serve and to be seen in a positive light. Further, by initiating and participating in activities the youths enjoyed, the police had an opportunity to see youth in a positive light.

Dr. Trevor Bennett has classified the various ways to consider community policing and has reduced them to three categories. First, he notes that there are arguments which refer to the intrinsic "goodness" of the general relationship between police and the community. Second, he recognizes relationships in which the police and the public work together to achieve common and specified goals, including the shared responsibility for crime control. Third, he acknowledges the need for police to take into consideration the wishes and concerns of the community. In Bennett's words:

> . . . [A] workable definition of a community policing philosophy might include the following basic elements: a belief or intention that the police should work with the public whenever possible in solving local problems and a belief that they should take account of the wishes of the public in defining and evaluating operational police policy. (Bennett, 1992: 7)

A second theme emphasizes *attacking the communities' problems on a broader front*—in effect, rejecting the exclusive focus on serious crime. The theme emerging from research is that much fear of crime is independent of victimization and that there are things the police can do to deal with fear (Bureau of Justice Statistics, 1988, 1992). Research findings and practice make clear that citizens use the police for many purposes other than crime control and that things other than crime are principal concerns (Alpert and Dunham, 1992: 2–3). Certainly, goals other than the reduction of serious crime should be emphasized when it is realized that crime control is not the principal or only objective of the police. In any case, the police cannot achieve the reduction of fear or crime by themselves. What the police can achieve is the independent goal of public or customer satisfaction.

A third theme emphasizes some important *changes in the way the police visualize their work and their methods.* In the traditional strategy of policing, the key unit of work is the "incident." That is, patrol officers respond to a specific incident, and it is the incident that becomes the focus of a criminal investigation. What we have recently learned, however, is that a large proportion of incidents emerge from a relatively small number of situations and locations. Moreover, analysis of the problems underlying many incidents reported to the police suggests that the police might be able to imagine and mount different kinds of intervention (Goldstein, 1990).

The concept known as problem-oriented policing emphasizes involvement of the police in community life. This strategy has police serve as community agents rather than adversaries with the community. Study group member Professor James F. Short suggests that police should not maintain their gatekeeper function and solve problems *for* the community but should be involved in solving problems *with* community support and assistance. In this way, police can help develop and promote a sense of community (Short, 1990: 225–26). Professor Short makes a critical link from the 1990s problem-oriented policing to the role of police in the Chicago Area Project during the 1940s. As he informs us, there are many similarities in police functioning then and what we are suggesting for the future. The vision was—

> . . . [T]he police as a resource for the community, aiding local residents and working with indigenous leaders to solve community problems, with special focus on the problems of young people. The goal in each of these programs is to promote the achievement of "functional communities," that is, communities in which family life, work, religion, education, law enforcement, and other institutional areas reflect and reinforce common values (Shoe, 1990: 226).

Although arrests of offenders remains an important tactic, the police repertoire must be widened to include a variety of civil actions, mobilization of citizens and other government agencies to change the conditions that generate crime or that will likely escalate deteriorating conditions. For example, the strategy of "Weed and Seed" is to eliminate drug-related crime and to restore economic vitality to inner cities through multi-agency cooperation and the use of community empowerment and resident involvement (Department of Justice, 1991). An important aspect of this third theme is that the police should become pro-active, interactive, and preventative in their orientation rather than rely solely on reacting and control.

A fourth theme focuses on *changes in internal working relationships.* That is, police agencies need to examine the potential strengths and weaknesses of decentralization of authority by seeking ways to guide discretion and police behavior generally through increasing reliance on values rather than rules and strict methods of accountability (Alpert and Smith, 1993). These ideas are central to the concepts of community policing, problem-solving policing and smarter policing. Incorporating these ideas into strategies of policing, we believe, would truly professionalize police rather than treat them as blue-collar workers. In addition to making police work more effective, these four strategies may increase job satisfaction—and most importantly—community satisfaction (Greene, Alpert and Styles, 1992).

These four themes combine to form the overarching principle of changed police-community relationships. Currently, police work revolves around serious crimes. The community participates by becoming the eyes and ears of the police; however, this strategy keeps the police outside and above the community. Police are summoned by the community through individual requests for service, and those requests are evaluated primarily in terms of whether an offense has been committed and a crime has been solved.

Creative, problem-oriented policing strategies place the community in a much different position than they have been in the recent past. Under this new paradigm, police work is oriented toward community satisfaction and the increase in human and social capital in the community. Satisfaction is determined not only by the police response to individual calls, but also by community members banding together to advise and consult with the police. Further, community institutions play the most important roles in changing community conditions that generate crime and in shaping police activities related to crime and other community conditions. Placing police and the citizens in communication with community leaders creates a dialogue and interaction. This removes the police from a hierarchical position and has the effect of increasing the accountability of the police to the community.

One of the crucial issues that must be faced by all concerned with community policing is the assumption that there is a community to organize. Some cities and suburbs have developed rapidly and have not formed what sociologists refer to as communities or neighborhoods. Similarly, some precincts or reporting areas may not be contiguous with natural neighborhoods or communities. Finally, some areas that have deteriorated or are in the process of deteriorating may be difficult to organize. Areas needing organization the least will be the easiest to assist, while less well-organized communities, particularly underclass areas of the inner city, will be the hardest to organize (Alpert and Dunham, 1988). However, examples of difficult and complicated organization are available.

One example of this community-building comes from Judge Thomas Petersen in Dade County, Florida. Judge Petersen was able to create a sense of community in several areas known for their lack of community spirit or allegiance. Judge Petersen, with assistance from the housing authority, law enforcement officials, and private industry, established three community stores that sold essential items in housing projects. In each, the housing authority found sufficient space and turned the space into grocery stores with supplies donated by private industry. The shelves were stocked with no up-front costs. Further, training for the people necessary to run the business was procured from professionals in the grocery business. Those who were hired to run the store were in need of child care, and the space and training for that service was provided by the housing authority.

After a short period of time, a group of people were working in the store, others were working in the child care center, and all were removed from public assistance. More important, however, was the sense of community created by the stores and child care centers. The stores became a focal point of the projects, and residents, police, and others involved in their establishment gained a mutual respect and trust for each other. Residents who had been scared to talk to other residents began to realize the importance of community spirit and the benefits of mutual assistance. The workers and residents began to identify with the operation of the store, and when anyone began to cause trouble or tried to sell drugs, the police were called immediately, and residents would point out the offender and work with the police to do justice. After a short period, the stores earned the reputation as establishments that would not only sell goods but also as the heart of the housing projects, serving as a rumor control center, a place to get assistance from others, and a place with respect for the police function.

This new-found respect for police spread very quickly through the projects and neighborhoods. Residents who once despised the police were now working with them to solve crimes and create an atmosphere where street criminals would not be tolerated. In many respects, Judge Petersen had *created* a community spirit that fit neatly into the community-oriented policing strategy (Petersen, 1993).

## Implications for Police Performance Measurement

As society and the police approach a new understanding of how each can contribute to the other, it is critical to develop new measures to determine how well the police perform. Measures of performance rely on the definition of what the police are expected to do and how they are expected to do it. The measures must not only reflect but also help to shape community expectations of the police. For example, consider how neatly the current enshrined measures of police performance fit the dominant current strategy of policing.

## Current Performance Measures as a Reflection of Professional Law Enforcement

Recall that the current strategy of policing emphasizes crime control through arrests and that arrests are produced by patrol, rapid response to calls for service, and retrospective investigation. Current police performance measures are linked directly to these tasks. First, the overall objective of police has traditionally been perceived as to reduce crime. It follows that the traditional measure of police performance is the level of reported crime measured by the Uniform Crime Reports. Another police task is apprehending offenders. This task is measured by arrests. Other traditional measures related to the crime rate include the ability to solve crimes (clearance rates—a very subjective measure) and the ability to get to crime scenes quickly (response times). These existing measures fit the traditional policing strategy perfectly, and they have become recognized as the important measures.

### What Is Missing from These Measures?

Limitations of the traditional policing strategy are also represented by the current performance measures. It is important that crime is measured in terms of reported crime, rather than through victimization surveys. Indeed, the police long resisted the development of criminal victimization surveys, concerned that they would reveal differential reporting and would be too subjective. This emphasis on reported crime left invisible many crimes such as domestic assault, child abuse, extortion by armed robbers and drug gangs, and other crimes in communities that did not trust or have confidence in the police (Bureau of Justice Statistics, 1992, and Federal Bureau of Investigation, 1992).

It is also important that the measures that could have revealed the fairness and economy within which the authority of the police was deployed got less attention than the question of police effectiveness. There was no routine expectation that the police would publish data on patrol allocations, response times, or crime solution rates across neighborhoods.

Similarly, no serious efforts were made to develop statistical evidence on the incidence of brutality, excessive use of force, discourtesy, or corruption. In principle, one could have collected information about these things by soliciting civilian complaints and taking them as indicators of problems, if not probative of individual officer misconduct (U.S. Civil Rights Commission, 1981). Again, the argument, albeit flawed, was that unlike official crime statistics, such information was suspect and too subjective. Thus, in this area as elsewhere, the commitment to fairness and discipline in the use of authority was less important than the claim of crime control effectiveness.

Further, there was no real way to capture the quality of the response that the police made to citizen calls other than those involving criminal offenses for which an arrest could be made. In fact, most of the operational indicators implicitly viewed responding to non-crime complaints as something to be avoided and resisted rather than taken seriously. Measures included a comparison between time out of service and time in-service. In-service meant being on patrol, while out-of-service included meal breaks but also included meeting citizens and responding to their calls for service. Similarly, time spent on high-priority calls was compared with time spent on "nuisance calls." The purpose was to reduce time on nuisance calls, despite the fact that it was these calls that could be used to build the relationship with the community that was necessary to make their current tactics effective in dealing with crime (Sparrow, Moore, and Kennedy, 1990).

Finally, there was no real way to account for or measure pro-active operations. The only way to do this was through monitoring specialized squads or units. Units were created to deal with particular problems, often on a temporary basis, without the establishment of a method to capture the nature or extent of the units' activities. Similarly, there was no attempt to determine how much of the organization's resources was being committed to such pro-active operations (Bureau of Justice Statistics, 1992).

## Reforming Police Performance Measures

***Orienting the agency to the community.*** Several options exist to reform police performance measures. First, existing measures could be improved to live up to the challenge of professionalism. This would include audited clearance and arrest rates and the development of statistical evidence on the use of force and the incidence of brutality, discourtesy, and corruption, among others. Second, performance measures could be linked more closely to action in the community, including the level of centralization and community-level programs. Under this structure, programs must be established that encourage calls to the police and evaluate calls to the police for service as well as concerns regarding criminal behavior. Measures should also include—

- police-related and inter-governmental activities that improve the social fabric of the community
- projects with the assistance of private industry that improve informal and formal social control in the community
- fear of crime
- victimization and police service programs that help promote community spirit in those neighborhoods where none existed.

Further, measures of the form and level of self-defense efforts by citizens and measures of trust and confidence in the police should be routinely taken and evaluated. Measures of the quality of service delivery by the police should be taken to improve departmental functioning and reveal the quality of individual officers as reported by the citizens with whom they come in contact (Furstenberg and Wellford, 1973, and U.S. Civil Rights Commission, 1981).

*Encouraging pro-active problem solving.* One of the biggest problems in accounting for the performance of police departments is to capture what is accomplished during pro-active and problem-solving activities. One way to measure this concept is to view each problem-solving initiative as a particular program to be evaluated for its immediate impact. A second way to measure the impact is to view each as equivalent to a criminal investigation or special operation. In this way, a file is created, activities are monitored, and results recorded and evaluated.

The problem, of course, is that the problems come in different sizes. Size can be measured in terms of—

1) total resources committed to the problem
2) amount of time taken to solve
3) the number of specialized resources required
4) the extent to which higher-ranking officers must mobilize and coordinate efforts within and outside the department to deal with the problem
5) its importance and scale within the community.

One way to deal with these concerns is to develop a tailored program for individual areas. In other words, do not assume that each community has the same concerns or problems or that each community should respond similarly to certain problems. One product that would result from the effort to create, deliver, and measure these community-oriented programs and surveys is a database on which a department or a division within a large department could customize a pro-active or interactive problem-solving approach. Pressure to build a portfolio of problems solved successfully and improved attitudes toward the police could become as intense as current pressures to maintain low crime rates and quick response times.

*Managing the transition to the new strategy.* One of the most difficult problems faced by police managers in the short run is the awkward period of transition to the new strategy. The new programs will not be up and operating, and the new measurement systems will not be working and widely accepted. Yet the police will still be accountable to the public. Thus, they will have to develop measures that can keep them accountable during the transition.

One method is to identify the particular investments and efforts that are required to implement the new strategy of policing and report progress on these activities. If new training is required, they can report on the development of the new curriculum and the number of participating officers. If the formation of community groups is identified as important, that progress can be monitored and recorded. If the development of a new call management system or a new scheduling system is required, that, too, can be monitored. The point is simply to identify and monitor the key organizational investments that are required. Unfortunately, no data sets exist on which to begin an analysis. The Bureau of Justice Statistics has compiled the most comprehensive data set (Law Enforcement Management and Administration Statistics—LEMAS) but its elements do not include many of the critical measures discussed in this chapter (Reeves, 1992).

## Toward a New Strategy

The urgent need today in measuring police performance is to move away from a sterile conversation about performance measurement as an abstract technical problem and to understand it as a device that can be used managerially to shape the future of policing. This is neither a question of the essential unchanging measures that finally capture the value of policing nor a discussion of outcomes versus outputs nor a discussion of single versus multiple measures of performance. Instead, it is a discussion about a strategy of policing that will work in the future and how to measure its effects. Current measures of policing are holding police departments in their current mold and are keeping them mired in the past. These current measures need to be supplemented by innovative policing and new ways to measure their successes.

Our suggestion has several organizational elements that must be added to the traditional components already existing in many police departments. The police initiative must stress the need to learn about the residents and business people in their neighborhoods and to see them in situations that are not always defined as negative or at best neutral. This increased role for the police must include two basic approaches. First, a method must be devised to solicit information from members of the community. This method can incorporate meetings or citizens' advisory and focus groups with the police and can be enhanced by community surveys to determine attitudes and suggestions concerning the police and the police role. Another important dimension of this information gathering is the analysis of what Skogan has found to be measures of neighborhood decline and disorder (Skogan, 1990). Second, the police must use this information to reduce isolation between police and the citizens. The strategy is to assign officers for an extended period, supervised by command staff and advised by community groups. This move toward stability will increase the identification of an officer with the residents, geography, politics, and other issues in a given neighborhood.

These operational elements require proper training, feedback mechanisms, and an institutionalized reward system. Additionally, it is important that these efforts are measured, analyzed, and evaluated by the police officers, command staff, and members of the public.

### Neighborhood Training

Neighborhood training involves two basic questions the police must answer according to the needs of each community or neighborhood: what to do and how to do it. In other words, the priority of police resources, whether fighting crime or providing social services, changes from neighborhood to neighborhood. Police officers must identify these needs from their own experiences and expectations, from the perspective of the consumers, and from that of the police administration. Neighborhood training can effectively inform the officer as to what he or she can expect from the residents, physical surroundings, or other influences. This in-service training can introduce officers to community characteristics while they are working the streets under a supervisor (in a way similar to a field training officer). What to do can be determined by problem-solving techniques. How to do it is the all-important style of policing that needs to be developed and supervised by command staff.

Distinct differences may exist among officers, administrators, and citizens concerning style. Matching the style of policing to community needs and requirements will improve both the police and the community. This can be achieved through training based upon knowledge of community values and beliefs as well as the attitudes and priorities of police officers. A necessary aspect of this is the continuous dialogue between residents and the police. Research on attitudes, expectations and evaluation of services of both the police and the members of the community is critical.

## Monitoring

The final component of this strategy includes institutionalized monitoring and a formal reward system. This requires an ongoing system to monitor both the community and the police. The needs of the community can be determined by periodic social surveys, which, if linked to census data and local planning information, can inform officials of the changing nature of a given neighborhood. While it is relatively easy to identify what constitutes negative behavior, it is difficult to specify exemplary behavior. The proper use of good research, including appropriate sampling and a panel design, could provide a clear snapshot of the needs expressed by a given community. Police officers and administrators can work together to identify critical questions and a research design that can answer them. A Blue-Ribbon Committee studying the Miami Police Department concluded that while crime-fighting activities are important, service activities are equally as important in term of the new paradigm. In the final report, the committee noted:

> It is our conclusion that a minor organizational change can have a major impact on community relations and on the interrelationships between citizens and police. We believe that confidence in the police will be enhanced if the police measure and make more visible the activities they perform. Moreover, police work is usually rewarded by the gratitude an officer receives from those whom he or she helps. Status in the department, promotions, raises, commendations, etc., rest largely on his or her crime-fighting activities, the number of arrests, crimes he or she solves, etc. As a result, the patrol officer may regard service calls as a necessary evil. (Overtown Blue Ribbon Committee, 1984: 199)

These creative data, together with traditional law enforcement information, will permit the development and maintenance of neighborhood profiles. Analyzing and monitoring these profiles can assist the police in improving their training, tactical decisions, effectiveness and efficiency.

### Rewarding the Officers

Most police departments provide incentives for their officers. These include traditional promotions, merit increases, and "officer-of-the-month" recognition. Many departments offer several opportunities for their officers to receive or earn rewards. Traditionally, these rewards have been based upon aggressive actions that led to arrest(s), the capture of a dangerous felon, or some other heroic activity. These criteria for rewarding police officers are important and serve to encourage similar actions from others. Yet other types of police behavior deserve recognition but remain lost and hidden behind the visible, aggressive activities of police officers. Activities that should receive more attention include exemplary service to the community and the reduction or diffusion of violence. Those who provide meritorious service may be recognized but often their actions are lost behind the brave shooting incident or heroic rescue. The local community needs to recognize officers who serve their "beat" or neighborhood in an exemplary fashion. A "Best Cop on the Block" recognition would be an important reward, if provided by local residents or merchants. When an officer avoids a shooting or talks a suspect into custody, his or her superiors may not find out; if they do, the officer may be labeled as a "chicken" or one who cannot provide needed back-up to his fellow officers. Nonaggressive behavior that reduces violence needs to be reinforced, rewarded, and established as the model for other officers to copy.

An institutional reward system should be established for officers who avoid or reduce violent situations and who avoid the use of force, especially deadly force, when avoidance is justifiable. When command officers, from the chief to the sergeants, support and reward violence reduction, private business and service groups can be enlisted to provide symbolic and monetary rewards for such behavior. The institutional support for the effective policing of a neighborhood can only encourage others to consider a change in priorities and style. While this is only one aspect of a neighborhood intervention and community evaluation model, it could serve as a successful step toward meeting the joint needs of the citizens and the police.

Data on these activities should be collected, assessed and evaluated to help determine police departments' performance to do justice and promote secure communities.

### Summary and Conclusion

Police departments around the country have instituted one or more of the foregoing organizational components into community policing programs, but we are not aware of any agency that has incorporated them all or that uses many of these nontraditional performance measures. The components of the suggested program need coordination and individual assessment as well as analysis as a total effect.

Effective neighborhood policing requires that police administrators acquire adequate information on the specific neighborhood, including knowledge of the informal control structure of the neighborhood, attitudes about the police, and policing strategies and styles. This information can be obtained from citizen surveys, census data, community advisory groups, and community leaders. After accumulating the information, police administrators can decide how to deal with any incongruence between the neighborhood context and police policies, strategies, and styles. Some of these differences can be reduced by campaigns to educate the citizens and change public opinion and attitudes. In other cases, discrepancies can be reduced by training programs for officers who are assigned to the areas. The training can focus on neighborhood-specific strategies, appropriate styles for the specific neighborhood, and placing priorities on tasks consistent with the neighborhood's expectations. Subsequent to appropriate neighborhood-based training, police administrators need to create and institutionalize a system of monitoring and rewarding police officers' behavior. The police officers assigned to the neighborhood provide the final link integrating the formal control system of the police with the informal system in the neighborhood. Officers must apply the training principles appropriately through their use of discretion.

From data collected from the neighborhoods, a good plan for neighborhood intervention and community evaluation can bring modern police work in line with our modern world. Moore and Kelling (1983: 65) have previously summarized these ideas quite well:

> Police strategies do not exist in a vacuum. They are shaped by important legal, political, and attitudinal factors, as well as by local resources and capabilities, all factors which now sustain the modern conception of policing. So there may be little leeway for modern police executives. But the modern conception of policing is in serious trouble, and a review of the nature of that trouble against the background of the American history of policing gives a clear direction to police forces that wish to improve their performance as crime fighters and public servants.

> The two fundamental features of a new police strategy must be these: that the role of private citizens in the control of crime and maintenance of public order be established and encouraged, not derided and thwarted, and that the police become more active, accessible participants in community affairs. The police will have to do little to encourage citizens to participate in community policing, for Americans are well practiced at undertaking private, voluntary efforts; all they need to know is that the police force welcomes and supports such activity. Being more visible and accessible is slightly more difficult, but hiring more "community relations" specialists is surely not the answer. Instead, the police must get out of their cars, and spend more time in public spaces such as parks and plazas, confronting and assisting citizens with their private troubles. This is mundane, prosaic

work but it probably beats driving around in cars waiting for a radio call. Citizens would surely feel safer and, perhaps, might even be safer.

Private citizens working together and through community institutions can have a profound impact on policing. Those community organizations and police agencies that have developed reciprocal relationships will enjoy more success than those attempting to work without the benefit of the others' knowledge and information.

The maintenance and analysis of administrative statistics can provide community members and police supervisors with performance outcomes that promote justice. Patrol officers can be in the best position to understand the varied and changing needs of the community, and with input from research and training, appropriate activities can be devised to do justice and promote safe communities and develop a new meaning for the phrase "professional policing."

---

### Table 1

The mission of the police consists of many diverse activities, not objectives in themselves but which are directed toward the protection of life. Goals include doing justice, promoting secure communities, restoring crime victims, and promoting non-criminal options.

**Police: Goals, methods, and performance indicators**
**Goals**
*Doing Justice.* Treating citizens in an appropriate manner based upon their conduct.

**Methods/activities**
Balancing formal and informal social controls, responding to calls for service, patrolling tactics, issuing traffic tickets, conducting investigations, writing reports, making arrests, and assisting in criminal prosecutions.

**Performance indicators**
Nature and type of patrolling strategy, number of traffic tickets issued, known crimes that are cleared by audit or arrest, quality of reports, analysis of who calls the police, evaluation of policies emphasizing values over rules, time invested and quality of investigations, number of known crimes cleared by conviction, arrests and arrests cleared by conviction, cases released because of police misconduct, citizen complaints, lawsuits filed, and results of dispositions and officer-initiated encounters.

**Goals**
*Promoting secure communities,* enabling citizens to enjoy a life without fear of crime or victimization.

**Methods/activities**
Preventing/deterring criminal behavior and victimization, problem-solving initiatives, training for community differences, assisting citizens by reducing fear of crime and victimization.

**Performance indicators**
Programs and resources allocated to crime prevention programs, inter-governmental programs, resources, both time and dollars dedicated to

problem-solving, rewards and monitoring of police, public trust and confidence in police performance, public attitudes toward police actions and public fear of crime, and home and business security checks.

**Goals**

*Restoring crime victims,* by restoring victims' lives and welfare as much as possible.

**Methods/activities**

Assisting crime victims to understand the criminal justice system, assisting crime victims with their difficulties created by the victimization, assisting crime victims to put their lives back together.

**Performance indicators**

Number of contacts with victims after initial call for assistance, types of assistance provided to victims, including information, comfort, transportation, and referrals to other agencies.

**Goals**

*Promoting noncriminal options,* by developing strong relationships with individuals in the community.

**Methods/activities**

Develop and assist with programs that strengthen relationships between police and members of the community and among community members, increase human and social capital in the community and linkages with private industry.

**Performance indicators**

Programs and resources allocated to strengthening relationships between police and the community and among community members, including traditional community relations programs, school programs and resources spent to meet with the public in a positive alliance. Innovative programs to develop a sense of community, organizational measures of decentralization, community storefront operations and officer contacts with citizens for positive relations and feedback on performance are aspects of developing strong relationships with members of the community.

---

# References

Alpert, Geoffrey, and Roger Dunham. *Policing Urban America.* Prospect Heights, IL: Waveland Press. 1992.

Alpert, Geoffrey, and Roger Dunham. *Policing Multi-Ethnic Neighborhoods.* New York: Greenwood Press. 1988.

Alpert, Geoffrey, and William Smith. "Developing Police Policy: Evaluating the Control Principle." *American Journal of Police.* (Forthcoming, 1993).

Bazelon, David. *Questioning Authority.* New York: Knopf. 1988.

Bennett, Trevor. *Community Policing in Britain.* Paper presented to the International Conference on Community Policing. Institute of Criminology, University of Heidelberg, Heidelberg, Germany. September 1992.

Bureau of Justice Statistics. *Crime and the Nation's Households, 1991.* Washington, DC: Bureau of Justice Statistics. 1992.

Bureau of Justice Statistics. *Sourcebook of Criminal Justice Statistics, 1991.* Washington, DC: Bureau of Justice Statistics. 1992.

Bureau of Justice Statistics. *Report to the Nation on Crime and Justice,* 2nd.ed. Washington, D.C.: Bureau of Justice Statistics. 1988.

Cole, George. *The American System of Criminal Justice.* Pacific Grove, CA: Brooks/Cole Publishing Co. 1992.

Department of Justice. *Operation Weed and Seed: Reclaiming America's Neighborhoods.* Washington, DC: U.S. Department of Justice. 1991.

DiIulio, John. *Rethinking the Criminal Justice System: Toward a New Paradigm.* Washington, DC: Bureau of Justice Statistics. December 1992.

Federal Bureau of Investigation. *Crime in the United States 1991.* Washington, DC: United States Department of Justice. 1992.

Furstenberg, Frank, and Charles Wellford. "Calling the Police: The Evaluation of Police Service." *Law and Society Review* 7:393–406 (1973).

Gallup, George. *The Gallup Poll Monthly,* Report No. 318. Princeton, NJ: The Gallup Poll. 1992.

Goldstein, Herman. *Problem-Oriented Policing.* New York: McGraw-Hill. 1990.

Greene, Jack, Geoffrey Alpert, and Paul Styles. "Values and Culture in Two American Police Departments: Lessons from King Arthur." *Journal of Contemporary Criminal Justice* 8:183-207 (1992).

Kelling, George. "Measuring What Matters: A New Way of Thinking About Crime and Public Order." *The City Journal* 2(Spring): 21–34 (1992).

Metro-Dade Police Department. *Survey of African-American Males 15–30 Years of Age.* Metro-Dade Police Department. Miami. 1992.

Metro-Dade Police Department. *"Jammin' with the Man" Project Summary.* Metro-Dade Police Department, Miami. 1993.

Moore, Mark, and George Kelling. "To Serve and to Protect: Learning from Police History," *The Public Interest* 70:49–65. 1983.

Overtown Blue Ribbon Committee. *Final Report.* City of Miami, 1984.

Petersen, Thomas. *Personal communication.* February 1993.

Reaves, Brian. *Law Enforcement Management and Administrative Statistics, 1990: Data for Individual State and Local Agencies with 100 or More Officers.* Washington, DC: Bureau of Justice Statistics. 1992.

Short, James F. *Delinquency in Society.* Englewood Cliffs, NJ: Prentice-Hall. 1990.

Skogan, Wesley. *Disorder and Decline: Crime and the Spiral of Decay in American Neighborhoods.* New York: Free Press. 1990.

Skogan, Wesley, and George Antunes. "Information, Apprehension and Deterrence: Exploring the Limits of Police Productivity." *Journal of Criminal Justice* 7 (1979).

Sparrow, M., M. Moore, and D. Kennedy. *Beyond 911: A New Era for Policing.* New York: Basic Books. 1990.

U.S. Civil Rights Commission. *Who's Guarding the Guardians?* Washington, DC: United States Government Printing Office. 1981.

Walker, Samuel. *The Police In America.* New York: McGraw-Hill. 1992.

Whitaker, Catherine. *Crime Prevention Measures.* Washington, D.C.: Bureau of Justice Statistics. 1986.

Wilson, O. W., and Roy McClaren. *Police Administration,* 4th ed. New York: McGraw-Hill. 1977.

# Section IV

## Police Deviance
### Corruption and Controls

There has always existed a concern about the control of the powers granted by the government to use force. Where power exists, there also exists the potential to abuse that power. Police corruption requires only two elements: opportunity and greed. This section covers traditional areas as well as newly defined areas of police corruption and the control of potential abuses.

In the first selection, "Breeding Deviant Conformity," Victor Kappeler, Richard Sluder, and Geoffrey Alpert describe how the real and exaggerated sense of the danger inherent in police work affects how the police picture the world and nurture a police subculture. This police subculture enforces many postulates that influence what are deemed as acceptable and unacceptable behaviors of police officers.

In their article, Professors Wagner and Decker have provided us with an up-to-date examination of the process that is initiated when a civilian complains against a police officer. They suggest that the police have failed to meet the challenge presented by citizen complaints. Perhaps when citizens complain, and police administrators respond, it is akin to shutting the barn door after the horse escapes. One way to discover areas that require more administrative oversight is to examine information included in complaints made about the police by citizens.

In the next selection, "Varieties of Citizen Review," Samuel Walker and Betsy Wright Kreisel specify some of the major variations among citizen review procedures. In addition, they discuss the implications of these variations for enhancing the accountability of the police and identify the need for more research in the area of citizen complaints.

In the final article of this section "Ethics and Law Enforcement," Joycelyn Pollock discusses the many ethical dilemmas that police officers frequently face. She also discusses various ways the police resolve these ethical dilemmas, such as by utilizing the Code of Ethics for Law Enforcement (IACP), traditional ethical rationales or some other ethical guidelines.

# 16

# Breeding Deviant Conformity
## Police Ideology and Culture

*Victor E. Kappeler*
*Richard D. Sluder*
*Geoffrey P. Alpert*

Police see the world in a unique fashion. They process information about people and events in a manner that is shared by few other occupational groups. Simply put, police have a unique worldview. The concept of *worldview* is the manner in which a culture sees the world and its own role and relationship to the world (Redfield, 1953, 1952; Benedict, 1934). This means that various social groups, including the police, perceive situations differently from other social or occupational groups. For example, lawyers may view the world and its events as a source of conflict and potential litigation. Physicians may view the world as a place of disease and illness. For the physician, people may become defined by their illness rather than their social character. Likewise, the police process events with similar cognitive distortion. The police worldview has been described as a working personality. According to Jerome H. Skolnick (1966: 42), "The police as a result of combined features of their social situation, tend to develop ways of looking at the world distinctive to themselves, cognitive lenses through which to see situations and events."

The way the police view the world can be described as a "we/they" or "us/them" orientation. Police tend to see the world as being composed of insiders and outsiders—police and citizens. Persons who are not police officers are considered outsiders and are viewed with suspicion. This "we/they" police worldview is created for a variety of reasons: the techniques used to select citizens for police service; the normative orientation police bring to the profession; an exaggeration of occupational danger; the special legal position police hold in society; and the occupational self-perception that is internalized by people who become police officers. Before citizens can become police officers they must pass through an elaborate employment selection process. In order to be selected for employment,

*Forces of Deviance: The Dark Side of Policing.* Prospect Heights, IL: Waveland (1994), pp. 97–121. Reprinted with permission.

police applicants must demonstrate that they conform to a select set of middle-class norms and values. Police selection practices, such as the use of physical agility tests, background investigations, polygraph examinations, psychological tests and oral interviews, are all tools to screen-out applicants who have not demonstrated their conformity to middle-class norms and values. Many of the selection techniques that are used to determine the "adequacy" of police applicants have little to do with their ability to perform the real duties associated with police work (Gaines, Falkenberg and Gambino, 1994; Paynes and Bernardin, 1992; Maher, 1988; Cox, Crabtree, Joslin and Millett, 1987; Holden, 1984). Often, these tests are designed merely to determine applicants' physical prowess, sexual orientation, gender identification, financial stability, employment history, and abstinence from drug and alcohol abuse. If police applicants demonstrate conformity to a middle-class life style, they are more likely to be considered adequate for police service. The uniform interpretation of psychological tests, based on middle-class bias, tends to produce a homogeneous cohort. As one researcher has noted "the usefulness of psychological testing for police officer selection is, at best, questionable. . . . no test has been found that discriminates consistently and clearly between individuals who will and who will not make good police officers" (Alpert, 1993: 100).

A consequence of the traditional police personnel system is that it selects officers who are unable to identify with many of the marginal groups in society. Therefore, the police process people and events in the world through cognitive filters that overly value conformity in ideology, appearance, and conduct. This conformist view of the world, based on a shared background, provides police a measuring rod by which to make judgments concerning who is deviant and in need of state control (Matza, 1969) and what is "suspicious" (Skolnick, 1966) and in need of police attention. The shared background of the police provides a common cognitive framework from which police process information and respond to events.

This homogeneous group of police recruits experiences formal socialization when it enters the police academy. The police academy refines the cohort again by weeding out those recruits who do not conform to the demands of paramilitary training. Police recruits soon learn:

> . . . that the way to "survive" in the academy . . . is to maintain a "low profile," by being one of the group, acting like the others. Group cohesiveness and mutuality is encouraged by the instructors as well. The early roots of a separation between "the police" and "the public" is evident in many lectures and classroom discussions. In "war stories" and corridor anecdotes, it emerges as a full blown "us-them" mentality (Bahn, 1984: 392).

In fact some have argued that the paramilitary model of police training and organization is inconsistent with humanistic democratic values, demands and supports "employees who demonstrate immature personality traits," and creates dysfunctional organizations (Angell, 1977: 105; Argyris, 1957: 1–24). The encouraged traits closely resemble attributes of the authoritarian personality. In short, police are further differentiated from the public

and become more homogeneous in their worldview through formal training.

As Skolnick (1966) has noted, danger is one of the most important
facets in the development of a police working personality. The relationship
between the "real" dangers associated with police work and the police perception of the job as hazardous is complex. While police officers perceive
their work as dangerous, they realize that the chances of being injured are
not as great as their preoccupation with the idea of danger. Francis T.
Cullen, Bruce G. Link, Lawrence F. Travis and Terrence Lemming (1983:
460) have referred to this situation as a "paradox in policing." Their
research in five police departments found that:

> . . . even though the officers surveyed did not perceive physical injury as an
> everyday happening, this does not mean that they were fully insulated
> against feelings of danger. Hence . . . it can be seen that nearly four-fifths of
> the sample believed that they worked at a dangerous job, and that
> two-thirds thought that policing was more dangerous than other kinds of
> employment.

The disjuncture between the potential for injury and the exaggerated sense
of danger found among police officers is best explained in the remarks of
David Bayley (1976: 171) who observes:

> The possibility of armed confrontation shapes training, patrol preoccupa-
> tions, and operating procedures. It also shapes the relationship between
> citizen and policeman by generating mutual apprehension. The policeman
> can never forget that the individual he contacts may be armed and danger-
> ous; the citizen can never forget that the policeman is armed and may con-
> sider the citizen dangerous.

Police vicariously experience, learn and relearn the potential for danger through "war stories" and field training after graduation from the police
academy. In fact, an inordinate amount of attention and misinformation
concerning the dangers of police work is provided to police recruits at
police academies. Since police instructors are generally former street
enforcement officers, they already have a similar cognitive framework
through which their occupational experiences and view of the world have
been filtered. Training instructors tend to draw on experiences and use stories to convey information to recruits. Thus, much of the material presented
to new police officers serves to reinforce the existing police view of the world
rather than to educate police recruits or to provide appropriate attitudes,
values and beliefs (Murphy and Caplan, 1993; Cohen and Feldberg, 1991;
Delattre, 1989).

Even though well intended, police instructors' ability to educate is
restricted because most police training curricula overemphasize the potential for death and injury and further reinforce the danger notion by spend-
ing an inordinate amount of time on firearms skills, dangerous calls, and
"officer survival." In fact, the training orientation often bears a resemblance
to being prepared to be dropped behind enemy lines to begin a combat

mission. This is not to dismiss the possibility of danger in police work. Certainly, police are killed and injured in the line of duty, but these figures remain relatively small in comparison to the time spent indoctrinating recruits with the notion that the world is a dangerous place—especially if you are a police officer (FBI, 1993; Kappeler, Blumberg and Potter, 1993).

Police training is dominated by an attempt to develop the practical rather than the intellectual skills of recruits. Not only is a substantial amount of time spent on the skills associated with officer safety, a large block of time is spent indoctrinating police on the basic elements of criminal law and the techniques to be used to detect criminal behavior. Little time is spent on developing an understanding of constitutional law, civil rights or ethical considerations in the enforcement of the law. Police instructors evaluate student performance by weighting certain areas more heavily than others. Differential importance is given to the use of firearms, patrol procedures, and how to use force in arresting and restraining citizens. These three areas are seen as the most critical functions by instructors and are given greater emphasis in scoring the performance of recruits in the police academy.

The real and exaggerated sense of danger inherent in police work indisputably forms a great part of the police picture of the world. This allows police to see citizens as potential sources of violence or as enemies. Citizens become "symbolic assailants" to the police officer on the street (Skolnick, 1966). The symbolic assailant is further refined in appearance by taking on the characteristics of marginal segments of society (Harris, 1973; Piliavin and Briar, 1964). The image of the symbolic assailant takes on the characteristics of the populations police are directed to control (*see for example,* Sparger and Giacopassi, 1992). To the cop in southern Texas, the young Hispanic man becomes the potential assailant; in Atlanta, the poor inner-city black man becomes a source of possible injury; and in Chinatown, the Asian becomes the criminal who may resort to violence against the police. The element of danger emphasized by the police culture does much to foster the "we/they" worldview; it also focuses police attention on selective behaviors of certain segments of society.

Skolnick (1966) noted that the authority vested in the police is an equally important characteristic in the development of the police working personality. The law shapes and defines interactions between people and grants social status to members of society (Black, 1976, 1970). The police, by virtue of their social role, are granted a unique position in the law. Police have a legal monopoly on the sanctioned use of violence (Reiss, 1971; Bittner, 1970; Bordua and Reiss, 1967; Westley, 1953) and coercion (Bittner, 1970; Westley, 1953) against other members of society. The legal sanctions that prevent citizens from resorting to violence are relaxed for police officers. Police often resort to violence or coercion to accomplish their organizational goals of controlling crime and enforcing the existing social order. This legal distinction between citizens and police sets officers apart from the larger culture and other occupations.

Since the primary tools used by the police are violence and coercion, it was easy for the police to develop a paramilitary model of training and organization (Bittner, 1970). In this military model, likeness of dress, action and thought is promoted; homogeneity of appearance, ideology and behavior is emphasized. This military model has done much to foster the "we/they" worldview of police. Such a model allows police to see themselves as a close-knit, distinct group and promotes a view of citizens as "outsiders and enemies" (Sherman, 1982; Westley, 1956). This feeling of separateness from the surrounding society is illustrated by the alienation felt by officers who are promoted within the organization to positions of management or by those who leave the profession. Such individuals often feel isolated from their reference group as their occupational membership changes. Police, who once shared the danger, fear and authority of the profession with their subcultural peers become isolated from their reference group when their organizational or occupational standing changes (Gaines, Kappeler and Vaughn, 1994).

Finally, the police worldview is jaded by the perception of policing as the most critical of social functions. As the process of socialization and culturalization continues, police begin to believe and project for the public the image that they are the "thin blue line" that stands between anarchy and order. "Brave police officers patrol mean streets" and are on the front lines of a war for social order and justice. The war for social order is seen by the police as so important that it requires sweeping authority and unlimited discretion to invoke the power of law and, if necessary, the use of force.

After all, that is what the police are trained to do—enforce the law and, when necessary, use force to gain compliance. Similarly, police believe in the goodness of maintaining order, the nobility of their occupation, and the fundamental fairness of the law and existing social order. Accordingly, the police are compelled to view disorder, lawbreaking, and lack of respect for police authority as enemies of a civilized society. "They are thus committed ('because it is right') to maintain their collective face as protectorates of the right and respectable against the wrong and the not-so-respectable. . . . Thus, the moral mandate felt by the police to be their just right at the societal level is translated and transformed into occupational and personal terms and provides both the justification and legitimation for specific acts of street justice" (Van Maanen, 1978b: 227). If law, authority and order were seen as fostering inequity or injustice, the police self-perception would be tainted and the "goodness" of the profession would be questioned by the public. Police could no longer see themselves as partners in justice, but rather partners in repression—a role most police neither sought nor would be willing to recognize. Police who begin to question the goodness of the profession, the equity of law or the criticality of maintaining the existing social order often flee or are forced out of the occupation for other careers, further solidifying the police social character of those who remain.

## The Spirit Of Police Subculture

The concept of *ethos* encompasses the fundamental spirit of a culture: sentiments, beliefs, customs and practices (Biesanz and Biesanz, 1964). Ethos often includes the ideas valued most by a subculture or occupational group. When this term is applied to the police subculture, three general ideas surface. First, the police value an *ethos of bravery*. Bravery is a central component of the social character of policing. As such, it is related to the perceived and actual dangers of law enforcement. The potential to become the victim of a violent encounter, the need for support by fellow officers during such encounters, and the legitimate use of violence to accomplish the police mandate all contribute to a subculture that stresses the virtue of bravery. The bravery ethos is so strong among police that two authors have remarked, "Merely talking about pain, guilt or fear has been considered taboo. If an officer has to talk about his/her personal feelings, that officer is seen as not really able to handle them . . ." To express such fears is viewed by coworkers "as not having what it takes to be a solid, dependable police officer" (Pogrebin and Poole, 1991: 398).

Also, the military trappings of policing, organizational policy such as "never back down" in the face of danger, and informal peer pressure all contribute to instilling a sense of bravery in the police subculture. It is common for training officers to wait until a new recruit has faced a dangerous situation before recommending the recruit be given full status in the organization. Peer acceptance usually does not come until new officers have proven themselves in a dangerous situation. More than anything else, training officers and others in the police subculture want to know how probationary officers will react to danger—will they show bravery?

The importance of bravery in criminal justice occupational groups was highlighted in James Marquart's participant study of the prison guard subculture. Following a confrontation that required the use of force, Marquart (1986: 20) found that:

> The fact that I had been assaulted and had defended myself in front of other officers and building tenders raised my esteem and established my reputation. The willingness to fight inmates was an important trait rewarded by ranking guards. Due to this "fortunate" event, I earned the necessary credibility to establish rapport with the prison participants and allay their previous suspicions of me. I passed the ultimate test—fighting an inmate even though in self-defense—and was now a trustworthy member of the guard subculture.

An *autonomy ethos* is also evident in the police subculture's use and concern over discretionary law enforcement. The nature of police work results in officers demanding, and normally receiving, autonomy in law enforcement and legal sanctioning. As the first line of the criminal justice process, police officers make very authoritative decisions about whom to arrest, when to arrest, and when to use force. To this extent the police are the "gatekeepers" to the criminal justice system (Alpert and Dunham,

1992). This desire for autonomy often exists despite departmental, judicial, or community standards designed to limit the discretion of street enforcement officers. The need for autonomy can contribute to a sense of personally defined justice by members of the police subculture. Depending on subcultural membership, personal interpretations of justice and personal preferences could lead to abuses of discretion. Still, police officers cling to their autonomy in the areas of law enforcement and when to use force. Any attempt to limit the autonomy of the police is viewed as an attempt to undermine the police authority to control "real" street crime and not as an attempt on the part of citizens to curb police abuses of authority.

A third ethos evident in police subcultures is the *ethos of secrecy.* William Westley (1953: 37), a leading scholar on policing, noted that the police "would apply no sanction against a colleague who took the more extreme view of the right to use violence and would openly support some milder form of illegal coercion." Similar conclusions were reached by William J. Chambliss and Robert B. Seidman (1971) in their consideration of police discretion. The police code of secrecy is often the result of a fear of loss of autonomy and authority as external groups try to limit police discretion and decision-making ability. A second factor supporting the development of a code of secrecy is the fact that policing is fraught with the potential for mistakes. Police feel they are often called upon to make split-second decisions that can be reviewed by others not directly involved in policing. This "split-second syndrome" rationalization, however, has been used by the police "to provide after-the-fact justification for unnecessary police violence" (Fyfe, 1993: 502). The desire to protect one's coworkers from disciplinary actions and from being accused of making an improper decision can promote the development of a code of secrecy.

The police code of secrecy is also a product of the police perception of the media and their investigative function. Some researchers suggest that police officers are very concerned with the manner in which the media report their actions (Berg, Gertz and True, 1984). This, coupled with a police perception of the media as hostile, biased and unsupportive, contributes to friction in police-media relations and to increased police secrecy. However, it is sometimes mandatory for officers to refrain from making media releases, having public discussion, or commenting on current criminal investigations in order not to endanger or hinder the process. This necessity is often interpreted by the media, citizens, and others as a self-imposed censorship of information. Perceptions of this nature can promote the separation of the public and the police and create the impression of a secret police society.

## Cultural Themes in Policing

The concept of *themes* in a culture is related to the belief systems or "dynamic affirmations" (Opler, 1945) maintained by its members. Themes help to shape the quality and structure of the group's social interactions.

Themes are not always readily complementary to one another; however, they do occasionally balance or interact. This fact becomes readily apparent in studying the police subculture's dominant themes of social isolation and solidarity.

*Isolation* is an emotional and physical condition that makes it difficult for members of one social group to have relationships and interact with members of another group. This feeling of separateness from the surrounding society is a frequently noted attribute of the American police subculture (Sherman, 1982; Harris, 1973; Manning, 1971; Westley, 1970, 1956, 1953; Reiss and Bordua, 1967; Skolnick, 1966). Social isolation, as a theme of police subculture, is a logical result of the interaction of the police "worldview" and "code of secrecy." The self-imposed social isolation of the police from the surrounding community is well documented (Swanton, 1981; Cain, 1973; Skolnick, 1966; Clark, 1965; Banton, 1964; Baldwin, 1962).

Social isolation reinforces both of the earlier discussed worldview perspectives and ethos. Persons outside the police subculture are viewed somewhat warily as potential threats to the members' physical or emotional well-being, as well as to the officer's authority and autonomy. According to James Baldwin (1962) and Jerome H. Skolnick (1966), police impose social isolation upon themselves as a means of protection against real and perceived dangers, loss of personal and professional autonomy, and social rejection. Rejection by the community stems, in part, from the resentment which sometimes arises when laws are enforced (Clark, 1965). Since no one enjoys receiving a traffic ticket or being arrested and no one enjoys being disliked, the police tend to look inward to their own members for validity and support. Therefore, the police often self-impose restrictions on personal interactions with the community.

Bruce Swanton (1981) examined the topic of police isolation. He pointed out that two primary groups of determinants promote social isolation. Swanton maintained that these determinants were either self-imposed by the police or externally imposed upon the police by the community. Self-imposed police determinants generally concerned work-related requirements of the police profession. These represent structurally induced determinants created by the organization and the police subculture. The most important of these include: administrative structures; work structures; and personality structures (Swanton, 1981: 18).

Swanton found that the traditional view of police work—enforcing the law, detecting and apprehending criminals—created a sense of suspiciousness in police officers. This suspiciousness led to a false belief that positive community interactions or kindness from citizens were designed to compromise the officer's official position. A further deterrence to the maintenance of relationships with members of the general community outside the police subculture is the ambiguity evident in the police officer's on-duty and off-duty status. Swanton (1981) noted that the long and often irregular working hours—a result of shift schedules and possible cancellation of days off or vacations—coupled with the community's perception of police work as socially unattractive contribute to the police officer's sense of isolation. Swanton's "publicly initiated determinants" of isolation include:

> . . . suspicion that police compromise their friendships with higher loyalty to their employer; resentment at police-initiated sanctions or the potential thereof; attempts at integration by those wishing to curry favor, which are resented by others; and personality of police perceived as socially unattractive, thereby reducing the motivation of non-police to form close relationships with them (1981: 18).

Using a different perspective of the police, Charles Bahn (1984: 392) summarized the problem appropriately when he stated "social isolation becomes both a consequence and a stimulus. . . . Police officers find that constraints of schedule, of secrecy, of group mystique, and of growing adaptive suspiciousness and cynicism limit their friendships and relationships in the non-police world."

The second theme evident in the police subculture is *solidarity* (Harris, 1973; Westley, 1970, 1956, 1953; Stoddard, 1968; Skolnick, 1966; Banton, 1964). Traditionally, the theme of police solidarity and loyalty was seen as the result of a need for insulation from the earlier mentioned perceived dangers and rejection of the community. Michael Brown (1981: 82) has noted the importance of loyalty and solidarity among the police. Consider his interpretation of one police officer's remarks.

> "I'm for the guys in blue! Anybody criticizes a fellow copper that's like criticizing someone in my family; we have to stick together." The police culture demands of a patrolman unstinting loyalty to his fellow officers, and he receives, in return, protection: a place to assuage real and imagined wrongs inflicted by a (presumably) hostile public; safety from aggressive administrators and supervisors; and the emotional support required to perform a difficult task. The most important question asked by a patrolman about a rookie is whether or not he displays the loyalty demanded by the police subculture.

Theodore N. Ferdinand (1980), however, has noted that solidarity and loyalty change in proportion to an officer's age and rank. He maintained that police cadets have the least amount of solidarity, and line officers have the greatest amount of solidarity. Ferdinand (1980) noted that until the age of forty, much of a police officer's social life is spent within the confines of the police subculture. However, solidarity declines as police move into higher ranks in the department. Members of the police administrative hierarchy are frequently seen by the line officers in much the same perspective as members of the community and other non-police characters—namely, as threatening to the welfare of the subculture.

Police solidarity, therefore, may be said to be an effect of the socialization process inherent to the subculture and police work. New members are heavily socialized to increase their solidarity with the group, and those who move away from the subculture, either through age or promotion, are gradually denied the ties of solidarity. This socialization, or cohesion, is based in part upon the "sameness" of roles, perceptions and self-imagery of the members of the police subculture.

## Postulates of Police Culture

*Postulates* are statements of belief held by a group which reflect its basic orientations (Opler, 1945). Postulates are the verbal links between a subculture's view of the world and their expression of that view into action. Because postulates and cultural themes may conflict, the degree to which they complement one another and are integrated is said to be indicative of the homogeneity and complexity of a culture. Postulates, then, are statements—expressions of general truth or principle that guide and direct the actions of subcultural members. Such statements enable one to understand the nuances of a subculture to a greater degree than do ethos or themes. Postulates act as oral vehicles for the transmission of culture from one generation to the next, and tend to serve as reinforcers of the subcultural worldview.

Postulates basic to an understanding of the police subculture have been collected and arranged into an informal code of police conduct. Elizabeth Reuss-Ianni (1983a), drawing from the research of many others (Manning, 1977; Rubinstein, 1973; Savitz, 1971; Stoddard, 1968; Skolnick, 1966; Westley, 1956, 1953), identified several police postulates (*also see*, Reuss-Ianni and Ianni, 1983b). Although she used these postulates to demonstrate the conflict between administrators and line officers, they can also be divided into three separate categories that reflect the culture of policing. Ruess-Ianni's work is important because it illustrates the influence that line officers have on the total organization. Her work shows that despite administrative efforts to produce organizational change, substantive change is difficult to attain without the collective efforts of group members. In the case of the police, Ruess-Ianni recognized the importance of informal work groups and the influence those groups have on structuring social relationships both in and outside of the police subculture. Hence, postulates are important in shaping not only the attitudes, values and beliefs of police officers but also a shared understanding of what are deemed to be both acceptable and unacceptable behaviors.

### Postulates Shaping the Ethos of Secrecy
### and the Theme of Solidarity

The first group of postulates identified by Ruess-Ianni reflects the ethos of secrecy that surrounds much of police work. This secrecy has many functions, three of which seem especially important. . . . First, the public is denied knowledge of many police activities because, in the eyes of the police, they have no "need to know." While it may be prudent to restrict access to certain types of sensitive information in law enforcement, the veil of secrecy that shields police from the public has the effect of minimizing public scrutiny of police activities and behaviors. Secondly, many of the postulates identified by Ruess-Ianni are guideposts which keep officers from relaying too much information to police supervisors. For first-line police officers, these postulates are seen as necessary protections to insulate police officers from what they see as unwarranted punishment or challenges to their autonomy. Finally, these postulates may be most important in the sense that taken together, they provide first-line police officers with a sense of solidarity. Some of the postulates indicative of the ethos of secrecy and the theme of police solidarity include:

- *"Don't give up another cop"* (Ruess-Ianni, 1983: 14). As perhaps one of the most important factors contributing to a sense of solidarity and secrecy, this postulate admonishes officers to never, regardless of the seriousness or nature of a case, provide information to either superiors or non-police that would cause harm to a fellow police officer. Ruess-Ianni notes that this postulate implicitly informs a police officer that abiding by this canon and never giving up another cop means others "won't give you up."

- *"Watch out for your partner first and then the rest of the guys working that tour"* (Ruess-Ianni, 1983: 14). This postulate tells police officers they have an obligation to their partners first, and then to other officers working the same shift. "Watching out," in this context, means that an officer has a duty not only to protect fellow officers from physical harm, but also to watch out for their interests in other matters. If, for example, an officer learns that another member of his or her squad is under investigation by an internal affairs unit, the officer is obligated to inform the officer of this information. As with the postulate listed above, the implicit assumption here is that if you watch out for fellow police, they will also watch out for you.

- *"If you get caught off base, don't implicate anybody else"* (Ruess-Ianni, 1983: 14). Being caught off base can involve a number of activities, ranging from being out of one's assigned sector to being caught for engaging in prohibited activities. This postulate teaches officers that if someone discovers their involvement in proscribed activities, officers should accept the punishment and not expose fellow officers to scrutiny or possible punishment. In essence, this rule of behavior advises police officers that if caught for misbehavior, accept the punishment, but do not involve others who might also be punished. This postulate insulates other police officers from punishment and reduces the possibility that organized deviance or corruption will be uncovered.

- *"Make sure the other guys know if another cop is dangerous or 'crazy'"* (Ruess-Ianni, 1983: 14). Police are caught in a double-bind if they become aware that one of their fellow members is unstable or presents a safety hazard. In this case, the secrecy dictum prohibits a line officer from informing police supervisors of another officer's instability or unsuitability. Yet at the same time, an officer has an obligation to watch out for his or her peers. In order to deal with such a contradiction, this rule of behavior tells an officer that if he or she is aware that another officer may be dangerous or crazy, there is an obligation to let other police know of the potential safety risks, but not to take formal action against the officer. This postulate allows "problem" officers to continue to operate within the profession and reduces the chances that they will be detected by the agency administration or the public. It does, however, allow informal sanctions of exclusion to be imposed.

- *"Don't get involved in anything in another cop's sector"* (Ruess-Ianni, 1983: 14). Ruess-Ianni notes that in older, corrupt departments, this dictum advised officers not to try to hedge in on another police officer's illegal activities. In essence, this rule informed police that officers "owned" certain forms of corruption in their sector. Today, this postulate teaches officers that they are to stay out of all matters in other officers' sectors. This rule of territoriality is believed necessary because officers are responsible for activities in their respective beats. This postulate serves to limit the spread of information making it easier for officers to deny knowledge of deviance, which in turn makes deviance appear to be a mere aberration.

- *"Hold up your end of the work; don't leave work for the next tour"* (Ruess-Ianni, 1983: 14–15). These postulates teach officers that if they neglect their work responsibilities, two results are likely to occur. First, other officers must cover for those who shirk their responsibilities. Second, malingerers call attention to everyone on a shift. Thus, there are pressures for all officers to carry their own weight. . . . If, however, an officer fails to follow this edict, other officers are expected to "cover" for the officer and to deflect attention away from the group.

- *"Don't look for favors just for yourself"* (Ruess-Ianni, 1983: 16). This dictum admonishes officers not to "suck up" to superiors. In essence, this rule tells officers that their primary responsibilities are to their peers and that attempts to curry favors with superiors will be looked down upon. This postulate prevents line officers from developing relationships with superiors that might threaten the safety of the work group.

## Postulates Supporting Police Isolationism

Ruess-Ianni has identified several postulates that are reflective of the "we/they" worldview that police develop. These postulates teach new officers that non-police simply do not understand the true nature of police work. As such, these pronouncements reinforce the notion that there are vast differences between police and citizens. Further, non-police will never be able to truly understand the unique problems inherent in policing. John Van Maanen (1978a) referred to these citizens as "know nothings" because of their characterization by the police. Ultimately, this we/they worldview increases police isolation from citizens. Postulates indicative of the we/they worldview and supportive of police isolationism include:

- *"Protect your ass"* (Ruess-Ianni, 1983: 15). As perhaps one of the most important postulates leading to a sense of isolation, this rule teaches police to be wary of everyone—including citizens and superiors. At the simplest level, the rule informs police that anyone who wants to cause trouble for an officer probably can. Hence, the rule teaches police that others can not be trusted. Because of this, officers must be vigilant and take all steps necessary to protect themselves from any possible threat. While these threats might include the possibility of physical harm, they would also include the possibility of disciplinary action by superiors and the potential for citizens to complicate the lives of police by filing complaints, making allegations, or uncovering deviance.

- *"Don't trust a new guy until you have him checked out."* (Ruess-Ianni, 1983: 14). Rookie police and officers who are new to a work group are not to be automatically accorded status as a trusted group member. Instead, outsiders are to be treated cautiously until information about them can be obtained, or until they have "proven" themselves. In some cases, rookie officers are "tested" to determine if they can be trusted. Those officers having a history with the department are checked out through the "grapevine" and are often intentionally placed in situations to see if they can be trusted.

- *"Don't talk too little or too much; don't tell anybody more than they have to know"* (Ruess-Ianni, 1983: 14–15). The themes of "don't talk too much," and "don't reveal more than necessary" inform new police officers that others—including citizens and supervisors—are not to be trusted. These dictates reinforce the notion not only that "loose lips sink ships," but also that there is no need to provide others with information beyond the minimum required. This is true because information can be distorted or used in other ways that are potentially harmful to police. At the same time, the dictate "don't talk too little" lets new police officers know that excessive silence or introversion will be seen as suspicious behavior by other officers. As Ruess-Ianni notes, the extremes of talking too much or too little are both viewed as suspicious behaviors by fellow officers. This postulate directs officers to maintain communications with the work group but to limit their exposure to administrators and citizens.

- *"Don't trust bosses to look out for your interests"* (Ruess-Ianni, 1983: 16). This maxim informs new police officers that when forced to make a choice, managers and administrators will look out for their own best interests rather than those of the officer. Whether true or not, this idea has the effect of further distancing officers from their superiors. Since line officers are taught that they can not depend on either citizens or superiors, they are forced to align themselves with the only group left for protection—fellow police.

## Postulates Indicative of the Ethos of Bravery

David H. Bayley and Egon Bittner (1989) have noted that a crucial part of a police officer's job is to take charge of situations and people. Taking charge, in this sense, involves developing a "presence" to handle incidents. In essence, this means that officers must be poised to take control regardless of the situation. Yet, it is crucial not to appear too ready, since overeagerness can escalate situations. In one officer's words, "Always act . . . as if you were on vacation." At the same time, however, "One must be keyed up but not 'choke'" (Bayley and Bittner, 1989:101). A couple of Ruess-Ianni's postulates strongly suggest that above all else, new officers must always show bravery in the performance of police work. These postulates are:

- *"Show balls"* (Ruess-Ianni, 1983: 14). Police themselves characterize their work as laden with danger and fraught with hazards. Accordingly, this postulate counsels police that they are never to back down from a situation. While this is especially true for incidents that occur in view of the public, it is also important for an officer to never back down from a situation where other officers are present. This postulate is important in the eyes of the police; backing down shows the public that the police are weak. All police, therefore, are believed harmed by the cowardice of an individual officer. Thus, the idea that if an officer gets into a situation, he or she must have fortitude to control the situation. A challenge to the authority of a single officer is seen as a challenge to the authority of the entire police group. These challenges must be accepted and dealt with.

- *"Be aggressive when you have to, but don't be too eager"* (Ruess-Ianni, 1983: 14). This postulate reflects the idea that while officers should always be alert, they should not go out of their way to seek trouble. This is partly because overeagerness, or having a "chip" on one's shoulder, will only bring unneeded complications. In a sense, the maxim "If you look for trouble, it will find you," applies here. Therefore, challenges to authority must be met and dealt with, but they should not be sought out. Police are to avoid acting in ways that cause the group to undergo unnecessary scrutiny. However, this postulate teaches an officer to meet a challenge or confrontation as aggressively as necessary to handle it effectively.

Through exposure to these and other postulates, new generations of police officers combine their experiences and perceptions of the world—all of which are filtered through the unique perspective of police officers' eyes. With these "truths," officers develop a belief system which dictates acceptable and unacceptable behavior. These postulates serve as reinforcers of the police worldview and act as part of the socialization process for members of the police occupation. Through these postulates, officers are taught to keep police business "secret," the necessity for solidarity among the ranks, and the belief that police are different and isolated from larger society. Violations of these canons may lead to immediate sanctions from fellow subculture members, frequently resulting in some form of expulsion from the security of the group. It is ironic that police who violate the precepts of the subculture are doubly isolated—first from the community by nature of the occupation and later by the police subculture, for violation of its informal norms of conduct. Police officers who do not conform to the postulates of the work group become outcasts who have been stripped of the benefits of group membership.

The occupational culture provides police with a unique working personality. This working personality includes the development of a worldview that teaches police to distinguish between insiders and outsiders (i.e. police/non-police)—in other words, those who are okay versus those who must be cautiously watched. This we/they perspective instills in officers a perpetual concern for the element of danger in their work. The police working personality reinforces the notion of "differentness" in three ways. First, police are taught that they are vested with the unique power to use force and violence in carrying out legal mandates. Second, the paramilitary nature of police work isolates police from others in society. Finally, police are indoctrinated with the idea that they are the "thin blue line" between anarchy and order.

Police ethos reflect the ideas valued most by the police. Some of the most important ethos transmitted by the police subculture are the ethos of bravery, the ethos of autonomy, and the ethos of secrecy.

Cultural themes are also a part of the police culturalization process. In this case, cultural themes are fairly specific rules of behavior that shape police interactions. A dominant cultural theme in policing is the idea that police are socially isolated from the rest of society. A second important cultural theme extols the need for police solidarity.

Finally, several postulates of the police culture were reviewed. Postulates are specific principles used to guide and direct the actions of subcultural members. Postulates that reinforce the need for police secrecy and solidarity include instructions to never "give up" another cop; to watch out for other police, especially one's partner; and if caught engaging in prohibited activities, never implicate other officers. Postulates that support police isolationism instruct police to "protect your ass" by being wary of everyone; not to trust new officers until they have proven themselves; and not to trust supervisors to look out for an officer's best interests. Postulates also instruct officers on the ethos of bravery: have fortitude and never back down in a situation; be aggressive but not overeager in handling situations.

## References

Alpert, G. P. (1993). The Role of Psychological Testing in Law Enforcement. In Dunham, R. G. and G. P. Alpert (Eds.). *Critical Issues in Policing: Contemporary Readings* (2nd ed.). Prospect Heights, IL: Waveland Press.

Alpert, G. P., & R. G. Dunham. (1992). *Policing Urban America* (2nd ed.). Prospect Heights, IL: Waveland Press.

Angell, J. E. (1977). Toward an Alternative to the Classical Police Organizational Arrangements: A Democratic Model. In L. K. Gaines and T. A. Ricks, (Eds.) *Managing the Police Organization*. St. Paul, MN: West Publishing Company.

Argyris, C. (1957). The Individual and Organization: Some Problems of Mutual Adjustment. *Administrative Science Quarterly* (June): 1–24.

Bahn, C. (1984). Police Socialization in the Eighties: Strains in the Forging of an Occupational Identity. *Journal of Police Science and Administration* 12(4): 390–94.

Baldwin, J. (1962). *Nobody Knows My Name*. New York: Dell Publishing Company.

Banton, M. (1964). *The Police in the Community*. London, England: Travistock.

Bayley, D. (1976). *Forces of Order: Police Behavior in Japan and the United States*. Berkeley: University of California Press.

Bayley, D. H., and E. Bittner. (1989). Learning the Skills of Policing. In R. Dunham and G. P. Alpert, (Eds.) *Critical Issues in Policing: Contemporary Readings*. Prospect Heights, IL: Waveland Press.

Benedict, R. (1934). *Patterns of Culture*. Boston: Houghton Mifflin Company.

Berg, B. L., M. G. Gertz, and E. J. True. (1984). Police-community Relations and Alienation. *Police Chief* 51(11): 20–23.

Biesanz, J., and M. Biesanz. (1964). *Modern Society* (3rd ed.). Englewood Cliffs, NJ: Prentice-Hall.

Bittner, E. (1970). *The Functions of Police in Modern Society*. Chevy Chase, MD: National Clearinghouse for Mental Health.

Black, D. (1976). *The Behavior of Law*. New York: Academic Press.

_____. (1970). Production of Crime Rates. *American Sociological Review* 35: 733–48.

Brown, M. K. (1981). *Working the Street: Police Discretion and the Dilemmas of Reform*. New York: Russell Sage Foundation.

Cain, M. E. (1973). *Society and the Policeman's Role*. London, England: Routledge and Kegal Paul.

Chambliss, W. J.,and R. B. Seidman. (1971). *Law, Order and Power*. Reading, MA: Addison-Wesley.

Clark, J. P. (1965). Isolation of the Police: A Comparison of the British and American Situations. *Journal of Criminal Law, Criminology and Police Science* 56: 307–19.

Cohen, H. S., and M. Feldberg. (1991). *Power and Restraint: The Moral Dimension of Police Work*. New York: Praeger.

Cox, T. C., A. Crabtree, D. Joslin, and A. Millet. (1987). A Theoretical Examination of Police Entry-level Uncorrected Visual Standards. *American Journal of Criminal Justice* 11(2): 199–208.

Cullen, F. T., B. G. Link, L. F. Travis, and T. Lemming. (1983). Paradox in Policing: A Note on Perceptions of Danger. *Journal of Police Science and Administration* 11(4): 457–62.

Delattre, E. J. (1989). *Character and Cops: Ethics in Policing*. Washington, DC: American Enterprise Institute for Public Policy Research.

Federal Bureau of Investigation (1993). *Law Enforcement Officers Killed and Assaulted*. Washington, DC: U.S. Government Printing Office.

Ferdinand, T. H. (1980). Police Attitudes and Police Organization: Some Interdepartmental and Cross-cultural Comparisons. *Police Studies* 3: 46–60.

Fyfe, J. J. (1993). The Split-second Syndrome and Other Determinates of Police Violence. In R. G. Dunham and G. P. Alpert, (Eds.) *Critical Issues in Policing: Contemporary Readings* (2nd ed.). Prospect Heights, IL: Waveland Press.

Gaines, L. K., and V. E. Kappeler. (1990). The Police Selection Process: What Works. In G. Cordner and D. Hale, (Eds.). *What Works in Policing?* Cincinnati: Anderson Publishing Company.

Gaines, L. K., P. Costello, and A. Crabtree. (1989). Police Selection Testing: Balancing Legal Requirements and Employer Needs. American *Journal of Police* 8(1): 137–52.

Gaines, L. K., S. Falkenberg, and J. A. Gambino. (1994). Police Physical Agility Testing: A Historical and Legal Analysis. *American Journal of Police*, forthcoming.

Gaines, L. K., V. E. Kappeler, and J. B. Vaughn. (1994). *Policing in America.* Cincinnati: Anderson Publishing Company.

Harris, R. (1973). *The Police Academy: An Insider's View.* New York: John Wiley and Sons.

Holden, R. (1984). Vision sTandards for Law Enforcement: A Descriptive Study. *Journal of Police Science and Administration* 12(2): 125–29.

Kappeler, V. E., M. Blumberg, and G. W. Potter. (1993). The *Mythology of Crime and Criminal Justice.* Prospect Heights, IL: Waveland Press.

Kraska, P. B., and V. E. Kappeler. (1988). Police On-duty Drug Use: A Theoretical and Descriptive Examination. *American Journal of Police* 7(1): 1–28.

Kuykendall, J.,and D. Burns. (1980). The Black Police Officer: An Historical Perspective. *Journal of Contemporary Criminal Justice* 1(4): 103–13.

Maher, P. T. (1988). Police Physical Agility Tests: Can They ever be Valid. *Public Personnel Management Journal* 17: 173–83.

Manning, P. K. (1977). *Police Work: The Social Organization of Policing.* Cambridge: The MIT Press.

_____. (1971). The police: Mandate, Strategies and Appearances. In L. K. Gaines and T. A. Ricks. (Eds.) *Managing The Police Organization.* St. Paul: West Publishing Company.

Marquart, J. (1986). Doing Research in Prison: The Strengths and Weaknesses of Full Participation as a Guard. *Justice Quarterly* 3(1): 20–32.

Matza, D. (1969). *Becoming Deviant.* Englewood Cliffs, NJ: Prentice-Hall.

Murphy, P. V., & Caplan, D. G. (1993). Fostering Integrity. In R. G. Dunham and G. P. Alpert, (Eds.). *Critical Issues in Policing: Contemporary Readings,* (2nd ed.). Prospect Heights, IL: Waveland Press.

Opler, M. E. (1945). Themes as Dynamic Forces in Culture. *The American Journal of Sociology* 51: 198–206.

Paynes, J., & Bernardin, H. J. (1992). Entry-level Police Selection: The Assessment Center is an Alternative. *Journal of Criminal Justice* 20: 41–52.

Piliavin, I., & Briar, S. (1964). Police Encounters with Juveniles. *American Journal of Sociology* 70: 206–14.

Pogrebin, M. R., & Poole, E. D. (1991). Police and Tragic Events: The Management of Emotions. *Journal of Criminal Justice* 19: 395–403.

Reaves, B. A. (1992a). *State and Local Police Departments, 1990.* Washington, DC: Bureau of Justice Statistics, U.S. Department of Justice.

_____. (1992b). *Sheriff's Departments 1990.* Washington, DC: Bureau of Justice Statistics, U.S. Department of Justice.

_____. (1989). *Police Departments in Large Cities, 1987.* Washington, DC: Bureau of Justice Statistics, U.S. Department of Justice.

Redfield, R. (1953). *The Primitive World and Its Transformations.* Ithaca, NY: Cornell University Press.

_____. (1952). The Primitive Worldview. *Proceedings of the American Philosophical Society* 96: 30–36.

Reiss, A. J. (1971). *The Police and the Public*. New Haven: Yale University Press.

Reiss, A. J., & Bordua, D. J. (1967). Environment and Organization: A Perspective on the Police. In D. J. Bordua (Ed.) *The Police: Six Sociological Essays*. New York: John Wiley and Sons.

Reuss-Ianni, E. (1983a). *Two Cultures of Policing*. New Brunswick, NJ: Transaction Books.

Reuss-Ianni, E., & Ianni, F. A. J. (1983b). Street Cops and Management Cops: The Two Cultures of Policing. In M. Punch. (Ed.) *Control in the Police Organization*. Cambridge: MIT Press.

Rubinstein, J. (1973). *City Police*. New York: Farrar, Strauss and Giroux.

Savitz, L. (1971). The Dimensions of Police Loyalty. In H. Hann, (Ed.) *Police In Urban Society*. Beverly Hills: Sage.

Sherman, L. (1982). Learning Police Ethics. *Criminal Justice Ethics* 1(1): 10–19.

Skolnick, J. H. (1966). *Justice Without Trial: Law Enforcement in a Democratic Society*. New York: John Wiley and Sons.

Sparger, J. R., & Giacopassi, D. J. (1992). Memphis Revisited: A Reexamination of Police Shootings After the Garner Decision. *Justice Quarterly* 9: 211–25.

Sullivan, P. S. (1989). Minority Officers: Current Issues. In R. G. Dunham and G. P. Alpert, (Eds.). *Critical Issues in Policing: Contemporary Readings*. Prospect Heights, IL: Waveland Press.

Swanton, B. (1981). Social Isolation of Police: Structural Determinants and Remedies. *Police Studies* 3: 14–21.

Van Maanen, J. (1978a). On Becoming a Policeman. In P. K. Manning and Van Maanen, J. (Eds.) *Policing: A View From The Street*. Santa Monica: Goodyear.

_____. (1978b). The Asshole. In P. K. Manning and J. Van Maanen, (Eds.) *Policing: A View From The Street*. Santa Monica: Goodyear.

Westley, W. A. (1970). *Violence and the Police: A Sociological Study of Law, Custom and Morality*. Cambridge: MIT Press.

_____. (1956). Secrecy and the Police. *Social Forces* 34(3): 254–57.

_____. (1953). Violence and the Police. *American Journal of Sociology* 59: 34–41.

# 17

# Evaluating Citizen Complaints Against the Police

*Allen E. Wagner*
*Scott H. Decker*

## Introduction

The rule of law constrains the behavior of public agencies in American society. In no other case is this more apparent than for law enforcement agencies. The police are constrained by a variety of factors as they endeavor to go about their job. Perhaps it is the irony that the police sometimes act outside the law, as they enforce the law, that makes police misconduct particularly troublesome in a democratic society. From a more pragmatic perspective, the police are dependent on citizen cooperation to successfully fulfill their crime control mandate. Absent such cooperation, the identification and apprehension of criminal suspects becomes a nearly impossible task.

When the police are subjects of complaints, the process of law enforcement begins to break down. The perception of the police as violators of the law and public trust inhibits their ability to carry out their instrumental functions, as well as limits public confidence. The allegation of a complaint against a police officer is indicative of the perception that policing has passed beyond its acceptable bounds and becomes an unwarranted intrusion into public consciousness.

This chapter will examine the process by which a civilian complaint against the police emerges and is resolved. It begins with a brief discussion of the "ambivalent" nature of the role held by American police. Against this backdrop, the issue of police misconduct, specifically those behaviors which generate citizen complaints, is considered. The complaint process itself is then examined, with a specific focus on a typology of complainants. This discussion concludes with an examination of guidelines for dealing with complaints filed against the police. Next, consideration is given to the

Prepared especially for *Critical Issues in Policing*, 3/E by Allen E. Wagner and Scott H. Decker.

various structures in the review process. A concluding section considers the prospects for reform in the future.

## The Police Role and Complaints

Goldstein cautions that "anyone attempting to construct a workable definition of the police role will typically come away with old images shattered and a new-found appreciation for the intricacies of police work" (1977:21). While definitions of the police role are divergent, Niederhoffer (1969:7) cites a list by then FBI Director J. Edgar Hoover:

1. protection of life and property;
2. preservation of the peace;
3. prevention of crime;
4. detection and arrest of violators of the law;
5. enforcement of laws and ordinances; and
6. safeguarding the rights of individuals.

This list of police goals (or one similar) has been taught to recruit officers for at least a generation, and no one seriously doubts their foundation in the law. But the goals, laudable as they are, do not accurately reflect the vagaries of the police role.

What, then, is the role? Walker (1983:56–57) posits that, however one defines role, it is complex and ambiguous and leads to role conflict within the individual officer and between the police and the public. Such conflicts often lead to the filing of a complaint against the police. Clearly, the diffuse and often contradictory roles of the police precipitate many police-citizen misunderstandings. Different expectations regarding the police role, differences that stem in part from the discretion exercised by officers, lead to citizen complaints.

This "discretionary" aspect of police work is sometimes at the cutting edge of dissonance between the police (indeed, individual police officers) and the public. Consider the citizen; the public has its own definition and expectations of the police role. These, as does police work itself, vary from community to community. Essentially, the general public believes that the police should enforce the law, prevent crime, and maintain order. But, as Ward points out, "a group of drug addicts might have different expectations than the local Chamber of Commerce with regard to the way policemen institute searches" (1975:215).

The officer, therefore, must learn to react to the situation and the individuals involved, keeping in mind the expected gains or losses. The officer must determine which of several options are open and then choose between one or more alternatives which may be at variance with the expectations of some of those concerned, including other police officers.

It can be easily observed that the ambiguous nature of the police role almost invites criticism. Such criticism, particularly by the public, may frequently result in formal complaints.

# Police Misconduct

In 1903, a New York City police commissioner turned judge noted that his court had seen numerous citizens with injuries received when the police effected their arrest. He felt that many of them had done nothing to deserve an arrest but most of them had made no complaint. Said the judge, "If the victim complains, his charge is generally dismissed. The police are practically above the law" (Reiss, 1970:57). Germann observes, almost three-quarters of a century later, that "police attitudes for the most part, indicate no responsibility for unnecessary or illegal police violence, or abuses of police authority" (1971:418).

The key word is "authority." The laws of most states, coupled with department regulations, usually define the extent to which force may be used by a police officer in the performance of official duties.

## Some Definitions of Police Misconduct

Field observers, working on a project for the Center of Research on Social Organization in the late 1960s, were given several guidelines to assist them in determining when police use of force was judged to be unnecessary or improper.

1. If a policeman physically assaulted a citizen and then failed to make an arrest; proper use involves an arrest.
2. If the citizen being arrested did not, by word or deed, resist the policeman; force should be used only if it is necessary to make an arrest.
3. If the policeman, even though there was resistance to the arrest, could easily have restrained the citizen in other ways.
4. If a larger number of policemen were present and could have assisted in subduing the citizen in the station, in lockup, and in the interrogation rooms.
5. If an offender was handcuffed and made no attempt to flee or offer violent resistance.
6. If the citizen resisted arrest, but the force continued even after the citizen was subdued. (Reiss, 1970:64)

Stark notes that a set of guidelines was also prepared by the International Association of Chiefs of Police (IACP). While the IACP directions were longer and more legalistic in appearance than were those given the CRSO observers, they were similar in content (1972:57).

The unnecessary or excessive use of force by the police (both of which fit under the label of "physical abuse"), especially when a citizen is seriously injured, is a most serious complaint. However, there are other abuses which, while they do not physically injure anyone, might be termed degrading, dehumanizing, or humiliating. Police departments around the country record these types of complaints under a variety of terms such as verbal abuse, discourtesy, harassment, improper attitude, and ethnic slur.

By the same token, Reiss discovered that citizens objected to, and complained about:

1. the way police *use* language (not necessarily the words they select);
2. the habit police officers have of "talking down" to them; and
3. the "harassing" tactics of the police—the indiscriminate stopping and searching of citizens on foot or in cars, commands to go home or to "move on." (1970:59–62)

In 1968, the National Advisory Commission on Civil Disorders (the Kerner Commission) reported the finding of similar abuses. While it noted that verbal abuse or discourtesy in urban areas was more likely to be directed at whites, such tactics were particularly distressing to blacks. Said the commission report, "In nearly every city surveyed, the Commission heard complaints of harassment of interracial couples, dispersal of social street gatherings, and the stopping of (blacks) on foot or in cars without obvious basis. These, together with contemptuous and degrading verbal abuse, have great impact in the ghetto . . ." (1968:299–322).

Reiss summarizes the ways in which police have traditionally dealt with certain citizens, particularly those in the lower class:

1. the use of profane and abusive language;
2. commands to move on or get home;
3. stopping and questioning people on the street or searching them and their cars;
4. threats to use force if not obeyed;
5. prodding with a nightstick or approaching with a pistol; and
6. the actual use of physical force or violence itself. (1970:59)

This behavior on the part of police officers frequently results in citizen attempts at redress. Such redress often takes the form of a complaint.

## Previous Studies in Police Misconduct

The President's Commission on Law Enforcement and Administration of Justice reported, although it admitted that it could not determine the extent of physical abuse by the police, that earlier studies had shown that it was a significant problem. Said the commission:

> The National Commission on Law Observance and Enforcement (the Wickersham Commission), which reported to President Hoover in 1931, found considerable evidence of police brutality. The President's Commission on Civil Rights, appointed by President Truman, made a similar finding in 1947. And, in 1961, the U.S. Civil Rights Commission concluded that "police brutality is still a serious problem throughout the United States." (1967:193)

The Commission stated that it did not feel that physical abuse was as serious a problem as in the past, saying "the few statistics . . . suggest small numbers of cases involving excessive use of force" (1967:193).

Black and Reiss submitted a research study to the same commission. It was based on seven weeks of observations of police-citizen interactions in Boston, Chicago, and the District of Columbia. The research was not particularly focused on physical abuse but on other forms of police abuse. The Black and Reiss study found that: (1) police tend to be hostile toward antagonistic citizens, offenders, intoxicated persons (in some instances), and in field interrogations; (2) permission of citizens was seldom requested before personal searches were made of subjects; searches were determined to be unnecessary as often as 86 percent of the time; and (3) black citizens objected the least to personal searches, were less apt to be taken to the station house and released without charge, and were less discriminated against, when antagonistic, than whites, at least in radio dispatch situations (1967:35–107).

In 1971, Reiss addressed the subject of excessive force. This study determined that: (1) more than three-quarters of the cases involving excessive force took place in a patrol car, precinct station or public place (primarily the streets); (2) almost all victims were offenders or suspects and were young, lower-class males from any racial group; and (3) persons regarded by the police as deviant offenders (drunks, homosexuals, drug addicts), or who were perceived (by the officer) to have defied the officer's authority, were the most likely victims of undue force (1971:1).

Reiss noted the disparity between his findings and popular opinion that black citizens are the primary victims of physical abuse. He suggested that, even though white officers might be prejudiced toward blacks, they did not discriminate in the use of excessive force. It is Reiss's contention that the *police culture* more readily explains the use of force than does prejudice (1971:76).

More recent studies have, however, shown that nonwhite citizens, especially blacks, *are* more often the victims of police misconduct. Hudson, in his study of complaints investigated by the Philadelphia Police Advisory Board, found that police encounters with nonwhite citizens more frequently led to altercations than did police encounters with white citizens. Nonwhite citizens also constituted 70 percent of the principal complainants in Hudson's study (1970:187). Wagner found that blacks constituted slightly more than two-thirds of those who filed complaints against the police (1980:249). Decker and Wagner determined that black complainants were more likely to have been injured in an incident which precipitated a complaint against the police and were also more likely to be arrested than their white counterparts (1982:116–7). Decker and Wagner also found that the incident which prompted the complaint was more likely to have occurred in police custody, out of public view, if the complainant was black (1985:111).

What are some of the reasons set forth for this situation? Chevigny observes that, "police recruits are much like other young men of a similar background; it is police mores and the police role that make them adopt police attitudes" (1969:137), and "the challenge to police authority continues as a chief cause of force in all urban police departments" (1969:60).

Niederhoffer asserts, "at first impression it would appear that above all other groups the police ought to be tied to the law, but because they learn to manipulate it, the law can become nothing more than a means to an end" (1969:97). All of these works point to the role of police culture as a primary source for misconduct. Thus, macro-level rather than micro-level (individual) concerns seem most appropriate when considering efforts to stem police behavior perceived offensive by citizens. This point was underscored by Friedrich's (1980) analysis of police use of force. He notes that classic characteristics of the setting were more closely related to the use of force by officers than were individual characteristics of the officers themselves. Skolnick and Fyfe (1993:90) add that police applicants do not see themselves as bullies, nor does the police literature suggest that the police service attracts authoritarian personalities. Both the written and unwritten rules of police departments combine to form a distinctive worldview that "affects the values and understanding of cops on and off the job . . . ." Thus, efforts to stem police misconduct seem most appropriately targeted at characteristics of the police culture—those norms which guide police work.

## Filing a Complaint

When a breakdown in the management of a police-citizen encounter has occurred, the citizen may file a complaint. Russell, in his study in England and Wales, found that those citizens who did decide to file a complaint against the police did so only after giving consideration to one or more of the following:

1. the citizen was advised that he might well succeed in his complaint;
2. he was able and prepared to make the effort to complain in the belief that justice would be done;
3. he believed that by complaining a policeman might be deterred from misbehaving in the future and that the result could only be in the public interest; and
4. the complaining citizen does not believe that any effort will be made by the officer or his associates to seek revenge. (1978:54)

The respondents in Russell's study did not indicate a personal revenge motive, nor did Russell explain *why* complainants have such beliefs.

An explanation concerning the decision to file a complaint against a police officer may also be found in the reasons for *not* filing a complaint. As enumerated by Russell, these are:

1. the advice of significant others;
2. the apathy of the potential complainant;
3. the apprehensiveness of the citizen;

4. the fatalistic approach that no effective action will be taken by the police;
5. the belief that police work is sufficiently difficult and hazardous without making it more so; and
6. an unawareness of the complaint procedure. (1978:52–53)

These reasons resulted in the following typology.

### The Advised

The advice not to complain against the police may be given by a professional (i.e., attorney, social worker), or by another governmental agency based on the facts given the individual or agency by the potential complainant. The advisor, perhaps more knowledgeable than the citizen, might "explain away" the basis for the citizen's feeling that the officer was not properly conducting himself or herself. Another "significant other" might well be a friend or relative, who, having previously filed a complaint, received no satisfaction. The advice of this individual (not to bother to file a complaint) contributes to the fatalistic posture described below.

### The Apathetic

Russell's survey of citizens disclosed that 14 percent were "apathetic potential complainants" who "could just not be bothered to become involved in the detailed procedures of making a complaint" (1978:52). The apathetic citizen has no other reason than a lack of desire to make a complaint.

Bayley and Mendelsohn found the same to be true in Denver. They discovered that there were minority persons in Denver who just did not want to take the time to complain. "People simply did not want to be bothered; the complaint was not as important as the time they would have to devote to it" (1969:132).

### The Apprehensive

Russell found some degree of apprehensiveness on the part of potential complainants in his survey. Citizens indicated that their fear of reprisals, whether by personal violence or extralegal means, precluded their filing a complaint.

The President's Commission learned that such apprehensiveness was sometimes well-founded. The commission noted that in one large eastern city "the police department used to charge many of those who filed complaints of police misconduct with filing false reports with the police" (1967:195). In another large city the practice was "to drop criminal charges against a person if he would agree to withdraw his complaint or agree not to file one" (1967:195).

More recently, the police have begun filing civil suits for libel and/or slander against complainants whose complaints are not substantiated by the police department investigation or who have filed civil suits against the police and lost. While the police argue that they are within their rights in suing a complainant, others feel that they are simply nuisance suits to harass and intimidate not only the present complainant but potential complainants as well.

The National Advisory Commission on Criminal Justice Standards and Goals also expressed knowledge of the problem when it asserted that "personal fear of reprisal or harassment, complex and cumbersome filing procedures, and the highlighted possibility of criminal prosecution for making a false report are three conditions that can discourage the public from making even valid complaints" (1973:471).

Reiss adds, "many citizens are reluctant to complain against agencies that hold power over them and could respond with punitive action" (1971:190).

## The Fatalistic

Russell describes the fatalistic person as "those citizens who do not utilize the complaints process because they believe that no effective action will be taken by the police . . ." (1978:53). The potential complainant who believes that nothing will really be done by the police dominates the literature. Bayley and Mendelsohn, for example, state that:

> [T]he evidence very clearly shows that people, regardless of ethnicity, do not complain against the police automatically when they feel aggrieved. People commonly accept what is done to them without trying to buck the system . . . . Willingness to complain seems to be a function of what happens to people and what they expect to be able to gain from it, and these factors are not class-specific." (1969:130)

## The Public Spirited

Russell's survey located a group of citizens who believed that the police have a difficult and hazardous job that would only become more difficult if citizens filed a complaint. This notion is not indicated in other literature.

## The Unaware

In contrast to the "public spirited," instances of potential complainants who either did not know how to initiate the complaint process or did not know that such a process existed are not unusual. The President's Commission commented that "the mechanics of receiving complaints often tends to discourage potential complainants from taking any action. Some procedures are so little known, so complex, or so hard to pursue that the ordinary citizen either gives up or never tries in the first place" (1967:196).

Repeating a recommendation of the National Advisory Commission on Civil Disorders some three years earlier, the Commission on Standards and Goals warned that this might be the result of a misunderstanding by the public. "If this is the case, it is incumbent on the police agency to educate the public in these areas" (1973:471).

# Police Accountability and the Citizen Complaint Process

The citizens of a democratic society should have the right to make complaints about the actions of public officials acting in their official capacity. Police officers should be no less accountable for their actions than the mayor or any other employee of a political subdivision.

## Positive Aspects of Citizen Complaints

Police administrators should look on citizen complaints as a barometer of police performance. Police officers have little supervision as they go about their duties, and fellow police officers are not likely to report their colleagues. Citizens can provide the police department with valuable information about how well the department is performing.

The United States Commission on Civil Rights believes that citizen complaints also provide another useful function, acting as "important indicators of public perception of the agency" (1981:50). Police departments, says the Commission, can use information obtained through citizen complaints to improve the public image and community relations of the department as they strive to provide better service to the community.

## Negative Aspects of Citizen Complaints

Actually making a complaint often takes a great deal of effort. The citizen may not know where to go to make the complaint. Even if he or she *does* know where to make the complaint, several obstacles exist.

First, the complainant may discover that there are no complaint procedures established for that police department; the citizen may, at best, be introduced to a ranking officer who will listen to the complaint but will take no formal action. (One of the authors will long remember the comment made to him by a member of a rural police department that "we don't accept complaints.") Second, the complainant may be required to go to the police department, a seemingly simple requirement which may actually be a hardship or an impossibility for the poor or disabled. Third, the citizen who goes to the police department to make a complaint against an officer may be greeted with any number of reactions. The literature is rich with evidence of the close-knit police fraternity. Accordingly, the complainant may be treated with courtesy and respect or may meet with intimidation, threats, and hostility. Caiden and Hahn point out, for example, that some departments require that the citizen complete a complaint form which states that the complainant is subject to prosecution for making false statements if the information is not substantiated (1979:171). Finally, the complainant may discover that the police department has an arbitrarily-assigned "statute of limitations" on citizen complaints; the complaint will not be accepted if it is made after a certain length of time following the precipitating incident.

The citizen who overcomes the obstacles to the process and files a formal complaint then learns, if it wasn't previously known, that the complaint will be investigated by officers of that police department. Whether the investigators will be one of the accused officer's supervisors or a member of an internal affairs unit, the complainant comes face-to-face with the reality that the police department is investigating itself, a fact which the complainant may find, at the least, disheartening. Whether or not the concern of the citizen that police investigating police will prove fruitless is justified, the police department must recognize that suspicion and take steps to avoid even the appearance that the investigation is anything but impartial. All of these considerations, both positive and negative, are best addressed within the framework of a formal, written citizen complaint procedure.

## Establishing a Citizen Complaint Process

In its 1981 report to President Ronald Reagan, the United States Commission on Civil Rights listed several reasons for "the continuous, thoughtful examination" of police conduct (1981:v). "Police officers possess awesome powers . . . protection of civil rights demands close examination of the exercise of police authority . . . police officers exercise their powers with wide discretion and under minimal supervision . . . a single occurrence or a perceived pattern of discriminatory and unjustified use of force can have a powerful, deleterious effect on the life of the community" (1981:v–vi). Finally, the Commission noted:

> Thus, there is ample reason for studying police conduct even without further justification. However, the volume of complaints of police abuse received by the Commission has increased each year, and the nature of the alleged abuse has become more serious. *Patterns of complaints appear to indicate institutional rather than individual problems.* (1981:vi, italic added)

The International Association of Chiefs of Police (IACP) contributed its prestige to a similar endeavor, publishing a detailed manual of rules and procedures for the management of effective police discipline. The lengthy IACP publication began with a sample policy statement which police departments might adopt. The model statement called for: "the establishment of a system of complaint and disciplinary procedures . . ." and "the prompt receipt, investigation and disposition of complaints regarding the conduct of members and employees of the Department . . ." (1976:40). The IACP policy statement also recognized the importance of citizen complaints in the management of a police department when it stated that:

> [T]he Police Department welcomes from the people of the community constructive criticism of the Department and valid complaints against its members or procedures. (1976:40–41)

The Police Executive Research Forum began its model police misconduct policy statement by asserting that, "the purpose of this policy is to improve the quality of police services" (1981:1). PERF then listed three ways in which the improvement could be accomplished:

1. through the provision of meaningful and effective complaint procedures, citizen confidence in the integrity of police increases and
this engenders community support and confidence in the police
department;
2. through disciplinary procedures that permit police officials to
monitor officers' compliance with departmental procedures;
3. by clarifying rights and ensuring due process protection to citizens
and officers alike. (1981:1)

All three of the documents, those of the U.S. Civil Rights Commission,
the International Association of Chiefs of Police, and the Police Executive
Research Forum, are remarkably similar. These similarities include:

1. the publication and distribution by the police department of written rules and regulations guiding the conduct of officers as they
perform the various duties required of them;
2. an emphasis on the importance of proper supervision as a means
of reducing and controlling police misconduct;
3. the establishment of an internal affairs unit (or individuals in a
small department) with written guidelines on the conduct of an
internal investigation;
4. the creation of a citizen complaint system which is not intimidating, is accessible, and accepts anonymous complaints;
5. the education of the public about the disciplinary process and how
complaints against the police may be filed;
6. the use of complaint forms on which citizen complaints would be
recorded and which would form the basis for an investigation (one
copy would go to the accused officer); the Civil Rights Commission
recommended, in addition, the use of bilingual forms;
7. a prompt investigation of the complaint; and
8. equally prompt notification of the complainant and the accused
officer as to the results of the investigation and what channels of
appeal are open.

## The Structure of the Police Review Process

Much of the debate about citizen complaints against the police has focused
on the structure of responses to such complaints. There is considerable evidence that police and citizens desire *different* structures to deal with such
complaints. There is also evidence to indicate that the structure, responsibility, jurisdiction, and staffing of such review boards have a significant
impact on their decisions.

West (1988) notes, however, that any determination about what form
the complaint process should take must consider all actors. While the system must, he says, be thorough and impartial, it must also be equally acceptable "to the officers themselves, to members of the public, and to those
elected political officials who are charged with the responsibility of ensuring

that police agencies are effectively and efficiently managed" (101–2). Dugan and Breda (1991:171) assert that the way that a police agency deals with criticism "will determine whether criticism is a positive management tool or a basis for low morale, cynicism, and nonprofessional behavior." We turn our attention now to the various structural aspects of the complaint process and their impact on the process.

The review of police conduct is a complex process. There are both formal and informal controls on police behavior, subjecting it to review from a variety of different sources. Most important in the review process is that review which comes from external social institutions. Such institutions include, most directly, judges, prosecutors, and police administrators. It is obvious that each of these are entrusted with the formal responsibility of review of police procedures, policies, and actions, many on a daily basis. In addition, the *potential* review by one or more of these agencies exerts a control on police behavior. In addition to these formal agencies entrusted with an oversight function, there are many groups and institutions, external to the justice system, that perform a similar function. Notable among these efforts are the media. Newspapers, radio, and television are all actively engaged in reviewing police conduct through reporting and editorials. As such, they "review" police behavior in such a way as is likely to have a widespread impact, perhaps greater than that of any aspect of the justice system.

The central issue in the consideration of the formal structure of the process is the extent to which citizens are involved. The review of police conduct provided by these external groups is significant, but it tends to lack the directness or focus of those formally entrusted with the direct responsibility of oversight of allegations of police misconduct. These institutions may take several forms, but crucial to their form is the extent to which citizens are involved in the group. The level of involvement by citizens in the formal police review process varies significantly. It is this level of involvement that distinguishes the several formal procedures now in use by police departments.

In its most frequently occurring form, the police review process excludes citizens from the process altogether. In their review of the administrative structure of police complaint procedures in the 1960s, Beral and Sisk (1964) found that the model in which only police were involved predominated. This was true into the 1980s, as the reviews of Terrill (1982) and Kerstetter (1985) indicated. They estimated that perhaps as many as 80 percent of all administrative structures are composed of only police officers.

Walker and Bumphus (1991) have shown, however, that since 1986 there has been an increase in the number of cities involving citizens at some stage of the complaint review process. They found that investigations of police misconduct in 18 cities (36 percent) were solely internal, that is, had no citizen involvement. Another 6 cities (12 percent) had minimal civilian involvement; usually the complainant was given the opportunity to appeal the final disposition to a board which included nonsworn personnel. The remaining 26 cities (52 percent) provided for greater involvement of citizen review.

Several arguments exist to support the police-only model. First is the expertise brought to a review process. Police officers are well-versed in matters of law and police procedure and, it is argued, are thus in the best position to render informed and competent decisions regarding citizen complaints. Supporters of this model also argue that the process lacks credibility among police officers when it includes citizens. The effectiveness of the process is enhanced when police are the sole arbiters in the process, and thus outcomes are likely to have more significant consequences. Further arguments include the well-accepted notion that bureaucracies and public sector organizations are responsible for solving their own problems. Citizen involvement in the process is evidence of the inability of the police organization to deal effectively with the shortcomings or misbehavior of its members. While this list is not an exhaustive one,[1] it provides the major arguments presented in support of review structures which include only police personnel.

The other major structural alternative includes citizens in some part of the review process. It should be noted that the review process is a truncated one involving many different decision points. Prominent among those are the receipt of complaints, evaluation, investigation, adjudication, and disciplinary recommendations. There is considerable variation among those structures which do allow citizen input as to what stages of the process allow that input. Kerstetter and Rasinski (1994) say, however, that their study of the Minneapolis police department underscores the value of even modest civilian participation in the process. We will examine each of the structures which allow citizen input, beginning with the least amount of involvement and stretching along a continuum to those which have full citizen involvement at each stage.

The structure which allows for the least input by citizens into the complaint process is that which includes citizens who are employees of the police department in a nonsworn capacity. These "police-civilians" represent the least involvement of outsiders into the complaint review process. Typically, models which utilize this approach involve the citizens in the earlier stages of the complaint process (i.e., the receipt and/or investigation of complaints), reserving the latter stages (adjudication and assignment of penalties) to police personnel.

The remaining three models all involve citizens from outside the police department. They do, however, vary considerably as to the extent of that citizen involvement. Kerstetter (1985) has identified three such complaint review models, which he refers to as the *civilian monitor, civilian input,* and *civilian review* structures. Each progressively involves citizens to a greater extent.

The first of the models, the *monitor,* is the weakest of the three, allowing citizen input into the complaint review process only after the complaint has been reviewed and a punishment determined within the police structure. Under this model, citizens provide a review of police decisions after the fact. The opportunity to have an impact on the process and outcome of any individual complaint is minimal. The next structure, *input*, allows citizen participation at the earliest stages of the complaint review process. In particular, citizen input is used at the stages of receipt and investigation of the complaint. However, the remaining stages (adjudication and punishment) are handed over to the police agency. The final model, *review*, is the strongest of the three in that citizens are involved in all of the meaningful stages of the complaint process—receipt, investigation, adjudication, and punishment.

In the first national survey of civilian review procedures in the United States, Walker and Bumphus (1991) found that 32 of the 50 largest cities had instituted civilian review procedures.[2] They observe that 17 of the 32, over half of the total, have been established only since 1986.

Walker and Bumphus found no two agencies whose civilian review procedures were identical. They divided the 32 systems according to the following criteria:

1. who does the initial investigation of a citizen complaint; and

2. who reviews the investigative report and makes a recommendation for action. (1991:1)

The models which emerged are classified as follows:

Class I. (a) Initial investigation and fact-finding by nonsworn personnel; (b) Review of investigative report and recommendation for action by nonsworn person or board consisting of a majority of nonsworn persons.

Class II. (a) Initial investigation and fact-finding by sworn police officers; (b) Review of investigative report and recommendation for action by a nonsworn person or board which consists of a majority of nonsworn persons.

Class III. (a) Initial investigation and fact-finding by sworn officers; (b) review of investigative report and recommendation for action by sworn officers; (c) opportunity by the citizen who is dissatisfied with the final disposition of the complaint to appeal to a board which includes nonsworn persons. (1991:1)

Walker and Bumphus (1991:3) note that the three classes are similar to Kerstetter's three models: Class III is similar to Kerstetter's "civilian monitor;" Class II is similar to "civilian input;" and Class I is the same as "civilian review."

As a result of their survey, Walker and Bumphus classified 12 (37.5 percent) of the 32 police agencies as Class I; 14 (43.7 percent) as Class II; and 6 (18.7 percent) as Class III. Thus, almost half of the 32 police departments with civilian review procedures have included some civilian input in the process.

While the Walker and Bumphus survey did not measure the effectiveness of civilian review procedures, the authors note (1991:1) that, "the spread of civilian review represents a new national consensus on civilian review as an appropriate method of handling citizen complaints about police misconduct."

There are many dilemmas which emerge as a result of this consideration of the structure of the complaint review process. The clearest distinction between structures can be made between those which include meaningful citizen participation and those which do not. An issue of primary significance to the resolution of complaints—credibility—cuts both ways. West (1988:108) observes that those who favor external review argue that the closed system, where police investigate the police, is contrary to "the rules of natural justice." Those opposed to external review say that such review threatens police morale and professionalism. It seems imperative that citizen involvement be integrated into the police structure, but in such a way as to preserve the ability of the police to monitor themselves. Kerstetter (1985) has argued that the emphasis on the resolution of complaints should be not on punishment but rather on conciliation, compensation, training, and assistance. This view, whatever merits it may have, ignores the obvious dilemma that in many departments a serious problem exists with many officers—as well as ignoring the prevailing norms regarding citizen treatment. These problems may require solutions of a punitive nature, rather than the re-integrative ones recommended by Kerstetter.

## Conclusion

This chapter has reviewed the citizen complaint process by placing it in a broader framework and attempting to see that process within the larger context of policing as an institution. The nature of police work, particularly the enforcement aspect of the role, is adversarial by nature. Such interactions are likely to generate disagreement and hostility. That complaints eventuate from such interactions is not surprising. Campaigns to recruit more sensitive or less aggressive police officers would appear to have little if any effect in reducing citizen complaints. The evidence reviewed in this paper points to the role of the police as an institution in fostering and in some ways encouraging those behaviors on the part of the police which are likely to generate complaints. Most commentators have pointed to the role of the police culture in shaping the actions that are most likely to result in citizen complaints. This suggests that an institutional change of some magnitude would be necessary to redirect police actions and reduce the number of complaints.

Perhaps more importantly, the results of this paper strongly suggest that the police as an institution have been unable to meet the challenge presented by citizen complaints. Absent in the operation of the complaint process has been a procedure, a well-defined mechanism for dealing with such allegations in a way that guarantees both due process for officers and accountability to the public. Certainly few bureaucracies are successful in institutionalizing an instrument of self-criticism. However, the tenuous position of the police in a democratic society demands that such institutionalization occur. To fail to do so jeopardizes the police enterprise.

## Notes

[1] For a more exhaustive list, see Terrill (1982), and International Association of Civilian Oversight of Law Enforcement (IACOLE) (1989).
[2] The number of cities with civilian review procedures was listed as thirty in the original report. It was updated to thirty-two cities in a February, 1992 addendum.

## References

Bayley, David H. and Harold Mendelsohn (1969). *Minorities and the Police*. New York: The Free Press.

Beral, Harold and Marcus Sisk (1964). "The Administration of Complaints by Civilians Against the Police." *Harvard Law Review*, Vol. 77.

Black, Donald J. and Albert J. Reiss, Jr. (1967). "Patterns of Behavior in Police and Citizen Transactions." *Field Surveys III, Studies in Crime and Law Enforcement in Major Metropolitan Areas*, Vol. 2, Washington, DC: U.S. Government Printing Office.

Caiden, Gerald and Harlan Hahn (1979). "Public Complaints Against the Police," in Ralph Baker and Fred A. Meyer, Jr. (eds.), *Evaluating Alternative Law-Enforcement Policies*. Lexington, ME: Lexington Books.

Chevigny, Paul (1969). *Police Power*. New York: Vintage Books.

Decker, Scott H. and Allen E. Wagner (1982). "Race and Citizen Complaints Against the Police: An Analysis of Their Interaction," in Jack R. Green (ed.), *The Police and the Public*. Beverly Hills: Sage Publications.

_____ (1985). "Black and White Complainants and the Police." *American Journal of Criminal Justice*, Vol. 10, No. 1.

Dugan, John R. and Daniel R. Breda (1991). "Complaints About Police Officers: A Comparison Among Types and Agencies." *Journal of Criminal Justice*, Vol. 19, No. 2.

Friedrich, Robert J. (1980). "Police Use of Force: Individuals, Situations, and Organizations." *Annals*, Vol. 452 (November).

Germann, A. C. (1971). "Changing the Police—The Impossible Dream?" *The Journal of Criminal Law, Criminology and Police Science*, Vol. 5112 (September).

Goldstein, Herman (1977). *Policing A Free Society*. Cambridge, MA: Ballinger Publishing.

Hudson, James R. (1970). "Police-Citizen Encounters That Lead to Citizen Complaints." *Social Problems*, Vol. 18, No. 2.

International Association of Chiefs of Police (1976). *Managing for Effective Police Discipline*. Gaithersburg, MD: International Association of Chiefs of Police.

International Association of Civilian Oversight of Law Enforcement (IACOLE) (1989). *Compendium of International Civilian Oversight Agencies*. Evanston, IL: IACOLE.

Kerstetter, Wayne A. (1985). "Who Disciplines the Police? Who Should?" in William A. Geller (ed.), *Police Leadership in America: Crisis and Opportunity*. Chicago: American Bar Foundation.

Kerstetter, Wayne A. and Kenneth A. Rasinski (1994). "Opening A Window into Police Internal Affairs: Impact of Procedural Justice Reform on Third-Party Attitudes." *Social Justice Research*, Vol. 7, No. 2 (March).

National Advisory Commission on Civil Disorders (1968). *Report of the National Commission on Civil Disorders*. New York: Bantam Books.

National Advisory Commission on Criminal Justice Standards and Goals (1973). *Police*. Washington, DC: U.S. Government Printing Office.

Niederhoffer, Arthur (1969). *Behind the Shield: The Police in Urban Society*. Garden City, NY: Anchor Books.

Police Executive Research Forum (1981). *Police Agency Handling of Officer Misconduct: A Model Policy Statement*. Washington, DC: Police Executive Research Forum

The President's Commission on Law Enforcement and Administration of Justice (1967). *Task Force Report: The Police*. Washington, DC: U.S. Government Printing Office.

Reiss Jr., Albert J. (1970). "Police Brutality—Answers to Key Questions," in Michael Lipsky (ed.), *Law and Order Police Encounters*. New Brunswick, NJ: Aldine Publishing.

_____ (1971). *The Police and the Public*. New Haven: Yale University Press.

Russell, Ken (1978). *Complaints Against the Police: A Sociological View*. Glenfield, Leicester, England: Milltak Limited.

Skolnick, Jerome H. and James J. Fyfe (1993). *Above the Law: Police and the Excessive Use of Force*. New York: The Free Press.

Stark, Rodney (1972). *Police Riots*. Belmont, CA: Wordsworth Publishing.

Terrill, Richard J. (1982). "Civilian Review Boards." *Journal of Police Science and Administration*, Vol. 10, No. 4.

U.S. Commission on Civil Rights (1981). *Who is Guarding the Guardians? A Report on Police Practices*. Washington, DC: U.S. Government Printing Office.

Wagner, Allen E. (1980). "Citizen Complaints Against the Police: The Complainant." *Journal of Police Science and Administration*, Vol. 8, No. 3.

Walker, Samuel (1983). *The Police in America*. New York: McGraw-Hill Book Company.

Walker, Samuel and Vic W. Bumphus (1991). *Civilian Review of the Police: A National Survey of the 50 Largest Cities*. Omaha, NE: Center for Public Affairs Research.

Ward, Richard H. (1975). "The Police Role: A Case of Diversity," in George G. Killinger and Paul F. Cromwell Jr. (eds.), *Issues in Law Enforcement*. Boston: Holbrook Press.

West, Paul (1988). "Investigation of Complaints Against the Police: Summary Report of a National Survey." *American Journal of Police*, Vol. 7, No. 2.

# Varieties of Citizen Review
## The Relationship of Mission, Structure, and Procedures to Police Accountability

*Samuel Walker*
*Betsy Wright Kreisel*

## Introduction

The videotaped beating of Rodney King by Los Angeles police officers in 1991 intensified public interest in the related issues of police brutality and citizen complaints about police misconduct. Citizen complaint procedures is an area of tremendous change in American policing. Many cities and counties have established external (or citizen) complaint review procedures (Walker and Wright 1995) as alternatives to traditional internal complaint procedure. Citizen review procedures vary considerably with respect to their mission, formal structure, and operating policies (Goldsmith 1991a; Walker 1995a; West 1988). The existing variations have introduced a number of unresolved problems related to the goals of citizen review.

This chapter specifies some of the major variations among citizen review procedures, discusses the implications of these variations for enhancing the accountability of the police, and identifies research needs in the area of citizen complaints.

## Police Misconduct and Citizen Complaints

Citizen complaints about police behavior, particularly the excessive use of force, is a major part of the police-community relations problem in America (Chevigny 1969; Geller and Toch 1995; NAACP 1995; National Advisory Commission on Civil Disorders, 1968; U.S. Commission on Civil Rights 1978, 1981a, 1981b). Civil rights groups have alleged that minorities are the victims of widespread police abuse and that internal police department complaint procedures fail to adequately investigate complaints and discipline officers (ACLU 1964, 1966, 1992; Chevigny 1969; Littlejohn 1981b).

Prepared especially for *Critical Issues for Policing*, 3/E by Samuel Walker and Betsy Wright Kreisel.

The National Advisory Commission on Civil Disorders (1968:310–12), for example, concluded that police abuse and inadequate complaint procedures were among the causes of the riots of the 1960s. The 1991 Rodney King incident indicated the persistence of these problems in the 1990s (NAACP 1995; Skolnick and Fyfe 1993; Walker, Spohn, and DeLone 1996).

Official data on citizen complaints provide some prima facie support for the allegations by civil rights groups. The Police Foundation study of police use of force found that African Americans represented 21.3 percent of city populations but 42.3 percent of persons filing complaints. Similar disparities are found in official data reported by individual police departments and citizen review procedures (New York CCRB 1993). The Police Foundation also found that African American complainants are less likely to have their complaints sustained than were white complainants. They represented 42.3 percent of all complaints filed with city police departments, but only 27.3 percent of all sustained complaints. Hispanic Americans, on the other hand, were underrepresented among persons filing complaints against the city police relative to the presence in the city populations (Pate and Fridell 1993:I, 95).

To remedy these problems, civil rights groups have demanded the creation of external, or citizen complaint review procedures.[1] Terrill (1991:294–5) observes, "Racial discrimination or allegations of it are usually at the heart of most movements to introduce a civilian oversight mechanism." Although proposals for citizen review were defeated in the 1960s (Terrill 1988; Kahn 1975), the concept spread rapidly beginning in the 1980s. The number of citizen review procedures increased from 13 in 1980 to more than 65 by 1995 (Walker and Wright 1995).[2] Bayley (1991:vi) argues that, with the exception of a few specialists, "few people are aware of how general this movement [toward citizen review] has been." The growth of citizen review procedures is but one part of a pervasive climate of change and ferment in policing, which includes community policing and demands for greater accountability of the police (Bayley 1995).

Citizen review procedures take several different forms. Goldsmith (1988), Kerstetter (1985), Perez (1994), and Walker and Bumphus (1991) classify citizen review procedures according to the nature and extent of citizen input in the complaint process. Other variations, some of which are explored in this study, also exist (Walker 1995a).

These variations have added a new complexity to both public policy debates and scholarly research on citizen review. Traditionally, the issue of citizen review has been framed in terms of a sharp dichotomy between internal and external forms of review. Advocates of citizen review have argued that it is a more independent and effective means of handling citizen complaints (ACLU 1964, 1966, 1992; Littlejohn 1981b; Luna 1994; NAACP 1995; Terrill 1990). Opponents argue that it is ineffective, wasteful, and an improper intrusion on the professional autonomy of law enforcement agencies (AELE 1982; IACP 1964; Perez 1994).

Given the existing variations, the traditional dichotomy is no longer an adequate framework for discussing complaint review systems. With respect to public policy, the choice is not a simple either/or question of whether or not to adopt citizen review. Rather, it is a question of which form of citizen review, if any, to adopt. With respect to evaluation research, it is no longer a question of the effectiveness of citizen review relative to internal review. Instead, it is a question of effectiveness of particular forms of citizen review relative to other forms and/or different forms of internal review.

It should also be noted that there appear to be great variations among internal police complaint review procedures. The literature on this subject, however, is far smaller than on citizen review (Chevigny 1969:264; Kappeler, Kraska, and Marron 1995; Mollen Commission 1994; Perez 1994; Sherman 1978).

## The Literature on Citizen Review

The literature on citizen review falls into four general categories. The first group consists of the polemical literature advocating (ACLU 1964, 1966, 1992; NAACP 1995) or opposing (AELE 1982; IACP 1964) the concept. Both sides rely primarily on anecdotal evidence about the effectiveness or ineffectiveness of different complaint review systems.

The second group includes studies of the political controversies surrounding citizen review in particular cities (Bellush 1971; Black 1968; Browning et al. 1984; Jones 1994; Kahn 1975; Littlejohn 1981a, 1981b; Terrill 1988). While rich in detail about local events, these studies have been relatively limited in their analytic framework. Only two studies have investigated the political dynamics surrounding the adoption or rejection of a citizen review proposal. Bellush (1971) analyzed voting data from the 1966 New York City referendum to investigate the sources of support and opposition to the Civilian Complaint Review Board. Browning et al. (1984:152–156) investigated the relationship between civil rights activity and the representation of African Americans in local government and the adoption of a citizen review procedure. This study was limited to a few cities in California, and the findings have been rendered out of date by subsequent developments in many of the cities studied.

The third group consists of descriptive studies of the formal administrative structure of citizen review agencies. The major focus has been on developing taxonomies based on the nature and extent of citizen input (Goldsmith 1988; International City Management Association 1992; Kerstetter 1985; Perez 1994; Walker and Bumphus 1991).

The fourth group of studies consists of attempts to evaluate the effectiveness of citizen review (Hudson 1972; Jolin and Gibbons 1984; Kerstetter 1985, 1995; Kerstetter and Rasinski 1994; Luna 1994; Perez 1978, 1994; Perez and Muir 1995; Sviridoff and McElroy 1988, 1989a, 1989b). However, these studies suffer from several limitations. Only two have attempted to compare internal and citizen review complaint procedures (Hudson 1972; Perez 1978, 1994), and both suffer from methodological weaknesses. All of the existing studies fail to take into account the highly problematic nature of official data on complaints (Adams 1995; Walker and Bumphus 1992; Walker 1995b). Only one (Sviridoff and McElroy 1988, 1989a, 1989b) evaluates citizen review in terms of more than one of its goals.

## Citizen Review and Police Accountability

Citizen review is designed to provide greater accountability of the police to the public. The core assumption is that the involvement of citizens in the complaint process will provide a more independent and therefore more effective review of complaints than internal review. Studies of the police subculture have found a strong element of group solidarity among the police, particularly in the face of external criticism, and a willingness to lie to cover up misconduct by other officers (Westley 1970).

The idea that citizen review is more independent and effective than internal review involves four closely linked propositions: that citizen involvement in the complaint process will produce (1) more objective and more thorough investigations; (2) a higher rate of sustained complaints and more disciplinary actions against guilty officers; (3) greater deterrence of police misconduct (through both general and specific deterrence); (4) higher levels of satisfaction on the part of both individual complainants and the general public.

These assumptions have never been tested. The individual propositions have not been critically examined, and the crucial linkages between propositions have not been studied. Moreover, there are few discussions of what constitutes an "independent" review of complaints (Terrill 1990), few meaningful discussions of what constitutes "thorough" investigation of complaints (Kappeler, et al 1995; Perez 1994), little discussion of the problems associated with the sustain rate (Walker 1995b; Walker and Bumphus 1992), and little research on the impact of different complaint review systems on citizen perceptions (Perez 1978). By the same token, it should be noted that the assumptions underlying the criticisms of citizen review—that non-sworn persons are unqualified to evaluate complaints, that citizen review undermines the professional autonomy of the police, etc.—are equally untested (AELE 1982; IACP 1964; Perez 1994).

This chapter specifies some important variations in the mission, structure, and policies of citizen review procedures and discusses the implications of these variations for the goal of enhancing the accountability of the police. It advances research on citizen review in three respects. First, it is based on a comprehensive sample of existing citizen review procedures, as opposed to the selective samples used in previous studies.[3] Second, it focuses on a wider range of administrative features of citizen review than previous studies. Third, it raises new questions about the relationship between administrative features and the larger goal of enhancing police accountability.

## Methodology

This chapter is based on an analysis of official documents related to 65 citizen review procedures in the United States.[4] It is believed that these 65 procedures represent the entire universe of citizen review procedures as of January, 1995. Previous studies have been based on small and highly selective samples of citizen review procedures.

There is much confusion over the terminology related to complaint procedures. Citizen review is defined here as a "procedure for handling citizen complaints about police officer misconduct that involves persons who are not sworn officers at some point in the process" (Walker & Bumphus 1991:1). The commonly used term "civilian review *board*" is inappropriate because some procedures do not involve a multi-member board, but are administrative agencies with a single executive director. The generic term citizen review *procedure* is used rather than agency because some complaint review systems are citizen-staffed procedures within the formal structure of the police department, while others are separate governmental agencies.[5] The term "civilian" is not used since it implies a "civilian/military" dichotomy that is inappropriate for domestic policing (Bittner 1970).

Capturing the universe of citizen review agencies poses a number of difficulties. No national-level agency monitors changes in police complaint procedures on an ongoing basis.[6] The International Association for Citizen Oversight of Law Enforcement (IACOLE), a professional association of citizen review staff and board members, has published two compendia describing citizen review procedures, but these documents are neither systematic nor current (IACOLE 1985, 1989).

Our study utilized a variety of techniques to capture the universe of citizen review agencies. Initially, the police departments in the 100 largest cities in the United States were surveyed by mail and asked to indicate whether or not they were subject to some form of citizen review. Citizen review procedures in smaller cities and in county governments were identified through a combination of other methods: (1) a review of the membership list, newsletters, and compendia published by IACOLE; (2) consultation with key informants (citizen review staff members, community activists, scholars) known to the authors to be knowledgeable about the subject; (3) a review of published surveys of citizen review agencies (New York City 1992; New York Civil Liberties Union 1993); (4) monitoring of selected national news media (e.g., *The New York Times, Law Enforcement News*).[7]

Once a citizen review procedure was identified, telephone inquiries to local officials were made to verify the existence of the procedure and to request copies of the relevant documents. The experience of this process dramatized the problems associated with mail and telephone inquiries

(Pate and Fridell 1993:I, 59–60). In several instances local officials (in police departments, mayor's offices, city councils) were either ignorant of or misinformed about existing citizen review procedures. In those cases, follow-up calls to other officials were necessary to verify the initial information.[8]

The official documents requested include: (1) enabling ordinances, statutes, and executive orders; (2) official rules and procedures; and (3) annual reports. These documents were analyzed in terms of the role and mission, organizational structure, and operating policies of each citizen review agency.

## Variations among Citizen Review Procedures

Table 1 presents the findings of the analysis of the official documents related to the 65 citizen review procedures. The findings and the implications for police accountability are discussed below.

### Role and Mission

The role and mission of citizen review has traditionally been defined as an independent mechanism for reviewing complaints against police officers on a case-by-case basis. However, this definition does not accurately describe existing citizen review procedures in three respects. First, many procedures are not fully independent because citizens do not conduct the initial fact-finding investigations. Second, some do not investigate individual complaints at all, while many others also have authority to review police department policies. Third, some procedures handle complaints against other public employees in addition to police officers.

*1. The Nature of Citizen Input.* Although citizen review is intended to enhance the accountability of the police through citizen involvement in the complaint process, there are significant variations in the nature of that involvement (Goldsmith 1988; Kerstetter 1985; Perez 1994; Walker and Bumphus 1991). Previous studies generally distinguish between procedures where (1) citizens or non-sworn persons conduct the initial fact-finding investigations on complaints; (2) citizens have some input in the review of complaints but do not conduct the fact-finding investigations; or (3) citizens monitor or audit the complaint process but do not review individual complaints.

Table 1 indicates that citizens conduct the initial fact-finding investigations in 34 percent of all citizen review procedures, provide input in 46 percent, and have a monitoring or auditing role in 20 percent.

*Discussion:* The above data have enormous implications for the assumptions underlying citizen review. As noted above, the core assumption is that it will provide a more independent review of complaints. Yet, in two-thirds of all citizen review procedures complaints are investigated by sworn officers. This raises serious questions about whether the related goals of citizen review (more complaints sustained, greater deterrence of misconduct, etc.) are likely to be attained. In short, the majority of existing citizen review procedures are less independent than is widely believed.

**2. *Case-by-Case Complaint Review vs. Policy Review.*** Citizen review is intended to provide an independent review of complaints against the police. The data in Table 1 indicate that 97 percent of citizen review procedures review individual citizen complaints. This is referred to here as the *case-by-case complaint review* function. At the same time, however, nearly two-thirds of all citizen review procedures are also authorized to review police department policies and to recommend changes where appropriate. This role is referred to here as the *policy review* function. Two citizen review procedures (3 percent of the total) engage only in policy review.

### Table 1  Organizational Features of Citizen Review
### n = 65

|  | Number | Percentage |
|---|---|---|
| Case-by-case complaint review | 63 | 97 |
| Case-by-case review only | 23 | 35.3 |
| Case-by-case review and policy review | 40 | 61.5 |
| Policy review only | 2 | 3 |
| Nature of citizen input |  |  |
| Conduct investigations | 22 | 34 |
| Provide input | 30 | 46 |
| Monitor, audit | 13 | 20 |
| Responsible for complaints against: |  |  |
| Police officers only | 54 | 83 |
| Police officers and other public employees | 11 | 17 |
| Agency with single director | 10 | 15 |
| Multi-member board | 55 | 85 |
| Average number of board members | 10 |  |
| With police officers as members | 15 |  |
| Authority to recommend: |  |  |
| Disposition of complaint only | 39 | 60 |
| Specific disciplinary action | 26 | 40 |
| Policies and procedures |  |  |
| Independent investigative power | 25 | 38 |
| Subpoena power | 25 | 38 |
| Public hearings | 30 | 46 |
| Legal representation | 21 | 32 |
| Full criminal trial model | 7 | 10.7 |
| Mediation | 13 | 20 |

*Discussion:* Case-by-case complaint review and policy review represent different strategies for enhancing police accountability. The case-by-case approach is consistent with the assumptions about citizen review identified above (more independent investigations, more sustained complaints, etc.). This approach is primarily a deterrence strategy. Policy review, on the other hand, represents a preventive strategy. Instead of punishing individual officers, it focuses on identifying and correcting underlying problems as a way of preventing future misconduct (Gellhorn 1966:191–3). Kerstetter (1985:180) argues that policy review should focus on the integrity of the complaint process. Bayley (1991:ix) argues that a citizen review procedure can use complaints to "determine recurrent problems in police operations that might lead to changes in policy, tactics, training, and supervision."

The question of which strategy is more effective in achieving police accountability is not addressed in the current literature on citizen review. No evaluations have investigated the deterrent effect of sustained complaints, either on individual officers or the police department as a whole. Meanwhile, there are no studies of the policy review function. It is not known whether citizen review procedures even utilize their policy review authority, whether policies they recommend are adopted by police departments, or whether such policies have any impact on policing. Thus, it is impossible to say whether the preventive strategy embodied in the policy review function is an effective means of achieving accountability, or whether it is relatively more or less effective than the deterrence strategy embodied in the case-by-case approach.

An important variation of the policy review function is referred to as the *auditor* approach. Two of the agencies reported in Table 1 (San Jose and Seattle) function as auditors. Since the initial research for this chapter was completed, the Los Angeles County Board of Supervisors have retained a private law firm for the purpose of auditing the complaint procedure of the Los Angeles County Sheriff's Department (Bobb 1996). The auditor approach is designed to review the operations of the police department's internal complaint review procedure. The process is somewhat similar to a traditional financial audit. Auditors file official reports identifying problems with the complaint procedure, making recommendations for change, and monitoring compliance with previous recommendations.

In short, citizen review procedures have embraced two different definitions of their role and mission, reflecting different strategies for achieving accountability. It is impossible at this point to draw any conclusion regarding their relative effectiveness.

**3. Jurisdiction.** Citizen review developed as a mechanism for achieving accountability of the police. Alleged misconduct on the part of other government officials has never generated equivalent demands for external scrutiny by citizen-dominated procedures (Gellhorn 1966:170–1). Yet, as Gellhorn (1966:185–6) points out, most people, particularly the poor, have more frequent contact "with welfare and educational authorities than with the police." The decisions made by these officials, while not as dramatic as an arrest or a shooting, have profound effects on the lives of ordinary people.

Table 1 indicates that 17 percent of existing citizen review procedures have jurisdiction over complaints against other public employees as well as police officers.

*Discussion:* Jurisdiction over complaints against other public employees has important implications for the role and mission of citizen review. First, it responds to the criticism that citizen review unfairly singles out the police for special scrutiny (Terrill 1991:294). Second, it embodies the principle that all public officials should be held to a high standard of accountability (Gellhorn 1966:186). In short, the broader jurisdiction embodied in some citizen review procedures offers a model for a more comprehensive approach to the accountability of public officials.

At present little is known about the activity of citizen review procedures with respect to complaints about public employees other than police. There is virtually no discussion in the literature on this aspect of the role and mission of citizen review. Nor are there any studies of the handling of complaints against non-police employees.

## Organizational Structure

Citizen review procedures differ significantly in terms of their formal organizational structure. The vast majority (85 percent) involve a multi-member board. This explains the popularity of the term, "citizen review board." The remaining 15 percent, however, are administrative agencies with a single executive director (Table 1). The 55 boards vary substantially in terms of their size and composition. They range in size from twenty-four to three members, with an average of ten. Some include sworn police officers, while others do not.

*Discussion:* The organizational structure of citizen review procedures has important implications for achieving the goal of greater police accountability. These implications are illuminated if we think in terms of abstract models of citizen review procedures.

Multi-member boards embody a *direct representation model* of accountability. This model assumes that police accountability is enhanced by directly involving representatives of diverse elements of the community, particularly racial and ethnic minorities, in the complaint review process. This approach is based on the prevalent view that police departments are isolated from the public, are resistant to external scrutiny, and are particularly alienated from racial and ethnic communities.

It should be noted that a variety of police reform efforts over the past thirty years have been based on a similar analysis of police problems. These reforms include police-community relations programs (U.S. Department of Justice 1973), team policing (U.S. Department of Justice 1977), foot patrol (Police Foundation 1981), and community policing (Eck and Spelman 1987; Greene and Mastrofski 1988). The direct representation model assumes that the appointment of minority group members to citizen review boards will help to overcome the conflicts between the police and minority communities.

Citizen review procedures with a single director represent an *administrative model* of accountability. This approach assumes that a given problem (e.g., police misconduct) is best addressed through a specialized bureaucratic agency. The agency itself is held accountable through the review of its director's performance by elected officials (e.g., the mayor, city council) who are answerable to the public through the electoral process.

The direct representation model leaves two important questions unresolved. First, which groups are entitled to representation on a citizen review board? Second, which individuals effectively represent a particular group?

With respect to the first question, anecdotal evidence suggests that the African American and Hispanic communities are represented on virtually all citizen review boards. In a few procedures, positions are reserved for the representatives of specific civil rights organizations. The issue of group representation on citizen review agencies has not received explicit discussion in the literature. There is no discussion of the appropriate level of minority group membership. The issue of "tokenism" has not been addressed. Nor has there been any discussion of the representation of other groups, including Native Americans, Asian Americans, women, gays and lesbians, and police officers. The latter two groups raise special issues.

The question of whether gay and lesbian people are entitled to representation on citizen review boards is a matter of great controversy. On the one hand, there is evidence that gay and lesbian people are frequent victims of police harassment and excessive use of force (Herek and Berrill 1992). On the other hand, some people regard homosexuality as morally offensive and oppose any official government recognition of gay and lesbian people.

The issue of police officer membership on citizen review boards raises particularly serious questions. As Table 1 indicates, fifteen (or 27 percent) of the 55 review boards have sworn police officers as members. The extent of police participation varies from a high of 75 percent to a low of 8 percent of all members, with an average of 37 percent.

Police officer membership, however, raises questions about the actual and perceived independence of citizen review boards on which they serve (Terrill 1990). Does the presence of police officers result in less thorough investigation of complaints and fewer sustained complaints than would otherwise be the case? Does police officer membership compromise the perceived independence of a citizen review board in the eyes of the community? Neither of these questions have been addressed in the literature on citizen review.

The second question raised by the direct representation model involves *which* individuals effectively represent particular communities. The issue of "tokenism" is an extremely sensitive one in American racial politics. As Guinier (1994) argues with respect to legislative districting, skin color does not guarantee a particular point of view on social and political issues. Similarly, it cannot be assumed that all African Americans hold the same viewpoint about their local police. A particular leader may have close ties to the political establishment (e.g., mayor, city council, police department, etc.), and gain appointment to a citizen review board as a result. It is not clear whether such a person is in fact independent of the police and is perceived as being independent. Such a person may tend to favor police officers when reviewing complaints on the basis of his or her general outlook on social and political issues (e.g., as a small business entrepreneur who wants strong police action against street crime). In short, mere skin color does not guarantee "independence" of the police as envisioned by the advocates of citizen review.

The same question arises with respect to police officer members of citizen review boards. The increased diversity of law enforcement personnel has resulted in the emergence of different points of view among officers and organizations representing different perspectives. An officer appointed to serve on a citizen review board, for example, could be the de facto representative of the local police union and, therefore, be hostile to the citizen review procedure. Alternatively, the appointed officer could be the representative of a racial or ethnic minority group organization and, therefore, be more favorably inclined toward complaints filed by minority citizens.

Similar questions arise with respect to the administrative model of citizen review. The goal of an independent review of complaints assumes that the agency director is both independent of the police and perceived as such. Anecdotal evidence suggests that some agency directors are retired law enforcement officers. It is an unresolved question whether such individuals are "independent" of the police, or are perceived as being independent.

At present there is no research on the composition of citizen review boards, the characteristics of citizen review agency directors, or the processes by which these persons are selected. In the literature on citizen review there is virtually no discussion of the question of which groups are entitled to representation on boards, the special issue of police officer membership, or the complex problem of determining who is sufficiently independent of the police. All of these issues are directly relevant to the basic question of the actual and perceived independence of citizen review.

## Operating Policies

Citizen review procedures differ with respect to many operating policies (Walker 1995a). The analysis here focuses on four procedures which have direct implications for police accountability: independent investigative power, subpoena power, public hearings, and legal representation. These four represent a *criminal trial model* of complaint investigation. The criminal trial model assumes that the investigation of complaints against the police should resemble, as nearly as possible, the traditional criminal trial. The crucial elements include, but are not limited to, an adversarial process, investigation of alleged wrongdoing by an independent authority, sufficient procedures for obtaining all relevant facts, adjudication in a public hearing, and a right to legal representation for all parties to the dispute.

The alternative to the criminal trial model is the *administrative investigation model*. This model resembles a standard internal personnel process: a closed, non-public procedure, with some limited due process protections for the employee.

As noted above, 34 percent of all citizen review procedures have independent investigative powers. Previous studies have regarded this power as the defining characteristic of the different types of citizen review (Goldsmith 1988; Kerstetter 1985; Walker and Bumphus 1991). This study places it in the context of the other policies designed to ensure independent and thorough investigation of complaints. Thirty-eight percent of citizen review procedures have subpoena power; about half (46.2 percent) conduct public hearings; and almost one-third (32 percent) allow legal representation for either the police officer, the citizen or both. Only 7, or 10.7 percent of all citizen review procedures, however, have all four elements of the criminal trial model. Two procedures, representing 3 percent of the total, have no elements of the criminal trial model. The vast majority (86 percent) are hybrids, with some features of the criminal trial model.

*Discussion:* The criminal trial model represents a strategy for achieving independent and thorough review of complaints. There are two reasons for questioning the viability of this model. First, as the data indicates, only 34 percent of all citizen review procedures have the most important element of the criminal trial model, independent review of complaints, and only 10 percent have the four key policies associated with the model. This raises serious questions about whether the vast majority of citizen review procedures have sufficient powers to fulfill the goals of the criminal trial model.

Second, there are good reasons for questioning whether the criminal trial model is appropriate for the complaint process. The criminal trial model is rarely found in the criminal process itself. It is a truism in the administration of criminal justice that few cases go to trial and that the criminal process is an administrative rather than an adversarial one (Bureau of Justice Statistics 1992; Packer 1968). The adversarial trial disappeared many decades ago, for many complex reasons (Heumann 1978). It is legitimate, therefore, to ask whether the criminal trial model is appropriate for the review of complaints against the police. Gellhorn (1966) and Kerstetter (1985) have questioned whether citizen review, as an adversarial proceeding, is capable of conducting more independent investigations, sustaining more complaints, and achieving the other related goals.

The criminal trial model is further limited by the fact that only a handful of citizen review procedures have the power to impose discipline on police officers; most can only make advisory recommendations to the police chief executive (Perez 1994; Walker and Bumphus 1991).[9] The scope of recommendations by citizen review procedures also varies. Forty percent of all citizen review procedures are authorized to recommend a specific disciplinary action in a given case (Table 1). The others only make recommendations about the disposition of the complaint (i.e., sustained, unfounded, not sustained, exonerated), leaving the decision about disciplinary action up to the chief executive. In short, the powers of citizen review procedures are far more limited than those of judges in the criminal process.

The appropriateness of the criminal trial model for citizen review of complaints has received only limited attention in the literature to date (Gellhorn 1966; Kerstetter 1985; Perez 1994). Two general possibilities merit consideration. If the criminal trial model is appropriate, it is important to specify the features necessary for effective performance. Those features are not necessarily limited to the ones discussed here, and would also include sufficient resources in terms of staff and budgets. There is little discussion and no research, however, on the question of what features are likely to guarantee effective achievement of the goals of citizen review.

If the criminal trial model is inappropriate, alternative models need to be explored. Several alternatives already exist in at least some limited form. One approach is the resolution of complaints through mediation. Mediation is regarded as less costly and time-consuming than an adversarial proceeding, and less likely to aggravate the polarization between citizens and the police. Sviridoff and McElroy (1989a:9) suggest that mediation is more consistent with the goals of complainants.

As Table 1 indicates, about 19 percent (12 out of 65) of citizen review procedures currently offer some form of mediation. To date, however, only one study examines mediation in a citizen review process, and it reaches no definitive conclusions regarding its effectiveness (Sviridoff and McElroy 1989a). More research is needed on the nature of mediation procedures in the handling of complaints against the police and its effectiveness relative to other procedures.

A second alternative is to abandon case-by-case review of complaints altogether in favor of policy review. As discussed above, this approach seeks to achieve police accountability through a preventive rather than a deterrent strategy. Some analysts believe that the auditor approach, for example, is a more effective and efficient way of improving the handling of complaints. It provides for the continuous monitoring of the internal complaint procedure with a capacity to report its findings to the public. It does not involve the creation of an entirely new complaint procedure which may not be as independent and effective as intended. The New York Civil Liberties Union (NYCLU) is a strong advocate of citizen review, but devotes much of its energy to monitoring and criticizing the existing Citizen Complaint Review Board (NYCLU, 1993). The Citizen Complaint Review Board in Washington, DC was abolished for financial reasons in 1995, but virtually all observers agree that it was extremely ineffective.

A third alternative is a hybrid approach, combining case-by-case review (perhaps limited to the most serious kinds of complaints) and policy review. As Table 1 indicates, this approach exists in nearly two-thirds of all citizen review procedures. The hybrid approach is consistent with Bayley's (1991:ix) suggestion that there should be different procedures for different kinds of complaints.

## Conclusion

Citizen review of complaints against police officers has emerged as an important new aspect of policing. Its rapid growth has produced a wide variety among procedures with respect to their mission, structure, and operating policies. It is no longer possible to speak of "citizen review" as an undifferentiated phenomenon. Many different forms currently exist. Future discussions of the subject, along with attempts to evaluate the effectiveness of complaint review systems, need to take into account these variations.

The assumptions underlying citizen review, meanwhile, also need critical examination. This article has highlighted the problematic relationship between the goals of citizen review and administrative features. Although citizen review is designed to provide an independent review of complaints, many existing procedures are not structured in ways that guarantee fulfillment of that goal.

Future research on citizen review needs to focus on three related issues. First, additional research is needed to specify in greater detail the variations among citizen review procedures. The field is in a state of nearly continuous change. New complaint procedures are created and old ones significantly revised every year. At the same time, additional research is needed on the variations among internal police complaint procedures. Second, the assumptions underlying citizen review need more critical assessment than they have received to date. Third, there is a need for rigorous comparative evaluations of complaint review systems which take into account the variations among both citizen review and internal police review procedures.

Citizen review of complaints against the police has spread rapidly in recent years, in the United States and in other countries. This change is only one part of a pervasive atmosphere of innovation in policing. Bayley (1995:101) argues that the present era may be "the most creative period in policing since the modern police officer was put on the streets of London in 1829." As an attempt to enhance the accountability of the police, citizen review is consistent with the goal of making the police more responsive to the public.

Additional research is needed to determine the relationship between citizen review and other innovative programs, such as community policing, designed to enhance police accountability and responsiveness to the public.

## Notes

[1] A wide variety of terms are used to describe these procedures: "external review," "civilian review," "civilian oversight," and "citizen review." This article uses citizen review.

[2]The more recent LEMAS data indicate that the number of citizen review procedures is over 80 (Bureau of Justice Statistics 1995). There are a number of errors in the LEMAS data, however, with a number of departments incorrectly reporting the existence of a citizen review procedure (Walker, research in progress).

[3]These surveys include: Goldsmith (1988), IACOLE (1989), International City Management Association (1992), Kerstetter (1985), New York Civil Liberties Union (1993), and Perez (1994). Only West (1988) is based on a systematic survey and it is out of date due to the rapid growth of citizen review.

[4]An earlier version of this research (Walker and Wright 1995) reported a total of 66 citizen review agencies. Albany, New York was incorrectly reported as having a citizen review procedure. The corrected total, reported here, is 65.

[5]There is considerable misunderstanding on this subject. Because the San Francisco Office of Citizen Complaints is under the jurisdiction of the San Francisco Police Commission, it is, in an official and legal sense, a part of the law enforcement agency. The San Diego County Citizens Law Enforcement Review Board, on the other hand, is a separate county agency.

[6]The *Law Enforcement Management and Administrative Statistics, 1993* (Bureau of Justice Statistics 1995) includes a question regarding citizen review. A follow-up investigation by the authors of this article currently in progress has tentatively found a number of errors where a law enforcement agency is incorrectly listed as having a civilian review board. For further criticisms of the LEMAS methodology and data, see Walker and Katz (1995).

[7]Some additional information came from journalists who contacted the lead author about developments related to citizen review in their area.

[8]The hazards of mail surveys are illustrated by the Police Foundation survey of the use of force (Pate and Fridell 1993:II, B-24) which produced an estimate of the number of citizen review procedures twelve times higher than the one reported here. The Police Foundation estimate that 5.3 percent of all municipal police departments have some form of citizen review yields a total of 636 procedures (.053 x 12,000). The estimate that 7 percent of all sheriffs departments have citizen review yields another 210 procedures (.07 x 3,000). The authors of the Police Foundation survey acknowledge the limitations of mail surveys (Pate and Fridell 1993:58–60).

[9]The exceptions are the San Francisco Office of Citizen Complaints, the Milwaukee Fire and Police Commission, Chicago Police Board, and the Detroit Police Commission. The police departments in these cities are governed by citizen commissions which have the ultimate authority to discipline police officers.

## References

Adams, K. (1995). "Measuring the Prevalence of Police Abuse of Force." In W. A. Geller and H. Toch, eds. *And Justice For All*. Washington: Police Executive Research Forum.

American Civil Liberties Union (1964). *Policy Guide*, Policy #204, "Civilian Review Boards." New York: ACLU.

_____ (1966). *Police Power and Citizens' Rights: The Case For an Independent Police Review Board*. New York: ACLU.

_____ (1992). *Fighting Police Abuse: A Community Action Manual*. New York: ACLU.

Americans For Effective Law Enforcement (1982). *Police Civilian Review Boards*. AELE Defense Manual, Brief #82–3. San Francisco: AELE.

Bayley, D. (1991). "Preface." In A. J. Goldsmith, ed. *Complaints Against the Police: The Trend to External Review*. Oxford: Clarendon Press.

_____ (1994). *Police For the Future*. New York: Oxford University Press.

Bellush, J. (1971). *Race and Politics in New York City*. New York: Praeger.

Bittner, E. (1970). *The Functions of the Police in Modern Society*. Washington, DC: National Institute of Mental Health.

Black, A. (1968). *The Police and the People*. New York: McGraw-Hill.

Bobb, Merrick (1996). *The Los Angeles County Sheriff's Department: Fifth Semi-annual Report*. Los Angeles: Los Angeles County.

Browning, R. P., D. R. Marshall, and D. H. Tabb (1984). *Protest is Not Enough*. Berkeley: University of California Press.

Bureau of Justice Statistics (1992). *The Prosecution of Felony Arrests, 1988*. Washington, DC: Government Printing Office.

_____ (1995). *Law Enforcement Management and Administrative Statistics, 1993*. Washington, DC: Government Printing Office.

Chevigny, P. (1969). *Police Power: Police Abuses in New York City*. New York: Vintage Books.

Cohen, B. (1972). "The Police Internal System of Justice in New York City." *Journal of Criminal Law, Criminology, and Police Science* 63 (March): 54–67.

Dugan, J. R. and D. R. Breda (1991). "Complaints About Police Officers: A Comparison Among Types and Agencies," *Journal of Criminal Justice* 19: 165–71.

Eck, J. E. and W. Spelman (1987). *Problem-Solving: Problem-Oriented Policing in Newport News*. Washington, DC: PERF.

Geller, W. A. and H. Toch (1995). *And Justice For All: Understanding and Controlling Police Abuse of Force*. Washington, DC: PERF.

Gellhorn, W. (1966). *When Americans Complain*. Cambridge: Harvard University Press.

Goldsmith, A. J. (1988). "New Directions in Police Complaints Procedures: Some Conceptual and Comparative Departures." *Police Studies* 11 (Summer): 60–71.

_____ (1991a). *Complaints Against the Police: The Trend to External Review*. Oxford: Clarendon Press.

_____ (1991b). "External Review and Self-Regulation: Police Accountability and the Dialectic of Complaints Procedures." In A. J. Goldsmith, ed., *Complaints Against the Police: The Trend to External Review*. Oxford: Clarendon Press.

Greene, J. and S. Mastrofski (1988). *Community Policing: Rhetoric or Reality?* New York: Praeger.

Griswold, D. B. (1994). "Complaints Against the Police: Predicting Dispositions." *Journal of Criminal Justice* 22 (No. 3): 215–21.

Guinier, L. (1994). *The Tyranny of the Majority*. New York: The Free Press.

Herek, G. M. and K. T. Berrill (1992). *Hate Crimes: Confronting Violence Against Lesbians and Gay Men*. Newbury Park: Sage.

Heumann, M (1978). *Plea Bargaining*. Chicago: University of Chicago.

Hudson, J. R. (1972). "Organizational Aspects of Internal and External Review of the Police." *Journal of Criminal Law, Criminology, and Police Science* 63: 427–32.

IACOLE (1985). *Compendium of Civilian Oversight Agencies*. Chicago: IACOLE.

_____ (1989). *International Compendium of Civilian Oversight Agencies*. Chicago: IACOLE.

IACP (1964). "Police Review Boards." *Police Chief* (February): 12–35.

International City Management Association (1992). "Police Review Systems." *MIS Report* 24 (No. 8, August).

Jolin, A. I. and D. C. Gibbons (1984). "Policing the Police: The Portland Experience." *Journal of Police Science and Administration* 12 (September): 315–22.

Jones, R. S. (1994). "Processing Complaints: A Study of the Milwaukee Fire and Police Commission." *Marquette Law Review* 77:489–519.

Kahn, R. (1975). "Urban Reform and Police Accountability in New York City: 1950–1974." In R. Lineberry and L. Masotti, eds., *Urban Problems and Public Policy*. Lexington: Lexington Books. Pp. 107–27.

Kappeler, V. E., P. B. Kraska, and J. E. Marron (1995). "Police Policing Themselves: The Processing of Excessive Force Complaints." Paper. Academy of Criminal Justice Sciences. Boston, MA. (March).

Kerstetter, W. A. (1985). "Who Disciplines the Police? Who Should?" In William A. Geller, ed., *Police Leadership in America: Crisis and Opportunity*. Chicago. American Bar Foundation.

_____ (1995). "A 'Procedural Justice' Perspective on Police and Citizen Satisfaction With Investigations of Police Use of Force: Finding a Common Ground of Fairness." In W. A. Geller and Hans Toch, eds. *And Justice For All*. Washington, DC: PERF. Pp. 223–32.

Kerstetter, W. A. and K. A. Rasinski (1994). "Opening a Window into Police Internal Affairs: Impact of Procedural Justice Reform on Third-Party Attitudes." *Social Justice Research* 7 (No. 2): 107–27.

Littlejohn, E. (1981a). "The Cries of the Wounded: A History of Police Misconduct in Detroit." *University of Detroit Journal of Urban Law* 58: 173–219.

_____ (1981b). "The Civilian Police Commission: A Deterrent of Police Misconduct" *University of Detroit Journal of Urban Law* 59 (Fall): 5–62.

Luna, E. (1994). "Accountability to the Community on the Use of Deadly Force." *Policing By Consent*, I (December): 4–6.

Mollen Commission (1994). *Commission Report*. New York: Mollen Commission.

NAACP (1995). *Beyond the Rodney King Story: An Investigation of Police Misconduct in Minority Communities*. Boston: Northeastern University Press.

National Advisory Commission on Civil Disorders (1968). *Report*. New York: Bantam Books.

New York CCRB (1993). *Annual Report*. New York: CCRB.

_____ (1992). *Survey of Civilian Complaint Systems*. New York: CCRB.

New York Civil Liberties Union (1993). *Civilian Review Agencies: A Comparative Study*. New York: NYCLU.

Packer, H. (1968). *The Limits of the Criminal Sanction*. Stanford: Stanford University Press.

Pate, A. M. and L. A. Fridell (1993). *Police Use of Force: Official Reports, Citizen Complaints, and Legal Consequences*. 2 Vols. Washington, DC: The Police Foundation.

Perez, D. W. (1978). *Police Accountability: A Question of Balance*. Berkeley: University of California.

_____ (1994). *Common Sense About Police Review*. Philadelphia: Temple University Press.

Perez, D. W. and W. K. Muir (1995). "Administrative Review of Alleged Police Brutality." In Geller and Toch, eds., *And Justice For All*. Washington, DC: PERF. Pp. 205–22.

Police Foundation (1981). *Newark Foot Patrol Experiment*. Washington, DC: The Police Foundation.

Sherman, L. W. (1978). *Scandal and Reform*. Berkeley: University of California Press.

Skolnick, J. H. and J. J. Fyfe (1993). *Above the Law*. New York: Free Press.

Sviridoff, M. and J. E. McElroy (1988). *Processing Complaints Against Police: The Civilian Complaint Review Board*. New York: Vera Institute of Justice.

_____ (1989a). *Processing Complaints Against Police in New York City: The Complainant's Perspective*. New York: Vera Institute of Justice.

Sviridoff, M. and J. E. McElroy (1989b). *The Processing of Complaints Against Police in New York City: The Perceptions and Attitudes of Line Officers.* New York: Vera Institute of Justice.

Terrill, R. J. (1982). "Complaint Procedures: Variations on the Theme of Civilian Participation." *Journal of Police Science and Administration* 10 (4): 398–407.

_____ (1988). "Police Accountability in Philadelphia: Retrospects and Prospects." *American Journal of Police* 7: 79–99.

_____ (1990). "Alternative Perceptions of Independence in Civilian Oversight." *Journal of Police Science and Administration* 17: 77–83.

_____ (1991). "Civilian Oversight of the Police Complaints Process in the United States: Concerns, Developments, and More Concerns." In A. J. Goldsmith, ed., *Complaints Against the Police: The Trend Toward External Review.* Oxford: Clarendon.

U.S. Commission on Civil Rights (1978). *Civic Crisis-Civic Challenge: Police-Community Relations in Memphis.* Washington, DC: Government Printing Office.

_____ (1981a). *Policing in Cincinnati, Ohio: Official Policy vs. Civilian Reality.* Washington, DC: Government Printing Office.

_____ (1981b). *Who is Guarding the Guardians?: A Report of Police Practices.* Washington: U.S. Commission on Civil Rights, October. Pp. 124–27.

U. S. Department of Justice (1973). *Neighborhood Team Policing.* Washington: Government Printing Office.

_____ (1977). *Improving Police/Community Relations.* Washington, DC: Government Printing Office.

Wagner, A. E. (1980a). "Citizen Complaints Against the Police: The Complainant" (1980) *Journal of Police Science and Administration* 8 (No. 3): 247–52.

_____ (1980b). "Citizen Complaints Against the Police: The Accused Officer." *Journal of Police Science and Administration* 8 (No. 4): 373–77.

Walker, S. (1995a). *Citizen Review Resource Manual.* Washington, DC: Police Executive Research Forum.

_____ (1995b). "Rethinking the Sustain Rate: Notes on the Proper Standard for Measuring the Effectiveness of Citizen Review of the Police." Presentation. Annual Meeting. American Society of Criminology, Boston, (November).

Walker, S. and V. W. Bumphus (1992)."The Effectiveness of Civilian Review: Observation on Recent Trends and New Issues Regarding the Civilian Review of the Police." *American Journal of Police* 11(No. 4): 1–26.

_____ (1991). *Civilian Review of the Police: A National Survey of the 50 Largest Cities.* Omaha: University of Nebraska at Omaha.

Walker, S. and C. M. Katz (1995). "Less Than Meets the Eye: Police Department Bias Crime Units." *American Journal of Police* 14(1): 29–48.

Walker, S., C. Spohn and M. DeLone (1996). *The Color of Justice: Race, Ethnicity and Crime in America.* Belmont: Wadsworth.

Walker, S. and B. Wright (1995). *Citizen Review of the Police—1994: A National Survey.* Washington, DC: Police Executive Research Forum.

West, P. (1988). "Investigation of Complaints Against the Police: Summary Report of a National Survey." *American Journal of Police* 7 (No. 2): 101–21.

Westley, W. A. (1970). *Violence and the Police.* Cambridge: MIT Press.

# 19

# Ethics and Law Enforcement

*Joycelyn M. Pollock*

*You are a police officer, riding "one-man" patrol. At approximately 10
P.M., you and one other vehicle are stopped at a red light. The light
changes and you and the other vehicle start driving. Suddenly you
observe the other vehicle weaving from lane to lane. You turn on your
lights and siren and after about an eight-block drive, the vehicle finally
pulls over. You exit your vehicle and find that not only is the driver very
intoxicated, but he is also your first cousin. What should you do?*

A "dilemma" can be defined as a difficult decision in which two or
more choices of behavior are possible. In the situation above, clearly the
"choice" is either to take formal action (for example, arrest) or deal with the
drunk driver in some informal way (call someone to come and get him,
park his car and take him home, or let him go, for instance). More specifically, it is an ethical dilemma, because it involves a decision made in one's
professional capacity that carries a judgment of "right" or "wrong." What is
the "right" answer for the officer in this situation? Is the only "ethical"
action to arrest one's cousin? Is the officer "unethical" if he or she does not
arrest?

Police officers face myriad dilemmas during the course of their
careers. What should they do when they stop a single mother with four children in the car who has outstanding misdemeanor warrants? What should
an officer do when his or her partner uses excessive force during an arrest
and an internal investigation ensues? When he or she knows of another
officer falsifying an overtime report? When a restaurant owner offers a free
or discounted meal? When a gift is proffered? Each of these involve decision making. Each decision can be judged using ethical rationales.

Ethical dilemmas exist in every profession—doctors make decisions
as to what form of medical treatment to employ, considering issues of risk
and cost, whether to prolong life in terminal cases, whether to use addictive
drugs to control pain, and so on; lawyers face ethical dilemmas when clients want them to pursue cases with no legal merit, when they must maintain confidentiality regarding a client's wrongdoing, or when certain tactics
may be very efficacious but contrary to the spirit and/or rules of profes-

Prepared especially for *Critical Issues in Policing*, 3/E by Joycelyn M. Pollock.

sional conduct. In fact, all of us will face ethical decisions related to our professions or occupations. These ethical dilemmas are typically contrasted to moral dilemmas, which are those decisions which take place in our private lives as opposed to our professional lives. Sometimes the two are overlapping. For instance, an individual may be tempted to have an extramarital affair—this is clearly a moral dilemma because it concerns personal, private behavior. However, if the affair involves a co-worker, subordinate or superior at the workplace (or a client, witness, or suspect for those in criminal justice professions), then the decision is not only a moral dilemma but also an ethical dilemma. Other decisions also may be private "moral" choices for other individuals but fall into "ethical" judgments for police officers because of the nature of public service.

Public servants typically have authority to make decisions over others and/or make decisions which influence the "public good," but, in return, have responsibilities to make those decisions fairly without bias or prejudice, and with appropriate objectives and values guiding their decision making (Delattre 1989). For this reason, public servants tend to be held to higher standards than the rest of us. We want our politicians, judges, and police officers to be honest, possess integrity, be fair, and have our interest at heart. In effect, we want them to be better than us. Is this justified? Probably. Public service is, after all, a choice the individual makes, and the power we entrust to public servants is quite awesome. For police, it is literally the power of life and death. Thus, when a group of off-duty police officers become drunk and disorderly during a night out, the public is outraged—much more so than when the local plumber's union gets a little rowdy after a football game. When police officers commit crimes or engage in other wrongdoing, it is typically front-page news. Some may complain that no other profession's members are as heavily scrutinized as police or held to such a high standard, but when one understands the nature of public service, it is clear that the nature of the profession creates greater expectations. Law enforcement is not just a "job;" it is an acceptance of the responsibility of "protecting" and "serving." Further, it is accepting the responsibility to uphold and protect the law.

Unfortunately, many view public service as enjoying a "double standard" rather than adhering to a "higher standard" (Delattre 1989). Thus, politicians routinely get honorariums and "fees" from those over whom they make decisions and pretend that such money is not a bribe. The executive branch have been discovered making "secret" deals with foreign powers that would be illegal if made by private individuals or corporations. Police officers routinely excuse themselves from some laws (such as speeding or public intoxication) even while enforcing such laws against the rest of us. Public service, in these instances, becomes not a sacred office but a special "club" where standard rules of right and wrong are redefined.

Even among public service, law enforcement holds an almost unique position in the ability to use legitimate force (Murphy and Moran 1981). The only other group given the authority to utilize deadly force is the military. Both of these arms of government are expected to utilize their power in not only a lawful manner, but also a just and ethical manner. Our concern with the ethics of law enforcement, and our scrutiny, is understandable when one looks to other countries where the coercive force of police power is subverted and police become not guardians of the law but rather enforcers of pure power. When police utilize their awesome power in a manner that ignores the law, tyranny is only a small step away.

## Ethical Dilemmas in Policing

As mentioned previously, the variety and multitude of ethical dilemmas in policing range from the extremely serious—whether or not to shoot can be considered an ethical decision—to relatively petty decisions—whether to take a free cup of coffee. Much of the available literature has been written about the complicated issues of the use of deception in undercover work. However, more police officers probably deal with such "mundane" issues in the use of discretion as to whether to ticket on a traffic stop, or whether to enforce minor warrants, or whether to try to talk a storeowner out of pressing charges in a shoplifting case. Each of these may not carry the weight of more serious ethical issues (such as whether to report and testify against a corrupt partner), but they are very pervasive and deserve the same level of scrutiny as the other more obvious ethical dilemmas. When asked to provide ethical dilemmas in training courses, police report dilemmas in the categories of use of discretion, extent of duty issues, honesty and loyalty issues, and gratuities (Pollock and Becker 1996).

### Discretion

Discretion can be defined as the power to make a decision. Obviously, all ethical dilemmas involve making a decision—however, in some cases, one course of action is definitely wrong (taking a bribe, for example). In their use of discretion, officers often run into situations where no clearly "right" action emerges—difficult domestic disturbance calls, shoplifting calls where the shoplifter deserves sympathy (because of age, poverty, exigent circumstances or some combination), or other "messy people problem" calls often create problems for the officer who doesn't see a clearly "right" way to resolve the problem. Some incidents involve the law and his or her sense of "justice." For instance, the following:

> *A department store calls for a wagon call. You get there and find a 70-year-old lady arrested for trying to steal hearing aid batteries. She is on a fixed income and unable to purchase the batteries. She even looks like your mother.*

In these cases, the officer feels torn between duty to enforce the law and a more sympathetic course of action. Decision making is sometimes constrained by the insistence of the complainant that the offender be prosecuted. Officers sometimes resolve the dilemma by persuading the storeowner not to press charges and/or paying for the items themselves. Other officers leave it to the courts to parcel out "mercy." In cases of traffic stops, no such complainant exists and therefore some officers utilize discretion and do not enforce the law for a variety of reasons. For instance, some officers feel torn when they stop a mother with children and no infant seats. They question the efficacy of giving a poor woman a ticket which will cost money, when she cannot afford the infant seats in the first place. Some officers will perceive their duty to include helping the woman with referrals to get infant seats; some see their duty more restricted to enforcing the law.

Another category of discretion involves family disputes. Police are often called when the true problem is more complicated than the formal legal system could ever resolve.

> You go to a disturbance at a residence. It is your third time there. The problem is the same each time. Father gets drunk; he then tells his son, daughter-in-law and their kids to leave his home. The son refuses to take his family and leave. The real problem is the father being drunk, yet the father has a legal right to tell his son's family to leave. What should you do?

There are no good answers as to how officers should respond to calls dealing with difficult interpersonal disputes. As in the other cases, some officers see their role in a fairly limited fashion with discretion limited to whether to enforce a law, while other officers see that a greater range of choices (with greater responsibilities) are open to them to resolve disputes.

Other decisions involve personal and/or professional loyalties, such as the dilemma opening this chapter, in which the officer stops his first cousin for DWI. Officers are often in the position of stopping other officers, family members or friends. They may respond to calls involving other officers in altercations at bars or other locales. Most officers report some difference in how they handle calls involving other officers. Is this ethical? Officers justify such different treatment with the belief that police officers get treated more harshly by courts and by their own department than do other people, or by the belief that they could not do their jobs in the department if they were known as someone who "burned" another cop. It is difficult, however, to find much justification for such a "double standard" by any traditional ethical system.

## Duty

Other dilemmas involve situations in which officers either do not know what their duty is or they know what they should do, but it is inconvenient, difficult or time-consuming. For instance:

> It is 10:30 P.M. and you are a late-shift unit heading into the station when you notice a large traffic jam. As you near the scene you observe that it is an accident involving two cars and a fixed object. Do you stop or take the back way to the station?

Obviously, the duty of a patrol officer is to stop and render assistance and it would be unethical to shirk one's duty. However, before we castigate the police officer who does detour past an accident so he or she does not have to put in several hours of overtime finishing the paperwork, remember that in every profession there are similar examples of things we should and should not do, tasks we leave for someone else to perform, and calls we choose not to make. Understanding the ethical nature of decision making is not to say that we will always make the right decision—sometimes we make the choice not to be ethical because the lapse is small, or because our rationalization is persuasive (at least to us). The danger is when our rationalizations become second nature and when we are no longer able to define the true character of our actions; in other words, when we do not realize that our actions are purely egoistic and cannot be justified under any ethical system.

Duty issues are almost always a conflict between doing one's duty and personal interest. At times, it is unpleasant, inconvenient, or dangerous to do "one's duty." A second category of duty issues arise in the expansive or restricted definitions of the duties that officers hold in their profession. "Crime fighters," for instance, would perceive their duty differently from those who define their role as "peace officers" when responding to a domestic call. Community policing redefines the duties of police officers in certain ways. These issues are discussed and debated at policy levels (what the goal, mission and objectives of police in our society are), but also at a very individual level (what my responsibility is to this person in need, even though there is no law to enforce).

## Honesty

Another type of dilemma involves honesty—three types can be distinguished. The first type of dilemma involves illicit personal gain—"found" money. Most officers probably flirt with the concept of keeping stolen money or drug money—it is certainly a stock theme in screenwriters' fantasies. Some officers actually do come into contact with large sums of money, and it is tempting to consider the ease in which it could be taken and the things it could buy. Officers are also quick to label anyone who actually takes such money a "thief." Officers are faced with more temptation than most of us—arriving at the scene of a burglary before the owner arrives; patrolling at night; being offered bribes, drug money, and so on; are all temptations for those who have weak moral and ethical codes. Some officers may be more tempted than others. Recruiters attempt to hire individuals who have strong internal codes of moral conduct, but there are no paper-and-pencil tests which measure future moral conduct.

Other honesty issues involve protecting oneself (for example, having an accident in a patrol car requires a report to be written, but the officer will be sanctioned even if the accident was minor or not his or her fault). It is tempting to ignore the accident and hope that the damage will be ignored or not attributed to his or her shift. One may distinguish lying for gain (overstating time on an overtime sheet) as somewhat different from lying to stay out of trouble; however, both are supported solely by egoistic rationales.

Another issue of honesty involves trying to secure a conviction through lying (perjury). An illegal search or lack of probable cause for an arrest may lead to the temptation to lie after the fact to save the arrest or make the conviction. In this case, the officer is not necessarily trying to help him or herself (although that could be part of it too), but he or she also might have the goal of protecting the public. Obviously, this type of lying is still unethical. Under any rationale, untruthful police officers are more harmful than letting one criminal go free. Even under utilitarian ethics, which are based on the "end" (as in "the end justifies the means"), the loss of credibility that ensues when officers lie far outweighs the potential benefit of any particular conviction.

Yet another type of honesty dilemma involves whistleblowing. Most officers will eventually find themselves in a situation where they observe or have knowledge of the wrongdoing of other officers. What is the ethical course of action?

> On a winter afternoon Officers A and B are riding patrol in a rough area of town. Officer A spots a possible burglar and stops. After a brief chase, the suspect is arrested. Officer B uses a little more force than is necessary. Officer A does not agree. What does he/she do?

> Officer A was an alcoholic and consumed alcohol very heavily on a day-to-day basis. Even while on duty A was highly intoxicated. Joe Blow, a concerned citizen who owned a liquor store in the beat, knew of A's situation, decided to call Officer B, and advised him to talk to A about the problem before it gets out of hand. What should Officer B do?

In these situations, officers are faced with conflicting duties—to the organization and society in general, and to their partners and colleagues. Remember, the issue of whistleblowing is not unique to law enforcement, nor is the "blue curtain" of secrecy—the so-called practice of protecting and covering up for each other. In medicine, one might call it the "white curtain" since many (if not most) doctors will not report or testify against each other in competence hearings or malpractice suits. Lawyers also rarely turn each other in for ethics violations, and in many other professions and occupations the person who "snitches" is ostracized. How many students who are aware of another student cheating will report that person to the professor? Is this not somewhat parallel to the officer faced with wrongdoing on the part of his or her friend and colleague?

In these situations, the conflict is between loyalty to one's friend/colleague and loyalty to the organization or to one's own integrity (Wren 1985, Ewin 1990). If one had no loyalty to friends, there would be no dilemma in turning them in; if one had no integrity or loyalty to the organization, there would be no inclination to do anything at all about the wrongdoing of a friend. Officers experience conflict only when they are loyal and also honest. Assuming all employees have some modicum of integrity, in those organizations that have not earned the loyalty of employees, loyalty to friends/colleagues eclipses loyalty to the organization and sets up a situation where officers will cover up for each other and allow unethical behavior to continue. It is clear that if a department expects police officers to police themselves, administrators must create an organization that demands and deserves loyalty.

One factor which influences officers' decision making is the character of the wrongdoing. Some police officers say they would never turn in their friends but then also say they would never have friends who did something that required them to come forward. No police officer would "cover up" for a child killer, rapist or like criminal on the force. Alternatively, very few police officers would report anyone who committed a minor breach of a technical rule. For the many forms of wrongdoing in between, the officer struggles with his or her conscience as to the gravity of the offense, and the "weighing" of friendship against that offense.

Honesty dilemmas are also discussed in the literature—specifically, the use of deception in undercover work (Skolnick 1982, Marx 1985). Here the issue is whether officers should lie during the investigative phase of police work (for instance, by using informants or going undercover). To what extent is lying acceptable? Should one lie to effect a confession (for example, telling the suspect that a co-conspirator had already confessed)? The trouble with lying at the investigative phase is that it sometimes leads to a temptation to lie at the trial stage of the prosecution. The officer may see no difference if the "end justifies the means." On the other hand, one can find some justification for such lying beyond mere egoism.

## Gratuities

Finally, there are those ethical dilemmas which involve gratuities. Gratuities can be defined as something given because of one's role or position as a matter of policy, while a gift may be defined as an item of value given to an individual as an individual. Sometimes it is not exactly clear whether the offered item is a gift or a gratuity.

*Officer A is new to his beat. Where he worked before, he would stop at a local convenience store and buy something to drink. He has learned from past experiences that if he accepts such items without paying, people always expect something in return. In this new beat, he stops by a store. The clerk refuses to accept payment. Officer A explains that he would prefer to pay. The clerk, now upset, accuses Officer A of trying to be better than the others and says he will tell the officer's supervisor, who also stops by. What should the officer do?*

*A guy's car broke down on the freeway. As an officer on duty, you stopped. You took him home since he only lived a short distance away in your beat. It was early in the morning and the man was very appreciative. He wanted to buy you breakfast to show his appreciation so he offered you five dollars.*

In the second situation, the person helped was offering a gift to a particular officer because of a kind act over and above the officer's duty. In the first situation, the clerk was offering something (indeed, insisting on the officer taking something) simply by virtue of the officer's uniform. One might conclude that the first situation would be wrong. Arguments against gratuities include the idea that there is an expectation of different or "special" service when gratuities are a store policy; officers come to expect them and may patrol differently because of these policies. Also, there is a perception of unfairness on the part of other store owners who may not be able to afford to give gratuities. For all these reasons, ethical systems offer little support for the practice. In the second example, it seems as if no harm has occurred; however, this type of gift is almost always against departmental policy and is defined as unethical as well. Why? There is always an ethical prohibition against receiving something of value from those about whom you make decisions (a politician who accept "gifts" from lobbyists comes to mind as the clearest example of this unethical practice). We do not trust decision makers to be objective when they receive value from a party over whom they make decisions. Another aspect to consider is the unethical nature of receiving value for something for which you are already receiving payment. The officer was on a city payroll and didn't need a "tip" from a citizen for doing his job (perhaps it could lead to a situation where public servants did not do their jobs unless they received "tips" or extra compensation).

In a more sophisticated analysis, we would want to look at motivation and intent, on the part of the officer and the giver (Kania 1988). The second scenario seems harmless because the officer evidently had a "good heart"—otherwise he wouldn't have gone out of his way to help the motorist; and the motorist was grateful for an act that already occurred, not offering something in return for a future favorable decision. Typically, however, rules cannot be written by taking into account "good intentions." A departmental rule manual cannot have a rule that states gratuities are acceptable as long as the giver and receiver do so with "good intentions" but are unacceptable otherwise; therefore most departments have official policies prohibiting gratuities entirely, yet informal departmental policy often accepts the taking of gratuities to lesser or greater extents and punishes only those who abuse the practice.

## Other Dilemmas and Officer Misconduct

There are many other dilemmas police officers may face in their professional lives that have not been discussed previously in this chapter. Other ethical issues which may be addressed include employee theft (use of supplies, personal long-distance calls), cheating on overtime, falsification of internal reports, cheating or overreaching on sick days, injury claims, misuse of computers, extra jobs interfering with work performance, sexual or racial discrimination, treating citizens with disrespect, blame shifting, and other practices.

Other than journalistic accounts exposing wide-scale corruption, there are only a few sources which detail police deviance (Barker and

Carter 1991). It is important to know what police view as serious misbehavior, as well as to what extent it occurs. Barker (1978), in a study of
officer misconduct, asked fifty officers in a small police department how
many of their number participated in the following types of misconduct.
Their responses are in parentheses after the behavior listed: sleeping on
duty (39.58 percent), engaging in sex on duty (31.84 percent), police brutality (39.19 percent), perjury (22.95 percent), and drinking on duty (8.05
percent). Since Barker's study is quite dated, the results must be interpreted with caution. Today, one might find that fewer officers, for instance,
believe other officers engage in brutality. One of the problems with studying
officer deviance is the issue discussed above—police are loathe to discuss
with others the unethical practices found in their departments. Thus, little
is known until major scandals erupt.

### Police Corruption

Thus far we have discussed situations of officers facing "ethical dilemmas." It is important to distinguish true ethical dilemmas from instances of
corruption. There have been several exposés of police corruption and some
academic literature which discusses the origin and reasons for the existence of such activities (Barker and Carter 1991, Souryal 1992, Murphy and
Caplan 1993). Corruption includes such illegal acts as "shopping" (taking
items from the scene of a burglary), bribery, and misuse of position. In
these cases, one should not define the decisions as ethical dilemmas. Theft
is a crime—not an ethical dilemma. Choosing to commit crime is no more
an ethical issue for a police officer than it would be for a criminal.

Examples of corruption occur with depressing regularity, and there
are a variety of explanations for the presence of corruption in police organizations. Some point to weaknesses in the recruiting and training practices
(Dorschner 1993), some point to the police subculture, and some to more
systemic elements of policing that set the groundwork for a network of corruption to exist. Rationalizations used by officers who engage in corruption
include: "The public thinks every cop is a crook—so why try to be honest?"
"The money is out there—if I don't take it, someone else will." "I'm only taking what's rightfully mine; if the city paid me a decent wage, I wouldn't have
to get it on my own" (Murphy and Moran 1981). But these are rationalizations, not explanations for why individuals feel they can engage in such
behavior, nor why others allow them to do so. Most agree that the strongest
correlate to the level of dishonesty among employees in an organization is
the level of dishonesty among administrators. If there is wide-scale corruption in a police department, inevitably that corruption has reached high levels of management which protected and even encouraged dishonesty on the
part of the rank and file.

## How to Resolve Ethical Dilemmas

When faced with an ethical dilemma, police officers may fall back on their
Code of Ethics, their academy training, the principles implicit in the "police

subculture," or traditional ethical rationales. Each of these approaches will now be discussed.

The Code of Ethics for Law Enforcement promulgated by the International Association of Chiefs of Police was written in 1956 and updated in 1991. It is an "aspirations" code, meaning that it promotes the model of a perfect police officer, one that mere mortals can only aspire to.

It is interesting that the Code has made few changes over the last twenty years, but one change that has been made has been to add the phrase "I will cooperate with all legally authorized agencies and their representatives in the pursuit of justice." This phrase brings into bold relief the dilemma of the officer who must choose between loyalty to colleagues and loyalty to the organization. There may be no issue more problematic in the application of the Code to day-to-day decision making by individual officers.

---

### Figure 19.1 Law Enforcement Code of Ethics

As a law enforcement officer, my fundamental duty is to serve the community; to safeguard lives and property; to protect the innocent against deception, the weak against oppression or intimidation and the peaceful against violence or disorder; and to respect the constitutional rights of all to liberty, equality and justice.

I will keep my private life unsullied as an example to all and will behave in a manner that does not bring discredit to me or to my agency. I will maintain courageous calm in the face of danger, scorn or ridicule; develop self-restraint; and be constantly mindful of the welfare of others. Honest In thought and deed both in my personal and official life, I will be exemplary in obeying the law and the regulations of my department. Whatever I see or hear of a confidential nature or that is confided to me in my official capacity will be kept ever secret unless revelation is necessary in the performance of my duty.

I will never act officiously or permit personal feelings, prejudices, political beliefs, aspirations, animosities or friendships to influence my decisions. With no compromise for crime and with relentless prosecution of criminals, I will enforce the law courteously and appropriately without fear or favor, malice or ill will, never employing unnecessary force or violence and never accepting gratuities.

I recognize the badge of my office as a symbol of public faith, and I accept it as a public trust to be held so long as I am true to the ethics of police service. I will never engage in acts of corruption or bribery, nor will I condone such acts by other police officers. I will cooperate with all legally authorized agencies and their representatives in the pursuit of justice.

I know that I alone am responsible for my own standard of professional performance and will take every reasonable opportunity to enhance and improve my level of knowledge and competence.

I will constantly strive to achieve these objectives and ideals, dedicating myself before God to my chosen profession . . . Law Enforcement.

Critics of the Code contend that it is so far removed from the everyday behavior practices of police officers that it has become irrelevant (Johnson and Copus 1981, Swift, Houston and Anderson 1993, Davis 1991). Officers may hear it once during their academy training and never have occasion to hear or read it again, much less use it as a model for conduct.

Officers typically identify several standard elements as important in being a "good officer." These elements include: legality (enforcing and upholding the law) service (protecting and serving the public), honesty and integrity (telling the truth, being honest in action), loyalty (to other police officers), and the Golden Rule (treating people with respect or the way one would like to be treated) (Pollock and Becker 1996). These elements seem to be universal with those officers who are committed to doing their best. They are not all that different from principles to live by in one's private life as well.

## The Police Subculture

The police "subculture," like all subcultures, is described as holding contrary, even anti-ethical, values to the formal organization. Larry Sherman (1982b) describes the subculture's values as including loyalty to colleagues, the idea that the public is the enemy, an acceptance of the use of force, belief in the right to employ discretion, and a protective use of the truth. Scheingold (1984) elaborates on the values of the subculture, including cynicism (everyone is a crook), the use of force (acceptable whenever a threat is perceived, even a threat to one's respect), and the idea that police are victims themselves (of poor pay, stigma, and inappreciativeness on the part of the public).

Obviously the police subculture, at least as described by most authors, and the Code of Ethics present contrary views of the "right" thing to do. Academy and in-service training may attempt to mediate these differences or emphasize them. Often one hears that the Field Training Officer (FTO) will start his or her training by first telling the rookie, "forget everything you learned in the academy. . . ." Academy training may be considered irrelevant and separate from the real world of policing. In-service classes may be a focus for resolving these differences or may be considered irrelevant, something to get through either by sleeping or maintaining the mere appearance of compliance.

Old guard officers describe younger officers as the "New Breed" or the "New School" if they earnestly employ the lessons learned from the Code and ethics classes in academies and in-service. In their eyes, these officers "sell out" other officers and do it for themselves so they will not get into trouble. The rationale that it is the "right" thing to do to police each other has not permeated all levels of some police departments because of competing, "older" subcultural values. Most police officers will admit that the "blue curtain" is still a potent force.

## Ethical Systems

An ethical system is an approach to resolving a problem. Issues of right and wrong are as old as time. If an individual is sincere in seeking the ethical course of action, often he or she applies broader principles of right and wrong. Most people employ either religion, utilitarianism, some form of deonotological ethics (which involves doing one's duty and respecting others' rights), or egoism when deciding upon a course of action. Egoism, according to most ethicists, is not an acceptable rationale for resolving ethical dilemmas. Police officers also tend to employ one or the other of these systems, or some combination, with utilitarianism perhaps being the most common one intuitively applied by criminal justice professionals (Swift, Houston and Anderson 1993).

---

**Figure 19.2   Ethical Systems**

**Religion**
 What is good is that which conforms to God's will.
 How do we know God's will?
 —Bible or other religious document
 —Religious authorities
 —Faith
**Ethical Formalism (deontological ethics)**
 What is good is that which conforms to doing one's duty and the categorical imperative.
 What is the categorical imperative?
 —Act in such a way that one would will it to be a universal law.
 —Treat each person as an end and not as a means.
**Utilitarianism**
 What is good is that which results in the greatest benefit for the greatest number.
 Act utilitarianism "weighs" the benefits of an act for just those people and just that incident.
 Rule utilitarianism "weighs" the benefits after determining the consequences of making that behavior a rule for the future.
**Egoism**
 What is good is that which results in the greatest benefit for me.
 Enlightened egoism, however, may reciprocate favors and be practiced by a "good" person (because it benefits the self to be nice to others).

---

Religion is not ordinarily employed when resolving professional ethical dilemmas. While religion certainly provides guidance in how to be a "good" person, more specific principles for resolving professional dilemmas are harder to identify. On the other hand most officers, when pressed to explain what makes a good officer, tend to come up with the basic idea that the good officer treats everyone with respect and "the way they would like to be treated," which is an application of the Golden Rule. Telling the truth, not stealing, and being one's brother's "keeper" are other ideals supported by religion.

Ethical formalism demands, first of all, that one do one's duty. All of us have a multitude of duties based on our roles. We may be students, teachers, police officers, probation officers (professional roles); mothers, fathers, daughters, sons, brothers, sisters (familial roles); and little league coaches, PTA presidents, committee chairpersons (other roles); and, of course, all of us are citizens. All of these roles have duties attached to them. The duties are categorical—one must do them regardless of external reward or consequences. If everyone lived up to their duties, it would be a perfect world. The second part of ethical formalism is to abide by the "categorical imperative." Again, there is no element of situational ethics here; one must abide by the principles in order to be ethical or moral. The principles involve acting according to universalism—in effect making sure one's behavior conforms to the rules of behavior by which one would want everyone to abide; and treating each person as an end and not as a means—not using people.

One problem with ethical formalism is understanding what one's duty is. For instance, in the situations described earlier where officers are faced with shoplifters who are more pathetic than criminal, is the duty to enforce the law or is there some larger duty to do "justice?" Other duty issues are more clear (for example, the accident scene where the officer will be extremely inconvenienced but will admit that his or her duty is to make the scene). Another way to approach these dilemmas is to apply universalism: whether an officer would want all officers to use individual judgment when deciding whether to arrest a shoplifter (the answer is probably yes); or whether he or she would want all officers to ignore accidents (the answer is probably no). The other element is, not using people as a means to an end. If you were helping the poor lady who stole hearing aid batteries so you could get your name in the paper in a local human interest story, then, of course, your action would not be ethical. The only thing that determines ethical action under this system is the "good heart," or the motivation for the action. In the gratuities example, the giver who had a "good heart" would be ethical while the giver who expected something in return would not be.

Utilitarianism defines good as that which benefits the many. Most of us resolve ethical issues using some elements of utilitarianism in our thinking. We intuitively understand that the individual is less important than the majority. Utilitarianism also is consequentialist, meaning that it looks to the end, not the means to determine "goodness." "Bad" means may result in a "good" end and therefore be redefined as "good" under utilitarianism. This ethical system is difficult to apply, however, in that there is a need to predict consequences. Is lying to gain a conviction "good" because we get one criminal off the street? Or is it "bad" because it results in a loss of credibility for police? We would have to have a crystal ball to predict the consequences of each behavior decision in order to apply utilitarianism accurately. Ethical formalism (or other deontological systems) needs no such prediction to determine goodness, since the definition of goodness lies in the essential nature of the action (for example, lying is bad because it violates the police officer's duty to uphold the law and it also violates the categorical imperative).

Egoism is also a consequentialist system but its measurement is more simple—what is good is that which benefits oneself. We all use egoism in many behavioral choices. The officer who drives by an accident, the officer who does not ticket speeding officers when anyone else would have received a ticket, the officer who loses his or her temper and uses excessive force on a suspect, the officer who cheats "a little" on overtime or court slips—all these officers have no ethical rationale for their actions except egoism. We reject egoism as an ethical rationale because it is internally illogical. How can it be right that each of us is correct in pursuing his or her own self-interest when inevitably our self-interests will collide? The analogy might be one of bumper cars at an amusement park. The "game" is to smash into as many other cars as one can for one's own enjoyment—no one moves very far or very fast. It would be more effective (if one was measuring distance traveled) if someone organized and said, "All right, everyone go this way and behave." That, of course, never happens because the fun is in the "bumping." But playing bumper cars is only a game; if we acted in a similar manner in real life we would "bump into" each other all the time and precious little would get accomplished. That is what egoism espouses, and that is why most ethicists reject it.

## Three Questions to Resolve Dilemmas

A final approach to resolving ethical dilemmas asks simple questions of the individual. The first can be called the "front-page test." How would you feel if your action appeared on the front page of the newspaper? If you would not like such exposure, then your action should be examined more closely. This may be simple but effective. Anyone in public office would do well to evaluate each behavior decision as if it might appear on the newspaper's front page tomorrow (because, indeed, it might!). The second question is related to the first: "How will you feel about your action when looking back on it?" Again, if you are not proud of your action or there are questionable ethics involved, you would probably want to forget the action. The final question is an application of the Golden Rule or universalism: "Would you consider your action fair if you were each of the other parties involved?" Another way of saying it is, "Did you treat others the way you would want to be treated?" These questions are sometimes overlooked when making day-to-day decisions. Thoughtful policing involves being sensitized to the ethical nature of decision making and, if being egotistic at times, at least recognizing such actions for what they are.

# "Good" Police Work and Being "Good"

Some issues of law enforcement ethics will continue to be complicated as long as there is confusion and disagreement over the nature of policing in a free society. If "good" police work is measured by the number of arrests, the surety of convictions, and the pure goal of catching criminals, then being a "good" officer may be contradictory to being a "good" person, and the good people who become officers may be distressed to find that being a good person is not "good enough." In many applications of professional ethics, one finds that these ethics are just a subset or smaller version of definitions of right and wrong in society. Typically we expect people to treat each other with respect. In most professions—medicine, law, teaching and others—this concept holds true in the particular aspects of that profession to the populace with which it interacts. We expect people to tell the truth. Again, this concept holds true in professional codes of ethics. However, in other cases we may "allow" behavior by officers that we would not allow from anyone else.

Much of what is defined as unethical on the part of officers is supported by the public itself. If the "end" of catching criminals becomes more important than the "duty" of protecting the sanctity of the law, then unethical actions are sure to follow because anything can be justified. If we accept unethical practices when they benefit us (requesting different treatment from officers because of who we are, accepting unethical means for removing street people and vagrants, agreeing that violating constitutional rights to catch drug dealers is acceptable, or offering gratuities so officers will frequent our place of business), then we can hardly cry out when unethical practices flourish and spread to other behavioral decisions. In the final analysis, police departments probably represent the communities they police. Cities torn by racial strife will also have a police department which plays racial politics. Communities where corruption is endemic among local politicians rarely escape similar corruption in their police departments. Communities that turn a blind eye to police violence (as long as it is visited upon less desirable groups) will probably have a police department marked by brutality. Individual officers, however, must hold themselves accountable for their own individual behavior. It is possible to be a "good" person and a "good" police officer when one takes time to define the terms, is aware of the ethical nature of decision making, and has the courage to live up to one's own principles.

## Expanded Bibliography

Barker, Thomas (1978) "An Empirical Study of Police Deviance Other Than Corruption." *Journal of Police Science and Administration* 6, 3:264–74.

Barker, Thomas and David Carter (1991) *Police Deviance*. Cincinnati, OH: Anderson Publishing Company.

Bedau, Hugo (1982) "Prisoners' Rights." *Criminal Justice Ethics* 1, 1:26–41.

Braswell, Michael, Tyler Fletcher and Larry Miller (1990) *Human Relations and Corrections* (3rd ed.). Prospect Heights, IL: Waveland Press.

Braswell, Michael, Belinda McCarthy and Bernard McCarthy (1991) *Justice, Crime and Ethics*. Cincinnati, OH: Anderson Publishing Company.

Callahan, Daniel (1982) "Applied Ethics in Criminal Justice." *Criminal Justice Ethics* 1, 1:1, 64.

Cederblom, J. and C. Spohn (1991) "A Model for Teaching Criminal Justice Ethics." *Journal of Criminal Justice Education* 2, 2:201–17.

Cohen, Howard (1985) "A Dilemma for Discretion." In W. Heffernan and T. Stroup (eds.), *Police Ethics: Hard Choices in Law Enforcement*, pp. 69–83. New York: John Jay Press.

_____ (1986) "Exploiting Police Authority." *Criminal Justice Ethics* 5, 2:23–31.

_____ (1987) "Overstepping Police Authority," *Criminal Justice Ethics* 6, 2:52–60.

Cohen, Howard and Michael Feldberg (1991) *Power and Restraint: The Moral Dimension of Police Work*. New York: Praeger Publishing.

Davis, Michael (1991) "Do Cops Really Need a Code of Ethics?" *Criminal Justice Ethics* 10, 2:14–28.

Davis, Michael and Frederick Elliston (1986) *Ethics and the Legal Profession*. Buffalo, NY: Prometheus Books.

Delaney, H. R. (1990) "Teaching the Applied Criminal Justice Ethics Course." In F. Schmalleger, *Ethics in Criminal Justice*, pp. 148–64. Bristol, IN: Wyndham Hall Press.

Delattre, Edwin (1989) *Character and Cops: Ethics in Policing*. Washington DC: American Enterprise for Public Policy Research.

Delattre (1989b) Ethics in Public Service: Higher Standards and Double Standards," *Criminal Justice Ethics* 1, 2:179–283.

Elliston, Frederick and Norman Bowie (1982) *Ethics, Public Policy and Criminal Justice*. Cambridge: Oelgeschlager, Gunn and Hain Publishers.

Dorschner, John (1993) "The Dark Side of the Force." In R. Dunham and G. Alpert (eds.), *Critical Issues in Policing* (2nd ed.), pp. 254–75. Prospect Heights, IL: Waveland Press.

Elliston, Frederick and Michael Feldberg (1985) *Moral Issues in Police Work*. Totawa, NJ: Rowman and Allanheld.

Ewin, R. E. (1990) "Loyalty and the Police," *Criminal Justice Ethics* 9, 2: 3–15.

Feibleman, James (1985) *Justice, Law and Culture*. Boston: Martinus Nijhoff Publishers.

Feinberg, Joel and Hyman Gross (1977) *Justice: Selected Readings*. Princeton: Princeton University Press.

Galvin, Richard (1988) "Limited Legal Moralism." *Criminal Justice Ethics* 7, 2: 23–37.

Haan, Norma, Eliane Aerts and Bruce Cooper (1985) *On Moral Grounds: The Search for a Practical Morality*. New York: New York University Press.

Heffernan, William and Timothy Stroup (1985) *Police Ethics: Hard Choices in Law Enforcement*. New York: John Jay Press.

Hyatt, W. D. (1991) "Teaching Ethics in a Criminal Justice Program." *American Journal of Police* 10, 2:77–86.

Johnson, Leslie (1982) "Frustration: The Mold of Judicial Philosophy." *Criminal Justice Ethics* 1, 1:20–26.

Johnson, Charles and Gary Copus (1981) "Law Enforcement Ethics: A Theoretical Analysis." In F. Schmalleger and R. Gustafson (eds) *The Social Basis of Crim-*

*inal Justice: Ethical Issues for the 80's*, pp. 39–83. Washington DC: University Press.

Kania, Richard (1988) "Police Acceptance of Gratuities," *Criminal Justice Ethics* 7, 2:37–49.

Kleinig, J. (1990) "Teaching and Learning Police Ethics: Competing and Complementary Approaches." *Journal of Criminal Justice* 18:1–18

Klockars, Carl (1983) "The Dirty Harry Problem." In C. Klockars, *Thinking About Police: Contemporary Readings*, pp. 428–38. New York: McGraw Hill.

_____ (1984) "Blue Lies and Police Placebos." *American Behavioral Scientist* 27, 4: 529–44.

Mackie, J. L. (1982) "Morality and the Retributive Emotions." *Criminal Justice Ethics* 1, 1: 3–10.

Malloy, Edward (1982) *The Ethics of Law Enforcement and Criminal Punishment.* Lanham, NY: University Press.

Marx, Gary (1985) "Who Really Gets Stung? Some Issues Raised by the New Police Undercover Work." In F. Elliston and M. Feldberg (eds.), *Moral Issues in Police Work*, pp. 99–129. Totawa, NJ: Rowman & Allanheld.

_____ (1992) "Under-the-covers Undercover Investigations: Some Reflections on the State's Use of Deception," *Criminal Justice Ethics* 11, 1:13–25.

Murphy, Jeffrie (1985) *Punishment and Rehabilitation.* Belmont, CA: Wadsworth Publishing Company.

Murphy, Patrick and Dean Caplan (1993) "Fostering Integrity." In R. Dunham and G. Alpert (eds.), *Critical Issues in Policing* (2nd. ed.), pp. 304–27. Prospect Heights, IL: Waveland Press.

Murphy, Paul and Kenneth Moran (1981) "The Continuing Cycle of Systemic Police Corruption." In F. Schmalleger and R. Gustafson (eds.), *The Social Basis of Criminal Justice: Ethical Issues for the 80's*, pp. 87–109. Washington DC: University Press.

Pollock, Joycelyn (1993) *Ethics in Crime and Justice.* Pacific Grove, CA: Brooks/Cole Publishing Company.

Pollock-Byrne, Joycelyn M. (1988) "Teaching Criminal Justice Ethics." *The Justice Professional* 3, 2:283–97.

Pollock, J. and R. Becker (1996) "Ethical Dilemmas in Police Work." In M. Braswell, B. McCarthy and B. McCarthy (eds.), *Justice, Crime and Ethics*, pp. 83–103. Cincinnati, OH: Anderson Publishing Company.

Pring, Robert (1988) "Logic and Values: A Description of a New Course in Criminal Justice and Ethics." *The Justice Professional* 3, 1:94–106.

Reiman, Jeffrey (1987) "The Marxian Critique of Criminal Justice." *Criminal Justice Ethics* 6, 1:30–50.

_____ (1990) *Justice and Modern Moral Philosophy.* New Haven: Yale University Press.

Scheingold, Stuart (1984) *The Politics of Law and Order.* New York: Longman.

Schmalleger, Frank (1990) *Ethics in Criminal Justice.* Prospect Heights, IL: Wyndham Hall Press.

Schmalleger, Frank and Robert Gustafson (eds.) (1981) *The Social Basis of Criminal Justice: Ethical Issues for the 80's.* Washington DC: University Press.

Schoeman, Ferdinand (1982) "Friendship and Testimonial Privileges." In F. Elliston and N. Bowie (eds.), *Ethics, Public Policy and Criminal Justice*, pp. 257–72. Cambridge: Oelgeschlager, Gunn and Hain Publishers.

Schoeman, Ferdinand (1985) "Privacy and Police Undercover Work." In William Heffernan and Timothy Stroup (eds.), *Police Ethics: Hard Choices in Law Enforcement*, pp. 133–53. New York: John Jay Press.

_____ (1986) "Undercover Operations: Some Moral Questions About S.804," *Criminal Justice Ethics* 5, 2:16–22.

Sherman, Lawrence (1981) *The Teaching of Ethics in Criminology and Criminal Justice.* Washington D.C.: Joint Commission on Criminology and Criminal Justice Education and Standards, LEAA.

_____ (1982a) *Ethics in Criminal Justice Education.* New York: The Hastings Center, Institute of Society, Ethics and the Life Sciences.

_____ (1982b) "Learning Police Ethics." *Criminal Justice Ethics* 1, 1:10–19.

_____ (1985a) "Becoming Bent: Moral Careers of Corrupt Policemen." In F. Elliston and M. Feldberg (eds.), *Moral Issues in Police Work*, pp. 253–73. Totawa, NJ: Rowman & Allanheld.

_____ (1985b) "Equity Against Truth: Value Choices in Deceptive Investigations." In William Heffernan and Timothy Stroup (eds.), *Police Ethics: Hard Choices in Law Enforcement*, pp. 117–33. New York: John Jay Press.

Skolnick, Jerome (1982) "Deception by Police." *Criminal Justice Ethics* 1, 2:40–54.

Souryal, Sam (1992) *Ethics in Criminal Justice: In Search of the Truth.* Cincinnati, OH: Anderson Publishing Company.

Souryal, Sam and Dennis Potts (1993) "What Am I Supposed to Fall Back On? Cultural Literacy in Criminal Justice Ethics." *Journal of Criminal Justice Education* 4:15–41.

Swift, Andrew, James Houston and Robin Anderson (1993) "Cops, Hacks and the Greater Good," Academy of Criminal Justice Sciences Conference, Kansas City, Missouri.

Williams, Gregory (1984) *The Law and Politics of Police Discretion.* Westport, CT: Greenwood Press.

Wren, Thomas (1985) "Whistle-Blowing and Loyalty to One's Friends." In W. Heffernan and T. Stroup (eds.) *Police Ethics: Hard Choices in Law Enforcement*, pp. 25–47. New York: John Jay Press.

# Section V

## Minorities in Policing

Recruiting minorities in police work has been an important issue facing police administrators for several decades. Unfortunately, there has not been a great deal of research or literature directed toward the problems faced by minority officers or toward the impact of hiring those officers. Yet, the calls for community-based policing strategies, which emphasize the integration of the formal control system of the police with the informal control system of the community, require minority participation in policing. Further, the values of affirmative action, equal opportunity and involvement of minorities all encourage the hiring and advancement of minorities in law enforcement.

This section about minorities and policing is included to respond to the lack of information available to students of police. We have asked both Kenneth Peak and Susan Martin to address the issue of minorities in policing. In addition, Nancy Herrington has provided some of her personal experiences to illustrate the research findings presented by Dr. Martin.

Kenneth Peak traces the development of African-American employment in the police workplace, suggesting that diversity is sorely needed and desirable in American police organizations. In addition, he contends that the police must work to improve the racial tensions between African-American community members and the police officers responsible for maintaining order in those communities.

Susan Martin, from the Police Foundation, examines the changes in the status of women in police work, the nature of the resistance of male officers to having women on the force, and the current research and policy issues related to women who choose police work. She concludes that the most blatant barriers to the recruitment of women in police work have fallen, and women are entering the profession in increasing numbers. However, female officers still face discriminatory treatment which limits their mobility and options for advancement.

Lieutenant Nancy Herrington explains some of the issues that have faced her as a successful woman in law enforcement. Her experiences demonstrate the problems faced by many women in what is still predominantly a male profession.

---

# African Americans in Policing

---

*Kenneth J. Peak*

## Introduction

Very little has been written about African Americans as police officers in this country. However, the extant literature indicates that African Americans have had neither a rapid nor facile access to the policing field. This article traces the development of African Americans in the police workplace. Included are discussions of the development of African-American policing in the United States, the unequal treatment and marginality that occurred during that development, contemporary issues and problems surrounding attempts to recruit African Americans into the police ranks, and some caveats that accompany endeavors to bring African Americans into those ranks. The general premise is tendered that diversity is sorely needed and is highly desirable in today's American police organizations, particularly as the community policing and problem-solving strategy expands and citizens are increasingly engaged in attempts to address neighborhood crime and disorder.

## The Development of African Americans as Police Officers

African Americans served as police officers as early as 1861 in Washington, D.C., yet 80 years later they still represented less than 1 percent of the country's police population (Johnson, 1947). Most black officers were first hired in large cities, and around the turn of the century they comprised 2.7 percent of the total of all "watchmen, policemen, and firemen" (Kuykendall and Burns, 1980:103). Then the number of black officers declined until about 1910, when there was less than 1 percent; the number increased slightly in the next decade and declined again, until in 1940 they were still only .9 percent of the total (Kuykendall and Burns, 1980:104). Even though blacks were increasingly hired into policing, there were substantial problems with respect to equal treatment by the departments, including such factors as

Prepared especially for *Critical Issues in Policing*, 3/E by Kenneth J. Peak.

powers of arrest, work assignments, evaluations, and promotions (Roberg and Kuykendall, 1993).

Perhaps typical of the unequal treatment of African-American police officers during the mid-twentieth century is the career of James S. Griffin, who, in 1941, with 55 other patrol officers (and only one other African American), was appointed to the St. Paul, Minnesota, police department. Griffin immediately received many undesirable assignments, such as beats on Skid Row, the jail, and rundown areas of the city. There was an unwritten rule against blacks riding in patrol cars, and these minority officers often were not allowed to wear uniforms for fear of offending members of the white community. Thirteen years would pass before Griffin was allowed to participate in a promotional exam. Today Griffin remembers the pain of his early policing experience:

> The police family, as with most families, has traditionally been homogenous. Newcomers quickly learn that to be part of the family, to feel certain of professional support, they must "fit in" with the workplace status quo. [African-American officers] have found that differences are not well tolerated within the family. Newcomers are expected to leave all cultural differences at the front door. (Griffin, 1997:102)

Griffin also noted that the situation facing the African-American officer has changed little today:

> The dilemma for the black police professional is how to blend the expectations of the profession with the coworkers' expectations and live harmoniously with her/himself. Black and white officers must carry out their duties to serve and protect an inequitable status quo, equitably. They are expected to mediate contact between their departments and the black community while enforcing laws that have been historically and demonstrably anti-African American. The rank and file minority officer often gets the more difficult and unpleasant assignments, usually in high crime areas where people having the lowest economic and educational levels are served and where the poorest housing and highest unemployment exist. Our black officers have been, and are, segregated in their own departments. (Griffin, 1997:102)

Griffin endured his initial problems with the white police world, ultimately serving for 42 years on the force, rising to the level of deputy chief in 1972 and retiring in 1983. Griffin's experiences of policing in the 1940s echo the findings in 1969 of Nicholas Alex in his classic study of Negro police officers. Alex found that the typical Negro police officer experienced "double marginality," being segregated from both the black and white societies and placed in a "special category by the department, his white colleagues, white civilians, and the lower-class Negro community" (Alex, 1969:210). Alex likened the African American's decision to become a police officer as "an effort to sail the narrow channel between Scylla and Charybdis, (since) no matter how professionally he acts, the realization that a Negro policeman is primarily a Negro is impressed upon him both by the department and by his white colleagues" (Alex, 1969:204).

Following World War II there was a steady, albeit slow, increase in the number of black officers. However, unequal treatment by their police superiors continued well into the 1950s. A 1959 survey of 130 cities and counties in the South found that 69 cities required black officers to call white officers when arresting white suspects, and 107 cities indicated that black officers patrolled only in black neighborhoods (Rudwick, 1962:8–14). Furthermore, in some southern towns African-American officers rode in cars marked "Colored Police" and were allowed to arrest only "colored" people (Sullivan, 1989:331). Indeed, as recently as 1966, a survey of southern states revealed that 28 police agencies still maintained restrictions on minority officers' arrest powers (*Ebony*, 1966:102).

The ghetto riots of the mid- and late 1960s were a major reason that an increased emphasis was placed upon the role of minorities in policing. The National Advisory Commission on Civil Disorders (known as the Kerner Commission), noted in 1968 that "Our nation is moving toward two societies, one black, one white—separate and unequal . . ." The Commission, and others of like nature during the same period, placed part of the blame for the riots and poor police-minority relations on the serious under-representation of blacks on police departments, saying that we must "Recruit more Negroes into the regular police force, and review promotion policies to insure fair promotion for Negro officers" (National Advisory Commission, 1968). In fairness to the police, however, it must be recognized that at this point in time many departments were far ahead of other government agencies, private businesses, and educational institutions in employing and promoting minorities (Goldstein, 1977).

Several developments affected the growth of African Americans in policing in the early 1970s, including federal reports (such as that from the U.S. Commission on Civil Rights), the 1971 Supreme Court decision in *Griggs v. Duke Power Company* (banning the use of intelligence tests and other artificial barriers that were not job-related), and Congressional legislation (such as the federal Equal Employment Opportunities Act of 1972). The mid-1970s witnessed the advent of the National Black Police Association and the National Organization of Black Law Enforcement Executives (NOBLE), advocating increased hiring of minority officers and improvement of community relations. In the 1980s, several lawsuits successfully challenged such requirements as height, age, weight, sex, and arrest records (Pursley, 1977).

Recently African-American police officers have slowly increased their representation in police agencies. For example, from 1987 to 1990 the percentage of African Americans in local police departments increased from 9.3 to 10.5 percent (U.S. Department of Justice, Bureau of Justice Statistics, 1993). Today about 11.3 percent of the 474,000 full-time employees of local police agencies are African American (U.S. Department of Justice, Bureau of Justice Statistics, 1996).

# Police Recruitment of African Americans:
## Methods and Problems

There are several compelling reasons why police agencies need to recruit, hire, and, hopefully, promote more people of color. First, it is essential due to the increasing diversity that is occurring generally across America. For example, during the 1980s the African-American population in the United States expanded from 26.5 million to nearly 30 million from 1980 to 1990, a 13.2 percent increase. This growth rate was about one-third higher than the national growth rate. African Americans now constitute about 12.1 percent of the total American population (U.S. Department of Commerce, Bureau of the Census, 1991). The recruitment of African Americans into police service is also essential for bridging the color gap that has traditionally existed, to provide role models for younger minority persons contemplating a career in policing, and for developing policies and procedures that will assist such officers in the future. Interaction that occurs among black and white officers reduces suspicion and distrust. And, finally, equal treatment is the touchstone for a truly democratic society.

Historically, however, there have been two broad reasons for the dearth of minorities in the police workforce. First are *institutional barriers*—the formal and informal barriers erected by police departments to dissuade minorities from seeking or continuing employment in the agency, such as complicated applications and the department's image regarding minorities (Gaines et al., 1997). The single most important step a police administrator can take to recruit minorities is to demonstrate unequivocally that he or she is working vigorously to ensure that the members of the department do not discriminate against them (Goldstein, 1977). Second are reasons of *personal preference* (lack of interest in a police career choice) (Gaines et al., 1997).

For these reasons, the recruitment of African Americans into police service remains a difficult task. Probably the single most difficult barrier has to do with the image that police officers still have in many minority communities. Unfortunately, police officers have often been seen as symbols of oppression or an army of occupation, as portrayed by James Baldwin (1961:65) in his classic description of how the police are viewed in the ghetto:

> Their very presence is an insult, and it would be, even if they spent their entire day feeding gumdrops to children. They represent the force of the white world . . . to keep the black man corralled up here, in his place. The badge, the gun in the holster, and the swinging club make vivid what will happen should his rebellion become overt.

Furthermore, many minorities view African-American police officers as people who have "sold out." For many of those African Americans in uniforms, there has existed a so-called "double marginality," where the African-American officers feel accepted neither by their own minority group nor by the white officers. However, one study of over one thousand African-American officers indicated that this problem, quite pronounced in the 1960s and 1970s, may no longer be a major problem with African-American officers' perceptions of their jobs (Campbell, 1980). Many African Americans view police work as an opportunity to leave the ghetto and enter the middle class. As one African-American police officer put it, "There were two ways to get out of my neighborhood and not end up dead or in prison. You either became or a minister or a cop. I always fell asleep in church so I decided to become a cop" (quoted in Sullivan, 1989:338).

Several recruitment strategies can assist in building a diverse police agency. First, recruiters must be carefully selected and trained for this task; they must develop the contacts, resources, and skills to be effective, and be committed to the goal of recruiting. They must also be provided the necessary budget and equipment to approach their mission, and have established guidelines (Shusta et al., 1995).

Next, it must be understood that recruitment must be done in an increasingly shrinking applicant pool, as qualified African Americans are also attracted to private industry, the armed forces, and other government positions. Police agencies must look in the right places and do the right things in order to attract African Americans as police applicants. Some smaller police agencies are forming consortiums and pooling their resources with other small agencies in order to have the necessary resources for recruitment advertising and initial testing of minority applicants. Clearly, the police must develop a recruitment strategy that will target people who are not usually recruited; this "alternative applicant pool" is defined as those people who are qualified for police work but who have no current intention of pursuing a police career (Bowers, 1990).

## Some Caveats Concerning Minority Recruitment

According to Steven Cox, there are several caveats to minority recruitment as well. Cox maintained that, in some cases, minority group members are recruited or promoted for reasons other than ability and competency; when this occurs, members of the dominant group are affected and a backlash may be expected. In some cases, in an effort to overcome past wrongs, we simply hire and promote personnel who should not have been hired or promoted. Cox argued that race, ethnicity, and gender should not be considerations when hiring or promoting police personnel. Eliminating these factors in the hiring and promotional process means developing tests that are not inherently biased in terms of such factors—a difficult task. Such tests are likely to be considerably different from those traditionally employed, and will likely be perceived as inferior to those tests previously taken by officers who were hired in the past. Of course, as Cox asserted, different does not necessarily imply inferior, either in testing or with respect to race, ethnicity, and gender (Cox, 1996).

## Summary and Conclusions

This article included an overview of the history of African Americans in police organizations. The slow development of their entry into and equal treatment within this workplace were demonstrated, as well as the general need for greater diversity in this occupation.

Ours is not a perfect world. Indeed, many African Americans remain convinced that America's criminal justice system—especially the police—are racist. The police must work to improve this situation. Furthermore, many police agencies must acknowledge that, because their past recruitment efforts have fallen short, they have more work to do.

Particularly as we approach the twenty-first century, with many police agencies adopting the community-oriented policing and problem-solving (COPPS) philosophy, it is essential that police departments better reflect the diverse nature of our society. COPPS dictates that police officers engage the community in resolving community crime and disorder (see Peak and Glensor, 1996). However, as one observer noted, "When police confront the black community, there's a lot of historical baggage confronting both groups. There are stereotypes and archetypes that exist in the minds of both. It plays itself out even when blacks and Hispanics are part of the police force" (Louis Wright, quoted in Benson, 1992:42).

Contemporary African-American police officers face problems similar to those of women who attempt to enter and prosper in police work: Until more African Americans are promoted and can affect police policy and serve as role models, they are likely to be treated unequally and have difficulty being recruited and promoted—a classic "Catch-22" situation.

Still, as we noted above, African Americans must not be recruited, hired, and/or promoted for the wrong reasons. The lowering of entrance standards will only create enmity and exacerbate an already delicate situation. Such a hiring preference even generated recent widespread dissatisfaction within the Federal Bureau of Investigation, with 69 percent of 3,000 FBI employees stating that they did not believe that the Bureau chose the best people for promotion (*Crime Control Digest*, 1991). It is clear that the effecting of diversity within the police service must be done with a view toward equality and empathy for all concerned parties.

## References

Alex, Nicholas (1969). *Black in Blue: A Study of the Negro Policeman*. New York: Appleton-Century-Crofts.

Baldwin, J. (1961). *Nobody Knows My Name*. New York: Dial Press.

Benson, K. (1992). "Facing the Issue of Race," *Police*, July: 40–43, 82.

Bowers, G. A. (1990). "Avoiding the Recruitment Crisis." *Journal of California Law Enforcement* 24(2): 64.

Campbell, V. (1980). "Double Marginality of Black Policemen: A Reassessment." *Criminology* 17:477–84.

Cox, S. M. (1996). *Police: Practices, Perspectives, Problems.* Boston, MA: Allyn and Bacon.

*Crime Control Digest* (1991). "White FBI Agents Upset by Minority Promotions," 25(25): 8, June 4.

*Ebony Magazine* (1966). "The Negro Handbook." Chicago, IL: Johnson Publishing.

Gaines, L. K., Kappeler, V. E., and Vaughn, J. B. (1997). *Policing in America* (2d ed.). Cincinnati, OH: Anderson Publishing Company.

Goldstein, H. (1977). *Policing a Free Society.* Cambridge, MA: Ballinger Publishing Company.

Griffin, James S. (1997). "African Americans in Policing." In Kenneth J. Peak, *Policing America: Methods, Issues, Challenges* (2d ed.). Upper Saddle River, NJ: Prentice Hall.

*Griggs v. Duke Power Company,* 401 U.S. 424 (1971).

Johnson, C. S. (1947). *Into the Mainstream: A Survey of Best Practices in Race Relations in the South.* Chapel Hill: University of North Carolina Press.

Kuykendall, J. and Burns, D. (1980). "The Black Police Officer: An Historical Perspective." *Journal of Contemporary Criminal Justice* 1:103–13.

National Advisory Commission on Civil Disorder (1968). *Report,* Chapter 11. Washington, D.C.: Government Printing Office.

Peak, K. J. and Glensor, R. W. (1996). *Community Policing and Problem Solving: Strategies and Practices.* Upper Saddle River, NJ: Prentice Hall.

Pursley, R. (1977). *Introduction to Criminal Justice.* Encino, CA: Glencoe Press.

Roberg, R. R. and Kuykendall, J. (1993). *Police and Society.* Belmont, CA: Wadsworth Publishing Company.

Rudwick, E. (1962). *The Unequal Badge: Negro Policemen in the South, Report of the Southern Regional Council.* Atlanta, GA: Southern Regional Council.

Shusta, R. M., Levine, D. R., Harris, P. R., and Wong, H. Z. (1995). *Multicultural Law Enforcement: Strategies for Peacekeeping in a Diverse Society.* Englewood Cliffs, NJ: Prentice Hall.

Sullivan, P. S. (1989). "Minority Officers: Current Issues." In R. G. Dunham and G. P. Alpert (eds.), *Critical Issues in Policing: Contemporary Readings* (Prospect Heights, IL: Waveland Press).

U.S. Department of Commerce, Bureau of the Census (1991). *1990 Census Profile: Race and Hispanic Origin,* Number 2:1–2.

U.S. Department of Justice, Bureau of Justice Statistics Bulletin (1993). "State and Local Police Departments, 1990," pp. 5, 11.

U.S. Department of Justice, Bureau of Justice Statistics Bulletin (1996). "Local Police Departments, 1993," p. 1.

# 21

# Women Officers on the Move
## An Update on Women in Policing

*Susan E. Martin*

For more than half a century after the acceptance of the first sworn female officer in 1910, women in policing were selected according to separate criteria from men, employed as "policewomen," and limited to working with "women, children, and typewriters" (Milton, 1972). It was only in 1972, with the passage of the 1972 Amendments to the Civil Rights Act of 1964, that women officers obtained the right to an equal opportunity in a law enforcement career. Since that date, many departments, often under court order, have eliminated discriminatory personnel policies. Despite these recent changes, however, women officers still face a variety of barriers to full occupational integration. This chapter examines: (1) the changes that have occurred in the status of women in policing in the past two decades; (2) the nature of the resistance of male officers to women in policing and the problems the women officers face as a result; and (3) current research and policy issues related to women in policing.

## Evidence of Change in Police Personnel Practices

Since 1972 many of the discriminatory practices that restricted the selection and deployment of women in policing have been eliminated and the number of female officers has grown. How adequate is the pace of change? Price (1982) asserts that the sexual integration of policing has not kept pace with changes in other male-dominated occupations, using the example of the increase of women law students from 8 percent in 1970 to 32 percent in 1980. Similarly, Reskin and Roos (1990), examining changes in occupational sex segregation between 1970 and 1988, categorized police work along with many blue-collar and craft jobs as those where women made disproportionately little headway. Fyfe, on the other hand, asserts that the

Prepared especially for *Critical Issues in Policing, 3/E* by Susan E. Martin.

changes in policing have been so dramatic that "the traditional view of polic-ing as a nearly exclusive white male occupation is quickly becoming out-moded . . . (in) virtually every population category and geographic region" (1987: 10). Moreover, 98 percent of the municipal departments serving populations greater than 50,000 had women officers assigned to field oper-ations (patrol) units (Martin 1990).

## Growth in the Number of Women Officers

The available evidence presents a mixed picture; there has been slow but steady growth in numbers of women officers and supervisors nation-wide and an expansion of their assignments into all aspects of policing. Nevertheless, women continue to be significantly underrepresented in police work according to data collected annually by the FBI since 1970. In 1971, prior to the change in the civil rights law, women comprised only 1.4 percent of the sworn personnel in municipal departments and 2.7 percent of the officers in suburban agencies. By 1975 they constituted 2.2 percent of the municipal personnel, with the largest increases occurring in depart-ments with populations between 250,000 and 1,000,000 (U.S. F.B.I. 1976). As shown in table 1, the proportion of women among all sworn offic-ers in municipal agencies was 3.8 in 1980, 6.2 in 1985, 8.3 in 1990, and 9.5 in 1994. Similar figures for suburban county agencies are 8.1, 9.7, 11.3, and 11.4, respectively. Thus, during the past two decades the pro-portion of women officers in city departments has grown steadily, with the greatest increases occurring in the larger cities. The representation of women in suburban agencies also grew, so that proportions were similar in city and suburban departments. However, women's representation in the smallest cities (i.e., those with less than 50,000 population) and rural agencies lags behind the more densely populated areas. Similarly, women constituted only 4.2 percent of sworn state police personnel in 1987 and 4.6 percent in 1990 (3.9 percent of whom were white)(U.S. Department of Justice 1992).

Data on the race, rank, and assignment of officers by sex until recently has been "shockingly limited" (Walker 1985). A recent study by the Bureau of Justice Statistics reported the race/ethnicity and sex of sworn local police. As shown in table 2, in 1993 white women comprised 5.7 per-cent of sworn police personnel, black women 2.2 percent, and women of other ethnic groups less than one percent. Looking at the ratio of women to men from each of the racial/ethnic groups, however, the table indicates that black women made up 19 percent of black sworn personnel while women comprised only 11 percent of Hispanic, and 7 percent of white and other ethnic sworn personnel.

**Table 1**
**Percentage of Women Employed as Sworn Officers**

|  | Year | | | |
|---|---|---|---|---|
|  | 1980[1] | 1985[2] | 1990[3] | 1994[4] |
| Total Cities | 3.8 | 6.2 | 8.3 | 9.3 |
| Cities with pop. > 250,000 | 4.6 | 8.6 | 12.6 | 14.2 |
| Cities with pop. 100,000–249,999 | 4.2 | 6.6 | 8.2 | 9.2 |
| Cities with pop. 50,000–99,999 | 3.1 | 4.5 | 6.2 | 6.9 |
| Cities with pop. 25,000–49,999 | 3.0 | 4.0 | 5.1 | 6.0 |
| Cities with pop. 10,000–24,999 | 2.9 | 3.8 | 4.3 | 5.2 |
| Cities with pop. < 10,000 | 3.2 | 4.7 | 5.5 | 6.4 |
| Suburban Counties | 8.1 | 9.7 | 11.3 | 11.4 |
| Rural Counties | 9.9 | 5.7 | 6.3 | 7.0 |

[1] Source: U.S. Federal Bureau of Investigation, 1981.
[2] Source: U.S. Federal Bureau of Investigation, 1986.
[3] Source: U.S. Federal Bureau of Investigation, 1991.
[4] Source: U.S. Federal Bureau of Investigation, 1995.

**Table 2**
**Race/Ethnicity of Full-Time Sworn Personnel in Local Police Departments, 1993**

| Race/Ethnicity | Total | Male | Female |
|---|---|---|---|
| White | 80.9% | 75.2% | 5.7% |
| Black | 11.3 | 9.1 | 2.2 |
| Hispanic | 6.2 | 5.5 | .7 |
| Other | 1.5 | 1.4 | .1 |
| Total | 100% | 91.2% | 8.7% |

Source: B. A. Reaves, 1996.

Data on the number of officers above the entry-level officer rank indicate that women's representation among supervisory personnel increased from less than 1 percent in 1978 to 3.3 percent of all supervisors in municipal agencies by the end of 1986 (including 2.3 percent white and 1 percent nonwhite women). Their representation decreases as one moves up the ranks; 3.7 percent of the sergeants, 2.5 percent of the lieutenants, and 1.4 percent of supervisory personnel of a higher rank are women (Martin 1990). According to a recent survey of the departments in the nation's 50 largest cities, women comprised 7.1 percent of supervisors, including 4.8 percent white women and 1.8 percent black women (Walker and Martin 1994). The fact that the proportion of women supervisors lags behind that of all per-

sonnel is not surprising since supervisors are selected from entry-level officers who are eligible for promotion after several years of service.

In sum, the statistics indicate both good news and bad news. On the
one hand, women have made steady numerical and proportional gains in
law enforcement agencies in all parts of the country. On the other hand,
they still comprise only a "token" (Kanter 1977) proportion of all sworn
police personnel and, like women in law and management,[1] are concentrated at the bottom of the police hierarchy but are virtually invisible in
high-level administrative posts. Although women were promoted to sergeant at a rate slightly higher than might be expected based on their representation among those eligible, the pace of their movement into
supervisory ranks suggests that women are not likely to assume departmental policy-making positions for many years.

### Changing Eligibility and Selection Criteria

The increase in female representation in policing is clearly related to
the development of a substantial body of law requiring nondiscrimination
on the basis of sex in terms and conditions of employment. More than two
decades ago police departments were brought under this legal edifice
through the Equal Employment Opportunity Act of 1972 (amending Title
VII of the Civil Rights Act of 1964), the Crime Control Act of 1973, the State
and Local Government Fiscal Assistance Act of 1976, numerous state
equal rights and fair employment practices laws and have been evolving
case law in interpreting these laws.

Much litigation has been related to height and weight standards that
eliminated most women and many Hispanics from eligibility for policing.
Departments' failure to substantiate their claims that height is predictive
of or correlated with superior job performance and the finding that there
is no correlation between height and performance (White and Bloch, 1975)
led courts to rule that the physical standards must be proved to be job relevant and necessary to safe and efficient job performance. In most cases
such proof has been lacking. Consequently, differential height and weight
eligibility requirements for male and female police applicants have been
virtually eliminated since 1972. By 1979 only 23 percent of the departments surveyed by Sulton and Townsey (1981) retained any height and
weight requirements for admission; by 1986 Fyfe (1987) found only 3.5
percent of the responding departments had minimum height standards
(mean = 63.7 inches) and 3.7 percent had minimum weight standards
(mean = 135.3 pounds).

Selection criteria also have changed. Most police departments use
several criteria for selecting eligible candidates. These include a written
examination, an oral interview, a psychological examination, a physical
agility test, and a background check. Formerly, most female candidates
were eliminated by the physical agility test and oral interview. The extent
to which otherwise qualified women are screened out by the oral interview

is unknown. The potential for bias is great unless interviewers are carefully screened, trained, and provided with structured interview formats. Increasingly, however, departments have moved toward structuring and standardizing the interview process as lawsuits have prohibited arbitrary practices. By 1981 Sulton and Townsey observed that oral interviews no longer appeared to disproportionately eliminate women candidates in large urban departments.

Physical agility tests have been a source of much litigation, due to differences between men and women in strength and agility, and the job relatedness of many of these tests has been questioned. The proportion of departments that use physical performance tests to assess fitness increased from 58 percent of responding agencies in 1982 to 76 percent in 1986 (Fyfe 1987:7), but most agencies changed the tests to conform with the law which prohibits such tests from eliminating a disproportionate number of women (unless such tests can be shown to be reasonably job related and have a valid purpose). In *Harless v. Duck* [1619 F.2d 611(1980)], for example, the court found that the physical agility test under question was invalid under Title VII, stating:

> Defendant did not meet their burden of proving that the test was valid and job-related. First, the job analysis does not specifically define the amount of physical strength required or the extent of physical exertion required. Second, the same type of tests never have been validated. Third, there is no justification in the record for the type of exercises chosen or the passing marks for each exercise.

Based on a survey of 246 municipal departments serving populations over 50,000, Martin (1990) found that 20 percent of the applicants were women; virtually the same proportion of those accepted (20.6 percent) and completing training (19.2) were women. Thus it appears that there is not systematic bias in the selection process; however, the wide variation among departments, in the proportion of applicants that were female and in the proportion of those women that were accepted, suggests that the recruitment and selection practices may favor women in some agencies and disadvantage them elsewhere. Furthermore, one of the factors that significantly reduced the rate at which women applied for police positions and at which those female applicants were accepted was the presence of a pre-training physical agility test.

## Evaluations of Women's Performance

Many of the barriers to equal opportunity for women in policing were based on the belief that women could not adequately perform in the basic police role as patrol officers. In the early 1970s, as legal pressures to assign women to patrol mounted, nine evaluation studies of women on patrol were conducted in departments widely divergent in size and geographical location.[2]

In all but the second phase of the Philadelphia evaluation, the evaluators concluded that women officers were equally effective as comparison males in performing patrol duties. At the same time, the studies found some gender differences in performance that have implications for policing, and observed that male officers and supervisors tended to hold negative attitudes toward women officers. They found that women were less aggressive, made fewer arrests, issued fewer traffic tickets, and were less likely to be involved in serious conduct unbecoming to an officer. The studies also found that the public was equally satisfied with male and female officers, that male supervisors rated the women as less effective than comparison men in handling violent situations. These nine studies undermined arguments that women are unable to perform patrol work adequately and that sex was a bona fide occupational qualification under Title VII. Consequently, they also contributed to the increased hiring of women officers.

A review of these evaluations (Morash and Greene, 1986) pointed out that despite findings generally favorable to women, gender biases were inherent in their evaluation designs. Most notable was the emphasis on traits stereotypically associated with "maleness" despite the lack of empirical evidence that the qualities evaluated were related to critical tasks performed by police. The study also indicated that there was a skewed sample of policing situations, two-thirds of which related to direct or potential violence, even though such incidents are far from frequent. In addition, the reports tended to assume that gender differences were the result of psychological or biological differences rather than the differences in the social experiences of the women officers in a workplace characterized by male officers' negative reactions to them. Although most studies observed differences in the treatment of the male and female officers and negative attitudes expressed by male officers and supervisors, they did not examine the intensity of these negative experiences nor consider their impact on women's performance.

Where the studies found differences in men's and women's behavior they did not consider the possibility that the women's style in resolving conflicts and disputes might have had a beneficial rather than a negative effect. For example, the women's lower arrest rates may mean that women were not taking enough initiative. Alternatively, it might indicate that women handled the situations better than male officers, if the latter caused incidents to escalate into confrontations which resulted in unnecessary arrests. A third explanation is that when a more experienced male patrolled with a female rookie, he tended to take charge of the situation and take credit for arrests more frequently than with male rookies. Thus, it is necessary to look beyond the numbers to an interpretation of their meaning.

# Barriers to the Integration of Women into Policing

The barriers to women in policing emanate from the structural characteristics of the occupation and the work organization, and the ways that cultural mandates and behavioral norms related to gender shape
interpersonal interaction in specific occupational contexts.

## Cultural and Structural Barriers to Gender Integration

In a study of men and women employed in corporations, Kanter
(1977) suggests that occupational behavior is shaped by three key structural features of the organization and the individuals' position in it: the
opportunity structure, the power structure, and relative numbers. These
variables constrain and shape possibilities for action and press people to
adapt to their situations.

Kanter observed that men and women behave differently in work
organizations because men have more real power and greater opportunities for mobility. Both men and women, when placed in powerless and
low-mobility situations, respond by lowering aspirations and developing
different patterns of occupational behavior from those with greater power
and opportunities. Blocked mobility leads to limited motivation which, in
turn, sets in motion a downward cycle of deprivation and discouragement.
Conversely, those with power and opportunities use these resources to
gain allies and supporters and prove themselves, triggering an upward
cycle of success. Although both cycles appear to be related to individual
motivation, in fact they arise in response to organizational factors.

In addition, Kanter noted that number affects occupational behavior
because minority individuals or "tokens" are treated differently than others
in three ways. First, because tokens are highly visible, they face performance pressures. Second, because tokens polarize differences between
themselves and dominants, they face heightened in-group boundaries and
social isolation. Third, because dominants distort and stereotype tokens'
characteristics, tokens are forced into stereotypic roles.

In addition to tokenism, sexism affects women workers. Even when
female tokens have job skills and work commitment they are harassed by
male co-workers and excluded from informal social networks, while male
tokens not only do not face similar discrimination (Kadushin, 1976;
Schreiber, 1979; Williams, 1989), but are the beneficiaries of advancement
up the "glass escalator" (Williams, 1992). Reskin (1988) identified three
additional practices that men adopt to prevent occupational equality when
women workers intrude into the men's occupational world: they type jobs
and tasks according to sex and give the less desirable and lower-paying
activities to women; they treat women in a paternalistic manner; and they
sexualize the workplace.

Paternalism involves men "helping" or "protecting" women by excus-
ing them from difficult or undesirable tasks in exchange for submissive or

dependent behavior. This "help," however, serves to control the women and deny them organizational rewards, stigmatizes them as inferior, and creates resentment by violating the men's sense of fairness (Jurik, 1985; Swerdlow, 1989; Padavic and Reskin, 1990).

The emphasis on women's gender includes sexual harassment which results in women experiencing psychological stress that contributes to higher turnover rates (MacKinnon, 1978; Gutek and Morash, 1982) as well as dilemmas in responding to co-workers (Martin, 1978; Swerdlow, 1989).

Occupational behavior also is guided by socially prescribed norms guiding the ways people "do" or enact gender within the context of larger social structures. Gender is not a fixed attribute of individuals but emerges or is enacted in interactions (West and Zimmerman, 1987; Martin and Jurik, 1996). Thus the way men display appropriate "masculine" and women show "feminine" behavior emerges through "doing" gender in everyday social interaction, including those in the workplace. Consequently, gender is a pervasive feature of all aspects of organizational life including the images, interactions, workers' identities, and policies that result in gendered divisions of labor and power relations in work organizations (Acker, 1990). For example, the extent to which definition of police work has become associated with the male gender is indicated by the merging of the word for the work and the gender of the worker (i.e., "policeman"). Because the norms and expectations of "appropriate" behavior for police (as well as for persons in other occupations historically dominated by men) are associated with enacting "masculine" behavior, women entering these occupations encounter dilemmas on the job. On the one hand, as police, they are expected to display "masculine" behavior and interact with fellow workers as peers and equals; on the other hand, as women, their male co-workers expect and pressure them to display "feminine" behavior (including deference to men) which is deemed inappropriate for an officer (Goffman, 1956). Thus, policewomen have to decide when and how to "act like a cop" and still "act like a lady" on the job.

**Police Work, the Police Culture, and Men's Opposition to Women Officers.** In addition to the barriers women face in a variety of nontraditional occupations, certain aspects of police work lead to unique problems for women officers. Police officers have enormous discretionary decision-making authority. Across the wide variety of policing tasks there is always the potential for violence and the authority to use coercive means to enforce the officer's definition of the situation. The police role as the representative of the coercive potential of the state and as a legitimate user of force in everyday life helps explain certain attitudes and behavioral characteristics of the police and their work culture. The presence of danger and the potential for violence lead to a generalized suspiciousness, isolation from the community, and a cohesive, informal occupational group with its own stratification system and norms. These, in turn, heighten the barriers to informal acceptance of anyone who is perceived as an "outsider" and, therefore, cannot be counted on to conform to group norms.

The men's opposition to women officers has been amply documented (Bloch and Anderson, 1974; Sherman, 1975; California Highway Patrol, 1976; Martin, 1980; Charles, 1981; Hunt, 1990). Most of the men's objections to women officers focus on their physical differences from men and are phrased in terms of concern for physical safety and women's alleged inability to deal with physical violence. Nevertheless, a variety of other concerns underlie their opposition. Women threaten to disrupt the division of labor, the work norms, the work group's solidarity, the insecure occupational status and public image, and the sexist ideology that undergirds the men's definition of the work as "men's work" and their identity as masculine men.

The use of women on patrol implies either that the men's unique asset, their physical superiority, is irrelevant (as it is on most assignments) or that the man working with a woman officer will be at a disadvantage he would not face in a physical confrontation working with a male partner. Moreover, the possibility that women officers reduce the likelihood of a physical confrontation or act appropriately by protecting their male partner is no comfort because it undermines the gender stereotypes that permeate the male officers' perceptual world. Women are not "supposed" to fight or to control other male citizens. At the same time, for a male officer, being "defended" by a woman is regarded as an affront to his manhood.

Women also threaten work-group solidarity. They raise the spectre of possible sexual intimacy between partners, fostering competition among the men and thus creating a competing set of loyalties. They also threaten the public image of police work and the mask of emotional detachment worn by male officers by exposing the fact that the day-to-day reality of policing does not revolve around crime fighting, but involves emotional labor and requires interpersonal skills. In addition, they inhibit men's use of crude language, their illicit on-the-job sexual activities, and the fringe benefit of enhanced masculinity that these confer.

Men's opposition to women in policing also reflects a "deeper concern about who has a right to manage law and order" (Heidensohn, 1992:215). In fact, according to Heidensohn, the view that "men 'own' order and have sole rights to preserve it" is the real but unstated issue underlying their assertions that women are unsuitable officers and will destroy men's solidarity. Instead, their resistance to women on patrol is better understood as emanating from a struggle over the ownership of social control. In sum, the men's opposition to women in their ranks stems from their threat to their definitions of the work, occupational culture, social status, and self-image as men's men which provides a psychological fringe benefit of the job.

***Structural Barriers: Equality versus Equity.*** Women enter policing at a disadvantage. Few went through an extensive anticipatory socialization process in which they vicariously rehearsed police roles. Compared with the men, fewer women have been in the military, had firearms training, or played team sports that involve physical contact and imbue the spirit of the team player.

At the training academy inequality may be fostered in several ways. An emphasis on meeting physical fitness standards that do not have to be maintained beyond the academy magnifies the importance of the physical differences between the sexes. Informal coddling of women by some physical education instructors who are protective or unable to deal with some women's manipulative efforts also negatively affects all the women. It allows some to move to the next stage of recruit training not fully prepared and fosters the expectation of those women that they can get along by being "different" rather than learning the lessons of group loyalty. It also undermines the confidence of male officers in women officers in general, and divides the women. At the same time, police training often fails to develop the interpersonal skills necessary to do the job well. These skills are usually more highly developed in women than in men, and their omission from the curriculum deprives the women of a job-relevant training opportunity in which they are likely to excel. Consequently, the new woman officer enters male turf on male terms with little recognition of the problems she will face, or acknowledgment of the interpersonal strengths she brings to the job.

The early months on the street are very important, since it is then that the reputation that follows an officer through a career is formed. Opportunities for learning and gaining self-confidence have a multiplier effect because once established, habits and reputations are difficult to change. Self-confidence grows with mastery of policing skills and positive feedback on performance. An officer who does not have, or does not take, opportunities to develop street patrol skills because of limited assignments, under-instruction, or overprotection is likely to act hesitantly, be viewed as a threat to others' safety, and be deprived of subsequent opportunities to handle situations.

Female rookies face several disadvantages on the street. They tend to have been sheltered from street life, and to be smaller and not as physically strong as the male rookies. They must overcome openly hostile attitudes of some of their trainers, supervisors, and partners; a dual standard of evaluation; and the performance pressures that "tokens" encounter.

Unless the timidity of some female rookies and the protectiveness of many of the men are consciously reversed, many women do not get opportunities to learn to act with decisiveness and confidence. Consequently, a self-fulfilling prophecy becomes a reality as they seek to manipulate others' expectations of them rather than altering their own behavior.

**Cultural Mandate and Interactional Barriers.** Women officers also face dilemmas in interacting with fellow officers and with citizens. As police officers, they are expected to interact with other police according to the norms governing relations among equals; as women they are expected to adhere to asymmetric norms governing male-female relationships where women are subordinates of men. Thus, in addition to dilemmas as "tokens," women officers must cope with norms that put them at a disadvantage in interactions with male officers.

Men's language keeps women officers "in their place" by constantly referring to them as "ladies" or "girls," (terms that suggest that they should be protected), or by calling those that do not conform to sex role stereotypes "lesbians," "broads," "bitches," or "whores."

Cursing also creates dilemmas. Many men are uncomfortable swearing in front of women officers but resent the inhibition on their expressiveness. Similarly, when women curse, men become offended and withdraw the deference they give to "ladies." If the women avoid cursing, however, their words are taken less seriously.

Frequent sexual jokes and gossip remind the women that they are desired sexual objects, visible outsiders, and feared competitors. In turn, this joking makes many of the women, concerned about even the appearance of impropriety, avoid interactions that might be viewed as having a sexual connotation. They maintain their moral reputation but sacrifice the opportunity to build close interpersonal relationships necessary for sponsorship and protection.

Gender stereotyping enables men to cast women into the roles that reflect in their linguistic categories, limit women's behavioral options, and have a negative impact on their work. Women either get pressed into enacting the "seductress," "maiden," "mother," or "pet" roles, or get labeled "lesbians" or "bitches" (Kanter, 1977). The former are deprofessionalized, protected from occupational demands, excluded from opportunities to develop occupational skills, and criticized for failing to fulfill their duties as officers. The latter are permitted to remain in the men's informal world, but their dangerous qualities are neutralized by defeminization and pejorative categorization.

Informal social exclusion and sexual harassment also remind the women that they are not "just officers." They are visible but excluded from career-promoting networks, vulnerable to harassment but held responsible for the outcomes of such interactions. They experience a more hostile interpersonal work environment than male officers as well as a unique group of work-related stresses. While the primary sources of stress for officers appear to be common to women and men (i.e., organizational and task-related concerns), both Wexler and Logan (1983) and Morash and Haarr (1995) have observed that women also endure an additional category of stressors. These include a lack of acceptance as officers; denial of information, sponsorships, and protection; and both sexual harassment and language harassment (i.e., deliberate exposure to profanity and sexual jokes).

***Relating to Citizens.*** All police officers face recurrent uncertainties in relating to citizens who may seek to disrupt normal interaction by disavowing the officers' identity, and by ascribing to them irrelevant statuses based on age, sex, or race (Goffman, 1961). While citizens usually defer to the police officer who usually has higher social status than persons he or she encounters (Sykes and Clark, 1975), some seek to base the interaction on the officer's "irrelevant" status characteristics, thereby reversing the flow. Although all officers occasionally face such deference reversals, these situations continually threaten women officers' interactions and force the women to find ways to turn them to their advantage, minimize their occurrence, and limit their effects on the officer's control of the situation.

In police-citizen encounters, four possible combinations of gender and social category may arise: male officers with male or female citizens, and female officers with male or female citizens. Each combination has different expectations and management problems as police relate to citizens by doing gender while they seek to control the situation or otherwise enact the police role.

In interactions with male citizens, male officers have status superiority by virtue of their office and expect citizens to defer and comply. On the basis of shared manhood, however, they are status equals. This shared manhood can sometimes be effectively used as a resource for doing gender since it is to the citizen's advantage, saying, in effect, "act like a man (i.e., control yourself) and I won't have to exert my authority as an officer to overpower you." It also benefits the officer by minimizing the necessity of using force and allows him to act as a "good guy," giving a little to gain compliance. When suspects or offenders try to define the situation in terms of shared manhood, however, officers may view the interaction as denying the deference due to their office. When a male officer relies too heavily on the authority of the badge or rejects a male citizen's effort to be treated "as a man," the result is a "duel of manhood" which has a high probability of a physical or verbal confrontation that might well have been avoided.

Male officers' double-status superiority over female citizens generally leads to few problems arising in such interactions, except those related to sexuality. Male officers may use the authority of their office to gain control or gain compliance by asserting, "act like a lady and I'll treat you like one." If invoking the rules of chivalry works, the officer gains control while enhancing his sense of manly generosity. If it fails, he can still treat the woman as a wayward "girl" on whom he will not waste his time, or he may use force.

Interactions between female officers and male citizens are problematic because police expect to take control of situations and be shown deference by citizens; men may defer to the office but resist being controlled by or deferential to a woman. For that reason expectations regarding how a man relates to a woman and to a police officer generally are different and sometimes often are in direct conflict. Women officers usually are given deference, either out of respect for the uniform or because compliance does not challenge a man's manhood if he chivalrously complies, whereas fighting a woman may cause a man to lose status, particularly when there are witnesses. However, the man's deference is revocable, particularly if the officer acts "unladylike" in carrying out her occupational role obligations. Since they often are at a physical disadvantage, female officers may have to rely on the deference of males as a control strategy. Although most women usually try to minimize rather than activate their gender status, they recognize that men seek to redefine situations so as to affirm men's status superiority but that they must retain control.

When women officers encounter sexist or sexual comments they usually ignore them or reply "you wouldn't say that to a male officer, would you?" They may also use a variety of verbal and nonverbal cues involving use of the voice, appearance, facial expression, and body postures which also convey the message that despite their small stature, as police they are to be taken seriously. Learning to transmit these messages, however, requires altering longstanding habits such as smiling, and learning literally to "stand up to people."

In dealing with women citizens, female officers get both greater cooperation and more "hassles" than male officers. While their common gender status implies a reduction of social distance, it revokes the special consideration that female citizens expect from (male) police, and for this reason, may arouse the female citizen's anger at not being able to flirt or cry her way out of a situation. Women also are more willing to fight female officers than male officers. Conversely, women officers often are viewed as more sympathetic and so are able to gain the cooperation of female citizens, particularly victims, who refuse to talk to male officers.

Effective officers of both genders appeal both to "gender-appropriate behavior" on the part of citizens, and to their respect for the officer's authority to gain cooperation. They use a citizen's expectations and values to their advantage, draw on mutually shared statuses to diminish social distance, and only rely on the authority of their office when necessary. Ineffective officers, on the other hand, either too rigidly rely on their formal authority or cannot transcend the limitations on their behavior posed by adherence to traditional norms for doing gender. For female officers this means failure to use the authority of their office and overreliance on deference to them as women; for male officers this means overemphasis on aggressive "macho" behavior that may result in an avoidable confrontation.

In sum, a woman officer faces barriers and handicaps that are built into both the formal and informal work structures. These culturally mandated patterns governing male/female interaction force her to "think like a man, work like a dog, and act like a lady" (Martin, 1980: 219).

## Issues for this Decade and Beyond

Have numerical increases and the passage of time required to achieve seniority and promotions reduced the barriers and limitations women officers face? What new problems challenge the women who move into supervisory positions, and the departments that hire women in greater numbers? These issues for future research will be addressed in the final section of this paper.

## Numbers: The Effects of Moving Beyond Token Status

Kanter (1977) observed that the proportion of minority individuals in work groups affects the manner in which minority members are treated. Her theory of tokenism suggests that members of a small minority suffer adverse conditions due solely to the small size of the subgroup. She distinguished four group types on the basis of proportional size of the minority: uniform groups with only one category of sex, race, or ethnicity; skewed groups in which minorities or "tokens" comprise up to 15 percent of the members; tilted groups typified by minority representation between 16 and 35 percent; and balanced groups. She asserts that minority members in tilted groups face barriers and constraints to acceptance that are less intense than in skewed groups because minorities can form coalitions affecting group culture.

An alternative minority proportion/inequality perspective, originating in race relations literature (Blalock, 1967; Marden and Meyer, 1973; Giles, 1977) asserts that minority individuals are less likely to be accepted by dominants when there are enough of them to threaten the economic and political security of the majority; thus, there is greater discrimination as the minority grows larger and more powerful.

In a test of these competing perspectives examining several work groups in a single organization where group membership ranged from highly skewed male to highly skewed female, South, et al. (1982) found some support for both perspectives. In measuring women's isolation from the work group they found no support for the hypothesis that token women have less contact with male workers and supervisors. However, consistent with the minority proportion hypothesis, female representation was negatively associated with the amount of encouragement for promotion women got from male supervisors. The proportion of women in a group was not significantly related to the quality of relations among women. The authors concluded that "token women are not found to face more severe organizational pressure than nontokens" (South, et al., 1982: 587) and that an increase in the number of minority workers without alteration in the relations between dominants and subordinates is not likely to improve the position of minorities substantially, and may even worsen relations.

Other studies also cast doubt on the assertion that an increase in number alone will relieve the problems of tokenism for women. In a study of the effects of proportions on women managers in two companies with 6 and 19 percent female managers respectively, Harlan and Weiss (1981) found that there was no simple linear relationship between the amount of gender bias or stereotyping and the percentage of women in management. The women in the 19 percent company faced more overt bias and harassment, and women in both companies felt that they had to work harder and face more challenges to their authority than male managers. Deaux and Ullman (1983) found the attitudes of males in the steel industry toward women were more negative in the company with more female employees than in the one with fewer. In a study of the automobile industry, Gruber and Bjorn (1982) found men's sexual harassment of women became more frequent and severe as the proportion of women increased. Thus, it is unclear whether the increase in the number of women in policing has reduced the occupational dilemmas posed by tokenism. While some of the performance pressures due to visibility may have diminished, the organizational structures embedded in a broader social system of gender inequality remain in place, and as women move up the organizational hierarchy, they again face the problems of "tokens" as well as challenges to their authority from men who may tolerate working with women but resist working for them.

## Assignments, Promotions and Women as Supervisors

For more than half a century women officers' assignments were limited to those viewed as compatible with their gender. Although women now are assigned to patrol just as men are, it appears that women officers continue to be disproportionately concentrated in support positions rather than line activities (Martin, 1990). Based on case studies of assignment patterns in three large agencies, it appears that, even with the same amount of time in policing, women have had more nonpatrol assignments than men and that a higher proportion of women than men hold staff support positions while men go into line units, such as special operations and traffic. These differences appear to arise from "pushes" away from patrol into "inside" assignments (Hunt, 1990) due to a hostile environment resulting from men's paternalism and harassment and from "pulls" toward assignments that offer more favorable hours and working conditions and that may reflect women's skills and interests. Similar questions arise with respect to racial patterns of assignments and how the combination of race and gender affect the occupational opportunities of minority women. The emerging literature on the intersection of race and gender suggests that because cultural images of white and black women differ, black women often are treated according to separate norms, are less often put on a pedestal or treated as "ladies," and afforded protection by white men (Martin, 1994). White women, particularly those who are physically attractive, appear to be more likely than black women to get inside assignments and protection on street patrol (Martin, 1994) and less likely to get recognition for superior performance (Belknap and Shelley, 1992).

Although it appears that women are gaining their "fair share" of promotions to sergeant in the large urban departments, questions arise with respect to opportunities for attaining higher rank, particularly top management positions that are based on political decisions rather than standardized examinations. Whether women in policing will be limited by a glass ceiling that women managers have encountered in other occupations remains an open question.

How have superiors and subordinates reacted to women supervisors? Limited interview data suggest that a woman sergeant's position is not an easy one. Like all new sergeants, they face problems adopting an effective supervisory style and "thinking like management." In addition, women sergeants face renewed difficulties as tokens, tend to lack mentors to help them, come in for more testing of their authority than new male sergeants, and face many of the problems observed from studies of women managers in other occupations.

Harriman (1985) asserts that although there were few differences in the attitudes, motivation, and behavior of effective women and men managers, the women's careers progressed more slowly than those of their male cohorts. A review of studies of leadership found no differences in behavior between the sexes after controlling for situational and other demographic variables (Nieva and Gutek, 1981); other studies have noted a tendency to identify effective leadership traits with masculine traits (Schein, 1975) and to regard women as less effective or successful leaders (Harriman, 1985; Statham, 1986).

Research on the relationship between gender and the use of power have found that successful managers of both sexes get and use power strategies effectively. However, the strategies and styles most associated with competence (i.e., direct rather than manipulative; concrete resource mobilization rather than personal) are also associated with masculinity. All styles may be effective if used by a man, but masculine styles were found not to be effective when used by a woman. Thus women supervisors face a dilemma: they can manipulate and be unrecognized or be direct and risk ineffectiveness and hostility.

All performance evaluations are subjective. Not only may rating systems involve categories or activities that are gender stereotyped, but the choice of words in a written evaluation—as well as what is omitted—may exert subtle influence. Although women were found to be no less competent than men in a number of studies, there were differences in the way their performance was perceived and evaluated which resulted in an overall pro-male bias in performance evaluations (Harriman, 1985). For example, women were rated less desirable candidates for university department chairmanships (Fidell, 1970), and identical work was rated higher by both males and females when it was attributed to a man rather than to a woman (Mischel, 1974). The effects of subtle differences in written evaluations was identified by Thomas (1987) in a study of promotion evaluations in the Navy. Women candidates whose numerical evaluation scores were as high as the men's were much less likely to have written comments commending for a position of commanding officer. Not only did supervisors' silence work against them, but the written comments focused on gender stereotyped feminine traits (e.g., well groomed, supportive, sensitive) that are valued less highly than the masculine terms (aggressive, logical, mature) in which males were described.

In a study of men and women managers and their secretaries, Statham (1986) found not only that men and women managers tended to have different management styles,[3] but that each was critical of the other's style. Men saw women managers as too hovering and unwilling to delegate; the women viewed the autonomy that men gave subordinates as "neglect." These findings have implications for women's success because most women managers are supervised and evaluated primarily by men who regard their style as inadequate. For women police officials the problem is compounded by having mostly male subordinates who may share with male supervisors resistance to a "feminine" management style. The anticipation of such opposition was suggested by a survey of women eligible for promotion (Wexler and Quinn, 1985) that found that nearly half the women stated that their greatest concern in being a sergeant was related to the negative reception they expected within the department.

## Turnover

Much of the literature on personnel turnover suggests that women in private industry have slightly higher turnover rates than men and that they leave jobs primarily due to family reasons, whereas men resign to accept other jobs. Others question these conclusions and suggest that women's turnover is related to their overrepresentation in jobs that are poorly paid, unsatisfying, and require a low skill level (Kanter, 1977) as well as to high levels of sexual harassment and discrimination (O'Farrell and Harlan, 1982; Jurik, 1985). Jacobs (1989) also found both an unexpectedly high proportion of women entering male-dominated jobs and a high turnover rate as well. This led him to conclude that the barriers to women's entry are lower than expected, but that employment in male-dominated occupations is less a permanent achievement for women than a temporary pass through a "revolving door."

The research on gender differences in turnover rates in policing is inconsistent. Women's turnover rate was found to be significantly higher than that of the men in the California Highway Patrol, the Royal Canadian Mounted Police (Linden and Minch, 1984), and one California sheriff's department troubled by a generally high turnover rate (Fry, 1983). Although women made up 6 percent of the sheriff's department's personnel, they accounted for 17 percent of those leaving the department in the three years prior to Fry's study. Their high turnover rate appeared to be related to their immediate assignment, however, since 71 percent of the women who resigned were assigned to the custody division (i.e., the jail) and 38 percent accepted employment with other law enforcement agencies. Another study (Sulton and Townsey, 1981) found that male and female turnover rates in municipal departments are similar. Martin (1990) found some support for both similarities and differences. Based on data from 303 municipal departments, women had a higher turnover rate during 1986 (6.3 percent) than men (4.6). The gender gap was even higher in state police agencies (8.9 percent for women versus 2.9 for men). At the same time, analysis of other factors affecting turnover indicated that in departments where women's turnover was high, men's separation rates also were high. The association between male and female turnover rates suggests that the same factors affect each group: internal policies that weed out officers who do not "fit" and alternative employment opportunities. Further research is needed on both turnover rates and reasons that officers leave a department.

## Pregnancy Policy: The Emerging Legal Issue

While the decade of the 1970s marked great strides in assuring legal equality for women, it also brought before the court the "harder" issue: how to deal equitably with biological differences between the sexes. Because only women can get pregnant, there is no way within our legal framework to treat men and women equally and equitably at the same time.

Underlying our legal framework are a set of assumptions and power relations that limit legal reasoning and affect decision making. One assumption is that men and women naturally and biologically occupy different roles in life. This has led to the view that being a worker and mother are incompatible and has resulted in maternity leave and other employment policies that put hardships on women.

In the 1970s in several cases the Supreme Court ruled that employers did not violate Title VII of the Civil Rights Act by denying sick-leave disability insurance or health insurance coverage to female employees to cover disabilities resulting from normal pregnancy. The court found no sex discrimination in California's disability insurance plan which excluded pregnancy from coverage but covered sex-linked disabilities such as prostate operations (*Geduldig v. Aiello*, 1976). Likewise, in *General Electric v. Gilbert* (1976), the majority held that sex discrimination occurs only when men and women are treated differently with respect to a shared situation or characteristic. Since men cannot become pregnant, it was not discrimination against women to deny them health benefits for pregnancy. The employer simply removed one condition from the list of covered conditions.

In response, Congress passed the Pregnancy Disability Act in 1978, broadening the definition of sex discrimination to encompass pregnancy, childbirth, and related medical conditions. It prohibited an employer from: (1) requiring a woman to take leave set arbitrarily at a certain time during pregnancy; (2) failing to grant full reinstatement rights; (3) failing to pay disability or sick leave for pregnancy in the same manner as it pays for other employee disability or sick benefits; and (4) protecting a woman employee from "reproductive hazards" without scientific evidence that a hazard actually exists.

While clarifying Congressional intent, the law left the equal treatment/special treatment question unresolved, as have two apparently contradictory Supreme Court decisions (*Wimberly v. Labor and Industrial Relations Commission of Missouri* and *California Federal Savings and Loan v. Guerra*). These rulings leave it up to each state to decide whether to give pregnant women more favorable treatment than other workers that are physically unable to work. Federal law only requires states to treat women as well or badly as their disabled co-workers; states are permitted—but not obligated—to require employers to give additional benefits without being discriminatory.

Because police work poses the risk of unpredictable physical violence or injury which many departments regard as a "reproductive hazard," pregnancy raises a number of policy questions for departments which often are not covered by bargaining agreements and municipal personnel policies. Although many departments have "light duty" policies that permit officers who are temporarily disabled to work in noncontact positions, there appear to be no uniform policies or common practices with respect to: (1) the point at which the pregnant woman becomes "disabled" and, thereby, "unfit" for patrol or other duties; (2) the person(s) who make the determination of whether the woman should be reassigned or forced to take extended leave; and (3) the assignments that are suitable for an officer on light duty. As the number of officers who are pregnant at the same time increases, a department's deployment problems grow, increasing the need for consistent and clearly articulated policies that assure both adequate protection of the community and of the rights of pregnant officers.

In conclusion, the status of women in policing today is uncertain. Clearly the most blatant barriers that kept women out of police work for more than half a century have fallen, and women are entering policing in increasing numbers. Gaining admission to the occupation, however, is only a first step. Women officers still face discriminatory treatment that limits their options and opportunities for advancement. Nevertheless, as more women enter the occupation, move slowly into positions of authority, and serve as role models and sponsors for other women, there is reason for guarded optimism about the future of women in law enforcement, as well as a large number of questions waiting to be addressed.

## Notes

[1] In 1985 only 2 percent of the top corporate executives of Fortune 500 companies were women (Powell, 1988:75) and 6 percent of law firm partners were women according to an ABA study (Goldberg, 1991).

[2] These studies assessed the Pennsylvania State Police (1973), Metropolitan Police of Washington, DC (Bloch and Anderson, 1974), the California Highway Patrol (California Highway Patrol, 1976), Denver (Bartlett and Rosenblum, 1977), Newton, Massachusetts (Kizziah and Morris, 1977), New York City (Sichel et al., 1978), and Philadelphia (Bartell Associates, 1978, Phases I and II) police departments.

[3] The women managers were described as "task-engrossed and person-oriented"; the men were "image-engrossed and autonomy-invested."

## References

Acker, Joan. 1990. "Hierarchies, Jobs and Bodies: A Theory of Gendered Organizations." *Gender & Society* 4:139–58.

Bartell Associates. 1978. "The Study of Police Women Competency in the Performance of Sector Police Work in the City of Philadelphia." State College, PA: Bartell Associates.

Bartlett, H. W. and A. Rosenblum. 1977. *Policewoman Effectiveness*. Denver: Civil Service Commission and Denver Police Department.

Belknap, J. and J. K. Shelley. 1992. "The New Lone Ranger: Policewomen on Patrol." *American Journal of Police* 12: 47–75.

Blalock, H. 1967. *Toward a Theory of Minority-Group Relations*. New York: Wiley.

Bloch, P. and D. Anderson. 1974. *Policewomen on Patrol: Final Report*. Washington: Urban Institute.

California Highway Patrol. 1976. Women Traffic Officer Project, Sacramento.

Charles, M. T. 1981. "Performance and Socialization of Female Recruits in the Michigan State Police Training Academy." *Journal of Police Science and Administration* 9:209–23.

Deaux, K. and R. Ullman. 1983. *Women of Steel*. New York: Praeger.

Fidell, L. S. 1970. "Empirical Verification of Sex Discrimination in Hiring Practices in Psychology." *Journal of Psychology* 25:1094–98.

Fry, L. 1983. "A Preliminary Examination of the Factors Related to Turnover of Women in Law Enforcement." *Journal of Police Science and Administration* 11:149–55.

Fyfe, J. 1987. *Police Personnel Practices, 1986*. (Baseline Data Report Volume 18, Number 6). Washington, DC: International City Management Association.

*Geduldig v. Aiello* 417 U.S. 125 (1976).

*General Electric v. Gilbert* 429 U.S. 125 (1976).

Giles, M. 1977. "Percent Black and Racial Hostility: An Old Assumption Reexamined." *Social Science Quarterly* 58:412–17.

Goffman, E. 1956. "The Nature of Deference and Demeanor." *American Anthropologist* 56:473–502.

———. 1961. *Encounters*. Indianapolis: Bobbs-Merrill.

Goldberg, S. B. 1991. "Token Women—The ABA Confronts its Glass Ceiling." *ABA Journal* 77:58–63.

Gruber, J. and L. Bjorn. 1982. "Blue-collar Blues: the Sexual Harassment of Women Autoworkers." *Work and Occupations* 9:271–98.

Gutek, B. and B. Morash. 1982. "Sex Ratios, Sex-Role Supervisors, and Sexual Harassment of Women at Work." *Journal of Social Issues* 38:55–74.

Harlan, A. and C. Weiss. 1981. *Moving Up: Women in Managerial Careers*. Wellesley, MA: Wellesley College, Center for Research on Women.

Harriman, A. 1985. *Women/Men/Management*. New York: Praeger.

Heidensohn, F. 1992. *Women in Control? The Role of Women in Law Enforcement*. New York: Oxford University Press.

Hunt, J. 1990. "The Logic of Sexism among Police." *Women and Criminal Justice* 1:3–30.

International City Management Association. 1972. "Personnel Practices in Municipal Police Departments." Urban Data Services.

Jacobs, J. 1989. *Revolving Doors: Sex Segregation and Women's Careers*. Stanford: Stanford University Press.

Jurik, N. 1985. "An Officer and a Lady: Organizational Barriers to Women Working as Correctional Officers in Men's Prisons." *Social Problems* 32:375–88.

Kadushin, A. 1976. "Men in a Woman's Profession." *Social Work* 21:440–47.

Kanter, R. 1977. *Men and Women of the Corporation*. New York: Basic Books.

Kelly, C. 1973. *Uniform Crime Report—1972*. Washington, DC: Government Printing Office.

Kizziah, C. and M. Morris. 1977. *Evaluation of Women in Policing Program: Newton, Massachusetts*. Oakland: Approach Associates.

Linden, R. and C. Minch. 1984. "Women in Policing: A Review." Unpublished manuscript. Ottawa, Canada: Ministry of the Solicitor General of Canada.

MacKinnon, C. 1978. *Sexual Harassment of Working Women*. New Haven: Yale University Press.

Marden, C. and G. Meyer. 1973. *Minorities in American Society*. New York: D. Van Nostrand.

Martin, S. E. 1978. "Sexual Politics in the Workplace: The Interactional World of Policewomen." *Symbolic Interaction* 1: 44–60.

_____. 1980. *"Breaking and Entering": Policewomen on Patrol*. Berkeley: University of California Press.

_____. 1990. *On the Move: The Status of Women in Policing*. Washington, DC: Police Foundation.

_____. 1994. "'Outsider within' the Station House: The Impact of Race and Gender on Black Women Police." *Social Problems, 41*, 383–400.

Martin, S. E. and N. C. Jurik. 1996. *Doing Justice, Doing Gender: Women in Law and Criminal Justice Occupations*. Thousand Oaks, CA: Sage.

Milton, C. 1972. *Women in Policing*. Washington, DC: Police Foundation.

Mischel, H. 1974. "Sex Bias in the Evaluation of Professional Achievements." *Journal of Educational Psychology* 66: 157–66.

Morash, M. and J. Greene. 1986. "Evaluating Women on Patrol: A Critique of Contemporary Wisdom." *Evaluation Review* 10: 230–55.

Morash, M. and R. Haarr. 1995. "Gender, Workplace Problems, and Stress in Policing." *Justice Quarterly* 12:113–40.

Nieva V. and B. Gutek. 1981. *Women and Work: A Psychological Perspective*. New York: Praeger.

O'Farrell, B. and S. L. Harlan. 1982. "Craftworkers and Clerks: The Effects of Male Coworker Hostility on Women's Satisfaction with Nontraditional Jobs." *Social Problems* 29: 252–65.

Padavic, I. and B. Reskin. 1990. "Men's Behavior and Women Interest in Blue-Collar Jobs." *Social Problems* 37: 613–28.

Pennsylvania State Police. 1973. "Pennsylvania State Police Female Trooper Study." Harrisburg: Pennsylvania State Police Headquarters.

Powell, G. 1988. *Men and Women in Management*. Beverly Hills: Sage.

Price, B. 1982. "Sexual Integration in American Law Enforcement." *The Future of Policing*, 205–13.

Reaves, B. A. 1996. *Local Police Departments, 1993*. (NCJ-148822) Washington, DC: Bureau of Justice Statistics.

Reskin, B. 1988. "Bringing the Men Back In: Sex Differentiation and the Devaluation of Women's Work." *Gender and Society* 2: 58–81.

Reskin, B. and R. Roos. 1990. *Job Queues, Gender Queues*. Philadelphia: Temple University Press.

Schein, V. 1975. "The Relationship between Sex Role Stereotypes and Requisite Management Characteristics among Female Managers." *Journal of Applied Psychology* 60: 340–44.

Schreiber, C. 1979. *Men and Women in Transitional Occupations*. Cambridge: MIT Press.

Sherman, L. J. 1975. "Evaluation of Policewomen on Patrol in a Suburban Police Department." *Journal of Police Science and Administration* 3:434–38.

Sichel, J. L., L. N. Friedman, J. C. Quint, and M. E. Smith. 1978. *Women on Patrol: A Pilot Study of Police Performance in New York City.* Washington, DC: National Institute of Law Enforcement and Criminal Justice.

Statham, A. 1986. "The Gender Model Revisited: Differences in the Management Styles of Men and Women." Unpublished manuscript. University of Wisconsin–Parkside.

Sulton, C. and R. Townsey. 1981. *A Progress Report on Women in Policing.* Washington, DC: Police Foundation.

Swerdlow, M. 1989. "Men's Accommodation to Women Entering a Nontraditional Occupation: A Case of Rapid Transit Operatives." *Gender and Society* 3: 373–87.

Sykes, R. and J. Clark. 1975. "A Theory of Deference Exchange in Police-Civilian Encounters." *American Journal of Sociology* 81: 584–600.

Thomas, R J. 1987. "Appraising the Performance of Women: Gender and the Naval Office." In B. Gutek and L. Larwood (eds.) *Women's Career Development.* Beverly Hills: Sage.

U.S. Department of Justice, Bureau of Justice Statistics. 1992. *State and Local Police Departments, 1990.* Bulletin NCJ-133284. Washington, DC: U.S. Department of Justice.

U.S. Federal Bureau of Investigation. 1976. *Uniform Crime Reports—1975.* Washington, D.C.: Government Printing Office.

_____. 1981. *Uniform Crime Reports—1980.* Washington, DC: Government Printing Office.

_____. 1985. *Uniform Crime Reports—1984.* Washington, DC: Government Printing Office.

_____. 1986. *Uniform Crime Reports—1985.* Washington, DC: Government Printing Office.

_____. 1991. *Uniform Crime Reports—1990.* Washington, DC: Government Printing Office.

_____. 1995. *Uniform Crime Reports—1994.* Washington, DC: Government Printing Office.

Walker, S. 1985. "Racial Minority and Female Employment in Policing: the Implications of 'Glacial' Change." *Crime and Delinquency* 31: 555–72.

Walker, S. And S. E Martin. 1994. "Through the Looking Glass Ceiling: Patterns in Hiring and Promotion by Race, Ethnicity and Gender in American Policing, 1982–1992." Paper presented at the Annual Meeting of the American Society of Criminology. Miami, FL, November.

West, C. and D. H. Zimmerman. 1987. "Doing Gender." *Gender & Society* 1:125–151.

Wexler, J. G. and D. D. Logan. 1983. "Sources of Stress among Women Police Officers." *Journal of Police Science and Administration* 11: 46–53.

Wexler, J. G. and V. Quinn. 1985. "Considerations in the Training and Development of Women Sergeants." *Journal of Police Science and Administration* 13: 98–105.

White, T. W. and R B. Bloch. 1975. *Police Officer Height and Selected Aspects of Performance.* Washington, DC: Police Foundation.

Williams, C. 1989. *Gender Differences at Work: Women and Men in Nontraditional Occupations.* Berkeley: University of California Press.

_____. 1992. "The Glass Escalator: Hidden Advantages for Men in the 'Female' Professions." *Social Problems* 39:253–66.

22

# Female Cops—1992

*Nancy L. Herrington*

It has taken nearly thirteen years, but I am finally growing comfortable with myself in my role as a female cop. Becoming a cop was, for me, not a lifetime pursuit. My idea and expectations of policing were incorrectly based on TV and the movies. My staying power and desire to be promoted have been due to my hardheadedness and persistence. My successes have been shared with a few police comrades but mostly family and nonpolice friends.

In law enforcement, competition is fierce and jealousy is very strong and visible if someone should do well. The veterans or those who don't believe women should be in police work can be nasty or sarcastic in their criticism. At a time when you would really appreciate the support of your peers and hearing their congratulations, you receive total silence and cold shoulders. A friend who was a rookie sergeant made lieutenant after his first try at testing. After only six years, he had jumped from officer to sergeant to lieutenant. He was considered a rookie by most and didn't "deserve" to be a lieutenant because he hadn't paid his dues. He shared with me his empty feelings in not having the support of his peers. That's why I've had to reserve talking about my successes and my good feelings and sharing them only with my family and nonpolice friends. They wanted me to do well, my police comrades didn't.

My route to the "World of Policedom" was different than for most. As an impressionable college student, I became a victim of crime. I had decided in 8th grade that I was going to be an architect. Even at that age I was destined to enter a nontraditional profession. The best thing going for me was I had supportive parents who never said, "No, you can't do that." When most girls my age were taking home economics, I was in drafting class. I knew I had to balance math and art. The math was easy, the true challenge came in funneling my creative side to be an artist. At age 14, I knew what college I wanted to attend—Arizona State University—because it had a nationally recognized school of architecture. When I got older, one

Prepared especially for *Critical Issues in Policing*, by Nancy L. Herrington.

**385**

of my sisters arranged for me to work for an architect to gain the valuable experience in my chosen career field. I had it all. I had a goal, I had direction, I had support and I had what it took to make it. I was also vulnerable to crime. In my second year of pre-architecture, I worked a part-time job near the campus at a local convenience store. Returning to my dorm late one night, I got out of my car and was approached by a young man who asked for a light. He introduced himself by way of an eight-inch knife and a stern warning not to say anything but to get back into my car. We left the secure campus of Arizona State University and travelled the road to Tucson—a direction that would change my life forever. Sharing this beginning with you is important because, unlike many people, being a cop was not a lifelong pursuit—just an opportunity for a job.

After the trauma of my kidnapping, my expectations were tainted. I moved back home, in confusion, and passed through one bad experience to another and then another. I no longer wanted to pursue being an architect. I didn't know what I wanted to do. That is the most difficult thing to do or be—indecisive. I did continue school and picked up a couple of electives in police science, mostly out of interest. Several years later I graduated with a degree in sociology. It was a far cry from an architectural degree. Then came the realization that one can't do a lot with a degree in sociology—maybe teach, maybe get a higher degree, maybe do government work. At the time I graduated, I was married to a cop and went looking for a job. Being a cop sounded like a fun job. Not a career, mind you, a job.

Throughout my tenure as a cop I have learned a great deal about the world and more importantly, about myself. I have grown up. I was the youngest and most spoiled child in our family, a pleasure I continue to enjoy. Thus, I lacked maturity and independence. The job quickly made me grow up in order to survive. I once heard a Dallas police officer describe his job as eight hours of the ten o'clock news. It may be that way in a "big city" police department, but for me, in the suburbs, it's just not that exciting. The focus is primarily serving the public, which can be pretty exacerbating for officers who would rather go out and kick ass. For me, there are just enough dead bodies, grotesque accident scenes, stress encounters and too many family disturbances, minor accidents, offense reports and barking dog complaints. The job has made me grow up.

Joseph Wambaugh has accurately described the police code of silence—that inbred culture that can lead to personal and professional success or suicide. I believe that for women, being accepted within that culture is difficult at best. Women must accept and endure constant sexual harassment and the continual challenge to personal values. Acceptance generally requires becoming one of the boys and sacrificing femininity to play the police role. A woman can maintain her stance, but she will suffer the slings and arrows of disapproval from her peers and supervisors. The only option other than endurance is quitting. Fighting back is not an option unless she is willing to live the rest of her professional life being ostracized. While an organization can legislate behavior, it can do nothing with attitudes that have chilling effects. I have constantly juggled between wanting to be accepted as just one of the guys to being obstinate and stalwart in my opinions and actions. Only now do I feel confident and truly comfortable with myself in my job.

The confidence came from my involvement in outside organizations and from the people who believed in me and what I was doing. I have at times tried to hide my profession from people because I was embarrassed to claim I was a female cop. In some places and circumstances, I felt I wasn't good enough. A prime example was my participation in a women's leadership program. I was one of eighty women selected statewide along with doctors, lawyers, successful entrepreneurs and corporate executives. In comparison to all of those talented, intelligent and powerful women, I felt pretty inadequate. I clearly remember, prior to our first leadership session, calling my parents long distance to say I didn't have the courage to face all of those women since I was only a cop. As always, my parents were encouraging. Dad said, "You get on down there, you are just as good as they are." Ironically, Dad was right. In fact, my career was so different that I became a real topic of discussion for my role in a nontraditional field. All of those bright and talented women wanted to know about my job and to hear police stories.

As a rookie officer, I remember one night at shift change asking for a portable radio from a male rookie officer. Exchanging equipment at shift change was our typical procedure. The best equipment generally went to the buddies who shared it with their buddies. On this particular night, I asked this officer for his portable radio. His response was, "I wouldn't let you lick the sweat off my balls if you were the last woman on earth." He then heartily laughed all the way into the station. I was devastated. It had been drilled into my head at the academy and with my field-training officers, you don't rat on another officer. Ironically, a few of the younger officers on my shift overheard the comment. Later in the shift, a couple of them approached me individually to encourage me to report the incident to my sergeant. Facing the fear of retaliation from my peers was not something I wanted to do. I did finally muster the courage to talk with my sergeant. Needless to say, I was scared to death. The offending officer was "talked to" and the incident was never brought up again—to my face. Today he's a high-ranking officer in the department.

Throughout my career, (and for other female cops I've known) I have been laughed at and not encouraged to do well. In this job, it is considered a real art of one-upmanship to speak with a sarcastic tongue. I have never understood why it is so funny to constantly berate people. I do know that the sarcasm can be very painful at times. I've been the brunt of rumors. Even though I was married, I was accused of "shacking up" with my sergeant who gave me preferential days off and beat assignments. In reality, those privileges were given because I was doing a good job. The shift lieutenant threatened to move me to another shift to "solve the problem." So, it was up to me to defend myself and to argue that the rumors were unfounded and were only acts of jealousy. I consistently led the shift in self-initiated activity with arrests and tickets while the other members of my shift chose to sleep on duty. I have been told to "settle down" by veteran officers because I might make them look bad. Looking back, I should have known it was going to be tough. Right after I passed the Oral Review Board to be hired, the personnel sergeant told me, "Well, we've got a year to get rid of you"—referring to the one-year work probationary period.

I've talked with other female cops about the way I've felt about the way I've been treated. The harsh treatment seems to be prevalent throughout law enforcement. One woman I met at a management training school told me that when she started with her department ten years ago, her training officer told her she wouldn't make it through the training program. When she asked why, he said, "Because you're black, you're female and you're a cop. I don't like blacks or females and the district you're working in, the people don't like cops." Another field-training officer told her he was only riding with her because he was being forced to. She was not to drive or speak to him. For three weeks she sat in the squad car and read a book.

Today, it's not very likely that those same blatant statements would be made to my friends or myself. Instead, they are made in the hallways or locker rooms or in more subtle tones and forms of behavior. You can't change attitudes through rules and regulations. Prejudicial feelings run deep and can only change through a slowly evolving process of education and generational levels. Young officers are more accepting of women and minorities because they grew up with them and do not view them as differently as the veteran officers.

At least as an officer I had one thing in common with my fellow officers, we all hated the "administration"—all of those supervisors who make our life hell and have forgotten everything they ever learned about police work. And then I became one of "them." Fortunately, because police officers are in state civil service, there are specific safeguards to eliminate discrimination. Promotions are based on standard written tests and then the successful completion of an assessment center test by independent observers. When I made sergeant, the real test of my staying power began.

The day an officer puts stripes on his or her uniform is the day he or she enters a world known as "kiss-ass." Suddenly, as if by decree, every subordinate becomes friendly and accommodating. Confronted by this sudden camaraderie on the one hand, there was still isolation on the other. My fellow sergeants could make decisions, impose disciplinary action and still be accepted. Whenever I did the same, I would be held accountable to a different standard and would have to justify my every move to my superiors. Speaking in staff meetings has always been forbidden. Either my supervisor would tell me not to say anything, or I would be sarcastically chastised by my peers. I soon learned never to do or say anything to embarrass the lieutenant.

It took me two tries to make lieutenant. There were supposedly two budgeted positions for lieutenant open. The first time I took the test, I missed second place by seven-tenths of a point. The second time, I placed first on the promotional list and left my closest competitor 100 points behind. (Oh how sweet the taste of revenge.) On the first test, I was left hanging on the list even though it was known that two lieutenants would be retiring within the year. On the second promotional list, they promoted the last guy hanging on the list even though there was no budgeted position and no one was known to be leaving. They literally "created" a new position miraculously on the day the promotional list was to expire. Something just doesn't seem fair about all of that. Unfortunately, my options have never changed. If I wanted to continue my career in policing, my most viable option was to overlook the discrimination and try to make a difference by example rather than by accusation—which would only isolate me further.

As a lieutenant, my peers support me on specific issues in the privacy of our offices behind closed doors, but won't support me in open staff meetings. In fact, one lieutenant in particular has said on several occasions, "I will never admit this to anyone else, but you are right."

As I have commanded new shifts, I openly share my philosophy about management. I am an advocate of participative management. The first goal of those in a leadership position should be to assess employees' needs. If employees are happy and feel appreciated in a comfortable working environment, they will like their jobs, come to work with enthusiasm, and serve the community better. Perhaps this philosophy originated because I am a woman. Unquestionably, it has become more firmly ingrained because my own experience (as you can infer from this article) has generally not been under such conditions. I have had young and veteran officers, male and female, tell me privately how much they appreciate my sincerity and efforts to make a difference. Not once have they openly acknowledged those same comments publicly before their peers or my supervisors. The higher a person rises in a police organization, the less recognition he or she receives for doing a good job. Supervisors tend to be called on the carpet more often than lower level officers. Because of my position in the organization, I see and hear more back stabbing among my peers—probably in an effort not to be left shouldering the blame. It seems the command rank officers bitch more about the "administration," even though we are one and the same, than the officers on the street. But, they don't have the fortitude to support and institute positive change to make a difference. If they would support participative management and work toward fostering an environment conducive to cooperation rather than assuming that rank is the most desirable structure, law enforcement would improve—both for professionals and for the people they serve.

Today, I am the only female supervisor and the highest ranking female staff member ever in a 130 commissioned member police department. I find that not much has really changed over the years. Having become more involved with the world outside of police work, I find that things for women are just about the same everywhere. I do have hope. There are a lot of talented and very bright women rising above the proverbial "Glass Ceiling" in nontraditional jobs. There is a new book out called *Megatrends for Women* that forecasts that the sheer magnitude in numbers of women coming into the workforce will in and of itself demand change.

Making positive change in law enforcement is a very slow and painful process. There is the ingrained tradition of law enforcement which is predominantly male-oriented. The military structure makes managerial and organizational change very complex and difficult at best. It is almost impossible to enact participative management with a ranked chain of command. The mere intimidation factor chokes true creativity in problem solving. Most police agencies I have seen have great intentions but lack a strong focus of their mission. Many efforts are being made to overcome these obstacles. However, it will take years of evolution to see any true improvement. The community will force police agencies to be more responsive. The large influx of women and minorities will give way to the implementation and evaluation of creative ideas in policing. We are already seeing the movement to community responsiveness with various forms of community-oriented policing. The old ways will no longer be the best ways. Many managers will have to conform or get out of the way.

What this means for women is more opportunities in law enforcement and less resistance to them being members of the career field. As with most other jobs, I catch more flack from the old guys than the younger guys. I have veteran officers tell me outright that women "got no place in police work." What's funny is that women tend to produce more, have fewer physical confrontations and fewer citizen complaints. We are better able to provide community service because of our nature to be more compassionate and understanding. The younger guys in police work have grown up, so to speak, with women working beside them, so it is only natural and easier for them to accept women in the job. With that fact alone, acceptance of women will continue to improve.

As for the kidnapping—yes, it dramatically changed the course of my life, and still subtly influences it. My time in police work has been very beneficial. I have grown up; I am now more confident. Knowing that "I can" is not an inspiration for me but a way of life. I survived the kidnapping without a physical scrape. I have lived, though, with the emotional scars that may have made me a better cop because I have been there and related to other victims.

# Section VI

## Community-Based Policing

The role of the community in the organization, maintenance and control of law enforcement has come full-circle since the police were first created as "organized watchers." In those early days of the police, it was the community or neighborhood which was the important focus of policing. Over the years, with the invention of two-way radios, automobiles, and computers, police work became impersonal and removed from the community level. However, in the 1990s, there has been an emphasis on reintegrating policing with the community and the neighborhood. In this section, we have included five articles that reflect the significance of community-based or community-oriented policing.

Professors Jack Greene and William Pelfrey have prepared an overview and history of police-community relations. In this selection, they use organizational theory to explain the relationship between police and the community. They note that it is essential that citizens become involved in assisting the police and that this assistance can take many forms. As crime is a by-product of many social, economic and political issues, its reduction requires a cooperative effort of formal and informal social control. That is, politicians, police and the public must cooperate to produce justice. Community policing means different things to different people. It is the methods by which these entities cooperate and the strategies utilized by the police that form what is known as community policing.

Article twenty-four, entitled "Broken Windows," by James Q. Wilson and George L. Kelling, is a classic article reviewing the impact of re-instituting foot patrols in Newark, New Jersey. It was concluded that re-instituting foot patrols had not reduced crime rates but that residents in foot patrolled neighborhoods felt more secure than residents of other neighborhoods. Drawing upon an historical analysis, Wilson and Kelling suggest a return to a focus on order-maintenance policing as opposed to the current preoccupation with crime control. However, these authors have been criticized for what Samuel Walker calls the misuse of history in recent police patrol analysis. Walker's criticisms are outlined in the next article, "Broken Windows and Fractured History: The Use and Misuse of History in Recent Police Patrol Analysis." Walker argues that Wilson and Kelling's policy proposals may be worth pursuing, but that they are grounded in a romanticized version of the history of policing and therefore need to be more fully developed.

**391**

In the next selection, "Community Policing," Gary Cordner discusses the four dimensions of community policing: tactical, philosophical, strategic and organizational. He notes that all the research on this topic focuses on the tactical dimension. Cordner suggests that since the evaluations thus far have been positive, research should now focus on the three other elements of community policing.

Article twenty-seven, "Underwriting the Risky Investment in Community Policing," discusses the commitment that society has made to community policing. David Kennedy and Mark Moore point out how hard community policing is to evaluate when it is more of a concept than a definitive strategy.

In the selection on problem-oriented policing, John Eck and William Spelman introduce another model of policing strategy which represents a significant evolutionary step in helping the police work smarter, not harder. Problem-oriented policing focuses on analyzing groups of incidents and deriving solutions that draw upon a wide variety of public and private resources.

# Shifting the Balance of Power Between Police and Community
## Responsibility for Crime Control

*Jack R. Greene*
*William V. Pelfrey, Jr.*

> Police work in the future is going to depend more upon public cooperation
> than it does at present. More and more of social life takes place in special-
> ist organizations or in groups of limited membership. Less and less can be
> controlled by a routine patrolman . . . . the police cannot regard public
> relations as something separate from the way they do their everyday work.
> (Banton, 1964: 261, 264)

These observations were made over 30 years ago by a British sociol-
ogist, Michael Banton, studying the police in Britain and the United States.
Among the chief concerns raised at that time was the insularity of the
police from the community and the growing tensions in police and community relations.

Many years have passed since Banton recorded his observations, yet
these issues remain today. The relationship between the police and those
policed has been a primary point of contention in American law enforcement and in many American communities. The precepts of democratic
governance require that the police be accountable to the body politic. How
that accountability is to be established, monitored, and evaluated, and by
whom, are issues which remain largely unresolved, and being unresolved
these issues contribute to increased tensions in police and community
relations.

The police as a social institution have become increasingly autonomous and politically independent over the years. Wrested from the "politics" of an earlier time (Walker, 1977), modern-day police departments
share the progressive ideology emphasizing political neutrality and administrative efficiency. Taking the "politics from policing" calls attention to the
partisan role the police have had in the past and the reforms of the police
that have occurred since the early 1900s.

Prepared especially for *Critcial Issues in Policing*, 3/E by Jack R. Greene and
William V. Pelfrey, Jr.

The new autonomy of the American police (Mastrofski, n.d.) has also produced potential negative effects. Among them is the further distancing of the citizens from public agency decisions. Are the police a "public institution" responsible for maintaining democratic values, or have they become a rigid bureaucracy, shielding themselves from public scrutiny and participation in policy making? What are the relationships between the police and the public; have they affected the formal organization of law enforcement or the way in which police behave in the community?

These questions and others like them arise consistently when we consider the role of the police in a democratic society and programs to improve police and community relations have been on the social agenda for many years. A resurgence of interest in police and community relations has most recently been associated with the trend towards the use of foot patrol and the stressing of a philosophy of community-oriented policing in many large, urban police departments. Do these programs overcome past problems, is the institution of policing changed by these efforts, or has policing itself resisted such changes?

## Police and Community Relations: What Level of Citizen Involvement?

Police and community relations (PCR) have been the subject of more than fifty years of law enforcement and civic effort presumably aimed at bringing the police and community into greater interaction and harmony. During this time, police-community relations have evolved from rather narrow and one-sided communication efforts, where the police talked to the community but rarely listened, to sophisticated programs which emphasize a strident citizen role in crime prevention and self protection. Frequently, police and community interaction programs have been couched in terms of police and community "co-production" of crime control and public safety services (Skolnick and Bayley, 1986).

Consistently, these programs have emphasized the consensual nature of citizen-government relations; the collaborative role of citizens and the police in crime prevention, social control and order maintenance; as well as the respective responsibilities of each (police and community). Further, police storefront offices have opened in many urban cities and the ability of the police to "reach out and touch" the community has generally been greatly enhanced in recent years. These programs, coupled with a return to foot patrol in many cities, have resulted in the belief among some that the fundamental strategy of the police is changing (Kelling and Moore, 1988). That strategy emphasizes "community" as the central attachment for the American police.

Despite such changes in programs, however, it remains unclear as to whether two-way interaction and communication between the police and the community have actually improved, or whether some of this "community-oriented effort" actually seeks to placate some of the most vocal citizens, while deflecting community concerns for greater police accountability. Are such "new" police and community partnerships substantive, or are they really designed to help further mystify the police role in democratic society (Manning, 1977; Klockars, 1988)?

Do the police seek out council from the community on matters affecting community safety, or do they simply "tell" the community how such problems are going to be addressed, albeit in a more politically sensitive way? What level of involvement will the police actually permit the community to have in policy making? If the community is to be a coproducer of crime control in neighborhoods, will that same community have co-equal status in the policy board room of the police? Are citizens provided the opportunity to initiate programs? Is this equality in initiative a myth, or is there a substantive role for the community in crime prevention? And, what level of involvement in organizational decisions do police officers themselves exercise? Are police officers also invited to the policy making to assist in setting the agenda for neighborhood safety? These questions draw our attention to the organizational obstacles confronting many police and community relations programs, including current efforts subsumed under the rubric of community or problem-oriented policing.

The ebb and flow of PCR programs has changed over the years. Prior to the mid-1960s these programs emphasized increased communication and a more open dialogue between the police and community residents. Many were directed at the issue of race relations. The urban turmoil of the 1960s resulted in the development of many action-oriented programs that emphasized some form of community participation, often through team policing strategies. Throughout the 1970s PCR changed direction, stressing community crime prevention rather than police and community relations. Programs aimed at reducing the opportunity to commit crime flourished. In the 1980s community crime prevention gave way to a raft of programs aimed at improving community social cohesion, many of which fell under the rubric of "community policing." In the 1990s PCR is said to have shifted the balance of power between the police and the community. Under this line of reasoning, the community is no longer expected to be passive in its relationship with the police or in its pursuit of neighborhood safety. Rather, problem-solving requires that the police and the community work together in identifying neighborhood problems, and that the community assume greater "guardianship" of the neighborhood. This shift in relationship between the police and the public is also suggested as part of a larger political and economic shift toward "community-centered" government.

The success or failure of community relations programs has been evaluated from many perspectives. The outcomes sought for community relations programs such as reduced crime and tension between the police and the public have not materialized in any direct sense (Radelet, 1986; 455–75). Evaluations of community crime prevention programs suggest that while we know more about crime prevention, "we may still not be able to do much about it" (Yin, 1986; 295). Reviews of community policing programs show mixed results (Greene and Taylor, 1988), attesting to problems in implementing and sustaining community-police coproduction of crime prevention services.

One of the natural outcomes of increasing community involvement in policing is the expectation by police departments that the community would take on more responsibility as their levels of independence, unity and investment rose following the programs initiated by the police. Thus one may have expected the balance of power between the police and the community to have shifted towards the community.

From the perspective of community involvement in police policy making, most PCR programs have failed. Citizens are no more a part of the police management and decision-making system today than they were in the past. Buerger (1994) suggests community and police partnerships are generally failures. Not only does the community get neglected in policy-making decisions, they are frequently misguided in the definition of "successful" programs. Rather than view significant crime reduction as the end, small successes become transposed as the perceived ends, ignoring larger scale problems such as the deterioration of the community infrastructure. Thus the police may in fact be attempting to solve only *their* problem (high crime rates) rather than the larger community problems. What accounts for these failures?

In explaining the development and direction of police and community relations programs, and the pitfalls that have beset these police innovations, we can turn our attention to the organization of policing. It is argued here that both the formal and social organization of policing has rendered many of these efforts ineffective. Ultimately we must also address the issue of the extent to which citizen involvement in the affairs of the police is really sought, and whether the balance of power concerning the initiation of police-community collaborations has shifted from the police towards the public as suggested by the rhetoric of community and problem-oriented policing.

Police and community relations can be viewed from an organizational perspective, wherein the objectives of police agencies themselves have dominated both the forum for police and community interactions as well as the programs that have evolved over the years. Greater participation of community residents, an avowed goal of most PCR programs, has been elusive, primarily because of the police organizational interests that have been imbedded in these programs. Similarly, participation of police officers themselves have been precluded by formal and social organizational issues. This chapter examines the organizational dynamics associated with the police and community relations movement and considers recent attempts to reorganize and redeploy police forces with greater community sensitivity.

# Organizational Theory and Police and Community Relations

In the logic of organizational analysis, all organizations seek to minimize the influence of the external environment on the internal operations of the focal organization (Thompson, 1967). The environment poses uncertainty for the organization and restricts the independent actions of managers (Dill, 1958). Changes in the environment of policing include shifting legal philosophies; gains and losses in municipal finance; as well as swings in public ideology toward law violation and lawbreakers. These changes can affect police agencies rather dramatically and directly (Greene, 1981a).

Changes in the law can force police agencies to change operational practices. This was the case in historic Supreme Court decisions regarding the right to counsel (*Miranda v. Arizona*), custody interrogations (*Escobedo v. Illinois*), search and seizure (*Mapp v. Ohio*), as well as court decisions surrounding the use of lethal force (*Garner v. Tennessee*). Changes in municipal finance have directly affected police forces, although they are generally in a better position politically to resist massive cutbacks (Greene, 1981a; Greene, Bynum and Cordner, 1986) in comparison to other municipal agencies.

Changes in public ideology also have great potential for affecting the management and operation of police agencies, such as when reform ideologies sweep new police chiefs into office; the public demands a "crackdown" on certain crimes; or public concern with police tactics becomes vocal. Each of these potential changes threatens the status quo within the organization, making organizational planning and goal development problematic.

Organizations, including police agencies, therefore seek to monitor the environment by identifying constraints, or fixed factors in the environment that affect organizational life, while attempting to predict contingencies, or the random fluctuations in the environment that may pose problems for the pursuit organizational goals (Thompson, 1967). Such a process helps to assure that the organization is in control of its resources and destiny.

Once organizational constraints and contingencies have been identified, the organization may attempt to counter these forces that pose uncertainty. Organizational resistance to environmental influence is accomplished through a variety of methods. Organizations in their transactions with the environment can buffer and level input transactions, thereby channeling and controlling demand for organizational services and client access. They can stockpile supplies and material to ward off dependence on the environment, or other specific agencies within the environment. Finally, they can control output transactions through distribution systems favorable to the host organization. Each of these activities seeks to minimize external influence on the policy making and internal rationalization of the organization.

The processes described above can be readily seen in business and economic organizations. Large-scale manufacturing organizations may actually buy or heavily invest in supplying firms to avoid external dependence. These economically motivated organizations have also affected client demand through advertising campaigns, planned obsolescence, and periodic model changes. Each of these activities more-or-less assures constant client demand for goods and services, thereby smoothing out economic uncertainty for these organizations. Finally, elaborate distribution systems have been developed wherein automotive manufacturing firms, for example, assure a marketplace for their products once produced.

Service organizations such as the police are also concerned with managing the environment. As rather closed and inwardly focused organizations, police agencies have historically been concerned with internal control and the projection of a professional public image. Police organizations present themselves symbolically to the public by emphasizing professionalism, bureaucratic control, crime effectiveness through the Uniform Crime Reports, technological innovation, and by invoking secrecy when necessary (Manning, 1977). These strategies influence public perceptions of the agency. In fact, current efforts at designing community-oriented policing programs have been criticized as yet another circumlocution of public law enforcement (see, Klockars, 1988).

Police and community relations programs have often been employed as an environmental management process, seeking to promote the organizational interests of the police. Police public relations programs, for example, have curried a favorable public image through a variety of police sponsored activities, including school programs, such as "Officer Friendly." These image enhancement programs, and slogans, such as "To Serve and Protect," all seek in part to control input—public support for the police. Other police and community relations programs such as Blockwatch and other forms of crime prevention may actually be more symbolic than substantive. Since little empirical evidence exists that such efforts have had a demonstrative effect on crime, the emotional attachments of these programs may loom more important for a police agency seeking to "manage" its environment. Similarly, storefront offices and the extended use of foot patrol may also be viewed in the context of image and environmental management as well.

Just as economic organizations seek to minimize environmental control, police agencies as public service organizations have also successfully engaged in leveling, buffering, stockpiling, and managing output transactions. Such efforts account for the fact that the police, as a public institution, are more able to ward off significant economic cuts and garner greater public support for resource expenditure, as compared to other public institutions (Greene, Bynum and Cordner, 1987).

Many of these behaviors can be understood in terms of the organizational imperative that has dominated much of law enforcement in this century. Such an analysis of the police organizational imperative sheds light on the reluctance of the police to engage in meaningful partnerships with the citizens they police.

## The Organizational Imperative

The role of the police in a democratic society has been the subject of general discourse and intellectual debate. Central to our system of government is the need for agencies of the law to operate within the limits of the law. The "means and ends" of law enforcement require that the police conform to the rule of law in the performance of their duties. The police as the most visible arm of the state have constantly been challenged as to the legality and con-stitutionality of their actions. For the police, then, the means and ends of law enforcement are of critical importance (Skolnick, 1966; Bittner, 1971; Goldstein, 1977; Greene, 1981b; Klockars, 1986).

The often "impossible mandate" of the police (Bittner, 1971; Man-ning, 1977) has arguably shifted the police organization to the posture of demonstrating the image of internal control, police professionalism, and an institutional commitment to community relations. Such a posture is also consistent with the practical need for the police organization to develop a positive external image while at the same time minimizing com-munity influence in police operations. Police and community relations pro-grams have provided the mechanism for mediating between the organizational control interests of the police agency and community con-trol issues imbedded in democratic theory.

Participation in police policy making has been successfully resisted in virtually all PCR programs; power sharing is not a central feature of PCR or other police agency programming (Brown, 1986). The "velvet glove" of police-community relations programs has at once provided a way for the police to gain broad public support, while at the same time masking the autonomy of action and decision making they exercise (Institute for the Study of Labor and Economic Crisis, 1982).

Citizen oversight of the police through such practices as civilian review boards or the political decentralization of police services has been successfully resisted in virtually every major American city (Caiden, 1977). Such successful resistance attests to the political autonomy of the police. As Walker (1977:170) has indicated:

In the 1960s, for example, the police attacked many police-community relations proposals advanced by blacks (or their white liberal supporters) on the grounds of political pressure. Opposition to both civilian review boards and court decisions were infringements on their professional autonomy. . . . In this and many other areas, black activists found that the rhetoric and techniques of professionalism, expertise and nonpartisanship [on behalf of the police] were used to frustrate their legitimate claims.

The police control-centered organizational model that historically and currently dominates much of police management also excludes the police themselves from the policy-making process. The downward flowing authority system and fragmented specialization that has occurred in polic-ing has contributed to minimizing the effect of police officers on the police organization. In virtually every proposal to move the police toward a com-munity or problem-focused mode of operation, there has been a corre-sponding claim to decentralize authority and de-specialize the police (Skolnick and Bayley, 1986; Alpert and Dunham, 1988; Goldstein, 1990; Trojanowicz and Bucqueroux, 1990; Sparrow, et al., 1990), so as to break the grip that the traditional control-centered police bureaucracy is pre-sumed to have on policing. The conflict that such a control emphasis has on policing is made manifest in many ways. Functionally, many police agencies have become "islands unto themselves," suboptimized through specialization. Another way is through competing ideologies within the institution of policing itself. Here the conflict stems from two ideologies of policing that are said to exist: one emphasizing the police street-level deci-sion making, the other management (Reuss-Ianni and Ianni, 1983).

Ideologically and functionally, then, the police have been able to resist the community participation goals of police and community relations pro-grams. Peripheral involvement by the community in police policy and deci-sion making has been maintained. Ideologically, too, the police have resisted the community. The two worlds of policing have also included "them" and "us."

## The Social Organization of Policing

In addition to the organization constraints placed on police and community relations programs, the social organization of policing also affects PCR issues. Policing has been called a "tainted occupation" (Bittner, 1971). That is, the very nature of public contacts that the police have with certain seg-ments of society are seen by many citizens as "dirty work."

Police work is also perceived by the police to be dangerous. The potential for danger, being what it is in law enforcement, often leads police officers to be suspicious and rather distrustful of people. Making the right decisions about who is dangerous and who is not has often led the police to err in favor of the conservative decision—that is, most contacts pose danger (Muir, 1977).

The environment of law enforcement contributes to the social isola-tion of police (Skolnick, 1966) and their use of violence to maintain respect for the law and individual officer authority (Westley, 1970; Stark, 1972). Such conditions hardly foster a close working relationship between the police and the public.

Moreover, while it is true that the "job satisfaction" of many officers who participate in some form of positive community interaction increases (Greene, 1989), it is not at all clear that this would be the case for all offic-ers so participating. That is, personality differences among officers, and the self-selection which often results in who eventually ends up in commu-nity relations-type police activities, may account more for these findings than do the interactions themselves. More importantly, community relations and/or community policing, for that matter, has often been relegated to the stature of but yet another organizational specialization, rarely touching the core elements of the police agency. The "grin and wave" squads, as they are called in many urban cities—referring to foot patrol and community policing—remain unattached to "real" police work in the minds of many police officials and police administrations. Such police cultural resistance to community contact efforts attests to the strong grip that the social organization of the police has on acceptable definitions of police and community relations. While many police appreciate the role the community can play in law enforcement, disparate officer views suggest these efforts are a waste of time (Carter, 1992).

While the environmental barriers to police and citizen interaction have been less visible in recent years, it is not at all clear that the police desire more contact with the public, or that the public desires more contact with the police (Manning, 1984). By minimizing contact with the citizenry, police officers reduce their exposure to physical danger and/or public criticism or complaint. While it is clear that police organizations may seek to influence the community response behavior of the police officer, Brown (1981:246) has suggested that police decisions to act are influenced by the police style found in the community and the officer's assessment of the risks and opportunities presented by such interactions.

The social organization of policing, then, may also resist the increased interactions thought necessary for effective police and community relations. Such a chilling effect poses serious problems for fostering the belief among the police and citizens that "the police are the public and the public the police."

## Police and Community Relations 1940–1996

The history of police and community relations begins, perhaps, in the 1940s with training developed by Joseph D. Lohman, emphasizing community dynamics and change, and by Gordon Allport, stressing intergroup relations. Lohman, a sociology lecturer at the University of Chicago, began in the early 1940s to teach courses in police-minority group relations to park police officers in Chicago. These courses applied the concepts developed in ecological sociology to police understanding of community dynamics, the migration patterns of rural blacks to the urban north, and the human relations aspects of the police officer's role (Lohman, 1947).

Allport, a professor at Harvard University, was training the Boston police in similar matters. Allport's courses included concern with crime causation and social disorder, as well as racial, religious and ethnic conflict between the police and the community (Radelet, 1986: 13–16).

While many of these early programs explored the dimensions of community life that affected police and public contact, they were also almost entirely police focused. That is, these programs rarely involved the citizens with whom the police were to interact. Information about community life and sentiment was, therefore, rather unidirectional—from the professor to the police. Despite the general non-involvement of minority communities in these programs about 30 police agencies in large cities employed such programming in 1952 (Senn, 1952).

These programs rarely affected the formal or social organization of law enforcement. Police departments throughout the United States specialized and compartmentalized police operations through the 1940–50 era (Fogelson, 1977). The "administrative era" in American policing rarely included the clients of policing (the citizens) in the policy and decision-making process. Police line officers were similarly excluded. Police and community relations were often relegated to an organizational specialty rather than being diffused throughout the police organization. With such specialization in PCR, line officers who worked the street often viewed community relations as someone else's job. Consequently, the early PCR effort was not effective in opening police agencies to community and police officer input.

Despite the emphasis of the social organization of policing at these times, it is not clear that such programs had a demonstrative effect. The post-World War II race riots of the late 1940s and early 1950s do not suggest that such effects were present.

During the 1940s and early 1950s human relations training for the police continued, but it was not until the mid-1950s that the form and focus of these programs changed. The National Institute on Police and Community Relations, a program of workshop training in human relations and community dynamics for police administrators and community leaders, began an era of more direct contact between the community and the police.

These programs provided the basis for police and community interaction on a wide array of topics. As Radelet (1986: 17) reports, the goals and objectives of these Police and Community Relations Institutes were:

1. To encourage police-citizen partnership in the causes of crime prevention.
2. To foster and improve communication and mutual understanding between the police and the total community.
3. To promote interprofessional approaches to the solution of community problems and to stress the principle that the administration of justice is a total community responsibility.
4. To enhance cooperation among the police, prosecution, the courts, and corrections.
5. To assist police and other community leaders to achieve an understanding of the nature and causes of complex problems in people-to-people relations and especially to improve police-minority group relations.
6. To strengthen implementation of equal protection under the law for all persons.

The National Institute on Police and Community Relations was conducted each year from 1955 to 1969, as a combined effort of Michigan State University and the National Conference on Christians and Jews. By the late 1960s, however, urban America was in turmoil. As Walker (1977: 171) indicates, "the initial police-community relations efforts of the 1940s were an impressive first stem but were woefully limited. The movement soon lost its initial momentum and the police-community relations problem reappeared with a vengeance in the mid-1960s."

In a study of police and community relations conducted by the International Association of Chiefs of Police and the U.S. Conference of Mayors in 1964, the strength of the community relations movement was assessed. The report, which surveyed cities with a population of 30,000 or more residents, determined that less than one-third had formalized police and community relations programs; two-thirds of the departments tried to cope with social unrest; cities with minority populations were not successful in recruiting nonwhite officers; the variety of programming was widely varied; and more than half of the police agencies responding were the object of complaints of police brutality and the unfair treatment of minority group members (International Association of Chiefs of Police and U.S. Conference of Mayors, 1964).

These findings suggest that despite the efforts by the National Institutes to focus police and community relations issues, minority group members felt as disenfranchised from the government as they had in the past, and police were seen as a brutalizing force. Clearly, participation in the policy-making process was not central to these times, and the quality of police-community relationships deteriorated rapidly in the late 1960s and early 1970s in most urban cities.

As the National Advisory Commission on Civil Disorders (1968: 157) reported:

> We have cited deep hostility between police and ghetto communities as a primary cause of the disorders surveyed by the Commission. In Newark, Detroit, Watts and Harlem, in practically every city that has experienced racial disruption since the summer of 1964, abrasive relationships between police and Negroes and other minority groups have been a major source of grievance, tension and ultimately disorder.

While the Commission went on to say that it was wrong to define the urban riots solely as a police-community relations problem, in 40 percent of the riots studied, police actions triggered the riot. Also, minority residents overwhelmingly believed police brutality and harassment were commonplace in minority communities; patrol practices, particularly "aggressive patrol styles," were more often found in minority communities; grievance systems against the police were ineffective; and communications between the police and the ghetto community were extremely poor.

Cumulatively, the urban riots of the 1960s and 1970s left much to be desired of police and community relations. As Radelet (1986: 20) suggests:

The assumptions of goodwill and commitment that had more or less motivated programs in police and community relations during the 1955–1967
period were abruptly called into question. The possibilities of developing
dialogue to build communications bridges across the chasms of intergroup
differences were brought into instant doubt. Traditional patterns of community organization (block committees, precinct councils, and so on) were
evidently not doing their job; many police officers and others began to ask
whether it was "worth the effort" and to ask, "What have we done wrong?"
There was widespread bewilderment. Some simply withdrew from further
efforts; many adopted a "get tough" philosophy.

Police and community programs of the late 1960s and early 1970s
took a different form. Due in part to the turbulence of the 1960s these programs focused more on the quality and quantity of police and citizen interactions in matters of crime prevention and control. The police were to be
more crime effective, while maintaining sensitivity to the community—a
criticism of the previous ten years.

Furthermore, these programs began to consider the police officer's
role in policy making. The police themselves felt disenfranchised from the
very organizations that employed them. Alienation and cynicism were rampant in many urban police departments (Niederhoffer, 1967), and the
quality of police organizational life had deteriorated considerably during
the riot years. Police officers were frustrated by what appeared to be complex, impersonal, and degrading organizational policies and practices.
These frustrations were evident in police treatment of citizens further contributing to the rapid decline in police and community tolerance.

Team policing was hailed as an alternative to the classic bureaucratic
arrangements that had so dominated police management practices (Angell,
1971). Team policing programs had tactical, community relations and
police officer job satisfaction components, making them complicated
indeed. Many programs were initiated in the late 1960s. Programs in Dayton; Detroit; New York City; Syracuse; Holyoke, Massachusetts; Los Angeles; and Richmond, California provided the basis for the first systematic
evaluation of the team concept (Sherman et al., 1973).

To overcome community complaints of police insensitivity, team
policing programs were designed for geographic stability in the provision
of police services, and greater interaction and communication between the
police and community residents. Here, the central theme was to emphasize
police officer familiarity with community circumstances and residents and
to create a sense of attachment to the community through constant assignment to the same geographic area (Sherman et al., 1973).

Patrol practices of the police had been the object of much community
complaint. Motorized patrol had taken the police from their community
context, and shift and staffing patterns rotated police officers through many
communities, thereby reducing any chance that officers could understand
the crime problems and resident needs in any particular neighborhood.
Geographic stability and increased community-police communications

were thought to greatly improve police and community relations as well as crime control efforts.

Team policing programs were also focused inwardly on the police organization. These programs were expected to reduce fragmented police service created by over-specialization, and to decentralize decision making by unifying police services, thus reducing the distinctions between police officers and investigators, and increasing police officer input into decision making. Each of these ideas required rather significant changes of the police organization, which had spent years increasing specialization; making sharp distinctions between patrol and investigative functions; and maintaining the power and authority of ranked (sergeants, lieutenants) versus nonranked (generally patrol) officers.

It was presumed that by blurring the lines of function between patrol and investigations, and between operations and supervision, the alienated police worker could be rejuvenated. Job enlargement, the process of giving police officers more breadth in their responsibilities, and job enrichment, the process of expanding decision making, were also imbedded concepts in team policing efforts.

In the end, team policing died at the hands of middle managers, police sergeants and lieutenants who resisted the loss of organizational power implied by such programs. In addition, since many team-oriented programs were demonstration projects, they were resisted by rank-and-file police officers as well. This resistance often stemmed from the additional organization prestige that was accorded team members over and above that accorded traditional patrol officers. The "elite" status of these team officers was not tolerated by others in the police organization, all of whom were struggling for status and recognition (Sherman et al., 1973: 93–94).

On the street team policing also encountered many obstacles. Many team officers received little training as to their new role assignment. Old police tactical practices were most used in the absence of new understandings. As Sherman, Milton and Kelly (1973: 73) noted:

> It was not long, however, before the team members noticed that their team policing hardly differed from the "policing" they had done before. In most cases, the style of police work changed very little under team policing. But it is impossible to say whether the organizational style of team policing failed to produce a new patrol style, or whether the organizational style of team policing was not, in those cases, created at all.

The legacy of team policing was not lost in the failure of early programs. Indeed, this model of police organization was to influence more recent efforts in the implementation of foot patrol and community policing.

Throughout the 1970s police agencies experimented with variations in the team approach. Cincinnati created the COMSEC program—Community Sector Team Policing (Schwartz and Clarren, 1977), which was a decentralized program conducted in one police district from 1973 to 1975. This program, based on the assumptions of increasing community interaction and organizational change outlined above, had much the same experience as earlier programs. The evaluators suggested:

> On the whole, over the 30-month experiment, police-community relations, already quite positive, changed only a little; burglary was reduced, and COMSEC dealt as well with other categories of Part 1 crimes as the centralized style of policing previously the norm in Cincinnati. The patrol officers involved were enthusiastic about team policing as an idea and as a practice, but they grew disenchanted as a result of what many officers perceived as undercutting of the program by headquarters. (Schwartz and Clarren, 1977: 5)

Concurrent with the drive to improve police reaction to crime through team policing, the 1970s also witnessed the expansion of crime prevention activities. These programs, while focused on preventing crime, particularly property crime, were also designed for greater citizen involvement.

Throughout the country "Operation Identification," a program to mark personal property; "Neighborhood Watch," a program to mobilize community residents to watch out for one another; and the use of home security surveys received greater police and community attention. In 1977 the federal government's Community Anti-Crime Program authorized $30 million for programs that encouraged "neighborhood groups to become actively involved in activities designed to prevent crime, reduce fear of crime, and contribute to neighborhood revitalization" (U.S. Department of Justice, 1978: 1).

Community crime prevention became a rallying point in many American police departments. Police organized community groups as Blockwatchers and Town Watch programs; promoted various identification programs from etching social security numbers on personal property to placing decals on automobiles; ran Police Explorer programs as adjuncts to the Boy Scout movement; organized community patrols; and increased communications linkages between the police and citizens through citizen crime reporting projects all under the rubric of community crime prevention. Communities also increased street lighting and altered environmental design in an effort to reduce crime and increase citizen perceptions of safety.

The crime prevention efforts undertaken at this time were to have reduced crime and improved police and community relations. The crime reduction results of most program evaluations are mixed, although certain techniques do appear to improve community relations. Operation identification programs have been plagued with low citizen enrollment (Heller et al., 1975), while security surveys have been associated with reduced victimization and improved police and community relations (International Training, Research and Evaluation Council, 1977). Citizen patrols often enjoy citizen support, although sustaining citizen participation can be difficult (Yin et al., 1977), while the community relations effects of citizen reporting programs remains uncertain (Bickman et al., 1977). Street lighting projects have not demonstrated a crime effect, although citizens in affected areas are reported to be less fearful (Tien et al., 1979).

Collectively, the crime prevention movement has opened up the idea that citizens have a legitimate role in police matters. This role, however, has generally been restricted; policy and decision making with police agencies have rarely been influenced by such programs. Rather the citizens become the "eyes and ears" of the police agency; watching has replaced walling and wariness as the central role ascribed for citizens in the crime control process (Sherman, 1983).

In the late 1970s and early 1980s team policing and community crime prevention yielded to a new patrol strategy—foot patrol and community policing. While community crime prevention is still quite active nationally, foot patrol and community-oriented police strategies have currently captured the imagination of the local police and the public. Police departments throughout the country are putting the police officer "back on the beat" and designing programs that emphasize decoupling the patrol-car response system from the 911 emergency communications system, decentralizing police decision making and authority, and involving the community in the coproduction of crime prevention services (Skolnick and Bayley, 1986). Most prominent of these approaches in recent years has been foot patrol.

From 1978 to 1979 an "experiment" in foot patrol was conducted in Newark, New Jersey by the Police Foundation. The Newark program emphasized "upgrading and stabilizing neighborhoods" (Police Foundation, 1981: 3), primarily through the use of foot patrol officers.

The idea for using foot patrol as a police intervention has crime control and community relations implications similar to those in team policing. In their article "Broken Windows," Wilson and Kelling (1982: 31) suggest that crime and social disorder are "inextricably linked." The general thesis is that declining social relations within communities open them to criminal invasion. A strong policing program emphasizing order maintenance and community/police interaction can support neighborhood social relations, thereby providing some hedge against social decay and ultimately crime. In a very real sense, then, this theory of police and community crime prevention implies a strong community relations effort.

In addition, putting the police "back on the beat" is thought to give the officer a community context—an understanding of the people in the community. Such a context is presumed to reduce officer alienation from the community, in the long term improving police officer job satisfaction (Hayeslip and Cordner, 1987).

The Newark foot patrol program embraced the "broken windows" concept by placing foot patrol officers in patrol beats in eight neighborhoods. Foot patrol officers were found to be more noticeable to community residents, who perceived a decline in street level activity and in the severity of crime in those areas. While citizen perceptions of safety, disorder and police presence changed, actual crime reporting and victimization were unaffected during the experiment.

The initial "success" of the Newark program fueled interest in foot patrol in other cities. Programs emphasizing some form of foot patrol intervention were conducted in Flint, Michigan (Trojanowicz, 1983), and Oakland, California (Reiss, 1985); a second program in Newark (1985), Houston, Texas (1987), and Boston, Massachusetts (1986). The results of these programs follow a similar pattern to those identified with the first Newark foot patrol program. In general, public relations between the police and the community improved, while crime rates were not affected. Oakland and Flint did report some crime control effects of foot patrol. Given several methodological problems in these studies, however, the validity of such effects remains at issue (Greene and Taylor, 1988). A recent conclusion from an analysis of the second foot patrol and community policing program conducted in Newark tends to summarize the research in this area (Skogan and Pate, 1987: 19):

> The evaluation indicates that, where the program was solely in the hands of the police, the area did not seem cleaner, and the level of public drinking, street harassment, gang activity, open drug use, vandalism, and the like, does not appear to have declined. However, there is substantial evidence that the Community Policing version of the program may have had more positive consequences. . . . fewer of those who were interviewed in the Community Policing area rated social disorder or physical decay as "big problems," and they felt safer and less worried about personal and property victimization.

Most of these programs involved foot patrol, but as Goldstein (1986) has indicated, foot patrol is only one strategy of community policing. For example, programs conducted in Baltimore, Maryland (1985), and Newport News, Virginia (1986) emphasize the philosophy of community policing described above, although foot patrol was not a major part of either effort. Rather, closer community contact and an orientation toward solving community problems was dominant in these latter two programs.

Skolnick and Bayley (1986) assessed police innovation in six American police departments. In Santa Anna, California, Community-Oriented Policing (COP) has been built in large measure on greater civilianization within the police department; the mobilization of communities by organizing some 150–250 block captains in each of the four community areas dividing the city; the use of police substations within local communities; and the revitalization of the downtown area. In Detroit, intensive community mobilization through organizing neighborhoods in crime prevention has been emphasized as the central feature of community policing.

Houston, Texas grew rapidly during the oil-boom years of the mid-1970s. Workers poured into Houston so rapidly that neighborhoods sprang up overnight. Houston's police, in attempting to cope with rapid growth and citizen estrangement accompanying this growth, developed the DART concept—Directed Area Responsibility Team. "Essentially, DART is team policing based on decentralized management and emphasizing community involvement" (Skolnick and Bayley, 1986:93). In Denver variations in patrol have been used to spark innovation and change, while community cooperation is stressed in police interactions with citizens.

In Oakland and in Newark, foot patrol became the mainstay of police operations. Keeping the police and community in closer contact and with greater interaction has been stressed.

Since the mid-1980s, community and problem-oriented policing has received a heightened level of attention by police policy makers and academics alike. (For example, see: Skolnick and Bayley, 1986; Eck et al., 1987; Alpert and Dunham, 1988; Greene and Mastrofski, 1988; Trojanowicz and Bucqueroux, 1990; Sparrow et al., 1989; Goldstein, 1990; Friedman, 1994.) This body of work has generally attempted to accomplish three interrelated ends in respect to thrashing out the appropriate relations between the police and the public.

First, as an emerging "strategy" for twenty-first century law enforcement, research on community policing has sought to define and describe how this "new approach" to law enforcement and community relations is taking root in police agencies. Consequently, several case studies have emerged to help clarify community and problem-oriented policing, as it is being experienced by the police and by the community.

Second, as a yet-evolving police and community relations concept, several scholars and nationally visible police leaders have taken advocacy positions in support of community policing as a "reform" to the ills of "traditional" policing, while others have taken the position of cautioning against over-expectation. In either case (advocacy or caution), the rhetoric of community policing has increased at a pitched pace and at times has eclipsed the substantive debate as to how the police and the citizenry are to interact (see Manning, 1984).

Third, if community policing is not to be criticized as being "old wine in new bottles," it must be distinguishable from past police institutional paradigms. That is, efforts to both shape and evaluate community and problem-oriented policing have found it necessary to be aware of the need to understand community policing as something different, in kind and function, from past law enforcement institutional practices and arrangements. This has resulted in several approaches to explicate the theoretical and practical dimensions of this, the newest model of policing and, by implication, to explicate a new and more harmonious relationship between officers and private citizens.

Among its many definitions, community policing has been variously labeled as "foot patrol" (Trojanowicz, 1983, 1986), as a strategy to reduce the fear of crime (Wycoff et al., 1985, 1985a, 1985b; Cordner, 1986), as a crime prevention strategy (Kelling, 1987), as a method to improve police officer job satisfaction (Hayeslip and Cordner, 1987), as a problem-solving process (Cordner, 1985, Eck and Spelman, 1987; Goldstein, 1990), as a process for greater police and community consultation and sharing of information and values (Wetheritt, 1983; Manning, 1984; Alpert and Dunham, 1988), as a method for changing the organizational and service delivery structures of the police (Manning, 1984; Skolnick and Bayley, 1986; Alpert and Dunham, 1993; Goldstein, 1990), and as a "reform" movement (Bayley, 1988; Mastrofski, 1988). While there are oftentimes overlapping themes in the definitions of community or problem-oriented policing, the central tendency is to define community policing in terms of organizational strategy, internal police reform, and greater civic accountability.

Common elements of community policing programs include a redefinition of the police role; greater reciprocity in police and community relations; area decentralization of police services and command; and some form of civilianization (Skolnick and Bayley, 1986). Each of these changes is viewed as a necessary condition to realizing greater police accountability to the community.

Role redefinition seeks to remove the police from narrow and traditional definitions of policing as crime fighting, to broader role definitions which view the police as problem solvers and community advocates. Reciprocity in police and community relations seeks to redress past practices of police talking "to" and not "with" the communities they are expected to serve and to make the police more law-abiding (Mastrofski and Greene, 1993). Decentralization of service and command seeks to bring the service "close to the customer," so that citizens and line-level police officers can have input into defining the services to be produced and in evaluating the quality and effectiveness of the services delivered (Greene, 1989). Finally, civilianization refers to the process of employing greater numbers of non-police personnel to work within the police bureaucracy, in part, to increase cost efficiencies, and, in part, to infiltrate and weaken the "blue-thin line" mentality often separating the police from the community.

Community and problem-oriented policing programs have sprung up all over the United States. Built on early fear reduction programs conducted in Newark, New Jersey (Pate et al., 1985) and Houston, Texas (Pate et al., 1986), as well as foot patrol programs carried out in Flint, Michigan (Trojanowicz, 1986), Oakland, California (Reiss, 1985), New York City (Ward, 1985), and Boston, Massachusetts (Bowers and Hirsch, 1986), among others, the newest of the community and problem-oriented policing programs are particularly focused on changing the style of policing within any given city (see Alpert and Dunham, 1993), and reducing the call-for-service dependence of the police on the public (see Eck and Spelman, 1987; Goldstein, 1990).

Claims and counterclaims not withstanding, research has been inconclusive in determining the full impact of community policing on police organizations and on the relationships between the police and the public. However, many of the projects assessed report favorable results, although much of the research surrounding these interventions remains anecdotal or marred by the traditional measurement problems associated with law enforcement research.

The general findings of these various studies have suggested that the police have some effect on perceptions of crime, if not on crime itself. Fear of crime is apparently affected by greater public visibility of the police, and programs that bring the police into greater interaction with the citizenry typically produce assessments that fear of crime is reduced through these interactions.

Other projects have examined the capacity of the police, working with the community, to produce innovative solutions to rather persistent community problems. Work conducted in New York City (Ward, 1985; Farrell, 1988; Pate and Shtull, 1994), Houston, Texas (Wycoff, et. al., 1985a, 1985b), Madison, Wisconsin (see Goldstein, 1990), Baltimore, Maryland (Cordner, 1985), Newport News, Virginia (Eck and Spelman, 1987), Cleveland and Toledo, Ohio (Ohio Crime Prevention Association, 1995), Lincoln, Nebraska (Nebraska Commission on Law Enforcement, 1994), Canada (Leighton, 1994), South Africa (van Rooyen, 1994) and Britain (Bennett, 1994), has suggested that such "innovative solutions" can be produced when the police seek to address "problems" rather than simply continue to respond to calls for police service. That is, there is evidence to suggest that the police, institutionally and individually, must become proactive community problem solvers, thereby reducing the magnitude and impact of incipient community problems while at the same time improving community trust of the police. This notion is indicated by Goldstein (1990), who suggests the responsibility for organizing activity must lie with the police.

Recent work in Chicago provides rare quantitative data demonstrating the relationship between the police and the community (Chicago Community Policing Evaluation Consortium, 1996). The Chicago Alternative Policing Strategy (CAPS) included beat meetings, where the police invited citizens to meet, interact with and inform the officers assigned to each beat. Researchers found the beats with the highest turnouts tended to be those with the highest crime rates. Those who attended the beat meetings were surveyed to determine how they addressed problems in their community. Most respondents (80 percent) contacted the police, while many (60 percent) brought the issue to the beat meeting. Further, a substantial minority of citizens (6 percent) stated they initiated a program to cope with the problem. Thus the citizen response in Chicago is a cooperative one, but only among those residents who attended the beat meetings to begin with, and rarely includes citizen initiated efforts.

In a few of the projects where there is community-focused data, such as the one conducted in Miami (Alpert and Dunham, 1988, 1993), it is clear that police sensitivity to community norms and their lack of conversancy with community expectations are, at once, longstanding complaints in minority communities, and changing this posture becomes an occupational prerequisite if the police are to become truly "community-oriented." This stance is substantiated by Buerger (1994), who notes officer efforts to organize the community are most needed where they are the least trusted, therefore a cyclical problem develops, and police efforts are unsuccessful. These findings suggest that police and community relations remain problematic in urban areas and that substantial police role change will be necessary to improve these relations in the future.

## Citizen Initiated Efforts

To address the question of whether the balance of power has shifted toward community initiated programs, one must consider the programs themselves. Although the majority of reported police-community programs studied are police initiated (Rosenbaum and Lurigio, 1994), important efforts have been introduced by citizens. In Houston (Wycoff, 1985), a community task force encouraged by the police became responsible for several neighborhood programs aimed at crime prevention and neighborhood security. In northeast Philadelphia, several communities began to experience an upswing in racially inflammatory vandalism. The problem culminated in several interracial fights and conflicts. A group of citizens, primarily from local townwatch and blockwatch groups, organized to form an interracial task force. They patrol parks and schools where racially motivated vandalism had occurred, developed education and mediation programs, and designed activities for the ethnically diverse communities, providing the residents an opportunity to "meet and greet" each other on neutral territory (Greene and Pelfrey, forthcoming). The police participate as advisors and service providers, but the program is led, funded, operated, and created by, concerned citizen leaders.

Following an increase in drug dealing in a certain area of Chicago, community leaders united to form a block club designed to combat the proliferation of dealers, buyers, and accompanying criminal element (Friedman, 1994). The members of this block club went to other cities to develop a perspective of effective community policing strategies, invited the police department to join them, and proceeded to illicit involvement from neighboring block groups. The group pressured landlords to evict drug dealing residents, and develop screening procedures for new residents. They persuaded the phone company to remove phones (or design them to only serve outgoing calls) which drug dealers were using to receive calls. While the police department provided a liaison and arrest support for the group, the block club was citizen initiated and directed.

In Los Angeles, a group of residents, business owners and local government recognized the rapidly deteriorating community infrastructure and sought to stabilize the community by involving a variety of city agencies (Margolis, 1994). By incorporating social services, the LAPD, and community activists, the team successfully provided the residents with a number of social and economic options.

Depending on the area of the city one is addressing, the principle constituents may be business or retail interests rather than residents. Efforts to create collaborations between the business people and the police can be as critical to community policing as community and police collaborations.

Through an assortment of tactics, a city can produce more effective and efficient responses to crime.

In Philadelphia, a contingent of city leaders and prominent members of the business community recognized a growing portion of Center City business was shifting to suburban markets. They determined this economic flight was due in large part to public perceptions of deterioration in the Center City area, formerly the most prominent business and retail section of Philadelphia. They organized to form the Center City District (CCD), funded by a tax on the 2100 businesses in Center City and the city itself.

The CCD recognized the growing crime problem and attempted to counteract it with the creation of a Center City Police Substation (Greene, Seamon, and Levy, 1995). This substation was subordinate to the two police districts which comprised Center City, and fielded two types of personnel. First, a contingent of footbeat officers worked the downtown area in day and evening shifts. Second, a group of Community Service Representatives (CSR) served as the "eyes and ears" of the police officers. The CSR's are uniformed (differently from police) and carry radios but are not sworn officers. They go through a training process, assist officers by gathering or providing information and can radio the substation if they spot a crime or a developing situation.

This initiative has proved a valuable tool in the revitalization of the Center City area, and has provided a forum for business and police interaction which had heretofore not existed. The collaborative efforts were initiated by the businesses, who fund the officers and CSR's that patrol their area.

A corporate partnership program was created in Montgomery County, Maryland, to coordinate resources between the police department and private security agencies in the area (Blair and Dowse, 1993). This partnership was designed to increase available options to both groups, train the private security groups in responding to crisis situations, and create a forum between the private sector and the police.

In Eugene, Oregon, the police department developed a community response team, in conjunction with local social service agencies and a health crisis team (Cooke, 1993). This team deals with minor injuries, suicide attempts, homeless cases, and other health issues which may not require an ambulance. This cooperative program utilizes and maximizes local resources through an innovative program, developed by both the police and local agencies.

These examples of citizen, private sector, local agency and police collaborations suggest there is room for cooperative initiatives, which may be grouped under the community policing umbrella. Although these are not unique stories, they are indicative of the success and creativity citizen initiated programs can entertain.

Although the citizen initiated program appears to be a minority when compared to the police initiate program, one must question whether there is an under-reporting bias in the police literature. Departments would clearly be more motivated to publicize their successes rather than the communities, and may feel police literature is not the appropriate forum for discussing community run programs. However, current available literature suggests the number of police created programs vastly outnumbers the citizen developed program.

## Lessons Learned

We return to the question that originally guided this inquiry: "Have police and community relations programs materially affected the formal and social organization of policing?"

In the evolution of community relations programs we can see a trend toward greater citizen involvement in the production of crime control services. Early programs either had no role for citizens or a limited and passive role. These changes are both internal and external to the police agency.

Internally, civilianization has become a cornerstone of progressive police management ideology. The use of public safety or community service officers, who are essentially civilians performing many citizen contact functions, is expected to reduce the social isolation of the community from the police.

Externally, community-oriented police programs have attempted to actively organize neighborhoods, increase citizen contact patrols and reopen community police stations, all with the view of more directly involving the citizen in prevention and suppression of crime and disorder (Sherman, 1986: 374–79).

Most community organizing programs, however, still fail to meaningfully involve the community in the policy making of the police agency itself. While there are programs which do effectively incorporate citizens, as discussed above, they tend to still be under the guidance and direction of the police. The citizen-initiated project appears to be the exception to the rule rather than the next step in the evolution of community policing.

Moreover, police mobilization of the community is differentially affected by the socioeconomic variation among communities. Part of the problem in developing and maintaining community organizations is in sustaining participation. The traditionally poor relationship between the police and the public must be overcome, but the process of incorporating citizens in new programs can be problematic (Grinc, 1994). When citizens are incorporated in police initiated programs, their roles are often cloudy or unspecified. Frequently they are simply asked to be the "eyes and ears" of the police. Grinc (1994), in an evaluation of eight community policing sites, found police administrators were frustrated because the community was dropping out of programs quickly, and failing to initiate their own programs. However, if the community is asked to fill such limited roles, they can hardly be faulted for failing to expand programs.

A review of citizen action and crime prevention programs (Greenberg et al., 1985: 137–48) suggests that citizen participation in community crime prevention organizations has varied widely from about 7 to 20 percent of the population, depending on the program studied. General awareness of crime prevention programs has been found to be substantially higher, from 20 to 55 percent, "suggesting that participation rates decrease with the 'aggressiveness' of the crime prevention program" (p. 138).

Citizen participation is also affected by the demographic characteristics of the citizens themselves. Middle-class citizens are more likely to participate in voluntary associations including crime prevention programs than are working and lower-class citizens, while blacks are more likely to participate (when economic status is controlled) than whites (p. 140). Emotional attachment to the local community is also associated with citizen participation in crime prevention programs, as is residence location—rural, suburban and urban residence, and type of neighborhood—loosely knit versus tightly knit (pp. 142–46). Strategies involving community participation, by consequence, must take into account the variation among neighborhoods and residents before a meaningful community-police program can be developed (Sherman, 1986: 379–81). As the Chicago research suggests, crime rate and type of crime within a community influences citizen participation (Chicago Community Policing Evaluation Consortium, 1996).

Blaming the community for failure to participate in police and community programs, however, would be shortsighted. If police departments fail to specify the role of citizens, or fail to provide citizens with the opportunity to create or expand their own roles, they may expect participation to be short-lived. Other police organizational factors may actually impede community organization and development.

Even the most elaborate programs ultimately hinge on the public becoming actively involved, and remaining involved over time. Community involvement is affected by many police organizational issues as well. In their assessment of the community's involvement in crime prevention programs, Garofalo and McLeod (1985: 18) suggested that the relationship between the police agency and the crime prevention programs was of critical importance; "Neighborhood Watch is a popular idea in many police departments at present, although in some cases its popularity stems from its perceived public relations value while in others it is really viewed as an effective way to deal with crime. . . ." Police agency commitment to a meaningful program, not one emphasizing "window dressing," is essential for sustained participation.

Where the policy and decision-making relationship is one-sided, police-to-community, we should not expect long-term involvement either. If the community has little voice in the determination of neighborhood problems and in assisting in the selection of police strategies for resolving those problems, then we might predict a decline in long-term participation. Furthermore, if community participation is solicited in times of crisis and allowed to recede when the immediate crisis is resolved or passes, again long-term participation should not be expected. This is especially true where the community participation is in response to a significant or highly publicized event.

We might also consider a different role for the police in crime and violence reduction programs; one that emphasizes less direct police control and a more supportive role for the police in mobilizing community resources.

> . . . if citizens believe that they themselves are the initiators rather than the recipients of "help" from outside professionals, and if those professionals—here the police—make themselves available for advice when needed, then the potential exists for more cooperation by citizens with police. This can result in more citizen reporting of crime, more tips on suspects, and improved police apprehension rates. Note that the means are not capital-intensive hardware and command-control policies imposed on the community by the police but labor-intensive citizen self-help supported by the police force.
>
> Of course, in inner-city communities where citizens and neighborhood groups are insufficiently organized to take the lead, we need to welcome whatever the police can do while we facilitate the development of community organizations. (Curtis, 1985: 216)

By whatever means community input and action is sought for crime prevention and community relations programs, the stakes are clearly political, and the central issue is the sharing of power (Brown, 1985).

By contrast, the informal side of policing has perhaps benefitted more from police and community relations programs than has the formal organization of policing. Where alternatives to the traditional police management structure have been employed, police officers have expressed more satisfaction with their jobs and with their contacts with the community.

In San Diego, a program to actively involve police officers in understanding the communities they police produced positive police officer attitudinal results (Boydstun and Sherry, 1975). In Baltimore, a problem-oriented approach to policing has resulted in improved police officer job satisfaction and in strengthened officer orientation toward resolving community problems (Hayeslip and Cordner, 1987). In Philadelphia, a community-police educational program, focused on communications and police-community problem solving, has demonstrated positive attitudinal results among participating police officers as well (Greene, 1989a; Greene and Decker, 1989). In addition, in Miami, Alpert and Dunham (1988: 119–20) reported:

> Neighborhood climate and the fluent interactions of people in close association are much more influential in forming attitudes toward the police . . . in a highly stratified, multiethnic metropolitan center like Miami, neighborhood climate not only varies tremendously, but strongly influences one's perceptions of the police . . . police officer effectiveness could be enhanced greatly if he received training specific to his district. This training would include knowledge concerning unique characteristics of the neighborhoods in the officer's district and the most appropriate and effective policing styles for those neighborhoods.

Those officers who function in community policing activities view their work as important and rewarding, and those in community policing roles tend to prefer their position over traditional roles (Greene and Pelfrey, forthcoming). Mastrofski, Worden and Snipes (1995) suggest officers with a pro-community policing philosophy approach arrest decisions differently than officers who are more traditional. These community policing officers are less likely to be influenced by a citizen's economic state and are more likely to address the needs of the victim. Thus officers in community policing roles and who advocate this philosophy are likely to be different from, and more satisfied than, regular patrol officers.

Collectively, then, police officer affective attachments to, and understanding of, the community have been enhanced in certain cities, as have officer role definitions as a result of police and community programs.

Officer participation in decision making remains a problem in many police departments; sharing power with police officers will be a major issue confronting police organizations in the future. Police role development and training are also essential features to improving community-based programs. If officers are to be given added community mobilization responsibilities, as they have in many American cities, then systematic preparation for these new roles needs to be developed. At present, the training component and selection of community policing officers in many community-policing programs is insufficient, which can produce less effective officers and frustration or jealousy between community policing officers and regular patrol officers (Dolan, 1994; Greene and Pelfrey, forthcoming b).

A current trend involves designating groups of officers as the community policing personnel, and placing the community policing responsibilities on their shoulders (Cooke, 1993; Dolan, 1994; Nebraska Commission on Law Enforcement, 1994; Ohio Crime Prevention Association, 1995). While this specialization philosophy has some advantages, there are significant problems. The separation may absolve other officers of any responsibility other than answering calls for service. Ways to avoid this issue include department wide training in community policing principles (Dolan, 1994) and clear policy statements from the chief (Ortiz and Peterson, 1994). Another option is to develop more specific areas of responsibility, and hold officers accountable for those sectors. This principle of sector integrity fell by the wayside during the era of professional policing, but may need to be revisited.

Without proper role training and role definition we may be condemned to repeat the mistakes of the team policing programs, failing to differentiate a new patrol style for community involvement.

## Conclusion

The importance of citizen involvement in providing public safety and security cannot be overstated. Resources for crime control have dwindled over the years. At the same time public demand for police services has increased. While citizen involvement in community-police programs is no cure-all for the problems of crime and social disorder, it is essential for the maintenance of democratic values. Furthermore, law enforcement agencies can hardly continue to exclude the clients and producers of police service from the policies and decisions affecting the "quality of life" in American communities. Although the process of recruiting and maintaining citizen involvement is difficult, it is currently a political and efficiency necessity.

Recently, there is evidence of a paradigmatic shift in policing. This shift appears to be moving away from the traditional "close-mindedness" of law enforcement bureaucracies toward a more participatory model of public safety. In certain cities, this change is thought to affect the entire style of policing (see Brown, 1991; Williams, Greene and Bergman, 1991). Some of these cities have developed unique initiatives which may be modeled in other cities. In other, if not most, cities, such changes have yet to be realized. Although most cities have now nominally begun the shift towards community policing, it is not yet evident whether this is an aesthetic shift or an actual change in policing philosophy.

Unfortunately, at the same time, there is also evidence of renewed and overt conflict between the police and the community. As a result of several factors, within national political ideologies and local economies, many police departments may be slipping back toward times when close and positive police and community relations were the exception rather than the rule. The role of the citizen in police-community collaborations remains unclear, and the likelihood of citizens initiating programs remains slim. The public spectacle of Los Angeles police officers beating an unarmed motorist named Rodney King remains vivid in the public consciousness, and indicates how tenuous the relationships between the police and the citizens, particularly minority citizens, actually are. Such evidence, repeated in several other American cities in the early 1990s, demands a continued vigilance both within and outside of police departments to help assure that past distinctions between police and community do not reemerge to the detriment of public safety and individual liberty.

## References

Alpert, G. P., and R. G. Dunham. 1988. *Policing Multi-Ethnic Neighborhoods*. New York: Greenwood Press.

_____. 1993. "Community Policing," in R. G. Dunham and G. P. Alpert (eds.) *Critical Issues in Policing* (2nd. ed.). Prospect Heights, IL: Waveland Press.

Angell, J. 1971. "Toward an Alternative to the Classic Police Organizational Arrangements: A Democratic Model." *Criminology* (August/November): 185–206.

Banton, M. 1964. *The Policeman in the Community*. London: Tavistock Publications.

Bayley, D. H. 1988. "Community Policing: A Report from the Devil's Advocate," in I. R. Greene and S. D. Mastrofski (eds.) *Community Policing: Rhetoric or Reality*. New York: Praeger.

Bennett, T. 1994. "Community Policing on the Ground: Developments in Britain," in D. P. Rosenbaum (ed.) *The Challenge of Community Policing: Testing the Promises*. Thousand Oaks, CA: Sage Publications.

Bittner, E. 1971. *The Functions of Police in Modern Society.* Washington, DC: National Institute of Mental Health.

Blair, B. R. and T. J. Dowse. 1993. "Promoting Corporate Community Partnerships." *Police Chief,* December, 28–32.

Bowers, W., and J. Hirsch. 1987. "The Impact of Foot Patrol Staffing on Crime and Disorder in Boston: An Unmet Promise." *American Journal of Police—Special Issue on Patrol and Community Policing* 4, 1 (Spring): 17–44.

Boydstun, I., and M. Sherry. 1975. *San Diego Community Profile: Final Report.* Washington, DC: Police Foundation.

Brown, L. 1985. "Police-Community Power Sharing," in W. Geller (ed.) *Police Leadership in America.* New York: Praeger.

_____. 1991. *Policing New York City in the 1990s: The Strategy for Community Policing.* New York: New York City Police Department.

Brown, L. and M. A. Wycoff. 1987. "Policing Houston: Reducing Fear and Improving Service." *Crime and Delinquency* 33, 1 (January): 71–89.

Brown, M. 1981. *Working the Street: Police Discretion and the Dilemmas of Reform.* New York: Russell Sage Foundation.

Buerger, M. E. 1994. "A Tale of Two Targets: Limitations of Community Anticrime Actions." *Crime and Delinquency,* 40, 411–36.

Caiden, G. 1977. *Police Revitalization.* Lexington, MA: Lexington Books.

Carter, D. 1992. "Community Alliance" in L. Hoover (ed.) *Police Management: Issues and Perspectives.* Washington DC: Police Executive Research Forum.

Chicago Community Policing Evaluation Consortium. 1996. "Community Policing in Chicago, Year Three." Chicago: Illinois Criminal Justice Information Authority.

Cooke, L. 1993. "Community Partnerships Increase Resources." *Police Chief* (December): 58–64.

Cordner, G. 1985. "The Baltimore County Citizen Oriented Police Enforcement (COPE) Project: Final Report." New York: Florence V. Burden Foundation.

_____. 1986. "Fear of Crime and the Police: An Evaluation of a Fear Reduction Strategy." *Journal of Police Science and Administration* 14(3): 223–33.

Curtis, L. 1985. "Neighborhood, Family and Employment: Toward a New Public Policy Against Violence," in L. Curtis (ed.) *American Violence and Public Policy.* New Haven: Yale University Press.

Dill, W. 1958. "Environment as an Influence on Managerial Autonomy." *Administrative Science Quarterly* 2 (March): 409–43.

Dolan, H. 1994. "Community Policing: Coping with Internal Backlash." *Police Chief* (March), 28–32.

Eck, J., and W. Spelman. 1987. *Problem-Solving: Problem-Oriented Policing in Newport News.* Washington, DC: National Institute of Justice and Police Executive Research Forum.

_____. 1987. "Who Ya Gonna Call: The Police as Problem Busters." *Crime and Delinquency* 33, 1 (January): 31–52.

Farrell, M. J. 1988. "The Development of the Community Patrol Officer Program: Community-Oriented Policing in the New York City Police Department," in J. R. Greene and S. D. Mastrofski (eds.) *Community Policing: Rhetoric or Reality.* New York: Praeger.

Fogelson, R. M. 1977. *Big City Police.* Cambridge: Harvard University Press.

Friedman, W. 1994. "The Community Role in Community Policing." in D. P. Rosenbaum (ed.) *The Challenge of Community Policing: Testing the Promises.* Thousand Oaks, CA: Sage Publications.

Garofalo, J., and M. McLeod. 1985. "Preliminary Results of a National Assessment of Neighborhood Watch." Paper presented at the annual meeting of the American Society of Criminology, San Diego, November.

Goldstein, H. 1977. *Policing a Free Society*. Cambridge: Ballinger.

____. 1979. "Improving Policing: A Problem Oriented Approach." *Crime and Delinquency* 25 (April): 236–58.

____. 1987. "Toward Community Oriented Policing: Potential, Basic Requirements and Threshold Questions." *Crime and Delinquency* 31, 1 (January): 6–30.

____. 1990. *Problem-Oriented Policing*. New York: McGraw-Hill.

Greenberg, S., W. Rohe, and J. Williams. 1985. *Informal Citizen Action and Crime Prevention at the Neighborhood Level: Synthesis and Assessment of the Research*. Washington, DC: U.S. Department of Justice.

Greene, J. R. 1981a. "The Environment of Criminal Justice Decision Making," in J. Hudzik et al., *Manpower Planning and Criminal Justice: An Overview*. Washington, DC: U.S. Government Printing Office, 180–208.

____. 1981b. "Changes in the Conception of Police Work: Crime Control versus Collective Goods," in K. Wright (ed.) *Crime and Criminal Justice in a Declining Economy*. Boston: Oelgeschlager, Gunn and Hain, Publishers, 233–56.

____. 1989a. "Community Policing and Cultural Change in Law Enforcement," unpublished. Richardson, TX: Southwestern Legal Foundation, Law Enforcement Institute.

____. 1989b. "Police Officer Job Satisfaction and Community Perceptions: Implications for Community Policing." *Journal of Research in Crime and Delinquency* 26, 2 (May): 169–83.

Greene, J. R., T. Bynum, and G. Cordner. 1987. "Planning and the Play of Power: Resource Acquisition and Use Among Criminal Justice Agencies." *Journal of Criminal Justice*.

Greene, J. R., and S. H. Decker. 1989. "Police and Community Perceptions of the Community Role in Policing: The Philadelphia Experience." *Howard Journal of Criminal Justice* 22, 8 (May): 105–23.

Greene, J. R., and R. B. Taylor. 1988. "Community-Based Policing and Foot Patrol: Issues of Theory and Evaluation," in J. R. Greene and S. D. Mastrofski (eds.) *Community Policing: Rhetoric or Reality*. New York: Praeger.

Greene, J. R., T. M. Seamon, & P. R. Levy. 1995. "Merging Public and Private Security for Collective Benefit: Philadelphia's Center City District." *American Journal of Police* 14, 3–20.

Greene, J. R. and W. V. Pelfrey, Jr. 1997. Forthcoming: "Job Attachment and the Acculturation of Community Policing Officers: A Survey of COPS AHEAD Officers."

____. 1997b. Forthcoming: "State of Community Policing in Philadelphia." Report to the National Institute of Justice.

Grinc, R. M. 1994. "'Angels in Marble': Problems in Stimulating Community Involvement in Community Policing." *Crime and Delinquency* 40, 437–68.

Hayeslip, D., and G. Cordner. 1987. "The Effects of Community-Oriented Patrol on Police Officer Attitudes." *American Journal of Police Special Issue on Foot Patrol and Community Policing* 4, 1 (Spring): 95–119.

Heller, N., Stenzel, W., and A. Gill. 1975. *National Evaluation Program Phase I Summary Report: Operation Identification Projects*. Washington, DC: Law Enforcement Assistance Administration.

International Training, Research and Evaluation Council. 1977. National Evaluation Program Phase I Summary Report: Crime Prevention Security Surveys. Washington, DC: Law Enforcement Assistance Administration.

Institute for the Study of Labor and Economic Crisis. 1982. *The Iron Fist and the Velvet Glove*, Third Edition. San Francisco: Crime and Social Justice Associates.

Kelling, G. L. 1987. "Acquiring a Taste for Order: The Community and Police." *Crime and Delinquency* 33(1): 90–102.

Kelling, G. L., and M. H. Moore. 1988. "From Political to Reform to Community," in J. R. Greene and S. Mastrofski (eds.) *Community Policing: Rhetoric or Reality*. New York: Praeger.

Klockars, C. 1985. *The Idea of Police*. Beverly Hills: Sage Publications.

_____. 1988. "The Rhetoric of Community Policing," in J. R. Greene and S. Mastrofski (eds.) *Community Policing: Rhetoric or Reality*. New York: Praeger.

Leighton, B. N. 1994. "Community Policing in Canada: An Overview of Experience and Evaluations" in D. P. Rosenbaum (ed.) *The Challenge of Community Policing: Testing the Promises*. Thousand Oaks, CA: Sage Publications.

Lohman, J. 1947. *The Police and Minority Groups*. Chicago: Chicago Park Police.

Manning, P. 1977. *Police Work: The Social Organization of Policing*. Cambridge: The MR Press.

_____. 1984. "Community Policing." *American Journal of Police* 3, 2 (Spring): 205–27.

Margolis, S. 1994. "Blythe Street Team Makes an Impact." *Police Chief* (October), 70–73.

Mastrofski, S. D. (n.d.) "The New Autonomy of American Police: Review aid Critique of a Contemporary Reform." Unpublished. Pennsylvania State University.

_____. 1988. "Community Policing as Reform: A Cautionary Tale," in J. R. Greene and S. Mastrofski (eds.) *Community Policing: Rhetoric or Reality*. New York: Praeger.

Mastrofski, S. D., and J. R. Greene. 1993. "Community Policing and the Rule of Law," in D. Weisburd and C. Uchida (eds.) *The Changing Focus of Police Innovation: Problems of Law, Order and Community*. New York: Springer-Verlag.

Mastrofski, S. D., R. E. Worden, and J. B. Snipes. 1995. "Law Enforcement in a Time of Community Policing." *Criminology* 33, 539–64.

Muir, W. 1977. *Police: Streetcorner Politicians*. Chicago: University of Chicago Press.

National Advisory Commission on Civil Disorders. 1968. *Report of the National Advisory Commission on Civil Disorders*. Washington, DC: U.S. Government Printing Office.

Nebraska Commission on Law Enforcement and Criminal Justice. 1994. "Partners in Planning: Community Planning Guide." Lincoln: Nebraska Crime Commission.

Neiderhoffer, A. 1967. *Behind the Shield*. New York: Doubleday.

Ohio Crime Prevention Association. 1995. The Guidebook to Community Policing in Ohio. Cleveland: Ohio Crime Prevention Association.

Ortiz, R. and M. Peterson. 1994. "Police Culture: A Roadblock to Change in Law Enforcement?" *Police Chief* (August), 68–71.

Pate, A. M., W. G. Skogan, M. A. Wycoff, and L. W. Sherman. 1985. "Reducing the 'Signs of Crime': The Newark Experience Executive Summary." Washington, DC: Police Foundation.

_____. 1986. "Reducing Fear of Crime in Houston and Newark: A Summary Report." Washington, DC: The Police Foundation.

Pate, A. M., W. G. Skogan, M. A. Wycoff, L. W. Sherman, and H. Williams. 1987. "Returning to First Principles: Reducing the Fear of Crime in Newark." *Crime and Delinquency* 33, 1 (January): 53–70.

Pate, A. M. and P. Shtull. 1994. "Community Policing Grows in Brooklyn: An Inside View of the New York Police Department's Model Precinct." *Crime and Delinquency* 40, 384–410.

Police Foundation. 1981. *The Newark Foot Patrol Experiment*. Washington, DC: Police Foundation.

Radelet, L. 1986. *The Police and The Community*, 4th ed. New York: Macmillan.

Reiss, A. 1985. *Policing a City's Central District: The Oakland Story*. Washington, DC: U.S. Department of Justice.

Reuss-Ianni, E., and F. Ianni. 1983. "Street Cops and Management Cops: The Two Cultures of Policing," in M. Punch (ed.) *Control in the Police Organization*. Cambridge: MIT Press, 251–74.

Rosenbaum, D. P. and A. J. Lurigio. 1994. "An Inside Look at Community Policing Reform: Definitions, Organizational Changes, and Evaluation Findings." *Crime and Delinquency* 40, 299–314.

Schwartz, A., and S. Clarren. 1977. *The Cincinnati Team Policing Experiment: A Summary Report*. Washington, DC: Urban Institute and Police Foundation.

Senn, M. 1952. *A Study of Police Training Programs in Minority Relations*. Los Angeles: Law Enforcement Committee of the Los Angeles Conference on Community Relations.

Sherman, L. 1983. "Patrol Strategies for Police," in J. Q. Wilson (ed.) *Crime and Public Policy*. San Francisco: Institute for Contemporary Studies Press.

_____. 1986. "Policing Communities: What Works?" in A. Reiss and M. Tonry, (eds.) *Communities and Crime*. Chicago: The University of Chicago Press.

Sherman, L., C. Milton, and T. Kelly. 1973. *Team Policing Seven Case Studies*. Washington, DC: Police Foundation.

Skogan, W., and A. Pate. 1987. "Reducing the Signs of Crime: Two Experiments in Controlling Public Disorder." Paper presented at the annual meeting of the American Political Science Association, Chicago, August.

Skolnick, J. 1966. *Justice Without Trial: Law Enforcement in a Democratic Society*. New York: John Wiley.

Skolnick, J., and D. Bayley. 1986. *The New Blue Line: Police Innovation in Six American Cities*. New York: Free Press.

Sparrow, M. K., M. H. Moore, and D. M. Kennedy. 1990. *Beyond 911: A New Era for Policing*. New York: Basic Books.

Stark, R. 1972. *Police Riots: Collective Violence and Law Enforcement*. Belmont, CA: Wadsworth.

Thompson, J. D. 1967. *Organizations in Action: Social Science Bases of Administrative Theory*. New York: McGraw-Hill.

Tien, J., V. O'Donnell, and A. Barnett. 1979. *National Evaluation Program Phase I Summary Report: Street Lighting Projects*. Washington, DC: Law Enforcement Assistance Administration.

Trojanowicz, R. T. 1983. "An Evaluation of the Neighborhood Foot Patrol Program: The Flint, Michigan Project." *Journal of Police Science and Administration* 11, 4: 410–19.

_____. 1986. "Evaluating a Neighborhood Foot Patrol Program: The Flint, Michigan Project," in D. Rosenbaum (ed.) *Community Crime Prevention: Does It Work?* Beverly Hills: Sage.

Trojanowicz, R. T., and B. Bucqueroux. 1990. *Community Policing: A Contemporary Perspective.* Cincinnati: Anderson Publishing.

U.S. Department of Justice, Law Enforcement Assistance Administration. 1978. *Got a Minute? You Could Stop a Crime.* Washington, DC: Ad Council.

van Rooyen, H. J. N. 1994. *Community Policing.* South Africa Press.

Ward, B. 1985. *The Community Patrol Officer Program.* New York: New York City Police Department.

Westley, W. 1970. *Violence and the Police.* Cambridge: The MIT Press.

Wetheritt, M. 1983. "Community Policing: Does It Work and How Do We Know?" in T. Bennett (ed.) *The Future of Policing.* Cambridge, Institute of Criminology.

Williams, W. L., J. R. Greene, and W. T. Bergman. 1991. "Strategic Leadership in a Big-City Police Department: The Philadelphia Story," Paper presented at the National Strategic Leadership Conference, sponsored by the Center for Creative Leadership, Greensboro, NC, July.

Wilson, J. Q., and G. Kelling. 1982. "The Police and Neighborhood Safety: Broken Windows." *Atlantic Monthly* 127 (March): 29–38.

Wycoff, M. A., and W. G. Skogan. 1985a. *Citizen Contact Patrol: The Houston Field Test.* Technical Report. Washington, DC: The Police Foundation.

_____. 1985b. *Police-Community Stations: The Houston Field Test.* Technical Report. Washington, DC: The Police Foundation.

Wycoff, M. A., W. G. Skogan, A. M. Pate, and L. W. Sherman. 1985. *Police as Community Organizers: Executive Summary.* Washington, DC: Police Foundation.

_____. 1985. *Citizen Contact Patrol: Executive Summary.* Washington, DC: The Police Foundation.

Wycoff, M. A. and W. G. Skogan. 1994. "The Effect of a Community Policing Management Style on Officer's Attitudes." *Crime and Delinquency* 40, 371–83.

Yin, R. 1986. "Community Crime Prevention: A Synthesis of Eleven Evaluations." in D. Rosenbaum (ed.) *Community Crime Prevention Does It Work?* Beverly Hills: Sage.

Yin, R., M. Vogel, and J. Chaiken. 1977. *National Evaluation Program Phase I Summary Report: Citizen Patrol Projects.* Washington, DC: Law Enforcement Assistance Administration.

# Broken Windows

*James Q. Wilson*
*George L. Kelling*

In the mid-1970s, the state of New Jersey announced a "Safe and Clean Neighborhoods Program," designed to improve the quality of community life in twenty-eight cities. As part of that program, the state provided money to help cities take police officers out of their patrol cars and assign them to walking beats. The governor and other state officials were enthusiastic about using foot patrol as a way of cutting crime, but many police chiefs were skeptical. Foot patrol, in their eyes, had been pretty much discredited. It reduced the mobility of the police, who thus had difficulty responding to citizen calls for service, and it weakened headquarters control over patrol officers.

Many police officers also disliked foot patrol, but for different reasons: it was hard work, it kept them outside on cold, rainy nights, and it reduced their chances for making a "good pinch." In some departments, assigning officers to foot patrol had been used as a form of punishment. And academic experts on policing doubted that foot patrol would have any impact on crime rates; it was, in the opinion of most, little more than a sop to public opinion. But since the state was paying for it, the local authorities were willing to go along.

Five years after the program started, the Police Foundation, in Washington, DC, published an evaluation of the foot-patrol project. Based on its analysis of a carefully controlled experiment carried out chiefly in Newark, the foundation concluded, to the surprise of hardly anyone, that foot patrol had not reduced crime rates. But residents of the foot-patrolled neighborhoods seemed to feel more secure than persons in other areas, tended to believe that crime had been reduced, and seemed to take fewer steps to protect themselves from crime (staying at home with the doors locked, for example). Moreover, citizens in the foot-patrol areas had a more favorable opinion of the police than did those living elsewhere. And officers walking

James Q. Wilson and George L. Kelling, as originally published in the March, 1982 issue of *Atlantic Monthly*. Reprinted with permission.

beats had higher morale, greater job satisfaction, and a more favorable attitude toward citizens in their neighborhoods than did officers assigned to patrol cars.

These findings may be taken as evidence that the skeptics were right—foot patrol has no effect on crime; it merely fools the citizens into thinking that they are safer. But in our view, and in the view of the authors of the Police Foundation study (of whom Kelling was one), the citizens of Newark were not fooled at all. They knew what the foot-patrol officers were doing, they knew it was different from what motorized officers do, and they knew that having officers walk beats did in fact make their neighborhoods safer.

But how can a neighborhood be "safer" when the crime rate has not gone down—in fact, may have gone up? Finding the answer requires first that we understand what most often frightens people in public places. Many citizens, of course, are primarily frightened by crime, especially crime involving a sudden, violent attack by a stranger. This risk is very real, in Newark as in many large cities. But we tend to overlook or forget another source of fear—the fear of being bothered by disorderly people. Not violent people, nor, necessarily, criminals, but disreputable or obstreperous or unpredictable people: panhandlers, drunks, addicts, rowdy teenagers, prostitutes, loiterers, the mentally disturbed.

What foot-patrol officers did was to elevate, to the extent they could, the level of public order in these neighborhoods. Though the neighborhoods were predominantly black and the foot patrolmen were mostly white, this "order-maintenance" function of the police was performed to the general satisfaction of both parties.

One of us (Kelling) spent many hours walking with Newark foot-patrol officers to see how they defined "order" and what they did to maintain it. One beat was typical: a busy but dilapidated area in the heart of Newark, with many abandoned buildings, marginal shops (several of which prominently displayed knives and straight-edged razors in their windows), one large department store, and, most important, a train station and several major bus stops. Though the area was run-down, its streets were filled with people, because it was a major transportation center. The good order of this area was important not only to those who lived and worked there but also to many others, who had to move through it on their way home, to supermarkets, or to factories.

The people on the street were primarily black; the officer who walked the street was white. The people were made up of "regulars" and "strangers." Regulars included both "decent folk" and some drunks and derelicts who were always there but who "knew their place." Strangers were, well, strangers, and viewed suspiciously, sometimes apprehensively. The officer—call him Kelly—knew who the regulars were, and they knew him. As he saw his job, he was to keep an eye on strangers, and make certain that the disreputable regulars observed some informal but widely understood rules. Drunks and addicts could sit on the stoops, but could not lie down. People could drink on side streets, but not at the main intersection. Bottles had to be in paper bags. Talking to, bothering, or begging from people waiting at the bus stop was strictly forbidden. If a dispute erupted between a businessman and a customer, the businessman was assumed to be right, especially if the customer was a stranger. If a stranger loitered, Kelly would ask him if he had any means of support and what his business was; if he gave unsatisfactory answers, he was sent on his way. Persons who broke the informal rules, especially those who bothered people waiting at bus stops, were arrested for vagrancy. Noisy teenagers were told to keep quiet.

These rules were defined and enforced in collaboration with the "regulars" on the street. Another neighborhood might have different rules, but these, everybody understood, were the rules for *this* neighborhood. If someone violated them, the regulars not only turned to Kelly for help but also ridiculed the violator. Sometimes what Kelly did could be described as "enforcing the law," but just as often it involved taking informal or extralegal steps to help protect what the neighborhood had decided was the appropriate level of public order. Some of the things he did probably would not withstand a legal challenge.

A determined skeptic might acknowledge that a skilled foot-patrol officer can maintain order but still insist that this sort of "order" has little to do with the real sources of community fear—that is, with violent crime. To a degree, that is true. But two things must be borne in mind. First, outside observers should not assume that they know how much of the anxiety now endemic in many big-city neighborhoods stems from a fear of "real" crime and how much from a sense that the street is disorderly, a source of distasteful, worrisome encounters. The people of Newark, to judge from their behavior and their remarks to interviewers, apparently assign a high value to public order, and feel relieved and reassured when the police help them maintain that order.

Second, at the community level, disorder and crime are usually inextricably linked, in a kind of developmental sequence. Social psychologists and police officers tend to agree that if a window in a building is broken *and is left unrepaired*, all the rest of the windows will soon be broken. This is as true in nice neighborhoods as in run-down ones. Window-breaking does not necessarily occur on a large scale because some areas are inhabited by determined window-breakers whereas others are populated by window-lovers; rather, one unrepaired broken window is a signal that no one cares, and so breaking more windows costs nothing. (It has always been fun.)

Philip Zimbardo, a Stanford psychologist, reported in 1969 on some experiments testing the broken-window theory. He arranged to have an automobile without license plates parked with its hood up on a street in the Bronx and a comparable automobile on a street in Palo Alto, California. The car in the Bronx was attacked by "vandals" within ten minutes of its "abandonment." The first to arrive were a family—father, mother, and young son—who removed the radiator and battery. Within twenty-four hours, virtually everything of value had been removed. Then random destruction began—windows were smashed, parts torn off, upholstery ripped. Children began to use the car as a playground. Most of the adult "vandals" were well-dressed, apparently clean-cut whites. The car in Palo Alto sat untouched for more than a week. Then Zimbardo smashed part of it with a sledgehammer. Soon, passersby were joining in. Within a few hours, the car had been turned upside down and utterly destroyed. Again, the "vandals" appeared to be primarily respectable whites.

Untended property becomes fair game for people out for fun or plunder, and even for people who ordinarily would not dream of doing such things and who probably consider themselves law-abiding. Because of the nature of community life in the Bronx—its anonymity, the frequency with which cars are abandoned and things are stolen or broken, the past experience of "no one caring"—vandalism begins much more quickly than it does in staid Palo Alto, where people have come to believe that private possessions are cared for, and that mischievous behavior is costly. But vandalism can occur anywhere once communal barriers—the sense of mutual regard and the obligations of civility—are lowered by actions that seem to signal that "no one cares."

We suggest that "untended" behavior also leads to the breakdown of community controls. A stable neighborhood of families who care for their homes, mind each other's children, and confidently frown on unwanted intruders can change, in a few years or even a few months, to an inhospitable and frightening jungle. A piece of property is abandoned, weeds grow up, a window is smashed. Adults stop scolding rowdy children; the children, emboldened, become more rowdy. Families move out, unattached adults move in. Teenagers gather in front of the corner store. The merchant asks them to move; they refuse. Fights occur. Litter accumulates. People start drinking in front of the grocery; in time, an inebriate slumps to the sidewalk and is allowed to sleep it off. Pedestrians are approached by panhandlers.

At this point it is not inevitable that serious crime will flourish or violent attacks on strangers will occur. But many residents will think that crime, especially violent crime, is on the rise, and they will modify their behavior accordingly. They will use the streets less often, and when on the streets will stay apart from their fellows, moving with averted eyes, silent lips, and hurried steps. "Don't get involved." For some residents, this growing atomization will matter little, because the neighborhood is not their "home" but "the place where they live." Their interests are elsewhere; they are cosmopolitans. But it will matter greatly to other people, whose lives derive meaning and satisfaction from local attachments rather than worldly involvement; for them, the neighborhood will cease to exist except for a few reliable friends whom they arrange to meet.

Such an area is vulnerable to criminal invasion. Though it is not inevitable, it is more likely that here, rather than in places where people are confident they can regulate public behavior by informal controls, drugs will change hands, prostitutes will solicit, and cars will be stripped. That the drunks will be robbed by boys who do it as a lark, and the prostitutes' customers will be robbed by men who do it purposefully and perhaps violently. That muggings will occur.

Among those who often find it difficult to move away from this are the elderly. Surveys of citizens suggest that the elderly are much less likely to be the victims of crime than younger persons, and some have inferred from this that the well-known fear of crime voiced by the elderly is an exaggeration: perhaps we ought not to design special programs to protect older persons; perhaps we should even try to talk them out of their mistaken fears. This argument misses the point. The prospect of a confrontation with an obstreperous teenager or a drunken panhandler can be as fear-inducing for defenseless persons as the prospect of meeting an actual robber; indeed, to a defenseless person, the two kinds of confrontation are often indistinguishable. Moreover, the lower rate at which the elderly are victimized is a measure of the steps they have already taken—chiefly, staying behind locked doors—to minimize the risks they face. Young men are more frequently attacked than older women, not because they are easier or more lucrative targets but because they are on the streets more.

Nor is the connection between disorderliness and fear made only by the elderly. Susan Estrich, of the Harvard Law School, has recently gathered together a number of surveys on the sources of public fear. One, done in Portland, Oregon, indicated that three fourths of the adults interviewed cross to the other side of a street when they see a gang of teenagers; another survey, in Baltimore, discovered that nearly half would cross the street to avoid even a single strange youth. When an interviewer asked people in a housing project where the most dangerous spot was, they mentioned a place where young persons gathered to drink and play music, despite the fact that not a single crime had occurred there. In Boston public housing projects, the greatest fear was expressed by persons living in the buildings where disorderliness and incivility, not crime, were the greatest. Knowing this helps one understand the significance of such otherwise harmless displays as subway graffiti. As Nathan Glazer has written, the proliferation of graffiti, even when not obscene, confronts the subway rider with the "inescapable knowledge that the environment he must endure for an hour or more a day is uncontrolled and uncontrollable, and that anyone can invade it to do whatever damage and mischief the mind suggests."

In response to fear, people avoid one another, weakening controls. Sometimes they call the police. Patrol cars arrive, an occasional arrest occurs, but crime continues and disorder is not abated. Citizens complain to the police chief, but he explains that his department is low on personnel and that the courts do not punish petty or first-time offenders. To the residents, the police who arrive in squad cars are either ineffective or uncaring; to the police, the residents are animals who deserve each other. The citizens may soon stop calling the police, because "they can't do anything."

The process we call urban decay has occurred for centuries in every city. But what is happening today is different in at least two important respects. First, in the period before, say, World War II, city dwellers—because of money costs, transportation difficulties, familial and church connections—could rarely move away from neighborhood problems. When movement did occur, it tended to be along public-transit routes. Now mobility has become exceptionally easy for all but the poorest or those who are blocked by racial prejudice. Earlier crime waves had a kind of built-in self-correcting mechanism: the determination of a neighborhood or community to reassert control over its turf. Areas in Chicago, New York, and Boston would experience crime and gang wars, and then normalcy would return, as the families for whom no alternative residences were possible reclaimed their authority over the streets.

Second, the police in this earlier period assisted in that reassertion of authority by acting, sometimes violently, on behalf of the community. Young toughs were roughed up, people were arrested "on suspicion" or for vagrancy, and prostitutes and petty thieves were routed. "Rights" were something enjoyed by decent folk, and perhaps also by the serious professional criminal, who avoided violence and could afford a lawyer.

This pattern of policing was not an aberration or the result of occasional excess. From the earliest days of the nation, the police function was seen primarily as that of a night watchman: to maintain order against the chief threats to order—fire, wild animals, and disreputable behavior. Solving crimes was viewed not as a police responsibility but as a private one. In the March, 1969, *Atlantic*, one of us (Wilson) wrote a brief account of how the police role had slowly changed from maintaining order to fighting crimes. The change began with the creation of private detectives (often ex-criminals), who worked on a contingency-fee basis for individuals who had suffered losses. In time, the detectives were absorbed into municipal police agencies and paid a regular salary; simultaneously, the responsibility for prosecuting thieves was shifted from the aggrieved private citizen to the professional prosecutor. This process was not complete in most places until the twentieth century.

In the 1960s, when urban riots were a major problem, social scientists began to explore carefully the order-maintenance function of the police, and to suggest ways of improving it—not to make streets safer (its original function) but to reduce the incidence of mass violence. Order-maintenance became, to a degree, conterminous with "community relations." But, as the crime wave that began in the early 1960s continued without abatement throughout the decade and into the 1970s, attention shifted to the role of the police as crime-fighters. Studies of police behavior ceased, by and large, to be accounts of the order-maintenance function and became, instead, efforts to propose and test ways whereby the police could solve more crimes, make more arrests, and gather better evidence. If these things could be done, social scientists assumed, citizens would be less fearful.

A great deal was accomplished during this transition, as both police chiefs and outside experts emphasized the crime-fighting function in their plans, in the allocation of resources, and in deployment of personnel. The police may well have become better crime-fighters as a result. And doubtless they remained aware of their responsibility for order. But the link between order-maintenance and crime-prevention, so obvious to earlier generations, was forgotten.

That link is similar to the process whereby one broken window becomes many. The citizen who fears the ill-smelling drunk, the rowdy teenager, or the importuning begger is not merely expressing his distaste for unseemly behavior; he is also giving voice to a bit of folk wisdom that happens to be a correct generalization—namely, that serious street crime flourishes in areas in which disorderly behavior goes unchecked. The unchecked panhandler is, in effect, the first broken window. Muggers and robbers, whether opportunistic or professional, believe they reduce their chances of being caught or even identified if they operate on streets where potential victims are already intimidated by prevailing conditions. If the neighborhood cannot keep a bothersome panhandler from annoying passersby, the thief may reason, it is even less likely to call the police to identify a potential mugger or to interfere if the mugging actually takes place.

Some police administrators concede that this process occurs, but argue that motorized-patrol officers can deal with it as effectively as foot-patrol officers. We are not so sure. In theory, an officer in a squad car can observe as much as an officer on foot; in theory, the former can talk to as many people as the latter. But the reality of police-citizen encounters is powerfully altered by the automobile. An officer on foot cannot separate himself from the street people; if he is approached, only his uniform and his personality can help him manage whatever is about to happen. And he can never be certain what that will be—a request for directions, a plea for help, an angry denunciation, a teasing remark, a confused babble, a threatening gesture.

In a car, an officer is more likely to deal with street people by rolling down the window and looking at them. The door and window exclude the approaching citizen; they are a barrier. Some officers take advantage of this barrier, perhaps unconsciously, by acting differently if in the car than they would on foot. We have seen this countless times. The police car pulls up to a corner where teenagers are gathered. The window is rolled down. The officer stares at the youths. They stare back. The officer says to one, "C'mere." He saunters over, conveying to his friends by his elaborately casual style the idea that he is not intimidated by authority. "What's your name?" "Chuck." "Chuck who?" "Chuck Jones." "What'ya doing, Chuck?" "Nothin'." "Got a P.O. [parole officer]?" "Nah." "Sure?" "Yeah." "Stay out of trouble, Chuckie." Meanwhile, the other boys laugh and exchange comments among themselves, probably at the officer's expense. The officer stares harder. He cannot be certain what is being said, nor can he join in and, by displaying his own skill at street banter, prove that he cannot be "put down." In the process, the officer has learned almost nothing, and the boys have decided the officer is an alien force who can safely be disregarded, even mocked.

Our experience is that most citizens like to talk to a police officer. Such exchanges give them a sense of importance, provide them with the basis for gossip, and allow them to explain to the authorities what is worrying them (whereby they gain a modest but significant sense of having "done something" about the problem). You approach a person on foot more easily, and talk to him more readily, than you do a person in a car. Moreover, you can more easily retain some anonymity if you draw an officer aside for a private chat. Suppose you want to pass on a tip about who is stealing handbags, or who offered to sell you a stolen TV. In the inner city, the culprit, in all likelihood, lives nearby. To walk up to a marked patrol car and lean in the window is to convey a visible signal that you are a "fink."

The essence of the police role in maintaining order is to reinforce the informal control mechanisms of the community itself. The police cannot, without committing extraordinary resources, provide a substitute for that informal control. On the other hand, to reinforce those natural forces the police must accommodate them. And therein lies the problem.

Should police activity on the street be shaped, in important ways, by the standards of the neighborhood rather than by the rules of the state? Over the past two decades, the shift of police from order-maintenance to law-enforcement has brought them increasingly under the influence of legal restrictions, provoked by media complaints and enforced by court decisions and departmental orders. As a consequence, the order-maintenance functions of the police are now governed by rules developed to control police relations with suspected criminals. This is, we think, an entirely new development. For centuries, the role of the police as watchmen was judged primarily not in terms of its compliance with appropriate procedures but rather in terms of its attaining a desired objective. The objective was order, an inherently ambiguous term but a condition that people in a given community recognized when they saw it. The means were the same as those the community itself would employ, if its members were sufficiently determined, courageous, and authoritative. Detecting and apprehending criminals, by contrast, was a means to an end, not an end in itself; a judicial determination of guilt or innocence was the hoped-for result of the law-enforcement mode. From the first, the police were expected to follow rules defining that process, though states differed in how stringent the rules should be. The criminal-apprehension process was always understood to involve individual rights, the violation of which was unacceptable because it meant that the violating officer would be acting as a judge and jury—and that was not his job. Guilt or innocence was to be determined by universal standards under special procedures.

Ordinarily, no judge or jury ever sees the persons caught up in a dispute over the appropriate level of neighborhood order. That is true not only because most cases are handled informally on the street but also because no universal standards are available to settle arguments over disorder, and thus a judge may not be any wiser or more effective than a police officer. Until quite recently in many states, and even today in some places, the police make arrests on such charges as "suspicious person" or "vagrancy" or "public drunkenness"—charges with scarcely any legal meaning. These charges exist not because society wants judges to punish vagrants or drunks but because it wants an officer to have the legal tools to remove undesirable persons from a neighborhood when informal efforts to preserve order in the streets have failed.

Once we begin to think of all aspects of police work as involving the application of universal rules under special procedures, we inevitably ask what constitutes an "undesirable person" and why we should "criminalize" vagrancy or drunkenness. A strong and commendable desire to see that people are treated fairly makes us worry about allowing the police to rout persons who are undesirable by some vague or parochial standard. A growing and not-so-commendable utilitarianism leads us to doubt that any behavior that does not "hurt" another person should be made illegal. And thus many of us who watch over the police are reluctant to allow them to perform, in the only way they can, a function that every neighborhood desperately wants them to perform.

This wish to "decriminalize" disreputable behavior that "harms no one"—and thus remove the ultimate sanction the police can employ to maintain neighborhood order—is, we think, a mistake. Arresting a single drunk or a single vagrant who has harmed no identifiable person seems unjust, and in a sense it is. But failing to do anything about a score of drunks or a hundred vagrants may destroy an entire community. A particular rule that seems to make sense in the individual case makes no sense when it is made a universal rule and applied to all cases. It makes no sense because it fails to take into account the connection between one broken window left untended and a thousand broken windows. Of course, agencies other than the police could attend to the problems posed by drunks or the mentally ill, but in most communities—especially where the "deinstitutionalization" movement has been strong—they do not.

The concern about equity is more serious. We might agree that certain behavior makes one person more undesirable than another, but how do we ensure that age or skin color or national origin or harmless mannerisms will not also become the basis for distinguishing the undesirable from the desirable? How do we ensure, in short, that the police do not become the agents of neighborhood bigotry?

We can offer no wholly satisfactory answer to this important question. We are not confident that there *is* a satisfactory answer, except to hope that by their selection, training, and supervision, the police will be inculcated with a clear sense of the outer limit of their discretionary authority. That limit, roughly, is this—the police exist to help regulate behavior, not to maintain the racial or ethnic purity of a neighborhood.

Consider the case of the Robert Taylor Homes in Chicago, one of the largest public-housing projects in the country. It is home for nearly 20,000 people, all black, and extends over ninety-two acres along South State Street. It was named after a distinguished black who had been, during the 1940s, chairman of the Chicago Housing Authority. Not long after it opened, in 1962, relations between project residents and the police deteriorated badly. The citizens felt that the police were insensitive or brutal; the police, in turn, complained of unprovoked attacks on them. Some Chicago officers tell of times when they were afraid to enter the Homes. Crime rates soared.

Today, the atmosphere has changed. Police–citizen relations have improved—apparently, both sides learned something from the earlier experience. Recently, a boy stole a purse and ran off. Several young persons who saw the theft voluntarily passed along to the police information on the identity and residence of the thief, and they did this publicly, with friends and neighbors looking on. But problems persist, chief among them the presence of youth gangs that terrorize residents and recruit members in the project. The people expect the police to "do something" about this, and the police are determined to do just that.

But do what? Though the police can obviously make arrests whenever a gang member breaks the law, a gang can form, recruit, and congregate without breaking the law. And only a tiny fraction of gang-related crimes can be solved by an arrest; thus, if an arrest is the only recourse for the police, the residents' fears will go unassuaged. The police will soon feel helpless, and the residents will again believe that the police "do nothing." What the police in fact do is to chase known gang members out of the project. In the words of one officer, "We kick ass." Project residents both know and approve of this. The tacit police-citizen alliance in the project is reinforced by the police view that the cops and the gangs are the two rival sources of power in the area, and that the gangs are not going to win.

None of this is easily reconciled with any conception of due process or fair treatment. Since both residents and gang members are black, race is not a factor. But it could be. Suppose a white project confronted a black gang, or vice versa. We would be apprehensive about the police taking sides. But the substantive problem remains the same: how can the police strengthen the informal social-control mechanisms of natural communities in order to minimize fear in public places? Law enforcement, per se, is no answer. A gang can weaken or destroy a community by standing about in a menacing fashion and speaking rudely to passersby without breaking the law.

We have difficulty thinking about such matters, not simply because the ethical and legal issues are so complex but because we have become accustomed to thinking of the law in essentially individualistic terms. The law defines *my* rights, punishes *his* behavior, and is applied by *that* officer because of *this* harm. We assume, in thinking this way, that what is good for the individual will be good for the community, and what doesn't matter

when it happens to one person won't matter if it happens to many. Ordinarily, those are plausible assumptions. But in cases where behavior that
is tolerable to one person is intolerable to many others, the reactions of the
others—fear, withdrawal, flight—may ultimately make matters worse for
everyone, including the individual who first professed his indifference.

It may be their greater sensitivity to communal as opposed to individual needs that helps explain why the residents of small communities are
more satisfied with their police than are the residents of similar neighborhoods in big cities. Elinor Ostrom and her co-workers at Indiana University compared the perception of police services in two poor, all-black
Illinois towns—Phoenix and East Chicago Heights—with those of three
comparable all-black neighborhoods in Chicago. The level of criminal victimization and the quality of police-community relations appeared to be
about the same in the towns and the Chicago neighborhoods. But the citizens living in their own villages were much more likely than those living in
the Chicago neighborhoods to say that they do not stay at home for fear of
crime, to agree that the local police have "the right to take any action necessary" to deal with problems, and to agree that the police "look out for the
needs of the average citizen." It is possible that the residents and the police
of the small towns saw themselves as engaged in a collaborative effort to
maintain a certain standard of communal life, whereas those of the big city
felt themselves to be simply requesting and supplying particular services
on an individual basis.

If this is true, how should a wise police chief deploy his meager
forces? The first answer is that nobody knows for certain, and the most
prudent course of action could be to try further variations on the Newark
experiment, to see more precisely what works in what kinds of neighborhoods. The second answer is also a hedge—many aspects of order-maintenance in neighborhoods can probably best be handled in ways that involve
the police minimally, if at all. A busy, bustling shopping center and a quiet,
well-tended suburb may need almost no visible police presence. In both
cases, the ratio of respectable to disreputable people is ordinarily so high
as to make informal social control effective.

Even in areas that are in jeopardy from disorderly elements, citizen
action without substantial police involvement may be sufficient. Meetings
between teenagers who like to hang out on a particular corner and adults
who want to use that corner might well lead to an amicable agreement on
a set of rules about how many people can be allowed to congregate, where,
and when.

Where no understanding is possible—or if possible, not observed—
citizen patrols may be a sufficient response. There are two traditions of
communal involvement in maintaining order. One, that of the "community
watchmen," is as old as the first settlement of the New World. Until well
into the nineteenth century, volunteer watchmen, not policemen, patrolled
their communities to keep order. They did so, by and large, without taking
the law into their own hands—without, that is, punishing persons or using

force. Their presence deterred disorder or alerted the community to disorder that could not be deterred. There are hundreds of such efforts today in communities all across the nation. Perhaps the best known is that of the Guardian Angels, a group of unarmed young persons in distinctive berets and T-shirts, who first came to public attention when they began patrolling the New York City subways but who claim now to have chapters in more than thirty American cities. Unfortunately, we have little information about the effect of these groups on crime. It is possible, however, that whatever their effect on crime, citizens find their presence reassuring, and that they thus contribute to maintaining a sense of order and civility.

The second tradition is that of the "vigilante." Rarely a feature of the settled communities of the East, it was primarily to be found in those frontier towns that grew up in advance of the reach of government. More than 350 vigilante groups are known to have existed; their distinctive feature was that their members did take the law into their own hands, by acting as judge, jury, and often executioner as well as policeman. Today, the vigilante movement is conspicuous by its rarity, despite the great fear expressed by citizens that the older cities are becoming "urban frontiers." But some community watchmen groups have skirted the line, and others may cross it in the future. An ambiguous case, reported in *The Wall Street Journal*, involved a citizens' patrol in the Silver Lake area of Belleville, New Jersey. A leader told the reporter, "We look for outsiders." If a few teenagers from outside the neighborhood enter it, "we ask them their business," he said. "If they say they're going down the street to see Mrs. Jones, fine, we let them pass. But then we follow them down the block to make sure they're really going to see Mrs. Jones."

Though citizens can do a great deal, the police are plainly the key to order-maintenance. For one thing, many communities, such as the Robert Taylor Homes, cannot do the job by themselves. For another, no citizen in a neighborhood, even an organized one, is likely to feel the sense of responsibility that wearing a badge confers. Psychologists have done many studies on why people fail to go to the aid of persons being attacked or seeking help, and they have learned that the cause is not "apathy" or "selfishness" but the absence of some plausible grounds for feeling that one must personally accept responsibility. Ironically, avoiding responsibility is easier when a lot of people are standing about. On streets and in public places, where order is so important, many people are likely to be "around," a fact that reduces the chance of any one person acting as the agent of the community. The police officer's uniform singles him out as a person who must accept responsibility if asked. In addition, officers, more easily than their fellow citizens, can be expected to distinguish between what is necessary to protect the safety of the street and what merely protects its ethnic purity.

But the police forces of America are losing, not gaining, members. Some cities have suffered substantial cuts in the number of officers available for duty. These cuts are not likely to be reversed in the near future. Therefore, each department must assign its existing officers with great care. Some neighborhoods are so demoralized and crime-ridden as to make foot patrol useless; the best the police can do with limited resources is respond to the enormous number of calls for service. Other neighborhoods are so stable and serene as to make foot patrol unnecessary. The key is to identify neighborhoods at the tipping point—where the public order is deteriorating but not unreclaimable, where the streets are used frequently but by apprehensive people, where a window is likely to be broken at any time, and must quickly be fixed if all are not to be shattered.

Most police departments do not have ways of systematically identifying such areas and assigning officers to them. Officers are assigned on the basis of crime rates (meaning that marginally threatened areas are often stripped so that police can investigate crimes in areas where the situation is hopeless) or on the basis of calls for service (despite the fact that most citizens do not call the police when they are merely frightened or annoyed). To allocate patrol wisely, the department must look at the neighborhoods and decide, from first-hand evidence, where an additional officer will make the greatest difference in promoting a sense of safety.

One way to stretch limited police resources is being tried in some public-housing projects. Tenant organizations hire off-duty police officers for patrol work in their buildings. The costs are not high (at least not per resident), the officer likes the additional income, and the residents feel safer. Such arrangements are probably more successful than hiring private watchmen, and the Newark experiment helps us understand why. A private security guard may deter crime or misconduct by his presence, and he may go to the aid of persons needing help, but he may well not intervene—that is, control or drive away—someone challenging community standards. Being a sworn officer— a "real cop"— seems to give one the confidence, the sense of duty, and the aura of authority necessary to perform this difficult task.

Patrol officers might be encouraged to go to and from duty stations on public transportation and, while on the bus or subway car, enforce rules about smoking, drinking, disorderly conduct, and the like. The enforcement need involve nothing more than ejecting the offender (the offense, after all, is not one with which a booking officer or a judge wishes to be bothered). Perhaps the random but relentless maintenance of standards on buses would lead to conditions on buses that approximate the level of civility we now take for granted on airplanes.

But the more important requirement is to think that to maintain order in precarious situations is a vital job. The police know this is one of their functions, and they also believe, correctly, that it cannot be done to the exclusion of criminal investigation and responding to calls. We may have encouraged them to suppose, however, on the basis of our oft-repeated concerns about serious, violent crime, that they will be judged exclusively on their capacity as crime-fighters. To the extent that this is the case, police administrators will continue to concentrate police personnel in the highest-crime areas (though not necessarily in the areas most vulnerable to criminal invasion), emphasize their training in the law and criminal apprehension (and not their training in managing street life), and join too quickly in campaigns to decriminalize "harmless" behavior (though public drunkenness, street prostitution, and pornographic displays can destroy a community more quickly than any team of professional burglars).

Above all, we must return to our long-abandoned view that the police ought to protect communities as well as individuals. Our crime statistics and victimization surveys measure individual losses, but they do not measure communal losses. Just as physicians now recognize the importance of fostering health rather than simply treating illness, so the police—and the rest of us—ought to recognize the importance of maintaining, intact, communities without broken windows.

# "Broken Windows" and Fractured History
## The Use and Misuse of History in Recent Police Patrol Analysis

*Samuel Walker*

A fresh burst of creativity marks current thinking about police patrol in the United States. This revival follows a period of doubt and disorientation in the late 1970s when recent research shattered traditional assumptions about patrol strategy. The most notable proposal for a reorientation of police patrol is set forth in "Broken Windows" by James Q. Wilson and George L. Kelling. Drawing partly on recent patrol experiments and partly on a re-thinking of police history, Wilson and Kelling propose a return to what they see as an older "watchman" style of policing (Wilson and Kelling 1982).

This selection examines the use of history by Wilson and Kelling in their proposal for reorienting police patrol. Because the historical analysis is central to their argument, its viability may well depend upon how well they have interpreted police history. Kelling develops his view of police history even more explicitly in a subsequent article co-authored with Mark H. Moore (Moore and Kelling 1983).

We shall argue here that Wilson, Kelling and Moore have misinterpreted police history in several important respects. Their proposal calls for a restoration—a return to a former tradition of police patrol. Joe McNamara, Chief of the San Jose police, has already responded to the "broken windows" thesis by arguing that the good old days weren't all that good (McNamara 1982). This selection elaborates upon that point and argues that the tradition of policing cited by Wilson, Kelling and Moore never existed. This does not necessarily mean that the broken windows thesis is completely invalid. But if there is merit in the style of police patrol

*Justice Quarterly* 1: 57–90 (1984). Reprinted with the permission of the publisher.

Wilson and Kelling propose, that style will have to be created anew. There is no viable older tradition to restore. Obviously, this is a far more difficult and challenging proposition than they have suggested.

## Policing and Broken Windows

Broken windows are a metaphor for the deterioration of neighborhoods. A broken window that goes unrepaired is a statement that no one cares enough about the quality of life in the neighborhood to bother fixing the little things that are wrong. While a broken window might be a small thing in and of itself, left unrepaired it becomes an invitation to further neglect. The result is a progressive deterioration of the entire neighborhood. Wilson and Kelling cite research in social psychology where abandoned cars were rapidly vandalized when some sign of prior vandalism invited further destructive acts (Zimbardo 1969).

Policing in America has failed, Wilson, Kelling and Moore argue, because it has neglected "the little things," the law enforcement equivalents of broken windows. This neglect is the product of the development of an efficiency-oriented crime control-focused style of policing over the past fifty years. Eric Monkkonen argues that the shift toward crime control began even earlier and was substantially complete by 1920 (Monkkonen 1981).

Two developments in the 1930s launched a radical reorientation of police patrol. The first was the greatly increased use of the patrol car, which took the patrol officer off the street and isolated him from the public. The second was the development of the Uniform Crime Reports system which then became the basic measure of police "success."

By themselves, these two developments might not have exerted such a profound effect on policing. The crucial difference was the influence of O. W. Wilson who forged a coherent theory of police management in the late 1930s. Wilsonian theory emphasized the suppression of crime as the primary mission of policing. Fulfillment of this mission depended upon maximizing the efficiency of patrol coverage. The automobile allowed a patrol officer to cover his beat more often during one tour of duty, and to do so in a more unpredictable fashion than foot patrol.

Wilson became the leading proponent of one-officer cars, claiming that two single officer patrol cars were twice as efficient as one two-officer car. He recommended that patrol beats should be organized according to a workload formula which distributed the work evenly among patrol officers. Finally, he concluded that rapid response time would increase apprehensions and generally enhance public satisfaction with police service (Walker 1977; Fogelson 1977).

Wilson tirelessly propounded his gospel of efficiency from the late 1930s onward. His text *Police Administration* became "the bible" of police management and instructed an entire generation of police executives (Wilson and McLaren 1977). Police departments converted almost entirely from foot to automobile patrol, invested enormous sums of money in sophisticated communications equipment, and encouraged members of the public to avail themselves of their service.

Lost in this process were the personal aspects of routine policing. The car isolated officers from the people in the neighborhoods, which became nothing more than a series of "beat assignments" to the officers. The most professionalized departments, in fact, took extra measures to de-personalize policing. Frequent rotation of beat assignments was adopted as a strategy to combat corruption.

The crime control orientation meanwhile caused the police to concentrate on more serious crimes—primarily, the seven felonies that comprised the Crime Index. Significantly, the police actively adopted the UCR system as the measure of their performance. It was not something imposed on them (Manning 1977). The police lost interest in lesser violations of the law and routine because they just did not count. These nuisances included drunks, loud and intimidating groups of teenagers, public drug dealing, and the like.[1]

According to Wilson, Kelling and Moore, these nuisances are the "broken windows," the little things that convey the message that no one cares about the quality of life in this neighborhood. Wilson, Kelling and Moore base much of their argument on the recent Newark Foot Patrol Experiment (The Police Foundation 1981). The presence of officers on foot patrol did not reduce crime, but did make people feel safer. Officers were able to establish and enforce informal rules of behavior for the neighborhood. It was alright to be intoxicated in public but not to pass out in the gutter, for example. Wilson and Kelling also cite with apparent approval the technique used by some Chicago police officers to maintain order in public housing projects: if groups of teenagers were troublesome, the officers would simply chase them away. "We kick ass," one officer explained (Wilson and Kelling 1982:35).

The "Broken Windows" article argues that policing should be neighborhood-oriented. More officers should be deployed on foot, and those officers should concentrate less on catching criminals and more on enforcing informal neighborhood norms of behavior. To a certain extent it advocates a form of team policing, although with some important differences.

Team policing experiments in the 1970s did not emphasize foot patrol, gave insufficient attention to street-level patrol tactics, and maintained the traditional crime control focus. Indeed, the incompatibility of some elements of team policing with the prevailing organizational structure and management philosophy was one of the factors in the failure of early team policing experiments (Sherman 1973; U.S. Department of Justice 1977; Schwartz and Clarren 1977).

"Broken Windows" offers an alternative model precisely because it focuses on what officers would actually do. It characterizes the recommended style of policing as a return to an earlier (pre-1930s) style of "watchman" or "constabulary" policing. At this point we turn our attention to the historical analysis that underpins this argument.

## The Historical Framework

The historical framework presented by Wilson, Kelling and Moore consists of three components: the near-term, which embraces the last fifteen years; the middle-term, which includes the last fifty years; and the long-term, which involves all of police history before the last fifty years.

Their reading of near-term history is excellent. One of the most important developments of the past fifteen years has unquestionably been the enormous expansion of our knowledge about all aspects of policing. We can now discuss in an informed fashion issues that were *terra incognita* to the staff of the President's Crime Commission (Walker 1983). The most important findings constitute a systematic demolition of the assumptions underlying O. W. Wilson's approach to police management. We have learned that adding more police or intensifying patrol coverage will not reduce crime and that neither faster response time nor additional detectives will improve clearance rates. Few authorities on policing today could endorse the basic Wilsonian idea that improved management in the deployment of patrol officers or detectives is likely to reduce the crime rate.

Wilson's, Kelling's and Moore's reading of the last fifty years of police history is mixed. They recognize the most significant developments in the period but misinterpret them in important respects. There are substantial implications of this misinterpretation for their proposed style of policing.

The development of American policing from the 1930s through the 1960s was a far more complex process than historians have lead us to believe. Wilson, Kelling and Moore can be excused in large part because they have simply drawn upon the available historical scholarship. We will focus here on two aspects of police history since the 1930s which have not received sufficient attention. The first involves the impact of the patrol car and the second concerns the crime control orientation of policing.

## The Technological Revolution

It is indeed true that American police departments largely converted from foot to automobile patrol between the 1930s and the present. We should, of course, be cognizant of the enormous variations that exist even today. Some departments are almost wholly motorized while others, primarily Eastern cities, still make heavy use of foot patrol (Police Executive Research Forum 1981). And it is also true that car patrols remove officers from the sidewalks, isolate them from casual contacts with ordinary citizens, and damage police-community relations. This analysis is part of the conventional wisdom about policing.

The impact of technology was paradoxical, however. The mid-century revolution in American policing involved not just the patrol car, but the car in conjunction with the telephone and the two-way radio. These served to bring police officers into far more intimate contact with people than ever before. While the patrol car isolated police officers in some respects, the telephone simultaneously increased the degree of contact in other respects. Let us examine this paradox in detail.

In the days of foot patrol, officers had extensive casual contacts with people. But they occurred primarily on the streets or in other public places. The police did not often obtain entry to private residences. The reason for this is obvious: there was no mechanism whereby the ordinary citizen could effectively summon the police. The telephone radically altered that situation with profound ramifications for both policing and public expectations about the quality of life. Stinchcombe (1963) has discussed the impact of privacy considerations on routine police work.

The telephone made it possible for the ordinary citizen to summon the police, and the combination of the two-way radio and the patrol car allowed the police to respond quickly. As we know, the more professional departments acquired a fetish for responding as quickly as possible to all calls. The development of the 911 telephone number was simply the logical conclusion of this effort to advertise and encourage people to use police service. People have in fact availed themselves of this service. The number of calls for service has escalated to the point where serious attention has been given to the idea of restricting or otherwise managing those requests in the last few years (Gay 1977).

Technology radically alters the nature of police-citizen contacts. Most of those contacts now occur in private residences. Albert Reiss reports that 70% of all police-citizen contacts occur in private places, 12% in semi-public, and 18% in open public places (Reiss 1971:16). The police not only gain access to private places, but observe the most intimate aspects of peoples' lives, and are asked to handle their most personal problems.

Research has confirmed that the bulk of police work involves domestic disputes and other problems arising from alcohol, drugs, mental illness, and poverty. Officers refer to all this as "bullshit" or "social work" because it is unrelated to what they believe to be their crime control mission.

Police-citizen contacts became increasingly skewed. The police lost contact with "ordinary" people and gained a great deal of contact with "problem" people, who included not just criminal offenders but those with multiple social problems. David Bayley and Harold Mendelsohn once observed that police officers had more direct knowledge about minorities than did the members of any other occupation. This knowledge was a direct product of the heavy demands upon police service placed by low-income and racial minorities (Bayley and Mendelsohn 1969:156).

Our understanding of the full impact of the telephone on policing remains problematic. Not all experts on policing accept the argument advanced here. Some argue that the police were indeed intimately involved in people's lives prior to the advent of the telephone.[2] Unfortunately, there is no empirical evidence that would permit the resolution of this question. Prior to the late 1950s, there were no observational studies of police patrol activities and thus we have no reliable evidence on what American police officers did on patrol in the pre-telephone era.[3]

## The Revolution in Public Expectations

One consequence of the technological revolution in policing has been a parallel revolution in public expectations about the quality of life. The availability of police service created and fed a demand for those services. The establishment of the modern police in the early nineteenth century was an initial phase of this process, which created the expectation that a certain level of public order would, or at least should, prevail (Silver 1967).

The technological revolution of the mid-twentieth century generated a quantum leap in those expectations. Because there was now a mechanism for getting someone (the police) to "do something" about minor disorders and nuisances, people came to expect that they should not have to put up with such minor irritations. Thus, the general level of expectations about the quality of life—the amount of noise, the presence of "strange" or "undesirable" people—has undergone an enormous change. Three generations of Americans have learned or at least have come to believe that they should not have to put up with certain problems.

The police are both the source and the victims of this revolution. They have stimulated higher levels of public expectations by their very presence and their policy of more readily available services. At the same time they are the prisoners of their own creation, swamped with an enormous service call workload. The recent effort to restrict or somehow manage this workload faces the problem of a public that expects rapid police response for any and every problem as a matter of right.

Documenting changes in public expectations concerning the police is difficult given the absence of reliable data about public attitudes or police practices prior to the late 1950s and early 1960s. Several indicators do provide evidence of short-term changes in public expectations. The development of three-digit (911) emergency phone numbers for the police increased the number of service calls. In Omaha, Nebraska, for example, the number of patrol car dispatches increased by 36% between 1969 and 1971, presumably as a result of a new 911 phone number (Walker 1983:110). These figures represent the dispatch of a patrol car, not the number of incoming calls. Omaha police officials estimate that about 35% of all calls do not result in a dispatch.

Additional evidence is found in data on the number of civilian complaints about police misconduct. In New York City, for example, the number of complaints filed with the Civilian Complaint Review Board (CCRB) increased from about 200 per year in 1960–62 to just over 2000 per year in 1967–68 and more than 3000 annually in 1971–74. It would be difficult to believe that the conduct of New York City police officers deteriorated by a factor of 10 or 15 during this period. Rather, the increase is probably the result of a lower threshold of tolerance for police misconduct on the part of citizens and the increased availability of an apparent remedy for perceived misconduct.

During the period under discussion, the procedures of the New York CCRB were reorganized several times. Each reorganization facilitated complaint filing and at the same time heightened public awareness of the availability of this particular remedy (Kahn 1975:113). The data on civilian complaints supports the argument made herein concerning police services generally: the availability of a service or remedy stimulates demand for that service, thereby altering basic expectations.

## The Mythology of Crime Control

The conventional wisdom states that police organize their efforts around the goal of crime control. Wilson, Kelling and Moore restate this conventional wisdom, but the matter is a bit more complex.

There is an important distinction between the self-image of the police and the day-to-day reality of routine policing (Goldstein 1977). The emphasis on crime control is and has been largely a matter of what the police say they are doing. Peter Manning argues persuasively that the police consciously created and manipulated this self-image as a way of establishing greater professional and political autonomy (Manning 1977).

As we have seen, however, the day-to-day reality of policing contradicted this self-image. The sharp contrast between the crime-fighting imagery of the police and the peacekeeping reality of police activities was one of the first and most important findings of the flood of police research that began in the 1960s. When Wilson, Kelling and Moore suggest that the police are completely crime control-oriented they seriously misrepresent the nature of contemporary policing.

The discrepancy between crime control imagery and operational reality also becomes evident when we look more closely at how police departments utilize their resources. The most recent Survey of Police Operational and Administrative Practices reveals enormous variations among departments (Police Executive Research Forum 1981). Many still distribute their patrol officers equally among three shifts, ignoring even the most rudimentary workload formulas, which were first developed by O. W. Wilson over forty years ago (Wilson and McLaren 1977: Appendix J). Departments typically do not revise the boundaries of their patrol districts on a regular basis. Districts remain unchanged for ten or twenty years, or longer. Meanwhile, the composition of the urban environment changes radically, as older areas are depopulated, new residential areas created, and so on.

## The Question of Legitimacy

The most important long-term development in American policing, according to Wilson, Kelling and Moore, has been the loss of political legitimacy. There can be little doubt that legitimacy, by which we mean acceptance of police authority by the public, is a major problem today.

The interpretation of police history offered by Wilson, Kelling and Moore, which purports to explain how that legitimacy was lost, is seriously flawed. The evidence completely contradicts the thrust of their argument.

The police in the nineteenth century were not merely the "adjuncts" of the machine, as Robert Fogelson (1977) suggests, but were central cogs in it. Wilson, Kelling and Moore maintain that this role offered certain benefits for the police, which reformers and historians alike have overlooked.

As cogs in the machine, the police served the immediate needs of the different neighborhoods. Political control was highly decentralized and local city councilmen or ward bosses exercised effective control over the police. Thus, the police carried out a wide range of services. Historians have rediscovered the social welfare role of the police, providing food and lodging for vagrants (Walker 1977; Monkkonen 1981). The police also performed political errands and were the means by which certain groups and individuals were able to corrupt the political process. These errands included open electioneering, rounding up the loyal voters, and harassing the opponents. Police also enforced the narrow prejudices of their constituents, harassing "undesirables" or discouraging any kind of "unwelcome" behavior.

Wilson, Kelling and Moore concede that there was a lack of concern for due process, but argue there was an important trade-off. By virtue of serving the immediate needs and narrow prejudices of the neighborhoods, the police gained an important degree of political legitimacy. They were perceived as faithful servants and enjoyed the resulting benefits. All of this was destroyed by the reforms of the twentieth century. The patrol car removed officers from the streets, while the new "professional" style dictated an impersonal type of policing. Legal concerns with due process denied officers the ability to use the tactics of rough justice by which they had enforced neighborhood community norms.

This historical analysis is central to the reorientation of policing presented in the "Broken Windows" article. Wilson, Kelling and Moore propose that the lost political legitimacy could be re-established by what they view as the older "watchman" style of policing. Unfortunately, this historical analysis is pure fantasy.

Historians are unanimous in their conclusion that the police were at the center of urban political conflict in the nineteenth century. In many instances policing was the paramount issue and in some cases the only issue. Historians disagree only on their interpretation of the exact nature of this political conflict. The many experiments with different forms of administrative control over the police (the last of which survives only in Missouri) were but one part of this long and bitter struggle for political control (Walker 1977; Fogelson 1977).

To say that there was political conflict over the police means that the police lacked political legitimacy. Their authority was not accepted by the citizenry. Wilson, Kelling and Moore are seriously in error when they suggest that the police enjoyed substantial legitimacy in the pre-technology era.

The lack of legitimacy is further illustrated by the nature of the conflicts surrounding the police. Non-enforcement of the various laws designed to control drinking was the issue that most often roused the so-called "reformers" to action. Alcohol consumption was a political issue with many dimensions. In some respects it was an expression of ethnic conflict, pitting sobersided Anglo-Saxons against the heavy-drinking Irish and Germans. Drinking was also a class issue. Temperance and, later, prohibition advocates tended either to come from the middle class or at least define themselves in terms of the values of hard work, sobriety, thrift and upward mobility (Gusfield 1963). When nineteenth century Americans fought over the police and the enforcement of the drinking laws, that battle expressed the deepest social conflicts in American society.

In one of the finest pieces of historical scholarship on the American police, Wilbur Miller explores the question of legitimacy from an entirely different angle (Miller 1977). The great difference between the London and New York City police was precisely the extent to which officers in New York were denied the grant of legitimacy enjoyed by their counterparts in London. Miller further argues that the problem of legitimacy was individualized in New York City. Each officer faced challenges to his personal authority and had to assert his authority on a situational level.

Miller does not argue that challenges to police legitimacy were patterned according to class, ethnicity or race. Thus, an Irish-American cop was just as likely to be challenged by a fellow countryman as he was by someone of a different ethnic background. To be sure, the poor, political radicals, blacks, and other people deemed "undesirable" were victimized more often by the police than were other groups, but it does not follow that the police enjoyed unquestioned authority in the eyes of those people who were members of the same class and ethnic groups as police officers.

## The Myth of the Watchman

With their argument that the nineteenth century police enjoyed political legitimacy, Wilson, Kelling and Moore have resurrected in slightly different garb the old myth of the friendly cop on the beat. They offer this older "watchman" style of policing as a viable model for contemporary policing. Quite apart from the broader question of political legitimacy, their argument turns on the issue of on-the-street police behavior.

Historians have not yet reconstructed a full picture of police behavior in the nineteenth century. At best, historians can make inferences about this behavior from surviving records. None of the historical accounts published to date presents a picture of policing that could be regarded as a viable model for the present.

What do we know about routine policing in the days before the patrol car? There is general agreement that officers did not necessarily do much work at all. Given the primitive state of communications technology, patrol officers were almost completely on their own and able to avoid effective supervision (Rubinstein 1974). Evidence suggests that evasion of duty was commonplace. We also know that corruption was the norm. Mark Haller (1976) suggests that corruption was possibly the primary objective of all of municipal government, not just the police department.

Wilbur Miller (1977), meanwhile, places the matter of police brutality in a new and convincing light. His argument that brutality was a response to the refusal of citizens to grant the police legitimacy speaks directly to the point raised by Wilson, Kelling and Moore.

Recently some historians have attempted to draw a more systematic picture of police law enforcement activities. The most convincing picture is drawn by Lawrence Friedman and Robert Percival (1981) in their study of the Oakland police between 1870 and 1910. They characterize police arrest patterns as a giant trawling operation. The typical arrestee was a white, working class adult male who was drunk and was arrested for intoxication, disturbing the peace, or some related offense. But there was nothing systematic about police operations. The people swept up into their net were simply unlucky—there was no reason why they should have been arrested rather than others whose behavior was essentially the same. Nor was it apparent, in Friedman's and Percival's view, that the police singled out any particular categories of people for especially systematic harassment.

The argument offered by Wilson, Kelling and Moore turns in part on the question of purpose: what the police saw themselves doing. Historians have established that police officers had a few purposes. The first was to get and hold the job. The second was to exploit the possibilities for graft that the job offered. A third was to do as little actual patrol work as possible. A fourth involved surviving on the street, which meant establishing and maintaining authority in the face of hostility and overt challenges to that authority. Finally, officers apparently felt obliged to go through the motions of "real" police work by arresting occasional miscreants.

We do not find in this picture any conscious purpose of fighting crime or serving neighborhood needs. That is precisely the point made by Progressive era reformers when they indicted the police for inefficiency. Wilson, Kelling and Moore have no grounds for offering this as a viable model for contemporary policing. Chief McNamara is right: the good old days were not that good.

The watchman style of policing described by Wilson, Kelling and Moore can also be challenged from a completely different perspective. The idea that the police served the needs of local neighborhoods and thereby enjoyed political legitimacy is based on a highly romanticized view of nineteenth century neighborhood life. Urban neighborhoods were not stable and homogeneous little villages nestled in the city. They were heterogeneous, and the rate of geographic mobility was even higher than contemporary rates. Albert Reiss (1971:209–210) in *Police and the Public* critiques recent "community control" proposals on these very grounds: they are based on the erroneous impression that neighborhoods are stable, homogeneous and relatively well-defined.

## Summary and Conclusions

In "Broken Windows," James Q. Wilson and George Kelling offer a provocative proposal for reorienting police patrol. Their argument is based primarily on an historical analysis of American policing. They propose a return to a watchman style of policing, which they claim existed before the advent of crime control oriented policing in the 1930s. This historical analysis is further developed in a subsequent article by Kelling and Moore (1983).

In this article we have examined the historical analysis used by these three authors. We find it flawed on several fundamental points.

First, the depersonalization of American policing from the 1930s onward has been greatly exaggerated. While the patrol car did isolate the police in some respects, the telephone brought about a more intimate form of contact between police and citizen by allowing the police officer to enter private residences and involving them in private disputes and problems.

Second, the crime control orientation of the police has been greatly exaggerated. Crime control is largely a matter of police rhetoric and self-image. Day-to-day policing is, on the other hand, primarily a matter of peacekeeping.

Third, there is no historical evidence to support the contention that the police formerly enjoyed substantial political legitimacy. To the contrary, all the evidence suggests that the legitimacy of the police was one of the major political controversies throughout the nineteenth century and well into the twentieth.

Fourth, the watchman style of policing referred to by Wilson, Kelling and Moore is just as inefficient and corrupt as the reformers accuse it of being. It does not involve any conscious purpose to serve neighborhood needs and hardly serves as a model for revitalized contemporary policing.

Where does this leave us? We should not throw the proverbial baby out with the bath water. The fact that Wilson and Kelling construct their "Broken Windows" thesis on a false and heavily romanticized view of the past does not by itself invalidate their concept of a revitalized police patrol. They correctly interpret the lessons of recent police research. Suppression of crime is a will-of-the-wisp which the police should no longer pursue. Enhancement of public feelings of safety, however, does appear to be within the grasp of the police. A new form of policing based on the apparent lessons of the Newark Foot Patrol Experiment, the failures of team policing experiments, and the irrelevance of most official police-community relations programs seems to be a goal that is both worth pursuing and feasible.

Our main point here is simply that such a revitalized form of policing would represent something entirely new in the history of the American police. There is no older tradition worthy of restoration. A revitalized, community-oriented policing would have to be developed slowly and painfully.

There should be no mistake about the difficulty of such a task. Among other things, recent research on the police clearly demonstrates the enormous difficulty in changing either police officer behavior and/or the structure and process of police organization. Yet at the same time, the history reviewed here does suggest that fundamental long-term changes in policing are indeed possible. Change is a constant; shaping that change in a positive way is the challenge.

## Footnotes

[1] James Fyfe argues that prosecutorial and judicial indifference to minor "quality of life" offenses is also responsible for neighborhood deterioration and that the police should not be singled out as the major culprits. By implication, he suggests that reorienting the police role would be futile without simultaneously reorienting the priorities of prosecutors and judges. Personal correspondence, James Fyfe to Walker.

[2] Lawrence W. Sherman accepts this view and dissents from the argument advanced in this article. Personal correspondence, Lawrence W. Sherman to Walker.

[3] The debate is conducted largely on the basis of circumstantial evidence. Sherman, for example, believes that literary evidence is a reliable guide to past police practices and cites *A Tree Grows in Brooklyn* as one useful example. Personal correspondence, Sherman to Walker.

## References

Bayley, D. and Mendelsohn, H. (1969) *Minorities and the Police*. New York: The Free Press.

Fogelson, R. (1977) *Big City Police*. Cambridge: Harvard University Press.

Friedman, L. M. and Percival, R. V. (1981) *The Roots of Justice*. Chapel Hill: University of North Carolina Press.

Gay, W. (1977) *Improving Patrol Productivity*, Vol. I, Routine Patrol. Washington, DC: Government Printing Office.

Goldstein, H. (1977) *Policing a Free Society*. Cambridge: Ballinger.

Gusfield, J. (1963) *Symbolic Crusade: Status Politics and the American Temperance Movement*. Urbana: University of Illinois Press.

Haller, M. (1976) "Historical Roots of Police Behavior: Chicago, 1890–1925." *Law and Society Review* 10 (Winter): 303–24.

Kahn, R. (1975) "Urban Reform and Police Accountability in New York City, 1950–1974." In *Urban Problems and Public Policy*, edited by R. L. Lineberry and L. H. Masotti. Lexington: Lexington Books.

McNamara, J. D. (1982) "Dangerous Nostalgia for the Cop on the Beat." *San Jose Mercury-News*, May 2.

Manning, P. K. (1977) *Police Work*. Cambridge: MIT Press.

Miller, W. (1977) *Cops and Bobbies*. Chicago: University of Chicago Press.

Monkkonen, E. (1981) *Police in Urban America, 1860–1920*. Cambridge: Cambridge University Press.

Moore, M. H. and Kelling, G. L. (1983) "To Serve and Protect: Learning from Police History." *The Public Interest* 70:49–65.

Police Executive Research Forum (1981) *Survey of Police Operational and Administrative Practices—1981*. Washington, DC: Police Executive Research Forum.

Police Foundation (1981) *The Newark Foot Patrol Experiment*. Washington, DC: The Police Foundation.

Reiss, A. (1971) *The Police and the Public*. New Haven: Yale University Press.

Rubinstein, J. (1974) *City Police*. New York: Ballantine Books.

Schwartz, A. I. and Clarren, S. N. (1977) *The Cincinnati Team Policing Experiment*. Washington, DC: The Police Foundation.

Sherman, L. W. (1973) *Team Policing: Seven Case Studies.* Washington, DC: The Police Foundation.

Silver, A. (1967) "The Demand for Order in Civil Society." In *The Police: Six Sociological Essays,* ed. by David J. Bordua. New York: John Wiley.

Stinchcombe, A. (1963) "Institutions of Privacy in the Determination of Police Administrative Practice." *American Journal of Sociology* 69 (September): 150–60.

U.S. Department of Justice (1977) *Neighborhood Team Policing.* Washington, DC: Government Printing Office.

Walker, S. (1983) *The Police in America: An Introduction.* New York: McGraw-Hill.

____. (1977) *A Critical History of Police Reform: The Emergence of Professionalization.* Lexington: Lexington Books.

Wilson, J. Q. and Kelling, G. L. (1982) "Broken Windows: Police and Neighborhood Safety." *Atlantic Monthly* 249 (March): 29–38.

Wilson, O. W. and McLaren, R. C. (1977) *Police Administration* (4th. ed.). New York: McGraw-Hill.

Zimbardo, P. G. (1969) "The Human Choice: Individuation, Reason, and Order versus Deindividuation, Impulse, and Chaos." In *Nebraska Symposium on Motivation,* edited by W. J. Arnold and D. Levine. Lincoln: University of Nebraska Press.

# 26

# Community Policing
## Elements and Effects

*Gary W. Cordner*

In less than two decades, community policing has evolved from a few small foot patrol studies to the preeminent reform agenda of modern policing. With roots in such earlier developments as police-community relations, team policing, crime prevention, and the rediscovery of foot patrol, community policing has become, in the 1990s, the dominant strategy of policing—so much so that the 100,000 new police officers funded by the 1994 Crime Bill must be engaged, by law, in community policing.

Despite all this activity, four complicating factors have made it extremely difficult to determine the effectiveness of community policing:

- *Programmatic complexity*—There exists no single definition of community policing nor any universal set of program elements. Police agencies around the country (and around the world) have implemented a wide array of organizational and operational innovations under the label "community policing." Because community policing is not one consistent "thing," it is difficult to say whether "it" works.

- *Multiple effects*—The number of intended and unintended effects that might accrue to community policing is considerable. Community policing might affect crime, fear of crime, disorder, community relations, and/or police officer attitudes, to mention just a few plausible impacts. The reality of these multiple effects, as opposed to a single bottom-line criterion, severely reduces the likelihood of a simple yes or no answer to the question "Does community policing work?"

- *Variation in program scope*—The scope of community policing projects has varied from single-officer assignments to department-wide efforts. Some of the most positive results have come from

This chapter is a substantial revision (revised especially for *Critical Issues in Policing*, 3/E) of an earlier article in *Police Forum* (July 1995).

projects that involved only a few specialist officers, small special units, or narrowly defined target areas. The generalizability of these positive results to full-scale department-wide implementation is problematic.

- *Research design limitations*—Despite heroic efforts by police officials and researchers, most community policing studies have had serious research design limitations. These include lack of control groups, failure to randomize treatments, and a tendency to measure only short-term effects. Consequently, the findings of many community policing studies do not have as much credibility as we might hope.

These complicating factors are offered not as excuses but rather to sensitize us to the very real difficulty of producing reliable knowledge about the effects of community policing. Additionally, they identify priority issues that need to be addressed in order to substantially improve what we know about the effectiveness of community policing.

# What is Community Policing?

Community policing remains many things to many people. A common refrain among proponents is "Community policing is a philosophy, not a program." An equally common refrain among police officers is "Just tell me exactly what you want me to do differently." Some critics, echoing concerns similar to those expressed by police officers, argue that if community policing is nothing more than a philosophy, it is merely an empty shell (Goldstein, 1987).

It would be easy to list dozens of common characteristics of community policing, starting with foot patrol and mountain bikes and ending with the police as organizers of, and advocates for, the poor and dispossessed. Instead, it may be more helpful to identify four major dimensions of community policing and some of the most common elements within each. These four dimensions of community policing are:

- The Philosophical Dimension
- The Strategic Dimension
- The Tactical Dimension
- The Organizational Dimension

## The Philosophical Dimension

Many of its most thoughtful and forceful advocates emphasize that community policing is a new philosophy of policing, perhaps constituting even a paradigm shift away from professional-model policing. The philosophical dimension includes the central ideas and beliefs underlying community policing. Three of the most important of these are citizen input, broad function, and personalized service.

*Citizen Input.* Community policing takes the view that, in a free society, citizens should have open access to police organizations and input to police policies and decisions. Access and input through elected officials is considered necessary but not sufficient. Individual neighborhoods and communities should have the opportunity to influence how they are policed and legitimate interest groups in the community should be able to discuss their views and concerns directly with police officials. Police departments, like other agencies of government, should be responsive and accountable.

Mechanisms for achieving greater citizen input are varied. Some police agencies use systematic and periodic community surveys to elicit citizen input (Bureau of Justice Assistance, 1994a). Others rely on open forums, town meetings, radio and television call-in programs, and similar methods open to all residents. Some police officials meet regularly with citizen advisory boards, ministry alliances, minority group representatives, business leaders, and other formal groups. These techniques have been used by police chief executives, district commanders, and ordinary patrol officers; they can be focused as widely as the entire jurisdiction or as narrowly as a beat or a single neighborhood.

The techniques used to achieve citizen input should be less important than the end result. Community policing emphasizes that police departments should seek and carefully consider citizen input when making policies and decisions that affect the community. Any other alternative would be unthinkable in an agency that is part of a government "of the people, for the people, and by the people."

*Broad Police Function.* Community policing embraces a broad view of the police function rather than a narrow focus on crime fighting or law enforcement (Kelling and Moore, 1988). Historical evidence is often cited to show that the police function was originally quite broad and varied and that it only narrowed in recent decades, perhaps due to the influence of the professional model and popular media representations of police work. Social science data is also frequently cited to show that police officers actually spend relatively little of their time dealing with serious offenders or investigating violent crimes.

This broader view of the police function recognizes the kinds of non-enforcement tasks that police already perform and seeks to give them greater status and legitimacy. These include order maintenance, social service, and general assistance duties. They may also include greater responsibilities in protecting and enhancing "the lives of those who are most vulnerable—juveniles, the elderly, minorities, the poor, the disabled, the homeless" (Trojanowicz and Bucqueroux, 1990: xiv). In the bigger picture, the police mission is seen to include resolving conflict, helping victims, preventing accidents, solving problems, and reducing fear as well as reducing crime through apprehension and enforcement.

*Personal Service.* Community policing supports tailored policing based on local norms and values and individual needs. An argument is made that the criminal law is a very blunt instrument and that police officers inevitably exercise wide discretion when making decisions. Presently, individual officers make arrests and other decisions based on a combination of legal, bureaucratic, and idiosyncratic criteria, while the police department maintains the myth of full or at least uniform enforcement (Goldstein, 1977). Under community policing, officers are asked to consider the "will of the community" when deciding which laws to enforce under what circumstances, and police executives are asked to tolerate and even encourage such differential and personalized policing.

Such differential or tailored policing primarily affects police handling of minor criminal offenses, local ordinance violations, public disorder, and service issues. Some kinds of behavior proscribed by state and local law, and some levels of noise and disorder, may be seen as less bothersome in some neighborhoods than in others. Similarly, some police methods, including such aggressive tactics as roadblocks as well as more prevention-oriented programs such as landlord training, may coincide with norms and values in some neighborhoods but not others.

Even the strongest advocates of community policing recognize that a balance must be reached between differential neighborhood-level policing and uniform jurisdiction-wide policing. Striking a healthy and satisfactory balance between competing interests has always been one of the central concerns of policing and police administration. Community policing simply argues that neighborhood-level norms and values should be added to the mix of legal, professional, and organizational considerations that influences decision-making about policies, programs, and resources at the executive level as well as enforcement-level decisions on the street.

This characteristic of community policing is also aimed at overcoming one of the most common complaints that the public has about government employees in general, including police officers—that they do not seem to care and that they are more interested in "going by the book" than in providing quality, personalized service. Many citizens seem to resent being subjected to "stranger policing" and would rather deal with officers who know them, and whom they know. Of course, not every police-citizen encounter can be amicable and friendly. But officers who generally deal with citizens in a friendly, open, and personal manner may be more likely to generate trust and confidence than officers who operate in a narrow, aloof, and/or bureaucratic manner.

## The Strategic Dimension

The strategic dimension of community policing includes the key operational concepts that translate philosophy into action. These strategic concepts are the links between the broad ideas and beliefs that underlie community policing and the specific programs and practices by which it is implemented. They assure that agency policies, priorities, and resource allocation are consistent with a community-oriented philosophy. Three strategic elements of community policing are re-oriented operations, geographic focus, and prevention emphasis.

*Re-oriented Operations.* Community policing recommends less reliance on the patrol car and more emphasis on face-to-face interactions. One objective is to replace ineffective or isolating operational practices (e.g., motorized patrol and rapid response to low priority calls) with more effective and more interactive practices. A related objective is to find ways of performing necessary traditional functions (e.g., handling emergency calls and conducting follow-up investigations) more efficiently, in order to save time and resources that can then be devoted to more community-oriented activities.

Many police departments today have increased their use of foot patrol, directed patrol, door-to-door policing, and other alternatives to traditional motorized patrol (Cordner and Trojanowicz, 1992). Generally, these alternatives seek more targeted tactical effectiveness, more attention to minor offenses and "incivilities," a greater "felt presence" of police, and/or more police-citizen contact. Other police departments have simply reduced their commitment to any form of continuous patrolling, preferring instead to have their patrol officers engage in problem solving, crime prevention, and similar activities when not handling calls and emergencies.

Many police agencies have also adopted differential responses to calls for service (McEwen, Connors, and Cohen, 1986). Rather than attempting to immediately dispatch a sworn officer in response to each and every notification of a crime, disturbance, or other situation, these departments vary their responses depending upon the circumstances. Some crime reports may be taken over the telephone, some service requests may be referred to other government agencies, and some sworn officer responses may be delayed. A particularly interesting alternative is to ask complainants to go in person to a nearby police mini-station or storefront office, where an officer, a civilian employee, or even a volunteer takes a report or provides other in-person assistance. Use of differential responses helps departments cope with the sometimes overwhelming burden of 911 calls and frees up patrol officer time for other activities, such as patrolling, problem solving, and crime prevention.

Traditional criminal investigation has also been reexamined in recent years (Eck, 1992). Some departments have de-specialized the activity, reducing the size of the detective unit and making patrol officers more responsible for follow-up investigations. Many have also eliminated the practice of conducting an extensive follow-up investigation of every reported crime, focusing instead on the more serious offenses and on more "solvable" cases. Investigative attention has also been expanded to include a focus on offenders as well as on offenses, especially in the form of repeat offender units that target high-frequency serious offenders. A few departments have taken the additional step of trying to get detectives to expand their case-by-case orientation to include problem solving and crime prevention. In this approach, a burglary detective would be as concerned with reducing burglaries through problem solving and crime prevention as s/he was with solving particular burglary cases.

Not all contemporary alternatives to motorized patrol, rapid response, and criminal investigation are closely allied with community policing. Those specific operational alternatives, and those uses of the freed-up time of patrol officers and detectives, that are consistent with the philosophical and strategic foundations of community policing can be distinguished from those that conform to other philosophies and strategies of policing (Moore and Trojanowicz, 1988).

*Geographic Focus.* Community policing strategy emphasizes the geographic basis of assignment and responsibility by shifting the fundamental unit of patrol accountability from time of day to place. That is, rather than holding patrol officers, supervisors, and shift commanders responsible for wide areas but only during their eight or ten hour shifts, community policing seeks to establish 24-hour responsibility for smaller areas.

Of course, no single officer works 24 hours a day, seven days a week, week in and week out. Community policing usually deals with this limitation in one or a combination of three ways: (1) community police officers assigned to neighborhoods may be specialists, with most call-handling relegated to a more traditional patrol unit; (2) each individual patrol officer may be held responsible for long-term problem solving in an assigned neighborhood, even though s/he handles calls in a much larger area and, of necessity, many of the calls in the assigned area are handled by other officers; or (3) small teams of officers share both call-handling and problem solving responsibility in a beat-sized area.

A key ingredient of this geographic focus, however it is implemented, is permanency of assignment. Community policing recommends that patrol officers be assigned to the same areas for extended periods of time, to increase their familiarity with the community and the community's familiarity with them. Ideally, this familiarity will build trust, confidence, and cooperation on both sides of the police-citizen interaction. Also, officers will simply become more knowledgeable about the community and its residents, aiding early intervention and timely problem identification and avoiding conflict based on misperception or misunderstanding.

It is important to recognize that most police departments have long used geography as the basis for daily patrol assignment. Many of these departments, however, assign patrol officers to different beats from one day to the next, creating little continuity or permanency. Moreover, even in police agencies with fairly steady beat assignments, patrol officers are only held accountable for handling their calls and maintaining order (keeping things quiet) *during their shift*. The citizen's question, "Who in the police department is responsible for *my area*, my neighborhood?" can then only truthfully be answered "the chief" or, in large departments, "the precinct commander." Neither patrol officers nor the two or three levels of management above them can be held accountable for dealing with long-term problems in specific locations anywhere in the entire community. Thus, a crucial component of community policing strategy is to create some degree of geographic accountability at all levels in the police organization, but particularly at the level of the patrol officer who delivers basic police services and is in a position to identify and solve neighborhood problems.

***Prevention Emphasis.*** Community policing strategy also emphasizes a more proactive and preventive orientation, in contrast to the reactive focus that has characterized much of policing under the professional model. This proactive, preventive orientation takes several forms. One is simply to encourage better use of police officers' time. In many police departments, patrol officers' time not committed to handling calls is either spent simply waiting for the next call or randomly driving around. Under community policing, this substantial resource of free patrol time is devoted to directed enforcement activities, specific crime prevention efforts, problem solving, community engagement, citizen interaction, or similar kinds of activities.

Another aspect of the preventive focus overlaps with the substantive orientation of community policing and problem-oriented operations. Officers are encouraged to look beyond the individual incidents that they encounter as calls for service and reported crimes in order to discover underlying problems and conditions (Eck and Spelman, 1987). If they can discover such underlying conditions and do something to improve them, officers can prevent the future recurrence of incidents and calls. While immediate response to in-progress emergencies and after-the-fact investigation of crimes will always remain important functions of policing, community policing seeks to elevate before-the-fact prevention and problem-solving to comparable status.

Closely related to this line of thinking, but deserving of specific mention, is the desire to enhance the status of crime prevention within police organizations. Most police departments devote the vast majority of their personnel to patrol and investigations, primarily for the purposes of rapid response and follow-up investigation *after* something has happened. Granted, some prevention of crime through the visibility, omnipresence, and deterrence created by patrolling, rapid response, and investigating is expected, but the weight of research over the past two decades has greatly diminished these expectations (Kelling, Pate, Dieckman, and Brown, 1974; Greenwood and Petersilia, 1975; Spelman and Brown, 1982). Despite these lowered expectations, however, police departments still typically devote only a few officers specifically to crime prevention programming, and do little to encourage patrol officers to engage in any kinds of crime prevention activity beyond routine riding around.

Moreover, within both informal and formal police cultures, crime solving and criminal apprehension are usually more highly valued than crime prevention. An individual officer is more likely to be commended for arresting a bank robber than for initiating actions that prevent such robberies. Detectives usually enjoy higher status than uniformed officers (especially in the eyes of the public), whereas, within many police agencies, crime prevention officers are seen as public relations functionaries, kiddie cops, or worse. To many police officers, crime prevention work is simply not real police work.

The preeminence of reactive crime fighting within police and popular cultures is understandable, given the dramatic nature of emergencies, crimes, and investigations. Much of police work is about responding to trouble and fixing it, about the contest between good and evil. Responding to emergencies and fighting crime have heroic elements that naturally appeal to both police officers and citizens. Given the choice, though, almost all citizens would prefer not being victimized in the first place to being dramatically rescued, to having the police successfully track down their assailant, or to having the police recover their stolen property. Most citizens would agree that "an ounce of prevention is worth a pound of cure." This is not to suggest that police should turn their backs on reactive handling of crimes and emergencies, but only that before-the-fact prevention should be given greater consideration.

A final element of community policing's preventive focus takes more of a social welfare orientation, particularly toward juveniles. An argument is made that police officers, by serving as mentors and role models, and by providing educational, recreational, and even counseling services, can affect peoples' behavior in positive ways that ultimately lead to reductions in crime and disorder. In essence, police are asked to support and augment the efforts of families, churches, schools, and other social service agencies. This kind of police activity is seen as particularly necessary by some in order to offset the deficiencies and correct the failures of these other social institutions in modern America.

## The Tactical Dimension

The tactical dimension of community policing ultimately translates ideas, philosophies, and strategies into concrete programs, practices, and behaviors. Even those who insist that "community policing is a philosophy, not a program" must concede that unless community policing eventually leads to some action, some new or different behavior, it is all rhetoric and no reality (Greene and Mastrofski, 1988). Indeed, many commentators have taken the view that community policing is little more than a new police marketing strategy that has left the core elements of the police role untouched (see, e.g., Klockars, 1988; Manning, 1988; Weatheritt, 1988). Three of the most important tactical elements of community policing are positive interaction, partnerships, and problem solving.

*Positive Interaction.* Policing inevitably involves some negative contacts between officers and citizens—arrests, tickets, stops for suspicion, orders to desist in disruptive behavior, inability to make things much better for victims, etc. Community policing recognizes this fact and recommends that officers offset it as much as they can by engaging in positive interactions whenever possible. Positive interactions have further benefits as well, of course: they generally build familiarity, trust, and confidence on both sides;

they remind officers that most citizens respect and support them; they make the officer more knowledgeable about people and conditions in the beat; they provide specific information for criminal investigations and problem solving; and they break up the monotony of motorized patrol.

Many opportunities for positive interaction arise in the course of call handling. Too many officers rush to clear their calls, however, often in response to workload concerns and pressure from their superiors, their peers, and dispatchers. As a result, they typically do a mediocre job of handling the immediate incident and make little or no attempt to identify underlying conditions, secure additional information, or create satisfied customers. The prime directive seems to be to do as little as possible in order to clear the call quickly and get back in the car and on the radio, ready to go and do little or nothing at the next call. Getting there rapidly and then clearing promptly take precedence over actually delivering much service or accomplishing anything. Community policing suggests, instead, that officers should look at calls as opportunities for positive interaction, quality service, and problem identification.

Even more opportunities for positive interaction can be seized during routine patrol, if officers are willing to exit their vehicles and take some initiative. Officers can go in and out of stores, in and out of schools, talk to people on the street, knock on doors, etc. They can take the initiative to talk not only with shopkeepers and their customers but also with teenagers, apartment dwellers, tavern patrons, and anybody else they run across in public spaces or who are approachable in private places. Police should insert themselves wherever people are and should talk to those people, not just watch them.

***Partnerships.*** Participation of the community in its own protection is one of the central elements of community policing (Bureau of Justice Assistance, 1994c). This participation can run the gamut from watching neighbors' homes to reporting drug dealers to patrolling the streets. It can involve participation in problem identification and problem solving efforts, in crime prevention programs, in neighborhood revitalization, and in youth-oriented educational and recreational programs. Citizens may act individually or in groups, they may collaborate with the police, and they may even join the police department by donating their time as police department volunteers, reserves, or auxiliaries.

Under community policing, police agencies are expected not only to cooperate with citizens and communities but to actively solicit input and participation (Bureau of Justice Assistance, 1994b). The exact nature of this participation can and should vary from community to community and from situation to situation, in keeping with the problem-oriented approach. As a general rule, though, police should avoid claiming that they alone can handle crime, drug, or disorder problems, and they should encourage individual citizens and community groups to shoulder some responsibility for dealing with such problems.

Police have sometimes found it necessary to engage in community organizing as a means of accomplishing any degree of citizen participation in problem solving or crime prevention. In disorganized and transient neighborhoods, residents are often so distressed, fearful, and suspicious of each other (or just so unfamiliar with their neighbors) that police have literally had to set about creating a sense of community where none previously existed. As difficult as this kind of community organizing can be, and as far from the conventional police role as this may seem, these are often the very communities that most need both enhanced police protection and a greater degree of citizen involvement in crime prevention, order maintenance, and general watchfulness over public spaces.

One vexing aspect of community organizing and community engagement results from the pluralistic nature of our society. Differing and often conflicting interests are found in many communities, and they are sometimes represented by competing interest groups. Thus, the elders in a community may want the police to crack down on juveniles, while the youths themselves complain of few opportunities for recreation or entertainment. Tenants may seek police help in organizing a rent strike, while landlords want police assistance in screening or managing the same tenants. Finding common interests around which to rally entire communities, or just identifying common interests on which to base police practices, can be very challenging and, at times, impossible.

It is important to recognize that this inherent feature of pluralistic communities does not arise because of community policing. Police have long been caught in the middle between the interests of adults and juveniles, landlords and tenants, and similar groups. Sometimes the law has provided a convenient reference point for handling such conflicts, but just as often police have had to mediate, arbitrate, or just take the side of the party with the best case. Moreover, when the law has offered a solution, it has frequently been a temporary or unpopular one, and one that still resulted in the police taking sides, protestations of "we're just enforcing the law" notwithstanding.

Fortunately, nearly all citizens want to be safe from violence, want their property protected, and want some level of orderliness in their neighborhoods. Officers can usually find enough consensus in communities upon which to base cooperative efforts aimed at improving safety and public order. Sometimes, apparently deep conflicts between individuals or groups recede when attention is focused on how best to solve specific neighborhood problems. It would be naive to expect overwhelming community consensus in every situation, but it is equally mistaken to think that conflict is so endemic that widespread community support and participation cannot be achieved in many circumstances.

**Problem Solving.** Supporters of community policing are convinced that the very nature of police work must be altered from its present incident-by-incident, case-by-case orientation to one that is more problem-oriented (Goldstein, 1990). Certainly, incidents must still be handled and cases must still be investigated. Whenever possible, however, attention should be directed toward underlying problems and conditions. Following the medical analogy, policing should address causes as well as symptoms, and should adopt the epidemiological public health approach as much as the individual doctor's clinical approach.

This problem solving approach should be characterized by several important features: (1) it should be the standard operating method of policing, not an occasional special project; (2) it should be practiced by personnel throughout the ranks, not just by specialists or managers; (3) it should be empirical, in the sense that decisions are made on the basis of information that is gathered systematically; (4) it should involve, whenever possible, collaboration between police and other agencies and institutions; and (5) it should incorporate, whenever possible, community input and participation, so that it is the community's problems that are addressed (not just the police department's) and so that the community shares in the responsibility for its own protection.

The problem solving process consists of four steps: (1) careful identification of the problem; (2) careful analysis of the problem; (3) a search for alternative solutions to the problem; and (4) implementation and assessment of a response to the problem. Community input can be incorporated within any or all of the steps in the process. Identification, analysis, and assessment should rely on information from multiple sources. A variety of alternative solutions should be considered, including, but not limited to, traditional enforcement methods. Typically, the most effective solutions are those that combine several different responses, including some that draw on more than just the police department's authority and resources.

A crucial characteristic of the problem-oriented approach is that it seeks tailored solutions to specific community problems. Arrests and law enforcement are *not* abandoned—rather, an effort is made in each situation to determine which alternative responses best fit the problem. Use of the criminal law is always considered, as are civil law enforcement, mediation, community mobilization, referral, collaboration, alteration of the physical environment, public education, and a host of other possibilities. The common sense notion of choosing the tool that best fits the problem, instead of simply grabbing the most convenient or familiar tool in the tool box, lies close to the heart of the problem solving method.

## The Organizational Dimension

It is important to recognize an organizational dimension that surrounds community policing and greatly affects its implementation. In order to support and facilitate community policing, police departments often consider a variety of changes in organization, administration, management, and supervision. The elements of the organizational dimension are not really part of community policing *per se*, but they are frequently crucial to its successful implementation. Three important organizational elements of COP are structure, management, and information.

**Structure.** Advocates of community policing often look at various ways of restructuring police agencies in order to facilitate and support implementation of the philosophical, strategic, and tactical elements described above. Any organization's structure should correspond with its mission and the nature of the work performed by its members. Some aspects of traditional police organization structure seem more suited to routine, bureaucratic work than to the discretion and creativity required for COP.

The types of restructuring often associated with community policing include:

- *Decentralization*—Authority and responsibility can sometimes be delegated more widely so that commanders, supervisors, and officers can act more independently and be more responsive.
- *Flattening*—The number of layers of hierarchy in the police organization can sometimes be reduced in order to improve communications and reduce waste, rigidity and bureaucracy.
- *De-specialization*—The number of specialized units and personnel can sometimes be reduced, with more resources devoted to the direct delivery of police services (including COP) to the general public.
- *Teams*—Efficiency and effectiveness can sometimes be improved by getting employees working together as teams to perform work, solve problems, or look for ways of improving quality.
- *Civilianization*—Positions currently held by sworn personnel can sometimes be reclassified or redesigned for non-sworn personnel, allowing both cost savings and better utilization of sworn personnel.

**Management.** Community policing is often associated with styles of leadership, management, and supervision that give more emphasis to organizational culture and values and less emphasis to written rules and formal discipline. The general argument is that when employees are guided by a set of officially sanctioned values they will usually make good decisions and take appropriate actions. Although many formal rules will still probably be necessary, managers will need to resort to them much less often in order to maintain control over subordinates.

Management practices consistent with this emphasis on organizational culture and values include:

- *Mission*—Agencies should develop concise statements of their mission and values and use them consistently in making decisions, guiding employees, and training new recruits.
- *Strategic Planning*—Agencies should engage in continuous strategic planning aimed at ensuring that resources and energy are focused on mission accomplishment and adherence to core values; otherwise,

organizations tend to get off track, confused about their mission and about what really matters.

- *Coaching*—Supervisors should coach and guide their subordinates more, instead of restricting their roles to review of paperwork and enforcement of rules and regulations.
- *Mentoring*—Young employees need mentoring from managers, supervisors, and/or peers—not just to learn how to do the job right but also to learn what constitutes the right job; in other words, to learn about ethics and values and what it means to be a good police officer.
- *Empowerment*—Under COP, employees are encouraged to be risk-takers who demonstrate imagination and creativity in their work—this kind of empowerment can only succeed, however, when employees are thoroughly familiar with the organization's core values and firmly committed to them.
- *Selective Discipline*—In their disciplinary processes, agencies should make distinctions between intentional and unintentional errors made by employees and between employee actions that violate core values versus those that merely violate technical rules.

**Information.** Doing community policing and managing it effectively require certain types of information that have not traditionally been available in all police departments. In the never-ending quality vs. quantity debate, for example, community policing tends to emphasize quality. This emphasis on quality shows up in many areas: avoidance of traditional bean-counting (arrests, tickets) to measure success, more concern for how well calls are handled than merely for how quickly they are handled, etc. Also, the geographic focus of community policing increases the need for detailed information based on neighborhoods as the unit of analysis. The emphasis on problem solving highlights the need for information systems that aid in identifying and analyzing community-level problems. And so on.

Several aspects of police administration under community policing that have implications for information are:

- *Performance Appraisal*—Individual officers can be evaluated on the quality of their community policing and problem solving activities, and perhaps on results achieved, instead of on traditional performance indicators (tickets, arrests, calls handled, etc.).
- *Program Evaluation*—Police programs and strategies can be evaluated more on the basis of their effectiveness (outcomes, results, quality) than just on their efficiency (effort, outputs, quantity).
- *Departmental Assessment*—The police agency's overall performance can be measured and assessed on the basis of a wide variety of indicators (including customer satisfaction, fear levels, problem solving, etc.) instead of a narrow band of traditional indicators (reported crime, response time, etc.).

- *Information Systems*—An agency's information systems need to collect and produce information on the whole range of the police function, not just on enforcement and call-handling activities, in order to support more quality-oriented appraisal, evaluation, and assessment efforts.
- *Crime Analysis*—Individual officers need more timely and complete crime analysis information pertaining to their specific geographic areas of responsibility to facilitate problem identification, analysis, fear reduction, etc.
- *Geographic Information Systems* (GIS)—Sophisticated and user-friendly computerized mapping software available today makes it possible for officers and citizens to obtain customized maps that graphically identify "hot spots" and help them picture the geographic locations and distribution of crime and related problems.

## What Do We Know?

Despite the programmatic and evaluation complexities discussed earlier, we do have a substantial amount of information from empirical studies of community policing. Table 1 summarizes the "preponderance of the evidence" on the effects of community policing based on a review of over 60 such studies (recent reviews have also been completed by Normandeau, 1993; Bennett, 1994; Leighton, 1994; and Skogan, 1994).

**Table 1**
**Preponderance of the Evidence on Community Policing**

| Effects/ Dimensions | Crime | Fear | Disorder | Calls for Service | Community Relations | Police Officer Attitudes | Police Officer Behavior |
|---|---|---|---|---|---|---|---|
| Philosophical: Citizen Input Broad Police Function Personal Service | | | | | | | |
| Strategic: Re-oriented Operations Geographic Focus Preventive Emphasis | | | | | | | |
| Tactical: Positive Interaction Partnerships Problem Solving | MIX | MIX | POS | MIX | POS | POS | MIX |
| Organizational: Structure Management Information | | | | | | POS | |

POS=positive effects (beneficial effects)
NEG=negative effects
MIX=mixed effects
blank=unknown (completely or substantially untested)

The first thing to note in Table 1 is that almost three-fourths of the 28 cells are blank, indicating that the effects are unknown (completely or substantially untested). Nearly all of the evaluations conducted to-date have focused on the tactical dimension of community policing, leaving us with little or no information on the effects of philosophical, strategic, and organizational changes. This gap in community policing research is undoubtedly caused by a combination of two factors: (1) most community policing efforts, at least until recently, have been limited programmatic and street-level initiatives rather than large-scale strategic or organizational-change initiatives; and (2) evaluation of narrowly-focused programmatic initiatives is much easier and more feasible than evaluation of philosophical and organization-wide change.

The most useful way to summarize the evidence on the effects of community policing is to scan the tactical row of Table 1.

## Crime

The evidence is mixed. Only a few studies have used experimental designs and victimization surveys to test the effects of community policing on crime; many others have relied on simple before-after comparisons of reported crime or single-item victimization questions drawn from community surveys. Overall, a slight majority of the studies have detected crime decreases, giving reason for optimism, but evaluation design limitations prevent us from drawing any authoritative conclusions.

## Fear of Crime

Again the evidence is mixed, but it leans more heavily in the positive direction. A number of studies have employed community surveys to make before-after comparisons of fear and related perceptions, some with experimental designs. Fear has typically been measured using a variety of survey items, lending the studies more credibility. The now widely-accepted view that community policing helps reduce levels of fear of crime and increases perceptions of safety seems reasonably well-founded, although some efforts have failed to accomplish fear reductions.

## Disorder

The impact of community policing on disorder, minor crime, incivilities, and signs of crime has not been subjected to careful testing as frequently as its impact on crime and fear. The available evidence suggests, though, that community policing, and especially foot patrol and problem solving, helps reduce levels of disorder, lending partial support to the "broken windows" thesis (Wilson and Kelling, 1982).

## Calls for Service

Community policing might reduce calls for service in several ways: problem solving might address underlying issues that generate calls; collaboration might increase call referrals to other government agencies; foot patrols and mini-stations might receive citizen requests directly, thus heading off calls to central dispatch; and workload management might find alternative responses for some types of calls. Although the ability of the last approach (workload management) to reduce the volume of calls dispatched to sworn units for immediate response has clearly been demonstrated (McEwen et al., 1986), the rest of the evidence on the effects of community policing on calls for service is mixed. Several studies have found positive effects but several others have not.

## Community Relations

The vast majority of the studies that have looked at the impact of community policing on citizens' attitudes toward the police have uncovered positive effects. Clearly, citizens generally appreciate mini-stations in their neighborhoods, foot patrols, problem-solving efforts, and other forms of community policing. These very consistent findings are all the more remarkable because baseline measures of citizen satisfaction with, and support for, their police are frequently quite positive to begin with, thus offering relatively little room for improvement.

## Police Officer Attitudes

A clear majority of the studies that have investigated the effects of community policing on officers' job satisfaction, perceptions of the community, and other related attitudes have discovered beneficial effects. Officers involved in community policing, especially if they are volunteers or members of special units, typically thrive on their new duties and responsibilities. Also, there is some evidence that organizing and managing officers differently (the so-called "inside-out" approach) can have positive effects on their morale and related attitudes (Wycoff and Skogan, 1993).

What is somewhat less certain, however, is (1) whether the positive effects of community policing on officers will survive the long term and (2) whether these benefits are as universal when *all* officers are required to engage in community policing. Whenever community policing is practiced only by specialists, as has generally been the case until recently in most departments, one condition that *is* nearly universal is conflict between the specialists and other members of the agency, frequently reflected in derogatory remarks about "the grin and wave squad."

## Police Officer Behavior

Significant anecdotal evidence suggests that foot patrol, problem solving, permanent assignment, mini-stations, and other features of community policing lead to changes in some police officers' behavior, but these behavioral effects have only been lightly documented thus far (Mastrofski, Worden, and Snipes, 1995). Evidence also suggests that many officers resist changing their behavior, out of opposition to the philosophical underpinnings of community policing, doubts that community policing really works, or just plain habit.

## Conclusion

A great deal of energy has been invested since 1980 in determining the nature of community policing and its effects. These efforts have paid off to the extent that the scope and variation of community policing is much better understood today and some of its effects have been fairly well documented. Since community policing has evolved significantly during this period, however, some of its elements have been more carefully evaluated than others. In addition, programmatic complexity, multiple effects, variations in scope, and research design limitations have hampered many of the community policing evaluations conducted thus far. Nevertheless, the tactical elements of community policing do seem to produce several beneficial outcomes for citizens and officers, and have the potential to impact crime and disorder. Whether the more philosophical, strategic, and organizational elements of community policing will become firmly rooted, and whether they will ultimately have beneficial effects, is yet to be seen.

## References

Bennett, Trevor. 1994. "Community Policing on the Ground: Developments in Britain." In Dennis P. Rosenbaum, ed., *The Challenge of Community Policing: Testing the Promises.* Thousand Oaks, CA: Sage, pp. 224–46.

Bureau of Justice Assistance. 1994a. *A Police Guide to Surveying Citizens and Their Environment.* Washington, DC: Bureau of Justice Assistance.

_____. 1994b. *Neighborhood-Oriented Policing in Rural Communities: A Program Planning Guide.* Washington, DC: Bureau of Justice Assistance.

_____. 1994c. *Understanding Community Policing: A Framework for Action.* Washington, DC: Bureau of Justice Assistance.

Cordner, Gary W. and Robert C. Trojanowicz. 1992. "Patrol." In Gary W. Cordner and Donna C. Hale, eds., *What Works in Policing? Operations and Administration Examined.* Cincinnati, OH: Anderson, pp. 3–18.

Eck, John E. 1992. "Criminal Investigation." In Gary W. Cordner and Donna C. Hale, eds., *What Works in Policing? Operations and Administration Examined.* Cincinnati, OH: Anderson, pp. 19–34.

Eck, John E. and William Spelman. 1987. *Problem Solving: Problem-Oriented Policing in Newport News.* Washington, DC: Police Executive Research Forum.

Goldstein, Herman. 1977. *Policing A Free Society.* Cambridge, MA: Ballinger.

Goldstein, Herman. 1987. "Toward Community-Oriented Policing: Potential, Basic Requirements, and Threshold Questions," *Crime & Delinquency* 25: 236–58.
_____. 1990. *Problem-Oriented Policing*. New York: McGraw-Hill.
Greene, Jack R. and Stephen D. Mastrofski, eds. 1988. *Community Policing: Rhetoric or Reality?* New York: Praeger.
Greenwood, Peter W. and Joan Petersilia. 1975. *The Criminal Investigation Process, Volume I: Summary and Implications*. Santa Monica: Rand Corporation.
Kelling, George L., Tony Pate, Duane Dieckman, and Charles E. Brown. 1974. *The Kansas City Preventive Patrol Experiment: A Summary Report*. Washington, DC: Police Foundation.
Kelling, George L. and Mark H. Moore. 1988. "The Evolving Strategy of Policing." *Perspectives on Policing* No. 4. Washington, DC: National Institute of Justice.
Klockars, Carl B. 1988. "The Rhetoric of Community Policing." In Jack R. Greene and Stephen D. Mastrofski, eds., *Community Policing: Rhetoric or Reality?* New York: Praeger, pp. 239–58.
Leighton, Barry N. 1994. "Community Policing in Canada: An Overview of Experience and Evaluations." In Dennis P. Rosenbaum, ed., *The Challenge of Community Policing: Testing the Promises*. Thousand Oaks, CA: Sage, pp. 209–23.
Manning, Peter K. 1988. "Community Policing as a Drama of Control." In Jack R. Greene and Stephen D. Mastrofski, eds., *Community Policing: Rhetoric or Reality?* New York: Praeger, pp. 27–46.
Mastrofski, Stephen D., Robert E. Worden, and Jeffrey B. Snipes. 1995. "Law Enforcement in a Time of Community Policing." *Criminology* 33, 4: 539–63.
McEwen, J. Thomas, Edward F. Connors III, and Marcia I. Cohen. 1986. *Evaluation of the Differential Police Responses Field Test*. Washington, DC: National Institute of Justice.
Moore, Mark H. and Robert C. Trojanowicz. 1988. "Corporate Strategies for Policing." *Perspectives on Policing* No. 6. Washington, DC: National Institute of Justice.
Normandeau, Andre. 1993. "Community Policing in Canada: A Review of Some Recent Studies," *American Journal of Police* 12,1: 57–73.
Skogan, Wesley G. 1994. "The Impact of Community Policing on Neighborhood Residents: A Cross-Site Analysis." In Dennis P. Rosenbaum, ed., *The Challenge of Community Policing: Testing the Promises*. Thousand Oaks, CA: Sage, pp. 167–81.
Spelman, William and Dale K. Brown. 1982. *Calling the Police: Citizen Reporting of Serious Crime*. Washington, DC: Police Executive Research Forum.
Trojanowicz, Robert and Bonnie Bucqueroux. 1990. *Community Policing: A Contemporary Perspective*. Cincinnati, OH: Anderson.
Weatheritt, Mollie. 1988. "Community Policing: Rhetoric or Reality?" In Jack R. Greene and Stephen D. Mastrofski, eds., *Community Policing: Rhetoric or Reality?* New York: Praeger, pp. 153–76.
Wilson, James Q. and George L. Kelling. 1982. "Police and Neighborhood Safety: Broken Windows," *The Atlantic Monthly* (March): 29–38.
Wycoff, Mary Ann and Wesley K. Skogan. 1993. *Community Policing in Madison: Quality From the Inside Out*. Washington, DC: National Institute of Justice.

27

# Underwriting the Risky Investment in Community Policing

## What Social Science Should Be Doing to Evaluate Community Policing

David M. Kennedy
Mark H. Moore

*America appears to have committed itself to a profound shift in its core policing strategy, from "reform policing" to "community policing." This shift has been propelled by a powerful historical critique of the reform strategy; by an operational movement in police departments; and by political forces. Still unanswered is the question of whether community policing "works"; that is, is a more valuable organizational strategy than the reform strategy. Social science and evaluation research are turning to this question. Implicit in the approach of community policing is a belief that the values of social science should guide social decision making; that this is a specialized task for trained outside evaluators; that "crime" is the most critical performance dimension; and that programs rather than organizations are the proper units of analysis. The authors argue that this framework may hinder the full development of community-policing departments as "learning organizations"; that dimensions other than crime are also important in recognizing the value that police departments contribute to cities; and that the successful evaluation of the community-policing movement requires attention to organizations as well as programs. They suggest a modified social science research agenda.*

With the passage of the 1994 crime bill and its elevation of community policing on the national agenda, it is fair to say that community policing has arrived, at least as a rhetorical and political commitment, if

Adapted with permission from the *Justice System Journal*, Vol. 17, No. 3, 1995, pp. 271–89.

not as an operational reality.[1] Community policing is now a *bona fide* movement. Few municipalities searching for new chiefs fail to make a commitment to community policing a condition for hiring; few chiefs fail to swear allegiance to the new school; few cities troubled by poor police performance and poor police/community relations fail to look to community policing for remedy. Society has, apparently, paid its money and made its choice.

## Betting on Community Policing

While not often acknowledged, this choice is a huge social bet. No one knows for sure whether the commitment to community policing will pay off in reduced victimization, or increased security. An important question is whether this bet is wise. As important, how can we organize ourselves to find out soon if we are on the right track? What roles should social science and the academy play in informing society of its choices on this major strategic decision? And do the differences between traditional policing and the emerging policing hold any implications for the assessment and evaluation tasks that typically form the core of the social science agenda on questions like these?

### Critique of the "Reform Strategy" of Policing

The principal justifications for betting on community policing have emerged from a historical and operational critique of our current strategy of policing, not from clear demonstrations that the alternatives would work. Accounts, and critiques, of the operational philosophy that has dominated American policing for most of this century—now called the "reform strategy," or the "law enforcement strategy"—are by now familiar.

Police departments committed to the reform strategy of policing see their principal goal as reducing crime through professional law enforcement. They think of themselves as the first step in the criminal justice system. They concentrate their attention on "serious" crime, primarily to ensure the most effective use of scarce resources, but also to limit their intrusions into private life. For some of the same reasons, they operate reactively, waiting until after a crime has been committed or they have received a call for service before intruding into private life. To produce the arrests that attack serious crime, they rely primarily on three operational tactics: (1) patrol (usually random, but sometimes directed toward particular places and times where offenses are likely to occur), (2) rapid response to calls for service, and (3) retrospective investigation.

Politically, police departments jealously guard their independence from political influence and control, establishing their legitimacy in society's need for fair and impartial enforcement of the law rather than in responding to local community concerns. Administratively, they organize themselves in highly centralized bureaucracies with power concentrated in a commissioner or chief at headquarters. They rely on paramilitary management and administration, with a heavy emphasis on hierarchy and strict supervision. And they grant special units, such as detective, narcotics, and SWAT teams, higher status than patrol officers.

Despite overall coherence and commonsense validity, this strategy over the last ten to fifteen years has come to be viewed with increasing dissatisfaction by both practitioners and scholars. The focus on serious crime led the police to devalue the interests of neighborhoods and communities in controlling fear, disorder, "minor" crimes like prostitution, and other insults to the quality of community life—with negative consequences for community morale, satisfaction with the police, and security.[2] The linkage to the criminal justice system meant that the police could only be as effective as the courts and prisons allowed them to be, which seemed less and less satisfactory as the capacity of many jurisdictions became increasingly overloaded. The emphasis on individual incidents made it difficult to get at underlying problems and forced a reactive rather than preventive posture. Experience and research alike revealed that rapid response failed to deliver on its crime control promise, and that motorized patrol generally failed either to deter crime or reassure the public.

Police departments' insistence on autonomy made them appear— and sometimes be—unaccountable and unresponsive; it also cut them off from potential allies and made them solely responsible for crime, fear, and safety problems they could not address alone. Centralized, paramilitary, command-and-control organization and management seemed to vest too much control at the top of departments, a long way away from communities' street-level concerns, and waste the creative potential of most police personnel. Policing's fascination with elite special units devalued the job of the patrol force, and with it the vast majority of the problems with which communities wanted help.

## The Alternatives:
## Problem-Solving and Community Policing

Two complementary approaches have emerged as alternative conceptions of better ways to police. One, *problem-solving policing*, enlists analysis and creativity in the service of addressing crime and other community concerns.[3] Problem-solving policing refocuses police attention from individual incidents to larger patterns of incidents that become community problems, and from the simple question of whether an arrest is justified by a particular incident, to the more complex question of what might be causing the incidents, and how they could be prevented in the future. Problem-solving policing works to identify why things are going wrong and to respond with a wide variety of often untraditional approaches. The other, *community policing*, explicitly recognizes the importance of communities' concerns and priorities in setting police priorities and the necessity of community support and partnerships if real progress is to be made in reducing victimization and restoring security.[4] Community policing increases police accountability to neighborhoods and communities, offers neighborhoods the kind of service and attention they desire, and crafts innovative working relationships.

In practice, the two approaches tend to become one: Problem solving, once begun, eventually forces police to attend to community concerns, and cultivate community allies, while community policing forces police to move beyond traditional tactics. *Community policing* has become the dominant label for the new policing, but most departments implementing community policing are in fact doing both, and we will use the term here as encompassing both approaches.

### Empirical Evidence of Effectiveness and Feasibility

The theoretical appeal of community policing currently constitutes the principal reason that society should bet on making it the dominant future police strategy. The theory gains increased weight, however, from evidence showing that particular kinds of police programs associated with community policing reduce victimization or enhance community security and that problem-solving approaches can reduce specific crime and security problems.[5] It is also clear that such programs are administratively feasible—that today's police departments can organize and sustain such activities, at least on some scale, and for some period of time. So, society's bet is not entirely ill founded.

Still, the potential of community policing is in no way conclusively established. This fact raises, in many quarters, quite sensible reservations. The historical critique alone is not sufficient reason to believe in community policing, and to make the kinds of investments in community policing that society is currently making. Nor, alone, are accounts of progress toward realizing community policing's new organizational forms, or of positive but isolated instances of success by community-policing-type programs against particular problems. The more commitment, inside and outside policing, to the new strategy, the more important it becomes to have evidence that community policing will work and will be more productive than reform policing or alternative approaches, such as strategic policing or investing in courts and prisons.

## Hedging the Bets:
## Learning from Experience

Evaluating the assumptions and operational success of the new philosophy of policing is a natural role for research-funding agencies and the academy, and is one that social scientists are eager to claim as their own. The results of their research and their informed opinions will be important to policing and to the judgments that the less expert in society make about policing. It is important, then, to think hard about this process. What are the right questions for society to be asking? How possible will it be to answer them? What studies or experiments should funding sources be commissioning? What issues should academics and social scientists try to address? Finally, given the common aspirations for improving conditions in the larger society, the profession of policing, and the state of knowledge, what is the right relationship among funding sources, social scientists, and the police profession?

This bundle of questions is important and unexpectedly challenging. In our view, the correct answer forces us to rethink some of our conventional ideas about how society should strike the balance between its desire to act only on the basis of confident knowledge (thereby avoiding errors of commission), and its desire to make progress and to experiment in areas where answers are unclear (thereby reducing errors of omission). It also forces us to rethink our ideas about what sorts of things can and should be the focus of empirical investigation. It also forces us to rethink conventional ideas about the relationship between academics and social scientists on one hand and practicing police professionals on the other.

## The Social Research and Development Model

The dominant frame for academic thinking on these questions is what one of the authors has elsewhere called the "social research and development" model.[6] This model attempts to place at the service of society the social scientists' strength, and a range of sophisticated methodologies, in identifying and ranking public problems; identifying their causes; devising and testing interventions; and disseminating protocols or ideal forms for proven interventions. The appeal of this model is obvious. In a world in which policy is often driven by aspiration, optimism, and fashion rather than by hardheaded analysis—and perhaps nowhere is this more true than in crime control policy—the social research and development model aspires to inform and discipline policy with hard facts and clear analysis. The riskier the bet society is contemplating, and the graver the stakes both for society and individuals, the stronger the claim that social science should set high standards for contemplated policies. And the more policy seems to be pulled along by faddish enthusiasm, the more appropriate that, in Lawrence Sherman's words, social science should provide protection against "self-delusion about success."[7]

A core feature of this model is the pride of place given to the *scientific testing of interventions* as the most important predicate for designing policy and taking action.[8] The strong version of this claim is that only the best experimental or evaluative methodologies, applied by outside specialists, are adequate tests for the effectiveness of operational approaches, and that only those operational approaches that pass the tests should be widely adopted. In, again, Lawrence Sherman's words,

> Business has a bottom line, but it also has the independent audit. Surgery has the patient's recovery, but it also has the second opinion. Academics write books, but they also must undergo book reviews. Each of these systems is a set of rules for evaluating the results of professional work. The rules may vary in fairness or accuracy of the assessments they produce,

but they all insure that the results are judged by someone independent of who did the work. Anything else is a conflict of interest.[9]

Progress in policing, according to this framework, should proceed slowly and carefully, brick by tested brick, as promising operational interventions are subjected to rigorous outside evaluation and gradually accrue into new and more effective strategies. Ideas about new strategies, particularly large and risky new strategies, should be subjected to early testing by the best social science methods. By implication, since social science does not now play this role in policing on any large scale, social science, practiced by outsiders, should gradually come to be a considerably more central and influential part of policing than is currently the case.

This is an attractive vision. Something very much like the social research and development model has indeed been a powerful element in the recent burst of soul searching and innovation in policing. Sophisticated social science applied to patrol, rapid response, and the detective function helped shake the profession's faith in the effectiveness of its core tactics, and set academics on the path for alternatives.[10] Rigorous experimental methodologies have tested model interventions against serious problems such as domestic violence; insightful qualitative analysis has shed important light on new strategies such as problem-solving policing.[11] Both the academy and the profession owe a great deal to the kind of structured, incremental contributions prized by adherents to the social research and development model. It is surely not obviously unreasonable to suggest that social science, and particularly rigorous outside evaluation, should play a more powerful and determinative role in the development of the new policing.

### Limitations of Social Research and Development

Still, we are hardly the first to notice that there are some difficulties with at least the stereotyped version of the social research and development model. It is not unreasonable to suggest, for example, that the world simply does not work like this: that large social and institutional changes do not occur because of, and are rarely subordinate to, social science findings. The initiative often comes, instead, from some combination of political ferment and professional experimentation at the edges of current capabilities. The reform model of policing developed in response to powerful political and professional currents, and its strategy was firmly fixed before rigorous analysis was ever brought to bear. It was justified by a series of reasonable, but untested and even unselfconscious, assumptions.[12] Social science insight and influence often pale beside such forces.

Nor are social science evaluations always as clear and dispositive as could be desired. Debate within policing about the credibility and import of George Kelling's classic Kansas City preventive patrol experiment is still heated. The apparently unambiguous, and widely influential, lessons of Lawrence Sherman's elegant Minneapolis test of mandatory arrest for domestic violence were confounded by his own replication of the experiment elsewhere.[13] Nor do conclusions about policy always flow seamlessly from even the best social science, even when its methods are put to work evaluating specific interventions. Sherman's domestic violence experiments are again instructive. The implications of his work are apparently clear: upper-class offenders should be arrested, since for them arrest reduces recidivism, while lower-class offenders should not, since for them arrest increases recidivism. But policy based on such principles can run afoul of notions of equity, of a desire to use sanctions to communicate a strong social stand against particular offenses, and of concerns about the civil liability of enforcement agencies. Such concerns have little to do with judgments about the *effectiveness* of the intervention on any particular dimension, and everything to do with what society does or should value. More or better evaluations will do little to resolve them.

It is also true that time is, at least occasionally, of the essence and that public policy cannot always wait for the fine but slow mill of social science to conclude its grinding. This is easy to accept when the urgency comes from some kind of crime or order problem: the beginning of a drug epidemic, for instance, or a newer offense like carjacking. In cases like this, the need to nip the problem in the bud, or the claim of public outrage and the need to demonstrate police responsiveness, can go far toward justifying a brisk, even if uncertain, response.

It is less easy to accept—it will indeed be unacceptable to many—that a "window of opportunity" forces us to act when the bet being made is a much larger one: a bet about the *profession* itself. Yet, it may well be that the current willingness of policing to entertain the prospect of major change is relatively fleeting. The field as a whole may not be as open to change as it is now for another generation. It may be that the best way to take advantage of this rare moment of ferment is to forge ahead of the accumulation of knowledge about what works, to maintain institutional momentum at the expense of precision and efficiency.[14]

Against the charge that precipitate action is inherently irresponsible, it is worth noting that the standards of the social research and development model are singularly strict ones, notably absent from, for instance, the private sector. There, the requirement that courses of action be justified by scientific proof—or the nearest possible equivalent—is replaced by the requirement that courses of action attract investment and perform well in the marketplace. Failure is *expected* in this realm and accepted as part of an ideology that supports ferment and experimentation as ultimately productive of better results than a more conservative, controlled, and rational process. Where public coin and public authority are being spent, where successful performance is less easily judged, and where none can escape the consequences of policy choices, a much different expectation applies. But if the range of possibilities locates unfettered entrepreneurism at one extreme and the social research and development model at the other, it is by no means clear that the proper standard for guiding an important innovation like community policing lies in following the path marked only by the bricks that science has been able to put in place.[15]

None of these considerations alone, nor all of them together, amount to a telling critique of the social research and development model. The world may not proceed according to state-of-the-art scientific advice, but perhaps it should, and perhaps we should do all we can to move in that direction, in part by endorsing and following the social research and development model. Professional biases and public norms may not be responsive to evaluation research, but perhaps they should be, or at least more so than they are now. It may sometimes be necessary to leap before we look, but perhaps those occasions are rare, or could be made more rare through additional investment in social science. Perhaps the only reasonable criterion for large public experiments like community policing is the social research and development test of strict scientific evaluation.

But we think the issues raised above do weaken the claim of the social research and development model. We think other issues, discussed below, do it a great deal more harm. One set of issues has to do with the *possibility*, at least at the moment, of testing community policing according to the social research and development model. Another set has to do with the *appropriateness and desirability* of doing so, at least as usually proposed.

In our view, evaluations of community policing pose significant problems for conventional models of program evaluations. The first problem is that it is by no means clear what interventions should be tested. What is community policing?[16] When can we say it is operating in a particular location? The second problem is that it is not obvious how the interventions should be evaluated. What would it mean for community policing to succeed? Given that the concept of community policing seeks to redefine the ends of policing as well as the means, and the new ends involve many long-term, intangible results such as restoring neighborhood morale, how can community policing be effectively evaluated? In short, social science is handicapped by difficulties in defining both independent and dependent variables. The difficulties are by no means insurmountable, but to evaluate community policing properly, some adjustments of the conventional model must be made.

## Problems in Evaluation: Defining Community Policing

We think of community policing as an overall strategy or philosophy of policing rather than any particular program. This makes it both similar to and different from the reform strategy of policing.

Like the reform strategy of policing, the strategy of community policing can be captured in a few guiding precepts. Yet, what makes the few simple precepts for community policing different from those for the reform strategy is that they prescribe general themes and ideas rather than define specific tactics.[17] In Herman Goldstein's words, the need that community policing responds to is for "a broad conceptual framework" that "helps the police build a strong, sensitive institution, with refined methods of operating, that can better transcend the crisis of the day, whether that crisis be labor-management strife, racial conflict, political protest, drugs, or some yet-to-be-identified social problem."[18] As we have written elsewhere, the changes leading to a new policing are designed "to initiate the conditions under which the police may *continue to be adaptive and innovative*" (emphasis in original).[19]

Thus, in our conception, community policing cannot be captured simply by listing tactics, such as foot or bicycle patrol. It cannot be captured by listing operations, such as disrupting street drug markets or focusing on hot spots. It is best captured through an accounting of a core set of historically distinctive beliefs: in the problem-solving approach; in partnerships; in accountability and responsiveness; in prevention; and in the creative potential of line personnel. The goal is to create departments that routinely employ analysis and creativity, learn from experience, adapt to new problems and environments, and develop effective operational approaches.

This is in fundamental contrast to the reform model, which relied almost entirely on essentially static organizations delivering a few interventions that were believed to be both powerful and generally applicable. The reform strategy of policing was based on the *strategic innovation* of committing police departments to the goal of crime fighting through the *program innovations* of motorized patrol and rapid response (plus the existing model of detective investigation).[20] It is worth noting that the operational programs that formed the core of the reform strategy were very large programs, both in the sense that they consumed a substantial portion of departments' operational assets and capabilities and in the sense that they were believed to constitute an effective operational response to the largest, the most urgent, and the widest variety of the problems to which the police were expected to respond. It is also worth noting that the problems to which the police committed themselves to responding could be aggregated into one relatively homogeneous category: serious crime, or, somewhat more broadly, criminal law violations.

This singleness of purpose and operations goes a considerable way toward explaining the power of the cluster of evaluations that in the late 1970s called into question the efficacy of patrol, rapid response, and investigations. The results of the Kansas City experiments could reasonably be, and *were*, construed as meaningful to the entire profession. Patrol activity, responses to calls for service, and investigations were, for all practical purposes, the primary activities of police departments. The range of variation within and among departments was so small that these tactics and the crime-fighting strategy were effectively one and the same. Inevitably, then, when the effectiveness of these core operational programs was called into question, the field became ripe for a strategic change.

The simplicity and generality of these programmatic activities may have led police departments to focus almost entirely on *routines* and *out-*

*puts* rather than *outcomes*. Police departments, in Herman Goldstein's famous phrase, had become like bus drivers that were so committed to keeping to their schedules that they had no time for picking up passengers.[21] His historic contribution to policing is the insight that this focus on routines is neither desirable nor inevitable. It is possible to create thoughtful, purposeful police departments that seek results through a corresponding operational Catholicism. It is even possible to imagine police departments that operate not with a Taylorist assembly-line framework, but as consistently innovative, continuously customizing job shops.[22]

In many ways, this philosophy and its core operational and administrative elements are incompatible with traditional policing's structure, management, and tactics. Making patrol officers responsible for problem solving, for example, means granting them status and discretion not easily combined with a tradition of ordering street officers around by radio from headquarters. Developing a departmental capacity to respond in a comprehensive fashion to community concerns—be they drugs, guns, or fear in public housing—cannot easily be combined with a structure that allows specialist squads to respond to problems as they see them, independent of geographic commands. The creativity, flexibility, and initiative that community policing demands cannot easily be combined with the paramilitary hierarchy and often draconian management style that mark traditional departments. Because the points of conflict are many and severe, departments that commit themselves to community policing, therefore, are committing themselves to major change. The cost in money, energy, and—if the thrust toward community policing is mistaken—opportunity will be considerable.

The implications of these points for the proper evaluation of community policing are several. First, while the evaluation of community-policing-like programs, such as foot patrol, neighborhood police stations, or police-led community attacks on graffiti and littering, may give us a clue about the potential of community policing as an overall strategy of policing, they cannot firmly establish the value of adopting community policing as an overall philosophy of policing. The effects of the individual programs could be more or less than the effect of embracing community policing as a philosophy. Trying to evaluate an organization committed to the philosophy of community policing by observing the effectiveness of one kind of operation is like trying to evaluate General Electric by the effectiveness of its lightbulb division viewed at one moment of time. What is valuable about General Electric is its broader capacity to innovate and respond, not the value of any individual project. And so it may be with a community-policing organization.

Second, to gauge the value of a police department committed to the strategy of community policing, we may have to wait awhile, because it will take some time to build organizations that are capable of implementing the strategy. Indeed, for all the rhetoric about community policing, one cannot find a single organization that is now fully committed to this way of doing police business. If we want to learn more quickly about the value of community policing as an overall philosophy, we may have to force the pace a bit by stimulating the more rapid development of organizations committed to this philosophy.

Third, to produce police organizations that are committed to the philosophy of community policing, we have to experiment a great deal with administrative innovations as well as program innovations. We have to develop new methods of selecting, training, and supervising patrol officers. We have to develop new systems for responding to calls and dispatching patrol officers. We have to find new ways of consulting communities about problems that concern them, and of treating those problems institutionally as important new units of work. We have to find ways of authorizing, administratively recognizing, and effectively evaluating problem-solving initiatives of different sizes undertaken by the department.

In sum, the successful evaluation of community policing as an overall strategy of policing requires evaluators to change their unit of analysis. Rather than focusing on particular programs, they must look at the more generalized capacity of an organization to continue to develop new responses to changing demands and circumstances, and at the aggregate performance of those responses. They have to wait for such organizations to develop, or force the pace. They have to learn how to evaluate administrative as well as programmatic innovations.

## Problems in Evaluation: Defining Success

Note that there is nothing about this vision of a new policing that necessarily implies a commitment to new ends for policing, an abandonment of traditional tactics, or the accountability and partnership outlook associated with community policing. It is entirely possible to imagine a "learning" police department that is solely interested in serious crime, predisposed toward enforcement and arrest, and has no truck with community partnerships.

Yet, in practice, the focus on responding to community concerns and actually achieving results that comes with problem solving tends to evolve over time into a corresponding focus on new ends and means (and vice versa). Indeed, the research and discussion surrounding the development of community policing has changed the frame of evaluation research regarding the *ends* of policing as well as regarding the kinds of operational programs and organizations we need to police our cities.

Implicit in the current call for assessing whether community policing "works" is whether it will control crime; crime then becomes our dependent variable. This is a very important question. It is not, however, the *only* important question.

Community policing has opened a new normative conversation. For the first time since the solidifying of the reform movement, the ends of policing are being actively debated. Community policing has expanded thinking about policing to include, at the very least, combating fear and disorder as critical elements of the police function. It has also expanded police thinking about (or, sometimes, served to remind police and scholars about) the values of accountability, responsiveness, economy in the use of force and authority, freedom from corruption and abuse, adaptability, and the acceptability of police behavior to communities. All of these are now credible candidates as dependent variables in evaluating the larger community-policing experiment, since the achievement of any one of these could at least partially justify a shift to an overall strategy of community policing.

We recognize that not all will support the movement to extend policing's ends beyond crime control, or if beyond crime control then beyond attacking fear and disorder. Our own view is that the dimensions we nominate for use in evaluating police performance are not irrelevant to the evaluation of police agencies—any police agencies. Nor can they be understood merely as means to an end. In our view, these dimensions are crucial to assessing whether a community is blessed with high-performing, or cursed with poorly performing, police. If community policing does no better than reform policing to prevent violent victimization, but reduces other sorts of fear and prevents disorder in troubled communities, that would be a net gain in public value—not the only gain we would like, but a gain nonetheless. If it does no better at preventing crime but proceeds in a manner more responsive to communities, less alienating of minorities, and less productive of corruption and brutality, that too would be a net gain, both for society and for policing as an institution.

It is a profound mistake to conclude, as some have, that community policing is not about crime; there is no serious support for community policing, in the profession or in the academy, that is not support for more effective crime fighting. But it is also a mistake to conclude that community policing is *only* about crime. And, in many important quarters, particularly in minority communities, interest in these other dimensions is as or more compelling as is interest in crime fighting.[23]

This creates a practical problem. We simply do not have the information systems at either the national or local level that would support comprehensive, routine measurement of the effectiveness of community-policing organizations in producing results on fear, disorder, corruption control, responsiveness, and the like. It is not difficult to imagine how to gather such information. One would have to rely on instruments such as community surveys; focus groups of police and public; after-action audits of problem-solving initiatives; increased police and prosecutorial attention to corruption, abuse of authority, and perjury; and the like.[24] But doing so, either intensively at the local level, or broadly at the national level, is a significant undertaking. It would be comparable in scale to the initial development of the uniform crime-reporting system, an effort that took a generation to complete.

It is important to recognize that the capacity of social scientists working alone without the aid of operational agencies is extremely limited. With the exception of special research projects of limited geographic and longitudinal scope, social science must rely, as it currently does for crime and victimization data, on the operating data of local police departments, and the statistics collected at the national level. Local departments and Washington will in practice establish the systems to collect the data relevant to routinely evaluating community policing only if community policing gains a wide foothold. The FBI's Uniform Crime Reports (UCR) and the Justice Department's victimization surveys followed (and helped to sustain) policing's general embrace of crime-fighting ideology. The UCR system depends on the voluntary expenditure of a considerable amount of local energy on the part of police departments; this is now routine and thus unremarkable, but it was not always so. The UCR system's establishment was controversial and for some time its data was of rather questionable quality.[25] The Justice Department's victimization effort is among the largest, if it is not the largest, and most expensive of continuing survey research endeavors, and was designed precisely to fill a need clearly defined by the nation's dominant law enforcement and public safety agenda; notably, the shortcomings of reported crime data, particularly underreporting from minority neighborhoods with high victimization rates.

The same will surely be true of information systems designed to support the new goals of community policing at local and national levels. The subject of performance measures and information-gathering methodologies appropriate to these goals is currently being vigorously debated in both professional and academic circles.[26] It will be some time before those issues are resolved, and longer still before systems covering the nation or even a large number of sites are functioning. The debate is occurring only because departments are forging ahead with community policing, and the systems will be deployed only if they continue to do so. The Justice Department's victimization survey's structure and methodology could be used to assess, for example, fear, perceptions of disorder, attitudes toward the police, and self-defense activities. At best, however, that will give a broad national picture, unsuitable, as it is now for victimization, for city-level, much less neighborhood-level, analysis. More local data must be supplied by routine departmental, or ad-hoc, project-based, data gathering. It will thus be some time before either national or local data are collected routinely. A certain progression is likely here, with particular community-policing experiments gathering some data, individual departments designing instruments and systems for more routine local monitoring, and a national system, or systems, following.

It is, of course, possible for this information to be gathered by individual departments without national agreement on dimensions and protocols, or a national effort akin to the UCR; this is, in fact, already occurring. They will do so, however, *consequent to* departmental commitments to community policing. It is extremely unlikely that the academy will be able to win funding, or cooperation from departments, for independent research of the scope necessary to evaluate the effect of community policing on fear, corruption control, and other noncrime dimensions absent a wide commitment to the new strategy. For the most part, information will be gathered on the new dimensions, and support for special academic research will be forthcoming, because of departments' prior decisions to move into community policing. The conundrum remains: the broad, numerous, and replicated studies necessary to *evaluate* community policing on these important new dimensions are dependent on prior political commitment and administrative actions to *implement* community policing.

## Toward an Evaluation Agenda for Community Policing

The emphasis on learning organizations holds important implications for the kinds of social science that would be most useful in helping society size up community policing and, whatever the verdict, helping to chart a course toward improved policing. This foregoing analysis suggests that, to the extent that the social research and development model is valid for assessing community policing, it has to date framed the evaluation task incorrectly. The evaluation community has acted as if community policing (the independent variable) can be located in particular operational innovations, and the effect of community policing tested by assessing the crime-control effect of those innovations (the dependent variable). We believe that this is mistaken. We believe that community policing is located in *creative and responsive organizations* and that the proper dependent variable is *these organizations' production of innovative operations that are, in aggregate, effective* not only in controlling crime but also in preventing crime, reducing fear, and increasing community confidence in the police.

Adding weight to this formulation is the tendency for community-policing departments to act in practice as if particular operational interventions, even if powerful, are unlikely to be generally applicable elsewhere, at least without significant customization. A program that works against street drug markets in one neighborhood, or one city, is likely to do so because it was carefully designed in accord with the problems and opportunities those sites presented and either will not work or will need adapting elsewhere.

This obviously weakens the reach of a social research and development model focusing on evaluating operational interventions, since the evaluation findings will only be as generalizable as the intervention itself. Things get worse. Community policing believes that problems are heterogeneous and disaggregated, rather than homogeneous and few; it sees not "rape," as reform departments did, but stranger rape, rape among intimates, date rape, rape associated with bars, rape by repeat offenders, and more; potentially, all these problems are affected in operationally meaningful ways by community sentiments, assets, and conditions.[27] It therefore believes in stacking up many customized, and perhaps small, interventions in the hope of making a large, overall impact. It seems in practice to "bundle" promising operational approaches into coordinated, overall interventions. And it seems in practice to let interventions evolve through implementation based on lessons learned in the doing.[28]

The operational requirements for a high-quality community-policing department thus require both police officers and managers to focus on achieving substantive results. They also require broad searches for solutions, not only at the outset of an initiative but continuously as they learn about results and, perhaps, as field conditions change. This focuses considerable attention on outcomes and on the examination of their operations as they proceed. The community-policing framework, therefore, creates conditions that promote assessments.

Note, however, that this kind of assessment does not require, and may hinder, the kind of effort necessary to establish *with authority* that any effects that may occur can be attributed with certainty to the intervention. This weakens the value of these internal assessments, not only for motivating behavior and holding people accountable, but also, more fundamentally, for establishing the validity of interventions as general technologies suitable for exporting to other jurisdictions, and as contributions to the fund of scientific knowledge. This loss has to be weighed against the gain that comes from allowing people the room to adapt as they go along and to keep their focus on achieving results rather than maintaining the consistency of an experiment.

There can be, unfortunately, a fundamental contradiction between what is likely to work and what is necessary to strong experimental designs and powerful statistical evaluations. This may seem an outrageous claim, but consider that evaluation research can only assess the different levels of certainty that attach to claims about *what happened* in carefully designed and/or carefully analyzed interventions. The best experiments are carefully controlled, test only one or a few interventions, and are strict implementations of a structured initial design. Strong statistical evaluations are possible only when artifactual or natural conditions approximate these same elements. It may be, however, and much of our experience with promising community-policing interventions suggests, that what works may not in practice follow this outline. It may be that what works follows more of a learning-by-doing model: that successful interventions change in process, based on experience and additional information and ideas that emerge during implementation, and bring new operational elements to bear as the intervention proceeds. If this is so, it will be next to impossible for even the most laborious evaluation research to parse out what has actually happened. It is possible, of course, to draw a large-enough frame around the intervention to dissolve this difficulty, to consider the *process* of designing, implementing, and modifying the intervention the independent variable. But the test is then one of "community policing" or "problem-solving policing," not of a particular operational intervention.

All of these considerations make evaluation research of particular operational interventions both more difficult and of less potential return. The more interventions there are, the harder it becomes to evaluate them all. The more complicated they are, the more difficult to disentangle the contribution of particular elements. The more they change during implementation, the more difficult the study design and the less meaningful the results.

It is also true, however, that this picture vastly decreases the risk associated with not having powerful external evaluations. Because the reach of most interventions is intended to be limited and local, and because learning-through-doing is—in theory, at least—designed into the process, it is not so important if departments use relatively weak methodologies, or go astray at particular points in the learning process. This appears to be a point where Lawrence Sherman went astray in his now-famous critique of the Gainesville convenience-store robbery-prevention project. Much of Sherman's outrage at the Gainesville Police Department's evaluation of its operation stems from his belief that it was a potentially "nationally influential conclusion about effective policing."[29] There seems little reason to believe, however, that either the department or Goldstein saw the operation in other than a local light. When such is the case, we can afford to foster enthusiasm, creativity, and organizational development with a tolerance for experimentation and an encouragement of internal evaluations. Much good will come of it, and little harm.

This formulation resolves, to a considerable extent, the tension between inside and outside evaluation expressed in Sherman's critique. It is essential, if police departments are to become learning organizations, that they cultivate an atmosphere that values and rewards innovation, tolerates failure, and fosters a strong commitment to assessing the results of operations. Individual departments have the responsibility to address conditions within their jurisdictions, and if the developing theory of community policing is correct, they will do so through the experimental and differentiated process we have described. It is clearly their job to evaluate their own efforts and to learn from those evaluations.[30]

These evaluations, however, even if performed by outsiders, cannot accrue to a test of whether community policing as such works. That question can be answered only by examining whether more or less fully transformed departments do, in fact, learn and produce effective interventions, which are in aggregate effective against the range of problems departments routinely face. This is, obviously, still a crucial matter for society and the profession, and one to which the contribution of social science is of central importance. How, then, are we to best answer it?

First, we would encourage the academy to support the design of *performance measures and monitoring systems* appropriate to the new strategies. This can begin with local projects and experiments and with systems for routine local monitoring and expand to national systems and routine national monitoring. Both the profession and the academy need good information on fear, disorder, police misbehavior, community attitudes toward the police, and self-defense behavior. This information will be crucial to individual jurisdictions and to the profession as a whole regardless of the course of the larger national community-policing experiment.

Second, there should be a concerted effort, probably a partnership between the profession, the academy, and the federal government, *to accelerate the development of leading-edge departments into fully fledged community-policing departments.* We simply cannot test the strategy until we have a sample of advanced departments. That sample should encompass a range of cities with some variation in size and type. This endeavor would allow for earlier testing of the strategy, offer guidance to departments at earlier stages of development, and produce a range of operational innovations that could be subjected to careful external evaluation. It would permit, within certain irreducible limits, testing of community-policing departments against other departments pursuing traditional or other new strategies.

Third, evaluation specialists should address themselves to the *administrative innovations and processes of institutional change* that support and promote effective community policing. It is important to know how line officers can be given latitude to exercise discretion without opening the door to corruption; how to create more productive alternatives to the paramilitary style; how to combine rapid response with problem solving; how to implement these and other steps toward the new strategy; and how accurate is the profession's instincts about what works managerially and administratively. The sample of departments suggested above would provide rich research ground, but there is enough ferment in the field as it stands that this work can begin immediately.

Finally, we would encourage external program evaluations of particular operational interventions that are likely to hold promise for the entire profession. We suggest that such evaluations be applied to interventions that are potentially both *powerful* and *robust*—that is, effective against a range of concerns and in a range of circumstances. It was a feature of the reform model of policing that it concerned itself almost exclusively with tactics it believed to be powerful and robust. To date, to our minds at any rate, no new tactics with the reach once adduced to patrol, rapid response, and investigation have presented themselves. But some may, and others with less but still considerable reach will surely arise. Operational approaches of such general applicability should be examined by evaluation researchers.

If we do these things, we will in fact be well on our way to discovering what works, and we will be moving alongside a profession that not only shares that concern, but is busy creating a wide range of new experience from which all can learn. Whatever the eventual verdict on community policing, society, the profession, and social science will be the better.

## Notes

[1] Whether the stated commitment to community policing is in fact matched by the bill's substance remains open to question. The administration's attachment to the

concept, and its apparent belief in the *popularity*, of community policing is unaffected by the answer.

[2] See Skogan, 1990.

[3] See, for example, Goldstein, 1990.

[4] See, for example, Sparrow, Moore, and Kennedy, 1990.

[5] For current evidence on the effectiveness of community policing, see Moore, 1994. For an account of several paradigmatic problem-solving operations, see Eck and Spelman, 1987.

[6] For a fuller account of this model, see Moore, forthcoming.

[7] Sherman, 1991:693. This article is one of the best statements of the thesis that strict social science standards should be applied to the new strategies of policing and an excellent example of the passions the subject can arouse.

[8] This is, it should be noted, not the same as carrying out basic scientific research, which is considerably further removed from practical and policy application.

[9] Sherman, 1991:693. Sherman himself is not always so demanding; later in this same article, at p. 706, he offers an interesting set of "sliding scales" for deciding when *outside social scientists*, as opposed to *social science principles*, should govern the evaluation of interventions.

[10] On patrol, see Kelling et al., 1974. On rapid response, see Kansas City Police Department, 1977–79; Scott, 1981; and Spelman and Brown, 1984. On detectives, see Greenwood, Chaiken, and Petersilia, 1977. For a seminal and enormously influential assessment of the implications of this work and an alternative strategy for policing, see Goldstein, 1979.

[11] On domestic violence, see Sherman, 1992. On problem solving, see Eck and Spelman, 1987.

[12] Even within science itself, historical analysis suggests that the scientific method and objective tests of evidence and explanatory power are often subordinated to social, professional, and generational dynamics. See, for example, Kuhn, 1973, and Feyerabend, 1993.

[13] See Sherman, 1992.

[14] For more on this, see Moore, forthcoming.

[15] One of the few places outside science itself that such strict standards can be found is the testing of new drugs for medical fitness. There, the possibility of serious harm, which may present itself only after some time; the possibility that ineffective treatments may supplant effective ones; and the strong demand for new and innovative treatments have led to high hurdles for acceptance. Interestingly, each of these concerns is weak or absent in policing. While bad policing policy can be very harmful, it will be so in a public and usually immediate way, and tends to be self-correcting. We have for most crime and order problems, few clearly powerful and effective current approaches making experimentation with new ones less irresponsible. There is, despite recent developments, weak demand for innovative approaches. Indeed, even new interventions that have been proven to be effective are not routinely taken up across the profession.

[16] Emphasizing, again, that for our purposes *community policing* encompasses problem-solving policing.

[17] It is precisely this fact that leads to such frustration on the part of both police officers and evaluation methodologists, both of whom wish to know precisely how to go about their business. To this we would reply that we do not believe that this abstraction makes it impossible either to specify or to measure community policing, points we have addressed elsewhere (see Sparrow, Moore, and Kennedy, 1990) and will develop further in the body of this article.

[18] Goldstein, 1990:xiii.

[19] Sparrow, Moore, and Kennedy, 1990:201.

[20] For a discussion of types of innovation in policing, see Sparrow, Moore, and Kennedy, 1990:198–201.
[21] Goldstein, 1979.
[22] See Moore, Sparrow, and Spelman, forthcoming.
[23] See, for example, "Report of the Independent Commission on the Los Angeles Police Department," July 9, 1991, Ch. 5.
[24] See, for example, Alpert and Moore, 1993.
[25] See, for example, Kelling and Stewart, 1991.
[26] See Alpert and Moore, 1993.
[27] For an account of the application of problem-solving policing to sexual assault in Madison, Wisc., see Goldstein and Susmilch, 1982.
[28] For an example of an operation illustrating the last two points, see Kennedy, 1993.
[29] Sherman, 1990:701.
[30] Sherman (1991:699–705) provides an admirable primer for thinking about how this might be done.

## References

Alpert, G., and M. H. Moore (1993). "Measuring Police Performance in the New Paradigm of Policing," in *Performance Measures for the Criminal Justice System.* Washington, DC: Bureau of Justice Statistics, Princeton Study Group on Criminal Justice Performance Measures.

Eck, J. E., and W. Spelman (1987). *Problem Solving: Problem-oriented Policing in Newport News.* Washington, DC: National Institute of Justice, Police Executive Research Forum.

Feyerabend, P. K. (1993). *Against Method: Outline of an Anarchistic Theory of Knowledge.* New York: Verso.

Goldstein, H. (1990). *Problem-Oriented Policing.* New York: McGraw-Hill.

_____. (1979). "Improving Policing: A Problem-oriented Approach," 25 *Crime and Delin quency* 236.

Goldstein, H., and C. E. Susmilch (1982). "The Repeat Sexual Offender in Madison: A Memorandum on the Problem and the Community's Response," vol. 3 of the Project on Development of a Problem-Oriented Approach to Improving Police Service. Photocopy, University of Madison Law School.

Greenwood, P. W., J. M. Chaiken, and J. Petersilia (1977). *The Criminal Investigation Process.* Lexington, MA: DC Heath and Company.

Kansas City Police Department (1977–79). *Response Time Analysis,* 3 vols. Kansas City, MO: Board of Commissioners.

Kelling, G. L., and J. K. Stewart (1991). "The Evolution of Contemporary Policing," in *Local Government Management.* International City Management Association.

Kelling, G. L. et al. (1974). *The Kansas City Preventive Patrol Experiment: A Summary Report.* Washington, DC: Police Foundation.

Kennedy, D. W. (1993). *Closing the Market: Controlling the Drug Trade in Tampa, Florida.* Program Focus Series. Washington, DC: National Institute of Justice.

Kuhn, T. S. (1973). *The Structure of Scientific Revolutions,* 2nd. ed. Chicago: University of Chicago Press.

Moore, M. H. (forthcoming). "Learning While Doing: Linking Knowledge to Policy in the Development of Community Policing and Violence Prevention in the United States," in H. P. Wickstrom (ed.), *Integrating Crime Prevention Strategies:*

*Motivation and Opportunities.* Stockholm: National Council for Crime Prevention.

_____. (1994). "Research Synthesis and Policy Implications," in D. P. Rosenbaum (ed.), *The Challenge of Community Policing: Testing the Promises.* Thousand Oaks, CA: Sage Publications.

Moore, M. H., M. Sparrow, and W. Spelman (forthcoming). "Innovations in Policing: From Production Line to Job Shop," in A. Altshuler and R. Behn (eds.), *Innovation in State and Local Government.* Washington, DC: Urban Institute.

Scott, E. J. (1981). *Calls for Service: Citizen Demand and Initial Police Response.* Washington, DC: U.S. Department of Justice, National Institute of Justice.

Sherman, L. W. (1992). *Policing Domestic Violence: Experiments and Dilemmas.* New York: Free Press.

_____. (1991). "Herman Goldstein: Problem-Oriented Policing," 82 *Journal of Law and Criminology* 693.

Skogan, W. (1990). *Disorder and Decline: Crime and the Spiral of Decay in American Neighborhoods.* New York: Free Press

Sparrow, M. K., M. H. Moore, and D. M. Kennedy (1990). *Beyond 911: A New Era for Policing.* New York: Basic Books.

Spelman, W. G., and D. K. Brown ( 1984). *Calling the Police: Citizen Reporting of Serious Crime.* Washington, DC: National Institute of Justice.

# 28

# Problem-Solving
## Problem-Oriented Policing
## in Newport News

*John E. Eck*
*William Spelman*

Every Friday and Saturday night, residents of a suburban neighborhood complain to the police about teenagers who come in from another part of town. The youths make noise, drink, and commit minor acts of vandalism.

The parking lots around a large manufacturing plant are a haven for thieves. Thefts from autos parked in these lots account for 10 percent of all crimes reported in the city.

An apartment complex is notorious for its high burglary rates. One of every four residents are burglarized each year; follow-up investigations—and occasional arrests—seem to do no good at all.

Patrol officers and detectives spend millions of hours each year responding to incidents like these. Despite their efforts—and despite the arrests, convictions, and incarcerations that sometimes result—the incidents persist.

Research results spanning two decades have converged on a new approach for delivering police services, aimed at solving persistent problems like these. It is called *problem-oriented policing*. Using this approach, police go beyond individual crimes and calls for service, and take on the underlying problems that create them. To understand problems, police collect facts from a wide variety of sources, from outside as well as from inside police agencies. To develop and implement solutions, police enlist the support of other public and private agencies and individuals.

*Problem-oriented policing is a department-wide strategy aimed at solving persistent community problems. Police identify, analyze, and respond to the underlying circumstances that create incidents.*

The Problem-Oriented Policing Project was conducted by the Newport News (Virginia) Police Department and the Police Executive Research

National Institute of Justice. *Research in Brief*, January, 1987.

Forum, with guidance and funding from the National Institute of Justice. In this summary, we describe the origins of problem-oriented policing, the approach that was designed and implemented in Newport News, and some of the problems officers have addressed. But first, in order to show why this approach is new, let us review current police practice.

## Incident-Driven Policing

Current police practice is primarily incident-driven. That is, most police activities are aimed at resolving individual incidents, rather than groups of incidents or problems. The incident-driven police department has four characteristics.

First, it is *reactive*. Most of the workload of patrol officers and detectives consists of handling crimes that have already been committed, disturbances in progress, traffic violations, and the like. The exceptions—crime prevention and narcotics investigations, for example—make up but a small portion of police work.

Incident-driven police work relies on *limited information*, gathered mostly from victims, witnesses, and suspects. Only limited information is needed because the police objectives are limited: patrol officers and detectives are only trying to resolve the incident at hand.

The primary means of resolving incidents is to invoke the *criminal justice process*. Even when an officer manages to resolve an incident without arresting or citing anyone, it is often the threat of enforcing the law that is the key to resolution. Alternative means of resolution are seldom invoked.

Finally, incident-driven police departments use *aggregate statistics* to measure performance. The department is doing a good job when the city-wide crime rate is low, or the city-wide arrest rate is high. The best officers are those who make many arrests, or service many calls.

No department is purely incident-driven; but this is what all agencies do, almost all of the time. Appropriately responding to incidents can be effective: victims are aided, serious offenders are caught, and citizens are helped every day. But too often it fails. Handling calls for service is time-consuming, and rarely produces a tangible result. Officers become frustrated after they handle similar calls time and again, with no sign of progress. Citizens become frustrated when the difficulties that provoked their calls remain unresolved. The constant repetition of similar calls indicates that the incident-driven police department has been unable to do anything about the underlying conditions.

## Problem-Oriented Policing

An alternative to incident-driven policing was described by Herman Goldstein in 1979. Goldstein contended that reacting to calls for service was only the first step. Police should go further, and attempt to find a permanent resolution of the problem which created the call. Goldstein called his alternative the "problem-oriented approach." Problem-oriented policing, as it has developed in Newport News, is a direct extension of Goldstein's approach.

The theory behind problem-oriented policing is simple. Underlying conditions create problems. These conditions might include the characteristics of the people involved (offenders, potential victims, and others), the social setting in which these people interact, the physical environment, and the way the public deals with these conditions.

A problem created by these conditions may generate one or more incidents. These incidents, while stemming from a common source, may appear to be different. For example, social and physical conditions in a deteriorated apartment complex may generate burglaries, acts of vandalism, intimidation of pedestrians by rowdy teenagers, and other incidents. These incidents, some of which come to police attention, are symptoms of the problem. The incidents will continue so long as the problem that creates them persists.

As described by Figure A, the incident-driven police agency responds by dealing with each incident. Like aspirin, this symptomatic relief is valuable but limited. Because police typically leave untouched the condition which created the incidents, the incidents are very likely to recur.

A problem-oriented police agency would respond as described in Figure B. Officers continue to handle calls, but they do much more. They use the information gathered in their responses to incidents, together with information obtained from other sources, to get a clearer picture of the problem. They then address the underlying conditions. If they are successful in ameliorating these conditions, fewer incidents may occur; those that

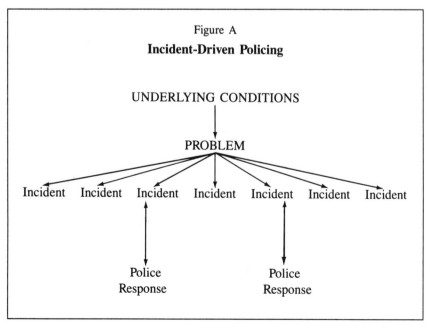

Figure A

**Incident-Driven Policing**

do occur may be less serious. The incidents may even cease. At the very least, information about the problem can help police to design more effective ways of responding to each incident.

Problem-solving is not new. Police officers have always tried to solve problems. But officers have received little guidance and support from police administrators. In fact, supervisors and other officers have often discouraged problem-solving; the more time officers spent dealing with problems, the less time was available for reacting to incidents.

Problem-oriented policing—the routine application of problem-solving techniques—is new. It is based on two premises. The first premise is that problem-solving can be applied by officers throughout the agency as part of their daily work. Previous problem-solving efforts have been confined to special projects or units. The second premise is that routine problem-solving efforts can be effective in reducing or resolving problems. The National Institute of Justice, the Forum, and the Newport News Police Department undertook this project to test these premises.

Although problem-oriented policing is new, it relies on twenty years of research on incident-driven policing.

## The Research Basis of Problem-Oriented Policing

Five areas of research contributed to the development of problem-oriented policing. The initial impetus for an alternative to incident-driven policing was contributed by research on police effectiveness.

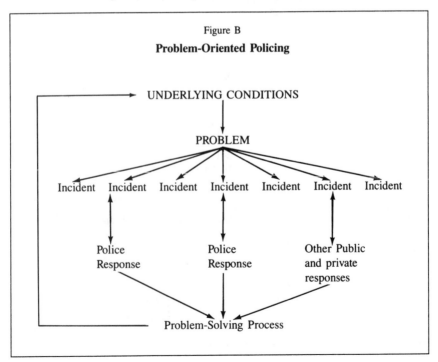

Figure B
**Problem-Oriented Policing**

## Effectiveness

Studies of preventive patrol, response time, and investigations showed that reacting to incidents had, at best, very limited effects on crime and public satisfaction. For many incidents, rapid patrol responses or lengthy follow-up investigations were not needed, suggesting that police managers could deploy their officers more flexibly without reducing effectiveness. Experiments in flexible deployment such as split force, investigative case screening, and differential response to calls confirmed that time could be freed up for other activities. To make better use of this time, managers turned to crime analysis. Crime analysis focused attention on groups of events, rather than single incidents. By identifying crime-prone locations, times, and offenders, crime analysts hoped to direct proactive, rather than reactive patrol and detective activities, thus using officer time more effectively. Crime analysis was restricted to crime problems, traditional police data sources, and criminal justice responses. Still, it marks the first attempt at routine problem-solving.

Crime analysis, directed patrol, and proactive investigations were an important advance over the incident-driven tradition, but the demands of the public and of officers themselves suggested that even bigger changes were needed. Community policing experiments and in-depth studies of public problems were influencing police to adopt a broader concept of their role; studies of police discretion and management were showing that changes in the police bureaucracy were needed, as well.

## Community

The riots of the 1960s made police aware of their strained relation with minority communities. Community relations units, stringent shooting policies, and civilian review boards were all attempts to reduce dissatisfaction with police among minorities. By the mid-1970s, police were going further, providing storefront police stations and foot patrols in an effort to improve public attitudes through increased personal contact with police officers. These programs increased communication between police and citizens. And as police began to recognize the vital role of citizen action in controlling crime and disorder, some agencies began to work closely with citizens to reduce crime and fear. Problem-oriented policing draws on experience showing that joint police/community activities are often the best methods for solving problems.

## Problem Studies

Over the last twenty years there have been a number of studies of problem areas that the police are called upon to handle. They aimed to develop a deeper understanding of the nature and causes of these problems, which would in turn lead to better police responses. The research of the late 1960s and early 1970s focused police attention on burglary, robbery, and other street crimes. In the later 1970s and the 1980s, research began to focus on problems that had not been considered central to police work: domestic violence, drunk driving, the mentally ill, and fear of crime, for example. Through these studies, researchers and practitioners learned that they would have to collect more information to understand these problems. It also became clear that other organizations needed to be involved if responses were to be effective. Finally, the variety of problems examined suggested that police needed to seriously consider many other issues besides crime.

## Discretion

In the 1960s, researchers called attention to the fact that police officers exercised much discretion. This raised questions about the equity and efficiency of police service delivery. It was apparent that discretion could not be eliminated; but police have succeeded in preventing abuses by structuring discretion. Through guidelines and policies, police agencies provide direction to their officers as to the best means of handling sensitive situations. But where do the guidelines and policies come from? In 1979, Herman Goldstein described what he called the "problem-oriented approach" as a means of developing these guidelines. Goldstein's approach is the core of problem-oriented policing.

## Management

While these studies were being conducted, the characteristics of American police officers were changing. More and more officers were getting college degrees and thinking of themselves as professionals. Like workers in private industry, officers began to demand a greater decision-making role in their agencies. Many police managers, recognizing that satisfaction and participation influence job performance, began to make better use of the skills and talents of their officers. Through job enrichment, managers gave their officers more interesting and challenging work, and made working conditions more flexible. And many departments made decision making more participative, by establishing task forces, quality circles, or management-by-objectives programs. Problem-oriented policing incorporates job enrichment, flexibility, and participative management, to make the fullest possible use of the skills and talents of street-level officers.

Problem-oriented policing applies findings from these five streams of research. As suggested by the effectiveness research, problem-oriented policing uses time management and thorough analysis to address groups of similar incidents, or problems. But it recognizes a broader role for police than just crime control, focusing on problems besides crime, and involving police with citizens, businesses, and other agencies to identify and resolve citizens' concerns. Finally, problem-oriented policing involves substantial changes in the police organization. It is a means for structuring discretion; it draws on the expertise of police officers and applies their desire to have decision-making roles.

## Designing Problem-Oriented Policing

This was the research background when the Problem-Oriented Policing Project began in Newport News. Some departments had implemented problem-solving approaches as part of special units or projects. But no department had implemented a problem-oriented approach agencywide. So an operational system had to be designed and tested. The National Institute of Justice required that the problem-solving system follow five basic principles:

- Officers of all ranks and from all units should be able to use the system as part of their daily routine.
- The system must encourage the use of a broad range of information, including but not limited to conventional police data.
- The system should encourage a broad range of solutions, including but not limited to the criminal justice process.
- The system should require no additional resources and no special units.
- Finally, any large police agency must be able to apply it.

Newport News was chosen to design and implement the system for several reasons. It is a moderately sized agency, with 280 employees serving a population of 155 thousand. So it was small enough that changes could be made in a reasonably short time, but served an urban population with many of the crime problems of big cities. Because Newport News was close to Washington, D.C., Forum staff could conveniently spend a great deal of time in the field. And its chief of police, Darrell Stephens, was well-versed in the background research, felt the project would be worthwhile, and was committed to its success.

To design the system, the Newport News Police Department assembled a task force of twelve department members, representing all ranks and units. As this group had no experience at solving problems, they decided to test the system they were designing on two, persistent problems: burglaries from an apartment complex, and thefts from vehicles. It was understood, however, that all subsequent problems would be handled by officers in their normal assignments.

As shown in Figure C, the Task Force designed a four-stage Problem Solving Process. During the *Scanning* stage, an officer identifies an issue and determines whether it is really a problem. In the *Analysis* stage, officers collect information, from sources inside and outside their agency. The goal is to understand the scope, nature, and causes of the problem. In the *Response* stage, this information is used to develop and implement solutions. Officers seek the assistance of other police units, other public and private organizations, and anyone else who can help. Finally, in the *Assess-*

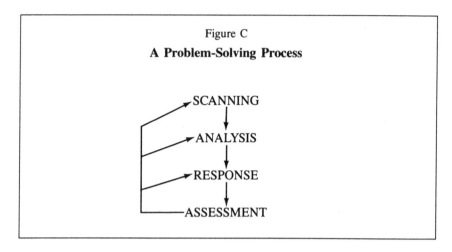

Figure C
**A Problem-Solving Process**

SCANNING

ANALYSIS

RESPONSE

ASSESSMENT

*ment* stage, officers evaluate the effectiveness of the response. Officers may use the results to revise the response, collect more data, or even to redefine the problem.

The heart of this process is the Analysis stage. To help officers analyze problems, the task force designed a *Problem Analysis Guide*. This guide (summarized in Table A) breaks the events that comprise a problem into three components:

1. *Actors*—victims, offenders, and others involved in the events;
2. *Incidents*—the social context, physical setting, and actions taken before, during, and after the events; and,
3. *Responses*—the perceptions and responses of citizens and private and public institutions to the problem.

The guide is a checklist of issues that officers should consider when they study a problem.

All officers of the rank of sergeant and above were trained in the use of the process and the guide, as well as on the research background of problem-oriented policing. The training also emphasized the need to encourage officer initiative in finding problems, collecting information, and developing responses. Officers throughout the department then began to apply the process and the guide.

## Problem-Oriented Policing at Work

There were two basic questions about this process that needed to be answered:

- Can officers use it routinely to solve problems
- Are these problem-solving efforts effective

To answer them, the Forum staff undertook an evaluation of problem-oriented policing in Newport News.

Table A

**The Problem Analysis Guide**
(List of topic headings)

**Actors**
*Victims*
Life-style
Security measures taken
Victimization history
*Offenders*
Identity and physical description
Life-style, education, employment history
Criminal history
*Third parties*
Personal data
Connection to victimization
**Incidents**
*Sequence of events*
Events preceding act
Event itself
Events following criminal act
*Physical context*
Time
Location
Access control and surveillance
*Social context*
Likelihood and probable actions of witnesses
Apparent attitude of residents toward neighborhood
*Immediate results of incidents*
Harm done to victim
Gain to offender
Legal issues
**Responses**
*Community*
Neighborhood affected by problem
City as a whole
People outside the city
*Institutional*
Criminal justice system
Other public agencies
Mass media
Business sector
*Seriousness*
Public perceptions
Perception of others

By June 1986, some two dozen problems had been identified, and were in various stages of analysis, response, and assessment. As Table B shows, officers considered a wide range of problems. Some problems affect citizens throughout the city; others are confined to neighborhoods. Some problems are criminal; others are related to the order maintenance, regulatory, or service roles of the police. Officers and their supervisors identified, analyzed, and responded to these problems during the course of their normal work by applying the process and guide. The number and diversity of problems tackled by department members shows that *police officers can solve problems routinely.*

The second test of the problem-solving process is the effectiveness of the responses. Three efforts have advanced far enough for us to judge their effectiveness. The results are encouraging:

- Burglaries in the New Briarfield Apartment complex were reduced by 35 percent;
- Robberies in the central business district were reduced by 40 percent;
- Thefts from vehicles parked outside Newport News Shipbuilding were reduced by 55 percent.

These results show that problem-solving efforts can be effective. To illustrate how problem-solving works, let us examine the first of these efforts below.

## Burglaries in the New Briarfield Apartments

Briarfield Apartments, a complex of 450 wood-frame units, was built in 1942 as temporary housing for shipyard workers. After World War II the postwar housing shortage was acute, so it remained standing. By 1984, the complex was generally regarded as the worst housing in the city. It also had the highest crime rate in the city: 23 percent of the occupied units were broken into each year. The Task Force decided to use Briarfield as a test of problem-oriented policing. Detective Tony Duke of the Crime Analysis Unit was assigned to study the problem.

To find out how residents felt, Duke arranged for patrol and auxiliary officers to survey a random sample of one-third of the households in January 1985. The residents confirmed that burglary was a serious problem. But they were equally concerned about the physical deterioration of the complex.

Indeed, as Detective Duke interviewed employees of city departments, he found that the burglary problem was related to the general deterioration of the complex. The fire department considered New Briarfield to be a firetrap. Public works was concerned about flooding because the complex had no storm sewers. Standing water rotted the floors, a cause for concern to the codes compliance department. Cracks around the door and window frames let in the cold and rain, and made breakins easy. And many

Table B

**Newport News Officers are Considering a Range of Problems**

| | Citywide | Neighborhood |
|---|---|---|
| **Crime problems** | Domestic homicides | Personal robberies (Central business district) |
| | Gas station driveoffs | |
| | | Commercial burglaries (Jefferson Avenue business district) |
| | Assaults on police officers | |
| | | Vacant buildings (Central business district) |
| | | Residential burglaries (New Briarfield Apts) |
| | | Residential burglaries (Glenn Gardens Apts) |
| | | Larcenies (Beechmont Gardens Apts) |
| | | Thefts from autos (Newport News Shipbuilding) |
| | | Drug dealing (32d and Chestnut) |
| **Disorder problems** | Runaway youths | Rowdy youths (Peninsula Skating Rink) |
| | Driving under the influence | Shot houses (Aqua Vista Apts) |
| | Disturbances at convenience stores | Disturbances (Marshall Avenue 7-Eleven) |
| | | Dirt bikes (Newmarket Creek) |
| | | Disturbances (Village Square Shopping Center |

units were vacant and uninhabitable, providing hiding places for burglars and drug users.

Immediately after the survey, the patrol officer responsible for the area around New Briarfield, Barry Haddix, decided to clean up the grounds of the complex. By working with the apartment manager and city agencies he was able to fix a variety of unsanitary and unsafe conditions. Trash and abandoned appliances were removed; abandoned cars were towed; the pot-holes were filled and the streets were swept.

Meanwhile, Detective Duke found that the owners of the complex were in default on a loan from the U.S. Department of Housing and Urban Development, and that HUD was about to foreclose. This presented the city with a possible solution. Duke wrote a report on New Briarfield, describing the crime problems, the views of the tenants, and the concerns of other city agencies. Chief Stephens used this report to mobilize other city agencies to make a joint recommendation to the city manager: help the tenants find better housing and demolish New Briarfield. The city manager accepted the recommendation. In June 1986, the city proposed that Briarfield be replaced with a new 220-unit apartment complex, a middle school, and a small shopping center. Negotiations are pending with HUD.

This long-run solution will take many months to implement. To hold the line until then, the police department assigned Officer Vernon Lyons to the full-time job of organizing residents of Briarfield and the surrounding neighborhood. Since January 1986, the New Briarfield Community Association has influenced residents to take better care of their neighborhood, and lobbied the resident manager and city agencies to ensure that the complex is properly maintained.

The activities of the police department and the community association have resulted in visibly better living conditions, and in a 35 percent drop in the burglary rate since the police began work.

## New Information, New Responses

One reason these efforts have been successful is that police managers have used the process and guide to encourage officers to gather more information, from a wider variety of sources than before. The survey of New Briarfield residents, and the extensive discussions with the apartment manager and public officials are examples. While studying other problems, officers have conducted literature reviews, interviewed prostitutes and thieves, surveyed businesses, held conferences with local public and private officials, photographed problem sites, and searched title and tax records.

As a result, the responses are more comprehensive than standard incident-driven reactions. This, too, is strongly encouraged by the depart-ment's managers. Some of the responses are improvements on standard tactics. For example, the department responded to the problems of downtown robberies and parking lot thefts by identifying, arresting, and incarcerating the most frequent offenders. But even in these examples, the involvement of people outside the criminal justice system was important. Other responses, such as the actions taken in New Briarfield, hardly involve the criminal justice process at all. While responding to other problems, officers have worked with businesses, the military, citizens' groups, state and federal agencies, and non-profit organizations. So the resources used are as diverse as the problems themselves.

## Implementing Problem-Oriented Policing

Problem-oriented policing involves a substantial change from current practice. The fully problem-oriented police agency will be different from present agencies in several ways.

- Problem-solving will be the standard method of policing, not just an occasionally useful tactic.
- Problem-solving efforts will focus on problems of the public, not police administration.
- When problems are taken on, police will establish precise, measurable objectives.
- Police managers will constantly look for ways to get all members of the department involved in solving problems.

These characteristics will be true of all agencies that have committed themselves to problem-oriented policing. As these agencies gain experience with problem-oriented policing, they should develop three additional characteristics:

- Officers will consistently undertake thorough analyses, using data from many sources.
- Officers will engage in an uninhibited search for solutions to all problems they take on.
- All members of the department will be involved in problem-solving.

Developing these characteristics will take time; police executives should plan to implement problem-oriented policing over a period of many years, rather than weeks or months.

As a result, there are no police departments with all seven of these characteristics yet. Newport News has the first four characteristics; several other departments will be initiating or increasing problem-oriented efforts over the next year. Nevertheless, problem-oriented policing represents an enormous change in the way officers think about their jobs, and in the way the entire department does business. While it will take a long time to develop, the Newport News experience has demonstrated that police executives interested in pursuing the problem-oriented approach can make their agencies more effective in a short time.

Problem-solving will be most successful if the department sets the stage by changing practices that may pose barriers to success. For example, many Newport News officers reported that time was a major constraint to their problem-solving activities. So the police manager should consider such tactics as differential police response and case screening. Use of crime analysis and proactive patrol and investigation tactics can also help the department get ready for less conventional activities. Constantly changing assignments and rotating shifts can make problem-solving activities inconvenient and difficult; police executives should consider stable assignments and shift schedules to remove these obstacles. A tough line on incidents of police corruption will show officers that the discretionary management style that problem-oriented policing requires is not an invitation to illegal or inappropriate behavior. Changes in promotion and reward procedures, implementation of management-by-objectives, and explicit training in effective problem-solving techniques can both motivate officers to solve problems and show them that the administration is serious about its efforts.

Getting support from institutions outside the police department is critical, since they provide information about problems and assistance in solving them. However, the problem-oriented approach may be difficult to sell to those outside policing: there is no unit, equipment, or other physical evidence to which the police can point; some will assume the police department has been solving problems all along. This puts a burden on police executives to begin teaching local government officials, members of civic organizations, the press, and others about the nature of the changes as soon as they decide to make them.

This process of educating the department and the public will continue once the police executive has committed the department to problem-oriented policing. Aside from education, the most important task for the police executive will then be to provide leadership and direction to street-level supervisors. Sergeants and lieutenants are especially important to the success of problem-oriented policing, because problem-solving efforts will rarely be cut-and-dried. Supervisors must be prepared to give their officers lots of discretion, assistance, and support, but they must also ensure that officers are putting in their best efforts. Supervisors must be patient, and emphasize performance; but they must also insist that officers keep at their work until they do what can reasonably be done. Under problem-oriented policing, the first-line supervisor's job becomes one of continually balancing conflicting objectives.

In the beginning, police managers at all levels will face a tension between the quantity of problems solved and the quality of problem-solving efforts. If they set standards too high or encourage officers to take on very large problems, they may scare others off; but if standards are set too low, problem-solving may appear trivial. Police executives will have to manage this tension carefully, although both quality and quantity are possible in the long run.

## Conclusions

The Problem-Oriented Policing Project was undertaken to test two premises: that officers throughout a police agency could apply problem-solving techniques as part of their daily routine, and that their problem-solving efforts could be effective. The Newport News experience suggests that these premises are correct. Many officers were able to get involved; their efforts were effective at reducing the size and seriousness of the problems they attacked.

This does not imply that all problem-solving efforts will be successful, of course, or even that all departments will be able to implement the problem-oriented approach. But it does demonstrate that problem-oriented policing can be successful, and that it deserves further experimentation. As other departments begin to adopt the approach, they will need to develop it further, fitting it to local conditions. If many departments adopt and develop the approach—if problem-oriented policing eventually replaces incident-driven policing as the basic organizing principle of American police work—its present stage of development will look primitive, indeed.

At base, however, it will remain the same. Problem-oriented policing emphasizes cooperation between the police, the public, and other agencies. It helps to ensure that police consider and respond to a wide variety of problems affecting the quality of life, not just crime. It gives line officers a chance to use their knowledge and experience to improve the communities they serve.

But it is much more than that. Problem-oriented policing represents a fundamental change from incident-driven policing. The Newport News Police Department—and other departments that adopt this approach—will continue to respond to incidents. But they will go beyond this first step, becoming much more than a crime control and emergency services agency. Instead, the Newport News experience suggests that the police department will become the front line in a comprehensive, human services system that includes the criminal justice system, other government agencies, private institutions, and private citizens themselves. The result will be more effective responses to crime and other troubling conditions.

# Section VII

## Use of Force

The authority to use force in the line of duty is one of the most controversial aspects of police work. While it is a necessary tool for officers in controlling crime and apprehending criminals, it also is the greatest source of police abuse of authority and citizen complaints. Police officers have the right to use force in certain specific situations, but questions are raised as to when it should be employed and how much force is necessary. The abuse of this authority is one of the most difficult problems facing police administrators today.

The beating of Rodney King in Los Angeles in 1991 provided an excellent example of the problems and consequences involved in the use of force. Regardless of the legal and policy-related responses to these events, the citizens of South Central Los Angeles made their opinions clear. Hopefully, this beating and the violent response to the not-guilty verdicts was a tragic but isolated incident. Unfortunately, there is no reason to believe that these events will not be repeated.

In article twenty-nine, "Controlling Police Use of Deadly Force: Assessing Two Decades of Progress," Professor Mark Blumberg discusses many of the changes that have taken place in statutes, administrative policies and practices regarding police use of deadly force. In addition, he examines the social context in which these changes have occurred. Professor Blumberg concludes that enormous progress has been made in the past twenty-five years with respect to controlling the unrestrained use of firearms by police officers.

Dr. James J. Fyfe distinguishes between police violence that is clearly extra-legal and violence that is simply the unnecessary result of police incompetence in article thirty, "The Split-Second Syndrome and other Determinants of Police Violence." He suggests that much of the problem with the excessive use of force is the result of officers being placed in situations that force the officer to make life and death decisions while under extreme time constraints or what he terms "the split-second syndrome." Dr. Fyfe concludes by proposing two principles that can be used to avoid the split-second syndrome: tactical knowledge and concealment.

Another use of deadly force is police pursuit driving. In earlier decades, pursuit was a widely accepted practice that was seen as necessary and appropriate. Today, police pursuit has taken on a new and deadly meaning. Pursuits must be limited to situations in which the need to immediately apprehend the suspect outweighs the risk to the public created by the pursuit. Dr. Geoffrey P. Alpert provides us with a critical look at this practice, which is similar to using a firearm—necessary but requiring significant controls and restrictions.

As a final article in this section, Victor Kappeler and Michael Kaune provide a critical review of police use of excessive force. These authors explain the use of force from a legal perspective and note the potential for civil liability. The effect of excessive force goes beyond legal exposure for the police officers involved and can have a devastating impact on the community and police everywhere.

# 29

# Controlling Police Use of Deadly Force
## Assessing Two Decades of Progress

*Mark Blumberg*

## Introduction

An unjustifiable killing by a police officer can have tragic consequences. As recent events in St. Petersburg, Florida demonstrate (Navarro, 1996:7), community outrage over a shooting that is perceived as unwarranted may lead to civil unrest resulting in property damage and further loss of life. In addition, the municipality may be forced to pay a large sum in civil damages; the officer may be terminated from the department (in extreme cases, criminally prosecuted as well); and the damage to police-community relations may take years to mend. Despite the harm that results from such incidents, it was only in recent years that any meaningful attempt to examine or control the use of deadly force by police officers was undertaken. Prior to the 1970s, police officers had wide discretion regarding the use of firearms; police departments often had poorly defined or nonexistent policies regarding this issue. Investigations into police shootings were sometimes conducted in a half-hearted manner, and police agencies often did not keep records of all firearm discharges by officers. In addition, social science research on this topic was practically nonexistent and no meaningful attempt to measure the incidence of police killings on a national basis had been undertaken.

This situation has changed dramatically in the last 25 years. First, many states have passed statutes which modified the common-law "fleeing-felon" doctrine that had allowed police officers to use deadly force for the purpose of apprehending any fleeing-felon who otherwise would escape. Second, the U.S. Supreme Court has ruled that shootings of unarmed, nonviolent fleeing felony suspects violate the Fourth Amendment to the Constitution.[1] Third, almost all major urban police agencies have enacted restrictive administrative policies regarding deadly force.

Prepared especially for *Critical Issues in Policing*, 3/E, by Mark Blumberg.
* The author would like to thank Dr. James J. Fyfe, who, over the years, has contributed valuable ideas and insights on many of the issues discussed.

Fourth, the U.S. Supreme Court has made it much less difficult for a citizen to file a lawsuit and collect civil damages as a result of a police action (including a questionable shooting).[2] Fifth, a substantial body of social science research has evolved which examines many aspects of the deadly force question, including such important concerns as the impact of departmental policy on the frequency of police shootings.

This article discusses many of the changes which have been outlined above and examines the social context in which they have occurred. The discussion begins with an examination of the more restrictive legal and administrative constraints which have been placed upon the use of police firearms in recent years. The rationale behind the common-law "fleeing-felon" doctrine is explored as well as the reasons why this doctrine is no longer valid as an appropriate justification for police use of deadly force. This is followed by an overview of the findings from the large body of research on police firearms usage which has accumulated over the last two decades. Special attention is devoted to three areas: (1) those studies which have policy implications; (2) studies which attempt to determine the number of killings by police officers in the United States; and (3) studies which examine the question of why African Americans are overrepresented as the victims of police shootings. In the concluding section, the effectiveness of various strategies for controlling the use of deadly force is examined. In particular, those strategies which have been demonstrated as being successful will be highlighted and suggestions regarding additional steps that police administrators may wish to consider in the hope of further reducing the level of police-citizen violence will be offered.

## Restricting Police Use of Deadly Force

### Legal Constraints

Unlike police officers in Europe (Rechtschaffen, 1985), law enforcement personnel in the United States have traditionally possessed enormous discretion regarding the use of deadly force. In addition to the right to use lethal force in self-defense (a right which is enjoyed by all citizens), police officers have historically been granted, under the "fleeing-felon" doctrine, the right to use deadly force to apprehend *any* fleeing felony suspect who could not otherwise be captured. This doctrine evolved during the Middle Ages in England and was transported to the thirteen colonies. It later became the law in almost all states.

At the time the "common-law" evolved, the "fleeing-felon" doctrine made sense. For one thing, all felonies were punishable by death in England during this period of time and courts did not devote as much attention as at present to safeguarding defendants' rights or to the presumption of innocence. Thus if deadly force was used, the felon was merely receiving the same penalty that would be imposed after trial. Today, the situation is quite different. Very few felons are put to death.[3] In fact, as a result of the U.S. Supreme Court's ruling in *Coker v. Georgia*,[4] it is unlikely that a state could constitutionally execute an individual for any crime other than murder. Therefore, the "common-law" as applied in twentieth century America no longer merely sanctioned the use of deadly force for the purpose of apprehending a felon who was likely to be executed. Instead, it allowed the use of deadly force to apprehend suspects who would be sent to prison if captured, or maybe even granted probation.

The second reason that the "fleeing-felon" doctrine is no longer appropriate pertains to the nature of the felony/misdemeanor distinction. At common-law, only the most serious offenses were classified as felonies (e.g., murder, mayhem, arson, rape, etc.). Today, there are literally hundreds of felonies. Many of these are statutorily created offenses which are *mala prohibita* in nature and proscribe conduct that poses no physical danger to anybody (e.g., income tax evasion, possession of a substantial quantity of marijuana, shoplifting expensive items, etc.). Consequently, a rule which originally gave the authorities the right to use deadly force when necessary to apprehend the most dangerous criminals was transformed into a statute that allowed its use against a wide variety of individuals who did not present a physical danger to either the police or the public.

The third distinction between the period in which the common-law developed and the present is that there was no communication between law enforcement agencies in the former period. Therefore, felons who escaped were likely to remain at liberty forever. This is no longer true in many cases. Today, sophisticated computer networks give police departments the ability to instantaneously retrieve information on wanted criminal suspects from the FBI. Consequently, the choice is no longer to shoot at a fleeing-felon or risk his permanent escape. In many cases, the choice is to use deadly force and perhaps kill the suspect in the process of apprehension or to let the individual escape and hopefully be apprehended at a later point in time.[5]

The fourth distinction between common-law times and the present also relates to changes in technology that have occurred. At the time that the "fleeing-felon" doctrine came into existence, there were no guns. Persons seeking to bring felons to justice were limited to the use of knives, swords, and other weapons that were effective only in hand-to-hand combat. With the invention of the handgun, the authorities were given the power through the "fleeing-felon" doctrine to stop individuals over a much greater distance, and at little risk to themselves.

Finally, it should be noted that felons had a greater incentive to resist arrest in common-law time. Because almost all felonies were punishable by death, suspects had every reason for using any method at their disposal to avoid capture. Under those circumstances, citizens (there were no municipal police agencies until the nineteenth century) needed the legal right to use deadly force if necessary. Today, because very few felons are at risk of being executed, the incentive to escape at any cost is greatly reduced as well as the justification for allowing the police to use deadly force to effect capture.

Nonetheless, the "fleeing-felon" doctrine remained the law in almost all American jurisdictions until the 1960s. Several factors coalesced during that decade which contributed to a reevaluation of these statutes. For one thing, the Civil Rights Movement opened the door to increased political participation by African Americans and other minorities in American society. Second, this was an era of heightened concern regarding the rights of criminal suspects.[6] Third, the latter part of the 1960s was a period of racial unrest and many American cities experienced riots which often resulted not only in property damage and injuries, but in loss of life as well. The President's Commission (1967) took note of the fact that in many of these urban disturbances, the precipitating event had been a questionable shooting by a police officer. The Commission recommended that police officers be forbidden from using deadly force to apprehend nonviolent fleeing felons (e.g., an unarmed burglar).

As a result of these social changes in American society, many states began to change their statutes so that police officers no longer had unbridled power to shoot at all fleeing-felons. Jurisdictions generally followed one of two approaches in limiting the use of deadly force. The most common modification was to limit the use of deadly force to situations in which the police sought to apprehend individuals who had committed so-called forcible felonies. Such felonies are generally limited to the more serious offenses involving either violence or the threat of violence (e.g., robbery). By the early 1980s, eleven states had taken this approach (Wukitsch, 1983).

Another common approach was to adopt the legal guidelines suggested by the Model Penal Code[7] for the control of deadly force. Under the Model Penal Code, a police officer may use deadly force only when the arrest is for a felony which involved the use (or threatened use) of deadly force or when the officer believes that the suspect will cause death or serious bodily injury if not immediately apprehended. By the early 1980s, ten states were following the recommendations of the Model Penal Code (Wukitsch, 1983).

Despite these reforms, almost half of the states in 1985 still subscribed to the common-law "fleeing-felon" doctrine when the U.S. Supreme Court handed down its decision in *Tennessee v. Garner*. In this case, the court ruled that the use of deadly force to apprehend a fleeing felony suspect who did not pose a significant threat of death or serious physical injury to the officer or others, violated the Fourth Amendment right to be protected against unreasonable search and seizure. The effect of this decision was to strike down as unconstitutional those statutes still in effect which gave police the legal right to use deadly force against nonviolent, unarmed fleeing-felons. The common-law "fleeing-felon" doctrine had at last been put to rest in the United States.

## Administrative Constraints

Police shootings tend to be a community concern in urban areas. State legislatures, on the other hand, are often dominated by conservative rural and suburban lawmakers. Consequently, many legislatures have been reluctant to restrict the use of deadly force by police officers. As already noted, almost half of the states still followed the common-law at the time the *Garner* decision was decided in 1985. Furthermore, only four state legislatures took action to change these unconstitutional statutes in the five-year period that followed *Tennessee v. Garner* (Fyfe and Walker, 1990). Therefore, the responsibility for developing and implementing sensible deadly force guidelines has become the responsibility of police administrators.

Police agencies always have the option of making their firearms policies more restrictive than state law. Obviously, they cannot make them less restrictive and give officers the right to use deadly force where state statute forbids it. By the early 1970s, police agencies had begun to draft administrative guidelines which restricted the use of deadly force by officers under their command. The guidelines generally paralleled the various types of revised state laws. Some departments prohibited the use of deadly force except in the apprehension of suspects who had committed a violent felony. Others prohibited its use except when the suspect was likely, in the officer's view, to endanger the safety of the community if not immediately captured. Finally, a few departments forbid officers from using their firearms except in the defense of life.

Not surprisingly, most police agencies that promulgated restrictive deadly force policies were urban departments. Because urban police administrators must be responsive to diverse interest groups, they are often under intense community pressure to minimize the use of firearms by officers under their jurisdiction. In a 1982 survey of seventy-five police departments that served populations of 100,000 or more, it was noted that only one agency allowed the use of deadly force to apprehend all fleeing-felons (Fyfe and Blumberg, 1985). On the other hand, a survey (undertaken in the early 1980s) which included county sheriffs' departments and police agencies serving a population of 20,000 or more indicated that slightly more than a third of the departments had no written policy whatsoever (Nielsen, 1983).

As a consequence, the *Garner* decision is likely to have its greatest impact on smaller police agencies (Fyfe, 1988). Nonetheless, a study of police departments in the 100 most populous cities of the United States conducted in 1988 reported that 30 percent of the agencies surveyed had to make changes in policy as a result of this decision (Walker and Fridell, 1992: 101). However, the researchers note that most of the changes were probably minor in nature.

## Overview of Research on Police Use of Deadly Force

### Introduction

Prior to 1970, Robin (1963) was the only empirical study of police deadly force reported in the social science literature. However, over the last 25 years, a substantial body of research has evolved. The findings of various studies have often provided guidance to police administrators who seek to make decisions that serve both the interests of law enforcement and those of the community. In the Supreme Court's *Garner* decision, the majority cited a number of social science studies in reaching its decision. In an *amici curiae* brief filed with the court, the Police Foundation (1984), joined by a number of police and criminal justice professional associations as well as law enforcement chief executives, was able to cite numerous studies which supported the conclusion that "laws permitting police officers to use deadly force to apprehend unarmed nonviolent fleeing felony suspects actually do not protect citizens or law enforcement officers, do not deter crime or alleviate problems caused by crime, and do not improve the crime-fighting ability of law enforcement agencies. . . . Moreover . . . laws permitting use of deadly force in those circumstances are responsible for unnecessary loss of life, for friction between police and the communities they serve resulting in less effective law enforcement, and for an undue burden upon police officers who must make and live with the consequences of hasty life-or-death decisions" (p. 11).

In this section, we present an overview of the social science research on police deadly force. It should be noted that a review of the findings of all previous studies is outside the scope of this article. That task has already been performed quite satisfactorily (Alpert and Fridell, 1992; Binder and Fridell, 1984; Geller and Scott, 1992). Instead, several important themes which have received attention in the literature are examined. The discussion begins with an overview of the various descriptive studies which have been conducted. This is followed by a review of studies which have policy implications for controlling police use of deadly force. Third, attention is directed to that body of research which attempts to measure the incidence of deadly force in the United States. Finally, empirical studies which seek to determine why African Americans are overrepresented as the victims of police shootings are examined.

## Descriptive Studies

Much of the early empirical research on the nature of police deadly force relied on the records from coroners' inquests (Harding and Fahey, 1973; and Knoohuizen, Fahey and Palmer, 1972) or newspaper accounts (Kobler, 1975a; and PILCOP, 1979). These sources are problematic for a couple of reasons. For one thing, records from coroners' inquests only contain reports on incidents in which citizens have been killed by the police. They do not include information on woundings or firearms discharges that do not hit their intended target. Second, the number and types of shooting incidents that are portrayed in newspaper accounts may be more a function of the editorial policy of the newspaper than the behavior of the police. In larger cities, the newspaper may not include accounts of all police shootings. For these reasons, many researchers have sought access to police department records pertaining to deadly force. Some of the most comprehensive descriptive studies of deadly force incidents have been the result of agency cooperation with these requests (Geller and Karales, 1981; Fyfe, 1978; and Milton, Halleck, Lardner, and Albrecht, 1977).

For the most part, descriptive studies of deadly force incidents have focused on the situational characteristics of police shootings (e.g., the precipitating event that brought the police into the situation, the time and place that the incident occurred, etc.) and the characteristics of the opponent (e.g., age, race, gender, whether or not the opponent had a weapon, etc.). After reviewing the available research, Geller and Karales (1981) note that a pattern seems to emerge which supports the following assertion:

> The most common shooting of a civilian by a police officer in urban America is one in which an on-duty, uniformed officer shoots an armed, black male between the ages of 17 and 30 at night in a public location, in connection with an armed robbery. Typically, the shooting is subsequently deemed justifiable by the police department following an internal investigation. Even if the officer is criminally prosecuted, a jury is unlikely to convict. . . . (p. 56)

Although this general pattern appears to be present in most cities, the research indicates that there are some differences across communities with respect to the situational characteristics of deadly force incidents (Blumberg, 1983). Readers wishing to examine the findings of previous studies in some detail are advised to consult Alpert and Fridell (1992), Geller and Scott (1992), Binder and Fridell (1984), and Geller (1982).

Despite the substantial body of research which has accumulated, Geller and Karales (1981: 74 76) correctly caution that studies conducted by different researchers are often not comparable to one another. For several reasons, it is risky to compare shootings across communities. First, varying definitions of what constitutes deadly force are utilized. Some studies examine only fatalities (Matulia, 1982); others include nonfatal hits (Geller and Karales, 1981; Milton, Halleck, Lardner, and Albrect, 1977), or nonfatal hits and "harmless discharges" as well in their definition of deadly force (Fyfe, 1978). This is problematic because research suggests that shootings which result in a fatality are qualitatively different from nonfatal hits and "harmless discharges" with respect to a number of important incident and suspect characteristics (Donahue and Horvath, 1991). Second, similar variables are often defined in a dissimilar manner (e.g., some researchers classify an opponent who tries to run down an officer with a vehicle as being "unarmed," others do not). Third, various studies examine different time periods. Finally, different limitations on the types of incidents that will be included in the data base are utilized by various researchers. These include differences with respect to the inclusion of accidental shootings, off-duty incidents, and those occurring outside of the officer's jurisdiction.

Much of the descriptive research is based on the view that police shootings are split-second decisions. Consequently, scholars have carefully examined the "final frame" in which officers actually decided to use deadly force. However, as Scharf and Binder (1983) have noted, many decisions to use deadly force are only one possible outcome resulting from a series of events, actions, and decisions which preceded the shooting. Furthermore, many shootings are averted even when officers have legal justification for using their firearm. Geller (1985) has proposed a methodology which could re-direct the focus of research away from the "final frame" and toward an analysis of "high-risk" encounters.[8] The intention would be to determine which factors are associated with officer restraint under these circumstances.[9] Fridell and Binder (1992) have utilized this approach in an analysis of potentially violent confrontations in four U.S. cities. The findings of this study suggest that situations resulting in police use of firearms are more likely to be characterized by ambiguity and surprise than those encounters where a shooting was averted.

## Controlling the Use of Firearms

Researchers have investigated the effectiveness of various strategies designed to reduce the level of deadly force employed by police officers. One possible means to achieve this goal is to change the applicable state statute. Another is to have police departments on their own initiative adopt more restrictive firearms policies. Third, a few studies have examined the question of whether it might be feasible to reduce the level of police-citizen violence by recruiting officers who have certain background characteristics. Finally, a number of authors have examined the impact of the *Garner* decision. The research in each of these areas is reviewed below.

### Statutory Change

Waegel (1984) has conducted the only systematic evaluation of the impact on police shootings resulting from a change in state law. He reports that a 1973 change in the Pennsylvania statute had little effect on police behavior. The number of shootings that were directed at nonviolent fleeing-felons did not decline despite the statutory change that prohibited this practice. Indeed, 19.9 percent (approximately one out of five) of the shootings that occurred after the law took effect appeared to violate the revised statute (p. 136). The author concludes that "in the absence of a clear message from the department administration to the effect that 'the new guidelines will be adhered to,' subcultural values defining certain uses of violence as serving positive ends appear to take precedence over legal responsibilities in guiding the behavior of some officers" (p. 137).

### Departmental Policy

A number of researchers have evaluated the impact of a more restrictive departmental firearms policy. The findings from these studies offer strong support for the view that departmental policy can be effective in reducing the number of police shootings, even in the absence of a change in state statute. Fyfe (1979) examined shootings by New York City police officers and concluded that a more restrictive policy did indeed reduce the number of shootings. Meyer (1980) observed that a more restrictive firearms policy was effective in reducing shootings by Los Angeles police officers. Binder, Scharf and Galvin (1982) reported a decline in the monthly shooting frequencies of three cities (Birmingham, Newark, and Oakland) following the introduction of a more restrictive policy. Although their findings were not statistically significant, this "result seemed due to the inadequacy of the data for the type of test rather than to absence of effect" (Binder and Fridell, 1984: 272). Geller and Scott (1992) report that the Dallas Police Department revised its shooting policy on two separate occasions during the 1980s. In each case, this change was accompanied by a decline in the number of intentional discharges. Finally, Sherman (1983) has reached the same conclusion regarding the effect of a more restrictive firearms policy in Atlanta and Kansas City (Missouri).

The research suggests not only that a tightened policy which is rigorously enforced will reduce the number of shootings, but that it will change their nature as well. Fyfe (1979) notes that in the period following the policy change in New York, a greater proportion of shootings were in defense of life than was previously the case. Likewise, Sherman (1983) concludes that the proportion of shootings involving unarmed fleeing-felons declined as a result of the policy changes that had been instituted in Atlanta and Kansas City (Missouri).

Policymakers do not seek to reduce the number of police shootings regardless of the costs involved. Consequently, the effect that restrictive firearms policies have on officer safety has received considerable attention in the literature. Fyfe (1979) reports that line-of-duty deaths actually declined in New York after the implementation of the more restrictive firearms policy. Although he does not necessarily attribute the decline to the adoption of the policy, it is clear that a more restrictive policy does not make the police officer's job more dangerous. Other researchers have examined data for Oakland and Los Angeles and also report no greater danger to police officers after the adoption of stricter shooting guidelines (Geller and Scott, 1992). In fact, Sherman and Cohn (1986) note that despite increasingly restrictive departmental firearms policies and despite the fact that the number of citizens killed by police officers was cut in half for the fifty largest cities between 1971 and 1984, the number of "citizen killings of police in those cities fell by two-thirds in the same fifteen year period" (p. 1). Clearly, restrictive firearms policies do not make a police officer's job more risky. They may even contribute to a safer working environment.[10]

Another question that has been posed is whether a policy that gives police officers a wide range of discretion with respect to the use of deadly force serves as a deterrent to crime. The available evidence suggests that it does not. Milton, et al. (1977) has observed that the rates of shooting vary across cities and that these rates are not explained by the index crime rate (p. 30) or the violent crime rate (p. 31). In other words, cities with a high rate of police shootings do not necessarily have either more or less crime than other communities. Likewise, Gain (1971) notes that an administrative policy which prohibited the use of deadly force against fleeing burglars had no effect upon the arrest rate for this crime. Finally, Fyfe (1981a) suggests that felons run a greater risk of being shot by their victims than by the police and because the actual probability of any particular felon being shot is so low,[11] a permissive deadly force policy is not likely to deter very many potential criminals.

### Recruiting Certain Types of Police Officers

If it could be demonstrated that officers possessing certain background characteristics were less likely to use firearms, police departments could vigorously recruit such applicants with the end result that the level of violence directed at citizens would be reduced. Unfortunately, there have been relatively few empirical studies on the relationship between police officer characteristics and the use of deadly force.

One of the few data sets that allowed analysis of these questions was made available to this author by the Kansas City (Missouri) Police Department. Demographic data were collected on a wide variety of characteristics for all officers who fired their weapons at citizens between 1972 and 1978. Identical information was also collected on a randomly selected control group representing all nonshooters who served with the department during this period of time (Blumberg, 1983). Because the research design incorporated data regarding the unit and beat of assignment for all officers, it was possible to examine the relationship between officer characteristics and deadly force while controlling for exposure to risk resulting from work assignment.

The findings indicated that most officer characteristics were not related to shooting behavior. Height, race, prior military service, marital status at appointment, officer education (Sherman and Blumberg, 1981), preservice officer experience with firearms, and whether or not the officer had been arrested prior to joining the department all failed to distinguish between shooters and nonshooters. Only officer age and length of police service were strongly related to the use of deadly force. Younger officers and those with fewer years of police experience were significantly more likely to be involved in a shooting, and to become involved in a repeat shooting than were older, more experienced officers (controlling for work assignment). The only other social characteristics that distinguished between shooters and nonshooters were gender and social class. Female officers and those from a middle-class background appeared to be less likely to shoot at citizens. However, the relatively small number of female officers in the sample[12] and the large number of missing cases[13] with respect to officer social class precluded a precise analysis of these relationships.

For the most part, these findings are consistent with other research on this topic. Geller and Karales (1981) and Fyfe (1981b) examined the relationship between officer race and shooting behavior. Both researchers noted that black officers have a higher shooting rate than white officers. Geller and Karales attribute this disparity primarily to a black overrepresentation in off-duty shootings (stemming in large measure from officer residence patterns). Because black officers are more likely to reside in high-crime neighborhoods, they are more likely to become involved in an off-duty shooting. There was no significant relationship between officer race and on-duty shooting incidents. Fyfe (1981b) did find racial disparities among both on-duty and off-duty shooting rates, but reports that when officer assignment and residence are controlled, most of the differences disappear. Clearly, it is not the race of the officer that is important in determining the probability that a shooting will occur; it is where the officer works (assignment) and where he or she lives (residence).

Grennan (1987) as part of a larger study examined the question of whether female members of male-female patrol teams in New York City fire their weapons as frequently as their male counterparts. His observation that they do not buttresses the tentative conclusion reached by Blumberg (1983) in Kansas City (Missouri). Both studies are consistent with findings from previous research that women approach patrol activities with a less aggressive style (e.g., they make fewer arrests) than male officers (Bloch and Anderson, 1974; Sherman, 1975).

Finally, Alpert (1984) has examined the relationship between officer age and shooting behavior in Miami. Although there was no relationship between officer age or length of police service and the use of firearms in this community (contrary to the findings reported by Blumberg [1983] for Kansas City [Missouri]), the author notes that younger, less experienced officers are more frequently involved in unintentional shootings. It has been suggested that at the time of this research, many of the Miami officers were so young that they were not at risk of intentional shooting because they were in training rather than on the street.[14]

The question arises, what are the implications of these findings for police administrators who seek to reduce the level of police-citizen violence? Several points should be noted. First, consistent with the findings of previous research that examined the use of nonlethal force by the police (Friedrich, 1980), there is little relationship between most officer background characteristics and deadly force. Second, there is some reason to believe that as female officers become more numerous in law enforcement agencies, they may have a salutary effect on the number of police shootings. Third, although police agencies are not likely to reduce the incidence of deadly force in the short term by hiring additional black officers, the long-term outcome of such a policy may be quite different. Walker (1985) notes that the infusion of minority (and female) officers into police departments may change the character of the prevailing police subculture. Although it would be difficult to measure, it is possible that a predominantly white department in a jurisdiction with a large black population would not have as harmonious a relationship with the community, and thus have a higher level of police-citizen violence, than would a department with a substantial number of black officers. Finally, police administrators may wish to consider various methods by which the number of shootings by younger officers could be reduced. Croft (1986), after observing that officers who use a high level of *nonlethal* force are more likely to be younger, appointed at an earlier age, and less experienced, proposes that the costs and benefits of the following strategies be examined: (1) raising the recruit entry age to 25; (2) giving younger recruits longer periods of training; (3) requiring younger recruits to work longer periods with older, more experienced officers; or (4) not immediately assigning younger officers to work alone on patrol.

## The Impact of *Tennessee v. Garner*

Several researchers have examined the impact of the U.S. Supreme Court's ruling in *Tennessee v. Garner*, which prohibited the use of deadly force to apprehend nondangerous fleeing felon suspects. It is perhaps appropriate that the effect of this decision, both within the state of Tennessee (Culliver and Sigler, 1995) and in the city of Memphis, has been analyzed (Sparger and Giacopassi, 1992).

Culliver and Sigler (1995) conducted a mail survey to determine what impact *Garner* had on law enforcement agencies serving Tennessee communities with a population over 5,000. They compared the number of reported firearms discharges by officers in 1982 and 1988 (three years prior to and three years after *Garner*). The researchers note that *Garner* did make a difference. The number of reported firearms discharges decreased from .0448 to .0268 per 100,000 population between these years. This finding is consistent with the view expressed earlier that this ruling is likely to have its greatest impact on smaller police agencies.

The *Garner* case initially grew out of a police shooting in Memphis, Tennessee, where an officer responding to a burglary call fatally shot and killed a fifteen-year-old suspect who was attempting to flee. For this reason, the Supreme Court's ruling was of special interest to members of this department. Sparger and Giacopassi (1992) have examined the impact on police use of deadly force of policy restrictions put in place in Memphis in response to this decision. They conclude that "both the overall shooting rate and the apparently discriminatory application of lethal force were reduced greatly as a result of the post-*Garner* deadly force policy" (p. 224). However, because officers on average made fewer violent felony arrests in the post-*Garner* period than in the comparable period preceding this decision (Sparger and Giacopassi, 1992: Table 2), one cannot be confident that the authors are correct in asserting that between "five and 15 lives were spared" as a result of the department's response to *Garner* (p. 224). Perhaps, fewer violent felony arrests means that there are fewer opportunities for officers to become involved in violent encounters with a citizen.

The only study that has attempted to evaluate the national impact of this ruling was conducted by Abraham N. Tennenbaum (1994). He utilized a complex statistical technique known as interrupted time series analysis to examine supplemental homicide reports. These data are collected by the FBI and include information on justifiable police homicides. The analysis indicated that *Garner* was indeed having a beneficial effect. As a result of this decision, there were approximately 60 fewer homicides per year by police officers in the United States (a reduction of more than 16 percent—p. 257). Furthermore, this decrease was not limited to jurisdictions where the deadly force statute had been declared unconstitutional.

Because almost all large urban police departments had already adopted guidelines prohibiting the use of deadly force against nonviolent unarmed fleeing felons, many researchers did not expect this ruling to have much of an impact (Walker and Fridell, 1992; Fyfe, 1988). It is therefore somewhat surprising that each of these studies found that *Garner* had some effect. The most plausible explanation for this may be Tennenbaum's (1994) assertion that law enforcement agencies responded to this decision by implementing shooting policies which went beyond the legal requirements set down by the Supreme Court.

## Measuring the Frequency of Police Deadly Force

Local, state and federal government agencies in the United States collect statistical data that encompasses a vast range of topics. For this reason, it is quite surprising to learn "that this country simply does not know how many of its own citizens it kills each year under the authority of the state" (Sherman and Langworthy, 1979: 553). There is simply no reporting system regarding police-caused homicides and no accurate count of how many citizens are shot or killed by the police each year in the United States.

In the absence of any centralized reporting system, a number of early studies relied on the *Vital Statistics of the United States* to measure the number of police-caused homicides (Kuykendall, 1981; Kobler, 1975b; and Takagi, 1974). These data are based on death certificates which have been completed by coroners (or medical examiners) and submitted to the state health department. In turn, the various state health agencies transmit these reports to the National Center for Health Statistics (U.S. Public Health Service) which publishes the information in the *Vital Statistics*. Because there is a category on the death certificate entitled, "death by legal intervention—police," these reports should provide an accurate count of the number of police homicides in the United States. Unfortunately, this is not the case.

According to the *Vital Statistics*, the number of police-caused homicides in the United States between 1965 and 1979 ranged from a low of 265 to a high of 412 per year (Binder and Fridell, 1984: 253). However, Sherman and Langworthy (1979) observed, based on an examination of data supplied by police agencies in thirteen jurisdictions, that the *Vital Statistics* may underreport the number of police killings by as much as 51 percent (p. 553). This system of reporting has so many flaws that the information generated is unreliable with respect to both the total number of police killings and the relative incidence of police-caused homicide from one city to another. It is ironic, as the authors note (Sherman and Langworthy, 1979: 560), that "while the police may have the most to gain by undercounting the number of citizens they kill. . . . it is the police that have provided the largest figures on the numbers of citizens killed."

More recent studies have relied on data voluntarily supplied by police departments to examine the number of police killings in urban communities (Sherman and Cohn, 1986; and Matulia, 1982). Each of these reports concluded that the level of police-citizen violence varies dramatically across departments. Sherman and Cohn (1986: 3) report that officers in New Orleans killed citizens (between 1980 84) at a rate fifty-two times higher than was the case in Honolulu. Large differences between cities persist regardless of whether population size, the number of police officers, or the overall general homicide rate in these communities is taken into account. Likewise, Milton, et al. (1977) observed that the variation in police officer shooting rates across cities is not explained by the population size (p. 29), police department size (p. 30), index crime rate (p. 30), or the violent crime rate (p. 31). Clearly, the evidence supports the conclusion that the substantial differences observed between various agencies with respect to the incidence of police shootings are due to policy considerations and not the crime rate.

Some researchers have attempted to determine the number of killings by police officers by examining the supplemental homicide reports filed by law enforcement agencies with the FBI's Uniform Crime Reporting Section. Although the bureau does not publish these data because of reservations with respect to their quality (Sherman and Langworthy, 1979: 547), they have generally been available to researchers.

Not all police agencies file these reports with the FBI (Geller and Scott, 1992). Consequently, it is not possible to utilize these data to calculate the number of justifiable homicides that occur annually in the United States. However, Geller and Scott (1992) have used these statistics to conclude that the 50 largest cities experienced a cumulative total of 142 killings, on average, each year during the period 1985–89 (p. 118).

Unfortunately, previous research suggests that there are wide disparities between homicide totals supplied by individual police agencies and those reported by the FBI for the same department (Fyfe, 1988). For example, the FBI data undercount by 49 percent the number of citizens killed in five of these large cities when the numbers are compared to statistics supplied by the individual agencies (Geller and Scott, 1992: 38). As a consequence, if the same pattern of undercounting exists in the other 45 large cities, there was actually "an aggregate annual average of 251 fatalities" (not 142) in the 50 largest cities during this period (Geller and Scott, 1992: 39).

Sherman and Cohn (1986) have reported that the number of justifiable homicides declined substantially in the largest 50 cities between the years of 1970 and 1984. Whether this trend continued into the late 1980s depends on whether the total number of justifiable homicides for these jurisdictions was closer to 142 or 251 (Geller and Scott, 1992). Although several police agencies have reported an increase in the number of shooting incidents during the late 1980s (as a result of the more violent climate in which their officers were working), Tennenbaum's national analysis concluded that the number of justifiable homicides declined after 1985. As a consequence, it is difficult to determine whether the number of killings by police officers is actually increasing or decreasing.

There are other factors that complicate research into this issue. For one thing, there has been a substantial increase in the number of armed private security officers in recent years. Because most shooting incidents involving these individuals are generally not counted by researchers,[15] any decline in the number of killings reported for public police may be offset by an increase in the number of killings that involve private police (Geller and Scott, 1992).

Second, not all shootings by police result in death. Some firearms discharges result in nonfatal injuries and others miss their intended target altogether. Nonetheless, the terms "justifiable homicide" and deadly force have sometimes been used interchangeably, even though there is no relationship between the number of fatalities and the number of deadly force incidents across communities. In fact, previous researchers have reported that not only does the proportion of incidents which result in death vary dramatically across jurisdictions (Geller and Scott, 1992), but there is little relationship between the rates of justifiable homicide and the firearms discharge rates among officers across departments (Fridell, 1989). For example, Sacramento had the lowest rate of justifiable homicide among 35 cities but ranked 14th in terms of the firearms discharged rate (Fridell, 1989: Table 1). The former ranking was attributable to the fact that only 2 percent of the discharges resulted in a death. On the other hand, the proportion in San Antonio was 46.5 percent.

The inescapable conclusion one must draw from the available evidence is that nobody knows how many times each year law enforcement officers in the United States fire their weapons at citizens, how many citizens are wounded or how many are killed as a result of police bullets. Furthermore, it is unclear whether the trend in recent years is toward fewer shootings or more. For these reasons, a number of authors have proposed that a national reporting system be established to gather these data (Geller and Scott, 1992; Sherman and Cohn, 1986). Not only would such a system be beneficial to researchers who are examining various issues surrounding police use of deadly force, it would also enable administrators, policymakers and citizens to assess how much restraint officers in a particular community are exercising relative to members of other departments who are working in comparable environments.

## Race and Police Firearms

Police shootings of African Americans under questionable circumstances have created friction between law enforcement agencies and African Americans in numerous communities. The National Advisory Commission (1968) reported that many of the urban disorders which plagued American cities during the 1960s were precipitated by white officers shooting black citizens. In the years since that period, controversial shootings involving African Americans have continued to periodically create mistrust between police departments and the citizens they serve. Birmingham, Dallas, Houston, Los Angeles, St. Petersburg, Miami and New York are among the cities that have experienced shootings which resulted in a storm of controversy, polarized the community and even led to violence in some cases. Thus, it is not surprising that a great deal of research has been directed toward examining the relationship between citizen race and police use of deadly force.

All studies are in agreement that African Americans are shot or killed by the police disproportionate to their numbers in the general population (Donahue, 1983; Binder, Scharf and Galvin, 1982; Matulia, 1982; Blumberg, 1981; Fyfe, 1981c; Geller and Karales, 1981; Meyer, 1980; Milton, Halleck, Lardner, and Albrect, 1977; Dallas Police Department, 1974; Jenkins and Faison, 1974; Takagi, 1974; Burham, 1973; Knoohuizen, Fahey and Palmer, 1972; and Robin, 1963). However, various researchers disagree about why this is the case. As noted by Goldkamp (1976), there are essentially two points of view. One perspective sees these high shooting rates of minority citizens as indicative of race discrimination by the police. The most strident proponent of this point of view is Takagi (1974: 30) who has argued that "the police have one trigger-finger for whites and another for blacks." Sherman (1980) is a more moderate spokesperson for this position. He argues that the higher rates of police killings for African Americans should be seen as suggestive of racial discrimination on a national basis. On the other hand, most researchers attribute the high number of African-American victims to their disproportionate arrest rates for crimes of violence (Binder, Scharf and Galvin, 1982; Matulia, 1982; Blumberg, 1981; Fyfe, 1981c; Milton, Halleck, Lardner, and Albrect, 1977; Dallas Police Department, 1974; and Harding and Fahey, 1973). These arrest rates are seen as reflecting a disproportionate participation by African Americans in violent criminal activity and therefore account for the relatively large number of African Americans shot by the police.

Analyzing the reason why African Americans are over-represented as the victims of police firearms is not a simple task. Consequently, researchers have relied on a number of strategies. The most common technique is to compare arrest statistics with shooting data to determine if African Americans are more likely to be the victims of police shootings than would be expected by their representation among those arrested for various types of criminal activity. Another relatively common technique is to examine the situational characteristics of shooting incidents to determine whether African Americans are shot or killed under circumstances that present less danger to the officer, and thus less justification, than incidents involving white victims. For example, a finding that a greater proportion of African-American than white shooting victims were unarmed would be considered evidence that racial discrimination on the part of the police was a factor in the disproportionate involvement of African Americans as shooting victims in a particular community.

In general, few studies which rely on arrest statistics report findings that are consistent with the notion that race discrimination on the part of the police explains the disproportionate representation of African Americans as shooting victims. Most researchers conclude that the proportion of African-American shooting victims is quite comparable to their representation among persons arrested for serious criminal activity (Donahue, 1983; Binder, Scharf and Galvin, 1982; Matulia, 1982; Geller and Karales, 1981; Fyfe, 1978; Milton, Halleck, Lardner, and Albrect, 1977; Dallas Police Department, 1974; Harding and Fahey, 1973; and Burnham, 1973). However, evaluation of arrest statistics is problematic for a couple of reasons. For one thing, there is the question of which arrest data are the appropriate comparative measure with which to examine the issue of racial discrimination in police shootings (Blumberg, 1981). Should the analysis focus on a comparison of the proportion of African Americans arrested for all offenses, index offenses, or only violent index offenses in a particular jurisdiction? Second, there is concern whether arrest statistics really are a valid indicator of the extent to which minority citizens commit crimes (Peirson, 1978). If arrest statistics themselves reflect discriminatory law enforcement by the police, they obviously have little value for addressing the question of whether shootings are the result of race discrimination by the police.

For these reasons, some researchers have compared the situational characteristics of shootings involving white and African-American victims. However, these studies do not always reach the same conclusion. Binder, et al. (1982) report that comparable proportions of white and African-American opponents were either attacking the officer or fleeing when shooting incidents are aggregated in four cities. Likewise, Blumberg (1981) observed that the situational characteristics of police shootings are similar in Kansas City (Missouri) and Atlanta regardless of opponent race. Contrary to these findings, Meyer (1980: 107) reports that shooting incidents involving African-American suspects in Los Angeles differ in circumstances from those involving others.

Unfortunately, this type of analysis also raises a troubling methodological issue. Because baseline data regarding all police-citizen encounters are generally not available, researchers cannot determine whether the police are more likely to shoot African Americans than whites under the same circumstances. Therefore, even if the data indicate that equivalent proportions of African Americans and whites were not armed, this still does not answer the question of whether unarmed African Americans are more likely to be shot since the relative number of unarmed whites and African Americans who come in contact with the police remains unknown.[16] One can only determine whether the situational characteristics of shooting incidents are similar for both races.

Fyfe (1982) was able to overcome this problem by calculating the rates at which police officers in New York and Memphis shot at unarmed white and African-American property crime suspects. His analysis indicated that Memphis police officers were 15 times more likely to shoot at African-American property crime offenders than at whites suspected of similar offenses (Fyfe, 1988: 194). However, in New York City, no evidence of racial discrimination was observed.

After reviewing the growing body of research on this topic, several observations are in order. For one thing, the question of why African Americans are disproportionately the victims of police shootings must be examined on a city-by-city basis. As the Fyfe (1982) study illustrates, what is true in one department may not be the case in another. Second, there is reason to believe that racial bias is more likely to be a factor in police shootings in those departments where officers are allowed to exercise a wide degree of latitude with respect to the use of deadly force (Fyfe, 1988). This view is supported by Sparger and Giacopassi (1992: 224), who report that "both the overall shooting rate and the apparently discriminatory application of lethal force in Memphis" were "reduced greatly as a result of the post-*Garner* deadly force policy." Finally, it is clear that until the society addressed the various social and economic inequalities that contribute to high rates of violent crime in many inner-city communities, African Americans are likely to remain over-represented, not only as victims of police firearms but in prisons and jails as well.

## Evaluation of Control Mechanisms

In this section, the effectiveness of various control strategies will be examined. The discussion will highlight those approaches which have been demonstrated to work, those which do not appear to be effective, and other steps which can be taken to further reduce the level of police-citizen violence.

### Criminal Law

Griswold (1985) has proposed that state statutes be amended to give the police the right to use deadly force only in self-defense. Fyfe and Blumberg (1985) have rejected this approach, arguing that the criminal law can only be effective in protecting citizens against the most egregious violations by police officers. The finding by Waegel (1984) that a change in state statute alone had little impact on police uses of deadly force would appear to support this contention.

The criminal law does not appear to be an effective means of reducing the number of police shootings for a number of reasons. For one thing, given the level of public anxiety over crime in American society, state legislatures are not going to want to be perceived as "further handcuffing the police" by passing statutes which restrict police firearms solely to defense-of-life situations. Such a statute would prevent law enforcement officers from even shooting to stop a mass killer if he were to drop his gun and flee after emptying his weapon into a group of citizens. Second, even if such statutes were passed, prosecutors are not likely to jeopardize their working relationships with police departments by charging officers with a crime for shooting a fleeing criminal suspect who has committed a violent crime. The evidence from previous studies is quite clear; very few officers face criminal charges as a result of on-duty shooting incidents (Waegel, 1984; Kobler, 1975b; and Knoohuizen, et al., 1972). Finally, even if prosecutors were willing to file charges under these circumstances, it is unlikely that juries would convict. Given the choice between taking the side of a police officer who may have acted in an overzealous manner to protect the public and a fleeing suspect who has committed a violent felony, there is little doubt which choice the jury will usually make. For these reasons, no state has seen fit to enact such a statute.

## Civil Liability

The U.S. Supreme Court has made it possible for victims of police misconduct (or their estates) to file suit against the municipality employing the officer under provisions of the federal civil rights statute.[17] The result has been that almost every shooting by a police officer culminates in a civil suit. Although juries may be very reluctant to convict law enforcement personnel of criminal charges, there is much less reluctance to award civil damages. Judgments in excess of one million dollars are not unknown. Because the award must be paid by the municipality, such lawsuits may create a strong financial incentive for police agencies to insure that their officers are carefully screened, properly trained and adequately supervised.

## Departmental Policy

The evidence is overwhelming that a restrictive firearms policy which is tightly enforced can be effective in reducing the number of police shootings. The task for police administrators in the "post-*Garner*" era is to decide how restrictive they want these policies to be. Three general options are available: (1) the *Garner* standard which allows the use of deadly force to apprehend any fleeing-felon who is armed with a weapon or who has committed a violent crime; (2) the standard proposed by the International Association of Chiefs of Police (IACP) which allows the use of deadly force to prevent the escape of a suspect who is reasonably believed to represent an *imminent* threat to public safety (Matulia, 1982); or (3) the strict defense-of-life standard favored by Sherman (1980). Whichever option is chosen, the policy should be framed in a manner that effectively guides officer behavior on the street (Alpert and Smith, 1994).

## Training

In far too many police agencies, officers receive extensive training to learn how to shoot but little attention is given to the ethical responsibilities such a decision entails. Furthermore, the mechanical training which is designed to give officers proficiency in the use of firearms is often unrealistic and inappropriate.

Traditionally, agencies have trained their officers to shoot by firing at fixed targets from a stationary position with adequate light. Because police-citizen confrontations rarely, if ever, occur under these circumstances, it is doubtful that this practice is helpful. More recently, police departments have adopted what is called the "Shoot—Don't Shoot" approach. Officers are presented with a series of vignettes and told to fire their weapons when they feel it is appropriate. Critics (Dade County Grand Jury, 1983) contend that this approach almost always results in the officer firing at the target, that it creates undue anxiety on the part of the officer, and that the focus is entirely on the "final frame." The series of decisions which lead up to the confrontation are ignored. In addition, the presentation of scenarios which are totally implausible serve no purpose except to create paranoia in the mind of the officer (e.g., a twelve-year-old child on a bike who suddenly draws a weapon on a police officer).

Scharf and Binder (1983) discuss a number of training strategies which have been adopted by various departments and which appear to hold more promise. For example, recruits in New York City discuss actual shooting incidents where the departmental guidelines are ambiguous. The Honolulu Police Department offers recruits training in the martial arts. Rochester, New York gives officers eight hours of training in the "ethics of using deadly force." Other departments require recruits to participate in role-playing situations which are designed to develop procedures for peacefully resolving dangerous situations. Many agencies now train officers in the skills of hostage negotiation. Some departments use what is referred to in Kansas City (Missouri) as "Operation 100" which is a carefully designed set of procedures for handling barricaded suspects. Unfortunately, not all agencies have adopted these sophisticated training procedures.

## Conclusion

In recent decades, enormous progress has been made with respect to controlling the unrestrained use of firearms by police officers. During this period, we have witnessed a number of important developments which have resulted in important changes within the police culture (Sherman and Cohn, 1986): firearms training has been improved, police departments have promulgated less permissive policies, social science researchers have amassed a large body of valuable information and the U.S. Supreme Court has issued a major ruling on this question. Although there is still considerable room for improvement in some areas, the record of the last two decades is clearly cause for optimism as we look to the future.

## Notes

[1] *Tennessee v. Garner*, 105 S.Ct. 1694 (1985).
[2] *Monell v. Department of Social Services*, 436 U.S. 658 (1978).
[3] Between 1977 and 1994, 257 persons were executed by judicial order upon conviction in the United States (Stephan and Snell, 1996: 10).
[4] *Coker v. Georgia*, 422 U.S. 584 (1977).
[5] Because clearance rates for many crimes are quite low, some have claimed that flee-

ing felons are not likely to be apprehended. However, as Silberman (1978) notes, these clearance rates are misleading. Because offenders generally commit many offenses, not just one, the likelihood of eventually being arrested is much greater.

[6] Many of the important decisions expanding the rights of criminal defendants (e.g., *Gideon v. Wainwright, Mapp v. Ohio, Miranda v. Arizona*, etc.) were handed down by the Warren Court during the 1960s.

[7] The Model Penal Code was drafted by the American Law Institute in 1962 as a guide which states may wish to follow when revising their criminal statutes and procedures.

[8] It is ironic that an earlier study undertaken in Chicago and co-authored by Geller is entitled, "Split-Second Decisions" (Geller and Karales, 1981).

[9] Hopefully, it will be possible to identify those types of situations which present a high risk of violence. Through proper training, officers can be encouraged to utilize procedures which reduce this risk.

[10] Because these restrictive policies in no way inhibit the officer from using deadly force in self-defense, it is not surprising that they do not adversely impact on officer safety.

[11] Fyfe (1981a: 381) has estimated that the police shot at a suspect in less than .02 percent (1 out of 5,000) of the reported cases in which a nonviolent felony occurred in the United States during 1978.

[12] There were forty-four female officers serving with the Kansas City (Missouri) Police Department on December 31, 1978, comprising only 4 percent of the agency's personnel.

[13] Officer social class was defined in terms of the father's occupation. Because many officers did not answer this question on their employment applications, information regarding social class was unavailable in many cases.

[14] Personal communication from Dr. James J. Fyfe, May 20, 1985.

[15] These incidents would be counted only if the security personnel were off-duty police officers employed on a second job.

[16] E.g., let us say that 50 percent of both white and African-American opponents were armed. It would still be argued by some that this does not eliminate the possibility that African Americans are more likely to be shot than whites under similar circumstances. Because baseline data with respect to the number of armed citizens of each race who come in contact with the police are not available, a definitive answer to this question is not possible.

[17] *Monell v. Department of Social Services*, 436 U.S. 658 (1978) and *Owen v. City of Independence*, 445 U.S. 622 (1980). In fact, the *Garner* decision grew out of a civil action that had been brought by the deceased boy's father.

# References

Alpert, Geoffrey P. 1984. *Police Use of Deadly Force: The Miami Experience*. Center for the Study of Law and Society, University of Miami.

Alpert, Geoffrey P. and Lorie A. Fridell. 1992. *Police Vehicles and Firearms: Instruments of Deadly Force*. Prospect Heights, IL: Waveland Press.

Alpert, Geoffrey P. and William C. Smith. 1994. "How Reasonable is the Reasonable Man?: Police and Excessive Force." *Journal of Criminal Law and Criminology* 85(2): 481–501.

Binder, Arnold and Lorie Fridell. 1984. "Lethal Force as a Police Response." *Criminal Justice Abstracts* 16(2): 250–80 (June).

Binder, Arnold, Peter Scharf and Raymond Galvin. 1982. "Use of Deadly Force by Police Officers." *Final Report*. Washington, DC: National Institute of Justice.

Bloch, Peter B. and Deborah Anderson. 1974. *Policewomen on Patrol: Final Report.* Washington, DC: Police Foundation.

Blumberg, Mark. 1983. "The Use of Firearms by Police Officers: The Impact of Individuals, Communities, and Race." Ph.D. dissertation, *School of Criminal Justice*, State University of New York at Albany.

_____. 1981. "Race and Police Shootings: An Analysis in Two Cities," in James J. Fyfe (ed.) *Contemporary Issues in Law Enforcement.* Sage Publications.

Burnham, David. 1973. "3 of 5 Slain by Police Here are Black, Same as the Arrest Rate." *The New York Times.* August 26.

Croft, Elizabeth Benz. 1986. "Police Use of Force: A Twenty Year Perspective." A paper presented at the *Annual Meeting of the Academy of Criminal Justice Sciences.* Orlando, Florida.

Culliver, Concetta and Robert Sigler. 1995. "Police Use of Deadly Force in Tennessee Following *Tennessee v. Garner.*" *Journal of Contemporary Criminal Justice* 11(3): 187–95.

Dade County Grand Jury. 1983. *Final Report.* Eleventh Judicial Circuit of Florida.

Dallas Police Department. 1974. *Report on Police Shootings.* Dallas, Texas: Center for Police Development, Southern Methodist University.

Donahue, Michael Eugene. 1983. "Halt . . . Police!: An Analysis of the Police Use of Deadly Force in a Large Midwestern City." Ph.D. dissertation, *Michigan State University.*

Donahue, Michael E. and Frank S. Horvath. 1991. "Police Shooting Outcomes: Suspect Criminal History and Incident Behaviors." *American Journal of Police* 10(3): 17–34.

Fridell, Lorie A. 1989. "Justifiable Use of Measures in Research on Deadly Force." *Journal of Criminal Justice* 17: 157–65.

Fridell, Lorie A. and Arnold Binder. 1992. "Police Officer Decisionmaking in Potentially Violent Confrontations." *Journal of Criminal Justice* 20:385–99.

Friedrich, Robert J. 1980. "Police Use of Force: Individuals, Situations, and Organizations." *The Annals of the American Academy of Political and Social Science* 452:82–97.

Fyfe, James J. 1988. "Police Use of Deadly Force: Research and Reform." *Justice Quarterly* 5(2): 165–205.

_____. 1982. "Blind Justice: Police Shootings in Memphis." *Journal of Criminal Law and Criminology* 83(2): 707–22.

_____. 1981a. "Observations on Police Deadly Force." *Crime and Delinquency* 27(3): 376–89.

_____. 1981b. "Who Shoots? A Look at Officer Race and Police Shooting." *Journal of Police Sciences and Administration* 9(4): 367–82.

_____. 1981c. "Race and Extreme Police-Citizen Violence," in R. L. McNeely and Carl E. Pope (eds.) *Race, Crime and Criminal Justice.* Sage Publications.

_____. 1979. "Administrative Interventions on Police Shooting Discretion: An Empirical Examination." *Journal of Criminal Justice* 7(4): 309–23.

_____. 1978. "Shots Fired: A Typological Examination of New York City Police Firearms Discharges 1971 1975." Ph.D. dissertation, *School of Criminal Justice*, State University of New York at Albany.

Fyfe, James J. and Mark Blumberg. 1985. "Response to Griswold: A More Valid Test of the Justifiability of Police Actions." *American Journal of Police* 4(2): 110–32.

Fyfe, James J. and Jeffery T. Walker. 1990. "*Garner* Plus Five Years: An Examination of Supreme Court Intervention into Police Discretion and Legislative Prerogatives." *American Journal of Criminal Justice* 14(2): 167–88.

Gain, Charles R. 1971. *Discharge of Firearms Policy: Effecting Justice Through Administrative Regulation.* Unpublished paper.

Geller, William A. 1985. "Officer Restraint in the Use of Deadly Force: The Next Frontier in Police Shooting Research." *Journal of Police Science and Administration* 13(2): 153–71.

_____. 1982. "Deadly Force: What We Know: A Practitioner's Desk Reference on Police-Involved Shootings." *Journal of Police Science and Administration* 10(2): 151–77.

Geller, William A. and Kevin Karales. 1981. *Shootings of and by Chicago Police.* Chicago Law Enforcement Study Group.

Geller, William A. and Michael Scott. 1992. *Deadly Force: What We Know.* Washington, DC: Police Executive Research Forum.

Goldkamp, John S. 1976. "Minorities as Victims of Police Shootings: Interpretations of Racial Disproportionality and Police Use of Deadly Force." *Justice System Journal* 2:169–83.

Grennan, Sean A. 1987. "Findings on the Role of Officer Gender in Violent Encounters with Citizens." *Journal of Police Science and Administration* 15(1): 78–85.

Griswold, David B. 1985. "Controlling the Police Use of Deadly Force: Exploring the Alternatives." *American Journal of Police* 4(2): 93–109.

Harding, Richard W. and Richard P. Fahey. 1973. "Killings by Chicago Police, 1969 1970: An Empirical Study." *Southern California Law Review* 46(2): 284–315.

Jenkins, Betty and Adrienne Faison. 1974. *An Analysis of 248 Persons Killed by New York City Policemen.* New York: Metropolitan Applied Research Center.

Kobler, Arthur L. 1975a. "Figures (and Perhaps Some Facts) on Police Killings of Civilians in the United States, 1965 69." *Journal of Social Issues* 31(1): 185–91.

_____. 1975b. "Police Homicide in a Democracy." *Journal of Police Issues* 31(1): 163–84.

Knoohuizen, Ralph, Richard Fahey, and Deborah J. Palmer. 1972. *The Police and Their Use of Fatal Force in Chicago.* Chicago Law Enforcement Study Group.

Kuykendall, Jack. 1981. "Trends in the Use of Deadly Force by Police." *Journal of Criminal Justice* 9(5): 359–66.

Matulia, Kenneth J. 1982. *A Balance of Forces.* Gaithersburg, Maryland: International Association of Chiefs of Police.

Meyer, Marshall W. 1980. "Police Shootings at Minorities: The Case of Los Angeles." *Annals of the American Academy of Political and Social Sciences* 452:89–110.

Milton, Catherine H., J. S. Halleck, J. Lardner, and G. L. Albrecht. 1977. *Police Use of Deadly Force.* Washington, DC: Police Foundation.

National Advisory Commission on Civil Disorders. 1968. *Report of the National Advisory Commission on Civil Disorders.* New York: E. P. Dutton.

Navarro, Mireya. 1996. "State of Emergency Declared after Rioting in Florida," *New York Times,* October 26.

Nielsen, Eric. 1983. "Policy on the Police Use of Deadly Force: A Cross-Sectional Analysis." *Journal of Police Science and Administration* 11(1): 104–8.

PILCOP. 1979. *Deadly Force: Police Use of Firearms 1970–78.* The Public Interest Law Center of Philadelphia.

Police Foundation, joined by Nine National and International Associations of Police and Criminal Justice Professionals, the Chiefs of Police Associations of two States, and Thirty-one Law Enforcement Chief Executives. 1984. *Amici Curiae Brief in* Tennessee v. Garner. United States Supreme Court 83–1035, 83–1070. Washington, DC: August 6.

President's Commission on Law Enforcement and Administration of Justice. 1967. *Task Force Report: The Police*. Washington, DC: U.S. Government Printing Office.

Rechtschaffen, O. H. 1985. "The Use of Firearms by the European Police." *Texas Police Journal* 33(2 March): 17–18.

Robin, Gerald D. 1963. "Justifiable Homicide by Police Officers." *Journal of Criminal Law, Criminology and Police Science* 54:225–31.

Scharf, Peter and Arnold Binder. 1983. *The Badge and the Bullet: Police Use of Deadly Force*. New York: Praeger.

Sherman, Lawrence W. 1983. "Reducing Police Gun Use: Critical Events, Administrative Policy, and Organizational Change," in Maurice Punch (ed.) *Control in the Police Organization*. Cambridge: MIT Press.

_____. 1980. "Execution Without Trial: Police Homicide and the Constitution." *Vanderbilt Law Review* 33(1): 71–100.

Sherman, Lawrence W. and Mark Blumberg. 1981. "Higher Education and Police Use of Deadly Force." *Journal of Criminal Justice* 9(4): 317–31.

Sherman, Lawrence W. and Ellen G. Cohn (with Patrick R. Gartin, Edwin E. Hamilton, and Dennis P. Rogan). 1986. *Citizens Killed by Big City Police, 1970–84*. Washington, DC: Crime Control Institute.

Sherman, Lawrence W. and Robert Langworthy. 1979. "Measuring Homicide by Police Officers." *Journal of Criminal Law and Criminology* 70(4): 546–60.

Sherman, Lewis J. 1975. "An Evaluation of Policewomen on Patrol in a Suburban Police Department." *Journal of Police Science and Administration* 3(4): 434–38.

Silberman, Charles E. 1978. *Criminal Violence, Criminal Justice*. New York: Random House.

Sparger, Jerry R. and David J. Giacopassi. 1992. "Memphis Revisited: A Reexamination of Police Shootings After the *Garner* Decision." *Justice Quarterly* 9(2): 211–25.

Stephan, James J. and Tracy L. Snell (1996). *Capital Punishment 1994*. Washington, DC: Bureau of Justice Statistics.

Takagi, Paul. 1974. "A Garrison State in a 'Democratic' Society." *Crime and Social Justice: A Journal of Radical Criminology* 5 (Spring–Summer): 27–33.

Tennenbaum, Abraham N. 1994. "The Influence of the *Garner* Decision on Police Use of Deadly Force." *Journal of Criminal Law and Criminology* 85(1), 241–60.

Waegel, William B. 1984. "The Use of Lethal Force by Police: The Effect of Statutory Change." *Crime and Delinquency* 30(1): 121–40.

Walker, Samuel. 1985. "Racial Minority and Female Employment in Policing: The Implications of Glacial' Change." *Crime and Delinquency* 31(4): 555–72.

Walker, Samuel and Lorie Fridell. 1992. "Forces of Change in Police Policy: The Impact of *Tennessee v. Garner*." *American Journal of Police* 11(3): 97–112.

Wukitsch, David J. 1983. "Survey of the Law Governing Police Use of Deadly Force." *New York State Bar Journal*, January.

# 30

# The Split-Second Syndrome and Other Determinants of Police Violence

Discussions of police violence are often blurred by the failure to distinguish between violence that is clearly extralegal and abusive and violence that is simply the unnecessary result of police incompetence. This distinction is important because the causes of these two types of violence, and the motivations of the officers involved, vary greatly. Extralegal violence involves the willful and wrongful use of force by officers who knowingly exceed the bounds of their office. Unnecessary violence occurs when well-meaning officers prove incapable of dealing with the situations they encounter without needless or too hasty resort to force.[1]

## Extralegal Police Violence

It is tempting but probably simplistic, to conclude that extralegal police violence results exclusively from the aberrations or prejudices of individual officers or their commanders. If this kind of violence were totally—or even primarily—attributable to officers who regard their badges as licenses to vent hostile and anti-social drives, we should be well advised to try to eliminate it by selecting and monitoring officers with greater care.

Certainly, these personnel processes are important, but it is probably useless to rely almost exclusively on them as the strategy for reducing extralegal police violence. First, our skill at predicting human behavior is not highly developed. Except in obviously extreme cases,[2] it is nearly impossible for personnel administrators to determine which police candidates for officers will eventually engage in extralegal violence. Second, as investigators of police corruption have suggested (City of New York, 1972), it is likely that characteristics of police work and police organizations, rather than characteristics of police officers, are the major determinants of police misconduct.[3]

Anne Campbell and John Gibbs, eds. *Violent Transactions*. New York: Basil Blackwell, 1986. Reprinted with permission of the publisher.

Klockars (1980) makes such an argument in his formulation of a police "Dirty Harry Problem." He argues that some police perceive the procedural limitations under which they work as arbitrary barriers to achievement of one of their most important goals: the protection of good folk through the apprehension and conviction of criminals. Such officers operate on a presumption of suspects' guilt, and become frustrated when legal processes result in acquittals of people who have, in fact, committed the crimes of which they have been accused. Subsequently, to serve what they (and much of the public) see as justice, these officers resort to "dirty means"—fabrication of evidence, intimidation and even torture—to circumvent such perceived barriers to justice as judicial exclusion of illegally obtained evidence, and to make sure that their suspects ultimately receive in court what the officers regard as their just due. Even though the actions of such officers may reflect a widely held view that there should be little distinction between factual guilt and legal guilt (Packer, 1968), they involve, Klockars asserts, wrongful moral choices by the officers themselves. The best way, according to Klockars, of preventing such wrongful choices is to punish the individual officers and the police agencies who make and tolerate them.

As Klockars acknowledges, however, his approach to this kind of violence is not entirely satisfactory. To penalize individual officers who have been trained and socialized by their employers to believe that policing cannot be done by the book and that abuse and misconduct are the most effective means of accomplishing police goals is probably unfair and would almost certainly be ineffective. Extralegal police violence is probably more closely attributable to politically expedient, but morally wrong, definitions of appropriate police conduct at the highest levels of police agencies than to the deviance of street-level officers. Thus, a better way to reduce such violence is to alter the organizational expectations and norms to which the officers who commit abuses conform.

For that reason, Klockars is much more persuasive in his suggestion that police *agencies* bear penalties for extralegal violence than in his qualified advocacy of individual punishment. Certainly, officers who apply wrongful definitions to their work may *deserve* to be punished. But such wrongful definitions are likely to survive them and to dictate the behavior of other officers unless their superiors—and the citizens whose taxes ultimately pay for disciplinary measures against the police—learn that the costs of encouraging or tolerating the use of dirty means to achieve good ends are intolerable.

Thus, as the United States Supreme Court indicated in *Monell* vs *New York City Department of Social Services,*[4] one way to correct high-level tolerance or encouragement of public officials' misconduct is to make citizens liable for their employees' misdeeds. Implicit in this approach is the theory that concerned citizens will then demand that officials behave in a manner that is more consistent with both law and their financial interests. But, because the citizenry usually does not comport with this neat theory, this approach is not totally satisfactory either.

Citizens are often apathetic rather than concerned about the operations of their officials, including the police. Many of them simply expect officials to be there when needed, and become concerned only when officials have failed to meet this responsibility, or when they have personally experienced or witnessed what they regard as a grave injustice at the hands of officials. Further, many of the most concerned citizens regard with great distaste and little empathy the people against whom the police employ extralegal violence. The citizens who have the time to devote to civic affairs belong to the middle and upper classes, who rarely are the victims of police abuse; but it is they who sit on the juries that determine whether police have exceeded the bounds of their authority and, if so, whether the citizens—themselves included—should compensate the victims.

There is probably no better way to reform the wrongful behavior of police officers than to hit in the pocket the citizens to whom they are accountable. But this tactic often fails because those same citizens determine whether and how hard their pockets should be hit, and because they often do not regard as peers the victims of police abuse. Consequently, reality demands that more operationally practicable means of reducing extralegal police violence be found.

One such method is simple but rare: the engagement of leaders willing to disabuse the citizenry of their unrealistic expectations of the police. In a democracy, rates of crime, levels of disorder and the safety of "good people" are more closely associated with social conditions than with the number of police or the willingness of the police to employ dirty means to achieve the good ends of order and public safety. Few elected officials or police chiefs, however, are willing to run the risk of appearing to be soft on crime by announcing to apathetic citizens that crime and disorder are *their* problems rather than police problems and that, unless they are willing to give up many of their freedoms, no level of police presence or toughness is likely to improve matters.[5]

Were more mayors and police chiefs willing and courageous enough to do so, the pressures upon them and their personnel to achieve ends that lie beyond their means would dissipate, as would the temptation to bend the rules in attempts to achieve the impossible.[6] Until we grow a new breed of elected executives and police chiefs who are somehow able to change unrealistic public expectations of the police, however, we will not remove the major source of extralegal police violence, but must expect it to continue, however dissipated by other, less direct, approaches.

## Incompetence and Unnecessary Police Violence

While extralegal police violence is egregious, it probably occurs far less frequently—and probably less frequently injures sympathetic and factually innocent victims—than does police violence emanating from simple incompetence. Such violence occurs when police lack the eloquence to persuade temporarily disturbed persons to give up their weapons, but shoot them instead. It occurs when, instead of pausing to consider and apply less drastic and dramatic alternatives, officers blindly confront armed criminals in the midst of groups of innocent people. It occurs when officers called to quell noisy but non-violent disputes act in a way that provokes disputants to violence to which the police must respond in kind. In short, it occurs when well-meaning police officers lack—or fail to apply—the expertise required to resolve as bloodlessly as possible the problems their work requires them to confront.

Much unnecessary violence occurs because many of us, including many police, have not adequately analyzed the role of the police or the problems they confront. Thus, we have not devised adequate solutions to these problems, and have instead settled for a standard of performance from the police that is far below what we should tolerate from other groups.

## The Role of the Police

A common conceptualization is that the police, along with the courts and correctional agencies, are a component of the criminal-justice system. This observation is true but, for two major reasons, it may lead to shallow analysis of the police and their problems. First, the courts (excluding civil courts) and correctional agencies devote their efforts exclusively to crime-related matters, but police officers do not. The clients of court personnel are those who have been charged with or victimized by crime; without exception, they are alleged criminals and their presumed victims. The people with whom the officials of correctional agencies interact most directly are those who are awaiting trial on criminal charges, or those who have been convicted of crime; without exception they are alleged or convicted criminals. But, in addition to bringing the alleged perpetrators and victims of crime to the attention of the courts, police regularly interact with people in circumstances in which criminal behavior is doubtful or clearly absent. The clientele of the police includes participants in minor disputes and traffic accidents, those who are lost and in need of travel directions, those who suffer sudden illness or injury, and many others whose problems have nothing whatever to do with crime, criminal law or criminal justice.

In addition, in many cases in which it is clear that some violation of criminal law has occurred, police possess greater discretion to devise informal and unrecorded dispositions of offenders than is true of any other criminal-justice officials. The police officer who sends a disorderly group of teenagers on their way on the grounds that it is more just—or more convenient—than arresting them may do so in the knowledge that no official record of his encounter with them will appear anywhere. What he does and says in such a case disappears into the ozone and, unlike a court or correctional-agency decision to release, cannot be objectively reconstructed by reference to any transcript or detailed official document.

In large measure, the police officer decides which of the people with whom he interacts shall come to the attention of the courts. He exercises a degree of discretion that is usually unrestricted by the prior decisions of any public official.[7] He cannot sentence offenders or impose harsh correctional conditions upon them, but he often has the power to choose between letting them go free and initiating a process likely to result in the imposition of penalties by other officials. He also has great power to impose upon his clientele penalties that do not require court agreement with his actions. Should he decide to arrest rather than to release, nothing a prosecutor, judge, defense attorney or correctional-agency official can do is likely to erase that arrest from the police record. Even when he recognizes that conviction is unlikely, the police officer knows that arrest will result in substantial inconvenience and cost.

But, as has been made clear in several attempts to define the police role, the police cannot be comprehensively discussed or understood in terms of their responsibilities to apprehend criminals or to enforce laws. Their job, Wilson (1968) suggests, includes the duty to see that popular conceptions of order are maintained. The police serve to prevent "behavior that either disturbs or threatens to disturb the public peace or that involves face-to-face conflict among two or more persons" (p. 16).

Goldstein (1977) concurs in part, arguing that law enforcement does not describe the role of the police, but instead defines only one of many methods that they may apply to achieve this goal. Bittner (1970) points out another method employed by police to maintain order: the use or threatened use of legitimate force (that is, as approved by both the government and most of the people served by the police) to coerce individuals to behave in accordance with society's expectations.

Still, the functions of the police are so complex that they are not adequately captured by even the broad "order-maintenance" descriptor. Just as many police tasks have little to do with crime or law, many have little to do with threats to public order, and many involve no coercion or threat or use of force. The police are on duty 24 hours a day, seven days a week, Sundays and holidays included, in order to tackle a variety of problems and crises. These range from tree-bound cats, through lost children and persons locked out of their homes, to people who have been horribly mangled in automobile accidents. In none of these cases is the quality of police response less critical for those concerned—the mother of a lost child, or the man whose femoral artery has been severed in a car crash—than in cases where the police are required to exercise their law-enforcement and order-maintenance responsibilities.

The breadth of police work is what makes Goldstein's definition of the role of the police the most comprehensive and satisfactory. He observes that

> The police function, if viewed in its broadest context, consists of making a diagnostic decision of sorts as to which alternative might be most appropriate in a given case. In this respect the total rule of the police differs little

from their role in administering first aid to sick and injured persons. (1977, p. 41)

Goldstein is correct. Police officers, like doctors, lawyers, psychologists and marriage counselors, are human-service workers. Like these others, police are paid to diagnose problems that befuddle the rest of us, to treat those within their competence, and to refer to more specialized agencies and officials those problems that they themselves cannot solve. Just as we call upon the doctor to investigate and treat internal complaints not responsive to our own treatment efforts, so we call upon the police to investigate and treat complaints deriving from certain external conditions that we cannot otherwise ameliorate—noisy neighbors, assault or robbery, the injury of a loved one by a hit-and-run driver.

Police officers, however, treat their clients and professional problems under conditions that do not affect most other human-service workers, and that greatly increase the potential for violence. Police-client interactions are uniquely *urgent, involuntary* and *public*. Unless we and the police fully appreciate the causal relations between these three conditions and violence, we inadequately diagnose police problems. The result is that we witness and experience violence that need not have occurred.

## Urgency of Police-Citizen Encounters

Police are generally unable to select the times at which they will perform their services. They are expected to respond to and resolve our problems *now*, while we routinely agree to wait until two weeks from Thursday to obtain help for our medical and legal dilemmas. In Bittner's terms, the police task consists of resolving problems *"that-ought-not-to-be-happening-now-and-about-which-somebody-had-better-do-something-now"* (1974, p. 30). As a consequence, police usually encounter their clients in circumstances analogous to those faced by hospital emergency-room personnel: they deal with people immediately after their problems have come to light, and must treat not only the substance of these problems, but also the shock that accompanies their clients' discoveries that suddenly all is not well.

## Involuntariness of Police-Citizen Encounters

The constraint of time usually denies police officers the luxury of picking and choosing their clientele from among those deemed in need of police attention, and places great limits on their ability to refer clients and problems to more highly qualified specialists. When we do get to see our family doctor, he may diagnose but decline to treat a problem that he views as most amenable to resolution by a more specialized colleague. But a police officer summoned to a late-night domestic dispute cannot withdraw with a referral to a better trained and more competent officer who does not come on duty until the morning. Regardless of his ineptness, and because his clientele includes the neighbors who cannot sleep because of the noise, he is duty-bound to establish at least temporary peace before he leaves, even if he has to coerce some of his clients to accept his prescriptions.

Therein lies another unique characteristic of police work: many of those who come to police attention do not seek it, but become unwilling clients through the intervention of third parties or of officers themselves. When this happens, just as officers cannot usually decline clients who come to their attention, so their clients cannot withdraw from treatment no matter how distasteful they find it. Given the choice, very few of the clients arrested or brought to book by the police would consent to this form of treatment.

## Public Setting of Police-Citizen Encounters

Unlike even emergency-room personnel, police officers are unable to choose the places in which they perform their services. The work of police patrol officers occurs not in private offices, but in public settings or other locations in which the problems of their clientele have come to light. As a result, police officers suffer the disadvantage of performing in places in which clients' behavior is not constrained by the formality and decorum of a professional setting and the realization that one is on another's territory. The clientele of the police are governed only by the behavioral rules of the street.

Another consequence of the public setting of police work is that officers must be attentive not only to the immediate problems of the clients they have been summoned to treat, but also to third-party reactions to their efforts. If they are to avoid criticism and even interference from bystanders, police officers summoned to restrain emotionally disturbed or drug-crazed persons on the street must do so in a way that is demonstrably proper and humane.

The police officers' concern with the *appearance* of propriety and humaneness is not shared by mental-health professionals who work in residential facilities, or who administer shock therapy to patients in the privacy of their clinics. Nor is it shared by others who must render their services in public places. Ambulance personnel, for example, often perform their work in public, but it rarely involves resolution of disputes or other competing interests, so they need not concern themselves with their audiences' perceptions of their fairness. In addition the work of ambulance personnel usually involves more distastefully gory and less intriguing and public problems than those of the police, so that bystanders watch the proceedings less closely. It is much easier, less nauseating and more interesting to watch the police subdue a street drunk than it is to watch a team of emergency medical technicians treat a man whose leg has been severed in an automobile accident. Finally, the techniques used by ambulance personnel are far more arcane than are those of the police: few bystanders have any experience or expertise in stanching the flow of blood or treating shock, but nearly everybody has attempted to resolve a dispute, calm an unreasonable or unruly person, and seen the ways in which television police subdue suspects. Consequently, few bystanders feel competent to judge or protest the work of ambulance personnel, but many view themselves as qualified to assess the work of the police. As can be seen from cases where riots have been precipitated by bystanders' dissatisfaction with police actions, some are even willing to demonstrate their disagreement violently and immediately.

Police officers must also be acutely aware that the presence of an audience of bystanders may affect their clients' behavior. In some cases, the embarrassment of having one's problems aired in public may cause—or increase—irrational behavior on the part of the client. In others—the crowd encouraging the young man poised to jump from a high roof comes to mind—bystanders may become direct actors in police encounters. In still others, as Muir observes, police respond to street disputes that are "played out on two levels—in the relationship between the two antagonists, and in the relationship of the crowd to the disputants. Police officers have to perceive both levels" (1977, p. 102). Muir describes a situation in which police arrived at a crowded recreation center and found a bat-wielding young man confronting an aide. This case, which superficially appeared to be an attack by an inner-city youth upon an older authority figure could be satisfactorily resolved only if the police took time to learn the antagonists' motivations and the importance of the crowd. Here, the young man suspected that the aide had raped his 13-year-old sister, so that

> From the point of view of the brother of the victim of the alleged rape, he was retaliating not only from a desire for retribution but to deter future marauders. . . . The brother was establishing face in the neighborhood, a reputation for dogged revenge; in thrashing his sister's rapist, he was making a harsh example for all the crowd to see. . . . He was publishing his message for those persons that really counted, those who might think they could push his family around. In the brutish neighborhood he and his family inhabited, the brother was making himself "a man of respect." . . .
>
> In the relationship between the crowd and the brother, the crowd's definition of honorable conduct became crucial. Depending on its expectations of him, his attack on the aide would have different meanings. . . . Anyone who had the talent to influence the crowd's philosophy in this matter could make a great deal of difference to what the brother felt he had to do to establish face. (pp. 102-3)

To summarize, then, a proper analysis of the police role requires acknowledgement of many unique characteristics of the work of street-level officers. Policing is a form of human-service work that requires officers to diagnose the problems they confront, and to decide which of several means of solving them—invoking the law, threatening to invoke the law, employing force or, as in Muir's example, attempting to persuade—is most likely to be successful. The broader discretion available to police officers than to other criminal-justice officials, however, is limited by several constraints unique to policing. There is an urgency about police work that does not affect court or correctional-agency officials or most others whose work involves diagnosis and treatment of human ills. The police cannot select the times or places at which they treat their clientele. They often must do so at odd hours and in very public places. Consequently, if they are to avoid criticism or adverse response by third parties, they must be greatly concerned not only with *doing* the right thing, but also with *appearing* to do the right thing. This compounds the difficulties of police work, because the people they treat are often adversaries rather than individuals who have come to the police for help. The people at the core of police problems often do not agree with police diagnoses of those problems or even that any problem exists. They do not see the police as individuals who have come to help them. Once the police have come, however, neither they nor the police may withdraw until the problem at hand is at least temporarily remedied.

The urgent, involuntary and public relationship between police officer and client creates a high potential for violence. To avert it, police must often apply considerable diagnostic skills, and must learn to manipulate these causal variables in ways that diminish the likelihood that violence will result. If urgency and time constraints sometimes lead to violence, it follows that police should slow the pace of their encounters with citizens so that cooled tempers and the restoration of reason may eventually lead to non-violent outcomes. If involuntariness sometimes leads to violence, it follows that police should attempt to diminish their clients' feelings that something is being done *to* them, by trying to win their confidence and devising problem solutions that at least appear to be collaborative rather than exclusively coercive. If the public settings of police-citizen encounters sometimes lead to violence, it follows that police should inject as much privacy as possible into these encounters.

There is evidence that attempts by police to manipulate time and involuntariness, and to make more private highly volatile encounters between police and citizens, do reduce violence. Recent police efforts to diagnose and plan for hostage situations and situations involving armed and barricaded persons have led to a high rate of bloodless resolution of these situations. The time-manipulative techniques employed in these situations include avoidance and delay of armed confrontation unless it is clear that lives are in imminent danger. Involuntariness is manipulated by trained negotiators who attempt to determine the motives and win the confidence of their subjects, and to convince them that surrender is in their own best interests. Privacy is introduced into these situations by carefully controlling media access to hostage-takers and *vice versa*, and by clearing the public from the immediate areas. These privacy techniques serve the multiple purposes of protecting uninvolved citizens, eliminating the audiences to whom hostage-takers may wish to play, reducing hostage-takers' loss of face at the time of surrender, and eliminating the possibility that the attention of bystanders or the media will encourage hostage-takers or barricaded persons to further rash actions (see, for instance, Schlossberg and Freeman, 1974).

Despite the apparent success of such defusing-techniques, many of us—and many police leaders—often encourage officers to think of themselves as rough and ready men and women of action whose prime function it is to show up quickly at emergencies and to make their diagnoses on the spot. Unless we more strongly encourage officers to develop the requisite diagnostic skills to deal with certain types of situations when they occur, we are likely to witness many more hasty and inaccurate diagnoses and many unnecessarily violent attempts to treat police problems.

## Police Diagnostic Expertise

As too many experiences have demonstrated, police often do not attempt diagnosis until they are in the midst of treating critical problems. The 1965 Watts riot began when, despite the violent reaction of a large and growing crowd drawn by the protests of the suspect's mother, two police officers persisted in their attempts to arrest a drunken driver whom they had already identified and could presumably retake later under quieter circumstances. The 1971 Attica prison riot resulted in the deaths of 39 inmates and hostages when New York State police officers, who usually work alone or in small groups in rural areas, were armed with shotguns and armor-piercing rifles and directed to storm and retake the tear-gas-filled, heavily-walled yard of a maximum-security prison inhabited largely by inner-city convicts. A block in Philadelphia burned down in 1985 when, in an attempt to evict a radical group, a police helicopter dropped onto the roof of an adjoining wooden house an incendiary device that had apparently never before been used by police in any field situation.

Looking back, it is easy to say that these decisions should not have been made. It would probably have been wiser for the police in Watts to have retreated, and to have returned to make their arrest in quieter and less public circumstances. In Attica and Philadelphia, continued negotiation or less drastic tactics probably would have better served the fundamental police responsibility to protect life than did the hastily devised tactics that were employed.

## The Split-Second Syndrome

It is difficult to define the factors that led well-meaning officials to make the bad decisions just reviewed, but it appears that they are reflections of what might be called a "split-second syndrome" that affects police decision-making in crises. This syndrome serves both to inhibit the development of greater police diagnostic expertise and to provide after-the-fact justification for unnecessary police violence. It also serves as a guide to many of the equally unfortunate low-visibility decisions made by individual police officers every day.

The split-second syndrome is based on several assumptions. First, it assumes that, since no two police problems are precisely alike, there are no principles that may be applied to the diagnosis of specific situations. Thus, no more can be asked of officers than that they respond as quickly as possible to problems, devising the best solutions they can on the spur of the moment. This, of course, places an extraordinary burden upon officers, who must make life-or-death decisions under the most stressful and time-constrained conditions.

Second, because of these stresses and time constraints, a high percentage of inappropriate decisions should be expected, but any subsequent criticism of officers' decisions—especially by those outside the police, who can have no real appreciation of the burdens upon officers—is an unwarranted attempt to be wise after the event. Thus, if we are to maintain a police service whose members are decisive in the crises to which we summon them, we had best learn to live with the consequences of the decisions we ask them to make. If we do not, we risk damaging police morale and generating a police service whose members are reluctant to intervene on our behalf.

Finally, the split-second syndrome holds that assessments of the justifiability of police conduct are most appropriately made on the exclusive basis of the perceived exigencies of the moment when a decision had to be taken. So long as a citizen has, intentionally or otherwise, provoked the police at that instant, he, rather than the police, should be viewed as the cause of any resulting injuries or damage, no matter how excessive the police reaction and no matter how directly police decisions molded the situation that caused those injuries or damages.

Thus, should police receive a report of an armed robbery in a crowded supermarket, they should be granted great leeway in their manner of response, because no two armed-robbery calls are precisely alike. If, in the course of responding, they decide that, to prevent the robber from escaping, the best course of action is to confront him immediately in the midst of a crowd of shoppers, they should not be told they should have acted otherwise. When they do challenge the alleged robber and he suddenly reacts to their calls from behind by turning on them with a shiny object in his hand, the only issue to be decided by those who subsequently review police actions is whether, at that instant, the suspect's actions were sufficiently provocative to justify their shooting him. That is so regardless of how the prior actions of the police may have contributed to their peril; regardless of how predictable it was that the suspect would be alarmed and would turn toward the police when they shouted to him; regardless of how many innocent bystanders were hit by bullets; and regardless of whether the reported armed robber was in fact an unhappy customer who, with pen in hand to complete a check for his purchase, had been engaged in a loud argument with a clerk during which he had said that the store's prices were "robbery."

The underpinning of the split-second syndrome, in short, is the assumption that the sole basis on which any use of force by the police needs to be justified is the officers' perceptions of the circumstances prevailing at the instant when they decide to apply force. The officers involved in the incident described above did, of course, possess much information that would lead them to believe that the subject of their call was a robber. When he turned on them, they were entitled, in the heat of the moment, to believe that their lives were in imminent danger. When they made the split-second decision to pull the trigger, they were also entitled to believe that no less drastic action would adequately protect their lives, so they were fully justified in shooting. Under the split-second syndrome, this shooting was a legitimate use of force under provocation.

But such an analysis lends approval to unnecessary violence, and to failure of the police to meet their highest obligation: the protection of life. Split-second analysis of police action focuses attention on diagnoses and decisions made by the police during one frame of an incident that began when the police became aware that they were likely to confront a violent person or situation. It ignores what went before. As the successful application of hostage techniques illustrates, it also ignores the fact that there are general principles that may be applied by officers to a variety of highly predictable, potentially violent situations.

It requires no great diagnostic ability to determine that the officers involved made a significant contribution to the bloody finale of the incident described above. Officers who respond to reports of robberies by charging through the front door and confronting suspects from exposed positions are almost certain to find themselves in great danger, real or perceived, and to face split-second decisions involving their lives, the lives of suspects and the lives of bystanders. Thus, instead of asking whether an officer ultimately had to shoot or fight his way out of perilous circumstances, we are better advised to ask whether it was not possible for him to have approached the situation in a way that reduced the risk of bloodshed and increased the chances of a successful and non-violent conclusion.

## Avoiding Split-Second Decisions

Even though most potentially violent situations encountered by the police are not as clear-cut as the one described in the previous section, opportunities usually do exist for officers to attempt to prevent the potential for violence from being realized. Police are usually assigned to the same geographic areas for long periods, but in my experience they are rarely encouraged to leave their patrol cars when there is little happening and to survey the places in which they might someday be asked to confront potentially violent situations. Were they to do so, they would be able to formulate tentative advance plans for dealing with reported supermarket robberies, warehouse burglaries and the like. Most often, police are directed by radio to scenes of potential violence (Reiss, 1971) and so are usually not on the spot at the time. Thus, even in the few minutes it takes them to get there, they have some opportunity to avoid split-second decisions by analyzing available information and planning their responses in advance of arrival. If they do not, and if they fail to structure their confrontations in a manner that is most likely to avert bloodshed, almost any violence that results is unnecessary, and should be condemned rather than rewarded with head-lines, honors and medals.

Two principles, tactical knowledge and concealment, may be useful diagnostic tools in deciding how to deal with potentially violent people and situations.[8] Tactical knowledge includes prior knowledge of the setting and actors involved. Most often, police officers summoned to potentially violent situations have far less tactical knowledge than is desirable. While they usually know only what they have been told over the radio, any potential adversaries know precisely what is happening, where it is happening and who is involved. Since this places officers at a great disadvantage, it is important that they employ techniques for enhancing their tactical knowl-edge before committing themselves beyond the point of no return. If they fail to do this, they may easily fall prey to the more knowledgeable violent subjects of their calls, or may misinterpret the actions of innocent per-sons—such as the outraged shopper with a pen—in a way that may create violence where none exists. Like the military, they must be expected to learn as much as possible about the settings in which they may have to intervene.

Concealment includes disguising one's intent or identity, as well as employing actual physical cover or shelter. Officers—especially those in uniform—are usually at a disadvantage where this factor is concerned. When they respond to scenes of potential violence (for instance, armed rob-beries in progress), they are readily identifiable, while the subjects of their calls (the robbers) usually are not. Consequently, officers should employ all possible means of concealing themselves or their presence until the moment of least hazard. Doing so generally involves confronting from posi-tions of concealment subjects who are temporarily without concealment. In the example of the reported supermarket robbery, this might mean that responding officers should avoid losing concealment by actually entering the supermarket, and should instead surreptiously take up positions of concealment outside it (for instance, behind parked cars) and wait for their suspect to come to them. The military knows that the safest way to con-front potential adversaries is to wait for the appropriate moment to ambush them from positions of concealment, but police are often encour-aged to charge up hills.

The use of concealment not only minimizes the risk of officers, bystanders and suspects, but may also prevent tragic mistakes. I can recount several occasions in which officers responding to such calls have neglected to seek concealment, have encountered armed individuals from positions of total exposure, have—with some justification—perceived imminent danger to themselves, and have shot persons later found to be plain-clothes police officers or crime victims who had armed themselves to pursue the actual perpetrators. Many of these tragedies might have been avoided if the officers involved had instead confronted these individuals from positions of physical cover. From such positions, officers make themselves near impossible targets, and are able to give their perceived adversaries opportunities to identify themselves or to drop their weapons without placing themselves in jeopardy.

Application of these principles requires that officers diagnose the most critical problems they face—those that may require the use of extreme force—*before* they occur, and that they attempt to apply to their resolution techniques of tactical knowledge and concealment. We demand that from the military and from the fire service, both of which spend considerable time diagnosing and planning for exigencies that we are someday likely to ask them to resolve. We do not tolerate it when their actions in emergency situations demonstrate that they have been taken by surprise and forced to react on the basis of instinct rather than of careful advance diagnosis and planning. But, when police resort to forcible means to resolve readily foreseeable problems that could have been peacefully resolved with advance diagnosis and planning, we not only tolerate but also often reward their behavior. The police officer who shoots and kills an armed robber is often rewarded for his efforts with a medal. Should he instead kill a shopper with a pen, he is likely to be viewed as the unfortunate victim of a shared tragedy who, under the circumstances, had no choice but to take the action he did.

We should pay less attention to the outcomes of potentially violent situations than to questions of whether officers respond to them in ways likely to reduce the potential for violence. If we do not, we fail to legitimize genuinely unavoidable provoked force, and we reward and encourage an operating-style that eschews advance diagnosis, planning and training, and relies on officers' ability to make the most critical decisions under the worst possible conditions. That operating-style can only lead to frequent bad decisions by officers, who in the heat of the moment cannot reasonably be expected to devise solutions of equal quality to those that could be reached through careful advance planning. These results are grossly unfair to the public and to street-level police officers.

Thus, to reduce unnecessary police violence, we must define the police as diagnosticians, and we must demand that they learn that role thoroughly long before they actually confront someone who they have reason to believe is armed and dangerous. As we have done where hostage situations are concerned, we must define as successful those encounters where the police have done everything reasonably possible to avoid violence, and we must cease rewarding easily avoided split-second violence.

## Footnotes

[1] As Bittner suggests, it is also necessary to distinguish between all types of violence and "the exercise of provoked force required to meet illegitimate acts" (1970, p. 36). There is little doubt that the police must be granted considerable license to employ such force, and, in our condemnation of what Bittner calls "provocative violence" by officials, we should be careful to avoid retracting the legitimacy of police authority

to employ necessary provoked force. The police simply cannot function without this authority. We should take care too to distinguish between legitimate provoked force and incompetence-related violence. The former is that *required* to put down threats against officers or other challenges to official authority. The latter is unnecessary, and occurs only because officers lack the expertise to employ readily available and less drastic means of putting down such threats and challenges.

[2] As a result of bureaucratic procedures or administrative apathy, guns and law-enforcement powers have sometimes been granted to, or not withdrawn from, officer candidates or in-service officers whom personnel investigations have shown to possess gross psychological instability or character flaws. I have reviewed police personnel folders that disclose that officers accused of misconduct had been hired by officials who knew that they had previously been excluded or dismissed from police service in other agencies because of congenital brain defects, extensive criminal records, long histories of drug abuse, assaults on supervisors and coworkers, or giving false sworn statements at previous official investigations of allegations that they had committed extralegal violence.

[3] Friedrich reports that the data he analyzed did "not support the notion that police use of force depends very much on the individual characteristics of the police" (1980, p. 89). Sherman's extensive survey (1980) of studies of police behavior found virtually no empirical support for assertions that individual officer characteristics are measurably related to any type of performance in office.

[4] The major import of the judgment in this case is that public agencies are liable when plaintiffs can demonstrate in court that they have suffered constitutional deprivations at the hands of public officials, and that the unconstitutional acts of these officials were directly caused by agency custom and practice. Thus, if an individual were able to demonstrate that he had been unconstitutionally beaten and arrested by a police officer, and that the police department involved had a history of encouraging or tolerating such misconduct, he would presumably be entitled to money damages from both the officer and the government agency that employed him.

[5] In addition, elected officials, who serve as intermediaries between citizens and police, may often be tempted to react defensively to judgments against police, regardless of whether such defensiveness is in the citizens' best interests. Consequently, citizens' ire may be redirected at what may be portrayed by elected officials as the arbitrariness of the courts, rather than at the police misconduct that gave rise to judgments against the taxpayers. For an elected mayor to acknowledge that his police department has operated unconstitutionally is not easy. It requires him to admit that the person he appointed as police chief (or who was otherwise determined to have been best qualified for that position) has performed his duties in a manner that violates the fundamental law of the land.

[6] See Manning (1977), who argues that the police have assumed—or been given—the "impossible mandate" of responsibility for crime control and order maintenance, and that most police are unwilling to admit that they cannot accomplish it.

[7] This is not to suggest that police currently operate with no *a priori* restrictions. As Goldstein (1977) points out, police operations are greatly influenced by legislators, and by the decisions made by prosecutors and judges in prior *similar* matters. My point is that police make decisions about specific individuals and situations before they have come to the attention of other officials.

[8] These principles were first articulated in a training-program I developed in 1976 while on the staff of the New York City Police Academy.

# References

Bittner, E. 1974. Florence Nightingale in Pursuit of Willie Sutton: A Theory of the Police. In H. Jacob (ed.), *The Potential for Reform of Criminal Justice*, Beverly Hills: Sage.

Bittner, E. 1970. *The Functions of the Police in Modern Society*. Rockville, Md: National Institute of Mental Health.

City of New York Commission to Investigate Allegations of Police Corruption and the City's Anti-corruption Procedures. 1973. *Commission Report*. New York: George Braziller.

Friedrich, R. J. 1980. Police Use of Force: Individuals, Situations and Organizations. *Annals of the American Academy of Social and Political Sciences*, 452, 82.

Goldstein, H. 1977. *Policing a Free Society*. Cambridge: Ballinger.

Klockars, C. 1980. The Dirty Harry Problem. *Annals of the American Academy of Political and Social Science*, 452, 33.

Manning, P. 1977. *Police work*, Cambridge: MIT Press.

*Monell vs New York City Department of Social Services*. 1978. 436 US 658.

Muir, W. K. 1977. *Police: Streetcorner Politicians*. Chicago: University of Chicago Press.

New York State Commission on Attica. 1972. *Attica*. New York: Bantam Books.

Packer, H. L. 1968. *The Limits of the Criminal Sanction*. Stanford: Stanford University Press.

Reiss, A. J., Jr. 1971. *The Police and the Public*. New Haven: Yale University Press.

Schlossberg, H. and Freeman, L. 1974: *Psychologist with a Gun*. New York: Coward, McCann and Geohagan.

Sherman, L. W. 1980. Causes of Police Behavior: The Current State of Quantitative RESEARCH. *Journal of Research in Crime and Delinquency*, 17, 69.

Wilson, J. Q. 1968. *Varieties of Police Behavior: The Management of Law and Order*. Cambridge: Harvard University Press.

# The Management of Police Pursuit Driving
## Assessing the Risks

*Geoffrey P. Alpert*

Actuarial statisticians and safety engineers have estimated the extent and costs of accidents, injuries and deaths for many activities and occupations for more than a century. While their facts and figures may deter some organizations and individuals from participating in risky tasks and activities, others continue to take risks, play the odds and enjoy the challenge.

A classic example of a cost-benefit analysis in the construction industry is the planning, insuring and building of the Bay Bridge from San Francisco to Oakland, California. The dangers of building an unprecedented suspension bridge, including job tasks and other types of risk, interrelationships among risk factors, as well as opportunities to reduce risk and error were analyzed and computed. The nature and extent of accidents, injuries and deaths were estimated and costs associated with those values were added to the construction costs. Obviously, the policymakers determined that the benefits of building the bridge were worth the expected and foreseeable human and financial losses.

The concept of calculated risk refers to the ratio of costs and benefits. The critical issue is to identify and measure accurately the costs and benefits. When the potential or anticipated benefits outweigh the risks, then a planned course of action will be acceptable (Krimsky and Golding, 1992). Risk analysis includes risk assessment and risk management; risk is best understood as "the likelihood of injury, harm, damage or loss multiplied by its potential magnitude" (Grose, 1987:25).

To understand risk analysis, the organizational contexts in which they exist must be understood. In the construction industry, the bottom line is (hopefully) the quality of the product and the financial profit. Other organizational contexts are more complicated. For example, police work includes many high-risk activities which move beyond financial consider-

This chapter is an updated version of what appeared originally in W. Bailey (ed.) *The Encyclopedia of Police Science*. Garland Publishing. 1993. Reprinted with permission.

ations and include the balance of law enforcement and public safety (Alpert and Fridell, 1992). Police administrators, policymakers and risk managers must accept, attempt to reduce or avoid physical risk and transfer financial risk. Too often these two types of risk are managed as separate entities, with the former controlled by administrators and the latter in the domain of an insurance carrier.

This actuarial approach to risk management and the probabilistic risk assessment approach can be applied to the analysis of risk in police activities. The actuarial approach as noted above, requires that the expected value of the event and the undesirable consequences be measured and evaluated. In the case of police pursuit driving, the number of events and undesirable consequences can be derived from research. The critical assumption is that the causal agents of the undesirable consequences or negative effects remain stable over time.

Probabilistic risk assessments attempt to predict the likelihood and foreseeability of safety failures of complex systems. That is, by the use of fault-tree or event-tree analyses, these assessments can reveal the failure probabilities for each component and link them to the system structure. The probabilities of success and failure generate a model of overall failure rate.

The success of these methods depends on the information used for estimating the elements of the events. Unfortunately, the lack of large-scale, complex and comparative data sets on police pursuit events reduces the ability to forecast disaggregated outcomes. These pursuit variables, including elements relating to the initiation and termination of the pursuit, the officers' and supervisor's functions, responsibilities of the communications center, traffic regulations, pursuit tactics, and issues concerning interjurisdictional pursuits will be discussed later. In addition, the contents of this chapter will review the risk elements of pursuit driving, the legal concerns and the policy and practices of police agencies.

## Pursuit Driving

Because of the complex nature of pursuit, the various actors, unpredictable actions and a lack of data, the risk assessment techniques perform better for the construction industry than they do for analyses of pursuit driving. One of the major impediments to accurate risk assessment is the unpredictable innocent bystander. When only the police officer and the suspect are considered, the actuarial and probabilistic assessments are powerful. However, these are only two of the three points on an interactive triangle, which has at its remaining corner the environment, including conditions, innocent drivers, passengers and pedestrians. A definition of pursuit and a discussion of the power and influence of each point of the interactive triangle follows.

A pursuit is an event in which the suspect is attempting to allude capture. His goal is to remain free and avoid arrest. Unless he has a death wish, the offender also wants to be safe and will run until he believes there is no chance of escaping or until he believes he is safe (Alpert et al., 1996). In either scenario, the offender will eventually surrender, return to a safe speed or become involved in an accident. It is the police officer and the supervisor who must decide, very quickly, whether to continue or terminate the pursuit.

The suspect, who has refused to heed the commands of the officer, has the primary responsibility to stop the chase by pulling over. The suspect is also directing the pursuit by selecting the course, speed and recklessness of the driving. However, the suspect is influenced psychologically by the police officer.

It is only the police driver who is subject to direct control during the course of police pursuit. The goal of the officer is to apprehend the suspect and make the arrest. Accordingly, it is the officer who must become aware of personal capabilities and take into account environmental conditions which may affect his or her ability to accomplish the mission of police—to protect lives. The officer's decisions must be based on information beyond personal safety and include the potential danger to the motoring public. The police officer must factor into the decision-making process the risk created by the suspect's driving, the potential actions of innocent bystanders, passengers and others who may become involved and how his or her driving influences the suspect's driving. In other words, the officer must understand that when a suspect refuses to stop for the emergency lights and siren, a routine encounter turns quickly into a high-risk and dangerous event. The officer must understand the effect of the "show of authority" by emergency equipment on the suspect's driving. If the suspect becomes reckless or refuses to stop, it is the officer and the officer's supervisor who must determine the value of continuing the pursuit and the risk of the pursuit to the officer, innocent bystanders, passengers and pedestrians. The officer and the supervisor must also understand the influence of the chase on the participants. The need to "win" and make that arrest is often influenced by the adrenaline rush felt by the officer. A pursuit is an exciting event and involves one person running to escape and another chasing to catch. If it continues, it resembles a drag race until one party terminates it or there is a crash.

One reason for this competition is the fact that police officers order thousands of motorists to pull over without complication. Most law-abiding citizens accept the warning or ticket or do not fight with the officer when an arrest is made. Certainly, the officer becomes used to compliance, and when a suspect does not submit to the wishes and orders of the officer, it is often perceived as "contempt of cop."

The final corner of the interactive triangle, the environment, including the innocent bystander, is uncontrollable. Yet, elements of this factor are predictable. Area of the chase, the likelihood of traffic, weather and other matters can be assessed to determine risk. However, an innocent bystander or passenger may not have knowledge of what is taking place and just may be at the wrong place at the wrong time. It is obvious that an officer is better able to control personal actions, reactions and communication than to change the weather, the area, population density or the abilities of the police cruiser. Unfortunately, most law enforcement driving programs view their mission as one of skill development and emphasize exercises designed to hone the trainee's mechanical skill to control the multi-ton guided weapon known as the police cruiser. The unfortunate reality is that much less effort is devoted to training *when* to use those acquired skills than *how* to use them. Comparatively, a pursuit is at least as dangerous to the public as the use of a firearm (Alpert and Fridell, 1992). The potential for physical and human injury becomes frightening where the kinetic energy of a 3,500 pound projectile is unleashed. Similarly, the danger of pursuit is multiplied with each vehicle encountered and frequent assessment of the risk of continuation is paramount (Alpert and Dunham, 1990; Alpert and Fridell, 1992).

Three factors are traditionally identified as comprising the police driving triangle, and it is clear that only one can be subject to control in the heat of the pursuit. Therefore, the police driver is the focus of effective pursuit policy and risk management. What we know about these factors specifically and pursuit in general has been learned from evaluation.

## Evaluation of Pursuit

A police pursuit is an attempt by a police officer to apprehend a suspect by ordering the suspect to halt by use of emergency equipment (lights and sirens). A pursuit is begun only after an officer initiates a traffic, felony or investigatory stop of a vehicle and the suspect refuses to obey the order to stop. Although there are other derivations of the definition, the basic elements of a pursuit, including a suspect fleeing to escape and a police officer chasing to apprehend, are the critical ones.

The evaluation of pursuit driving has only a brief history. Precious little research was conducted on pursuit until the 1980s when pursuit driving was seriously questioned by victims, concerned citizens and progressive police administrators (Alpert and Fridell, 1992). In the 1980s, police pursuit was identified as "the most deadly weapon" (Alpert and Anderson, 1986). Most recently, individual agencies are conducting their own data collection efforts and evaluating their findings. The specific numbers and conclusions from many of these studies have been reviewed elsewhere (Alpert et al., 1996; Alpert and Fridell, 1992). In 1997, it is appalling that only a few states require agencies to collect and analyze data on pursuit. In any case, it must be emphasized that the originating crime in most pursuits remains a traffic offense. Also, it is important to understand that pursuits in urban areas pose far greater risks than those conducted in rural areas and on freeways. Therefore, aggregate statistics mask the very real danger of urban pursuits and those conducted on streets where they are likely to encounter traffic. All the research conducted on pursuit points to the same issue: the balance between the enforcement of laws and the safety of the public. In other words, it is an accepted fact that pursuit driving is a dangerous police tactic and presents risk to the public. Driving on the public streets at excessive speeds or in an erratic manner is dangerous to all involved, officer and suspect, and to those who are in the path, passengers and innocent bystanders. The main question is whether it is worth enforcing the law for which the suspect is wanted compared to the risk created by that process. Stated in a different way, pursuit driving must be evaluated by balancing the need to immediately apprehend the suspect with the likelihood of accident or injury (risk). To understand pursuit is to understand both of these concepts.

It is clear that both the goals of law enforcement and public safety are significant. Unfortunately, to achieve one goal, the other may have to be sacrificed. On the one hand, if the enforcement of a particular law were treated to the exclusion of public safety, then any cost of pursuit driving would be justified. On the other hand, if public safety were considered paramount and laws were to be enforced only when there was no risk to the public, no pursuit would be justified. Obviously, neither of these two extremes is acceptable. Proper police conduct must balance the two goals after considering the mission of police: to protect life. Although no one has seriously advocated taking firearms away from the police, the trend has been to restrict their use to defense or preservation of life situations. Similarly, it would not be in society's best interest to take the ability to pursue criminals from the police, but as in the use of firearms, there is a trend to restrict its use (Alpert and Fridell, 1992). There exists a need to balance these two critical social demands: the need to immediately apprehend a suspect and the risk to the public created by a pursuit.

## The Need for Immediate Apprehension

The argument is clear: police have the duty to enforce the law, and one aspect of that duty is to arrest known violators. A police officer has the authority if not the duty to issue citations for traffic violations. Upon observation or reasonable suspicion of such a violation, the officer may initiate a traffic stop (*Delaware* v. *Prouse*, 1979). Similarly, if an individual suspected of a criminal act is observed in a vehicle, then the officer may initiate a "felony" stop. The initiation of these traffic and felony stops is a routine task expected, if not demanded, of police officers. As noted, most citizens acknowledge the request by an officer to stop and pull off the road when the officer turns on emergency lights and the siren. In the infrequent situation when the suspected law violator decides not to stop and increases speed or takes evasive actions, in other words, initiates a chase, the officer must do everything possible to stop the violator from creating havoc on the roadway, without driving recklessly himself. The only other option would be to terminate the attempt to make a traffic or felony stop and hope the law violator will not commit some heinous act.

There is legal support for the continued pursuit of law violators as long as the police officer does not drive recklessly. The theme among these cases is that the police should not be responsible for the outcome of the reckless behavior of the pursued and that the police should not be the insurer of this highly irresponsible person. In one of the earliest and most cited cases, the Kentucky Court of Appeals (then Kentucky's highest court) heard *Chambers* v. *Ideal Pure Milk Co.* (1952) where a traffic violator was pursued, drove recklessly and was involved in an accident with an innocent third party. The court ruled that even if a police officer *causes* a violator to increase his or her level of recklessness, the officer should not be responsible.

> Charged as they (the police) were with the obligation to enforce the law, the traffic laws included, they would have been derelict in their duty had they not pursued him. The police were performing their duty when Shearer, in gross violation of his duty to obey the speed laws, crashed into the milk wagon. To argue that the officers' pursuit caused Shearer to speed may be factually true, but it does not follow that the officers are liable at law for the results of Shearer's negligent speed. Police can not be made insurers of the conduct of the culprits they chase (pp. 590–91).

In another interesting case, *West Virginia* v. *Fidelity Gas and Casualty Co. of New York* (1967:90-91) noted:

> Even with the [emergency] warnings, however, the driver must operate the [police] vehicle with due regard for the safety of all persons. The majority holds whenever a high-speed chase results in a collision between the person pursued and a third party, the pursuing officer has, as a matter of law, met the "due regard" standard . . . by merely turning on his warning signals. . . . There are numerous scenarios where an accident is caused by one not a party to a collision.

Both the *Chambers* and *West Virginia* cases were used as precedents in one of the most cited decisions from a state court, *Thornton* v. *Shore* (1983). This case, from the Kansas Supreme Court, has become essential for municipal defense attorneys as it uses as its rule, only the actual driving of the officer as a measuring rod, and it relies upon the deterrence theory which suggests that all violators will flee if they are not chased. In this case, the trial court issued a summary judgment for a Kansas University Police Department officer who was sued pursuant to a chase that resulted in the death of two law-abiding motorists. The plaintiffs in this lawsuit argued that the police officer should have terminated the pursuit based on the extreme reckless behavior of the individual being pursued and should have recognized the foreseeability of an accident and likelihood of injury. The defendant police officer argued that he was immune from liability pursuant to the state law permitting him to disregard certain traffic laws but not to disregard the duty to drive with due regard for the safety of all persons. The trial court ruled that the officer's driving was reasonable and granted summary judgment. On appeal, the Kansas Supreme Court affirmed the summary judgment for the officer.

In the dissenting opinion of *Thornton* is a more modern and likely scenario for the 1990s. Justice Herd's dissent in *Thornton* (1983:668) exemplifies a more contemporary view:

> Even with the [emergency] warnings, however, the driver must operate the [police] vehicle with due regard for the safety of all persons. The majority holds whenever a high-speed chase results in a collision between the person pursued and a third party, the pursuing officer has, as a matter of law, met the "due regard" standard . . . by merely turning on his warning signals. . . . There are numerous scenarios where an accident is caused by one not a party to a collision. It is a question of causation.

While there are numerous other cases from a variety of jurisdictions which could be cited, they would add precious little and would basically repeat the arguments made above (Alpert and Fridell, 1992; Urbonya, 1991; Alpert, 1991). These arguments for the need to continue a pursuit and immediately apprehend the law violator focus on:

1. the officers' obligation and duty to apprehend suspects;
2. the dereliction of duty if the police do not pursue;
3. the police should not be responsible for the outcome of the reckless behavior of the pursued; and
4. the police should not be the insurer of this highly irresponsible person.

The decisions state directly or infer that information known about pursuit indicates that the law violator who is aware that an officer will terminate the pursuit simply will increase speed or recklessness to avoid capture. Interestingly, these cases acknowledge that the police officer may cause a violator to increase his or her level of recklessness and the general risk to the officer, law violator and motoring public, but for the sake of law enforcement, some danger or risk is necessary. One example of this philosophy has been stressed by the California Highway Patrol (1983). The general opinion of the California Highway Patrol (CHP), based upon its data, is that pursuits are worth the inherent risks; the CHP report concluded:

> Attempted apprehension of motorists in violation of what appear to be minor traffic infractions is necessary for the preservation of order on the highways of California. If approximately 700 people will attempt to flee from the officers who participated in this six-month study, knowing full well that the officers would give chase, one can imagine what would happen if the police suddenly banned pursuits. Undoubtedly, innocent people may be injured or killed because an officer chooses to pursue a suspect, but this risk is necessary to avoid the even greater loss that would occur if law enforcement agencies were not allowed to aggressively pursue violators. (1983:21)

In fact, a recommendation made in the Report of the California Highway Patrol reads: "[A] very effective technique in apprehending pursued violators may be simply to follow the violator until he voluntarily stops or crashes" (1983:17).

## The Need for Public Safety

The argument is clear: life is more important than property, and public safety is more important than the immediate apprehension of a law violator. Certainly, the public is better served by minimizing risks and maximizing police tactics that permit the safe apprehension of law violators or permit them to escape. Perhaps these issues have best been summarized in a 1992 Florida Supreme Court case, *Brown* v. *City of Pinellas Park* (1992:1227):

> Solely because a man ran a red light, suddenly the innocent citizens of Pinellas County were subjected to a threatening stream of publicly-owned vehicles hurtling pell-mell, at breakneck speed, down a busy roadway in one of Florida's most densely populated urban areas. . . . In the balance, the desire to bring Deady [suspect] to justice for running a red light is far less important than the lives of the Brown sisters. . . . Experience and foresight support the conclusion that Deady engaged in such reckless conduct primarily because he was being chased by police, and that this misconduct would have ceased had the police discontinued the pursuit.

In other words, when the risks of pursuit driving become so great that an accident or injury becomes likely, then it is more important to reduce the risks and terminate the pursuit than to apprehend the violator. Of course, if the violator is a known serial murderer, the risks can be increased in a pursuit beyond that of a traffic offender, but the murderer is likely to take more risks to escape than the minor offender, and this willingness to escape must be considered.

Another recent example comes from the Texas Supreme Court decision in *Travis* v. *City of Mesquite* (1992). The case involved a familiar fact pattern. The police engaged in a chase and the pursued vehicle collided with a third party. The issues included whether the police should be responsible for their decision to engage in a pursuit, regardless of the risks involved and whether, as a matter of law, the police officers' decisions both to initiate and continue the chase were the proximate cause of the collision. The court reported that "the decision to initiate or continue pursuit may be negligent when the heightened risk of injury to third parties is unreasonable in relation to the interest in apprehending suspects" (1992:99). The court noted that "police officers must balance the risk to the public with their duty to enforce the law to choose an appropriate course of conduct. Public safety should not be thrown to the winds in the heat of the chase" (1992:98).

In a recent federal case, *Groves* v. *United States of America* (1991), Judge Sporkin wrote in an unpublished opinion (1991:8 fn. 2):

> The principle of proportionality cannot be ignored in this case. A police officer cannot be allowed to risk the lives of innocent people traveling the public roads simply to pursue a car that runs a red light. There is no doubt that a number of traffic regulations should be waived when an emergency vehicle needs to make its way through the streets to protect lives. But the police must remember that the traffic regulations themselves exist to pro-

tect lives, and they cannot be hastily ignored when the police witness a minor infraction.

The critical issue is one of foreseeability. Common sense, supported by empirical research, indicates that traffic congestion, weather, area of the chase, speed, recklessness, likelihood of apprehension and other conditions and circumstances help determine the risk of pursuit driving. Even when an officer is exempt from the laws regulating traffic flow (stop signs and traffic lights) and is authorized to drive faster than the speed limit, by state statute, he or she must drive with *due regard* for the safety of all persons using the roads. This regulation arguably places a special responsibility on the driver of an emergency vehicle who chooses to exercise this privilege. The driver of the emergency vehicle may be held to a higher standard than a citizen, as he or she is a professional, assumed to have the proper training and experience to warrant the special exemption. The due regard criterion is not always limited to situations where police are directly involved in accidents and may extend to the totality of the situation and the driving of the offender as well as the officer. In other words, physical force used by the officer who crashes into another vehicle is likely to violate the "due regard" criterion. In addition, psychological force, or pressure placed on a suspect to flee may be considered as a violation of "due regard" for the safety of the motoring public. It is an officer's driving and its impact which will be judged by the reasonable man who is faced with the question: Should this pursuit have taken place the way it did, with the risks it created and for the potential results it could have yielded?

## Balancing Law Enforcement with Public Safety

The purpose of pursuit is to apprehend a suspect within the mission of police—to protect lives. Tactics and activities undertaken must consider apprehension secondary to public safety. One way to help officers understand this balance is to have them apply the same standards used in weighing the alternatives to firing a weapon in a situation where innocent bystanders may be endangered. Whenever an officer fires a weapon, he or she must be concerned that the bullet may accidentally hit an unintended target. By comparison, in pursuit, the officer has not only his or her vehicle to worry about but also must consider the pursued vehicle creating dangerous situations as well as other vehicles creating danger by attempting to get out of the way.

Pursuit driving has been available to the police in the fight against crime. Unfortunately, the inherent nature of pursuit creates a significant danger to the officers, law violators and general public. Whether or not this danger and the resulting injuries and deaths are worth the benefits is the question police administrators and policymakers have been examining for years. As in other applications of force, the courts have been establishing standards of proximate cause and reasonableness as the acceptable parameters for pursuit driving.

Police officials must determine whether they want to restrict pursuit by the type of offense known to the officer or by some other criterion. Some jurisdictions have rules and regulations that do not permit pursuit of a suspect who has only committed a traffic offense. Other jurisdictions limit pursuit to violent felons. Still other agencies do not permit pursuits for any offense without a supervisor's permission. However, most departments permit pursuit for most offenses but require the officer (and supervisor) to balance the need to immediately apprehend the suspect with the risk created by the pursuit. Pursuit policies are categorized into the following scheme (see alpert and Fridell, 1992: 118–19):

1. Judgmental: allowing officers to make all major decisions relating to initiation, tactics and termination;
2. Restrictive: placing certain restrictions on officers' judgments and decisions; and
3. Discouragement: severely cautioning against or discouraging any pursuit, except in the most extreme situations.

Police departments operating under regulations which emphasize judgmental decision making provide only guidelines for their officers. Usually, these warnings require officers to weigh various factors before initiating a pursuit, to consider their safety and the safety of others during a pursuit and to terminate a chase when it becomes too risky.

Departments that operate under restrictive regulations or specific rules limit individual officer's discretion. For example, these orders can restrict officers from initiating pursuits when the law violators are juveniles, traffic offenders or property offenders. Similarly, in-pursuit driving behavior may be regulated. Specific speed, distance or time limitations may be ordered. Additionally, a rule may restrict some types of driving such as going the wrong way on a one-way street, driving over curbs or on private property.

Discouragement policies only allow pursuit driving under specific conditions. Examples include chasing a known murder suspect or a suspect who has been observed committing a violent crime by the officer. These policies are very specific and leave little room for discretion.

In other words, there exists a policy continuum, ranging from detailed and controlled to general and vague. The latter emphasizes officer discretion and the former has reduced the discretionary decisions made on the street and provides the officers with more structure. Discretion, whether controlled by the command staff through policies and procedures or left up to the line officer, must be reasonably exercised within the rule of law and the expectations of the community.

One way to understand the balance between the need to immediately apprehend the suspect and the risk created by the pursuit is displayed in figure 1. The horizontal axis in figure 1 represents the risk of the pursuit to the officer, public and suspect. The vertical axis represents the degree to which the suspect must be apprehended immediately. The ninety-degree policy line represents the appropriate balance between these two factors.

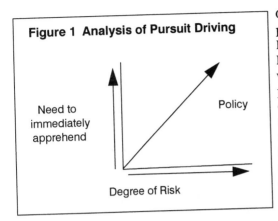

**Figure 1  Analysis of Pursuit Driving**

Need to
immediately
apprehend

Policy

Degree of Risk

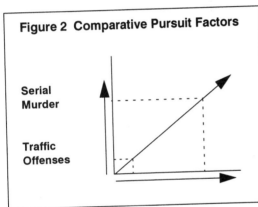

**Figure 2  Comparative Pursuit Factors**

Serial
Murder

Traffic
Offenses

On the one hand, if the police were chasing Jeffrey Dahmer, the need to apprehend him immediately would be represented by a point at the top of the vertical axis. Therefore, the authorized risk, which corresponds to the need to immediately apprehend the suspect would be at the far end of the horizontal axis. On the other hand, if police were chasing a traffic offender, which would be represented by a point on the bottom of the vertical axis, then a balanced policy would permit very little risk. The lines in figure 2 represent these two extreme examples.

## A Real-World Example

One example of how courts evaluate a constitutional claim involving a pursuit comes from a 1996 Ninth Circuit Court decision: *Lewis v Sacramento County* (1996). In this decision, the court reversed a summary judgment for a sheriff's deputy which was granted by a federal district court. In its decision, the court concluded that "deliberate indifference to or in reckless disregard for, a person's right to life or personal security" is the appropriate degree of fault to be applied to a high-speed chase (1996: 7). The chase involved a motorcycle driven by two teenagers, without helmets, being pursued by a Sacramento County deputy. This pursuit began when two officers responded to a call to break up a fight. As the officers were returning to their cars after handling the call, Deputy Smith (Sacramento County Sheriff's Deputy) saw Officer Stapp (Sacramento Police Officer) turn his emergency lights on and yell something at two boys riding a motorcycle. Although the city officer tried to drive his patrol car closer to the deputy's car to keep the motorcycle from leaving, its driver went between the two police cars and sped away. Deputy Smith accelerated after the motorcycle, chased it for less than two minutes through four stop lights and reached speeds up to 100 miles per hour. Deputy Smith was 100–150 feet behind the motorcycle and was driving beyond the range of his headlights.

The chase ended when the driver of the motorcycle went over a crest in the road, failed to make a sharp left-hand turn and skidded to a stop. Deputy Smith came over the crest of the hill, slammed on his brakes and hit Mr. Lewis.

The Sacramento County Sheriff's Department's pursuit policy required its deputies to balance the seriousness of the offense with the risks of the pursuit and to terminate a chase when the hazards of continuing outweigh the benefits of an immediate apprehension. The court noted (1996:7), ". . . Smith apparently only 'needed' to apprehend the boys because they refused to stop. . . . (and) there was no apparent danger involved in permitting the boys to escape. There certainly was risk of harm to others in continuing the pursuit." The court also noted (1996:8), "The simplest means of negating any danger the boys posed to the public would have been for Smith to discontinue the pursuit."

The court determined the need to immediately apprehend the two boys was minimal but listed significant risks (1996:8):

> Indeed, the dangers created by the chase were great. At least two cars and one bicyclist were forced off the road during the course of the chase. The pursued vehicle was a motorcycle, offering no protection to its riders. Both boys were minors. Neither was wearing a helmet. The chase was at night, in a residential area, and hit speeds of up to 100 miles per hour. Smith could not have stopped his car within the range of his headlights. Finally, even though Officer Smith was familiar with the area, he crested a hill blindly at a speed of about 65 miles per hour.

The court also stated that a reasonable officer should have known that this chase placed those on the motorcycle and members of the public in great danger (1996:12). In this case, it is clear what factors the court reviewed and how it assessed their value. Returning to figures 1 and 2, one can determine if the need to apprehend the suspect justified the risks taken by the police officers or whether the risks were unreasonable. The next section of this chapter will explore the various elements that are often found in pursuit policies.

## Pursuit Policy: General Principles and Specific Rules

The purpose of a policy is to reduce officer discretion and can include specific requirements and prohibitions as well as general guidelines. The restriction of specific actions, such as limiting the offenses for which officers can chase, the maximum speed and the duration of a pursuit, can all be controlled by specific rules, which will be discussed below. Similarly, these actions can be considered within the context of other variables, depending upon the type of policy which is desired and the type of training provided. The following are variables to be considered for a pursuit policy:

## 1. When to Continue (Initiate) a Pursuit

Officers must consider:
a. seriousness of originating offense
b. public and officer safety
c. state laws and any restrictions imposed (e.g. jurisdictional limits). pedestrian and vehicular traffic (patterns and volume)
e. location of pursuit (residential, commercial)
f. speeds (relative speeds compared to location)
g. weather
h. road conditions
i. capabilities of vehicles (muscle cars, motorcycles, police cars)
j. quality of communications

## 2. Police Units Authorized to Participate and Their Roles

a. number and type of units, roles and plan for apprehension
b. closing down intersections
c. other functions (channeling, road blocks)

## 3. Supervisory Roles and Responsibilities

a. duties—ensure that emergency equipment is on
b. communication with primary officer
c. requesting information to assess pursuit, determine limits and plan
d. terminating chase—confirmed by officers, ensure emergency equipment is off
e. number of units involved in pursuit and their activities
f. accountability for decision to continue or terminate
g. continued balance between risk and need to pursue or justification of risk
h. interjurisdictional considerations
i. post-pursuit control

## 4. Multi-Jurisdictional Pursuit Issues

a. whose policy controls
b. which agency is in charge

## 5. Driving Tactics

a. speed
b. passing other units
c. caravanning (number of units in chase—total, not per agency)
d. driving against traffic flow

## 6. Permissible and Impermissible Exceptional Tactics

a. justification for exceptional tactics
b. roadblocks (by type and permissible usage)
d. ramming and other contact maneuvers
e. boxing in
f. use of firearms

### 7. Air Support
    a. role of air units
    b. communication
    c. illumination of suspect vehicle
    d. impact of air unit on suspect
    e. impact of air unit on police vehicle (ground units turn off emergency equipment) and speed of ground units with air support

### 8. Termination
    a. protection of public
    b. definition of termination (all emergency equipment off and return to speed limit or come to a stop). factors which prohibit continuation of pursuit
    d. other units response when pursuit terminated
    e. communication

### 9. Capture of Suspect
    a. who is to take suspect into physical custody (secondary unit officers if possible)
    b. discipline
    c. use of force continuum
    d. obtaining medical support
    e. interjurisdictional considerations

### 10. Reporting and Post Pursuit Analysis
    a. completing pursuit reporting form
    b. accountability—formal review process
    c. progressive sanctions for policy violations

The policy can help create tactical knowledge and advance preparation, which involves knowing as much as possible about a situation before taking or continuing action to resolve it. The pursuing officer may be familiar with the area and may even be familiar with the likelihood of pedestrian or vehicular traffic but does not make the decision regarding the exact route to be taken or the spontaneous driving maneuvers taken by the law violator. A strong policy and training, however, can control the overall risk, the most critical factor of a police pursuit.

All pursuits involve risk. Fortunately, there are specific ways to decrease and control the omnipresent risk. Improving knowledge and preparation can achieve this goal and the following elements are necessary parts of a plan:

1. a clear and understandable *policy* delineating departmental requirements within the context of state laws and the police mission;
2. specific *training* to the policy, using examples of risk assessment;
3. a detached supervisor, trained in risk assessment, who takes *control* over the pursuit, who assumes its *supervision* and who will terminate it when it becomes too risky; and
4. *accountability*, by requiring officers to complete pursuit critiques

and having the forms reviewed individually to determine if the pursuit driving was within policy and collectively to provide information to trainers and policymakers; additionally, officers must receive feedback on the appropriateness of their pursuit driving.

One of the most perplexing and frustrating issues relating to pursuit is the inability of a police officer to convince a law violator to stop voluntarily. After a police officer uses his or her emergency lights and siren as a "show of authority," he or she must rely on the law violator to pull over and stop voluntarily. If that authority is challenged, and the law violator refuses to stop, there is nothing the officer can do, short of an application of deliberate physical force, such as a spike belt, rolling roadblock, or stationary roadblock to get the person to stop. This question of ability to apprehend must always be in the mind of the officer and supervisor and integrated into policy and training. A simple question or two in a policy supplemented by training is necessary:

1. What is your plan to get the law violator to stop?
2. What makes you think the violator is going to stop?

Research has demonstrated that most violators who flee from the police will continue to flee as long as the police are chasing with emergency equipment (show of authority). Once that equipment is turned off, these offenders are *likely* to slow down, attempt to blend into traffic or ditch the car and attempt to escape on foot. Once the officer has removed the show of authority, the law violator will likely slow down in a relatively short distance, unless he has a death wish. One of the issues to consider is whether getting a law violator to slow down and to thereby remove him as a threat to the public safety is a more important goal than his immediate apprehension.

It is essential to stress that officers can NOT assume that an individual observed for a traffic violation MUST be involved in something more serious because he or she is fleeing. Officers must rely on what they know, not what they think or sense. Increasing risks during a pursuit can only be justified by what is known (Alpert and Smith, 1991).

The purpose of pursuit is to apprehend a suspect. Within the mission of police, to protect lives, this purpose must be kept in mind at all times and all tactics or activities undertaken must be with safety and apprehension in mind. It is necessary for officers and supervisors to ask themselves, if this pursuit results in an injury or a death, or even property damage, would a reasonable person understand why the pursuit occurred, why it was continued or why it was necessary? This question will ultimately be asked, and it is appropriate to have it in the guidelines. A policy should include the warning that the officers' behavior will likely be reviewed and analyzed by a "common man" mentality. Will the officer be able to convince a group of nonpolice that his or her behavior and the risks he or she took were reasonable under the conditions?

# Termination of the Pursuit

The need to immediately apprehend a suspect must be balanced against the danger created by the pursuit. When the dangers or risks of a pursuit, or the foreseeability or likelihood of a collision outweigh the need to immediately apprehend the suspect, the lead officer or the supervisor must terminate it. This is usually dictated by the nature of the offense for which the law violator is wanted and the extent of the driver's recklessness.

Terminating a pursuit is defined as the officer turning off all emergency equipment, and slowing to the posted speed and returning to a normal patrol mode. When this occurs, the fleeing suspect will likely be aware of the status of the pursuit and react accordingly. Again, research findings indicate that the most likely reaction of the driver of the fleeing vehicle will be to slow down and reduce the risk to himself and the public.

# Defensible Training: Translating Policy into Practice

Pursuit training must provide more than mere lip service to the principles embodied in the policy. Similarly, departmental disciplinary actions must reflect any differences between the actions taken in pursuit and the mandates of the policy, even if no accident or injury results. Any officer who violates policy must be disciplined and must receive further training and education. Results of current police litigation stress that courts look not only to the existence of training but to its sufficiency. The holdings in cases such as *City of Canton* v. *Harris* (1989) demonstrate that the management of police pursuit risks requires an in-depth analysis of the elements of the pursuit. That is, tactics authorized by the agency for its officers must be a critical and integral part of the training process as well as policy. For example, to authorize by policy the use of roadblocks or "ramming" techniques without corresponding training is a grievous invitation to a "deliberate indifference" claim if injury to a suspect or officer should occur.

At the heart of defensible pursuit training is instruction in risk identification and assessment. The training must not be delivered from a purely theoretical standpoint but must integrate practical illustrations of risks which are unacceptable under agency policy. It must also be understood by the risk manager that the restrictiveness of the policy will help determine the degree of risks which will be taken. Officers must, by second nature, come to recognize which offender and environmental factors should trigger a decision to terminate a chase. Split-second decisions made by police officers must be reduced.

The training must integrate all departmental responsibilities, even those which may be mandated under directives or policies other than the pursuit policy. Obvious examples are departmental communications directives and deadly force policies (Alpert and Fridell, 1992).

Finally, training must address the need to modify unacceptable pursuit behavior and to create an awareness of the needs and expectations of the public. It is an axiomatic truth that policing is a balance of law enforcement and public safety. Unnecessary risk to the public violates the nature of the police mission. Training can help control the adrenaline-created disregard for public safety that, in some instances, accompanies the pursuit and the overreaction that is exhibited in its culmination when a suspect is taken into custody (Alpert and Smith, 1991).

## A Concluding Observation

Pursuit driving is one tactic that police have relied upon for the apprehension of suspects. Until the 1980s, very little was known about the risks and benefits of pursuit. The current trend of balancing the enforcement of laws with the safety of the public, has resulted in a number of restrictions being placed on pursuit. In fact, the more that is learned about pursuit, the more control is placed on it. The analogy of a pursuit to the use of a firearm has demonstrated the potential deadly consequences. Recently, the International Association of Chiefs of Police (1990) has published a Model Policy and a Policy Concepts and Issues Paper evaluating pursuit driving. While they have maintained a middle-of-the-road posture, they have summarized the need for reform (1990:1–2):

> The policy issue confronting law enforcement and municipal administrators is a familiar one of balancing conflicting interests: on one side there is the need to apprehend known offenders. On the other side, there is the safety of law enforcement officers, of fleeing drivers and their passengers, and of innocent bystanders. . . . The model policy is relatively restrictive, particularly in prohibiting pursuit where the offense in question would not warrant an arrest. Most traffic violations therefore, would not meet these pursuit requirements. It is recognized that many law enforcement officers and administrators may find this prohibition difficult to accept and implement, particularly where a more permissive policy has been traditionally accepted.

> But in this critical area of pursuit driving, law enforcement administrators must be prepared to make difficult decisions based on the cost and benefits of these types of pursuit to the public they serve.

## Cases

*Brown* v. *City of Pinellas Park*, Supreme Court of Florida, 604 So.2d 1222 (1992).
*City of Canton* v. *Harris* 109, S. Ct. 1197 (1989).
*Chambers* v. *Ideal Pure Milk Co.*, 245 S.W. 2d 589, 590-591. (Ky. 1952).
*Delaware* v. *Prouse*, 440 U.S. 648 (1979).
*Groves* v. *United States of America*, 778 F. Supp. 54 (D.D.C. 1991).
*Lewis* v. *Sacramento County*, ___F3rd___(1996).
*Travis* v. *City of Mesquite*, 830 SW 2d 94(1992).
*Thorton* v. *Shore* 666 P. 2d 655 (Kan. 1983).
*West Virginia* v. *Fidelity Gas and Casualty Co. of New York* 263 F. Supp 88, 90–91
    (D. W. Va. 1967).

## Bibliography

Abbott, Les. 1988. "Pursuit Driving." *FBI Law Enforcement Bulletin*, November: 7–11.

Alpert, Geoffrey P. 1987. "Questioning Police Pursuit in Urban Areas." *Journal of Police Science and Administration* 15:298–306.

———. 1991. "Analyzing Police Pursuit." *Criminal Law Bulletin*, 27:358–67.

Alpert, Geoffrey and Patrick Anderson. 1986. "The Most Deadly Force: Police Pursuits." *Justice Quarterly*, 3:1–14.

Alpert, Geoffrey P. and Roger Dunham. 1988. "Research on Police Pursuits: Applications for Law Enforcement." *American Journal of Police*, 7:123–31.

———. 1990. *Police Pursuit Driving: Controlling Responses to Emergency Situations*. Westport, CT: Greenwood Press.

Alpert, Geoffrey P. and Lorie Fridell. 1992. *Police Vehicles and Firearms: Instruments of Deadly Force*. Prospect Heights, IL: Waveland Press.

Alpert, Geoffrey P. and William Smith. 1991. "Beyond City Limits and into the Wood(s): A Brief Look at the Policy Implications of *City of Canton v. Harris* and *Wood v. Ostrander*." *American Journal of Police*, 10:19–40.

Alpert, Geoffrey P., Dennis Kenney, Roger Dunham, William Smith and Michael Cosgrove, *Police Pursuit and the Use of Force. A Final Report to the National Institute of Justice*. Washington, DC. (93-IJ-CX-0061) 1996.

Auten, James. 1990. "An Analysis of Police Pursuit Policy." *Law and Order* 38:53–54.

California Highway Patrol. 1983. *Pursuit Study*. Sacramento: California Highway Patrol.

Charles, Michael, David Falcone and Edward Wells. 1992. *Police Pursuit in Pursuit of Policy: The Pursuit Issue, Legal and Literature Review, and an Empirical Study*. Washington, DC: AAA Foundation for Traffic Safety.

Comment. 1986. "High-Speed Pursuits: Police Officers and Municipal Liability for Accidents Involving the Pursued and an Innocent Third Party. *Seton Hall Law Review*, 16:101–26.

Farber, William. 1985. "Negligent Vehicular Police Chase." *American Jurisprudence Proof of Facts*, 41(2): 79–132.

Fennessy, Edmund, Thomas Hamilton, Kent Joscelyn and John Merritt. 1970. *A Study of the Problem of Hot Pursuit by the Police*. Washington, DC: U.S. Department of Transportation.

Glines, Carroll. 1980. *Jimmy Doolittle: Master of the Calculated Risk*. New York: Van Nostrand Reinhold Co.

Grose, Vernon. 1987. *Managing Risk: Systematic Loss Prevention for Executives*. Englewood Cliffs, NJ: Prentice-Hall.

International Association of Directors of Law Enforcement Standards and Training. 1990. *National Law Enforcement Driver Training Reference Guide*. Washington, DC: D. Green Publishers.

Urbonya, Katheryn. 1991. "The Constitutionality of High-Speed Pursuits Under the Fourth and Fourteenth Amendments." *St. Louis Law Review*, 35:205–88.

# 32

# Civil Liabilities for Police Use of Excessive Force

*Victor E. Kappeler*
*Michael Kaune*

Police officers must sometimes resort to the use of force to subdue violent arrestees, to prevent escape, or to protect themselves and innocent victims from injury. During their law enforcement careers, most officers have had to use physical force to effect an arrest—far fewer have had to use deadly force. Unfortunately, there are no national statistics that describe how often police officers misuse force or even how often they justifiably use force. As a consequence, it is difficult to determine how many people are killed or wounded by the police each year. Researchers have had to rely on data collected for other purposes as well as on information that has voluntarily been supplied by police departments in order to estimate the annual number of police killings.

According to *Vital Statistics*, there were an average of 360 deaths due to legal intervention in the United States each year between 1970 and 1975. One of the most comprehensive studies ever undertaken included information collected from police departments and was designed to examine the rate of police killings during a 15-year (1970–1984) period in the 50 largest cities of the United States. This research reported that in no year did the police in America's 50 largest cities kill more than 353 people. Although these researchers report enormous variations in the rate at which police officers kill citizens, clearly these are relatively rare events (see Kappeler, Blumberg and Potter, 1996).

Not only did the Sherman and Cohn study show that police killings are rare events, it also concluded that they are becoming less frequent. The study found that the number of persons killed by big city police officers declined from 353 in 1971 to 172 in 1984. In effect, law enforcement personnel were killing about half as many people in 1984 as they were in 1971.

*Critical Issues in Police Civil Liability*, 2/E. Prospect Heights, IL: Waveland Press (1997), pp. 59–74. Reprinted by permission.

Even though police shootings of citizens are rare, these events have obvious and serious consequences. One of these consequences—and an important consideration in the decision to use deadly force—is the possibility of civil liability. Whenever a police officer kills or injures a citizen, there is a high probability that a civil lawsuit will be filed against the officer and the employing police department. The lawsuits can end in enormous damage awards against the police.

Historically, court decisions regarding the civil liability of police officers who use excessive force seemed to lack a sense of logical cohesiveness. There were differing legal standards of proof and interpretations of liability for excessive force. Plaintiffs would file cases under a number of different amendments. These often included the Fourth, Eighth, and Fourteenth Amendments. However, two Supreme Court decisions, *Tennessee v. Garner* (1985) and *Graham v. Conner* (1989), have produced guidelines that clarify some of the issues surrounding police liability for the use of excessive force. In this chapter, the difference between deadly and non-deadly force is distinguished. The two major avenues of suing the police—state torts and federal actions—are explored in the context of police use of force. Finally, the major Supreme Court decisions governing police use of force are analyzed and their importance is highlighted.

---

**Figure 4.1**
**Two Brooklyn Men Awarded $76 Million in Police Brutality Case**

---

A jury in New York City on March 8 awarded two Brooklyn men more than $76 million in damages in a police brutality suit, determining that five officers fired at the men and beat them for no reason in 1986 on a Coney Island street. Lawyers and the presiding judge in the two-week jury trial that ended March 7 called the award—to be split by plaintiffs Gerard Papa and James Rampersant—the largest in a civil case in Brooklyn history. It also was believed to be the highest award in a police brutality case in New York State.

The two men, driving Papa's blue Lincoln Continental, were cornered by five plainclothes police officers in two unmarked cars near West 33rd Street and Bayview Avenue in Coney Island on March 12,1986. Papa, who is white, and Rampersant, who is black, tried to drive away as the officers opened fire and then pulled the pair out of the vehicle and beat them. Police originally had said that the two men matched the description of muggers who had stolen $10 in a purse snatching days earlier.

The jury "felt it went beyond mistaken identity. That was pure alibi on the cops' part," said Harvey Weitz, Papa's attorney. "The officer's own statement admitted that these men were doing nothing illegal, nothing suspicious. This jury finally did what the Brooklyn district attorney and Police Department's internal affairs should have done a long time ago: begin to punish the police for this type of conduct," Papa said.

Source: (1990). *Crime Control Digest*, (March 19):10.

---

## Deadly and Non-Deadly Force Defined

Excessive force can occur when an officer uses deadly or non-deadly force. For an act to constitute excessive force, it need not result in death. Excessive force is any force that is unreasonable. Excessive force is a matter of judicial interpretation. If the force is legally determined to be excessive, the officer is liable for the consequences of its use. If the force is reasonable and required to achieve a legally justifiable goal, normally the force employed is not excessive, and an officer is said to be justified in using it. There are some incidents of police misconduct that clearly cannot be excused as justifiable under any interpretation.

---

**Figure 4.2**
**Honolulu Pays $100,000 To Settle Police Brutality "Toad Bobbing," Urination Suit**

---

The City of Honolulu has paid $100,000 to settle a police brutality suit filed by a man who said he was urinated on by two police officers and then forced to bob for toads in a drainage ditch eight years ago, it was revealed Dec. 21, 1989. The out-of-court settlement was reached with Scott Sabey, who sued the city and Bernard DeCoito and Francisco Tagalicod Jr., two former police officers sentenced to prison in 1983 for violating Sabey's civil rights. Sabey was arrested by Military Police in Waikiki for having beer cans in his car Nov. 22, 1980. He was released and taken by DeCoito and Tagalicod to a water-filled ditch near the Waikiki Shell concert hall.

Prosecutors said the officers urinated on Sabey, handcuffed him and ordered him at gun-point to bob for the toads. DeCoito and Tagalicod denied being at the scene and said they were drinking coffee at a Waikiki restaurant at the time. The jury, however, convicted both veteran officers.

U.S. District Judge Harold Fong called them a "disgrace" to law enforcement when he sentenced DeCoito to a six-year prison term and Tagalicod to a four-year term. DeCoito was later sentenced to another six-year term for beating a handcuffed man in a car in Waikiki in January 1980.

The Honolulu City Council approved the out-of-court settlement of Sabey's Federal court lawsuit earlier this year. Sabey's attorney, Michael Wilson, said the settlement would "send a message" to other police officers and the department that the rights of citizens should be respected. Honolulu First Deputy Corporation Counsel Ronald Mun also said the settlement was fair. He said a larger sum might have had to be paid if the case had gone to trial. "Obviously, the police officers involved weren't going to be sympathetic parties," he said.

Source: (1989). *Crime Control Digest*, (January 9):9–10.

---

*Deadly force* is defined as "force likely or intended to cause death or great bodily harm" (Black, 1990, p. 398). *Non-deadly force* is that force which is not likely nor intended to result in death or great bodily injury. Obviously, the use of deadly force does not always result in death or great bodily harm. Conversely, non-deadly force can result in lethal consequences. In this chapter, deadly force generally denotes the use of firearms with fatal consequences. Non-deadly force will refer to the use of other police equipment and control techniques that do not end in a fatality or serious injury.

## State and Federal Claims

Lawsuits alleging the use of excessive force, brutality, assault, and battery can be filed in state or federal courts either as state tort actions or as Section 1983 claims. Each jurisdiction requires different elements of proof, uses different cases of precedent, and relies on different legal standards for determining civil liability. The major distinction between state and federal actions is the element of constitutional deprivation. To be successful in a federal action, the plaintiff must prove that the officer's actions caused the deprivation of a constitutionally guaranteed right.

The required proof of constitutional deprivation is a product of legal history. The Supreme Court in the 1960s began to employ a seldom-used section of the United States Code for deciding lawsuits brought against the government. Title 42 of the United States Code, Section 1983-Civil Action for Deprivation of Civil Rights requires the plaintiff to prove: that the conduct complained of was committed by a person acting under color of state law; that this conduct deprived a person of rights, privileges or immunities secured by the Constitution or laws of the United States; and that the violation reached a constitutional level. Because of the reliance on this section of the United States Code, many of the lawsuits brought against police officers are called Section 1983 suits.

Until recently, there was some confusion over which constitutional right was being deprived when officers used excessive force. Most courts relied on the "due process" guarantee of the Fourteenth Amendment when determining legal liability (*Johnson v. Glick*, 1973; *Schillingford v. Holmes*, 1981; *Gumz v. Morrissette*, 1985) while other courts followed the Fourth Amendment's prohibition against unreasonable searches and seizures. A few courts would allow claims to be brought under the Eighth Amendment's prohibition against cruel and unusual punishment. Still other courts eschewed the use of a specific guarantee and proposed that Section 1983 alone was a source of substantive rights (*Graham v. Conner*, 1989).

James Fyfe's (1983) observation before the Supreme Court's decision in *Tennessee v. Garner* is insightful. He stated:

> Perhaps because of the seeming analogy between deaths caused by police shootings of fleeing felons and deaths effected by the system by executions after trial, plaintiffs' attorneys and scholars have frequently argued that fleeing felon police shootings are punishment and should be subject to Eighth Amendment protections. There are faults in this analogy, however, because execution is a court-ordered final disposition of an offender who has been given all the benefits of due process, and who has been found guilty beyond a reasonable doubt of a capital offense. Shootings to appre-

hend felony suspects, by contrast, occur earlier in the process, and are a last resort means of seizing suspected offenders. Thus, they are clearly subject to Fourth Amendment restrictions (p. 528).

The exact guarantee used is important because how the court interprets the guaranteed right dictates its determination of police liability. For example, a claim of excessive force brought under the Fourth Amendment would require the plaintiff to show that the force used was unreasonable, and a claim under the Eighth Amendment would require showing that the force used inflicted cruel and unusual punishment. The same case brought under the provisions of the Fourteenth Amendment would require a demonstration that the force used violated the due process clause to the extent that it shocked the conscience.

Since many claims of police use of excessive force do not reach the level of a constitutional deprivation (*Dunn v. Denk*, 1995; *Hinton v. City of Elwood, Kansas*, 1993), either because they were not the product of deliberate indifference to the violation or because they did not result in a (judicially determined) meaningful injury (*Cathey v. Guenther*, 1995), excessive force claims are often brought in state courts. The federal courts are split on the issue of whether a plaintiff must sustain serious injury before they can succeed in a Section 1983 suit. Several courts have, however, required that the plaintiff must have suffered a meaningful injury before police liability can be imposed (*Palmer v. Williamson*, 1989; *Hinton v. City of Elwood, Kansas*, 1993). For example, merely shoving, pushing, restraining or using a stun-gun on a suspect is not always actionable under federal law (*Trout v. Frega*, 1996; *Hinton v. City of Elwood, Kansas*, 1993; *Brown v. Noe*, 1989; *Eberle v. City of Anaheim*, 1990; *Evans v. Hawley*, 1990). In fact, courts are fond of remarking that "not every push or shove, even if it later seems unnecessary in the peace of a judge's chambers, subjects defendants to Section 1983 liability for excessive force (*Trout v. Frega*, 1996, p. 121). On the other hand, courts have held that a claim of improper use of handcuffs, slamming someone onto the ground, or twisting a suspect's arm causing stress or the need for medical attention can serve as viable claims of excessive force (*Brown v. Glossip*, 1989; *Harsen v. Black*, 1989; *Browning v. Snead*, 1995). As the United States Court of Appeals for the Fourth Circuit recently remarked, "The suggestion that . . . constitutional rights are transgressed only if he suffers [serious] physical injury demonstrates a fundamental misconception. . . . Police can violate a suspect's constititional rights . . . without leaving" a visible sign of any beating (*Riley v. Dorton*, 1996, p. 117).

Further confounding the issue of what type of injury is required to claim excessive force in federal court is the ruling in *Martin v. Board of County Commissioners* (1990). In Martin, the court ruled that although police officers never touched the plaintiff-patient, serving a warrant on her and subsequently forcing her to be removed from a hospital despite medical professionals' advice against it, could constitute unreasonable and therefore excessive force on the part of the police officers. At the other extreme, one court has held that the actions of a police officer who placed a gun in the plaintiff's mouth and threatened to blow his head off did not meet the "significant injury" requirement (*Wisniewski v. Kennard*, 1990).

The United States Supreme Court addressed the issue of just how severe an injury must be to form the basis of a Section 1983 lawsuit. In *Hudson v. McMillian* (1992) the Court granted certiorari to decide "whether the use of physical force against a prisoner may constitute cruel and unusual punishment when the inmate does not suffer serious injury" (p. 1). In *Hudson*, an inmate who had been handcuffed and shackled was kicked and punched repeatedly by correctional officers. During the beating, the correctional officers' supervisor "merely told the officers 'not to have too much fun'" (p. 1). As a result of the beating the inmate sustained "minor bruises and swelling of his face, mouth and lips. The blows also loosened Hudson's teeth and cracked his partial dental plate. . . ."

After concluding that the correctional officers' use of force was unnecessary and constituted the wanton infliction of pain, the Court reasoned that, "When prison officials maliciously and sadistically use force to cause harm, contemporary standards of decency are always violated. This is true whether or not significant injury is evident" (p. 6). Unfortunately, the Supreme Court's decision was grounded in the Eighth Amendment's cruel and unusual punishment clause rather than under the protections of the Fourth Amendment. Therefore it is not certain that such a ruling would apply to police officers when they use force to seize free citizens. One can only infer that the Court would grant an equal and consistent standard to free citizens who suffer from excessive force at the hands of police officers. Some courts, however, still cling to the serious injury requirement in police cases (*Dunn v. Denk*, 1995; 1996).

Lawsuits claiming improper use of force are often filed in state courts as torts of assault and battery or wrongful death. When actions are brought against the police in state court they are governed by existing state statutes or tort law. Normally, the degree of injury sustained by the plaintiff does not bar a state tort action for assault and battery. Again, a tort is a civil wrong in which the action of one person causes injury to the person or property of another, in violation of a legal duty.

The standard of proof in a state case is less restrictive than that needed in a federal lawsuit. Having to prove the deprivation of a constitutional right based on deliberate indifference is a high legal hurdle. Despite the difficulty of a federal action, most excessive force lawsuits are filed in federal court. There are a number of reasons for this—the major one being that attorney's fees may be included in the judgment and are not deducted from the settlement, as is true of many alternative actions. In other words, a million-dollar award in a federal suit actually goes to the plaintiff. The attorney's fees, often significant, are "tacked on" in addition to the award. In a similar state tort, the attorney's fees are first subtracted from the award and the plaintiff retains the balance. Therefore, while the requirements for successfully litigating a Section 1983 lawsuit are restrictive, the potential rewards are high.

## Federal Standards Governing the Use of Deadly Force

*Tennessee v. Garner* (1985) is the definitive Supreme Court decision on the use of deadly force by the police. Briefly, the facts of the case are that a Memphis police officer shot and killed an unarmed fifteen-year-old burglar who was fleeing the scene of a residence. The officer was "reasonably sure" that the suspect was unarmed and he stated that he shot the suspect to prevent escape. The officer's actions were thought justifiable under an existing state fleeing felon statute that authorized the police to use deadly force to prevent the escape of felony suspects.

Garner's father filed a lawsuit in federal court following the incident. The original *Garner* suit alleged violations of the Fourth, Fifth, Sixth, Eighth, and Fourteenth Amendments. The Sixth Circuit Court of Appeals concluded that the officer's actions amounted to a seizure and the officer's actions were governed by the provisions of the Fourth Amendment which requires that all seizures be reasonable. The United States Supreme Court also adopted this interpretation. The Supreme Court ruled that the police officer used excessive force when he seized Garner by gunshot and was thus liable for his actions.

In *Garner*, the Court introduced a new standard—the balancing test—for determining liability. The balancing test requires a court to "balance the nature . . . of the intrusion on the individual's Fourth Amendment interests against . . . the governmental interests alleged to justify the intrusion" (p. 8). The principle of the balancing test is fairly straightforward. Imagine the scales of justice; with the individual's interests on one end, and the government's interests on the other. If the citizen's rights and interests outweigh the government's interests, liability for use of force probably exists. Conversely, if the government has a substantial reason for using force, the citizen has no grounds for alleging liability.

The interests of a citizen are simple but substantial; he or she does not wish to die from a police bullet. To overcome this significant interest, the Court held that the officer may seize the suspect by using deadly force only when the officer "believe[s] that the suspect poses a threat of serious physical harm, either to the officer or to others" (*Tennessee v. Garner*, 1985, p. 11). A threat of serious harm is evident in two situations: first, when there is immediate and serious danger to the officer or bystanders; and second, when the suspect demonstrates dangerousness by the previous use or threatened use of force. These two elements or justifications for the use of deadly force are cornerstones of the *Garner* decision and warrant some consideration.

## Immediate and Serious Danger

There are two points to consider in determining immediate danger: the nature of the danger and the immediacy of the threat. A dangerous suspect is, generally, an armed suspect who can inflict serious physical harm. To date, suspects armed with guns, knives, flashlights, or those who use a vehicle as a weapon have been determined by the courts to be dangerous (*Pittman v. Nelms III*, 1996; *Butler v. City of Detroit*, 1985; *Ealy v. City of Detroit*, 1985; *Rhiner v. City of Clive*, 1985). In each case, it was determined that the suspect was capable of inflicting serious physical harm with the weapon at hand. Courts are less willing to recognize other items as constituting a danger to police officers. In one case, a police officer shot a criminal suspect for brandishing fingernail clippers (*Zuchel v. Spinarney*, 1989). Although the officer testified that he believed that the suspect had a knife, the court held that the jury could reasonably conclude that the officer's actions were not reasonable under the circumstances. Therefore, the cornerstone of immediate danger requires that the target of legal force be armed and capable of inflicting serious physical injury.

The second consideration is the immediacy of the threat posed by the suspect. Even if a suspect is armed and has the physical capability to inflict damage or serious injury, a police officer is not automatically legally justified in using deadly force. In one case, a federal court ruled that even though a suspect was armed and refused to heed police commands to drop his gun, "there appear[ed] to be some doubt as to whether the decedent's hand was raised in a shooting position" (*York v. City of San Pablo*, 1985). This factor led the court to conclude that the shooting was an act of police excessive use of force. In other cases, courts have held that "imminent danger" exists when a suspect turns and points the weapon at the officer, brandishes a weapon, is under physical assault by a number of suspects, or where a suspect has just completed an act of violence (*Pittman v. Nelms III*, 1996; *Rhoder v. McDannel*, 1991; *Merzon v. County of Suffolk*, 1991).

The issue of immediacy, however, has caused conflict among the courts. The case of *Hegarty v. Somerset County* (1995) illustrates how two courts, considering the same set of facts can reach different conclusions about the immediacy of a physical threat to police officers. Shortly after midnight Katherine Hegarty was shot and killed in her secluded cabin by police officers attempting a warrantless arrest. Katherine Hegarty was known for her marksmanship. Several campers trespassed on Hegarty's property by setting up a campsite about 75 yards from her cabin. Hegarty confronted the campers asking who gave them the key for the gate that was supposed to block their entry onto her property. The campers thought Hegarty was either intoxicated or mentally unstable. She told the campers that they were invading her privacy. After several verbal exchanges, the campers said they would leave in the morning. Hegarty went into her cabin, got a gun, and fired shots in the air from her front porch. One of the campers asked if they could leave, and she said she would follow them so they could get through the gate. The campers called the police from a truck stop.

Reserve Deputy Giroux responded to the call; familiar with Hegarty's reputation, he assumed that she was the person firing the shots, Giroux was joined by Deputies Guay and Crawford, Sergeant Hines, and State Trooper Wright. The officers collectively decided to arrest Hegarty, hoping to get her to leave the house. If these efforts failed, however, Wright warned "just because she's a woman, if things go bad, don't hesitate." When the officers arrived at the cabin, they heard music playing. Identifying himself as a police officer, Giroux yelled to Hegarty that he wanted to speak to her. There was no response. Hines knocked on the cabin door, still there was no response.

Using his flashlight, Crawford peered into Hegarty's bedroom and saw her lying on her bed with the rifle. Seeing the light, Hegarty turned the music down and asked who was at the window. Rather than informing Hegarty that she was the suspect of their investigation, the officers told her that they were investigating burglaries in the area and wanted to talk to her. Hegarty then asked them to leave her property. The officers asked Hegarty to come out of the cabin, but she refused.

About this time, Officer Guay told Hines "go." Hines then kicked in the front door, entered the cabin, and heard Guay yelling, "She's got a gun. Don't go." According to the officers, once Hines was inside, Hegarty started to point her rifle. Guay and Wright yelled to Hegarty to put down her gun. When she did not do so, Hines, Wright, and Guay shot and killed her.

John Hegarty brought a claim in a Maine federal district court pursuant to Section 1983, alleging that the four officers violated his wife's constitutional rights under the Fourth and Fourteenth Amendments. The officer defendants moved for summary judgment asserting qualified immunity because they were fearful of personal injury. The district court concluded that Wright, Guay, Hines, Crawford, and Giroux were not entitled to qualified immunity. The court reasoned "such fears were unreasonable under these facts. In fact, several officers have stated that, just prior to the entry, Hegarty posed no immediate danger to themselves or anyone else. Hegarty repeatedly asked the officers to leave, but she neither threatened them nor did she fire any shots while the officers were present. In fact, the officers decided to enter Hegarty's home forcibly only after it appeared that she had put down her rifle. Hegarty did not threaten injury to herself at any time, nor were there other individuals in danger . . ." (*Hegarty v. Somerset County*, 1994, p. 257).

The defendants appealed the district court's decision challenging the ruling that no competent police officer could have formed an objectively reasonable belief that "exigent circumstances" justified a forcible, warrantless entry for the purpose of effecting Hegarty's arrest and the subsequent use of force. Reconsidering the case, the court held that it was reasonable to believe that Hegarty "posed an imminent and unpredictable threat to their safety, and to herself" (*Hegarty v. Somerset County*, 1995, p. 1367). The court went on to note once the officers were committed to the operation they could have reasonably believed that she represented an imminent physical threat to their safety. Consequently, the court vacated summary judgment and entered judgment for the officers.

## Past Dangerousness

Deadly force may be justified when officers reasonably believe that a suspect has committed a crime involving the use or threatened use of serious physical harm. Under these circumstances, officers may use deadly force in the absence of an immediate threat. Problems arise, however, in determining what crimes are dangerous. For the moment, the courts have recognized murder, bank robbery, and armed robbery (*Trejo v. Wattles,* 1987; *Ford v. Childress,* 1986; *Ryder v. City of Topeka,* 1987) as crimes that are considered dangerous enough to warrant police use of deadly force. Conversely, however, burglary and swerving at police officers during a car chase does not justify the use of deadly force (*Kibbe v. City of Springfield,* 1985; *Tennessee v. Garner,* 1985). Officers must recognize that all seemingly violent crimes do not justify the use of deadly force in the eyes of the judiciary. A simple assault would not meet the requirements of past dangerousness so as to allow a police officer to use deadly force to effect a seizure.

An interesting issue, not yet directly addressed by the courts, is the idea of temporal proximity. In other words, how close in time to the commission of the dangerous crime must the use of force be? Can an officer use deadly force to apprehend an unarmed fleeing murder suspect who committed the crime days or even months earlier? One court came close to addressing the issue in the case of *Wright v. Whiddon* (1990). In *Wright,* the police-shooting victim was charged with armed robbery and had been incarcerated in a county jail. Wright was transported to court for a probation revocation hearing and the transporting officer failed to handcuff or adequately supervise the prisoner. During the court session, the officer received a call of a crime in progress and left the prisoner in the care of a seventy-year-old bailiff. Wright escaped the courthouse and dashed into the street. Officers pursued the escaping prisoner who was unarmed and made no threatening movements toward the officers or any other people. Just as the escapee was about to elude the officers on foot, one of the officers fired a single shot, mortally wounding the escapee. A Section 1983 lawsuit was filed against the officer who argued that the escapee's past dangerousness constituted a serious threat to other persons and therefore justified the use of deadly force. Unmoved by the defendant-officer's argument, the court pointed out that several "previous attempts to apprehend Wright were successfully accomplished without the need to use force whatsoever," and in each of those incidents Wright was armed (p. 699–700). Also in previous encounters where Mr. Wright had escaped, officers were able to track him down within a matter of hours and "capture him without incident" (p. 700). These facts coupled with the officer's failure to handcuff the escapee and leaving him with a seventy-year-old bailiff led the court to conclude that legal judgment for the officer was inappropriate.

# Standards Governing the Use of
# Non-Deadly Force

The *Garner* decision clarified many important issues concerning deadly force litigation. It effectively did away with common-law fleeing felon doctrines and ruled that the Fourth Amendment was the applicable standard in cases alleging the unreasonable use of deadly force by the police. The question remained as to its applicability to all circumstances in which police use force. In other words, was *Garner* applicable to cases of excessive non-deadly force? In *Graham v. Conner* (1989), the United States Supreme Court answered this question and others. There are three important conclusions from the *Graham* decision:

1. all claims of police excessive force are to be analyzed under the Fourth Amendment;
2. the proper legal standard to use in applying the Fourth Amendment is the "objective reasonableness" standard; and,
3. four specific factors or circumstances in the act of force are to be considered when determining liability.

Briefly, the facts of *Graham* are: Graham, a diabetic, had asked a friend to drive him to a nearby convenience store to purchase some orange juice to stave off an oncoming insulin reaction. At the store, Graham decided that the lines to the cashier were too long and opted to go to a friend's house for the needed orange juice. A Charlotte, North Carolina police officer observed Graham's rather furtive movements in the store and his hasty departure. The officer became suspicious and stopped Graham and his companion when they left the store. The officer then called for backup assistance. During this time, Graham exited his vehicle and passed out at the curbside. In the ensuing confusion of arriving backup, Graham was handcuffed. Officers then placed him on the hood of his friend's vehicle. Graham regained consciousness during this interlude and requested the officers verify his condition with the diabetic decal he carried in his wallet. He was told to "shut up" and was then thrown head-first into a squad car. As a result of these actions, Graham suffered a broken foot, cuts on his wrists, a bruised forehead, an injury to the shoulder, and continued to suffer from incessant ringing in his right ear. He later filed a Section 1983 suit, alleging that the officers used excessive force during the investigatory stop.

The Fourth Circuit Court of Appeals affirmed a lower court decision that the force used was not excessive. Upon appeal, however, the Supreme Court reversed the decision and ruled that the lower courts had applied the wrong legal standard—a substantive "due process" standard based on the Fourteenth Amendment—and ordered reconsideration based on the Fourth Amendment's "objective reasonableness" standard. The Court used strong language to make it clear that in the future:

all claims that law enforcement officers have used excessive force—deadly or not—in the course of an arrest, investigatory stop, or other "seizure" of a free citizen should be analyzed under the Fourth Amendment and its [objective] "reasonableness" standard (p. 1871).

The objective reasonableness standard is a two-part rule. The first consideration is a reprimand against using subjective interpretations in excessive force cases. The Court discards the old substantive due process standard, used by the lower courts, which required the defendant to prove that the officer acted sadistically and maliciously when using force. In the future, decisions should be made without regard to the officer's intent or motivation. In addition, such decisions should be made "from the perspective of a *reasonable* officer on the scene, rather than with the 20/20 vision of hindsight" (p. 1872 [*emphasis added*]). As a result, future decisions are to be based only on the objective facts of the case—no "mind reading" is allowed.

The second consideration is the reasonableness of the seizure. Determining the reasonableness of a seizure requires "a careful balancing" of the individual's interests and those of the government. In other words, the reasonableness standard is the balancing test of *Garner*. In *Graham*, however, it appears that the conflict between individual and governmental interests is not as dramatic as is the case in deadly force situations. Thus, additional factors can enter into the equation when determining liability in these cases. The Court stated that while "reasonableness . . . is not capable of precise definition or mechanical application" (p. 1871), a number of factors require careful consideration. These factors include:

1. whether the suspect poses an *immediate* threat to the officer or others;
2. the *severity* of the crime;
3. whether the suspect is *actively resisting* arrest; and,
4. whether the suspect is *attempting to escape* custody.

The first two factors were noted by the Supreme Court in the *Garner* decision. If the suspect poses a threat or the crime is of sufficient severity, it appears that the officer may use force to detain the suspect. In addition, if this type of suspect actively resists or attempts to escape, the officer may be justified in using force. However, a cautious interpretation of these factors should be taken.

It must be noted that *Graham* involves the use of non-deadly force. As a result, it may be imprudent to apply the four factors to situations involving deadly force. The *Garner* decision explicitly dealt with the use of deadly force; *Graham* did not. If *Graham* were applied to deadly force cases, it would seem that the Court has modified its position and now may condone the use of deadly force to prevent escape during an investigatory detention. Such a conclusion may be foolhardy, considering the facts of the case and the history of Section 1983 jurisprudence. A prudent interpretation would be that the four factors will carry varying weights under specific circumstances. For example, the presence of the first three factors would normally justify the use of deadly force, whereas the presence of only the fourth factor would limit an officer's use of force to non-deadly force. Courts, however, sometimes confuse the two standards for the application of force (see *Reynolds v. County of San Diego*, 1996). It will be interesting to note future decisions in this area of law. As mentioned earlier in the case of *Wright*, the escapee had been charged with a serious and dangerous crime, but the court felt that there was not an immediate threat posed to the officer or the general public. Therefore, courts will probably continue to base their decisions on the above-mentioned factors as well as on the totality of the circumstances surrounding the use of force by police officers.

## Summary

Knowing when to use force is an integral part of the street officer's career. Although the use of deadly force is something that officers seldom confront, the use of force is a principal tool in police work. The use of force can have grave consequences both socially and legally. There are rules which control the amount of force used and the circumstances under which it can be used. Officers must be mindful of these rules. One way the courts enforce those rules is by imposing civil liability. Until recently, it appeared that the courts lacked a sense of logical consistency regarding application of varying rules. Two decisions by the United States Supreme Court—*Garner* and *Graham*—have begun to clarify the Court's position on civil liability suits alleging excessive use of force by the police. While questions regarding the use of force by police officers remain, these two decisions have served to clarify many of the concerns surrounding police civil liability for use of excessive force.

Based on these rulings, one may conclude that using force to detain a citizen is a seizure and is thus governed by the Fourth Amendment. Such a seizure must be reasonable. To be reasonable, governmental interests served by the seizure must outweigh the interests of the seized citizen. When deadly force is used, the interests of the government are predicated on the potential of serious physical harm to the officer or to others. In instances where non-deadly force is used, the factors of escape or active resistance to arrest may also be considered but are not definitive.

## Sources

Black, H. C. (1990). *Black's Law Dictionary*, Sixth Edition. St. Paul, MN: West Publishing Co.
*Brown v. Glossip*, 878 F.2d 871 (5th Cir 1989).
*Brown v. Noe*, 711 F.Supp. 1114 (N.D.Ga. 1989).
*Browning v. Snead*, 886 F.Supp. 547 (S.D.W.Va. 1995).
*Butler v. City of Detroit*, 386 N.W.2d 645 (Mich.App. 1985).
*Cathey v. Guenther*, 47 F.3d 162 (5th Cir. 1995).
*Dunn v. Denk*, 54 F.3d 248 (5th Cir. 1995).
*Dunn v. Denk*, 79 F.3d 401 (5th Cir. 1996).
*Ealy v. City of Detroit*, 375 N.W.2d 435,438 (Mich.App. 1985).

*Eberle v. City of Anaheim*, 901 F.2d 814 (9th Cir. 1990).

*Evans v. Hawley*, 559 So.2d 500 (La.App. 2 Cir. 1990).

*Ford v. Childress*, 650 F.Supp. 110 (D.C.Ill. 1986).

Fyfe, J. J. (1983). Fleeing felons and the Fourth Amendment. *Criminal Law Bulletin*, 19(6): 525–28.

*Graham v. Conner*, 109 S.Ct. 1865 (1989).

*Gumz v. Morrissette*, 772 F.2d 1395 (7th Cir. 1985).

*Harsen v. Black*, 885 F.2d 642 (9th Cir. 1989).

*Hegarty v. Somerset County*, 53 F.3d 1367 (1st Cir. 1995).

*Hegarty v. Somerset County*, 848 F.Supp. 257 (D.Me. 1994).

*Hinton v. City of Elwood, Kansas*, 997 F.2d 774 (10th Cir. 1993).

*Hudson v. McMillian*, 112 S.Ct. 995 (1992).

*Johnson v. Glick*, 481 F.2d 1028 (2nd Cir. 1973).

Kappeler, V. E., Blumberg, M. and Potter, G. (1996). *The Mythology of Crime and Criminal Justice*, Second Edition. Prospect Heights, IL: Waveland Press.

*Kibbe v. City of Springfield*, 777 F.2d 801 (1st Cir. 1985).

*Martin v. Board of County Commissioners*, 909 F.2d 402 (10th Cir. 1990).

*Merzon v. County of Suffolk*, 767 F.Supp 432 (E.D. W.Y. 1991).

*Palmer v. Williamson*, 717 F.Supp. 1218 (W.D. Texas 1989).

*Pittman v. Nelms III*, 87 F. 3d 116 (4th Cir. 1996).

*Reynolds v. County of San Diego*, 84 F.3d 1162 (9th Cir. 1996).

*Rhiner v. City of Clive*, 373 N.W.2d 466 (Iowa 1985).

*Rhoder v. McDannel*, 945 F.2d 117 (6th Cir. 1991).

*Riley v. Dorton*, 93 F.3d 113 (4th Cir. 1996).

*Ryder v. City of Topeka*, 814 F.2d 1412 (10th Cir. 1987).

*Schillingford v. Holmes*, 634 F.2d 263 (5th Cir. 1981).

Sherman, L. W. and Cohn, E. G. (with Garten, Hamilton and Rogan) (1986). *Citizens Killed by Big City Police, 1970–84*. Washington, DC: Crime Control Institute.

*Tennessee v. Garner*, 471 U.S. 1 (1985).

*Trejo v. Wattles*, 654 F.Supp. 1143 (D.Colo. 1987).

*Trout v. Frega*, 926 F.Supp. 117 (N.D. Ill. 1996)

*Wisniewski v. Kennard*, 901 F.2d 1276 (5th Cir. 1990).

*Wright v. Whiddon*, 747 F.Supp. 694 (N.D. Ga. 1990).

*York v. City of San Pablo*, 626 F.Supp. 34 (N.D. Cal. 1985).

*Zuchel v. Spinarney*, 890 F.2d 273 (10th Cir. 1989).

# Section VIII

## Hazards of Police Work

Police work incorporates several job characteristics that present police officers with an unusual and unique set of personal hazards. Of course there is the real danger of being killed or assaulted while carrying out one's duties as an officer. In addition, there is an unusual degree of stress involved in police work, which has been associated with the ever-present threat of danger to oneself or to others and with the potential or actual use of (deadly) force. This unusual degree of stress has been linked to the frequent occurrence of divorce, alcoholism and suicide among police officers. Over the past decade, law enforcement administrators have increasingly become concerned about the personal hazards of police work and have focused on the identification and treatment of these problems.

Lorie Fridell and Tony Pate present information on police officer homicides. Fridell and Pate focus on what is known about police killings and especially those officers who are the victims of criminal homicide. They also discuss police officers killed accidentally.

The final article, "Police Suicide," examines the relationship between policing, stress and suicide. Bruce Arrigo and Karyn Garsky recommend stress reduction and management techniques, counseling sessions, and police mentoring be incorporated into the overall training curriculum. They argue that these kinds of intervention services will benefit the overall system of American policing institutions.

# 33

# Death on Patrol
## Killings of American Law Enforcement Officers

*Lorie A. Fridell*
*Antony M. Pate*

In the early afternoon of June 14, 1990, a Big Horn County (Montana) deputy sheriff was dispatched to respond to a bank alarm. Upon arrival, the deputy was given a description of the perpetrator's vehicle and gave chase. She was joined in the pursuit by another officer in a backup vehicle. The first officer's vehicle collided with the suspect's vehicle, causing both cars to stop. Gunfire ensued, leaving the female deputy dead from a gunshot wound from a .357 magnum in the abdomen below her body armor. The assailant was killed by the backup officer, the husband of the slain deputy.

According to research conducted by the National Law Enforcement Officers Memorial Fund, more than 12,500 law enforcement officers have been killed on duty in the history of the United States (Clark, 1992). As indicated in reports submitted to the Federal Bureau of Investigation, 3,280 law enforcement officers were killed between 1973 and 1994, including 1,945 (or 60 percent) who were killed feloniously, like the deputy described above, and 1,335 (40 percent) who were killed in accidents (FBI, 1976–1991). Thus, a police officer is killed about once every three days in this country.

In fact, American police officers are significantly more likely to be the victims of criminal homicide than Americans in general (Guralnick, 1963; Peterson and Bailey, 1988), and with regard to the vulnerability of Americans specifically *at work*, the National Institute for Occupational Safety and Health (NIOSH, 1996) places the occupations of "sheriff/bailiff" and "police and detective—public service" as second and third, after "taxicab driver/chauffeur," in terms of rates of workplace homicides. Lester (1980) found that U.S. officers have a much higher rate of criminal homicide than officers in sixteen selected industrial nations.

In this chapter we explore what is known about police killings, paying particular attention to the duty-related *felonious* deaths of law enforcement officers in the United States and its territories. That is, our focus is on those

Prepared especially for *Critical Issues in Policing*, 3/E by Lorie A. Fridell and Antony M. Pate.

officers who are the victims of criminal homicide while acting in a law enforcement capacity. We shall discuss the extent of the problem; the trends over the last two decades; the characteristics of agencies and jurisdictions which are associated with high rates of these deaths; and the characteristics of the incidents, the victim officers, and the offenders. Toward the end of the chapter, we provide information about the accidental deaths of on-duty officers—a subject about which much less is known than felonious killings.

Most of the studies on police killings have relied upon the data compiled by the Uniform Crime Reporting (UCR) Program of the Federal Bureau of Investigation (FBI). The UCR collects information concerning *all* these deaths nationally and within the U.S. territories and publishes annually the *Law Enforcement Officers Killed and Assaulted* (LEOKA). These data were first collected by the FBI in the early 1960s; general compliance with the voluntary system was achieved in the early 1970s. The amount and quality[1] of data regarding these incidents have improved progressively since that time and are considered the most reliable of all data collected in the UCR (Vaughn and Kappeler, 1986). Nevertheless, these data are based on police records and therefore represent a law enforcement interpretation of events.

The incidents included in the FBI data involve persons who were sworn law enforcement officers with full arrest powers. The deaths occurred while these law enforcement officers were acting in a duty-related capacity. (This includes officers who were officially "off duty" when they intervened in an incident in their law enforcement capacity.) In all instances, the offenders intended to harm the officers and/or resist the officers' interventions.

## Extent of the Problem

According to the data collected by the Uniform Crime Reporting Program, as shown in figure 1, the number of law enforcement officers who were feloniously killed fell from a high of 134 in 1973 to below 100 per year in the early 1980s, then fell again in the late 1980s. Officer slayings have fluctuated between 66 (1990) and 76 (1994) in the early 1990s. This represents a decline of about 50 percent since the 1970s.

Because the number of officers has actually *increased* significantly in the last two decades, the *rate* at which officers have been killed has declined quite significantly, as well. The rate of police killings (per 10,000 officers) fell from approximately 3.4 in 1973 to about 1.6 in 1983 to approximately 1.1 per 10,000 in 1993. The reasons for this decline cannot be precisely determined, although a number of contributing factors can be identified. For example, it is clear that the introduction of soft body armor in the 1970s led to a notable decrease in the chances of officers being killed as a result of wounds to the torso (U.S. Congress, Office of Technology Assessment, 1992a). In addition, many police departments have adopted

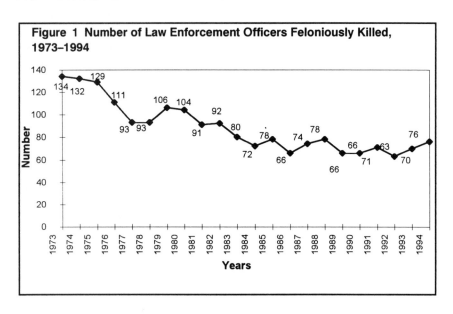

Figure 1  Number of Law Enforcement Officers Feloniously Killed, 1973–1994

sophisticated training procedures during the last two decades aimed at enhancing police officers' safety (Fyfe, 1987; Alpert and Fridell, 1992). Further, many agencies have revised their policies and procedures to ensure that officers are less likely to put themselves in dangerous circumstances (see e.g., Alpert and Fridell, 1992). It is also interesting to note that, according to NIOSH, overall workplace homicide declined between 1980 and 1993.

Although we have experienced a decrease in the felonious killings of law enforcement officers since the mid-1970s, we still are losing to criminal homicide 60 to 75 law enforcement officers each year. As part of our attempt to understand who is killed and under what circumstances, we describe below the agency and jurisdictional context of police shootings, followed by descriptions of the circumstances of the events, characteristics of the victims, and characteristics of the offenders.

## Agency and Jurisdiction Characteristics

A number of researchers have looked at the relationship between police killings/assaults and crime rates, poverty, income inequality, population ethnicity, and other social/cultural features of cities or states. Two of the early studies found that rates of police killings were positively correlated with city size, the "political climate," and violent crime rates (Cardarelli, 1968; Lester, 1978a).

Lester (1982) attempted to identify the city characteristics associated with high rates of police murders. He found that high rates of police murders were positively associated with gun ownership, southern locations, percent black population, percent of the population below the poverty level, gun ownership per capita, and the index crime rate including the murder and manslaughter rates (Lester, 1978b and 1982). By using state-level data for the years 1977 through 1984 and multivariate statistical techniques, Peterson and Bailey (1988) found significant associations between police killings and poverty and a measure of social disorganization. No relationship was indicated between police killings and income inequality, percentage of black population, or urbanization. Interestingly, they reported no relationship between the rate of police killings and serious crime rate (violent crime, property crime, total index crime).

## Region

As noted above, Lester found that police slayings were most likely to occur in the southern region of the country. This has been supported by other researchers (e.g., Cardarelli, 1968), though Peterson and Bailey only found a regional relationship for four of the eight years they studied (1977–1984).

Starting in 1987, the FBI included in its annual reports a regional comparison of police killings. For each of the years 1987 through 1994, the percentages of the officers killed in the West, Midwest, South and Northeast were compared to the percentages of all law enforcement officers nationwide employed within each region, as well as the percentage of the national population residing in each region. For seven of the eight years, the southern officers comprised a disproportionate percentage of all police killings relevant to the proportion of officers employed, as well as to the total population within the region. For instance, as indicated in figure 2, officers in the South accounted for 44 percent of all of the police officers feloniously killed in 1993, though they comprised only 37 percent of the total number of law enforcement officers employed nationwide and were policing only 37 percent of the total U.S. population. These data on police killings correspond with the criminological literature indicating a disproportionately high rate of homicide in the southern states (Porterfield, 1949; Kowalski, Dittmann, and Bung, 1980). A supposed "predisposition to lethal violence" (Gastil, 1971:412) in the South has been linked by some criminologists to a "subculture of violence" (Gastil, 1971; Hackney, 1969; Messner, 1983), as well as to the greater absolute poverty, and/or to the economic inequality in the southern states (see e.g., Loftin and Hill, 1974; Blau and Blau, 1982). Consistent with this is the NIOSH data indicating that the rates of workplace homicide during the period 1980–1992 were highest in the South (NIOSH, 1996).

## Agency Type and Size

Figure 3 provides insight into the rates of felonious killings of the various types of agencies—municipal, county, state police/highway patrol, and Police of Puerto Rico—and into the trends in those rates since the early 1970s. Federal agencies are excluded because of the lack of information

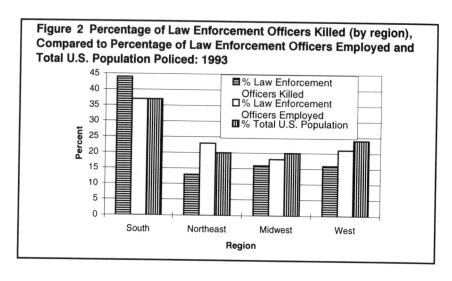

**Figure 2** Percentage of Law Enforcement Officers Killed (by region), Compared to Percentage of Law Enforcement Officers Employed and Total U.S. Population Policed: 1993

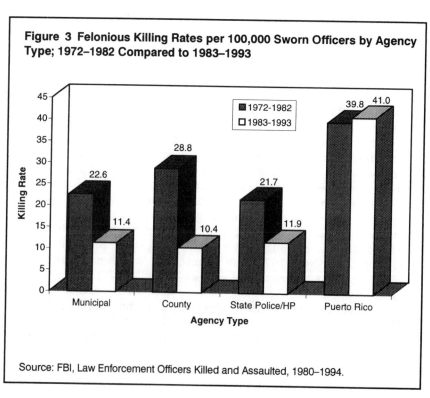

**Figure 3** Felonious Killing Rates per 100,000 Sworn Officers by Agency Type; 1972–1982 Compared to 1983–1993

Source: FBI, Law Enforcement Officers Killed and Assaulted, 1980–1994.

regarding the number of full-time officers they employ. Puerto Rico is included because officer deaths in that U.S. territory contribute significantly to annual U.S. totals, but their officers do not fit into the categories of municipal, county, or state police.

Clearly, Puerto Rico had the highest rate of officers slain per 100,000 sworn officers for both the 1972–1982 and 1983–1993 time periods at 39.8 and 41.0. This high rate across both time periods contrasts greatly to the large decreases in rates over time in the municipal, county, and state police agencies. County agencies had the second highest rate during the early time period with 28.8 officers slain per 100,000 sworn officers. However, the rate during the 1983–1993 time period fell by 64 percent to 10.4, the lowest rate of the four agency types.[2] During both time periods, municipal agencies and state agencies had similar rates and, consistent with this, similar declines across time periods.

Table 1 provides a comparison of the felonious killings rates within municipal and county agencies, by type and jurisdiction size, for the periods 1972–1982 and 1983–1993, the change in rates between those two periods, and the percentage change in those two rates. During the earlier time period, rural counties had the highest rate of felonious killings (45.5 per 100,000). However, a 77 percent decrease brought the rate down to one comparable to those of the other types of jurisdictions during the second time period.[3] During the more recent time period, the smallest cities (that is, cities with populations between 25,000 and 99,999 and cities with less than 25,000) have had the lowest rates of police killings (8.2 and 9.6, respectively).

**Table 1**

**Felonious Killing Rates by Agency Type and Jurisdiction Size for Municipal and County Agencies: 1972–1982 Compared to 1983–1993**

| Agency Type | Killing Rate 1972–1982 | Killing Rate 1983–1993 | Change | Percent Change |
|---|---|---|---|---|
| Cities 250,000 and Up | 23.2 | 13.4 | -9.8 | -42.3 |
| Cities 100,000–249,999 | 20.8 | 16.0 | -4.8 | -23.0 |
| Cities 25,000–99,999 | 15.9 | 8.2 | -7.7 | -48.2 |
| Cities Under 25,000 | 27.6 | 9.6 | -18.0 | -65.1 |
| Surburban Counties | 21.8 | 10.6 | -11.3 | -22.6 |
| Rural Counties | 45.5 | 10.3 | -35.2 | -77.4 |

## Characteristics of Incidents

Fridell and Pate (1995) coded incident characteristics from the narratives contained in the FBI's annual *Law Enforcement Officers Killed and Assaulted* publications to provide more detailed information than that provided by the UCR statistics. This was done for the 713 officers killed during the period 1983 to 1992.

For instance, Fridell and Pate determined the way in which each encounter was initiated, because Scharf and Binder (1983) argue that the mode of initiation may have ramifications for subsequent developments within a police-citizen encounter. Of the 713 officers killed during the years 1983 through 1992, one-third (34 percent) of them were dispatched to the incident in which they were killed. Another one-third (31 percent) of the officers proactively initiated the contact with the opponent as a result of observations.

Twenty percent of the officers were on assignment at the time of the incident. They were, for instance, serving a warrant, questioning a witness, or conducting surveillance. Some of the officers who were working security jobs were "on assignment" at a bank security desk. (Patrol was not defined as an assignment.) In 6 percent of the incidents, police action was "unanticipated." This category included the situations in which the officers "walked in" on crimes that they were unaware were taking place, or had the crimes "walk in" on them. For instance, one slain officer was on break conducting a transaction at his bank when a robbery took place. Similarly, some situations involved on-duty or off-duty officers walking into establishments, unaware that crimes were talking place within. Finally, 51 of the incidents, or 8 percent, involved ambushes of the officer. That is, the assailant sought out a particular officer to kill, usually as a result of some previous police action involving the assailant, or an assailant killed an officer only because of his/her status as an officer.

In 4 of every 10 incidents, the first interaction of the officer with the assailant was the fatal attack, that is they were "killed at entry." The remaining 60 percent of the officers had some sort of interaction (such as pursuit, communication) with the suspect prior to their attacks.

The coding scheme documented both the officer action and crime type for each incident to assess the nature of the incident to which the officer's attention was directed at the time of his/her death. The largest group of officers (33 percent) was intervening in an ongoing crime (or the immediate escape from a crime) when slain. In another 16 percent of the incidents, officers were making or attempting to make arrests in situations other than those in which the crime was ongoing (such as on warrants). In 13 percent of the incidents, officers were issuing citations and in another 13 percent they were investigating suspicious persons or circumstances.

Officers slain while intervening in ongoing crimes were most frequently intervening in domestic disturbances (24 percent) or robberies (22 percent). A plurality (47 percent) of the officers slain while investigating a completed crime were investigating a nonviolent crime other than burglary or drugs. Ninety-four percent of the situations involving citations, were traffic related. Four out of five officers (83 percent) slain while executing a search were searching for people or evidence related to drug offenses. Nine of every ten of the slain undercover officers were working on drug cases.

Many officers classified by the FBI as being feloniously killed in the line of duty during incidents involving the crime of robbery, were in situations where they themselves were being victimized (such as while off duty or on assignment in plainclothes) or found themselves inside commercial establishments when robberies took place. In fact, of the 81 incidents in which an officer was feloniously killed in the course of a robbery, 42 of these, or 52 percent were the type of victimizations described above. Two-thirds of those 42 incidents involved personal victimizations of the officers. The remaining one-third involved victimizations of establishments where the officers happened to be. Nearly three-fourths of these officers were off duty and 17 percent were working undercover. One was working as a detective and two were on special assignment.

The degree of danger associated with domestic disturbance calls has been a subject of debate in the police killings/assaults literature. Garner and Clemmer (1986) reviewed the history of this debate and noted that early misperceptions of the dangerousness of domestic violence were the result of misunderstandings regarding the types of incidents included under the FBI heading of "disturbance" in the LEOKA reports. Until the FBI split the "disturbance" category into two subgroups ("family quarrels" and "bar fights, man with gun, etc."), many criminal justice practitioners and researchers believed that the single category was mainly comprised of *domestic* disturbances. This led to overestimates of the proportion of officers who were killed responding to domestic violence situations.

Also leading to misconceptions regarding the danger associated with domestic disturbances was that conclusions were being drawn on the basis of raw numbers and percentages instead of rates. As Garner and Clemmer (1986) point out, to assess the relative danger of types of calls requires base rate information on the frequency of the types of calls. For instance, to assess the relative dangerousness to police of responding to domestic violence versus robbery calls we would need to know not only how many officers in a particular jurisdiction died responding to each type of call, but also, how many times officers in that jurisdiction responded to each type of crime. Using hypothetical data, if over a fifteen-year period, five officers in a city were killed responding to domestic violence calls and three officers were killed responding to robberies, we could *not* conclude that police were in more danger responding to domestic violence than to robbery. To draw conclusions, we would need to know how many times police in the city responded to domestic violence calls and how many times they responded to robbery calls during that 15-year period in order to calculate rates. If this city responded to 60,000 domestic violence calls and 7,500 robbery calls over the 15-year period, the rates would be .83 officers killed per 10,000 domestic violence calls and 4 officers killed per 10,000 robbery kills. Clearly, the likelihood of being killed is greater for a robbery call.

Garner and Clemmer (1986) relied on two earlier studies which measured police activity to estimate the relative risks (in terms of deaths and assaults) of types of police activity. Consistently, robbery calls ranked as the most dangerous in terms of risk per incident. Other researchers have also found that robbery-related calls, instead of domestic disturbance calls, are the most dangerous (for example, see Margarita, 1980; Konstantin, 1984; and Little, 1984). Just one published study (Uchida, Brooks, and Kopers, 1987) has found a higher "danger rate" (relative probability of assault) for police responding to domestic violence calls than for any other category of activity.

## Time and Distance

Various researchers examining other factors related to police killing incidents have looked at the time of the incident (for example, see Moorman and Wemmer, 1983; and Boylen and Little, 1990) and the distance between victims and perpetrators (see, for example Margarita, 1980).

According to the FBI data, approximately half of the felonious killings of police took place during the 8-hour period between 8 P.M. and 4 A.M. The period between 8 P.M. and midnight accounted itself for almost one-third of the killings. The fewest killings occurred between 4 A.M. and noon (FBI, 1994).

Over half (56 percent) of the slain officers were within 5 feet of their assailants; another 20 percent were between 6 and 10 feet from their assailants. Slightly more than 13 percent of the officers were between 11 to 20 feet of their opponents and the remaining 11 percent were over 21 feet from their opponents (FBI, 1980–1994).

## Location

Just under one-half of the officers killed during 1983 to 1992 were roadside when they were killed, another one-fourth were outside, but not roadside. Most of the officers who were inside structures when attacked were in residences, as opposed to commercial establishments (Fridell and Pate, 1995).

## Number of Suspects and Fellow Officers

Two-thirds of the slain officers faced a single threatening opponent at the time of their deaths. Another 20 percent faced two opponents. Just under 2 percent faced 5 or more suspects (Fridell and Pate, 1995).

Two-thirds of the officers slain during 1983 through 1992 had no law enforcement support in their *immediate* vicinity at the time of their deaths (Fridell and Pate, 1995). That is, though there may have been other officers on the scene, in two-thirds of the incidents no other officer was close enough to the victim officer to be in immediate danger him/herself or in a position to provide live-saving assistance.

## Weapons Used

According to the information reported to the FBI concerning officers killed during the period from 1975 through 1994, 92 percent of the police killings were committed with firearms, including 70 percent with handguns, 14 percent with rifles, and 8 percent with shotguns. The remaining killings involved officers being knifed, struck by cars, beaten to death, pushed to their deaths, killed by explosives, or killed by the use of "personal weapons," such as hands and feet (FBI, 1975–1994).[4]

During the period 1980 through 1994, 141 officers were feloniously killed with their own firearms (FBI, 1980–1994). This accounts for 12 percent of all officers feloniously killed during that period. The proportion of officers feloniously slain with their own firearms has not declined significantly since the early 1970s despite increased emphasis in training on weapon-retention techniques and the widespread adoption of holsters designed to prevent offenders from disarming the officers.

## Characteristics of Incidents by Officer Assignment

It is not unreasonable to assume that the characteristics of incidents in which officers are feloniously killed differ across various categories of law enforcement roles. For instance, it is likely that the particular dangers faced by municipal officers are different than those faced by state officers because of the differing activities and responsibilities of each type of officer. Similarly, it is likely that an officer working undercover faces different potentially lethal situations than those faced by foot patrol officers. It is also possible that the characteristics of incidents which lead to officers' deaths vary by the type and location of the jurisdictions for which the officers work. As part of the overall study, Fridell and Pate (1995) assessed the characteristics of the fatal incidents in terms of the officers' assignments, the type of agencies for which the officer worked, the region of the country in which the agency was situated, and the size and type of the jurisdiction for which the officer worked.

In this chapter, we describe selected findings for the analyses by assignment type. Of the 713 slain officers studied by Fridell and Pate (1995) over the ten year period (1983–1992), 360 (or 50 percent) were one-officer vehicle patrol officers, 84 (or 12 percent) were two-officer vehicle patrol officers, 31 (or 4 percent) were detectives, 105 (or 15 percent) were officers on special assignment, 30 (or 4 percent) were undercover officers, 96 (or 14 percent) were off-duty officers, and 7 (or 1 percent) were foot patrol officers.[5] (See figure 4.)

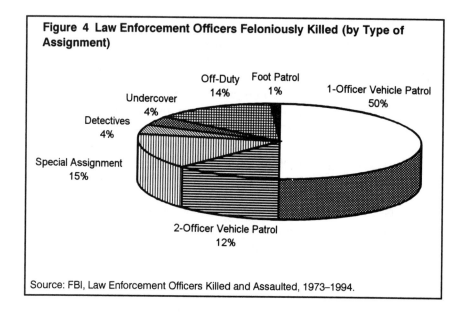

**Figure 4 Law Enforcement Officers Feloniously Killed (by Type of Assignment)**

Source: FBI, Law Enforcement Officers Killed and Assaulted, 1973–1994.

## One-Officer Vehicle Patrol Officers

In the early hours of February 4, 1991, a patrolman with the Philadelphia Police Department stopped a vehicle he suspected was stolen. The driver of the stopped vehicle exited his car and jumped onto the hood of the patrolman's vehicle, pointing a semiautomatic handgun at the officer. The patrolman attempted to dislodge the man by throwing the car into reverse. His opponent jumped off the car, ran alongside the cruiser, and fired into the cruiser. The 21-year-old officer, with 1 year of law enforcement experience died as a result of a shot to the head. (FBI, 1991)

Approximately one-half of the officers slain during 1983 through 1992 were, like the officer described above, one-officer vehicle patrol officers. Along with the two-officer vehicle patrol officers, more of these officers than officers on other assignments were *dispatched* to the incidents which led to their deaths. Just under half of the one-officer patrol officers were dispatched to the incidents compared to less than 20 percent of the officers on non-patrol assignments. A relatively small proportion (37 percent), compared to other assignments, were "killed at entry," that is, for officers "killed at entry" their first interaction with the opponent was the fatal attack. A plurality of the incidents (45 percent) occurred in residential areas and a relatively large proportion of the killings of these officers (57 percent), compared to the other assignments, occurred—like the incident described above—outside at the side of roads. As with two-officer vehicle patrol officers and off-duty officers, a relatively large proportion of one-officer vehicle patrol officers (33 percent) were intervening in ongoing crimes at the time of their deaths. The proportion of this officer group which was issuing citations (21 percent) at the time of their deaths exceeds the corresponding proportions in the other assignment groups. Consistent with this, more of this category of officers (25 percent) than the other groupings were attending to traffic-related incidents. A relatively large proportion (15 percent) of patrol officers (both one-officer and two-officer patrol), compared to other officer assignments, were killed while responding to domestic disturbance incidents. A small proportion (5 percent) of patrol officers were ambushed compared to undercover and off-duty officers. Similar proportions of one-officer patrol (73 percent), two-officer patrol (71 percent), detectives (80 percent) and special assignment (73 percent) officers faced only one opponent at the time of the attacks. As with other categories, the one-officer vehicle patrol officers were most often killed with handguns (69 percent). Relatively large proportions of these officers, compared to officers on other assignments, were disarmed (23 percent) and killed with their own weapons (19 percent). One-officer vehicle patrol officers were second only to off-duty officers in terms of their likelihood of being without immediate assistance at the incidents which led to their deaths (78 percent).

---

**One-Officer Vehicle Patrol Officers**

- Relatively small proportion ambushed
- More likely than other assignments to be dispatched
- Plurality occurred in residential areas
- Majority occurred outside at the side of roads
- Relatively small proportion "killed at entry"
- Plurality intervening in ongoing crimes
- Primarily one opponent
- Relatively large proportion disarmed and killed with their own weapons
- Likely to be without immediate assistance

---

## Two-Officer Vehicle Patrol

On the afternoon of September 12, 1991, a two-officer vehicle patrol team of the New York City Police Department responded to a man-with-a-gun call. The two officers interviewed a witness and obtained a description of the suspect as well as information regarding which direction he had headed on his bicycle. While searching the area, the officers observed the suspect who dumped the bicycle and attempted to escape on foot. Both officers chased the suspect into the courtyard of a building where the suspect turned and fired a revolver at them. While attempting to take cover behind a staircase, one of the officers, who was only wearing the front panel of his protective vest was shot six times. The 26-year old officer who had five years of experience died 4 hours later at the hospital. (FBI, 1991)

The circumstances of the killings of the 84 two-person vehicle patrol officers were similar to the circumstances of the one-person vehicle patrol officer killings except that the two-officer vehicles were more likely to be dispatched (55 percent)—as in the case described above, more likely to be killed indoors (24 percent), more likely to be intervening in ongoing crimes (42 percent) (and less likely to be issuing citations, 10 percent), more likely to be killed with handguns (81 percent), less likely to be disarmed (15 percent) and killed with their own weapons (12 percent), and, of course, much less likely to be without immediate assistance (11 percent).

---

**Two-officer Vehicle Patrol Officers**

Similar to one-officer vehicle patrol except:
- Even more likely to be dispatched
- More likely to be killed indoors
- Even more likely to be intervening in ongoing crimes
- More likely to be killed with handguns
- Less likely to be disarmed
- Much less likely to be without immediate assistance

---

## Detectives

In the early evening of August 28, 1985, a 14-year veteran of the New Jersey State Police joined other state and local officers in a raid of an apartment house where drugs were allegedly being manufactured. The veteran officer and others were admitted into the apartment by a male. As this male was being placed under arrest, another male emerged from a closet and fired a shotgun at the police, killing the 36-year-old State Police Officer. (FBI, 1985)

As in this case, killings of detectives were most likely to occur in residential neighborhoods (60 percent) and equal proportions were killed inside structures (37 percent) or by the sides of roads (37 percent). Compared to the other assignment categories, more detectives—like the one above—were killed while attempting arrests (32 percent) or while executing search warrants (25 percent). As with undercover officers and special assignment officers, a relatively large proportion of the detectives (30 percent) were killed while conducting law enforcement activities related to drug offenses.

More detectives (63 percent) than any other group were killed at entry. (In just under one-half of these incidents, the detective was executing either a search warrant or an arrest warrant.) More of the attacks against detectives (39 percent) than the other assignment groups occurred during the hours of 9 A.M. and 3 P.M.

A larger proportion of detectives (80 percent), than any other group, faced a single opponent at the time of attack. Along with special assignment officers, detectives were more likely than the other categories of officers to be shot with rifles (16 percent) or shotguns (13 percent). Relatively few of the detectives (3 percent) were disarmed and shot with their own weapons

(3 percent). Except for the undercover and off-duty officers, detectives were the least likely (13 percent) to be wearing soft body armor when slain. Just over half (55 percent) had law enforcement assistance in the immediate vicinity at the time of the attacks. Consistent with the finding that a large proportion of detectives were shot at entry is the finding that the final actions of many of these officers were to approach suspects (21 percent) or enter buildings or rooms (24 percent). These percentages were larger for detectives than for any other assignment group.

---

### Detectives

- Most likely to be killed in residential environments
- Most likely to be "killed at entry"
- Relatively large proportion were attempting arrests or executing search warrants
- Relatively large proportion were killed enforcing drug laws
- Most likely to face a single opponent
- Least likely to be wearing soft body armor
- Over half had assistance

---

## Special Assignment Officers

The Critical Incident Management Team of the San Joaquin County (California) Sheriff's Department was attempting to serve a narcotics search warrant on the morning of October 20, 1989. While most of the team were attempting to gain entry into the trailer they were to search, one deputy went to the rear of the trailer and broke a window with his flashlight to create a diversion. A rifle was fired from within the trailer and killed the deputy with a shot to the forehead. The 10-year veteran of the department was 35 years old. (FBI, 1989)

The 105 officers on special assignment included officers working in jails, working on special teams (like the deputy above), assigned to execute arrest and/or search warrants, and so forth. This group had the highest percentage of unarmed officers, 9 percent. They were primarily inside structures and primarily in residential areas. One-fifth (21 percent) were making an arrest at the time of the attack and another one-fifth (20 percent) were executing search warrants. They were second only to detectives in terms of the proportion of officers who were killed at entry (45 percent). As with detectives and undercover officers, a plurality of the slain special assignment officers (21 percent) were involved in incidents related to drug offenses. A relatively large proportion of these officers (73 percent) were facing a single opponent. Compared to the other groups, officers on special assignment were least likely to be killed with handguns (57 percent) and most likely to be killed with rifles (19 percent). A relatively large proportion (12 percent) were killed with shotguns. They were not more or less likely than the other groups to be disarmed (18 percent), killed with their own weapons (15 percent), or wearing body armor (32 percent). Two-thirds of the officers on special assignment had immediate assistance at hand when they were attacked. This proportion was second only to two-officer vehicle patrol officers, 90 percent of which had immediate assistance. The final action of one-fifth of the officers on special assignment was to enter a building or room. No other final action accounted for a larger proportion of these officers' final actions.

---

**Special Assignment Officers**

- Primarily inside structures and primarily in residential areas
- Relatively large proportion "killed at entry"
- A plurality were enforcing drug laws
- Relatively large proportion facing a single opponent
- Least likely to be killed with handguns; most likely of the officer groups to be killed with rifles
- High proportion had assistance

---

## Undercover Officers

A detective with the Baltimore Police Department was negotiating an undercover drug transaction in a third-floor apartment the evening of December 3, 1984. As planned, other detectives and Drug Enforcement Administration (DEA) agents entered the building to execute both arrest and search warrants. As they entered, they heard gunshots from the upstairs apartment. The 36 year old, 13-year department veteran was killed by shots with a handgun to his upper body. (FBI, 1984)

All of the 30 slain undercover officers studied by Fridell and Pate (1995) were armed and none were physically identifiable as law enforcement officers when attacked. A plurality (35 percent) of these officers were, like the one above, killed while inside structures and one-third (31 percent) were killed while roadside. Most were in residential areas and most were working drug-related assignments. These officers were relatively unlikely to be killed at entry. As with off-duty officers, a relatively large proportion (17 percent) of this group compared to the other assignment types was ambushed. The proportion of undercover officers killed during their own robbery victimizations (26 percent) exceeded that even of off-duty officers (20 percent); and a very large proportion of the undercover officers, relative to the other groups, faced more than one opponent when attacked. In only one-half of the incidents did it appear as if the opponent knew that his/her victim was a law enforcement officer. None of the slain undercover officers were disarmed and killed with their own weapons. Relatively few (7 percent) were wearing body armor and relatively few (35 percent) had the immediate assistance of other officers when attacked. The final action of one-fifth (20 percent) of the undercover officers, for whom there were data, was talking; another one-fifth (20 percent) were killed immediately upon entering a building or room.

---

**Undercover Officers**

- Relatively large proportion ambushed
- Plurality killed inside structures
- Most killed in residential areas
- Relatively unlikely to be "killed at entry"
- Most enforcing drug laws
- Highest proportion killed during their own robbery victimizations
- Relatively large proportion faced more than one opponent

---

## Off-Duty Officers

In the evening of March 2, 1990, an off-duty sergeant with the Police of Puerto Rico entered a store, unaware that a robbery was taking place. Two armed suspects approached the officer and demanded the keys to his car. The 51-year old resisted and, unable to access his ankle holstered weapon, was shot in the face. (FBI, 1990)

As in the above scenario, the 96 incidents involving off-duty officers were more likely than the incidents involving officers of other assignments types to involve situations where police action was unanticipated. That is, a situation "walked in" on the officer or the officer "walked in" on it. One-third of the incidents (32 percent) were initiated in this manner, and another one-third (36 percent) were officer initiated. All but three (96 percent) of the off-duty officers were armed during the incidents which led to their deaths. One-fourth were identifiable as police officers. (For the most part, these identifiable officers were going to work, returning from work, or working off duty as security in uniform.) A plurality (48 percent) were killed during the hours of 9 P.M. and 3 A.M. This percentage is higher than any other group. The off-duty killings were not distinctive in terms of occurring inside or outside, but a relatively large proportion (56 percent) of these killings occurred in commercial environments.

Two-thirds of the off-duty officers intervened in ongoing crimes and in half (48 percent) of the incidents, the crimes being attended to were robberies. A full 91 percent of the robberies in which off-duty officers "intervened" involved personal victimizations of the officers or victimizations of the establishments the officers were visiting. Thus, in a full one-third of *all* of the incidents during which off-duty officers were slain, these officers were "intervening" either in their own personal robbery victimizations (20 percent) or in the robberies of the establishments they were visiting (13 percent).

As with undercover officers, a relatively large percentage (19 percent) of the off-duty officers were ambushed, compared to other officer assignments. In a vast majority of these situations, the assailants set out to kill the particular officers as a result of some previous interaction with those officers. Half (44 percent) of the off-duty officers faced more than one opponent, and yet very few (less than 10 percent) had immediate assistance at the scene. Not surprisingly, just 4 (4 percent) of the 96 officers slain off duty were wearing body armor.

---

**Off-Duty Officers**

- Relatively large proportion ambushed
- Police action was unanticipated
- Relatively large proportion occurred in commercial environments
- Most intervening in ongoing crimes
- Many intervening in their own robbery victimizations
- Half faced more than one opponent
- Few had immediate assistance

---

## Officer Characteristics

As indicated in table 2, most of the officers killed between the years of 1980 and 1994 were male (97 percent) and white (87 percent). One-third (33 percent) of the officers were 30 years of age or younger. Their average age was 29 and their average number of years of service was 9. Seventy percent were in an official police uniform at the time of the killing and one-fourth of the slain officers were wearing protective body armor at the time of their deaths (FBI, 1980–1994).

The disproportionate representation of young, less experienced officers in the group of officers feloniously killed is a function, at least in part, of the greater proportion of younger police officers working patrol. That is, because younger officers compared to older officers are more likely to be working patrol, they are, of course, more likely to be attacked by citizens.

Konstantin (1984), using the FBI data and data on law enforcement personnel, found that black officers were disproportionately the victims of police killings relative to their representation nationally as law enforcement officers. Specifically, Konstantin found that, whereas approximately 6 percent of the law enforcement officers in the United States in 1978 though 1980 were black, they comprised 10.7 percent of the law enforcement officers feloniously killed in the line of duty. Fully one-third of the black officers killed were off duty at the time of the incident, compared to only 10.4 percent of the white officers. Geller and Karales (1981), who

## Table 2
## Profile of Victim Officers 1980–1994
### (*N* = 1,146)

|  | Percent |
|---|---|
| **Sex** |  |
| Male | 97 |
| Female | 3 |
| **Race** |  |
| White | 87 |
| Black | 13 |
| Other races | <1 |
| **Age** |  |
| Average age | 29 |
| Under 25 years of age | 8 |
| 25 through 30 years of age | 25 |
| 31 through 40 years of age | 38 |
| Over 40 years of age | 29 |
| **Years of Service** |  |
| Average years of service | 9 |
| Less than 1 year | 5 |
| From 1 through 4 years | 29 |
| From 5 through 10 years | 31 |
| Over 10 years | 35 |
| **Uniform** |  |
| In uniform | 70 |
| Out of uniform | 30 |
| **Body Armor** |  |
| Wearing protective body armor | 26 |
| Not wearing, unknown | 74 |

studied incidents in which shots hit Chicago officers between 1974 and 1978, also found that black officers were disproportionately represented among those who were shot both on duty and off duty.

These findings are consistent with research on police use of deadly force that indicates that black officers are disproportionately more likely to use deadly force (Fyfe, 1978, 1981; Geller and Karales, 1981). In both areas—killings of police officers and killings by police officers—authors have suggested that these findings might be due to the nature of the assignments of the on-duty black officers and the location of the residences of the black officers. Assignments and residences of black officers, compared to those of white officers, are more frequently in high crime areas (see, for example, Fyfe, 1978; Geller and Karales, 1981).

## Soft Body Armor

Soft body armor, designed to protect the torso from shotguns and small-caliber handguns while being comfortable enough for routine wear under a uniform, was first patented in 1972 (U.S. Congress Office of Technology Assessment, 1992a:2). Since that time, the wearing of such armor has become widespread, even mandated in some agencies. Fridell and Pate (1995) surveyed 1,111 county sheriffs' departments, county police departments, municipal police departments, and state law enforcement agencies and determined that over two-thirds of the agencies of each type provided their officers with body armor. Another 3 to 7 percent provided officers with a cash allowance to cover the purchase of body armor. Most departments of all types made the wearing of body armor optional, not mandatory, for their officers (Fridell and Pate, 1995).

In a recent survey, conducted by the John Jay College of Criminal Justice for the Allied Signal Corporation, a body armor manufacturer, over 72 percent of "front-line" officers indicated that they wore body armor "all of the time" (John Jay College, 1991). An additional 19 percent of these officers said that they wore protective vests "some of the time." Five percent said they never wore such armor. Since the data were collected by means of self-administered questionnaires, rather than by observations, the wear rate reported in the survey may be higher than it actually is.

The need for soft body armor is indicated by the fact that 562 (53 percent) of the 1,054 officers who were killed with firearms between 1980 and 1994 were killed as a result of wounds in the torso area (FBI, 1989, 1990). Of these 562, over 450 were *not* wearing soft body armor when they were killed; it seems reasonable to expect that a significant number of these officers' lives might have been saved had they been wearing body armor. However, estimating the actual number of officers whose lives have been saved because they were wearing soft body armor is extremely difficult. Despite the limitations, the Office of Technology Assessment, using evidence from the military indicating that approximately 43 percent of shots to the torso are fatal, estimates that about 10 officers per year are saved from death by gunfire because they were wearing vests (U.S. Congress Office of Technology Assessment, 1992b:29).

Fridell and Pate (1995) had the departments responding to their survey provide information regarding the outcome of firearms assaults to the torso against officers who were wearing and officers who were not wearing body armor for the period 1987 through 1992. As indicated in figure 5, among sheriffs' departments, one-fourth of the deputies who were not wearing body armor when shot in the upper torso died from their wounds. In contrast, less than 1 percent of the deputies who were wearing body armor when they were shot in the upper torso area—the area that soft body armor is designed to protect—were killed. This reflects a death ratio of 25 to 1 for officers not wearing body armor to officers wearing body armor. The ratio of deaths among persons shot in the torso for officers not wearing and wearing body armor was 5 to 2 among municipal agencies and 2 to 1 among state agencies. A similar FBI study (FBI, 1994) combining all types of officers, found that an officer shot in the torso while *not wearing* body armor was 14 times more likely to die, than an officer shot in the torso who *was wearing* body armor.

It is worth noting that body armor is divided into two general categories, that suitable for routine full-time wear and that suitable for terrorist threat and tactical use when weight and bulk are less important relative to the probability of danger. The former type can be made concealable and is designed for protection from handgun bullets but not from the higher velocity bullets or edged or pointed weapons such as knives or ice picks. The latter type is not concealable and is designed for protection from high velocity rifle bullets, as well as those fired from pistols. Although both types are commonly called "bulletproof vests," there is no guarantee that even a bullet which a type of garment is designed to stop will not kill the wearer since much of the body is not covered by the protective panels of a particular type of armor.

Thus, although no police officer has been documented to have been killed by a bullet that pierced armor designed to stop it, the data collected by the FBI indicate that, as shown in table 2, for the period between 1980 and 1994, 26 percent of the officers feloniously killed were wearing protective body armor at the time of the attack (FBI, 1980–1994). Of the officers feloniously killed while wearing body armor between 1985 and 1994, 60 percent suffered gunshot wounds to the head, one-fourth (61 officers) suffered gunshot wounds to the upper torso, just under 10 percent received

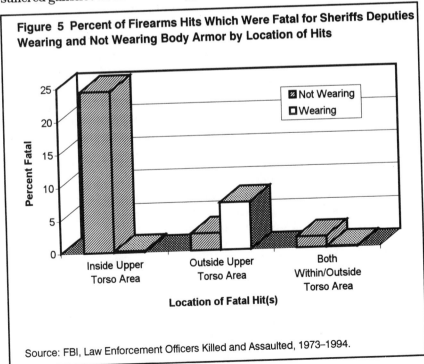

Figure 5 Percent of Firearms Hits Which Were Fatal for Sheriffs Deputies Wearing and Not Wearing Body Armor by Location of Hits

Source: FBI, Law Enforcement Officers Killed and Assaulted, 1973–1994.

gunshot wounds below the waist. Eight were intentionally struck by vehicles, 3 were stabbed, 1 was beaten, and 1 was struck on the head. Of the 61 instances wherein officers wearing body armor died from their wounds to the upper torso, in 51 instances the bullets entered areas outside the coverage of the vest (for example, at the side panels, armholes, or neck area) and in 11 instances the bullet penetrated the armor (FBI, 1994). In all of those 11 incidents, the vest was *not designed* to stop the particular ammunition involved.

## Characteristics of the Offender and Their Perspectives of the Incidents

As indicated in table 3, most of the persons identified as the perpetrator of a police killing during the years 1980 through 1994 were between 18 and 29 years of age (53 percent), male (96 percent) and white (54 percent) (FBI, 1980–1994).

Of offenders who perpetrated their killings between 1980 and 1994, almost three-fourths (72 percent) had a prior criminal arrest, just over half had a prior criminal conviction (53 percent), and one-third (38 percent) had a prior arrest for a crime of violence. One-fourth (24 percent) were on parole or probation at the time of the killing.

In 1992, the FBI-UCR published the results of an in-depth study of felonious killings of law enforcement officers to supplement the data collected on an annual basis (FBI, 1992b). The researchers selected 51 incidents of officer deaths, which involved 54 law enforcement officers and 50 offenders, most of which occurred during the period 1975 through 1985. One aspect of this in-depth study consisted of interviews with the offenders regarding their backgrounds and the slayings. From these interviews, the FBI learned that, on average, these offenders committed their first criminal offenses at the age of 12. Just under half indicated they had murdered or attempted to murder someone prior to the slayings of the officers and just under 20 percent indicated that they had previously assaulted an officer or resisted arrest.

Three-fourths of the offenders reported that they carried handguns regularly. The average age at which these persons started carrying guns was 18. One-third of the killers had been shot at some time in their lives. Several who mentioned this, also indicated that they had vowed never to be shot again, and instead, that they would shoot first.

The researchers conducted or accessed files from previously conducted psychological evaluations of the killers. Most of the killers studied were found to have some sort of personality disorder. Encountered most frequently were the antisocial personality and the dependent personality.

In the in-depth FBI interviews, three-fourths of the offenders reported that they were "engaged in drug or alcohol activities" at the time the officers were killed (FBI, 1992b:12). That is, they were either using, buying, or sell-

Table 3
**Profile of Suspects Identified in the Felonious Killing
of Law Enforcement Officers, 1980–1994
(*N* = 1,560)**

|  | Percent |
|---|---|
| **Total Number** | 100 |
| **Age** | |
| Under 18 years of age | 9 |
| From 18 through 29 | 53 |
| **Sex** | |
| Male | 96 |
| Female | 4 |
| **Race** | |
| White | 54 |
| Black | 44 |
| Other race | 2 |
| **Prior Criminal Record** | |
| Prior criminal arrest | 72 |
| Convicted on prior criminal charge | 53 |
| Prior arrest for crime of violence | 38 |
| On parole or probation at time of killing | 24 |
| Prior arrest for murder | 5 |
| Prior arrest for drug law violation | 24 |
| Prior arrest for assaulting an officer or resisting arrest | 12 |
| Prior arrest for weapons violation | 38 |

ing drugs or alcohol. Over half of the offenders indicated that the officers they killed were unprepared or surprised during the encounters. However, just about half of the killers said that there was nothing that their victim officers could have done to prevent their own deaths. Just under 10 percent indicated that the officers might have acted more "professional" and been spared, though the researchers point out that "none of these offenders was able to articulate what was meant by being 'professional'" (FBI, 1992b:13).

Even when specifically asked, none of the offenders indicated that the race of the officer had any effect on his/her decision to kill. Interestingly, however, 7 of the offenders, all males, indicated that they would not have killed the law enforcement officers if the officers had been female.

## Accidental Killings

As mentioned earlier, during the period 1980–1994, 1,335 law enforcement officers were killed accidentally while acting in the line of duty, accounting for 40 percent of all law enforcement officers killed in the line of duty during that period. Figure 6 provides information about the number of officers who were killed accidentally and feloniously between 1973 and 1994. The dotted line in that figure indicates that the number of accidental killings reported to the FBI rose between 1973 and 1975, dropped in 1976, rose consistently and dramatically between 1976 and 1989, and fell back to the level of the late 1970s during the period 1990–1994.

What figure 6 makes clear is the strikingly different trends reported for the two types of killings. While the number of accidental killings increased during the 1970s, reported felonious killings fell. As a result, although there were two to three times as many felonious, as compared to accidental, killings reported in the 1970s, there have been approximately equal numbers of both types since the mid-1980s. The reasons for these differences require further attention before they can be understood. It may simply be, for example, that police departments began systematically reporting felonious killings earlier than they did accidental killings. Or, there may have been systematic changes occurring in the policing world that account for these differences.

As indicated in figure 7, almost one-half of these accidental deaths were due to automobile accidents. Other circumstances included being struck by vehicles (22 percent), aircraft accidents (13 percent), accidental shootings (7 percent), motorcycle accidents (7 percent), and "other" (6 percent), such as deaths from falls or drownings.

Geller and Karales (1981) found that one-fifth (21 percent) of all of the police shootings (on and off duty) in Chicago during the five-year period they studied were accidentally self-inflicted. These incidents involved accidental discharges during "non-combat" handling of weapons and accidental firings during the course of arrest attempts. Eleven percent of all the officers shot in Chicago between 1974 and 1978 were accidentally shot by

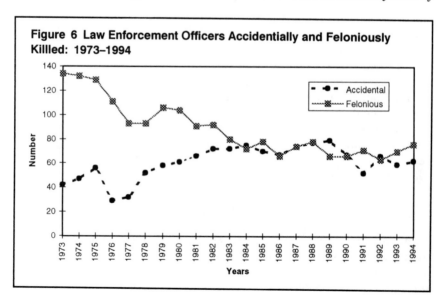

**Figure 6 Law Enforcement Officers Accidentially and Feloniously Killled: 1973–1994**

**Figure 7 Law Enforcement Officers Accidentally Killed, Circumstances of Death: 1980–1994**

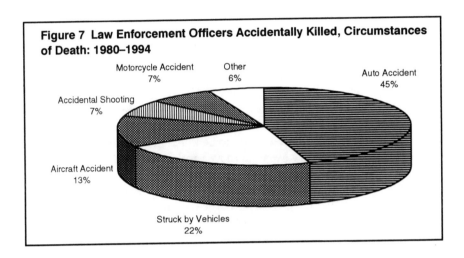

other officers. Specifically, of these 20 shootings, 16 were accidental gun discharges, two were stray bullets, and two involved mistaking officers for suspects. Fyfe (1978) found a similar situation in New York City during 1971 through 1975. He states that police in New York "are at least as likely to be killed by themselves, their acquaintances or their colleagues as by their professional clientele" (1978:476).

## Summary

Policing is a dangerous occupation. Law enforcement officers are feloniously killed while on the job at a rate second only to taxi drivers. The Federal Bureau of Investigation reports that 3,280 law enforcement officers were killed between 1973 and 1994, including 1,945 who were killed feloniously and 1,335 who were killed accidentally. There has been a general decrease, however, in the number of officers feloniously killed, dropping from a high of 134 in 1973 to fewer that 80 per year in the 1990s. There has been an even greater decline in the *rate* at which officers are feloniously killed.

The rate at which police officers are killed has consistently been highest in the southern states. There is also evidence that police killings are more likely in large cities and in jurisdictions with high levels of violent crime, high rates of gun ownership, and high levels of poverty. The Police of Puerto Rico have consistently had the highest rate of felonious killings compared to other agency types (municipal, county, and state).

From an in-depth analysis of incidents, we learned that most of the slain officers were on vehicle patrol and that half of the officers were slain while intervening in an ongoing crime or otherwise making an arrest, for instance, pursuant to a warrant. Many officers classified by the FBI as being feloniously killed in the line of duty during incidents involving the crime of robbery, were in situations where *they themselves* were being victimized. For 4 of every 10 slain officers, their first interaction with the opponent was the lethal attack itself. Two-thirds of the officers were without immediate assistance when they were slain.

Incident characteristics varied by assignment type. For instance, more detectives than any other group were killed at entry, special assignment officers were most likely to be killed indoors, and off-duty officers were more likely than any other group to be killed in commercial establishments. At least one of every five undercover and off-duty officers were slain while intervening in their own robbery victimizations.

Most of the officers killed were white males, with an average of nine years of law enforcement experience. Three-fourths were not wearing body armor. Most of the persons identified as having killed police officers were between 18 and 29 years of age, male, white, and had at least one prior criminal arrest.

Since 1973, according to the FBI, approximately 40 percent of all officers killed in the line of duty were killed accidentally. By far the largest number of these deaths were due to automobile accidents. In the early 1970s, the number of such accidental killings was only about one-third that of felonious killings. While the reported felonious killings decreased, however, the number of reported accidental killings rose. By the mid-1980s, there were approximately as many accidental as felonious killings.

## Conclusion

In this chapter, we have reported on the research which has been conducted on the deaths of law enforcement officers killed in the line of duty. Our focus has been primarily on those officers killed feloniously. The purpose of this research is to provide policy makers with the information they need to produce a safer working environment for our law enforcement professionals. In fact, over the years many of the researchers have suggested policy modifications and/or training improvements based on their findings and many of the suggestions have been implemented to some extent within police departments. It is possible that these recommendations have contributed to the decline in the number of officers feloniously killed each year.

One suggestion was to implement special procedures and training as they relate to traffic stops, effective use of "cover," dealing with hostages, searching suspects after arrest, and so forth. Many of the more recent suggestions also advocated enhancing training to promote officer safety. Konstantin (1984), for instance, suggested improved training of police with regard to officer-initiated encounters. He claimed, "officers caught in such situations are inadequately prepared to plan their approaches to the scene, and are instead plunged into the middle of ongoing and very dangerous events" (p. 42). Sherman et al. (1989) suggested that rehearsing each drug raid could reduce the danger to police in drug-related circumstances.

The FBI, too, made a number of training and policy recommendations following their in-depth study of 51 incidents where officers were feloniously killed. The researchers noted that in a significant number of the incidents studied, officers made tactical errors such as approaching improperly a suspect or vehicle, or failing to conduct a thorough search of the suspect for weapons. Increased training was recommended in those areas as well as in the general handling of traffic stops, weapon retention, handcuff use, and teamwork. The FBI also recommended the development of procedures to guide officers who become victims of robbery while off duty and, not surprising, recommended the use of body armor by all uniformed field officers.

Continued research and analysis, such as that described in this chapter, are required to enhance the safety of the persons in this country who put their lives on the line each day in their efforts to enforce the law.

## Notes

[1] The varying quality and consistency of data within categories of information over time explains the use of various reference periods in this article. We attempt, for each category of data, to provide the longest meaningful reference period for which there were quality data reported in consistent categories.

[2] It is important to note, in interpreting these rates, that a change in definitions by the U.C.R. in 1983 led to a 123 percent increase in the reported number of officers employed in sheriffs'/rural agencies between 1982 and 1983. Part of the reduction in rates must be attributed to this increase.

[3] As discussed above, this change must be interpreted in light of the fact that a change in the definition by the U.C.R. of sheriffs'/rural agencies occurred between 1982 and 1983.

[4] A recent study conducted by Handgun Control, Inc. (1995) claims that "assault weapons and guns sold with high capacity magazines" are involved in 13 percent of the incidents in which officers are killed, though these weapons apparently account for less than 1 percent of the firearms owned by persons in the U.S.

[5] We exclude the seven foot-patrol officers from the coverage in this section, as there are too few to allow for meaningful comparisons with the other groups.

## References

Alpert, G. P. and L. A. Fridell (1992). *Police Vehicles and Firearms: Instruments of Deadly Force.* Prospect Heights, IL: Waveland Press.

Blau, J. R. and P. M. Blau (1982). "The Cost of Inequality: Metropolitan Structure and Violent Crime." *American Sociological Review* 47(1): 114–29.

Boylen, M. and R. Little (1990). "Fatal Assaults on United States Law Enforcement Officers." *The Police Journal* 64(1): 61–77.

Cardarelli, A. P. (1968). "An Analysis of Police Killed by Criminal Action: 1961–1963." *The Journal of Criminal Law, Criminology, and Police Science* 59(3): 447–53.

_____ (1976). *Police Murders and Effective Countermeasures.* Santa Cruz: Davis.

Cardarelli, A. P. (1986). *Cops, Killers and Staying Alive: The Murder of Police Officers in America*. Springfield, IL: Charles C. Thomas.

Clark, C. (1992). *The Making of a Memorial: The People Behind the National Law Enforcement Officers Memorial Fund*. Washington, DC: National Law Enforcement Officers Memorial Fund.

Federal Bureau of Investigation (1971–94). *Uniform Crime Reports: Law Enforcement Officers Killed and Assaulted*. Washington, D.C.: U.S. Department of Justice.

_____ (1992). *Killed in the Line of Duty: A Study of Selected Felonious Killings of Law Enforcement Officers*. Washington, D.C.: Uniform Crime Reports Section, Federal Bureau of Investigation, U.S. Department of Justice.

Fridell, L. and Antony Pate (1995). *Death on Patrol: Felonious Homicides of American Police Officers*. Report submitted to the National Institute of Justice (#91-IJ-CX-K025) by the Police Foundation.

Fyfe, J. J. (1978). Shots Fired: A Typological Examination of New York City Police Firearms Discharges, 1971–1975. Ph.D. Dissertation, State University of New York at Albany.

_____ (1981). "Race and Extreme Police-citizen Violence." In *Race, Crime and Criminal Justice*, edited by R. McNeely and C. Pope, pp. 89–108. Beverly Hills: Sage.

_____ (1987). The Metro-Dade Police/Citizen Violence Reduction Project. An unpublished report submitted to the Metro-Dade Police Department by the Police Foundation.

Garner, J. and E. Clemmer (1986). "Research in Brief: Danger to Police in Domestic Disturbances—a New Look." Washington, D.C.: U.S. Department of Justice, National Institute of Justice, November. Reprinted in *Critical Issues in Policing: Contemporary Readings*, edited by Dunham, R. G. and G. P. Alpert (1989) pp. 517–30. Prospect Heights, IL: Waveland Press.

Gastil, R. D. (1971). "Homicide and a Regional Culture of Violence." *American Sociological Review* 36(3): 412–27.

Geller, W. A. and K. J. Karales (1981). *Split-Second Decisions: Shootings of and by Chicago Police*. Chicago, IL: Chicago Law Enforcement Study Group.

Guralnick, L. (1963). "Mortality by Occupation and Cause of Death Among Men 20-64 Years of Age: United States, 1950." *Vital Statistics, Special Reports* Vol. 53(3). Bethesda, MD: US Department of Health, Education, and Welfare.

Hackney, S. (1969). "Southern Violence." *American Historical Review* 74(3): 906–25.

Handguns, Inc. (1995). *Cops Under Fire: Law Enforcement Officers Killed with Assault Weapons or Guns with High Capacity Magazines*. Washington, DC: Author.

John Jay College of Criminal Justice (1991). *National Body Armor Survey Summary*. New York: John Jay College.

Konstantin, D. (1984). "Homicides of American Law Enforcement Officers." *Justice Quarterly* 1(1): 29–45.

Kowalski, G. S.; R. L. Dittmann; and W. L. Bung (1980). "Spatial Distribution of Criminal Offenses by States, 1970-1976." *Journal of Research in Crime and Delinquency* 17 (Jan.): 4–25.

Lester, D. (1978a). "A Study of Civilian-caused Murders of Police Officers." *International Journal of Criminological Penology* 6:373–78.

_____ (1978b). "Predicting Murder Rates of Police Officers in Urban Areas." *Police Law Quarterly* 7(3): 20–25.

Lester, D. (1980). "The Murder of Police Officers: Comparative Studies, Part I." *Police Studies* 3(2): 54–57.

_____ (1982). "Civilians Who Kill Police Officers and Police Officers Who Kill Civilians: A Comparison of American Cities." *Journal of Police Science and Administration* 10(4): 384–87.

_____ (1984). "The Murder of Police Officers in American Cities." *Criminal Justice and Behavior* 11(1): 101–13.

Little, R. (1984). "Cop-killing: A Descriptive Analysis of the Problem." *Police Studies: The International Review of Police Development* 7(2): 68–75.

Little, R. and M. Boylen (1990). "Facing the Gun: The Firearms Threat to Police Officers." *Journal of Police Science and Administration* 17(1): 49–54.

Loftin, C. and R. H. Hill (1974). "Regional Subculture and Homicide: An Examination of the Gastil-Hackney Thesis." *American Sociological Review* 39 (October): 714–24.

Margarita, M. (1980). "Killing the Police: Myths and Motives." *Annals of the American Society of Political and Social Science* 452 (November): 63–71.

Messner, S. (1983). "Regional and Racial Effects on the Urban Homicide Rate: The Subculture of Violence Revisited." *American Journal of Sociology,* 88(March): 997–1007.

Moorman, C. B. and R. C. Wemmer (1983). "Law Enforcement Officers Murdered in California: 1980-81." *The Police Chief* May: 42–44, 54.

National Institute for Occupational Safety and Health (1996). *Violence in the Workplace: Risk Factors and Prevention Strategies.* Washington, DC: Author.

Peterson, R. D. and W. C. Bailey (1988). "Structural Influences on the Killing of Police: A Comparison with General Homicides." *Justice Quarterly* 5(2): 207–33.

Porterfield, A. L. (1949). "Indices of Suicide and Homicide in States and Cities: Some Southern-non-southern Contrasts with Implications for Research." *American Sociological Review* 14 (August): 481–90.

Scharf, P. and A. Binder (1983). *The Badge and the Bullet: Police Use of Deadly Force.* New York: Praeger Publishers.

Sherman, L. W. (1980). "Perspectives on Police and Violence." *Annals of the American Academy of Political and Social Science* 452(November): 1–12.

Sherman, L. W.; C. DeRiso; D. Gaines; D. Rogan; and E. Cohn (1989). *Police Murdered in Drug-Related Situations, 1972–1988.* Washington, DC: Crime Control Institute.

Swanton, B. (1983). "Shootings of Police Officers: American and Australian Hypotheses." *Police Studies* 8:231–40.

Uchida, C. D.; L. W. Brooks; and C. S. Kopers (1987). "Danger to Police During Domestic Encounters: Assaults on Baltimore County Police, 1984–86." *Criminal Justice Policy Review* 2(4): 357–71.

U.S. Congress, Office of Technology Assessment (1992a). *Police Body Armor Standards and Testing: Volume I,* OTA-ISC-534. Washington, D.C.: U.S. Government Printing Office.

_____ (1992b). *Police Body Armor Standards and Testing: Volume II: Appendices,* OTA-ISC-535. Washington, D.C.: U.S. Government Printing Office.

Vaughn, J. B. and V. E. Kappeler (1986). A Descriptive Study of Law Enforcement Officers Killed: 1974–1984. Paper presented at the Academy of Criminal Justice Sciences, Orlando, Florida.

Violanti, J. M.; J. E. Vena; and J. R. Marshall (1986). "Disease Risk and Mortality Among Police Officers: New Evidence and Contributing Factors." *Journal of Police Science and Administration* 14(1): 17–23.

# Police Suicide
## A Glimpse Behind the Badge

*Bruce A. Arrigo*
*Karyn Garsky*

There are few documented studies on police suicide and its determinants. This paucity of research is a result of problems in the accurate identification of potentially suicidal officers as well as concerns for adverse departmental press and public scrutiny. In order to advance the literature in this area, the present study explores how certain social, psychological, and interpersonal experiences relate to a law enforcement agent's proclivity to commit suicide. In particular, the authors examine how occupational stress, a non-supportive family structure, and alcoholism, may contribute to serious suicidal ideation. The article concludes by speculating upon training techniques in the police academy. The authors maintain that the overall instructional aim must focus upon prevention and detection of self-destructive behavior. In addition, strategies that address these training concerns are discussed in the context of routine law enforcement practice and ongoing administrative police policy setting.

## Introduction

The duties performed by the police are alternatively seen by many as brave and heroic or tedious and demanding. These are the public's perceptions, incomplete as they may be. Indeed, although we may feel inconvenienced when pulled over by a state trooper, we do not realize the ongoing stress officers confront; stress which lurks behind the badge. The visible aspects of policing, such as the shoot-outs, the hostage situations, and the common bar fights, are clearly physically dangerous—at times they are even deadly. However, the unseen and unheard social, psychological, and interpersonal strains on today's law enforcement agents can be equally deadly. Beyond the stress and the build-up of tension, looms the possibility of suicide. To date, however, meager attention has been given to policing and the factors which may bring an officer to engage in such self-destructive behavior.

Prepared especially for *Critical Issues in Policing*, 3/E by Bruce A. Arrigo and Karyn Garsky.

The problem of police suicide is not new (e.g., Friedman, 1967; Skolnick, 1975; Lester, 1983; Hill and Clawson, 1988), nor is its considered seriousness as a leading cause of accidental death among officers (e.g., Violanti, Vena and Marshall, 1986; Law Enforcement News, 1995). These studies show that suicide is more prevalent for law enforcement agents than for workers in other occupations.

Early research conducted in the New York Police Department found that between 1950 to 1967, the suicide rate averaged twenty-two per 100,000 deaths a year (Friedman, 1967). What is so disturbing about this statistic is that, during the same reporting period, the average rate of death by suicide for all males was only seventeen per 100,000 (Friedman, 1967). In a related study, researchers found that from a sample of 2,662 police officers, there was an average of one suicide every 2.5 years between 1950 to 1979 (Violanti and Vena, unpublished). Using the same sample, the suicide rate increased to one death every 1.25 years for the reporting period of 1980 to 1990 (Friedman, 1967). Violanti (1995) contends that such data help explain the persistent and acute upward trend in police suicides.

Additional investigations indicate that officers have the second highest suicide rate from among a field of thirty-six occupations (Labovitz and Hagehorn, 1971; Violanti, 1995). These findings confirm the suspicion that persons employed in law enforcement are more likely to commit suicide than those in other professions (Hill and Clawson, 1988). And, most recently, the National Fraternal Order of Police (FOP) published its findings from an ongoing study on accidental deaths among police agents. For this study, data was collected from 92 FOP lodges representing 24 states. Researchers affiliated with the FOP's Center for Criminal Justice Studies conducted the investigation. They concluded that between 1992–1994, 17 out of 46 deaths (37 percent) were the result of suicide (Law Enforcement News, 1995:1). This figure represented the number one cause of accidental death among officers for the reporting period.

Studies like those mentioned above raise important questions related to self-destructiveness and police behavior. To address this broad concern, this chapter conceptually explores the nature and likelihood of police suicide by examining three of its key determinants: occupational stress; the lack of adequate family networks of support; and alcoholism among officers. We investigate these determinants and how they can (and sometimes do) affect an officer's career. We conclude by speculating upon their implications for both police academy training and general policy setting. In order to better situate our study, we begin with an overview of stress and suicide relevant to contemporary policing in American society.

## Background on Stress, Suicide, and Policing in Society

As Wagner and Brzeczek (1983, p. 10) suggest, "suicide denotes all behavior that seeks and finds [as its] . . . solution to an existential problem . . .

[the] attempt on the life of the subject." As their definition implies, there are many reasons why officers choose to take their own lives. For some, it is about harboring extremely hostile feelings that are turned inward on the self. Such feelings are stimulated by unresolved life problems or existential dilemmas. The emotional scarring that one confronts may include self-hatred or the hatred of life itself. Continuous negative emotional feelings involving shame, hopelessness, guilt, or dependency may also plague a suicidal mind and are likewise related to deep-seated, unsettled issues.

In their analysis of policing in society, Wagner and Brzeczek (1983:10) further indicate that "suicide may result from external social factors, internal psychological factors, and internal biological factors." These factors are varying categories of stress which, when operationalized as forms of social, psychological, and interpersonal trauma, can escalate to crisis, suicidal ideation, and the termination of life.

In relationship to law enforcement practice, external social factors may include the everyday interaction with the chronic criminal, the vagrant, the prostitute, or the juvenile delinquent. The constant contact with such troubled individuals in unsavory places can bring about additional stress and can create a very negative view of the world (Hartsough, 1991:131). In addition, the police organization itself can be viewed as an external social factor. The demanding rules of the profession, disagreeable job assignments, and limited employee promotion opportunities contribute to stress in the police organization which in turn differentially affect individual officers (Kroes, Hurrell and Margolis, 1974). Dissatisfaction with the criminal justice apparatus per se is an example of an internal psychological factor related to stress and suicidal ideation. Following an attitudinal survey conducted by Wexler and Logan in 1983, several commentators concluded that frustration with and cynicism over the criminal process and the court system were the two highest sources of stress perceived by all officers (as cited in Bartol, 1992:249).

Further support for the futility that officers experience with the criminal justice system can be linked to trial outcomes that seemingly ignore the danger the police confront when engaged in routine law enforcement practice. As Coman, Evans and Stanley (1992:432) explain:

> [The police] perception that the justice system is excessively lenient toward criminals also contributes to officers' feelings of cynicism. Cynicism is heightened when, having placed themselves at personal risk to apprehend criminals, officers see the latter subsequently freed or given light sentences.

In addition to frustration and cynicism regarding the criminal justice apparatus, on-duty police officers encounter a constant and divergent barrage of citizen sentiment which can be psychologically stressful, if not altogether devastating. Adjusting to the emotional pushes and pulls of the work are psychically depleting. Whether negotiating the release of a hostage, breaking up a barroom brawl, or comforting a lost child, the experience of riding an emotional roller coaster can produce persistent work-related tension for many officers.

Related to frustration with the judicial system and the psychic demands of routine police work are the feelings of isolation and stigmatization which many officers confront. It is very difficult for law enforcement personnel to become detached from their uniforms. Even while off-duty, friends and family may still perceive them as officers. Hagerman (1978:402) suggests that the pressure of being on-duty 24 hours a day induces stress and forces officers to identify coping mechanisms. As one commentator insists, "it would be difficult to find an occupation that is subject to more consistent and persistent tension, strain, confrontations and nerve wracking than that of the uniform patrolman" (Milanovich, 1980:20).

The third clustering of factors related to police suicide identified by Wagner and Brzeczek are biological in nature. Serious disease is among the leading organic conditions which can lead to self-destructive behavior. Indeed, a recent study exploring disease, risk factors, and mortality rates among officers reports some rather startling figures and correlations relevant to suicide (Marshal, Vena and Violanti, 1986). According to the research team and its identification of risk factors for suicide among the study's police officer participants, 48 percent smoked, 15 percent had high cholesterol, 86 percent had little to no exercise regimen, and 25 percent were at least 25 percent overweight. The investigators concluded that all of these factors were indicative of self-destructive behavior (Marshal, Vena and Violanti, 1986).

The research team also examined how, if at all, such risk factors among officers contributed to the development of heart disease and other health-related problems. Irregular eating habits due to shift work, frequent interruption of meals following a dispatcher's call for assistance, and a sensitive or nervous stomach (including loss of appetite) related to the nature of police work, were all shown to be linked to serious digestive disorders. Myers (1983:332) has even suggested that the stress of police work can in fact cause cancer. For example, persistent lack of exercise can produce colon cancer. The common use of alcohol and the occurring digestive disorders can cause esophagus and stomach cancers respectively. Indeed, following a study of 20 police suicides in Chicago, research findings indicated that six officers were already dealing with serious health problems (Wagner and Brzeczek, 1983:11).

In sum, there is a correlation between external social, internal psychological, and internal biological factors of stress and an officer's proclivity to engage in self-destructive (i.e., suicidal) police conduct. In the next several sections, we examine more closely these stress factors. Our position is that they can be redefined and more appropriately (and concretely) understood as social, psychological, and interpersonal determinants.

# Determinants of Police Suicide:
# A Preliminary Assessment

## Occupational Stress

The nature of police work as an occupation is very stressful. Routine exposure to danger, confronting unknown assailants, dealing with unpredictable situations, and negotiating citizen hostilities are all physically and mentally draining (Martelli, Martelli and Waters, 1989:267). It is this level of anxiety which has led some police commentators to contend that such occupational stress can "cause significant personal distress" (Coman, Evans and Stanley, 1992:429). How officers cope or adjust to the demands of the job while engaged in law enforcement practice is therefore important to understanding more about the nature of police work and the likelihood of police suicide.

In order to explore the suggested linkages, two illustrations are utilized. The first example addresses a suicide crime scene. The second illustration relates to police training for vehicular stops. Both are events described by officers.

> I pushed open the door, and this guy is sort of sitting up on the bed, and he had a hunting rifle, and he was barefoot, with his toe by the trigger. He was still holding onto the barrel, and there was nothing left of his head. Blood was everywhere. Brains and pieces of brain and skull were all over the place. For some reason, to this day I don't know why, I felt for a pulse. I guess it's a habit that [with] every first-aid call you go on, you feel for a pulse. You just c[a]n't believe somebody could do something like this (Poole and Pogrebin, 1991: 401).

In the statement above an officer describes a suicide scene in which a man put a shotgun in his mouth and pulled the trigger. The officer who recounts the incident has become emotionally detached. The circumstances, although tragic, appear to be routine. The second example is as follows:

> . . . for several days, we put the group through every conceivable situation in which they could get hurt or deceived. . . . They were lied to, argued with and shot . . . not one situation involved an honest person. (Southward, 1990:22)

In this scenario, an officer describes a class on vehicle stops which he taught. His instructional goal was to educate trainees based upon the worst imaginable occurrences. Preparation for uncertainty, confrontation, and death were the essentials of this training exercise.

Although in many ways different, these narratives illustrate how the occupation of policing is about living with danger. Officers are supposed to assume a calm presence and to be professional in the face of this danger. This expectation endures, despite the tragedy and/or despite the victim. After witnessing the most heinous of murder acts and crimes committed against young children, police officers "are expected to maintain a poised presence " (Poole and Pogrebin, 1991:395).

Another form of occupational stress can be found in the organization of the police force. Martelli, Martelli and Waters (1989:268) have considered how the authoritarian structure and management practices of police departments contribute to stress. Unpleasant job assignments and excessive disciplinary action alter the morale and communication of the department as well. The authoritarian structure of police organizations is further evidenced when officers are unable to participate in decisions that affect them. Orders are passed down from rank to rank and, typically, little input is sought from patrol personnel.

Another organizational stressor includes restricted police activity following major court decisions. Inciardi (1993:247), for example, notes that the decision in *Weeks v. U.S.* in 1914 limited officers' behavior by implementing the exclusionary rule. Following the ruling, any evidence illegally seized in a federal case could be suppressed in court. A decision such as this greatly affects the manner in which police and detectives collect evidence. Frustrated officers believe that some criminals are released on technicalities. Similar departmental problems can be linked to the decisions in *Escobedo v. Illinois* (1964) which ensures the presence of counsel during police interrogation and *Miranda v. Arizona* (1966) which requires that police make suspects aware of their rights before any questioning occurs.

Additional forms of organizational stress can be traced to departments that are targets of negative press. "Performing duties under the scrutiny of the public, press, and courts demands competence and decisiveness . . . mastery of these skills does not come without a potential price" (DiVasto and Saxton, 1992:12). There are many rules and report procedures that function to merely protect the department from criticism. Many times, however, an officer of the law must assume a false attitude (for example, being "nice" or ingratiating to the press in order to avoid departmental criticism). Not only does this false attitude conceivably create even more stress, but, as Myers (1983:331) reports, such stress has been found to decrease the immune system which increases the likelihood of health related problems. Again, in order not to tarnish the reputation of one's department, officers, subjected to the pressure of a media campaign, incorporate this false identity into their persona. The potential harm to the officer can be devastating.

Related to the nature of police work and the organizational structure of departments which generate stress, is the unavoidable psychological scarring. Psychic trauma is caused by constant suppression or repression of anxiety-producing events experienced by police officers. Following a shooting in which an on-duty officer was paralyzed, the officer's wife (also a police agent) described the experience of her husband's tragedy and how she copes with her life-long sorrow:

> Sometimes when I lie in bed at night I just want to get up and run out the front door screaming, because I can see my life stretching on like this forever. I know things are improving and it has gotten considerably better, but sometimes I just think I would like to have somebody to go play with every

now and then. I would like to have a normal loving relationship (Poole and Pogrebin, 1991:398).

Suppressing stress or keeping it "bottled up" inside can alter one's mood, impair effective cognitive processes, and dramatically change personality (Coman, Evans and Stanley, 1992:429–30). Some studies have shown that the immediate consequence of such stressors create higher levels of hopelessness and feelings of lack of control which are both primary determinants of suicide (Coman et al.:430).

The variable of hope or hopelessness is considered to be crucial to one's decision to choose suicide (Wagner, 1983:10). When one's ability to cope with stressful situations is affected by such constant suppression or repression, feelings of depression, anxiety, and desperation occur. A common police coping response is that of cynicism. Cynicism has been described as a "mocking disbelief of the police system" (Howe, Marshal and Violanti, 1985:107). Through cynicism, the officer lessens the impact of job demands by simply disbelieving them. With so many indicators of potential psychological trauma and mental deterioration, it would seem apparent that additional emotional support would need to be made available to officers. However, many times the department subculture denies such assistance. The following vignette as chronicled by Poole and Pogrebin (1991:399) amply demonstrates this point:

> A young officer was chasing a drunk driver who hit another car and killed a young woman. The police officer involved in the chase was very upset when he saw the woman lying on the road by her car. I was on the scene right after the accident. I could tell right off he was pretty shaken up. I called the station and told the shift lieutenant that this officer needs to be ordered out of the scene. I remembered the lieutenant saying, "He'll get over it." And he never did anything.

In addition to hopelessness and cynicism as manifestations of job-related psychic scarring and deteriorating police coping strategies, is the interpretation of minor events as extremely stressful. For example, Southward (1990:20) reports that a Virginia police officer described feeling "keyed up, apprehensive and aggressive" while trying to teach his daughter how to drive. The father's response to the daughter's driving error was to admonish her as follows: "If you do that again, you won't drive for a month!" As Southward comments, this was the same response the father made to a traffic violator a few years prior as a trooper (Southward, 1990:20). Clearly, the two events were different. Clearly, the affected participants (daughter versus traffic violator) were different. The behavioral response from the father/officer, however, was the same.

Coupled with the frustrating vagaries of police work, organizational demands, and feelings of hopelessness and cynicism as contributing to occupational stress in the police force, are the expectations of department employers. Pugh (1986:1) has examined the qualities, roles, and concepts related to being a "good" police officer. He lists several criteria which can be (and are) used for hiring and evaluation purposes. These criteria include:

1. React quickly and effectively to problem situations.
2. Exhibit initiative, problem solving capacity, effective judgment, and imagination in coping with complex situations.
3. Demonstrate mature judgment (common sense) in deciding to make an arrest, give a warning, or use of force.
4. Tolerate stress in a multitude of forms.
5. Maintain a balance perspective in the face of constant exposure to the worst side of human nature.

The first three criteria seem commonplace for an employer to expect from his/her employee. However, the fourth and fifth points are not typical job requirements. Police work is socially constructed as anxiety-producing and its participants (suspects and the general public) are perceived as dark, vile, and vicious. Framed as such, these understandings only invite stress in an officer's already tension-filled work routine.

There are also various roles one assumes as a police officer. Individuals function as law enforcers and public servants. They have the responsibility of maintaining social order and keeping peace in neighborhood streets. All of these roles are regarded as primary when considering applicants for the police profession. However, these various duties may lead to role conflict and may result in problems for individual police officers. The conflict the officer confronts and its resolution is related to employer expectations of how best to remedy the dilemma. In his analysis of the "good" police officer, Pugh (1986: 3) defines four types of role conflict:

1. *Internal Role Conflict*—An individual has internalized a role that includes contradictory expectations or when he occupies two or more positions that carry incompatible role expectations.
   *Example:* A homicide detective elicits a confession from a ruthless killer without mirandizing the suspect. The officer internally wrestles with the demands of following appropriate criminal procedure (enforcing the defendant's rights) while ensuring that the public is protected.
2. *External Role Conflict*—An individual is confronted with incompatible expectations from two or more persons in his position network.
   *Example:* The precinct sergeant wants the patrol team to work desk duty but the supervising officer of the patrol team wants you and your squad car out in the field.
3. *Extra-Role Conflict*—An individual perceives that others hold different expectations for him as an incumbent of a single position.
   *Example:* An officer feels she needs to be more proactive in her policing; be especially alert while patrolling. Fellow precinct officers believe that the officer is overly aggressive and should be more restrained while on patrol.
4. *Inter-Role Conflict*—An individual perceives that others hold different expectations of him as the incumbent of two or more positions.
   *Example:* The public wants their neighborhood officers to be more

community oriented while patrolling and more aggressive when engaged in arrests. The precinct chief wants field officers to be more problem oriented in the community and less aggressive while engaged in arrests.

What Pugh's typology suggests is that the everyday discretionary decisions in which officers engage can create role conflict. This, in turn, can produce occupational stress. Our contention is that it is this stress, particularly when internalized and coupled with the other forms of job-related anxiety as described above, which functions as a catalyst for suicidal ideation and self-destructive behavior.

## Family Stress

Success on the job does not always equate with success on the home front. This is true for many professions. It appears especially applicable to contemporary policing. According to Southward (1990:20), "the traits and dispositions that make exceptional police officers unfortunately make very poor spouses, parents, and friends." Patterned responses called "dispositions," help police to act quickly and without conscious thought of similar events. "Without dispositions, every event would have to be evaluated [individually] to decide the best course of action or think how to perform each action" (Southward, 1990).

Although these dispositions save many lives during patrol work, they become destructive when brought home. Southward's (1990) work on policing provides an excellent illustration of this point. An officer's wife was trying to get her son to do the dishes one night. While the two continued to argue, the off-duty officer walked into the kitchen, evaluated the situation, and immediately took control. The officer admonished his wife for being bossy, talked to his son about responsibility, and told everyone else to leave the room so that the dishes could get washed. In other words, the officer "issued a warning, dispersed the participants in the dispute, and got the job done" (p. 21). Even though the officer (a state trooper) did get the boy to do the work, the problem was that he could not simply drive away in his patrol car. He had to live with these same people. In this situation, the officer's disposition embarrassed his wife, undermined her authority, and alienated him from the entire family.

The spouse in a police marriage often undergoes stress from the police organization as well which in turn places extra stress on the police officer. There are some types of stress which are "inherent in the nature of [police] work . . . . [T]hey come with the territory" (Hartsough, 1991:131). Some of these inherent aspects include shift work, unpredictable absences from home (such as for court appearances), and the long, irregular hours a police officer usually works. Maynard and Maynard (1982:309) report that given police work schedules, spouses and family members often forgo making vacation plans for the near future. Husbands and wives of police officers also undergo psychological stress. Threats to the officer's safety can create emotional fatigue for a spouse. These threats can reach a critical incident level when the officer is fired upon, severely injured, or taken hostage (Hartsough, 1991:131).

A debilitating injury or death is also mentally challenging for family members. However, officers are more routinely "emotionally distant and moody" if a life-altering injury or loss of life befalls a fellow officer (especially a partner) (Hartsough, 1991:132). Following such traumatic incidents, police personnel can become preoccupied with the tragic event and incapable of concentrating on their own lives, their work, or their families.

In addition to patterned responses, spousal attitudes toward organizational demands of police work, and job-related injury or death as features of family stress, is the activity of *defusing at home*. Hartsough (1991:132) describes this phenomenon as follows:

> Letting off steam about the workday is a healthy practice, especially if family relationships are supportive. The officer gets to ventilate feelings, and the family gets a more realistic sense of life on the job. This practice is a two-edged sword, however, because defusing at home can also become a source of stress for the family, especially if the emotions are mostly negative, the complaints prolonged, and the family becomes frustrated when nothing changes.

When an officer (especially a young one) becomes totally engulfed in and preoccupied with law enforcement, the officer's spouse and family may feel left out of his/her life. The husband/wife may feel that they are second to the officer's job and may become jealous and resentful. In Maynard and Maynard's (1982:309) longitudinal study of stress in police families they found that there was a 70 percent divorce rate within the first five years for the department they observed. Fifty-seven percent of the spouses felt they were not as important as their husbands' or wives' occupations. Fifty-five percent felt the department had a negative attitude toward marriage and families. Forty-five percent of the spouses felt the department did not meet the needs of the family. Almost 52 percent of the spouses had given up other job opportunities and 60 percent were discouraged from making plans too far ahead in the future.

Another experience of stress in the family context occurs when the officers are trained in the academy to remain detached from the situations in which they are involved (Southward, 1990:22). The competing and emotionally wrenching demands of law enforcement work do not make it possible (let alone wise) for officers to become fervently invested in every situation they encounter. It would be personally devastating if they were so involved. The officer would lose all objectivity and would not be able to function effectively for the public, for the department, or for his or her partner.

Notwithstanding, it can be destructive when this level of emotional detachment is brought into the home. Southward (1990:22) relates an incident in which a police officer describes his feelings when his wife's mother died. As the officer states,

I wanted very much to comfort her, but all I felt was impatience with the whole matter. As hard as I tried, I could not empathize with her pain, and I knew she could feel my impatience and detachment.

This professional attitude is crucial when trying to maintain control while on duty; however, it is not appropriate in the context of familial living. Indeed, the impact such sentiments could have on the spouse and how this impact could then subsequently affect the officer are potentially disastrous.

Channeling this police professionalism to the home front is not addressed in academy training. As McCreedy (1983:37) reports, "the purpose of recruit training is to adequately prepare today's police candidates for the rigorous demands of a changing profession." However, even with such academy programs as field training where candidates are taught how to deal with complex situations and dangerous criminals, they are never instructed on how to decompress, go home, and enjoy the warmth and support of their families. Police professionalism can keep family and friends at a distance. Both may even feel that the law enforcement officer is unapproachable. One officer's daughter admitted knowing "when to keep her distance" when her father first came home from work (Southward, 1990:19). The same father described a situation at home in which he misplaced his hairbrush. He found himself interrogating each family member as if he was conducting a criminal investigation. He responded like a "trooper," not like a husband and father (Southward, 1990: 22–23). When an officer feels his family is unsupportive (real or imagined), s/he may lose all sense of intimacy with them. This can produce feelings of hopelessness which is a lethal elixir for suicidal thoughts.

Munchausen's Syndrome has been found to be prevalent in law enforcement and can also be linked to suicide. Munchausen's Syndrome falls into the category of mental illness known as factitious disorders (DiVasto and Saxton, 1992:11). A common illustration of Munchausen would include something like the following: an individual self-inflicts illness or injury (or complains of illness) and then defies medical treatment by remaining ill, despite the best efforts of doctors. An officer acquires this illness for two main reasons. The first reason is the need for sympathy. "An officer, faced with overwhelming interpersonal stress or threat of loss, creates an incident in which he is the victim, and occasionally, the hero" (DiVasto and Saxton, 1992:13). In an attempt to be the focus of sympathy, care, and concern, an officer may inflict an injury (such as a laceration from a knife) to become the center of attention. Feeling unsupported from a spouse, sensing the bitter end of a marriage, experiencing alienation from a son or daughter may, in the context of work-related stress, produce this factitious disorder.

The second reason an officer may be subjected to this disorder relates to the configuration of the police organization as compatible with a college sorority/fraternity. "The rookie officer who has not been exposed to danger may feel the need to invent such an incident to achieve credibility" (DiVasto and Saxton, 1992:13), and hence acceptance into the police subculture. The need to be a member of the group may be so crucial to new officers, that they might adopt behavioral patterns that can only be described as unnecessarily dangerous.

## Alcoholism and Stress

A high suicide rate among alcoholics appears to be unquestionable (Wagner and Brzeczek, 1983:14). Alcohol can be used as a relaxing device or even as a sleeping aid for those who work long, irregular hours of shift work. Drinking is commonly practiced in order to numb or deaden feelings of depression. However, whatever one feels while sober, one is more likely to act upon those feelings while intoxicated (Myers, 1983:167). Feelings of hopelessness and worthlessness become exaggerated when alcohol is consumed. In a study conducted in Chicago on alcoholism, suicide, and policing, alcohol abuse was indicated in 12 of the 20 officer suicides (Wagner and Brzeczek, 1983: 10). In addition, 9 of the 12 suicide cases had a substantial quantity of alcohol in their bodies at the time of death (Wagner and Brzeczek, 1983).

In the police subculture, alcohol consumption is not only accepted but is encouraged and reinforced (Stege, 1986). Within the rhythms, customs, and practices that constitute policing, alcohol maintains a high recreational value. It is not only used for socializing, but also for stress reduction (Stege, 1986: 83). When asked to describe the place of alcohol consumption within the routine function of policing, a recovering alcoholic exclaimed the following: "After a particularly terrible night shift, it is not uncommon for the officers to get together for a [drinking] party" (Dietrich and Smith, 1986:302).

For novice officers and the other new hires of a department, alcohol may serve as a test of trustworthiness, loyalty, and masculinity. As one officer commented, "when you hang out with police officers, all they do is drink and talk about work . . . . [It's an] easy thing to fall into" (Dietrich and Smith, 1986: 303). This behavior is easily camouflaged within the subculture. The new workers are socialized so that drinking patterns become the norm. Thus, the behavior associated with these newly formed norms is not viewed by others within the police reference group as deviant.

There is also a great deal of uniformity within the structure of the police organization. It is not surprising to find such uniformity within the police subculture in relation to alcohol as well. This concept of uniformity is best expressed in the following statement made by an officer describing membership in the police milieu: "either you drank or you didn't belong" (Dietrich and Smith, 1986: 302–3).

As previously discussed, there are many occupational stressors linked to police work. Not only do these stressors lead to suicidal tendencies in themselves, they also lead to alcoholism which has a dramatic impact on suicidal ideation. In their research on non-medical uses of drugs and alcohol by officers, Dietrich and Smith (1986:303) identify four occupational demands which relate significantly to police stress and, thus, indirectly affect alcohol consumption. The first is what they term *depersonalization*. This is the process whereby officers learn to react unemotionally to the numerous unpleasant work situations they come in contact with on a daily basis. Depersonalization occurs when there is an apparent role conflict between job-related objectives and real human emotions. The second occupational demand which may drive an officer to drink is called *authoritarianism*. When an officer's behavior is based upon and structured by a list of legal and organizational guidelines, then authoritarianism exists. Here, it is the absence of control which induces the officer's stress. *Organizational protection* is a third occupational demand leading to alcohol abuse, according to Dietrich and Smith. It is defined as a network of departmental or precinct rules and reports that serve to protect the organization from criticism. *Danger preparation* is the fourth and final job-related demand which impacts on police drinking behavior. The realization that life-threatening risk or extreme personal jeopardy persists throughout one's on- (and off-) duty interaction is a stressor that continues everyday throughout an officer's career.

Another factor related to alcohol abuse among law enforcement personnel is found in their coping strategies. Cynicism, or a mocking disbelief, helps officers manage by discounting the demands of the police force. One method for controlling such deep-seated cynicism is through (excessive) drinking. Associated with cynicism is the strategy of secrecy. When deliberately withholding information or surreptitiously disobeying a directive from a supervisor, one's sense of autonomy increases. But these heightened feelings of independence come with a cost. For example, cultivating a scheme where the effect is that an officer does not report to a department psychologist to discuss job-related stress may promote feelings of toughness, coolness, and pride; however, the same officer may be alleviating unresolved anxiety through on-duty alcohol consumption. Lavish or otherwise, alcohol consumption while on the job is in direct violation of organizational rules. However, by being deviant, the strains of the occupation are somewhat lessened (Dietrich and Smith, 1986:304).

The use of alcohol among police officers not only serves as a vehicle for socialization and stress reduction, it also functions to promote questionable life management and faulty life adjustment skills. As Myers (1983:335–39) suggests, when conventional coping strategies fail (e.g., aerobic exercise, relaxation, and social support), one must find alternatives or one cannot go on living. In the case of police officers, the most common elective is alcohol which can also discourage someone from living (Myers, 1983). The profound demands placed on law enforcement officers are undeniable. Unfortunately, at times, such demands lack the requisite community appreciation and foster deleterious reactions from a community's officers. It is our contention that excessive drinking and its attendant features function as important determinants to police suicide.

Thus far we have provisionally explored how exaggerated levels of job dissatisfaction, non-supportive family structures, and alcohol consumption may work to effect police suicides. We have suggested that these determinants are more specific manifestations of social, psychological and interpersonal stress-related variables. Much of our commentary has been based upon speculation following the available, though limited, literature. In an effort to further expand our knowledge on this under-examined, albeit important, social problem, we now consider what preliminary steps might be taken in academy training and administrative policy setting which would more adequately prepare prospective police candidates and police departments for the demands of the profession.

## Police Training and Policy Setting: Considerations for the Future

There are three broad suggestions we believe are warranted in the context of policing in society, stress, and suicide. These recommendations are based upon the absence of *any* meaningful procedures incorporated into general academy training. While the suggestions seem obvious and straightforward, they are not usually recognized as important features of one's readiness to assume a position as a police officer. Following the identification and discussion of our recommendations, we consider their overall likelihood for promoting an ongoing climate of suicide prevention and detection within departments. Further, we address how, if at all, policy setting within precincts can and must include on-going staff development designed to address stress related to police work, family life, and alcohol use.

### Stress Management and Stress Reduction Techniques

The curricula for most police academy training facilities do not include any classes on decompression practices or procedures. Yet understanding how to cope with the pressures of police work is pivotal to job satisfaction, a good home life, and a healthy attitude toward alcohol. We contend that stress management and reduction extend beyond access to the gym. Physical exercise is a mechanism to channel stress. It is not, however, the entire solution. We recommend that a mandatory class explaining how to cope with and abate anxiety needs to be incorporated into all academy programs. Aspects of the course would include nutrition and dieting practices; physical health, fitness, and exercise routines; mental wellness, imaging, and relaxation techniques; recreational, leisure, and outdoor activities; and humor, play, and amusement strategies.

### Group "Rap" or Process Sessions

Conventional police practices make psychological services available to officers experiencing job-related pressure. On occasion, group sessions are held for individuals coping with similar problems (e.g., the effects of using deadly force, the aftermath of a partner killed in the line of fire). Officers tend not to be enamored with therapeutic assistance. Often, participation in counseling is perceived by the individual as a statement of his/her weakness, troubled conscience, or ineffectiveness. The attitude of other officers can communicate these same sentiments. We suggest that exposure to group sessions as a mechanism of peer support must occur early in the candidate's training and regularly while on the job. We maintain that by instituting group process or "rap" sessions as a part of routine police work, the perception of what counseling is all about becomes demystified.

The focus of the sessions can vary depending on the needs of the participants. The aims, too, can vary but would essentially include: (1) to identify and explore individual officer concerns regarding all aspects of policing; (2) to listen to and counsel individual officers through peer support; and (3) to foster and acknowledge greater understanding of officers' shared concerns as a way of furthering departmental esprit. Developing the appropriate training balance between this more introspective and self-revealing dimension of policing and the more instinctual and deterministic aspects of law enforcement would need to be worked out in various academy curricula.

### Police Mentoring

Neophyte officers learn about policing twice over: while in the academy and then again while in the field. During exposure to both, however, critical decisions are made routinely. How choices are elected becomes a matter of both obedience and responsibility to the profession as well as discipline and respect for oneself and others. Officers learn a great deal about doing the right thing and owning their decisions. They do not learn nearly as much about how to appreciate themselves and others as fully as possible. This is what discipline and respect teach us. They remind us of the importance of the process; that is, finding meaning and purpose in our work as situated in *how* we do it, not in the work itself. When police outcomes are not satisfying, discipline and respect enable us to see that the way we went about our job may have included principles of unparalleled integrity. Conversely, when police outcomes are satisfying, discipline and respect signal that what we effected may have been tarnished by how we went about our work. Skilled mentoring teaches us about obedience and responsibility as well as discipline and respect. We maintain that this type of instruction deserves a place not only in academy training but also as a outlet for staff development. Granted, senior patrol partners indoctrinate junior patrol partners. We are questioning the quality of that indoctrination and recommending that such mentoring can influence policing, stress build-up, and even suicidal ideation.

The recommendations of stress management and reduction, group counseling sessions, and police mentoring are designed to prevent suicide attempts. In other words, these are precautionary strategies that arguably help to create a climate in which officers feel more comfortable speaking out when frustrations concerning police work materialize. As academy training components, officers would be better equipped to confront the daily job-related demands. In addition, we contend that such preparedness would affect the quality of one's home life and one's relationship to alcohol consumption.

In the context of general police policy setting, departments need officers who can function effectively. It would seem that mechanisms that reduce stress which, when intensified, may lead to self-destructive behavior, offer precincts a way of preserving otherwise skilled and dedicated individuals. Clearly, this is advantageous for everyone concerned. To ignore or dismiss such on-going preventive and detection practices in a profession where job-related anxiety, family stress, and alcohol abuse runs rampant, is to knowingly damage the system, short-change the public, and betray the officers who protect and serve.

# Conclusions

This chapter conceptually explored the relationship between policing, stress, and suicide. Despite the dearth of research available, we suggested that several social, psychological, and interpersonal stressors were clearly implicated in the nature and likelihood of an officer's self-destructive behavior. We provisionally examined how the determinants of occupational stress, inadequate networks of family support, and alcohol abuse tell us more about policing in society and officer suicide. We also considered the relevance of our analysis in the context of police training. Here, too, our treatment was essentially exploratory. We recommended that as a matter of police training and on-going policy, efforts structured to foster suicide prevention and detection were most essential. Accordingly, we argued for the importance of incorporating stress reduction and management techniques, group counseling and process sessions, and police mentoring into the overall training curriculum. Our position was that these training outlets would re-orient officers' outlook on policing in ways that decreased stress and identified those factors that precipitate suicide. Further, we suggested that such instruction should be recognized as integral to continued staff development at all precincts. We argued that as a matter of policy, departments would do well to consider the viability of these intervention services as a way of benefiting the overall system, improving relations with the public, and preserving otherwise exemplary officers.

# References

Bartol, M. (1992). "Small-town Women Police." *Criminal Justice and Behavior*, 19, 246–49.

Coman, G. J., Evans, B. J., and Stanley, R. O. (1992). "The Police Personality: Type A Behavior and Trait Anxiety." *Journal of Criminal Justice*, 20, 429–41.

Dietrich, J., and Smith, J. (1986). "Non-medical Use of Drugs and Alcohol by Police." *Journal of Police Science and Administration*, 14, 300–6.

DiVasto, P., and Saxton, G. (1992). "Munchausen's Syndrome in Law Enforcement." *FBI Law Enforcement Bulletin*, 11–13.

*Escobedo v. Illinois*, 378 U.S. 478 (1964).

Friedman, P. (1967). "Suicide Among Police." In E. Schneidman (Ed.), *Essays in self-destruction*. New York: Science House.

Gentz, D. (1991). "The Psychological Impact of Critical Incidents of Police Officers." In J. T. Reese, J. M. Horn, and C. Dunning (Eds.), *Critical Incidents In Policing* (pp. 119–23). Washington, DC: U.S. Department of Justice.

Hagerman, M. (1978). "Occupational Stress of Law Enforcement Officers and Marital and Familial Relationships." *Journal of Police Science and Administration*, 6, 402–16.

Hartsough, D. M. (1991). "Stresses, Spouses, and Law Enforcement: A Step Beyond." In J. T. Reese, J. M. Horn, and C. Dunning (Eds.), *Critical Incidents In Policing* (pp. 131–35). Washington, DC: Department of Justice.

Hill, K. and Clawson, M. (1988). "The Health Hazards of 'Street Level' Bureaucracy: Morality Among the Police." *Journal of Police Science and Administration*, 16, 243–48.

Howe, B., Marshal, J. R., and Violanti, J. M. (1985). Stress, Coping, and Alcohol Use: The Police Connection." *Journal of Police Science and Administration*, 10, 302–14.

Inciardi, J. A. (1993) (2ed). *Criminal Justice*. New York: Worth Publishers.

Kroes, W., Hurrell, J., and Margolis, B. (1974). "Job Stress in Policemen." *Journal of Police Science and Administration*, 2, 145–55.

Labovitz, S. and Hagehorn, R. (1971). "An Analysis of Suicide Rates Among Occupational Categories." *Sociological Inquiry*, 41, 67–72.

*Law Enforcement News*. (1995). "National FOP Looks at Police Suicide and How to Prevent It." Vol 21 (422): 1, 8.

Lester, D. (1983). "Stress in Police Officers: An American Perspective." *The Police Journal*, 56, 184–93.

Lester, D. (1992). "Social Correlates of Opportunity Based Suicide Rates." *Psychological Reports*, 70, 154–59.

Lippert, W. W. (1991). "Police Officer Suicide or Homicide: Treating The Affected Department." In J. T. Reese, J. M. Horn, and C. Dunning (Eds.), *Critical Incidents In Policing* (pp. 180–84). Washington, DC: U.S. Department of Justice.

Marshal, J. R., Vena, J. E., and Violanti, J. M. (1986). "Disease, Risk, and Mortality." *Journal of Police Science and Administration*, 14, 17–23.

Martelli, J., Martelli, T. A., and Waters, L. K. (1989). "The Police Stress Survey." *Psychological Reports*, 64, 267–73.

Maynard, P. E., and Maynard, N. E. (1982). "Stress in Police Families." *Journal of Police Science and Administration*, 10, 302–14.

McCreedy, K. (1983). "Entry Level Police Training." *Police Chief*, 50, 22–58.

Milanovich, C. (1980). "The Blue Pressure Cooker." *Police Chief*, 47, 18–29.

*Miranda v. Arizona*, 384 U.S. 436 (1966).

Myers, D. G. (1983) (2ed). *Exploring Psychology*. New York: Worth Publishers.

Poole, E. D. and Pogrebin, M. R. (1991). "Police and Tragic Events: The Management of Emotions." *Journal of Criminal Justice*, 19, 395–403.

Pugh, G. M. (1986). "The Good Police Officer: Qualities, Roles, and Concepts." *Journal of Police Science and Administration*, 14, 1–3.

Skolnick, J. (1975). *Police in America*. Boston: Educational Associates.

Southward, N. (1990). "Taking the Job Home." *FBI Law Enforcement Bulletin*, pp. 19–23.

Stege, H. W. (1986). "Drug Abuse by Police Officers." *Police Chief*, 53, 53–83.

Violanti, J. (1995). "The Mystery Within Understanding Police Suicide." *Law Enforcement Bulletin*, 64, 19–23.

Violanti, J. (1984). "Police Suicide on The Rise." *New York Trooper*, Jan.: 18–19.

Violanti, J. M., and Vena, J. E. (unpublished) Epidemiology of police suicide. NIMH Grant MH47091-02.

Violanti, J., Vena, J. and Marshall, J. (1986). "Disease, Risk, and Morality Among Police Officers: New Evidence and Contributing Factors." *Journal of Police Science and Administration*, 14, 17–23.

Wagner, M. and Brzeczek, R. J. (1983). "Alcoholism and Suicide: A Fatal Connection." *FBI Law Enforcement Bulletin*, pp. 8–15.

# Index